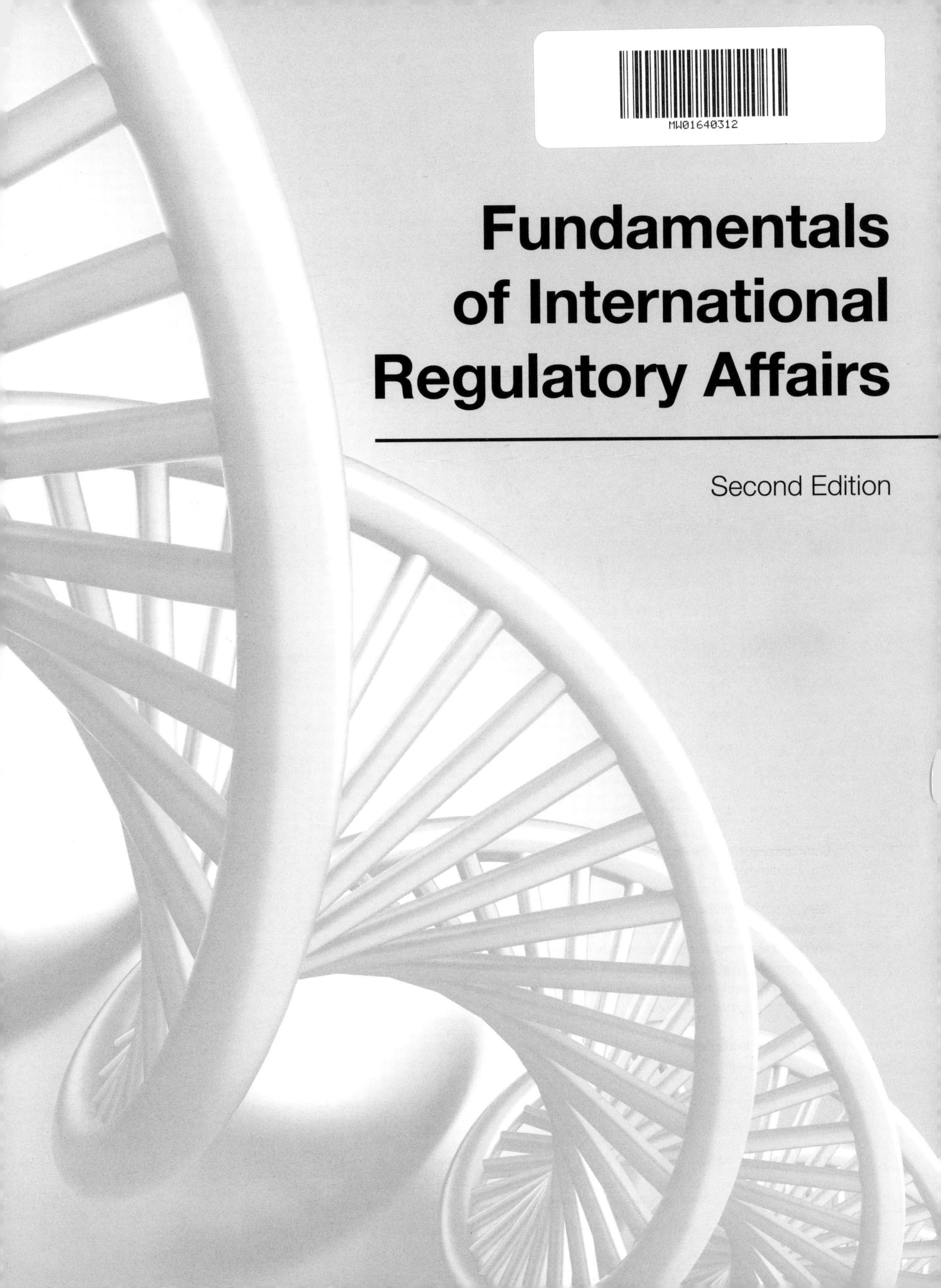

Fundamentals of International Regulatory Affairs

Second Edition

ISBN: 978-0-9898028-0-2

Every precaution is taken to ensure accuracy of content; however, the publisher cannot accept responsibility for the correctness of the information supplied. At the time of publication, all Internet references (URLs) in this book were valid. These references are subject to change without notice.

RAPS Global Headquarters
5635 Fishers Lane
Suite 550
Rockville, MD 20852
USA

RAPS.org

Foreword

Since the first edition of *Fundamentals of International Regulatory Affairs* was published in 2010, much has changed on the global scene. There continue to be significant developments in the harmonization of requirements and regulations by international bodies such as the International Conference on Harmonisation (ICH) for pharmaceuticals and biologics, the relatively new International Medical Device Regulators Forum (IMDRF), which supplanted the Global Harmonization Task Force, and the World Health Organization (WHO). Other organizations working to streamline the development and registration procedures include the Pharmaceutical Inspection Convention and Pharmaceutical Inspection Cooperation Scheme (PIC/S), the International Organization for Standardization (ISO) and the International Cooperation on Harmonisation of Technical Requirements for Registration of Veterinary Products (VICH).

This second edition has been significantly expanded to cover additional topics, with new chapters on:

- Crisis Management
- Heath Technology Assessment
- Clinical Trials: GCPs, Regulations and Compliance
- In-Country Representation
- Counterfeit Deterrence
- Stability Test Requirements
- Device Quality Systems
- Active Implantable Medical Devices
- Software
- Vaccines
- Products Manufactured From Human Blood or Plasma
- Combination Products
- Botanical and Natural Health Products

The book is organized into five sections:

- **Section I:** General Information—topics relating to multiple product lines and overarching issues
- **Section II:** Pharmaceuticals—information on premarket requirements, submission, testing, quality and postmarket requirements for prescription drugs, generic products and nonprescription drugs
- **Section III:** Medical Devices—topics covering the entire medical device lifecycle, quality system requirements, in vitro diagnostic devices, active implantable devices and software
- **Section IV:** Biologics—information on high-risk biotech products, biosimilars and vaccines
- **Section V:** Other Product Classifications—blood and plasma products, orphan products, combination products, cosmetic, food supplements, veterinary products and botanical/natural health products

The text is accompanied by a matrix of applicable laws and regulations, a glossary and an extensive index. *Fundamentals of International Regulatory Affairs, Second Edition*, is an excellent reference for those involved in multinational product development and marketing at all levels—from those new to the regulatory profession to more experienced professionals looking for information on a less familiar product. It also can serve as a study tool for those planning to sit for the Global Regulatory Affairs Certification (RAC) exam, in conjunction with other study materials.

Pamela A. Jones
Senior Editor

Acknowledgements

The Regulatory Affairs Professionals Society (RAPS) extends its thanks to the following individuals for their contributions to this book, sharing their expertise to further the regulatory profession and assist their colleagues.

Marcelo de Moraes Antunes, RAC (Global)
Regulatory Affairs Strategy Consultant
SQR Consulting
São Paulo, Brazil

Rajaram Balasubramanian, PGDOM, RAC (US, EU)
Director—RA & QA
Elekta
Chennai, India

Nicole Beard, MSc, PhD
Managing Director, Head Regulatory Affairs Europe & International
BiogECHO S.A.R.L.
Geneva, Switzerland

Shailesh S. Dewasthaly
Vice President, Toxicology
Intercell AG
Vienna, Austria

Hoss A. Dowlat, PhD
Vice President, Regulatory Affairs EU-USA, Global Strategy
PharmBio Consulting
Freiburg, Germany

Jethro Ekuta, DVM, PhD, RAC, FRAPS
Vice President and Global Head, Pharmacovigilance Analytics & Insight and International Pharmacovigilance Global Medical Organization
Janssen Research & Development LLC
Horsham, PA, USA

Heidi Feik, MSc, RAC
Senior Consultant
Michor Consulting e.U.
Vienna, Austria

Renee Hardley, RAC
Manager, Quality and Regulatory Affairs
Boston Scientific Pty Ltd.
Sydney, Australia

Birgit Hausberger, Mag. rer. nat.
Regulatory Affairs Specialist
Baxter Innovations GmbH
Vienna, Austria

Julia Hilscher, Dr
Junior Consultant
Michor Consulting e.U.
Vienna, Austria

Sofina M. Jain, MS, RAC
Regulatory Affairs Associate
Par Pharmaceutical
Irvine, CA, USA

Alexander Krieg, PhD, RAC
Regulatory Affairs Manager
Tecan Schweiz AG
Zurich, Switzerland

Mukesh Kumar, PhD, RAC
Senior Director, Regulatory Affairs and Quality Assurance
Amarex Clinical Research
Germantown, MD, USA

Robert Laughner, MS, RAC (US, EU, CAN)
Regulatory Science
Cook Incorporated
Bloomington, IN, USA

C. David Lim, PhD, RAC, ASQ-CQA
President, CEO and Principal
Regulatory Doctor
Riner, VA, USA

Salma Michor, PhD, RAC
CEO & Principal Consultant
Michor Consulting e.U.
Vienna, Austria

Shekhar Natarajan, MSc, MRSC, MTOPRA
Director, Regulatory Informatics and Submission Management
Global Regulatory & Quality Assurance
Merck Serono
Darmstadt, Germany

Philipp Novales-Li, DMedSc, PhD, DPhil (Oxford), RAC
Director, Global Regulatory Affairs
Novartis Vaccines and Diagnostics Inc.
Emeryville, CA, USA

Robert G. Peterson, MD, PhD, MPH
Clinical Professor of Pediatrics
University of British Columbia Faculty of Medicine
Vancouver, British Columbia, Canada
Chair, Canadian Drug Expert Committee

Moulakshi Roychowdhury, PharmD, JD
Director of Global Advertising & Labeling, Regulatory Affairs
Forest Laboratories Inc.
New York, NY, USA

Marcela Saad, MSc, PharmD, RAC (Global)
President & Senior Consultant
MarcM Consulting Canada
Kitchener, Ontario, Canada

Jasmina Savic, MSc, RAC
Global Regulatory Affairs Manager
Grünenthal GmbH
Aachen, Germany

Siegfried Schmitt, PhD
Principal Consultant
PAREXEL Consulting
Braintree, Essex, UK

Anna-Veronika Schrodt, Mag. phil.
Senior Regulatory Affairs Specialist
Baxter Innovations GmbH
Vienna, Austria

Chander Sehgal, MD, MBA
Director, Common Drug Review and Optimal Use of Drugs
Canadian Agency for Drugs and Technologies in Health
Ottawa, Canada

Sharad Mi Shukla, MSc, RAC (US, EU)
Manager, Regulatory Affairs
Johnson & Johnson
Delhi, India

Michael Siano, MA
Global Regulatory Specialist
Emergo Group
Austin, TX, USA

Evelyn A. Steele, MTOPRA
Director, Global Regulatory Affairs
GlaxoSmithKline Consumer Healthcare
Weybridge, Surrey, UK

Manuel Urena, RAC
Senior Regulatory Affairs Manager
Smith & Nephew USD Ltd.
Dubai, UAE

Erik Vollebregt
Partner
Axon Lawyers
Amsterdam, The Netherlands

Table of Contents

Section I: General Information

Section II: Pharmaceuticals

Section III: Medical Devices

Section IV: Biologics

Section V: Other Product Classifications

Appendices

Figures

Tables

Chapter 1

Introduction to Regulatory Affairs

By Salma Michor, PhD, RAC

OBJECTIVES

- ❑ Learn why healthcare regulations for medicinal products and devices were established
- ❑ Discover the key historical milestones leading to today's healthcare regulations
- ❑ Clarify the importance of global harmonization

LAWS, REGULATIONS AND GUIDELINES COVERED IN THIS CHAPTER

US

- ❑ The *Federal Food, Drug, and Cosmetic Act* of 1938 (*FD&C Act*), as amended by the *Food and Drug Administration Modernization Act* of 1997 (*FDAMA*) (Public Law 105-115)

EU

- ❑ Commission Directive 2003/32/EC introducing detailed specifications as regards the requirements laid down in Council Directive 93/42/EEC with respect to medical devices manufactured utilising tissues of animal origin
- ❑ Council Directive 93/42/EEC of 14 June 1993, concerning medical devices
- ❑ MEDDEV 2.12-1 rev 6., *Guidelines on a Medical Device Vigilance System* (December 2009)
- ❑ Regulation (EC) No. 1829/2003 of the European Parliament and of the Council of 22 September 2003 on genetically modified food and feed

ICH

- ❑ *Pharmacovigilance Planning E2E*, (Current Step 4 version, November 2004)

GHTF

- ❑ GHTF/SG2/N54R8:2006, *Medical Devices Post Market Surveillance: Global Guidance for Adverse Event Reporting for Medical Devices* (18 December 2006)
- ❑ GHTF/SG5/N2R8:2007, *Clinical Evaluation*, May 2007, pp 4-12

Introduction

The main aim of drug regulation is to keep unsafe products off the market. Drug regulation entails granting of marketing authorization licenses to place products (considered to be relatively safe) on the market after a thorough evaluation by Competent Authorities. It must be stressed, however, that no medicinal product is 100% safe. Tests carried out on a population of limited size, under controlled conditions during clinical trials may fail to identify critical issues and adverse events. When drugs are placed on the market for the first time, little is really known about side effects that may first come to light when used by millions in the population at large. Previously unknown adverse events may occur, or known adverse events may occur at a higher frequency than expected. Hence, regulations require medicinal product monitoring in the postauthorization and marketing phases.

In addition to medicinal product regulation, most countries worldwide have enacted regulations for medical devices, food and food supplements and cosmetic products.

In some countries, such as the US and Canada, laws to regulate food and drug products were established in the 19th century. The evolution of modern healthcare in Canada began with the *British North American Act* of 1867, which gave individual provinces jurisdiction over most health services.[1] The *Vaccine Act* of 1813 was the first federal law in the US dealing with consumer protection and therapeutic substances.[2] Food regulations in the US and Europe have an even longer history, while regulations covering cosmetics and medical devices have been developed more recently. In the EU, healthcare regulations became firmly established during the second half of the 20th century.[3] Other regions, such as Asia and the Pacific, Middle East and Africa and the Americas have introduced drug and medical device regulations to greater or lesser extents and at various points.

In developing countries, drug regulations may be more difficult to implement and monitor; hence, the danger of drug and food adulteration may be higher there than in other regions of the world.

The history of medicinal product registration in much of the industrialized world has followed a similar pattern, which can be described as: "Initiation, Acceleration, Rationalization and Harmonization."

The realization that it was important to have a critical evaluation of medicinal products by Competent Authorities before they are allowed on the market was reached at different times in different regions. The "initiation" of stricter controls was triggered by human disasters such as the tragic mistake in the formulation of a children's syrup in the 1930s in the US, which led to the introduction of the product authorization systems; in Europe, the trigger was the thalidomide tragedy of the 1960s.

Most countries saw a rapid increase ("acceleration") in laws, regulations and guidelines for reporting and evaluating safety, quality and efficacy data on new medicinal products in the 1960s and 1970s. Even though different regulatory systems were based on the same fundamental obligations of evaluating product quality, safety and efficacy, the detailed technical requirements diverged over time. This resulted in the duplication of effort involving time-consuming evaluations and expensive test procedures. Eventually, the rising costs of healthcare paved the way for "rationalization" and "harmonization."[4]

It must be understood that many different stakeholders are involved in the regulatory process, including healthcare providers, industry and consumers. The aims of these interest groups may differ: providers and reimbursement bodies may aim to minimize costs; consumers crave a large variety of low-cost, good-quality medicines; while industry desires easy, inexpensive market access.

Before Regulations

Before regulations were in place, drugs and other critical products could be sold like any other consumer product. In the US, for example, medicines were initially patented to protect trade secrets. These medicines were uncontrolled products ranging from harmless mixtures to toxic combinations of narcotics and other substances.[5]

Lack of control not only allowed marketing of products that were not controlled or tested for efficacy, safety and tolerability, but also led to the possible sale of adulterated products. Adulteration was a problem in both the healthcare and food sectors, and governments began to impose laws and regulations to combat adulteration and ensure safety. Commonly adulterated foods included alcohol, milk and bread. Practices that make drugs and foods adulterated include using ingredients of inferior quality and making false claims on labels. Legislation designed to prevent the sale of unsafe or unwholesome food is one of the oldest forms of governmental or societal intervention in the food and agricultural system.[6]

Ethical considerations were also major contributors to stronger regulations.[7]

The need for ethical standards has its foundation in the inhumane practices of infamous Nazi physician, Josef Mengele, during the second world war. During World War II, doctors in Nazi Germany conducted horrifying research on prisoners in concentration camps, which resulted in the Nuremberg Code being created in 1948.[8]

Many unethical clinical research trials were also carried out in the US and the UK during the same period. President Franklin Roosevelt created an Office of Scientific Research and Development to combat diseases such as dysentery, influenza and malaria, and other diseases that commonly affect soldiers. Trials were carried out on orphans, mentally retarded individuals in institutions and prisoners, with the justification that it was necessary for some sacrifices to be made to benefit the whole of society. Negative publicity paved the way for healthcare regulations to protect public safety.

The introduction of stricter regulations in certain major economies has led the way to stricter regulations in other parts of the world.

Start of Regulation

Realization of the importance of drug evaluation was reached at different times in different regions.[9] The first food and drug laws aimed to prohibit commerce in misbranded and adulterated foods, drinks and drugs. In the US, initially, laws regulating product labeling rather than requiring a premarket assessment of safety or efficacy were implemented. The regulatory framework that evolved over the years imposed increasingly stricter control. Sulfanilamide is one example of a drug that was placed on the market without safety testing.[10] Following the introduction in 1937 of a liquid version of sulfanilamide that contained diethylene glycol (a poisonous solvent), 107 people in the US died from ingesting the elixir. The public outrage over the sulfanilamide tragedy led to the rapid passage of the *Federal Food, Drug, and Cosmetic Act* (*FD&C Act*) of 1938,[11] which required drugs to be cleared for safety before being introduced on the market.[12] In Japan, government regulations requiring all medicinal products to be registered for sale started around 1950.[13]

Stricter regulations came into force in the 1960s as a consequence of the thalidomide tragedy in Europe and Canada. Contergan, a product containing the active ingredient, thalidomide, was used to treat morning sickness in pregnant women. The teratogenic potential of thalidomide was not adequately characterized during development. As a result, thousands of babies were born with a rare malformation known as phocomelia.[14]

Other cases calling for stricter regulations include the potential transmission of bovine spongiform encephalopathy (BSE, mad cow disease) and transmissible spongiform encephalopathy (TSE, Creutzfeldt-Jakob disease) to humans via medicinal products containing bovine-derived materials. The BSE/TSE crisis in the early 1990s led to stricter control of drugs containing or derived from bovine material (e.g., Commission Directive 2003/32/EC of 23 April 2003 introducing detailed specifications as regards the requirements laid down in Council Directive 93/42/EEC with respect to medical devices manufactured utilizing tissues of animal origin in the EU[15]). Although the origins of such scandals have their roots in certain geographic regions, the impact has been felt worldwide. Other sectors, such as food, cosmetics and medical devices also came under closer scrutiny.

Globally, the 1960s and 1970s saw a rapid increase in laws, regulations and guidelines for reporting and evaluating the data on new medicinal products' safety, quality and efficacy. During this period, the industry was starting to become more international and globalization began. Registration of medicines, medical devices, cosmetic products and foods, however, remained a national responsibility in most cases. Although different regulatory systems were based on the same fundamental obligations to evaluate quality, safety and efficacy, the detailed technical requirements for each country and/or region were significantly divergent.

Harmonization

Nonharmonized registration regulations meant that it was necessary to duplicate efforts to obtain approvals in different regions, which was time-consuming and expensive. The drive to rationalize and harmonize regulations was impelled by concerns over rising healthcare costs, escalating R&D costs and the need to meet public expectations.[16] In addition, life-saving medicines need to reach patients with minimum delay.

Initiation of International Conference on Harmonisation (ICH)

Work on harmonizing regulatory requirements began in the 1980s. It was pioneered by the European Community (EC) with the aim of developing a single market for pharmaceuticals. The success achieved in Europe demonstrated that harmonization was feasible.[17] The desire to have international harmonized standards and trilateral discussions among the EC, Japan and the US led to specific plans for action during the World Health Organization (WHO) International Conference of Drug Regulatory Authorities (ICDRA) in Paris in 1989. The authorities of Europe, Japan and the US approached the International Federation of Pharmaceutical Manufacturers & Associations (IFPMA) to discuss a joint regulatory authority-industry initiative on international harmonization, and ICH was conceived. ICH was born at a meeting in Brussels in April 1990, hosted by the European Federation of Pharmaceutical Industries and Associations (EFPIA).

Initiation of International Cooperation on Harmonisation (VICH)

The International Cooperation on Harmonisation of Technical Requirements for Registration of Veterinary Medicinal Products (VICH), a trilateral program (EU, Japan, US), is an ongoing program to harmonise technical requirements for marketing authorizations for veterinary medicinal products in the regions concerned.[18] It was officially launched in April 1996.

The Global Harmonization Task Force (GHTF)

GHTF was conceived in 1992 in an effort to achieve greater uniformity across national medical device regulatory systems. As with ICH and pharmaceuticals, the main aim of GHTF was to enhance patient safety while increasing access to safe, effective and clinically beneficial medical technologies worldwide.

GHTF was comprised of five Founding Members—EU, US, Canada, Australia and Japan—and represented a partnership between regulatory authorities and industry. In February 2011, the International Medical Device Regulators Forum was founded to replace GHTF.[19] This forum is a voluntary group of medical device regulators worldwide that discusses future directions in medical device regulatory harmonization. These regulators have come together to build on the strong foundational work of GHTF, and to accelerate international medical device regulatory harmonization and convergence.

Monitoring

Stricter regulation of drugs has continued from the 1960s through 2000 and beyond. This has been driven by a series of major adverse drug reactions. For example, subacute myelo-optic-neuropathy (SMON) was found to be caused by ciloquinol. While this drug was first marketed in the early 1930s, its side effects only became apparent in the 1970s when ciloquinol was linked to severe neurological reactions as a result of stricter pharmacovigilance and surveillance regulations.

Other examples include practolol, which after five years on the market was linked to oculomucocutaneous syndrome. In the 1980s, several drugs were linked to serious side effects: ticrynafen and benoxaprofen were found to cause deaths from liver disease. Zomepirac, a nonsteroidal anti-inflammatory drug, was associated with an increased risk of anaphylactoid reactions.[20]

The list goes on: suprofin was found to cause acute flank pain and reversible acute renal failure, and isotretinoin was almost removed from the US market because of its link to birth defects. Over the past few years, crises concerning the use of several drugs have arisen. Examples include allegations of ischemic colitis from alosetron; rhabdomyolysis from cerivastatin; arthralgia, myalgia and neurologic conditions from Lyme vaccine; multiple joint symptoms from anthrax vaccine; and heart attack and stroke from rofecoxib, to name a few.[21]

The results of such severe drug adverse events have in some instances led to recalls. In the US alone, more than 22 different prescription drug products have been removed from the market since the 1980s.[22]

Pharmacovigilance/Vigilance

Drugs

Vigilance requirements for both drugs and medical devices have increased in recent years. The decision to approve a drug is based on a satisfactory benefit:risk within the conditions specified in the product labeling.[23] The decision to approve a drug or device application is based on information available at the time of approval. However, as noted above, tests carried out during the preclinical and clinical testing phases may fail to detect critical issues. A product's safety profile can change significantly through use in a much larger number of patients. Thus, it is vitally important that drugs and devices placed on the market be closely monitored, especially during the early postmarketing period.

ICH has published *Pharmacovigilance Planning E2E*.[24] Better and earlier planning of pharmacovigilance activities is needed before a product is approved or a license is granted. This guideline has been developed to encourage harmonization and consistency, and to prevent duplication of effort. The guideline could be of benefit to public health programs throughout the world as they consider new drugs in their countries.[25] The guideline recommends several pharmacovigilance activities including:

- passive surveillance
- stimulated reporting
- active surveillance
- comparative observational studies
- targeted clinical investigations
- descriptive studies

Medical Devices

In GHTF's (now IMDRF's) *Medical Devices Post Market Surveillance: Global Guidance for Adverse Event Reporting for Medical Devices*, the objective of "vigilance" is:

> "to improve protection of the health and safety of patients, users and others by disseminating information which may reduce the likelihood of, or prevent repetition of adverse events, or alleviate consequences of such repetition."[26]

Medical device manufacturers placing products on the market are required to notify regulatory authorities of any adverse events. Different regions may implement more or less strict rules and each may have regional and/or national guidelines and regulations. The EU, for example, has published *Guidelines on a Medical Device Vigilance System* (MEDDEV 2.12-1 rev. 6).[27]

For incidents/adverse events to be reportable to national Competent Authorities, the following are assumed:

- An event has occurred.
- The manufacturer's device is associated with the event.
- The event led to one of the following outcomes:
  - death of a patient, user or other person
  - serious injury of a patient, user or other person
  - no death or serious injury occurred, but the event might lead to the death or serious injury of a patient, user or other person if it recurs

It is important that regulatory authorities communicate with counterparts in other countries to stay informed about incidents that have not occurred locally.[28] WHO follows standard operating procedures for issuing alerts among member states and may also work with IMDRF to assist in disseminating information to countries as appropriate.

Foods, Food Supplements and Cosmetics

Less-critical products such as foods, food supplements and cosmetics do not require formal vigilance reporting, but follow regular monitoring via formal inspections. Food quality is becoming increasingly important and food manufacturers need to ensure strict hygiene and quality standards in their manufacturing facilities.

Stricter Authorization Requirements

Today, the drug and medical device approval processes in most countries require preclinical and clinical testing. In most developed countries, drug trials comprise preclinical testing followed by three phases of clinical testing:

- Phase 1—usually carried out by clinical pharmacologists on a small number of healthy volunteers to determine drug metabolism, a safe dosage range and tolerability
- Phase 2—also carried out by clinical pharmacologists on a small number of patients with the target disease; here, information about the drug's pharmacokinetic properties, safety and efficacy is gathered
- Phase 3—carried out by clinical investigators on a larger population to evaluate efficacy and to test for toxicity; at least one Phase 3 study needs to be a randomized clinical trial, in which some patients receive the trial drug and others receive a placebo or standard treatment[29]

For medical devices, the approach to clinical testing (now also being applied to drugs) is to have the clinical evaluation as an ongoing process throughout the life of the device.[30] More emphasis is placed on collecting appropriate information via:

- literature reviews
- clinical experience
- clinical investigations

The manufacturer is responsible for identifying data relevant to the device and deciding what and how much data need to be collected during the investigation to prove the device's safety.

Other Products

Veterinary Products

Veterinary products are regulated in more or less the same manner as medicinal products for humans. The main difference is that drugs for animal populations need to conform to maximum residue limits since they may end up in the food chain. In the US, premarket approval is not required for medical devices intended for animal use; FDA does not require submission of a 510(k) or formal premarket approval for devices used in veterinary medicine.[31] In the EU, medical device law does not include veterinary products. That means such products as special drug delivery systems cannot be CE marked, and fall under drug regulations.

Abridged Applications

Less critical products, such as those of well-established use, traditional herbal medicinal products and generic drugs, may not require preclinical and clinical tests if their safety can be shown based on information in the public domain or by reference to originator products. Over-the-counter (OTC) products containing new chemical entities must be treated as full applications even though their active ingredients may not warrant prescription status.

Orphan Drugs

An "orphan drug" can be defined as a pharmaceutical agent that has been developed specifically to treat a rare medical condition, referred to as an "orphan disease."

In the US, a law regulating such drugs was enacted in 1983 (*Orphan Drug Act* (*ODA*)). The EU's definition of an orphan condition is broader than that of the US, in that it also covers some tropical diseases found primarily in developing nations.[32] Since financial incentives for manufacturing and marketing orphan drugs are low, many Competent Authorities have created initiatives and financial support for companies that engage in orphan drug research.

Food, Dietary Supplements and Cosmetics

In general, food, dietary supplements and cosmetic products do not need premarket controls. However, the manufacturer must be able to show that its products meet the minimum safety standards regarding composition, packaging and information. It is generally the manufacturer's responsibility to implement a market surveillance system both to ensure safety and in case the need for a batch recall arises.

Some countries require Genetically Modified Organisms (GMOs) entering the food chain to be closely monitored, and traceability needs to be ensured. For example, in the EU, clear systems for tracing and labeling GMOs (Regulation 1830/2003/EC) and for regulating the marketing and labeling of food and feed products derived from GMOs (Regulation 1829/2003/EC[33]) have been established.

Product Innovations

Technological advances have made many novel therapies available, including biologics, blood products and advanced therapy medicinal products (ATMPs). It is important that regulations evolve to keep abreast of advances in science and technology. Innovative product developers may both benefit from and exploit the existence of a "regulatory vacuum."[34] In such instances, manufacturers may be more informed than officials of the Competent Authority and could share their expertise by becoming involved in defining the regulatory framework for the new area, influencing public and agency opinion.[35]

Public Health and Economic Resources

Initially, science and public health protection were the motivating factors and primary drivers in healthcare regulation. In recent years, economic considerations have also begun impacting healthcare regulation development.[36,37]

In many countries, healthcare systems rely on products reimbursed by national health systems. In this respect, public health is highly dependent on the availability of high-quality reimbursed products. It is in the interest of local governing bodies to have access to high-quality medicines at affordable prices, necessitating price controls. In countries where the healthcare costs are borne by individual consumers, access to affordable medicines is even more critical.

Stakeholders and the Availability of Information

In today's world of electronic media such as the Internet, it is almost impossible to hide any critical issues related to any product from the general public. Information is available to virtually anyone, even in very remote parts of the world. Industry must ensure that only safe products are placed on the market and act responsibly if any critical issues arise. To maintain public confidence in the healthcare system, timely and appropriate regulations that ensure medicinal/healthcare product(s) quality, safety and efficacy, and clear instructions for use, are necessary.[38]

Healthcare regulations must balance the interests of patients, manufacturers, regulatory authorities, insurance companies and others in a fast-moving and complex environment.[39] Such regulatory systems need to be robust and quickly adaptable in the face of advancing technology.

At the global level, it is imperative that laws regulating critical healthcare products and standards become more harmonized to ensure worldwide patient safety. Mutual Recognition Agreements between various geographic regions ensure that quality standards are harmonized, which also avoids duplication of efforts. In this respect, the work carried out by harmonization bodies such as ICH and IMDRF is becoming increasingly important in defining and shaping the worldwide industry.

Last but not least, regulations continue to be a moving target. Regulatory professionals and the life science industry need to keep abreast of national, regional and global regulatory changes to ensure that safe, reliable and good-quality medicines reach patients at the right time.

References

1. Regulatory Affairs Professionals Society. Chapter 1, History of Canadian Food and Drug Regulation. In: *Fundamentals of Canadian Regulatory Affairs, Third Edition*. Rockville, MD. 2011:1–6.
2. Regulatory Affairs Professionals Society. Chapter 1, FDA and Related Regulatory Agencies. In: *Fundamentals of US Regulatory Affairs Eighth Edition*. Rockville, MD. 2013: 1–10.
3. Regulatory Affairs Professionals Society. Chapter 1, EU Regulatory Affairs—An Historic Perspective. In: *Fundamentals of EU Regulatory Affairs Sixth Edition*, Rockville, MD. 2012:1–16.
4. ICH History. ICH website. http://www.ich.org/about/history.html. Accessed 15 July 2013.
5. Op cit 2.
6. Op cit 1.
7. Op cit 3.
8. Kiefer J. "The History and Importance of Informed Consent in Clinical Trials." Bryn Mawr website. http://serendip.brynmawr.edu/biology/b103/f01/web2/kiefer.html. Accessed 15 July 2013.
9. Op cit 4.
10. Grigg W. "1938–1988: The 50th Anniversary of the Federal Food, Drug and Cosmetic Act." *FDA Consumer.* January 1989: 28–32.
11. The *Federal Food, Drug and Cosmetic Act* of 1938, as amended by the *Food and Drug Administration Modernization Act.* 1997 (Public Law 105-115). GPO website. http://www.gpo.gov/fdsys/pkg/PLAW-105publ115/html/PLAW-105publ115.htm. Accessed 15 July 2013.
12. Op cit 2.
13. Op cit 4.
14. Op cit 3.
15. Commission Directive 2003/32/EC of 23 April 2003 introducing detailed specifications as regards the requirements laid down in Council Directive 93/42/EEC with respect to medical devices manufactured utilising tissues of animal origin. Eur-Lex website. http://eur-lex.europa.eu/LexUriServ/LexUriServ.do?uri=OJ:L:2003:105:0018:0023:EN:PDF. Accessed 15 July 2013.
16. Op cit 4.
17. Ibid.
18. What is VICH? VICH website. http://www.vichsec.org/. Accessed 16 March 2013.
19. About IMDRF. IMDRF website. http://www.imdrf.org/about/about.asp. Accessed 15 July 2013.
20. Op cit 15.
21. Ibid.
22. Ibid.
23. ICH, *Pharmacovigilance Planning E2E* (Current Step 4 version, November 2004). ICH website. http://www.ich.org/fileadmin/Public_Web_Site/ICH_Products/Guidelines/Efficacy/E2E/Step4/E2E_Guideline.pdf. Accessed 15 July 2013.
24. Ibid..
25. Ibid.
26. GHTF SG2-N54R8:2006, *Medical Devices Post Market Surveillance: Global Guidance for Adverse Event Reporting for Medical Devices* (December 2006). IMDRF website. http://www.imdrf.org/docs/ghtf/final/sg2/technical-docs/ghtf-sg2-n54r8-guidance-adverse-events-061130.pdf. Accessed 15 July 2013.
27. MEDDEV 2.12-1 rev 6, *Guidelines on a Medical Device Vigilance System* (December 2009). EC website. http://ec.europa.eu/health/medical-devices/files/meddev/2_12_1-rev_6-12-2009_en.pdf. Accessed 15 July 2013.
28. WHO, *Medical Device Regulation: Global Overview & Guiding Principles* (2003), pp 44–45.
29. Ibid.
30. GHTF, SG5-N2R8:2007, *Clinical Evaluation* (May 2007), pp 4–12.
31. US FDA, "How FDA Regulates Veterinary Devices." FDA website. www.fda.gov/AnimalVeterinary/ResourcesforYou/ucm047117.htm. Accessed 15 July 2013.
32. "Definition of Orphan Disease." Medterms website. www.medterms.com/script/main/art.asp?articlekey=11418 . Accessed 15 July 2013.
33. Regulation (EC) No. 1829/2003 of the European Parliament and of the Council of 22 September 2003 on genetically modified food and feed. Eur-Lex website. http://eurlex.europa.eu/LexUriServ/site/en/oj/2003/l_268/l_26820031018en00010023.pdf. Accessed 15 July 2013.
34. Op cit 3.
35. Ibid.
36. Ibid.
37. Strom BL. Chapter 1, What is Pharmacoepidemiology? In: Strom BL and Kimmel SE, eds. *Textbook of Pharmacoepidemiology*. Chicester, England: John Wiley & Sons, Ltd; 2006:3-11.
38. Op cit 3.
39. Ibid.

Chapter 2

Crisis Management for the Medical Product Industry

By Mukesh Kumar, PhD, RAC

OBJECTIVES

- Learn about types of crises that arise in the medical product industry
- Understand the basics of crisis management
- Recognize the regulatory perspectives on crisis
- Learn about public resources available to assist with crisis management

Introduction

Crisis is defined as an event or series of related events that is, or is expected to lead to, a difficult, dangerous, unstable and negative situation affecting an individual or a company. A crisis event, if not managed adequately and timely, could negatively affect the economics, public image and security of the affected party. Most crises arise from internal or external factors that happen with little or no warning and require immediate decisions. Most are multi-dimensional and require the involvement of diverse resources within a given organization. Additionally, most crises require a change in organizational practices as the existing system is deemed to have failed.[1] The crises described in this chapter are ones inherent to the medical product industry and do not include those caused by natural disasters and other universal human factors, such as rumors, workplace violence, terrorist attacks or man-made disasters.

Unlike risk management, which involves managing potential and known threats of narrow scope, crisis management involves managing unknown threats during and after their occurrence. An organization also can build broad crisis management policies to address situations that potentially could lead to a crisis, similar to that of risk management. It is possible to prepare for potential situations by learning from similar organizations' experiences. Most common crisis management policies and plans include emergency management and business-continuity management, which address global existential issues. However, medical product companies have to deal with additional issues, such as stagnant product pipelines, unplanned regulatory hurdles and unexpected safety issues with marketed products for which most companies do not or cannot plan ahead. Since these situations usually are caused by a combination of internal and external factors, the task of finding solutions requires managing the internal causes and controlling external reactions.

Crises can happen regardless of an organization's size, its location, available resources and employee skill levels. In all cases, early identification and management of crises are vital for the organization's survival. Crisis management involves methods to respond to a crisis, establishing metrics to deal with crises and developing possible response mechanisms. A crisis management plan should include possible worst-case scenarios and solutions in the form of a contingency plan. This chapter looks at crisis situations in the context of the life sciences industry and provides a list of resources available to the industry to assist in addressing events before, during and after they happen.

Types of Crises Specific to the Medical Product Industry

The medical product industry is unique in terms of its reliance on biological science and human response to its products. The time, investment and risk of failure due to poorly definable and unpredictable events are unparalleled. Products developed by the industry have to go through one of the most extensive testing, review and approval processes of any other industry, much of which is highly transparent to the public. Products range from simple chemical drugs to complex biological products and sophisticated life-saving machines, from those that have been around for centuries to cutting-edge, state-of-the-art technology. The regulations governing the industry are changing constantly , often as knee-jerk reactions by regulators to isolated crisis events. The global market for medical products leads to additional issues related to international business and regulatory, legal, financial, logistical and social affairs. The industry is very diverse in terms of the profiles of the companies that compete side by side in the same market, from large multi-billion dollar corporations with thousands of employees and worldwide operations, to small businesses with one or few products, very few employees and small revenues. Companies constantly have to maintain their public perception and be prepared to respond to negative media reports.

With the above complex issues at play, there are three broad categories of crisis unique to the medical product industry:

1. technological crisis
2. regulatory crisis
3. organizational crisis

Technological Crises

A technological crisis could involve either urgent events that require immediate attention or long-term events that have been in the making for an extended period of time and require a company to implement substantial operational and policy changes. Examples of this type of crisis are unexpected issues with the safe use of a given product or failure of research and development activities to replenish dwindling product pipelines.

New Safety Concerns for Product

Despite extensive testing of medical products in experimental systems (*in vitro* and *in vivo*) and human subjects, it is almost impossible to predict all the possible adverse events that could be caused by the consumption of a drug or the use of a biologic product or medical device. The best case scenario is when early studies with an investigational product provide a clear indicator of a safety issue, and further development is halted. However, the discovery of new, unexpected and unanticipated product safety issues during late stage clinical trials, or worse still, after marketing approval, could lead to a major crisis in terms of managing the adverse event and making decisions about educating consumers or withdrawing the product from market.

There are several guidance documents from regulators in the US and EU regarding the management of safety events during the investigational phase and after marketing approval.[2,3] During the investigational phase, the safety profile of a drug, biologic or medical device is monitored closely, and adjustments can be made to the development process as new safety information becomes available. Hence, finding new unanticipated adverse events late in the development phase of a product generally is considered an accepted risk of developing a medical product. Rejection of a product late in development may be an existential event for a small company with one or few products in development; however, the crisis practically can be averted by diversification of the pipeline and judicious planning. The US Food and Drug Administration (FDA) and the European Medicines Agency (EMA) provide numerous opportunities to interact with regulators in various ways to discuss how to address safety issues identified during development. Hence, premarket safety events generally do not meet the definition of a crisis situation.

The safety events identified after obtaining marketing approval, on the other hand, indeed can lead to a crisis. Regulatory authorities expect companies to establish robust pharmacovigilance programs to identify and report safety events in a timely fashion. Failure to comply could lead to crisis. Not all adverse events associated with a medical product lead to a crisis. Crisis is defined as an event that requires product withdrawal, consumer warnings and management of exposure to the product.

Managing Postmarketing Safety Events

FDA and EMA guidance documents[4,5] require the following elements for pharmacovigilance:

- planning of pharmacovigilance activities throughout the product lifecycle
- science-based approach to risk documentation
- effective collaboration between regulators and industry
- applicability of the pharmacovigilance plan across the three ICH regions

Planning a pharmacovigilance program starts with the safety profile established during a product's investigational phase. This includes the anticipated adverse events based on preclinical and clinical testing conducted in support of the marketing approval application. Certain populations typically are not included in the investigational phase, such as children, pregnant women, patients with relevant co-morbidity (such as hepatic or renal disorders), patients with disease severity different from that studied in clinical trials, sub-populations carrying known and relevant genetic polymorphism and patients of different racial and/or ethnic origins. Such populations are likely to be exposed to the product once it is available in the marketplace and hence define the potential or unknown risk of a given product. The pharmacovigilance program should document a given product's anticipated, potential and unknown risks followed by expedited or periodic safety reporting to regulatory agencies.

Pharmacovigilance should involve a combination of passive and active reporting, observational studies and even targeted clinical trials, depending on a given product's safety profile. The safety crisis can be managed via an effective pharmacovigilance plan associated with an event management plan. Safety events should be addressed promptly, completely and transparently. Event management should include a public relations exercise whereby the company makes the public aware of its risk management practices and the actions taken to safeguard consumers.

Two case studies are used to highlight event management practices: the Johnson & Johnson Tylenol episode is an example of good safety event management, and the Merck Vioxx episode is an example of bad safety management. These examples can be used in creating and evaluating the adequacy of safety crisis management programs.

Declining R&D Productivity

Despite huge advances in scientific, technological and managerial practices in the last 20 years, the number of new products developed by the industry per billions of dollars spent on R&D activities has steadily declined. By some estimates, 95% of drugs under development fail to meet the safety and effectiveness criteria, and could cost anywhere from $350 million for a small company developing a single product, to up to $5 billion per product for a large company working simultaneously on multiple candidates.[6] The severe decline in R&D productivity has created a crisis in terms of diminishing product pipelines and frustrated development programs. It has been suggested that this R&D decline is due to improper development programs that lack focus and adequate planning, and involve resource mismanagement.[7] Another hypothesis for this decline is an over-conservative and risk-averse culture that stifles innovation.[8]

The management of R&D-related crises requires long-term planning and a change in a company's core policies and competencies. It has been suggested that a development program should have realistic goals, with a view toward the current regulatory expectations. Adding additional financial resources to failing projects without initially analyzing and troubleshooting the core reasons for failure is not helpful. Products targeted for development should be based on a thorough review of available evidence and a critical evaluation of the claims made for the product's potential to succeed in the market.

Regulatory Crises

For a company in the medical product industry, the worst kind of crisis involves a major dispute with regulators regarding a decision for granting marketing approval or requiring a product recall postapproval. However, disputes can happen at any stage in a given product's lifecycle, starting with the investigational phase. Both FDA and EMA have well-defined processes for dispute resolution between regulators and sponsors. In most other parts of the world, disputes among regulators and sponsors are addressed in less publicly described processes on a case-by-case basis.

Regulatory Crises During the Investigational Phase of Development

Most issues that arise during clinical trials and at the time of marketing approval application submission can be discussed in meetings with regulators. There are well-defined processes for meeting with FDA reviewers;[9] similar processes are in place for meetings with EMA reviewers. FDA meetings provide a sponsor with an opportunity to discuss with the reviewers any anticipated, potential or unknown risks of a development plan and to troubleshoot issues before they happen. Meetings with regulators should incorporate the following rules:

1. Provide specific questions supported by sufficient background information.
2. Provide potential answers to your questions and ask for concurrence; address any objections.
3. Ask questions relevant to the given product under discussion's stage of development.
4. Encourage scientific discussion, counter arguments and defend proposed rationale.
5. Involve individuals with direct roles in discussion with regulators.

Dispute Resolution Process

Postmarketing disputes with regulators usually lead to legal proceedings resulting in extensive costs, time and public relations situations. However, several regulatory processes are available whereby a sponsor can address disputes with FDA.[10–12] Ideally, a sponsor should attempt to address disputes using FDA's internal processes before taking legal action. Following FDA's ombudsman processes does not close the legal resource; however, the reverse is not true. When resolving disputes with FDA, a company should remember the following rules for discussion:[13]

1. Regulatory history of a given product is cumulative—FDA considers all information and documents submitted to it throughout the life of a project. FDA does not like to ignore information previously submitted directly by the sponsor or from other public sources unless the sponsor presents a justification deemed acceptable by agency reviewers.
2. All data available for a given product is relevant to FDA's scientific review—All data submitted to FDA for a given product by a manufacturer plays a role in the agency's final decision about that product. FDA reviews applications using a scientific rationale, where all available information is considered while making a decision.

3. All human experience data for a given product should be used in FDA applications—Human experience with a given product from non-US regions or published literature could provide an important rationale to support the product's safety and efficacy claims and should be used by the sponsor. Such data can be collected in a retrospective analysis of patient experience in ex-US or non-IND and non-IDE clinical trials.
4. All commitments made to FDA during previous discussions should be kept—FDA expects sponsors to keep all promises made. Regulatory often has been called a "moving target," where policies, review guidelines, criteria for review, etc., change over time as new products are reviewed by FDA.
5. Periodic discussions with FDA are a must for all programs—The dispute discussion should not be the only time a sponsor talks to FDA. FDA meetings are, perhaps, among the most valuable tools available to a manufacturer to increase the likelihood of securing a product's approval. These meetings can be used to address issues such as trial design, procedures, study parameters, statistical methods for data analysis and pharmacovigilance plans to avoid a dispute in the first place. Regulatory strategy always should be confirmed directly with the agency before or early in implementation.
6. Conflict resolution should be systematic—Try to work with the reviewers to address their concerns about data validity by providing additional information before taking more aggressive action. If the data from a given application are challenged based on scientific rationale, there are only two ways to resolve it: 1) initiating a scientific peer-to-peer discussion between your subject matter experts and FDA reviewers to understand their concerns and provide explanation and 2) identifying the key missing data and filling those gaps with newly generated data in further clinical trials or using other methods discussed above.
7. FDA is neutral about your product—FDA is mandated to protect US patients and consumers and make sure all products available to patients have adequate justification for safe and effective use. FDA reviews are neutral with regard to a product's commercial success or failure. So, when FDA reviewers have comments about a product, manufacturers are served better by listening and trying to resolve scientific issues.

Organizational Crises

Unlike the previous two categories of crisis management, where companies have to deal with issues partially under their control, organizational crises are due almost entirely to deficiencies in the company's management, quality processes and resources. These crises can erode a company's credibility with regulators and investors and damage its public image. Most of these events become crises due to the failure of a company's internal processes and are avoidable.

Negative Findings from FDA audits

FDA audits are detailed reviews of an organization's quality systems and are unavoidable events for all medical product companies. A successful FDA audit is considered highly beneficial for an organization's credibility and public image.[14] Most FDA audits are announced in advance to give the organization a brief time to prepare; the audits are based on FDA's inspection manual available on the agency's website. FDA auditors make frequent public presentations and speeches highlighting the key elements of an audit. With all the available resources and guidance, it is inexcusable for an organization to be ill-prepared for an FDA audit, or even worse, to be noncompliant. An example of what negative FDA findings and noncompliance can do to an organization is the Ranbaxy Pharmaceuticals' experience. Ranbaxy was found to have conducted several repeated acts of fraud, misrepresentation and illegal activities.[15] Most of these findings were based on deliberate acts of misconduct, leading to a fine of more than $500 million from FDA; in addition, several similar legal proceedings occurred in other countries, and the company lost revenue due to public backlash to its products overall.

Clinical Trial Risks

As is the case with audits, numerous resources are available to help understand, plan, avoid and troubleshoot clinical trial risk management. Clinical trials can run over budget rapidly and exceed timelines through mismanagement. Common issues with clinical trials' management include failure to recruit subjects, compliance issues with clinical sites, mishandling of investigational products and loss of biological samples due to improper shipping and storage. All these issues can be planned and addressed by implementing a clinical trial risk management plan, which should include crisis identification, timely review and appropriate corrective and preventive actions.

Off-label Use and Whistle Blowers

Illegal marketing of off-label uses of medical products is a punishable offence. Several companies recently have been fined by FDA for such marketing practices.[16–18] Most were fined because they promoted off-label uses of their products intentionally. Many of these cases were brought to FDA's attention by whistle-blowers within the companies. There are formal legal processes for a sponsor to promote additional uses of its products, such as through implementation of a process to train sales staff. Such processes can help avoid this crisis while still allowing free speech and scientific discussion.

Medical Product Industry Needs Specific Crisis Management

In comparison to other areas of management, crisis management is a relatively new field. Crisis management incorporates elements of risk management, including such proactive activities as forecasting potential crises and planning how to deal with them. Since many crisis situations cannot be anticipated, any crisis management plan should be generic. Companies should develop policies for addressing common themes across all kinds of crises. In general, crisis management should be based on the following core principles:

1. Create a crisis management policy—A company should create broad principles or practices to be used in all events that meet the definition of a crisis. The policy should define the role of senior management, designate responsibilities and establish timelines for addressing issues. A crisis profile that includes expected, potential and less-likely crisis events is helpful in training personnel; it can be beneficial to learn from experiences at similar organizations.
2. Define the crisis management team—This core team should consist of personnel from different departments in a company based on the identification of all possible and probable crises. Such a plan also should allow for unforeseen situations and unexpected crises. The plan should include roles and responsibilities of the individuals involved in crisis preparation and mitigation.
3. Communication—Effective communication is vital in any crisis situation. Any crisis plan should have an efficient and detailed communication strategy. Companies should ensure an adequate infrastructure is in place to support rapid communication with both internal and external stakeholders in times of crisis.
4. Training—Training is an important part of crisis management. This ensures organizational preparedness for facing the crisis and usually is carried out in the form of mock drills. Many companies have regular fire drills, which, while usually a bother, form part of a wider crisis management plan.
5. Surveillance—Establish processes and practices for constant surveillance of internal and external activities and monitoring the regulatory environment, news and industry trends to forecast potential events and plan contingencies.

Conclusions

Crises are multi-dimensional events that require a similarly multi-dimensional approach for mitigation. Although most specific events are hard to predict, one can learn from industry trends and predict potential risk. Crisis management for the medical product industry builds on the general principles of crisis management accepted across all industries and can be customized to the special conditions that exist within the industry.

References

1. Venette S J. (2003). Risk communication in a High Reliability Organization: APHIS PPQ's inclusion of risk in decision making. Ann Arbor, MI: UMI Proquest Information and Learning.
2. FDA Guidance, *ICH E2E, Pharmacovigilance Planning* (April 2005).
3. "The European Union regulatory network incident management plan for medicines for human use," EMA/351583/2012.
4. Op cit 2
5. Op cit 3,
6. "The Cost Of Creating A New Drug Now $5 Billion, Pushing Big Pharma To Change." *Forbes*, 12 August 2013. http://www.forbes.com/sites/matthewherper/2013/08/11/how-the-staggering-cost-of-inventing-new-drugs-is-shaping-the-future-of-medicine/. Accessed 21 August 2013.
7. Scannell JW, Blanckley A, Bolden H and Warrington B. "Diagnosing the decline in pharmaceutical R&D deficiency," (2012). *Nat Rev Drug Discover*. 11:191-200.
8. "Culture as a culprit of pharma R&D crisis." *Forbes*, 19 April 2012. http://www.forbes.com/sites/brucebooth/2012/04/19/culture-as-a-culprit-of-the-pharma-rd-crisis/. Accessed 21 August 2013.
9. Kumar M. "Meeting With FDA Can Increase the Probability of Product Approval." *Regulatory Focus*, October 2010, pp. 22-27.
10. Kumar M. "Resolving Scientific Disputes with FDA: Regulatory Processes and Practical Tips." *Regulatory Focus*. March 2011, p. 22-25.
11. FDA Guidance: Formal Dispute Resolution Appeals Above the Division Level. http://www.fda.gov/downloads/Drugs/GuidanceComplianceRegulatoryInformation/Guidances/UCM079743.pdf. Accessed 21 August 2013.
12. FDA-CDRH guidance: Resolution of Difference of Opinion. http://www.fda.gov/AboutFDA/CentersOffices/OfficeofMedicalProductsandTobacco/CDRH/CDRHOmbudsman/ucm113713.htm. Accessed 21 August 2013.
13. FDA Not Fully at Fault, Manufacturer Made Mistakes too. http://www.medicaldevicesummit.com/Main/Blogs/72.aspx. Accessed 21 August 2013.
14. Kumar M, Kazempour, K, and Breisch S. "An FDA Audit is good for you", Regulatory Focus, October 2011, p. 8-11.
15. Dirty Medicine: The Ranbaxy Story. Fortune 13 May 2013. http://features.blogs.fortune.cnn.com/2013/05/15/ranbaxy-fraud-lipitor/. Accessed 21 August 2013.
16. Evans D. "Pfizer Broke the Law by Promoting Drugs for Unapproved Uses. Bloomberg website. http://www.bloomberg.com/apps/news?pid=newsarchive&sid=a4yV1nYxCGoA. Accessed 21 August 2013.
17. "Fines unlikely to end off-label drug marketing." NBC news website. http://www.nbcnews.com/id/32694936/ns/business-us_business/t/fines-unlikely-end-off-label-drug-marketing/. Accessed 21 August 2013.
18. Rubin R. "Pfizer fined $2.3 billion for illegal marketing in off-label drug case." USA Today website. http://usatoday30.usatoday.com/money/industries/health/2009-09-02-pfizer-fine_N.htm. Accessed 21 August 2013.

Chapter 3

Health Technology Assessment

By Robert G. Peterson, MD, PhD, MPH and Chander Sehgal, MD, MBA

OBJECTIVES

- ❑ Review the basic principles underlying Health Technology Assessment (HTA) in three representative countries where reimbursement decisions by public payers or decision makers are closely tied to HTA
- ❑ Understand the differences between a regulatory assessment and an HTA
- ❑ Understand the opportunities for HTA and regulatory assessment requirements to converge to improve efficiencies

Introduction

Health Technology Assessment (HTA) is intended to translate research-derived knowledge into both clinical and economic terms that are relevant and understandable to healthcare decision makers. Although HTA as a discipline is not new, its acceptance as a mainstream mechanism in healthcare decision making has steadily increased across the globe over the last decade. Moreover, while the use of HTA in reimbursement decisions for medicines is at a relatively mature stage, there is an increasing interest in the application of HTA for decision making in other health technologies such as medical and surgical devices, along with medical and surgical procedures.

HTA was first introduced as a concept decades ago and has been adopted by many jurisdictions with publicly funded or subsidized healthcare. The reported high cost of drug development has seemingly led to a demand for price premiums that has put enormous pressure on the finite and shrinking healthcare budgets across most jurisdictions. Jurisdictions are looking to move toward the concept of purchasing health outcomes rather than simply purchasing medicines.

In the recent past, access to medicines was synonymous with regulatory, or market, authorization. Today, this is no longer the case. In part, this is because the cost of drug development has resulted in price increases that often place new drugs beyond the means of self-pay, creating a similar pressure for public and private drug payment programs to demand value for price. This has occurred *pari passu* with global acceptance of evidence-based medical practice and has created a threshold for a new paradigm of "value-based medicine," i.e., relying on evidence not only for drug outcome, but also for the highest affordable health outcome.

There are numerous mature HTA programs both for medicinal and non-medicinal treatment options. The general characteristics of a successful HTA program are discussed in this chapter, with a focus on pharmaceuticals. Brief summaries are provided of national HTA programs in three jurisdictions with longstanding publicly funded healthcare: the UK, Australia and Canada. Requirements for these three HTA programs and the mechanisms for their application vary. These summaries will provide an understanding of the potential scope of an HTA program.

Regulatory requirements, the "first hurdle" for success in a drug development program, vary somewhat internationally, but have achieved greater harmonization and consequent predictability than found in HTA programs. Rigorous standards are defined by regulatory agencies for efficacy and manufacturing (quality) standards. Arguably, regulatory standards for safety are rigorous, but less so than for efficacy and quality in that clinical trials are typically designed to support an unbiased comparison of a pre-declared clinical outcome between the new drug and a "clean" comparator (often a placebo to limit confounding);

outcomes are powered to provide reliable estimates of differences in efficacy under the conditions of the clinical trial. Safety is often a secondary outcome, and when pre-declared as such, represents discrete measures of safety, rather than "safety" in general. Hence, by design, clinical trials provide regulators with strong evidence in support of the new drug's therapeutic claim, at least within the parameters of the clinical trials, provides some evidence of safety as observed during the trials and requires high intrinsic validity. Often, postmarketing regulatory requirements address the safety shortcomings of those clinical trials. It typically has not been the case that an application for market authorization be based on a direct head-to-head comparison with another marketed product; however, there are increasing instances where a new product claim includes a "safer than…" statement that relies on such comparisons. Those clinical trials with active comparator arms supporting regulatory authorization have an evidence base that further supports an HTA application.

Health technology assessors look at the "same" clinical trials as regulators and have similar requirements for rigorous internal validity in proof-of-concept for a new drug's therapeutic claim. However, the true value of these clinical trials to the health technology assessor is not just the statistically inferred difference between the treatment arms, but rather, the reliability of the clinical trial to predict the future benefits and harms of the new treatment across the patient horizon, i.e., how well the clinical trials can be extrapolated to all patients who will subsequently receive the new drug outside the defined parameters of the clinical trials. Often, the high intrinsic validity of a clinical trial is determined by strict inclusion and exclusion criteria and by measuring outcomes using methods available to clinical researchers, but not generally used in the practice of medicine. Such trials, while rigorous, have been criticized as measuring irrelevant outcomes in patient populations not typically found in the routine practice of medicine. There are increasing examples of the regulatory requirements for relevance of measured outcomes and the generalizability of clinical trials across the patient horizon.[1] HTA is focused on external validity as the evidence from clinical trials is used as inputs to pharmacoeconomic models that estimate proof-of-value of a new medicine. Furthermore, HTA absolutely requires evidence comparing the clinical outcomes between therapeutic options and often faces challenges in merging clinical trials without direct head-to-head active comparisons to create the necessary inputs to pharmacoeconomic models. Basically, decision makers who rely on recommendations from an HTA report seek evidence of both clinical- and cost-effectiveness that supports the comparative benefits and harms of the new product in relation to those currently subsidized by the decision maker. Cost-effectiveness for the purpose of this discussion is the ratio of monetary cost of the treatment divided by a value known as the quality-adjusted life-year (QALY), which is the arithmetic product of life expectancy and a measure of the quality of the remaining life-years.[2-4] The National Institute for Health and Care Excellence (NICE) defines the QALY as a "measure of a person's length of life weighted by a valuation of their health-related quality of life."[5]

Absent clinical trials with active comparator arms, for the HTA to have a "clean bottom line," independent clinical trials (vs. placebo) for appropriate comparator drugs (and potentially non-drug therapeutic options) need to be designed with similar inclusion/exclusion criteria, identically defined clinical outcomes and, ideally, head-to-head comparisons within the same trials. Deprived of such trials (more common than not), methods employing meta-analysis are relied on to estimate such comparisons. Newer methods employ Bayesian as well as frequentist statistical methods in mixed treatment comparisons[6] where drugs can be compared using randomized clinical trials of individual drugs vs. placebo, direct head-to-head comparisons and even evidence from observational studies. In similar clinical trials, these methods can provide valuable evidence for the health technology assessor as inputs to pharmacoeconomic models. All too often, however, restrictive parameters of clinical trials that create high intrinsic validity limit the ability of the meta-analysis to meet standards for reliable systematic reviews.

Examples of three HTA programs are provided to demonstrate the potential scope of HTA at the jurisdictional level.

England

NICE is a special health authority identified as an "arms length body" that is funded by the UK Department of Health. It was established in 1999 to "reduce variation in the availability and quality of NHS treatments and care." NICE meets this obligation by producing public health guidance reports on medicines and other health treatment options. These reports are directed to the National Health Service (NHS) in England, but are widely read and acknowledged by international health sectors.[7] The National Health Service requires NICE to produce reports based on comparisons of therapeutic options, unique or "breakthrough" treatments and to make recommendations that are based on a threshold pharmacoeconomic model that estimates incremental costs per QALY. NICE recommends the adoption of a new treatment in terms that suggest good economic value for payment by the public payer, uncertain value or less than good value. Independent expert committees comprised of clinicians, pharmacists, patients and health economists create guidance documents that are subsequently reviewed by the NICE Guidance Executive. The NICE Citizens Council advises on the public perspective for social and moral issues arising from NICE guidance reports.

NICE is asked to appraise "significant new drugs" and devices for their clinical benefits and harms and their cost effectiveness. Similar appraisals are conducted locally within NHS, but the intent of the NICE guidance is to create a more-national approach to appropriate utilization of treatment options. Once published, the NICE guidance is expected to supersede local advice and practice, although there is not a formal mandate that limits funding of alternative treatments.

The NICE pharmacoeconomic model is based on a league table approach and has been criticized for not having sufficient latitude to incorporate societal (or ethical) values in its final determination of value.[8] Proponents argue that the league table approach (start expending available resources to meet the lowest cost/QALY options and proceed to higher cost/QALY options until financial resources are exhausted) is an excellent model for economic value, and other factors such as those that society may place on vulnerable populations with unmet medical needs should be applied only after the cost/QALY has been estimated within the economic model.

An alternative economic approach has been linked to value-based pricing, where a higher price could be contemplated for a product that targets a well-defined, at risk or "in need" population, but only a substantially lower price would be accepted if the target population is less defined, i.e., larger.[9] The NHS has indicated that it will incorporate value-based pricing into its decision making by the end of 2013:

> "Under the new system of value-based pricing, the Government would apply weightings to the benefits provided by new branded medicines, which would imply a range of price thresholds reflecting the maximum they are prepared to pay for medicines. These thresholds or maximum prices would be adjusted to reflect a broader range of relevant factors that are not fully taken into account by the current system of using Quality Adjusted Life Years (QALYs) by NICE so they could be used to calculate the full value of a new product.
>
> The Government proposes that the price threshold structure is determined as follows:
>
> 1. There would be a basic threshold, reflecting the benefits displaced elsewhere in the NHS when funds are allocated to new medicines
> 2. There would be higher thresholds for medicines that tackle diseases where there is a greater "burden of illness": the more the medicine is focused on diseases with unmet need or which are particularly severe, the higher the threshold
> 3. There would be higher thresholds for medicines that can demonstrate greater therapeutic innovation and improvements compared with other products
> 4. There would be higher thresholds for medicines that can demonstrate wider societal benefits."[10]

Australia

The Pharmaceutical Benefits Scheme (PBS) is an Australian government initiative that provides affordable access for all residents to effective and cost-effective medicines.[11] This public drug payment plan relies on HTA reports produced by external contractors. Recommendations, based on those reports, are made by an independent expert advisory committee known as the Pharmaceutical Benefits Advisory Committee (PBAC). PBAC advises the Australian federal minister of health, who decides whether a new drug product will be added to PBS.

PBAC meets four times per year to review HTA reports that include economic evaluations based on a price submitted by the manufacturer when applying for a PBS listing (public subsidy) recommendation. The pharmacoeconomic analysis relies on the submitted price and input from assessments of the comparative benefits and harms of the new product in relation to other products that are paid for by PBS. When a cost-effectiveness comparison is unfavorable, the PBAC chair may communicate this to the product manufacturer who may indicate a willingness to negotiate a price (and/or interpretation of the pharmacoeconomic analysis) in order to obtain a favorable recommendation.

The federal health minister reviews PBAC recommendations. In addition, if a drug is expected to incur expenditure of more than $5 million per year, it is reviewed by the Commonwealth Department of Finance and Administration. If a drug is expected to incur expenditure of more than $10 million per year, it is reviewed by the Australian federal cabinet.

According to the Australian Department of Health and Aging website, PBAC takes the following into account when reviewing submissions:

1. The conditions for which the Therapeutic Goods Administration has approved the drug for use in Australia—PBAC only recommends the listing of a medicine for use in a condition that is in accordance with the Australian Register of Therapeutic Goods, i.e., the Australian product label.
2. The conditions in which use has been demonstrated to be effective and safe compared to other therapies.
3. The costs involved—PBAC is required to consider that the budget spent in subsidizing medicines by PBS represents cost-effective expenditure of taxpayers' funds.
4. A range of other factors and health benefits—these factors may include costs of hospitalization for adverse events and/or other medical or surgical treatments that may be incurred, as well as measures of quality of life.
5. In making its recommendations, PBAC also may recommend maximum quantities and restrictions that should be considered for the medicine to be subsidized by PBS.

PBAC has guidance documents stipulating that an applicant must submit evidence to support a review of comparative effectiveness and cost relative to alternative treatments (which may be non-pharmacologic).[12] Any drug submitted for a listing recommendation that is substantially more costly than alternatives must justify the price with evidence developed in the population for which the subsidy is being requested. Subsequent to the submission, PBAC uses external contractors to evaluate the product manufacturer's submission. This evaluation is then further subjected to appraisal by subcommittees to verify and comment on the external report. These subcommittees may be comprised of representatives from a number of health research disciplines, including epidemiologists, health economists, statistical analysts and others. Both the external report and the subcommittee evaluation are provided to the manufacturer for comment prior to the PBAC meeting, and manufacturers' comments are considered along with the reports.

A recent update on PBAC activities in 2005–10 reported that the initial recommendations on major submissions were successful from 49% (2008) to 56% (2010) of the time.[13] Factors that PBAC identifies as relevant to recommendations are comparative cost-effectiveness, comparative health gain, financial implications for PBS and financial implications for government health budgets. While cost/QALY is considered in the cost-effectiveness models, no fixed threshold has been declared for a positive recommendation. Thus, PBAC has the opportunity to consider the severity of the condition, available alternative treatments (or lack thereof), equity and what has been referred to as a "Rule of Rescue." This rule relates to life-threatening conditions where evidence may not be sufficiently developed to support the cost, but there may be a willingness to pay on the part of government.

Canada

Unlike NHS in England or PBS in Australia, Canada does not have a national pharmaceutical strategy with a common purchaser of medicines. Rather, Canada has brought together nine of the ten provinces, their territories and six targeted federal drug plans into the Common Drug Review (CDR) program that provides advice to participating drug plans to guide their decisions on listing a new medicine for payment on their respective public drug plans. The CDR was founded in 2002 and started accepting submissions in 2003. Recommendations are nonbinding, and the participating drug plans base their decisions on additional factors such as budget impact as well as local political and social values. HTA is completed by the Canadian Agency for Drugs and Technologies in Health (CADTH), and recommendations are provided to provinces and other interested parties through the published recommendations of the independent Canadian Drug Expert Committee (CDEC, formally CEDAC). CDEC is comprised of physicians (specialists and general practitioners) and pharmacists. In addition, there are two full voting public members. External clinical experts and health economists are consulted as needed. Recommendations and reasons for the recommendations are shared in draft form with provinces and the applicant manufacturer prior to publication. During this "embargoed period," the manufacturer may provide reasons for a reconsideration of the recommendation that would go back to CDEC. Once final, the recommendations and their reasons are publicly available on the CADTH website.

In Canada, manufacturers use published guidance documents to apply for a CDEC recommendation. These applications are similar in content to those described for the Australian procedure. In addition to providing published and unpublished clinical trial results, the manufacturers must submit pharmacoeconomic models that support the proposed (typically confidential) price. When head-to-head trials are not submitted, the manufacturer will rely on indirect comparisons to support its product's cost-effectiveness on the Canadian market. When noninferiority trials are relied on for head-to-head comparison, the economic analysis often will consist of a cost minimization analysis against comparator products already listed by one or more Canadian provincial public drug plans.

Once an application has been received by CADTH, a public notice invites patient organizations to file a submission using a standard template for CDEC to consider as part of its deliberations. Typically, several patient groups may file submissions, which the CDEC public members summarize. The public members typically present the patient input submissions during the CDEC meeting prior to clinical or economic reports so the committee may have patient group-identified unmet needs "on the table" during its full consideration of the product application.

Alternatively, participating drug plans may initiate a request for advice to CDEC, asking for advice on specific questions with regard to a previous recommendation. A request for advice may result in either a changed recommendation or a letter of advice from the CDEC chair to the participating drug plans.

In reviewing submissions to CDR, CADTH will formalize a QUORUM flowchart providing reasons why some clinical trials may or may not be included in their HTA report. The draft HTA report (called a CDR Clinical and Pharmacoeconomic Review Report) from CADTH is shared with the applicant prior to formal consideration at a CDEC meeting. Manufacturers' responses to this draft report are limited to 10 pages, but their comments and the response by CADTH reviewers are provided to CDEC members in advance of their meetings. CDEC meets 10 times per year. No formal Cost/QALY threshold has been published by CADTH; rather recommendations from

Table 3-1. Acceptable CADTH Formats

Recommendation Options	Description and Considerations
List	• A drug* demonstrates comparable or added clinical benefit and acceptable cost/cost-effectiveness relative to one or more appropriate comparators.†
List With Clinical Criteria and/or Conditions	Examples include: • A drug* demonstrates comparable or added clinical benefit and acceptable cost/cost-effectiveness relative to one or more appropriate comparators in a subgroup of patients within the approved indication. In such cases the subgroup is specified through "clinical criteria." • A drug* demonstrates added clinical benefit, but the cost/cost-effectiveness relative to one or more appropriate comparators† is unacceptable. In such cases, a "condition" may include a reduced price. • A drug* demonstrates comparable clinical benefit and acceptable cost/cost-effectiveness relative to one or more appropriate comparators.† In such cases, a "condition" may include that the drug* be listed in a similar manner to one or more appropriate comparators. Examples of clinical criteria include, but are not limited to: • characteristics that identify a patient subgroup (e.g., comorbidity status, inadequate response or intolerance to appropriate comparator[s]) • characteristics of the care setting (e.g., prescribed by or under the care of an experienced clinical team) • starting and stopping rules (e.g., response to treatment). Examples of conditions include, but are not limited to:†† • pricing considerations • reimbursement limits (e.g., number of doses supported by clinical and cost-effectiveness evidence) • formulary listing status of one or more appropriate comparators (e.g., a drug plan that already lists an appropriate comparator may consider listing the drug under review with the same criteria) **Note:** The use of "and/or" in the "List with clinical criteria **and/or** conditions" allows for three subcategories of this listing category: • clinical criteria and conditions • clinical criteria only • conditions only
Do not List at the Submitted Price	An example of a scenario that typically fits this listing category includes: A drug* demonstrates comparable clinical benefit, but the cost/cost-effectiveness relative to one or more appropriate comparators† is unacceptable. **Note:** The "Of Note" section in the recommendation may provide additional context around price, comparator(s), patient subgroups to whom the drug might be restricted and other relevant considerations.
Do not List	• A drug* does not demonstrate comparable clinical benefit relative to one or more appropriate comparators.†

**Refers to a drug under review.*

†An appropriate comparator is typically a drug listed by one or more CDR participating drug plans for the indication under review.

††Although not listed as conditions, evidence gaps and the need for evidence development may be highlighted in the the CDEC Recommendation document as needed.

CDEC follow a publically vetted format and may be one of those in **Table 3-1**.

A recent report of the outcomes of CDEC recommendations issued from 2011–12 has identified the success rate for a Listing or a Listing with Conditions or Requirements to be in the range of 50–58%.[14]

General Discussion Regarding HTA Requirements

A substantial gap exists between regulatory decisions to provide market authorization for new medicines and recommendations from HTA agencies regarding payments for the same medicines. This can be attributed in part to the added analysis during HTA that takes economic factors into account. Just as there are differences between regulatory authorities in market authorization decisions, there are differences in HTA recommendations.

Typically, all regulators and all HTA organizations consider the "same" clinical trial evidence. Reasons for variance in outcomes between regulators have been attributed to variance in the practice of medicine in different jurisdictions. Variance in HTA recommendations may be linked to similar factors but, in addition, may reflect differences in the acceptance of comparators used in pharmacoeconomic models, varying pricing and reliance on traditional explicit or implicit thresholds for cost-effectiveness. NICE has stated a cost/QALY threshold of £30,000/QALY, but often refers to this as a typical threshold for decision making. Other HTA organizations such as Canada and Australia do not stipulate a threshold for recommendation purposes. In general, a cost/QALY of $50,000/QALY is accepted as a threshold, below which treatments are generally considered good value. Therefore, it is not surprising that manufacturers seek to provide pharmacoeconomic models that estimate cost/QALY below $50,000 (£30,000). Often, such pharmacoeconomic models are sensitive to input parameters that are subject to varying interpretation. For example, a time horizon of 50 years in a model for a medicine that will be used largely in elderly patients, when subjected to sensitivity analysis using a shorter time horizon, may yield substantially increased cost/QALY estimates.

The greatest challenge in HTA has been the lack of high quality comparative evidence to support a proof-of-value claim. Clinical trials rarely incorporate active comparators in superiority designs. Noninferiority trial designs often have been criticized by regulators for lack of assay sensitivity.[15] Similar concerns exist within HTA; however, there also may be stricter requirements for noninferiority margins expressed in HTA reviews.[16] For example, a noninferiority margin of greater than 10% may not be accepted by HTA where there is an unwillingness to "give away" more than one in 10 patient responses to the old, less expensive drug. In addition, support for any price increment that is based on noninferiority data is significantly challenged by the question: "Why pay more for a drug that is shown to be "almost as good as" its comparator?"

In the past, indirect comparisons of new drug versus existing drug(s) have relied on naïve assumptions across trials of comparable placebo populations and, therefore, differences in drug versus placebo from individual trials are submitted. This often ignores variance in "placebo effect" across trial populations as well as substantial variances that may be present across trials with respect to inclusion and exclusion criteria and definition of outcomes that are reported.

More recently, newer methods utilizing Mixed Treatment Comparisons (MTC) in network meta-analysis have provided more sophisticated estimates of drug comparisons.[17] To be successful, the estimates of comparative benefits of the drugs studied must be based on strict rules regarding heterogeneity of the trial designs, populations studied, similar outcome measures (and exact definitions of them), thus MTC can be limited by inadequate data inputs.

The advantage of performing an MTC of published trials over a noninferiority designed trial itself is debatable. In the case of a noninferiority design, equivalence is measured by noninferiority margin (statistically, Drug A is almost as good as Drug B) and can lead to a value estimate largely being based on pricing. The manufacturer of the new drug positions its product as the same price or less expensive than a known price comparator, based on a claim of equivalence in clinical benefit. While this can be a successful strategy, it is subject to acceptance of the comparator drug and its quoted price. Not infrequently, less expensive comparators may be identified during HTA, and acceptance of the declared noninferiority margin may be disputed.

MTC offers the possible outcome of a superior product being identified. By virtue of a claim of superior benefit (or safety), a pharmacoeconomic model may be constructed that supports a price premium or a preferential listing decision between comparators.

Often, the manufacturer acknowledges that high quality comparative data may not exist to support a premium price structure for a new product. In these circumstances, application for a product listing (or subsidy) for the price may be supported by a request to provide a listing recommendation as a second- or third-line treatment where less expensive options have not provided benefit. This strategy attempts to remove comparators from consideration since they will have been "declared ineffective" in the population to be treated, and at times suggests reimbursement for patient subpopulations that are either outside the label approved by regulators or for whom clinical data are not available to support the clinical benefit claims in the proposed subpopulations. A cost-effectiveness argument must still be provided, but this strategy introduces the concept of "unmet need" to support the premium price. While this is sometimes the basis for a Listing with Criteria and/or Conditions recommendation in Canada, it typically is reserved for serious or life-threatening outcomes.

Unfortunately, data to support the second- or third-line treatment often are not provided in the application. For this application strategy to be successful, the manufacturer must present data from clinical trials in patients where a first- and/or second-line, less-costly treatment, has been tried and failed to provide benefit. Absent this, the HTA deals with significant uncertainties and relies on a "leap of faith" that the new treatment will not simply be a further futile expense that does not lead to the desired health outcome.

Possible Convergence in Regulatory and HTA Requirements

A general harmonization of regulatory requirements for new drug applications has resulted in improved predictability and uniformity in regulatory decisions. No similar global guidance is available for HTA applications, although there are numerous initiatives to seek this end.[18,19]

Until HTA requirements become unified, challenges remain in pursuing harmonization between regulators and HTA organizations.

One of the most compelling areas for the convergence of HTA and regulatory requirements is the external validity of clinical trials. While internal validity drives clinical trial design in proof-of-concept of benefit, the trial's external validity supports proof-of-value across the greater population to be treated. This has been referred to as the benefit-to-harm profile across the patient horizon.[20] While this concept is important to both the regulator and the payer, all too often the benefit-to-harm profile is developed through postmarketing commitments (more often than not linked to postmarket risk mitigation strategies, not demonstration of benefit in broader populations). The regulator will depend on health providers' decisions on "value in prescribing" a new drug and gaining "experience" with the new drug outside the clinical trial environment. When this is reduced to passive reporting of adverse events in largely uncontrolled populations, the challenge in identifying the ongoing benefit-to-harm of a new drug is evident.

HTA is commissioned to identify proof-of-value prior to decisions on health expenditure for the product. As such, unless the clinical trials leading to market authorization decisions have high external validity, i.e., are strongly predictive of benefits and harms across the patient horizon, the HTA recommendation often will be more restrictive than a general subsidy or listing that might be indicated by the product label. Hence, several large randomized controlled trials (RCTs) that measure direct clinical benefits and harms will have greater convergence between regulatory and HTA evidence requirements than will several small, short trials that rely on surrogate endpoints for demonstrating a statistically significant demonstration of efficacy.[21]

A recent publication from the European Medicines Agency (EMA) summarizing reasons for non-approval of new medicines is revealing in terms of that regulator's evidence requirements for external validity.[22] Non-approval of drug registration applications was impacted both by clinical outcome and clinical relevance. Moreover, careful identification of target population during drug development was an important factor in clinical relevance. While not addressing the further economic considerations that HTA would examine, the EMA analysis of success in new drug applications has identified evidence requirements common to both HTA and regulatory agencies regarding clinical relevance.

Currently, convergence of evidence requirements is not led by economic considerations in most countries where HTA and regulatory functions are mandated independently. However, clinical data to support the clear definition of the target population, the ability of the clinical trials to predict benefit and harm over the patient horizon and, therefore, requirements for external validity of trials submitted in support of marketing authorization applications for, along with regulatory authorities' expectations that superiority trials versus placebo will be accompanied by active comparator studies are all areas where HTA and regulatory assessments can overlap.

Summary

HTA is presented from the perspective of three jurisdictions that have mature, longstanding national programs. Each of these jurisdictions has a strong component of publicly funded drug subsidy or full payment programs. Sustainability of publicly funded healthcare is a challenge as escalating costs in many areas of public funding (infrastructure, education and job creation, among others) compete with the rapidly inflating costs of new medicines. The expiration of patent protection for many longstanding profit drivers for the pharmaceutical industry may be good news for public drug plans; however, serious unmet therapeutic needs persist, which are dependent on innovation. The fact that public drug plan budgets are challenged by expensive new medicines can be regarded as a threat to innovation; however, the development of cost-effective new medicines can clearly mitigate such uncertainties. Healthcare decision makers must choose wisely in expenditures but are consistently seeking innovative therapeutic options for unmet patient needs. **Table 3-2** summarizes the key HTA factors.

HTA, as defined and described in this chapter, is a definite reality that challenges the development of new medicines. Regulators embrace many of the evidence requirements of the HTA process. While traditionally, clinical trials with high internal validity against a placebo arm would suffice for market authorization, a product lifecycle approach to regulating new medicines addresses benefits and harms across the patient horizon. The greater the ability of a clinical trial to predict the behavior of the new medicine across the patient horizon, the greater assurance there may be of lifecycle events. Regulators would like this assurance prior to market approval; HTA agencies would like this prior to making recommendations regarding drug expenditures.

When evidence in support of a defined target population is accrued during new drug development and is supported by clinical outcomes that have high clinical relevance in comparison to other treatment options, the economic analyses become much more straightforward. A careful drug development program that culminates in clear proof-of-value will provide a level of predictability not only for regulatory applications, but for HTA as well. In the end, patients will benefit foremost from such success.

Table 3-2. Factors Key to HTA

1. External Validity of clinical trials
    a. The value of a clinical trial is how well it will predict the behavior (benefits and harms) across the Patient Horizon.
    b. Strict inclusion/exclusion criteria weaken the generalizability of the clinical trial and will limit scope of payment recommendations.
    c. Complex outcome measures, not easily assessed in the routine practice of medicine, will weaken the case for proof-of-value.
2. Comparative evidence
    a. Direct head-to-head comparisons with an active comparator
        i. Often placebo trials will be "discounted" in favor of the direct comparison trials.
        ii. Non-inferiority margins may be stricter for HTA acceptance.
    b. Indirect comparisons using network meta-analysis applies strict rules for homogeneity of included RCTs.
3. Pharmacoeconomic models
    a. Cost-effectiveness thresholds and inclusion of societal values vary across HTA agencies.
    b. Pharmacoeconomic models always subjected to sensitivity analysis.
        i. Assumptions in the models require justification
        ii. Factors that cause the model to be unstable are to be avoided.
4. Pricing and Budget impact
    a. Vary across HTA agencies.
        i. Not all HTA considers budget impact, just cost-effectiveness
        ii. Pricing may be complex with product listing agreements involving many factors such as ceiling expenditures, or value based pricing schemes.
5. Risk assessment of both benefits and harms
    a. Risk of a harm and health cost of the harm.
    b. Risk of not achieving the benefit and cost of health outcome.
        i. Large number needed to treat (NNT) may cause benefits to be discounted.

References

1. Upton GJG and Lee RD. "The Importance of the Patient Horizon in the Sequential Analysis of Binomial Clinical Trials." *Biometrika* 63:No. 2 (August 1976), pp. 335–342.
2. Drummond MF, Sculpher MJ, Torrance GW, O'Brien BJ, Stoddart GL. *Methods for the Economic Evaluation of Health Care Programmes.* Oxford: Oxford University Press, 2005. 3rd edition.
3. Weinstein MC, Torrance G, and McGuire A. "QALYs: The Basics." *International Society for Pharmacoeconomics and Outcomes Research* (ISPOR) Volume 12 (Supplement 1), 2009, pp. S5–S9.
4. Weinstein MC, Stason WB. "Foundations of cost-effectiveness analysis for health and medical practices." *N Engl J Med,* 1977;296:716–21.
5. NICE. Measuring effectiveness and cost effectiveness: the QALY. NICE website. www.nice.org.uk/newsroom/features/measuringeffectivenessandcosteffectivenesstheqaly.jsp. Accessed 4 March 2013.
6. Spiegelhalter DJ, Myles JP, Jones DR and AbramsKR. "Bayesian methods in health technology assessment: a review." *Health Technology Assessment,* 2000; Vol. 4: No. 3, pp. 1–136.
7. NICE. Who we are. NICE website. www.nice.org.uk/aboutnice/whoweare/who_we_are.jsp. Accessed 4 March 2013.
8. Adab P, Rouse AM, Mohammed MA and Marshall T. "Performance league tables: the NHS deserves better." *BMJ* 324:12 January 2002, pp. 95–98.
9. Claxton K. Value based pricing for the NHS. University of York website. www.york.ac.uk/media/che/documents/papers/presentations/VBP%20iHEA%20110711%20(16.45%20session%20final%20slides%20kc).pdf. Accessed 5 March 2013.
10. 20:20 Selection. VALUE BASED PRICING (VBP)—How the NHS will purchase drugs. 20:20 Selection website. www.2020selection.co.uk/value-based-pricing.asp. Accessed 4 March 2013.
11. Australian Department of Health and Ageing. About the PBS. Department of Health and Ageing website. www.health.gov.au/internet/main/publishing.nsf/Content/health-pbs-general-faq.htm-copy2. Accessed 4 March 2013.
12. Australian Department of Health and Ageing. PBS Publication, Guidelines for preparing submissions to the PBAC (December 2008). www.health.gov.au/internet/main/publishing.nsf/content/pbacguidelines-index. Accessed 5 March 2013.
13. Pretium Drug Tracker Trend Report. www.pretium.com.au/drug-trackerPDF/Drug%20Tracker%20-%2012%2001.pdf. Accessed 19 April 2013.
14. Wyatt Health Management. CDR has issued 5 more reviews. Wyatt Health website. www.wyatthealth.com/custom2/cdr-has-issued-5-more-reviews. Accessed 4 March 2013.
15. Temple R and Ellenberg SS. "Placebo-controlled trials and active-control trials in the evaluation of new treatments." *Ann Int Med,* 133:455-470, 2000.
16. Pocock S. "The pros and cons of noninferiority trials." *Fundamental & Clinical Pharmacology* 17:483–490, 2003.
17. Song F, Loke YK, Walsh T, Glenny AM, Eastwood AJ and Altman DG. "Methodological problems in the use of indirect comparisons for evaluating healthcare interventions: survey of published systematic reviews." *BMJ* 2009;338:b1147.
18. Health Technology Assessment international website. www.htai.org. Accessed 4 March 2013.
19. Centre for Innovation in Regulatory Science (CIRS). HTA Programme webpage. CIRS website. http://cirsci.org/hta-programme. Accessed 4 March 2013.
20. Op cit 1.
21. Op cit 16.
22. Putzeist M, Mantel-Teeuwisse AK, Aronsson B, et al, "Factors influencing non-approval of new drugs in Europe." *Nature Reviews Drug Discovery* 11:903-904;2012.

Suggested Further Reading

- Sutton AJ, Cooper NJ, Abrams KR, Lambert PC and Jones DR. "A Bayesian approach to evaluating net clinical benefit allowed for parameter uncertainty." *Journal of Clinical Epidemiology* 2005; 58: 26-40.
- Jansen JP, Crawford B, Bergman G and Stam W. "Bayesian Meta-Analysis of Multiple Treatment Comparisons: An Introduction to Mixed Treatment Comparisons." *International Society for Pharmacoeconomics and Outcomes Research* (ISPOR) Volume 11:Number 5, 2008, pp. 956-964.

Chapter 4

Clinical Trials: GCPs, Regulations and Compliance

By Jasmina Savic, MSc, RAC

OBJECTIVES

- ❑ Understand clinical trials and why they are conducted
- ❑ Understand principles of Good Clinical Practice (GCP)
- ❑ Become familiar with legislation and regulatory prerequisites for clinical trial commencement, conduct and finalization
- ❑ Understand pharmacovigilance and reporting requirements
- ❑ Understand regulatory compliance principles

LAWS, REGUILATIONS AND GUIDELINES COVERED IN THIS CHAPTER

ICH & OTHERS

- ❑ ICH, *Guideline for Good Clinical Practice E6(R1)*
- ❑ World Medical Association, Declaration of Helsinki
- ❑ ICH, *General Considerations for Clinical Trials E8*
- ❑ ICH, *Structure and Content of Clinical Study Reports E3*
- ❑ ICH, *Clinical Investigation of Medicinal Products in the Pediatric Population E11*
- ❑ ICH, *Ethnic factors in the Acceptability of Foreign Clinical Data E5(R1)*
- ❑ ICH, *Development Safety Update Report E2F*
- ❑ ICH, *Clinical Safety Data Management: Definitions and Standards for Expedited Reporting E2A*

EU

- ❑ Regulation (EC) No 1901/2006 of the European Parliament and of the Council od 12 December 2006 on medicinal products for paediatric use and amending Regulation (EEC) No 1768/92, Directive 2001/20/EC, Directive 2001/83/EC and Regulation (EC) No 726/2004
- ❑ Directive 2001/20/EC of the European Parliament and of the Council of 4 April 2001 on the approximation of the laws, regulations and administrative provisions of the Member States relating to the implementation of good clinical practice in the conduct of clinical trials on medicinal products for human use, Official Journal of the European Union, 2001

US

- ❑ *Food and Drug Administration Safety and Innovation Act (FDASIA)* of 2012.
- ❑ FDA, Code of Federal Regulations Title 21, Part 312, *Investigational New Drug Application*

CANADA

- *Food and Drug Regulations*, Division 5, *Drugs For Clinical Trials Involving Human Subjects*, Canada, October 2012

AUSTRALIA

- Australian Government, Department of Health and Ageing, Therapeutic Goods Administration, *Access to Unapproved therapeutic goods, Clinical Trials in Australia*, October 2004

Introduction

Drug development is a complex, lengthy process that consists of many phases. After the nonclinical development and the basic toxicological and pharmacological data required to evaluate a new drug's safety are available, human clinical trials may commence.

Although clinical trials are regulated nationally, there are generally accepted principles that are respected globally. Good Clinical Practice (GCP) comprises international ethical and scientific guidelines developed by the International Conference on Harmonisation (ICH) that describe standards for designing, conducting, recording and reporting trials involving the participation of human subjects.[1]

Compliance with GCP standards gives assurance that subjects' rights, safety and well-being are respected as stated in the *Declaration of Helsinki*.[2] Compliance with these principles also is a prerequisite for good clinical trial conduct and approval of the drug marketing authorization application.

Clinical Trials—Basics

A clinical trial or study is any investigation in human subjects intended to discover or verify the clinical, pharmacological or other pharmacodynamic effects of an investigational product(s); or identify any adverse reaction(s) to an investigational product(s); or study absorption, distribution, metabolism and excretion of an investigational product(s) with the object of ascertaining the product's safety and/or efficacy. The terms clinical trial and clinical study are synonymous.[3]

Before a trial is initiated, the product's foreseeable risks and inconveniences should be weighed against its anticipated benefit for the individual trial subject and society. A trial should be initiated and continued only if the anticipated benefits justify the risks.[4]

Each medicine needs to go through the same set of clinical trial phases to prove its safety, efficacy and quality. Phases of clinical trials are developed based on the stage of product development, endpoints of the trial, targeted population (healthy volunteers or patients) and number of subjects enrolled. Some trials have characteristics of two types of clinical trial phases and are therefore categorized as such (e.g., Phase 2/3).

Clinical trial phases are stratified as follows:[5]

- Phase 1—First-in-man trials are intended primarily to establish the drug's safety, tolerability and pharmacokinetic properties and establish a possible dose[6] using mainly placebo and/or double-blind techniques. These studies usually involve a few (20–80) healthy subjects. This phase also can include bioequivalence trials when comparing the Investigational Medicinal Product (IMP) with the reference product in healthy volunteers. In this case, a randomized, two-period, two-sequence single dose crossover design is recommended.[7] In certain cases, it might not be ethical to enroll healthy volunteers since the IMP's risk:benefit ratio is too high (because of the IMP's toxicity). This is usually the case with anti-cancer drugs.
- Phase 2—This phase usually involves several hundred (200–500) patients in whom efficacy is tested while a more definitive therapeutic dose also is determined. In Phase 2, randomized, placebo-controlled studies are the standard design. These trials also are referred to as "therapeutic exploratory" trials.

  There is also sub-categorization to Phase 2a and Phase 2b trials. Phase 2a trials usually are referred to as "pilot trials" and investigate dose-response, type of patient and frequency of dosing. Phase 2b trials usually are referred to as "pivotal trials" and serve to more prominently demonstrate a medicine's efficacy.
- Phase 3—These trials use primarily double-blind, randomized, placebo- and/or active-controlled techniques to test for efficacy, benefits and possible side effects. The larger population (1,000–5,000 patients) and the approach allow for more statistically significant and conclusive results. These trials also are referred to as "therapeutic confirmatory" trials.

  The results of these clinical trials (especially Phase 3) are vital in supporting applications for marketing authorization approval.

  Phase 3b or so-called "peri-approval" trials are trials performed after the application for a marketing authorization approval is submitted but before approval is granted and the product is placed on the market. These trials serve to complement earlier trials or may be used to collect different kinds of information (e.g., Quality of Life).
- Phase 4—These studies are performed after a license has been granted and only involve approved indications and conditions. Such postapproval trials are becoming increasingly important in allowing proper monitoring and detection of long-term effects of approved products, especially in terms of previously unknown or inadequately measured adverse reactions and potential risk factors. Phase 4 studies that

are observational can be also called "postmarketing surveillance" trials.

- Phase 5—Postmarketing surveillance is sometimes referred to as Phase 5. The surveillance trials are often utilized when the authorities consider that the use of the medicine should be studied after the approval is granted in a broader population than the clinical trial setting. These trials can be limited to only one country (at the request of that country's authorities) or be multinational.

GCPs and Clinical Trial Conduct

ICH's *Guideline for Good Clinical Practice E6(R1)* describes the responsibilities and expectations of all participants involved in the conduct of clinical trials, including investigators, monitors, sponsors and Institutional Review Boards (IRBs) and covers aspects of clinical trial monitoring, reporting and archiving.

GCP covers:

- clinical trial design
- clinical trial conduct
- roles and responsibilities of involved parties
- recording
- reporting

Basic GCP principles usually are transposed into national laws and represent binding legislation. Guidance on how to comply with GCPs is given in the form of regulations, guidances or communications, which are tools applicants can use to reach high levels of compliance.

Since each authority worldwide regulates clinical trials in its own territory and does not necessarily harmonize its standards with other countries or regions, applicants conducting multinational, multi-center clinical trials might face different requirements, possible lack of standardization in applying GCPs and Good Manufacturing Practices (GMPs) and different national application and approval processes.

Before any clinical trial can commence, it is mandatory to obtain a Competent Authority authorization and Ethics Committee opinion(s). The time needed to obtain positive opinions varies among countries and regions (from 60 days in the EU to up to few months in China).

Once a trial commences, any change in the conduct of the study or planned analyses should be reported to the Competent Authority and/or Ethics Committee. The time(s) and reason(s) for the change(s), the procedure used to decide on the change(s), the person(s) or group(s) responsible for the change(s) and the nature and content of the data when the change was made should be described. Whether the change was documented as a formal protocol amendment also should be noted.[8] Any protocol amendment must be approved before implementation in a trial except when necessary to eliminate an immediate hazard to subjects or when the change involves only logistical or administrative aspects of the trial. This is important because any changes could affect the interpretation of the study results.

The ICH guideline, *Structure and Content of Clinical Study Reports E3*,[9] is intended to allow the compilation of a single core clinical study report that is acceptable to all regulatory authorities in the ICH regions. It is important that sponsors provide information and justification regarding the sample size, including statistical considerations or practical limitations.

ICH has published a number of guidelines pertaining to clinical testing and expedited reporting under "Efficacy."[10]

Clinical Trial Responsibilities

Clinical trial key personnel who must follow GCPs based on the ICH's *Guideline for Good Clinical Practice E6(R1)* are:

- sponsor (including Contract Research Organization (CRO))
- investigator
- Institutional Review Board (IRB) or Independent Ethics Committee (IEC)

The most important obligation of all personnel involved in clinical trials is to fully respect trial subjects' rights, safety and well-being. Other responsibilities are presented in the following paragraphs.

Sponsor Obligations[11]

The sponsor is the individual, company, institution or organization that takes responsibility for the initiation, management or financing of a clinical trial. The sponsor bears the ultimate responsibility for the quality and integrity of the trial data, although some or all activities can be outsourced to other parties (e.g., CROs).

Other responsibilities of the sponsor include:

- financing clinical trial conduct
- quality assurance and quality control (with internal audits included) to ensure the trial is conducted in compliance with the protocol, GCP and regulatory requirements
- ensuring all clinical trial personnel are adequately qualified and trained
- ensuring adequate trial design is developed utilizing qualified experts
- using qualified experts to supervise the trial conduct, to handle the data, to verify the data, to perform statistical analysis and to prepare the trial report
- providing a clear clinical trial protocol
- providing the Investigator's Brochure (IB) with all previous nonclinical and clinical experience with the investigational drug
- selecting appropriately trained and experienced investigator(s) or institution(s) to conduct the trial

- ensuring the clinical trial is authorized by the Competent Authority(s) and favorable opinion received from IRBs or IECs
- ensuring investigational product(s) is manufactured, packed and labeled in accordance with GMPs
- supplying investigational product(s) to investigator(s) or institution(s) after all documentation is obtained and maintaining system for tracking, retrieval and disposition of the used and unused product(s)
- ensuring trial monitoring
- establishing a scientific Independent Data Monitoring Committee (IDMC), if needed, consisting of appropriate independent experts
- providing insurance coverage for subjects entering the trial, if applicable under the regulatory requirements
- ensuring all clinical trial information is recorded, handled, kept confidential and processed in accordance with written SOPs and GCPs
- ensuring direct access to source data or documents for the investigator(s) or institution(s) for trial-related activities and ensuring subjects are adequately informed about this
- ensuring proper safety monitoring and expediting reporting in accordance with applicable regulatory requirements
- ensuring retention of all sponsor-specific essential documents in conformance with the applicable regulatory requirement(s) and informing investigator(s) or institution(s) in writing of the need for record retention
- preparing a clinical trial report after the trial has ended
- maintaining compliance and promptly reacting to any noncompliance

Investigator Obligations[12]

The investigator is the person responsible for the conduct of the clinical trial at a trial site. Responsibilities of the investigator are:

- having the proper education, training and experience to comply with the applicable regulatory requirements in order to assume responsibility for the proper conduct of the trial
- providing a written application for the trial to the IRBs or IECs, providing all necessary documents and information, progress reports and, in general, communicating with the IRBs or IECs during the trial conduct
- obtaining and documenting informed consent and fully informing subjects of all aspects of the trial
- following the protocol and procedures described therein (not deviating unless necessary to eliminate an immediate hazard(s) to the subjects)
- being responsible for all trial-related medical decisions
- immediately reporting all Serious Adverse Events (SAEs) as defined in the protocol to the sponsor
- reporting all unexpected Serious Adverse Drug Reactions to the regulatory authority(ies) and the IRB or IEC as per regulatory requirements
- providing adequate medical care to trial subjects
- permitting sponsor monitoring and auditing and inspections by the authorities
- ensuring proper trial commencement, conduct and finalization within the agreed timeframe
- ensuring proper number of qualified staff and facilities to conduct the trial
- ensuring proper staff training
- ensuring investigational product(s) accountability at the trial site
- keeping delivery, inventory, use, return or disposal of any used or unused investigational product(s) records
- ensuring the use of the investigational product(s) as per the protocol
- keeping, maintaining and retaining all records related to the trial (e.g., source documents, case report forms)
- making direct access to the trial-related information available to monitors, auditor, IRBs or IECs and the regulatory authority, upon request

IRB and IEC Obligations[13]

The IRB or IEC is an independent body (a review board or committee, institutional, regional, national or supranational) comprised of medical professionals and non-medical members. It is responsible for ensuring human subjects' rights, safety and well-being are protected and providing public assurance of that protection by, among other things, reviewing and approving or providing favorable opinion on the trial protocol; the suitability of the investigator(s) and facilities; and the methods and material to be used in obtaining and documenting informed consent of the trial subjects.

Additional responsibilities of IRBs and IECs are:

- ensuring the review of the clinical trial (protocol, informed consent and documents to be given to the subjects, IB) within the specified timeframe and provide an opinion
- ensuring decision making is documented in writing
- reviewing each trial at least annually
- ensuring all payment methods are adequate and stated in the written documents provided to the subjects

- having written procedures in place and membership lists
- retaining written records and making them available upon request

Pediatric Clinical Trials

Drug development legislation is constantly changing as a result of new findings, new information and new experiences. As a result, direct or indirect impact on specific product development can be expected.

One example is the introduction of pediatric legislation in the US (1997)[14] and the EU (2007)[15] that aims to improve medical product research in children and the availability of high quality, safe and effective treatments for children. As a result, each sponsor needs to create a pediatric plan early in product development to ensure that when the marketing authorization application in these regions is submitted, the pediatric plan is fully in place.

A pediatric plan should cover all pediatric subpopulations (from pre-term newborn infants to adolescents) and should scientifically discuss all aspects and the prevalence of a disease in children, current treatments available, age-appropriate formulations, posology and duration of treatment. If the disease for which a drug is under development does not occur in children, a sponsor may obtain a waiver.

In addition, in some cases, clinical trials in children are deferred until more information from adult development is available. This is primarily to safeguard the safety of children.

There are special ethical aspects when planning and conducting clinical trials in children. The main principle is to try to expose the least possible number of children to the IMP and clinical trial procedures associated with the investigation. It is generally expected that children enrolled should gain some benefit from the investigation (except for special cases, e.g., non-therapeutic trials).[16]

All these aspects need to be discussed with authorities early enough in product development to allow the strategy for pediatric development to be agreed upon in time to ensure smooth overall product development.

If sponsors encounter any difficulties during pediatric development, they are encouraged to contact authorities in a timely manner and discuss those issues to find the best possible solution.

Acceptance of Foreign Clinical Data

Development of new pharmaceuticals is increasingly becoming a global effort. For a number of reasons,[17] companies tend to conduct multinational, multicenter clinical trials across the globe. The authorities have recognized this and are trying to set a number of standards to ease the acceptance of clinical data between the countries and regions (**Figure 4-1**).

ICH has provided guidance with objective of:

- describing regulatory and development strategies that will permit adequate evaluation of the influence of ethnic factors while minimizing duplication of clinical studies and supplying medicines to patients expeditiously
- describing the characteristics of foreign clinical data that will facilitate their extrapolation to different populations and support their acceptance as a basis for registration of a medicine in a new region
- describing the use of bridging studies to allow extrapolation of foreign clinical data to a new region[18,19]

ICH regions (US, EU and Japan) and non-ICH regions have developed their own local guidelines on this topic, bearing in mind this ICH guideline. For example, Asian countries (Japan, China and Korea) also are working on creating and maintaining a Tripartite Cooperation to ease clinical trial conduct and data gathering on a regional level.[20]

Clinical Trial Registry

To ensure that a complete view of research is accessible to all those involved in healthcare decision making, the World Health Organization (WHO) established the International Clinical Trial Registry Platform (ICTRP). The goal of this platform is to improve research transparency and ultimately strengthen the validity and value of the scientific evidence base.[21]

The need for such a registry was expressed during the Ministerial Summit on Health Research (November 2004) and later during the 58th World Health Assembly, where participants called for "a voluntary platform to link clinical trials registers in order to ensure a single point of access and the unambiguous identification of trials with a view to enhancing access to information by patients, families, patient groups and others."[22]

This registry contains data sets from Data Providers, which are national clinical trial registries from the following countries: Australia, China, Republic of Korea, US, India, Cuba, EU, Germany, Iran, Japan, Africa, Sri Lanka and the Netherlands.[23] Also, the International Standard Randomised Clinical Trial Number (ISRCTN) register is recognized as a Data Provider. The ISRCTN is a simple numeric system for the unique identification of randomized controlled trials worldwide.[24]

Information provided to the WHO ICTRP must fulfill WHO registry criteria.[25]

There is an increasing need to improve the transparency of clinical research conducted worldwide and nationally, which can improve general knowledge on the ongoing research for certain diseases or pharmaceuticals.

Sponsors usually are asked to provide minimal information to the national or regional registries about their clinical trials. Examples of national and regional databases

Figure 4-1. Acceptance of Foreign Clinical Data

Assessment of the clinical data package in the new region
Question 1: Meets regulatory standards?
Question 2: Extrapolation of foreign data available?
Further clinical study(ies) needed for acceptance by the new region
Acceptability in the new region?
Original CDP including foreign clinical data
YES
YES
No further clinical study needed
YES
NO
Study(ies) needed to bridge
NO
YES
Additional clinical study(ies) to meet regulatory standards
NO
NO
Clinical study(ies)
• To meet regulatory requirements
• To bridge
Clinical Data Package for the new region
Additional Clinical Study(ies)
Bridging Study(ies)

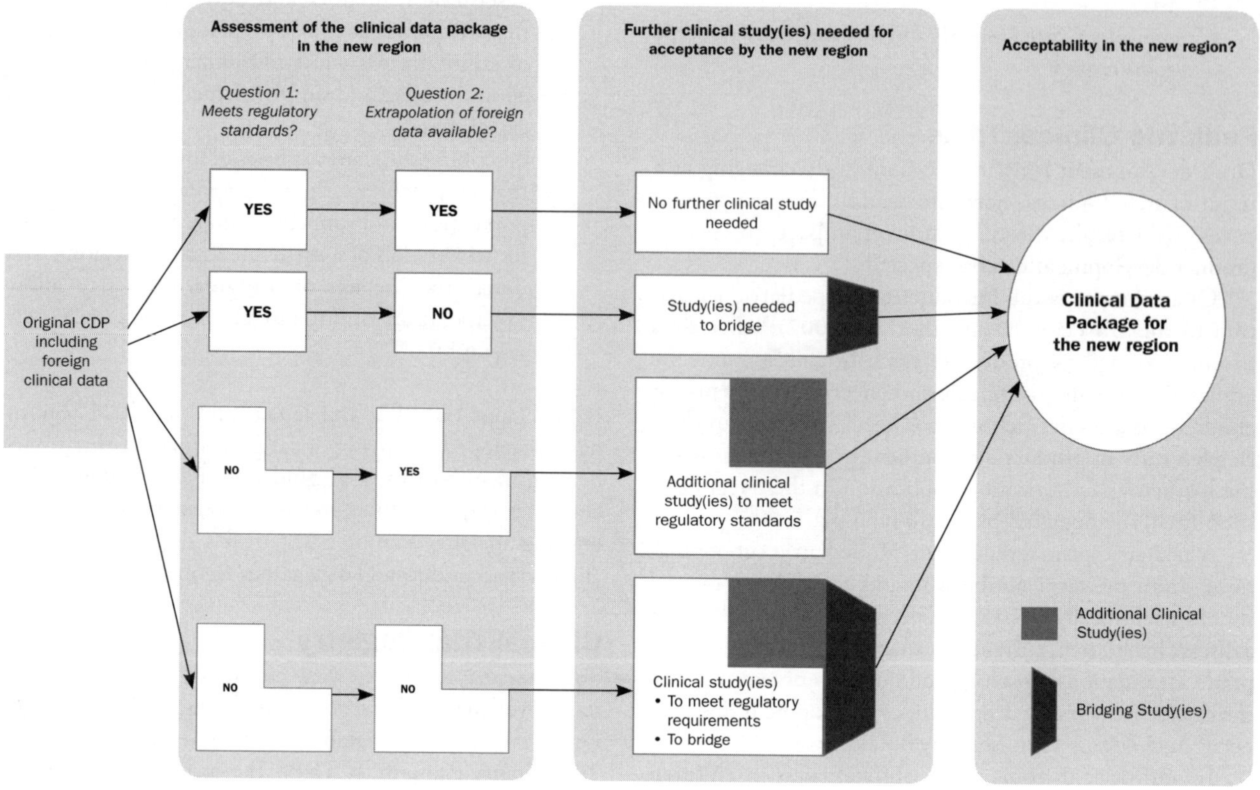

*Souce: ICH, *Ethnic factors in the Acceptability of Foreign Clinical Data E5(R1)*

are ClinicalTrials.gov in the US and clinicaltrialsregister.eu in the EU.

The information in these databases is publically available and is also transposed into the WHO ICTRP.

Pharmacovigilance

Development Safety Update Report (DSUR)

During the clinical development of pharmaceuticals, the safety information obtained from the clinical trials must be tracked and periodically assessed in order to evaluate the risk to trial subjects. It is also important to inform regulators and Ethics Committees of the analyses performed and their outcomes.

According to the ICH guideline, sponsors are required to submit annual Development Safety Update Reports (DSURs) in the ICH regions. A DSUR is a harmonized report in terms of content, format and timing of the report submission so all countries have the unique, high-quality, comprehensive report.[26] A DSUR is submitted within 60 days of the anniversary date on which the first clinical trial was approved.

Reporting Obligations

Besides periodic safety reporting in the form of the DSUR, sponsors must act on important clinical safety information obtained during the course of clinical development.[27]

Certain standards set at the international level define what should be reported and the timeframes for reporting.

This is called "expedited" reporting. The purpose of expedited reporting is to make regulators, investigators and other appropriate parties aware of new, important information on serious reactions. Therefore, such reporting generally will involve events previously unobserved or undocumented.[28]

The following require expedited reporting:[29]

- single cases of serious, unexpected adverse drug reactions (ADRs)
- other events that might influence the benefit:risk assessment:
    - o expected serious ADRs with an increased rate of occurrence
    - o a significant hazard to the patient population (e.g., lack of efficacy for treatment of life-threatening disease)
    - o a major safety finding from an animal study (e.g., carcinogenicity)

Reporting timeframes are as follows:[30]

- Fatal or life-threatening unexpected ADRs—These cases fall under a very rapid reporting scheme. Regulatory agencies should be notified (e.g., by telephone, fax or in writing) as soon as possible but no later than seven calendar days after first knowledge by the sponsor that a case qualifies, followed by a report with more information within eight additional calendar days.
- Other serious, unexpected ADRs—These cases that are not fatal or life-threatening must be filed as soon as possible but no later than 15 calendar days after first knowledge by the sponsor that the case meets the minimum criteria for expedited reporting.

Responsibilities for communicating these events are (see **Figure 4-2**):

- sponsor is required to notify all participating investigators of the serious and unexpected ADRs and any new safety findings from animal studies
- sponsor is required to notify regulatory authorities and Ethics Committees of any serious and unexpected ADRs as per regulatory requirements
- investigator is responsible for communicating any ADRs that may be caused by, or probably caused by the drug (If ADRs fall under category of serious and unexpected, the reporting should be done immediately to the sponsor and the Ethics Committee.)

Clinical Trial Regulatory Compliance

Compliance with GCPs during the trial guarantees that all trial subjects' well-being, rights, safety and integrity are fully respected. GCPs guarantee that the trial will be managed by appropriately trained and qualified personnel, that the trial will be continuously monitored and any new information adequately communicated and acted upon.

Noncompliance can arise on many levels; therefore, preventing noncompliance should be the main target when planning the trial. One efficient tool for preventing noncompliance is proper training and information sharing among all stakeholders. Adequate and repeated training on the protocol, SOPs and GCPs can raise awareness of compliance principles and can lead to easier and quicker noncompliance identification.

According to GCP principles, the sponsor, the investigator or institution and the IRB or IEC are all responsible key players in ensuring the protection of subjects in clinical trials. Institutions are responsible for individual investigators and Ethics Committees. Institutional noncompliance is a systemic failure to implement practices and procedures under which they are required to operate and are registered under the applicable national regulations.[31]

Although the most frequent source of noncompliance is the investigator, the other parties mentioned above also have responsibilities and the sponsor is ultimately accountable for ensuring that subjects' well-being, safety and rights are protected.[32]

Noncompliance with the protocol, SOPs, GCPs or applicable regulatory requirement(s) by an investigator or institution or by member(s) of the sponsor's staff should lead to prompt action by the sponsor to secure compliance.[33] Depending on the severity of noncompliance issues, the actions needed to bring the situation into the compliance state differ. The actions needed should follow careful analysis of the consequences caused by the noncompliance. All measures should be taken immediately to ensure subjects' safety and well-being.

If the monitoring or auditing identifies serious or persistent noncompliance on the part of an investigator or institution, the sponsor should terminate the investigator's or institution's participation in the trial. When an investigator's or institution's participation is terminated because of noncompliance, the sponsor should promptly notify the regulatory authority(ies).[34]

Common noncompliance issues include: failure to report unanticipated adverse events, falsified data, plagiarism of study results, implementation of significant changes to the protocol without first informing the authorities, enrolling subjects who do not meet the inclusion criteria, failure to make timely reports to the Competent Authorities and IRBs, misuse of Informed Consent Forms, etc.[35]

Regulatory authorities and Ethics Committees use inspections and audits to check the compliance of sponsors, institutions and investigators. Preapproval inspections (PAI) are part of this system. (For further information on PAIs, please see Chapter 10.) In addition, sponsors use internal and external audit systems to ensure their internal systems, partners and contractors comply with the above-mentioned principles. During the course of a clinical trial, the sponsor utilizes monitoring visits to regularly check whether the investigator, the staff and the investigational site comply with the protocol, SOPs and GCPs.

Each country has set its own system for checking compliance, but all are based on the basic principles of inspections and penalties for noncompliance.

One recent US example of noncompliance was the case of Cetero Research (contract bioanalytical laboratory, Houston, TX, USA). The US Food and Drug Administration (FDA) found significant violations of bioequivalence and bioavailability requirements of local regulations in bioanalytical studies conducted by Cetero Research. FDA concluded that the data generated at Cetero from 1 April 2005 to 15 June 2010 were unreliable. As a result, all the sponsors who had samples analyzed at Cetero as a part of their studies to support NDAs needed to reassess their data, conduct third-party audits or provide an explanation of why the data could be accepted.[36]

In addition, the European Medicines Agency (EMA) conducted its own separate analysis of the data for all Marketing Authorisations that had studies that had been outsourced to Cetero Research in their dossiers. As a result, Marketing Authorisations for seven medicines were suspended until adequate data are made available.[37]

Furthermore, Cetero Research filed for bankruptcy protection in March 2012 and was sold and renamed as the PRACS Institute.

This example shows how large an impact noncompliance can have on the company itself and other partners and contractors. It also shows that the influence is not necessarily limited to only one country or region, but can have global consequences.

Country-specific Information

Although the exact procedure for clinical trial application varies from country to country, most procedures would involve the following steps:

- Ethics Committee (Institutional Review Boards in the US) approval
- application to the Competent Authority
- clinical trial initiation
- clinical trial closure

The same or similar information needed to support the clinical study conduct in human subjects is usually requested by all authorities. The documents needed for a clinical trial application (CTA) normally include:

- cover letter
- application form
- clinical trial protocol
- investigator's brochure (IB)
- Investigational Medicinal Product Dossier (IMPD)

In certain instances, a pre-CTA meeting can be arranged between the clinical trial sponsor and the Competent Authority to discuss any issues. Due to the complexity of the subject, implementation of GCPs has been somewhat less straightforward than GLPs. In the US, no single set of regulations covers GCPs. Rather, several regulations apply and must be considered together, for example, protection of human subjects (21 CFR Part 50) and financial disclosure by clinical investigators (21 CFR Part 54). Also, in the EU, implementation of the *Clinical Trial Directive* (Directive 2001/20/EC of the European Parliament and of the Council of 4 April 2001 on the approximation of the laws, regulations and administrative provisions of the Member States relating to the implementation of good clinical practice in the conduct of clinical trials on medicinal products for human use) has been a challenge for all parties involved such as Ethics Committees, Competent Authorities and pharmaceutical companies.[38]

US

In the US, the clinical development process usually starts with the submission of the Investigational New Drug application (IND) to FDA. The process is described in Title 21 of the Code of Federal Regulations (CFR) Part 312.[39]

Submission of an IND is required in the following cases:

- new chemical entity (NCE)
- approved drug
  - o new indication
  - o new dosage form
  - o new doses
  - o new route of administration
  - o new dosage regimen

The IND is actually a request for an exemption from the federal law that prohibits distribution or transportation of an unapproved drug across state lines. FDA does not actually approve INDs. The IND is "in effect" in 30 calendar days after the submission to FDA (i.e., 30 days after the submission is registered in FDA's Document Control Room).

The IND must contain information in three areas:[40]

- animal pharmacology and toxicology studies
- manufacturing information
- clinical protocols and investigator information

One IND can contain a number of studies conducted with the same drug but with a different dose, pharmaceutical formulation, route of administration, etc.

During the IND review, FDA can ask for further clarifications at any time during the review cycle. The sponsor should diligently address all comments received and rapidly provide the missing information to FDA. If issues are not resolved and FDA finds that the study protocol for the investigation is clearly deficient in design to meet its stated objectives, or human subjects are or would be exposed to an unreasonable and significant risk of illness or injury, it can place a study on clinical hold.

A clinical hold is an order issued by FDA to the sponsor to delay a proposed clinical investigation or to suspend an ongoing investigation. The clinical hold order may apply to one or more of the investigations covered by an IND. When a proposed study is placed on clinical hold, subjects may not be given the investigational drug.[41]

There are three IND types:[42]

- Investigator IND—investigator is the one initiating and conducting the study
- Emergency Use IND—used in emergency situations when there is no time to submit an IND
- Treatment IND—used for treatment of patients with a serious or immediately life-threatening disease condition who are not in a clinical study while the final clinical work is conducted and the FDA review takes place[43]

Figure 4-2. Responsibilities for Communicating ADRs

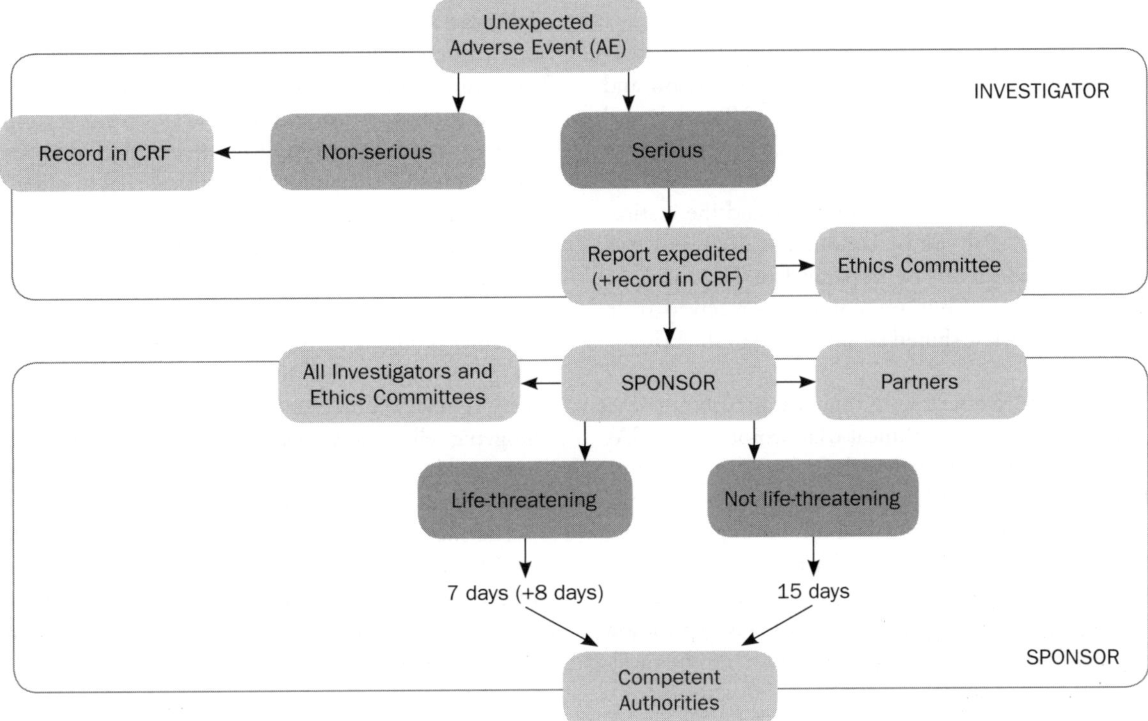

There are two IND categories:[44]

- Commercial (sponsored)
- Research (non-commercial)

After the 30-day period has expired and if no issues are raised by FDA, the sponsor can proceed with the submission of documents to the IRBs and IECs that are located in the concerned hospitals. Only after IRB or IEC approval, may the study commence.

Once the IND is in effect, there might be significant changes to certain aspects of a study that need to be reported to FDA and the IRBs and IECs. Only after the information is submitted to FDA and approval is obtained from the IRBs or IECs can the amendments be implemented.

The sponsor also is obliged to submit annual reports to FDA within 60 days of the anniversary of the date the IND went into effect. An annual report should contain a brief report of the progress of the investigation.[45]

If no subject is enrolled into clinical study for a period of two years or all investigations under an IND are on clinical hold for one year or more, FDA will put the IND on inactive status.

Canada

To conduct clinical studies in Canada, sponsors must submit a CTA to Health Canada.[46] A CTA is required for NCEs and new indications or an unauthorized dose, route of administration, dose regimen, etc. of an already approved drug.

Health Canada reviews the application within a 30-day period and issues a Non-objection Letter (NOL) at the end of the review process.

Before the study can commence, the approval of the local or institutional Research Ethics Board at each institution must be obtained.[47]

Changes to a previously authorized CTA must be submitted to Health Canada either as a CTA-Amendment or a notification, depending on the impact of change on the subjects' safety and the drug's quality and efficacy.

Australia

There are two main routes for conducting clinical studies in Australia:[48]

- Clinical Trial Notification Scheme (CTN scheme)
- Clinical Trial Exemption Scheme (CTX scheme)

Under the CTN scheme, all material relating to the proposed trial, including the trial protocol, is submitted directly to a Human Research Ethics Committee (HREC) by the investigator at the sponsor's request. The Therapeutic Goods Administration (TGA) does not review any data relating to the clinical trial. The TGA "Notification of Intent to Conduct a Clinical Trial" form (the CTN Form) signed by the Chairman of the HREC and Authoring Authority (based in the institution that will conduct the trial) is submitted by the sponsor to TGA.

Under the CTX scheme, a sponsor submits an application to conduct clinical trials to TGA for evaluation and comment. A sponsor cannot commence a CTX trial until written advice has been received from TGA regarding the application, and approval for the conduct of the trial has been obtained from an Ethics Committee and the institution at which the trial will be conducted. A clinical trial application can be submitted in parallel to TGA and the HREC for assessment, but any comments received from TGA during the review should be submitted to the HREC, as well.

It is important to note that the application submitted to TGA does not include the clinical trial protocol(s). TGA's primary responsibility is to review the safety of the product's use; the HREC is responsible for considering the scientific and ethical issues of the proposed clinical trial protocols.

The review period for the CTX scheme can be 30 or 50 working days, depending on the data submitted. A 30-working day period for evaluation of a CTX application applies when the supporting data relate only to chemical, pharmaceutical and biological issues. A 50-working day period applies for applications supported by chemical, pharmaceutical and biological, pharmacotoxicological and clinical data.

Japan

In Japan, the regulating body is the Pharmaceuticals and Medical Devices Agency (PMDA), which reviews Clinical Trial Notifications (CTNs), but the final review is done by the Ministry of Health, Labour and Welfare (MHLW).

Information submitted to support the application is essentially the same as in other countries. The sponsor should consider the translation of documents needed for the submission (one example is the Investigator's Brochure, which is required to be in Japanese).

The review process lasts 30 days, including the review cycles by both PMDA and MHLW. There is no approval letter issued and the sponsor can commence the trial once the 30 day period has elapsed. Approval from the Ethics Committees also should be obtained before the trial starts.

After the trial has begun, it is possible to file an amendment to the protocol or study conduct. It should be noted that if significant changes are proposed, PMDA may request that the previous CTN be withdrawn and a new one submitted.

EU

Directive 2001/20/EC[49] is the main legal basis for clinical trial principles and conduct in the EU. In order to apply for clinical trial authorization, a sponsor must be established in the EU or have a legal representative located there.

Before the application is submitted, the sponsor must obtain a unique EudraCT number from the EU database. This number uniquely identifies the trial protocol.[50]

The sponsor must submit a CTA to the Competent Authority and Ethics Committees in each EU Member State where it intends to conduct the clinical trial in order to get clinical trial authorization from the Competent Authority and a positive opinion from the Ethics Committees.

The usual review time is 60 calendar days for both Competent Authorities and Ethics Committees. For medicinal products involving gene therapy or somatic cell therapy or those containing genetically modified organisms, the review timeframe can be 90 days. In the case of xenogenic cell therapy, there is no pre-set review timeframe. These timelines may be shorter or longer in each Member State, depending on the national procedures.

The submission documentation must be compiled for each Member State, since each has its own requirements in addition to the usually required documents mentioned at the beginning of this section. During the review process, Competent Authorities and/or Ethics Committees can request further explanations and additional information. The review clock is then stopped until the sponsor provides the additional information.

Once the trial has started, it might be necessary to make amendments to the clinical trial protocol or conduct procedures. Amendments can be classified as substantial or nonsubstantial.

Substantial amendments require submission to the Competent Authorities and/or Ethics Committees and require prior approval before their implementation. Amendments are regarded as substantial when they are likely to have a significant impact on patients' safety or mental or physical integrity, the trial's scientific value, conduct or management or the IMP's quality or safety.

Nonsubstantial amendments do not require notification to the Competent Authorities and/or Ethics Committees. These amendments should be recorded, archived and made available for inspection purposes. Examples of nonsubstantial amendments are typographical corrections in the protocol, IB update, etc. Commission Communication 2010/C82/01 provides guidance on the differentiation between substantial and nonsubstantial amendments.[51]

During clinical trial conduct, the sponsor must report all suspected serious unexpected adverse reactions (SUSARs) that are fatal or life-threatening to the Competent Authorities and Ethics Committees immediately and within seven days, followed by a written report within an additional eight days. Other SUSARs can be reported within 15 days.

In addition, a Development Safety Update Report (DSUR) should be submitted within 60 days from the anniversary of the date on which the first clinical trial was approved.

The sponsor should notify the concerned Competent Authority and Ethics Committee(s) when the last subject has completed the study in that specific country and when the last patient in the complete trial has completed his or her last visit. This is referred to as End of Trial notification (EoT), which should be submitted within 90 days from the last patient/last visit (LPLV).

Since the current EU clinical trial approval process is not harmonized and sponsors struggle with the different interpretations of Directive 2001/20/EC among different Member States, the EU Heads of Medicines Agencies is working toward creating a harmonized process for clinical trial review and approval. They formed the Clinical Trials Facilitation Group (CTFG),[52] which has the following goals:

- sharing scientific assessments of multinational clinical trials
- harmonizing processes, practices and assessment relating to clinical trials mainly in the fields of CTAs, clinical trial amendments and safety procedures
- developing data sharing and participating in the improvement of information systems
- developing communication with stakeholders and cooperating with other EU working groups

One of the major goals of the CTFG was to develop a Voluntary Harmonisation Procedure (VHP),[53] which is intended to provide a coordinated assessment of multinational, multicenter clinical trials across the EU Member States. This procedure is conducted in two steps:

- First Step: 30-day assessment of core documents. At the end of the 30-day period, a positive opinion is issued or a request for further information (RFI) is send to the sponsor. In the latter case, the sponsor has 10 days to respond. A positive opinion is then issued at Day 60.
- Second Step: 10-day national phase where each Member State should issue a clinical trial approval.

It is important to note that the VHP is applicable only to Competent Authorities, not to Ethics Committees. Submission to Ethics Committees should be done in parallel.

Current experience with the VHP shows that the procedure has its benefits, including shorter review timelines and consolidated health authority feedback. Acceptance of the VHP is increasing as is the number of VHP applications, which will lead to a more harmonized EU clinical trial authorization environment.[54]

Conclusion

Although clinical trials are regulated nationally, there are generally accepted principles that are respected globally. Good Clinical Practices (GCPs) provide the basic principles for clinical trial conduct and protection of subjects enrolled in trials. Compliance with GCPs is the main key for ensuring clinical trial data validity and acceptance for drug registration purposes.

Each country has incorporated the GCP principles into its national laws and regulations that regulate clinical trial conduct in its territory.

Although there are national differences regarding the documents needed to support clinical trial authorization, there are core documents, without which a clinical trial cannot be approved, that are required to be submitted in every country. National expertise is needed to identify the requirements on the local level and to provide the input in a timely manner.

Continuous follow up on global and national regulation developments also is needed to adequately adjust clinical development plans and to ensure the maximum patient protection and, consequently, successful product development.

References

1. ICH, *Guideline for Good Clinical Practice E6(R1)* (Current Step 4 version, June 1996). ICH website. www.ich.org/fileadmin/Public_Web_Site/ICH_Products/Guidelines/Efficacy/E6_R1/Step4/E6_R1__Guideline.pdf. Accessed 1 November 2012.
2. World Medical Association, Declaration of Helsinki. WMA website. www.wma.net/en/30publications/10policies/b3/. Accessed 1 November 2012.
3. Op cit 1.
4. Ibid.
5. ICH, *General Considerations for Clinical Trials E8* (Current Step 4 version, July 1997). ICH website. www.ich.org/fileadmin/Public_Web_Site/ICH_Products/Guidelines/Efficacy/E8/Step4/E8_Guideline.pdf. Accessed 1 November 2012.
6. *Fundamentals of Canadian Regulatory Affairs, Third Edition*, Chapter 19: Clinical Trial Applications. Copyright © 2011 by Regulatory Affairs Professionals Society, Rockville, MD. pp 133-144.
7. EMA, *Guideline on the investigation of bioequivalence*, CPMP/EWP/QWP/1401/98 Rev. 1/ Corr, 20 January 2010. EMA website. www.ema.europa.eu/docs/en_GB/document_library/Scientific_guideline/2009/09/WC500003011.pdf. Accessed 1 November 2012.
8. ICH, *Structure and Content of Clinical Study Reports E3* (Current Step 4 version, November 1995). ICH website. www.ich.org/fileadmin/Public_Web_Site/ICH_Products/Guidelines/Efficacy/E3/E3_Guideline.pdf. Accessed 1 November 2012.
9. Ibid.
10. International Conference on Harmonisation, Efficacy guidelines. ICH website. www.ich.org/products/guidelines/efficacy/article/efficacy-guidelines.html. Accessed 1 November 2012.
11. Op cit 1.
12. Ibid.
13. Ibid.
14. US Food and Drug Administration Safety and Innovation Act (FDASIA) of 2012. GPO website. www.gpo.gov/fdsys/pkg/BILLS-112s3187enr/pdf/BILLS-112s3187enr.pdf. Accessed 1 November 2012.
15. Regulation (EC) No 1901/2006 of the European Parliament and of the Council od 12 December 2006 on medicinal products for paediatric use and amending Regulation (EEC) No 1768/92, Directive 2001/20/EC, Directive 2001/83/EC and Regulation (EC) No 726/2004. EUR-Lex website. http://eur-lex.europa.eu/LexUriServ/

LexUriServ.do?uri=OJ:L:2006:378:0001:0019:en:PDF. Accessed 1 November 2012.

16. ICH, *Clinical Investigation of Medicinal Products in the Pediatric Population E11* (Current Step 4 version, July 2000). ICH website. www.ich.org/fileadmin/Public_Web_Site/ICH_Products/Guidelines/Efficacy/E11/Step4/E11_Guideline.pdf. Accessed 1 November 2012.
17. Savic J., "Regulatory Concerns for Pharmaceutical Product Development. Going Global: Choice or Necessity?" *Pharmaceutical Compliance Monitor,* September 2012. Pharmaceutical Compliance Monitor website. www.pharmacompliancemonitor.com/regulatory-concerns-for-pharmaceutical-product-development-going-global-choice-or-necessity/3113/. Accessed 1 November 2012.
18. ICH, *Ethnic factors in the Acceptability of Foreign Clinical Data E5(R1)* (Current Step 4 version, February 1998). ICH website. www.ich.org/fileadmin/Public_Web_Site/ICH_Products/Guidelines/Efficacy/E5_R1/Step4/E5_R1__Guideline.pdf. Accessed 1 November 2012.
19. ICH, *Questions and Answers: Ethnic factors in the Acceptability of Foreign Clinical Data E5 Q&A(R1),* June 2006. ICH website. www.ich.org/fileadmin/Public_Web_Site/ICH_Products/Guidelines/Efficacy/E5_R1/Q_As/E5_Q_As__R5_.pdf. Accessed 1 November 2012.
20. Pharmaceuticals and Medical Devices Agency (PMDA), Concept Paper, *Research Project on ethnic factors in clinical data from three countries China-Japan-Korea,* Working Group on Drug Clinical Trials, 28 December 2010. PMDA website. www.pmda.go.jp/kokusai/file/101228_clear.pdf. Accessed 1 November 2012.
21. WHO, *International Clinical Trial Registry Platform (ICTRP).* WHO website. www.who.int/ictrp/en/. Accessed 1 November 2012.
22. WHO, *International Clinical Trial Registry Platform (ICTRP), About the WHO ICTRP.* WHO website. www.who.int/ictrp/about/en/. Accessed 1 November 2012.
23. WHO, *International Clinical Trial Registry Platform (ICTRP) Search Portal.* WHO website. http://apps.who.int/trialsearch/. Accessed 1 November 2012.
24. ISRCTN Register. ISRCTN website. http://isrctn.org/. Accessed 1 November 2012
25. WHO, *International Clinical Trial Registry Platform (ICTRP), WHO Registry Criteria.* WHO website. www.who.int/ictrp/network/criteria_summary/en/index.html. Accessed 1 November 2012.
26. ICH, *Development Safety Update Report E2F* (Current Step 4 version, August 2010). ICH website. www.ich.org/fileadmin/Public_Web_Site/ICH_Products/Guidelines/Efficacy/E2F/Step4/E2F_Step_4.pdf. Accessed 1 November 2012.
27. Op cit 1.
28. ICH, *Clinical Safety Data Management: Definitions and Standards for Expedited Reporting E2A* (Current Step 4 version, October 1994). ICH website. www.ich.org/fileadmin/Public_Web_Site/ICH_Products/Guidelines/Efficacy/E2A/Step4/E2A_Guideline.pdf. Accessed 1 November 2012.
29. Ibid.
30. Ibid.
31. Fundamentals of US Regulatory Affairs, *Seventh Edition*, Chapter 7, Clinical Trials: GCPs, Regulations and Compliance. Copyright © 2011 by Regulatory Affairs Professionals Society, Rockville, MD. pp 73-90.
32. Op cit 1.
33. Ibid.
34. Ibid.
35. Op cit 31.
36. FDA, *Notification to Pharmaceutical Companies: Acceptance of third-party data integrity audit for Cetero studies conducted from March 1, 2008 to August 31, 2009.* FDA website. www.fda.gov/Drugs/DrugSafety/ucm265559.htm. Accessed 1 November 2012.
37. EMA, *Medicines studied at Cetero Research facility.* September 2012. EMA website. www.ema.europa.eu/ema/index.jsp?curl=pages/medicines/human/referrals/Cetero_Research_facility/human_referral_000324.jsp&mid=WC0b01ac05805c516f. Accessed 1 November 2012.
38. Michor S. "Product Lifecycle Management: A European Perspective." *Regulatory Focus,* Vol. 13, No. 8, August 2008, pp 18-27.
39. FDA, Code of Federal Regulations Title 21, Part 312, *Investigational New Drug Application.* FDA website. www.accessdata.fda.gov/scripts/cdrh/cfdocs/cfcfr/cfrsearch.cfm?cfrpart=312. Accessed 1 November 2012.
40. FDA, *Investigational New Drug (IND) Application.* FDA website. www.fda.gov/drugs/developmentapprovalprocess/howdrugsaredevelopedandapproved/approvalapplications/investigationalnewdrugindapplication/default.htm. Accessed 1 November 2012.
41. FDA, Code of Federal Regulations Title 21, Part 312.42, *Clinical holds and requests for modification.* FDA website. www.accessdata.fda.gov/scripts/cdrh/cfdocs/cfcfr/CFRSearch.cfm?fr=312.42. Accessed 1 November 2012.
42. Op cit 40.
43. FDA, Code of Federal Regulations Title 21, Part 312.320, *Treatment IND or treatment protocol.* FDA website. www.accessdata.fda.gov/scripts/cdrh/cfdocs/cfcfr/CFRSearch.cfm?fr=312.320. Accessed 11 January 2013.
44. Op cit 40.
45. FDA, Code of Federal Regulations Title 21, Part 312.33, *Annual reports.* FDA website. www.accessdata.fda.gov/scripts/cdrh/cfdocs/cfCFR/CFRSearch.cfm?CFRPart=312&showFR=1&subpartNode=21:5.0.1.1.3.2. Accessed 1 November 2012.
46. Health Canada, Food and Drug Regulation, Division 5, *Drugs For Clinical Trials Involving Human Subjects.* Health Canada website. www.hc-sc.gc.ca/dhp-mps/compli-conform/clini-pract-prat/reg/1024-eng.php. Accessed 1 November 2012.
47. Health Canada, *Clinical Trial Application (CTA).* Health Canada website. www.hc-sc.gc.ca/dhp-mps/prodpharma/applic-demande/guide-ld/clini/cta_background-eng.php. Accessed 1 November 2012.
48. Australian Government, Department of Health and Ageing, Therapeutic Goods Administration, *Access to Unapproved therapeutic goods, Clinical Trials in Australia,* October 2004. TGA website. www.tga.gov.au/pdf/clinical-trials-guidelines.pdf. Accessed 1 November 2012.
49. Directive 2001/20/EC of the European Parliament and of the Council of 4 April 2001 on the approximation of the laws, regulations and administrative provisions of the Member States relating to the implementation of good clinical practice in the conduct of clinical trials on medicinal products for human use. EUR-Lex website. http://eur-lex.europa.eu/LexUriServ/LexUriServ.do?uri=OJ:L:2001:121:0034:0044:en:PDF. Accessed 1 November 2012.
50. Fundamentals of EU Regulatory Affairs, Fifth Edition, *Chapter 14 Medicinal Product Clinical Trials.* Copyright © 2011 by Regulatory Affairs Professionals Society, Rockville, MD. pp 129-140.
51. Commission Communication 2010/C 82/01 Detailed guidance on the request to the competent authorities for authorisation of a clinical trial on a medicinal product for human use, the notification of substantial amendments and the declaration of the end of the trial (CT-1). Official Journal of the European Union. EUR-Lex website. http://eur-lex.europa.eu/LexUriServ/LexUriServ.do?uri=OJ:C:2010:082:FULL:EN:PDF. Accessed 1 November 2012.
52. Introduction to Clinical Trial Facilitation Group (CTFG). HMA website. www.hma.eu/78.html. Accessed 1 November 2012.
53. CFTG. *Guidance document for a Voluntary Harmonisation Procedure (VHP) for the assessment of multinational Clinical Trial Applications, Version 2,* March 2010. HMA website. www.hma.eu/fileadmin/dateien/Human_Medicines/01-About_HMA/Working_Groups/CTFG/2010_03_VHP_Guidance_v2.pdf. Accessed 1 November 2012.
54. CFTG Activity Report for period 2010-11, 20 November 2011.

Chapter 5

In-Country Representation

By Michael A. Siano, MA and Heidi Feik, MSc, RAC

OBJECTIVES

- ❑ Learn the function of an in-country representative
- ❑ Understand the practical reasons for in-country representation requirements
- ❑ Gain insight into diversity of qualifications for in-country representatives among different countries
- ❑ Understand global requirements for in-country representation
- ❑ Understand pros and cons of third-party representatives versus distributor representatives

LAWS, REGULATIONS AND GUIDELINES COVERED IN THIS CHAPTER

EU/GHTF

- ❑ Council Directive 93/42/EEC of 14 June 1993 concerning medical devices
- ❑ Council Directive 90/385/EEC of 20 June 1990 on the approximation of the laws of the Member States relating to active implantable medical devices
- ❑ Directive 98/79/EC of the European Parliament and of the Council of 27 October 1998 on *in vitro* diagnostic medical devices
- ❑ MEDDEV 2.5/10, January 2012, *Guideline For Authorised Representatives*
- ❑ GHTF/SG1/N055: 2009, *Definitions of the Terms Manufacturer, Authorised Representative, Distributor and Importer*
- ❑ Directive 2001/83/EC of the European Parliament and of the Council of 6 November 2001 on the Community code relating to medicinal products for human use (as amended)

Australia

- ❑ *Therapeutic Goods Act* 1989
- ❑ Therapeutic Goods (Medical Devices) Regulations 2002
- ❑ Australian Regulatory Guidelines for Medical Devices (ARGMD), 2011

Canada

- ❑ *Food and Drug Act*
- ❑ *Medical Devices Regulations* (SOR/98-282)
- ❑ *Radiocommunication Regulations* (SOR/96-484)
- ❑ Spectrum Management and Telecommunications—Radio Standards Procedure: RSP-100 Radio Equipment Certification Procedure ("RSP-100")

Japan

- ❑ *Pharmaceutical Affairs Law* of 2002
- ❑ Yakushokuhatsu No. 0709004 of 2004
- ❑ MO 135 for GVP (good vigilance)
- ❑ MO 136 for GQP (good quality)

US

- ❑ 21 CFR 807—Establishment Registration and Device Listing for Manufacturers and Initial Importers of Devices
- ❑ 21 CFR 207—Registration of Producers of Drugs and Listing of Drugs in Commercial Distribution

Introduction

The definition of an in-country representative differs broadly across the spectrum of jurisdictions—where one is required—ranging from an established business entity licensed as the medical device or medicinal product importer, to a natural person residing in the country.

With the notable exception of Canada, most countries require a local establishment for the commercialization of medical devices in their territories. For medicinal products, this also is a prerequisite in most countries.

The requirements for an in-country representative generally can be met in several ways. Most common among these are establishing a local branch of the parent company, assigning a distributor or importer or employing a third-party professional representative service.

Functions and Purpose of an In-Country Representative

In general, an in-country representative acts as a liaison between a foreign manufacturer and the local Competent Authority. To facilitate identification of the appropriate local entity for product questions and/or complaints, the in-country representative's name and contact information often is required to appear on the label. The in-country representative is available to receive user complaints, forward these to the manufacturer and submit the required reports to the regulatory authority.

In-country representatives also generally are expected to maintain device and/or drug technical information and compliance documentation so these can be furnished to the regulatory authority upon request.

In practical terms, an in-country representative eliminates the need for regulatory authorities to communicate with a foreign entity, possibly in a different language and time zone, about important safety and compliance information for the devices and/or drugs on their markets. In some markets, the in-country representative bears responsibility for the safety of the product, including taking any necessary legal actions.

In-country representatives bear varying degrees of legal responsibility, depending on the region and on the contract agreement with the manufacturer.

The official title of the in-country representative differs from country-to-country, with the EU and GHTF (IMDRF) term, "Authorized Representative" (AR) commonly used generically. For drugs, the term is usually "license holder" or "local representative."

Qualifications of an In-Country Representative

The qualifications for an in-country representative vary significantly from country to country. The basic qualification, of course, is a local presence. This often can be either a real or legal person (i.e., an individual or a business entity). For business entities, normal business licenses generally are required. Additionally, many countries require the in-country representative to obtain special licenses through the Ministry of Health (or other health authority) and have specially qualified staff.

Global Examples

The following examples, taken from some of the world's largest economies, with well-developed regulatory systems, illustrate a spectrum of requirements for in-country representation.

US

Overview

The US Food and Drug Administration (FDA) requires foreign manufacturers without a place of business in the US to appoint a US agent to represent them. Unlike many countries where only the legal medical device manufacturer is required to have in-country representation, foreign contract manufacturers also must have a US agent.

The definition of a US agent is given in Title 21 Code of Federal Regulations (CFR), Volume 8, Part 807(r) as:

> United States agent means a person residing or maintaining a place of business in the United States whom a foreign establishment designates as its agent. This definition excludes mailboxes, answering machines or services, or other places where an individual acting as the foreign establishment's agent is not physically present.

In the US, unlike many other markets, market authorization (clearance/approval/exemption) is granted to the medical device manufacturer rather than the local representative, and a foreign manufacturer can submit 510(k) submissions or Premarket Approval (PMA) applications on its own behalf without the involvement of the local representative.

The manufacturer can change the US agent without prior agreement or authorization from the US agent, unless stipulated by prior agreement.

Foreign manufacturers (repackers, relabelers and control laboratories involved in the manufacture, preparation, propagation, compounding, processing or testing of human or veterinary drugs and human biological products, including the manufacturer of active pharmaceutical ingredients) whose drugs are imported into the US are required to register with FDA and submit a listing of every product in commercial distribution in the US (Section 510 of the *Food, Drug, and Cosmetic Act* (*FD&C Act*) and 21 CFR Part 207).[1]

Drug products must be listed with FDA before they may be imported for commercial distribution in the US. Additionally, foreign manufacturers and importers are required to register with FDA within five days of submission of a New Drug Application (NDA) or Abbreviated New Drug Application (ANDA) and to identify only one US agent. The name, address and phone number of this US agent must be submitted as part of the initial and updated registration information.

Qualifications

A US agent must be a person residing or maintaining a place of business in the US. Staff must be physically present in the US and available by phone during normal business hours. There are no special requirements for staff or facilities.

Responsibilities

The US agent must assist FDA in communicating with the foreign manufacturer, assist in scheduling establishment inspections and provide information to FDA on the products on the US market. FDA may serve documents on or supply information to the US agent, which is considered equivalent to providing said documents or information to the manufacturer itself. In the US, the medical device or drug manufacturer, rather than the in-country representative, is responsible for adverse event and pharmacovigilance reporting.

Registration

The US agent is not responsible for device or drug listing in the US, although the US agent may perform this function. Foreign manufacturers must list the name and address of their US agents in their establishment registrations.

Liability

The manufacturer maintains legal responsibility for the device or drug on the US market.

Postmarket Surveillance (Vigilance)/Pharmacovigilance

The US agent is not responsible for postmarket surveillance activities or for adverse event reporting; these responsibilities fall to the manufacturer instead.

EU

Overview

Council Directive 93/42/EEC of 14 June 1993 concerning medical devices (the *Medical Devices Directive*, or *MDD*) establishes the requirement for an in-country representative (Authorized Representative) in Article 14:

> Where a manufacturer who places a device on the market under his own name does not have a registered place of business in a Member State, he shall designate a single authorised representative in the European Union.

The definition of an authorized representative according to the EU medical devices directives and GHTF guidance is:

> 'authorised representative' means any natural or legal person established in the Community who, explicitly designated by the manufacturer, acts and may be addressed by authorities and bodies in the Community instead of the manufacturer with regard to the latter's obligations under this Directive;

The *MDD* is largely silent on specifics of the Authorized Representative's role; however, many of the holes left by the *MDD* are filled in by MEDDEV guidance document 2.5/10.

For drugs (Directive 2001/83/EC, as amended), a Marketing Authorization may be granted only to an applicant established in the European Community. Foreign manufacturers need to appoint a legal representative in the EU to act as the Marketing Authorization Holder (MAH). The definition of such a representative is given in Directive 2001/83/EC:

> The person, commonly known as local representative, designated by the marketing authorisation holder to represent him in the Member State concerned.

All foreign manufacturers must have an Authorized Representative in order to commercialize medical devices or drugs in the EU. Additionally, an Authorized Representative is required for a foreign manufacturer to undertake clinical trials in the EU. The name and address of the Authorized Representative, in addition to that of the manufacturer, must appear on the device or drug labeling.

For devices, a manufacturer may engage multiple Authorized Representatives for multiple products or product models; however, the same device model cannot be assigned to multiple Authorized Representatives. Thus, a one-to-one relationship must exist between product models and Authorized Representatives. The same requirements apply to medical devices and active implantable devices; however, this is not the case for IVDs.

The directives for devices and drugs do not define the roles and responsibilities of an Authorized Representative in detail. This, instead, is left to contractual agreements between the manufacturer and the Authorized Representative, in which a broad range of duties can be either delegated or withheld from the Authorized Representative. Thus, when engaging an Authorized Representative in the EU, it is important to clearly define the expectations of each party in their respective roles. It is also important to note that national law may include additional requirements for Authorized Representatives that reside in their territories over the requirements stipulated by the directives.

Qualifications

An Authorized Representative must be an established business entity within a member country of the European Free Trade Association (EFTA). Unlike other countries, there are no personnel qualification requirements.

Responsibilities

The Authorized Representative is required to maintain and provide upon request certain regulatory documentation to the Competent Authority for the purpose of market surveillance, including the Declaration of Conformity and Technical File for devices. Implicit in the requirement for Authorized Representatives to furnish documentation to authorities upon request is the need for the information to be up to date.

The Authorized Representative also is required to promptly communicate information from the Competent Authority to the manufacturer.

For drugs, technical files or dossiers need to be submitted for prior approval to the Competent Authority. This documentation must be kept on the premises of the legal representative.

Registration

Device registration requirements vary from one Member State to another. Where device registration is required, this can be delegated to the Authorized Representative. For drugs, registration is not required since each drug can only be marketed after issuance of a license by the Competent Authority.

Various activities require registration in the EU, including clinical trials for drugs and devices in addition to performance evaluations of IVDs and the marketing of IVDs, Class I devices, registration of Class IIa, Class IIb and Class III medical devices and custom-made devices. Intent to perform clinical investigations can be notified to the Competent Authorities by either the manufacturer or Authorized Representative; however, registration for IVDs, Class I devices and custom-made devices must be done by the Authorized Representative.

Liability

The directives are largely silent on the respective degrees of liability between the Authorized Representative and manufacturer for devices placed on the EU market. However, because the directives generally treat the manufacturer and Authorized Representative as equivalent entities (making reference to "the manufacturer or Authorized Representative"), and because the Authorized Representative is an easier target for legal action than a foreign manufacturer, the practice that has developed—and generally been supported by the courts—is one in which the Authorized Representative is fully liable for the device on the EU market.

For drugs, the MAH shall be responsible for marketing the medicinal product. The designation of a representative shall not relieve the MAH of legal responsibility.

Postmarket Surveillance (Vigilance)/Devices

The directives' required postmarket reporting activities do not address the respective responsibilities of the manufacturer and Authorized Representative. In MEDDEV 2.12/1 (on Medical Devices Vigilance System), the manufacturer and Authorized Representative are given equal standing in most respects.

This necessitates a clear contractual understanding between the medical device manufacturer and Authorized Representative as to the respective roles in postmarket vigilance activities.

Pharmacovigilance/Drugs

For drugs, the MAH should ensure that an appropriate pharmacovigilance system is in place, assume responsibility and liability for its products on the market and ensure that appropriate action will be taken when necessary. The MAH, therefore, should ensure that all information relevant to a medicinal product's benefit:risk balance is reported to the Competent Authorities and any other agency fully and promptly in accordance with the legislation.

When submitting a Marketing Authorisation Application, the applicant, in preparation for the role and responsibilities as MAH, should submit a description of the pharmacovigilance system and proof that the services of a Qualified Person Responsible for Pharmacovigilance (QPPV) are in place.

The MAH should have a QPPV residing in the EU, permanently and continuously at its disposal.

National regulations in some Member States require a nominated individual in that country who has specific legal obligations with respect to pharmacovigilance at a national level. One such individual may also act as the QPPV for the whole EU. Alternatively, the QPPV for the EU may be a separate person, in addition to meeting requirements under the relevant national regulations.

Australia

Overview

To supply a drug or a medical device to the Australian market, foreign manufacturers are required to appoint an Australian Sponsor. The definition of a Sponsor, according to the *Therapeutic Goods Act* of 1989, is:

a. a person who exports, or arranges the exportation of, the goods from Australia; or
b. a person who imports, or arranges the importation of, the goods into Australia; or
c. a person who, in Australia, manufactures the goods, or arranges for another person to manufacture the goods, for supply (whether in Australia or elsewhere);

but does not include a person who:

d. exports, imports or manufactures the goods; or
e. arranges the exportation, importation or manufacture of the goods; on behalf of another person who, at the time of the exportation, importation, manufacture or arrangements, is a resident of, or is carrying on business in, Australia.

The Australian Register of Therapeutic Goods (ARTG) listing is granted to the Australian Sponsor, and the Sponsor maintains control over the market authorization in Australia.

Qualifications

The Australian Sponsor must be either a legal resident of Australia or a company established in the country, with a representative of the company residing in Australia.

Responsibilities

The Australian Sponsor is required to maintain regulatory documentation showing compliance with Australian regulations and liaise with the Therapeutic Goods Administration (TGA) on behalf of the manufacturer.

Registration

Listings in the ARTG must be submitted by the appointed Australian Sponsor.

Liability

The Australian Sponsor is considered equivalent to the manufacturer and carries a high degree of liability for the drug or device on the Australian market.

Postmarket Vigilance

Postmarketing vigilance requirements fall to the Sponsor. These include adverse event reporting for events occurring in Australia, recalls and maintenance of distribution records.

Japan

Overview

Manufacturers intending to manufacture drugs or medical devices in foreign countries and export them to Japan are required to be accredited by the Minister of Health, Labour and Welfare (MHLW) as an "Accredited Foreign Manufacturer," specified in Article 13-3 of *Pharmaceutical Affairs Law* (*PAL*), in the same way a Japanese manufacturer is licensed. The accreditation must be renewed every five years.

A foreign manufacturers should have either a local operating affiliate or an in-country representative in order to import and commercialize medical devices and drugs in Japan. This function is known as the Japanese Marketing Approval Holder (MAH).

Before applying for accreditation, the Japanese MAH needs to submit a "Business Number Registration Form," with information on the foreign applicant's business and manufacturing establishments.

A company that has a local partner with a valid importing license can be considered temporarily accredited.

Qualifications

The MAH must be a licensed business entity that has passed inspection for Good Quality Practice (GQP) and Good Vigilance Practice (GVP) and must be licensed by the MHLW to act as an MAH.

Staff must include a general manager, quality manager and safety manager as full-time employees. These personnel must meet minimum education requirements, depending on the class of devices with which they work.

Responsibilities

The MAH assumes full responsibility for the drug or device on the Japanese market. Additionally, the MAH has a role in the importing process to conduct a regulatory release assessment for each international shipment.

For many foreign medical device manufacturers, the MAH is an actual customer; this relationship is similar to a medical device company and its distributors in other countries. In many instances, the MAH is then responsible for the distribution of the medical device onto the market in Japan.

Registration

Drugs and medical device submissions, certifications and approvals must be submitted by the MAH

Liability
The MAH has legal liability for the drug or device on the Japanese market.

Postmarket Vigilance
All postmarket activities required fall to the MAH.

Canada

Overview
Canada is one of the few countries with a well-developed regulatory system for drugs and medical devices where a local representative is not required to market a product within its borders.

Foreign manufacturers can register and market their drugs and devices in Canada without a local representative, except in the case of devices containing wireless technology.

Manufacturers of devices containing wireless technology are subject to the requirements of the *Radiocommunication Regulations* (SOR/96-484) overseen by Industry Canada and must appoint a local representative in order to obtain the required wireless licenses to market in Canada as outlined in the Spectrum Management and Telecommunications—Radio Standards Procedure: RSP-100 Radio Equipment Certification Procedure (RSP-100).

Representative Types

In most markets that require in-country representation, there are three general entity types that can serve this function: a local branch (daughter company) of a foreign manufacturer, a local distributor/importer or a professional representation service. Each of these alternatives comes with various tradeoffs, which often differ by market.

Because the in-country representative generally maintains control of the drug or device approval in the market, conferring this control to a distributor or importer creates a potential for conflict of interest between the manufacturer and distributor should the relationship sour.

Where a daughter company of the manufacturer is established in a given market, the local branch can act as in-country representative and avoid the need to cede control of the product approval—and thus, market access—to a distributor or importer. In certain markets, the staff qualifications may make this approach impractical. For example, in some markets, the entity holding device registration is required to have highly qualified staff, such as a biomedical engineer.

A third alternative is the use of professional representation services. These are third-party firms who fulfill the in-country representation requirements on behalf of manufacturers without local offices. These services are available in many of the larger markets. Although these services come at a cost, they allow manufacturers to maintain control of their registrations in foreign markets without the need to establish a branch office in the country or relinquish the product approval to a distributor. An additional consideration in appointing a third-party representative over a distributor is the ability to maintain greater control over technical information, as this would not need to be supplied to the distributor.

Conclusions

The preceding examples provide a brief overview of in-country representation requirements in some of the major markets. Additionally, in almost every regulated market throughout the world, some type of local representation is required to commercialize a medicinal product or medical device.

In areas where regulatory systems are not well developed and/or not codified or transparent, there is essentially a de facto requirement for local representation since in-person interactions are often necessary for product approval and/or customs clearance.

In-country representation must be considered in any global regulatory strategy. It is important to understand the options available for representation and plan accordingly. In many cases, the local representative will hold significant power over market access for the drug or device and, thus, it is vital to identify trustworthy partners for in-country representation and establish agreements that optimize a manufacturer's control over market authorization licenses.

It is also important to consider the ability to transfer market authorization licenses between entities, whether multiple entities can register the same device and whether multiple distributors can be authorized based on a single market authorization. The selection of a suitable in-country representative is more important in countries where one can get "locked" into a commercial relationship, e.g., in countries where it is difficult to transfer licenses and/or appoint multiple distributors.

References

1. 21 CFR 207—Registration of Producers of Drugs and Listing of Drugs in Commercial Distribution.

Chapter 6

Regulation of Global Advertising and Promotion

Updated by Moulakshi Roychowdhury, PharmD, JD

OBJECTIVES

- ❑ Understand the necessity for regulation of pharmaceutical advertising and promotion worldwide
- ❑ Review the two main models of regulation: industry self-regulation and government regulation
- ❑ Learn the basic global concepts and necessary components of promotion
- ❑ Understand the relationship between advertising and providing gifts and samples to healthcare providers
- ❑ Understand the impact of social media and Internet promotion
- ❑ Understand the need for monitoring

REGULATIONS AND GUIDELINES COVERED IN THIS CHAPTER

- ❑ Directive 2004/27/EC of the European Parliament and of the Council of 31 March 2004 amending Directive 2001/83/EC on the Community code relating to medicinal products for human use
- ❑ European Federation of Pharmaceutical Industries and Associations (EFPIA), European Code of Practice on the Promotion of Medicines, Update 2007
- ❑ International Federation of Pharmaceutical Manufacturers and Association (IFPMA), *Code of Pharmaceutical Marketing Practices*
- ❑ 21 CFR 314.550 Promotional materials (drugs)
- ❑ 21 CFR 601.45 Promotional materials (biologics)
- ❑ World Health Organization (WHO), Resolution WHA41.17, *Ethical Criteria for Medicinal Drug Promotion*
- ❑ WHO Technical Report Series, No. 722, *The Selection and Use of Essential Medicines*

Introduction

The regulation of advertising and promotion of prescription drugs, and in many cases, medical devices, is a topic that is frequently in the global media, and is a major focus of enforcement, with levels of control varying from region to region. This is a complicated area undergoing constant scrutiny because, while pharmaceuticals are inherently a business, and hence, the industry's profits are tied to marketing and promotion of its products, pharmaceuticals have a direct impact on patient healthcare and overall healthcare costs. Due to this impact on patient health, advertising and promotion generally are held to higher ethical standards as determined by each region. It is imperative that the advertising of regulated products, such as drugs and medical devices, be controlled to protect public health.

However, depending on the region, the regulation of pharmaceutical advertising and promotion may be heavily self-regulated by industry (through the application of voluntary industry codes and guidelines) and/or through direct government oversight. This chapter reviews the regulatory powers of each region and their potential interactions and provides a few illustrative examples.

The exact definition of advertising as it relates to medicinal products or medical devices is different across regions but generally is understood as the provision of any form of information, including door-to-door advertising, or any activity that aims to promote the prescription, supply, sale or consumption of such products.

While the regulation of advertising and promotion is predominantly a national issue that lies within the purview of local governmental authorities and industry self-regulation, harmonization has been promoted primarily by the development of voluntary codes of practice by pharmaceutical and other international organizations such as the World Health Organization (WHO),[1] the International Federation of Pharmaceutical Manufacturers Association (IFPMA)[2] and the European Federation of Pharmaceutical Industries and Associations (EFPIA),[3] among others. Harmonization of regulations and standards is intended to promote the free movement of goods across national boundaries. Such codes provide minimum standards that could be adapted[4] across jurisdictions that have varying laws and different enforcement levels.

Advertising and Promotion—Understanding the Terms and Overarching Principles

Advertising

As noted above, the exact definition of advertising is different across regions, but generally is considered to be the provision of information to promote the use of a product.

Several types of advertising exist and usually are categorized as follows:

- advertising of medicinal products, such as non-prescription drugs, which are freely available to the general public, whether over-the-counter or off-the-shelf
- advertising of prescription-only drugs including products containing psychotropic or narcotic substances
- advertising to the general public
- advertising to healthcare professionals[5]

Although advertising restrictions are determined at the national level, in general, prescription-only medicinal products—especially those containing psychotropic or narcotic substances—usually may be advertised only to healthcare professionals who are qualified to prescribe or supply those products.[6]

Promotion

World Health Assembly Resolution WHA41.17 defines "promotion" as all informational and persuasive activities by manufacturers and distributors, the effect of which is to induce the prescription, supply, purchase and/or use of medicinal drugs.

Only drugs legally available in a country should be promoted, and any promotional activities should comply with national health policies and regulations.[7] Any promotional claims should be accurate, truthful, informative, up to date and should be substantiated. Drug promotion should not try to make unjust or unsubstantiated comparisons to put competitors at a disadvantage.

Overarching Principles[8]

Overall, the majority of laws/regulations governing pharmaceutical advertising and promotion include the following criteria:

1. should be consistent with product information and labeling approved by governmental agencies
2. should be truthful and not misleading

Some regions may have further requirements for the provision of risk information or a "fair balance" of information.

Regulation of Advertising and Promotion

Industry Self-Regulation Versus Government Regulation

In many countries, while laws on pharmaceutical advertising and promotion exist, regulation is predominantly self-executed through the use of industry organizations and voluntary industry codes and guidelines. These organizations have created codes of conduct and often have set methods of addressing breaches of conduct. In certain countries, these industry organizations may have the ability to issue fines; approaches vary by country with respect to standards, sanctions and corrective actions.[9,10] The majority of complaints regarding code or legal violations generally stem from competitor companies. If the codes or guidelines are based on law, and the violations are severe, governmental authorities may step in and enforce the laws.[11]

In many jurisdictions, while the advertising and promotion of drugs and biologics for human use are regulated, the materials are not subject to preapproval by governmental authorities. Instead, manufacturers use a self-regulating mechanism in most jurisdictions in conjunction with postmarket monitoring by governmental authorities. Authorities should ensure, however, that there are adequate and effective methods, which may be based on prior evaluation, to monitor the advertising of medicinal products.

Some EU Member States, including the UK, Germany, France and Italy, have regulations that require prior evaluation and/or other restrictions for some product types.[12] In France, any advertising intended for the general public must be authorized by the French regulatory authority (ANSM) before release, while advertising intended for healthcare professionals must be submitted to the agency no more than eight days after its release.[13] In the US, manufacturers and/or license holders are required to submit a copy of all advertising materials and a current package insert or other labeling to the US Food and Drug Administration (FDA), although pre-clearance of promotional labeling and advertising is only done in "extraordinary circumstances."[14]

In all instances, regulators can penalize companies that use noncompliant advertising materials; therefore, manufacturers are well advised to impose internal controls and processes to ensure compliance with local laws and regulations.

International Organizations

IFPMA

IFPMA is a global nonprofit, nongovernmental organization representing the research-based pharmaceutical, biotech and vaccine industries.[15] In 2013, its members comprised 31 leading international companies and 50 national and regional industry associations in both developed and emerging countries.

The pharmaceutical industry is responsible for ensuring that product information, including any advertising and promotional materials, is accurate and not misleading. In the early 1980s, Health Action International, a group of consumer health organizations, expressed concerns about inappropriate marketing in developing countries and requested that a code for the promotion of pharmaceuticals be developed.[16]

To this end, IFPMA published its *Code of Pharmaceutical Marketing Practices*, adopted in 1981, as a form of self-regulation. It has since been updated several times. The IFPMA *Code of Practices*, supplemented by member association and company codes, has helped set standards for self-regulation and the ethical promotion of medicinal products. However, a large percentage of the country members have country-specific codes, and in these instances, the country codes supersede the IFPMA codes.

According to IFPMA, promotional activities must meet high ethical standards while also conforming to all relevant laws and regulations. Any claims made for therapeutic indications and conditions of use must be based on valid scientific and clinical evidence. Any side effects, contraindications and precautions also must be presented in a form that is clearly understandable to the end user.

WHO Ethical Criteria for Medicinal Drug Promotion

Following the November 1985 World Health Organization (WHO) Conference of Experts on the Rational Use of Drugs in Nairobi, WHO prepared a revised drug strategy addressing the establishment of ethical criteria for drug promotion. This strategy was based on updating and extending the ethical and scientific criteria previously established in Resolution WHA21.41 (1968).[17] In May 1988, the 41st World Health Assembly adopted Resolution WHA41.17, the main objective of which was to establish ethical criteria for medicinal drug promotion and to support and encourage the improvement of healthcare through the rational use of medicinal products.[18] The resolution acknowledged that interpretation of what is ethical varies in different regions and societies and established a baseline for the honest and truthful promotion of medicinal products.

The resolution's ethical criteria constitute general principles for standards applicable to both prescription and nonprescription drugs. These principles could be adapted by governments to meet their local political, economic, cultural, social, educational, scientific and technical situations, according to their national laws and regulations.[19] However, while all United Nations' (UN) member states have passed resolutions supporting the WHO ethical criteria, the criteria is under-utilized around the world.

Major elements of the WHO ethical criteria include: that promotion should not be "disguised as an educational or scientific activity, that undue advantage should not be taken of people's concern for their health and that generally Direct-To-Consumer Advertising (DTCA) of prescription medicines should not be permitted."[20, 21]

While the WHO ethical criteria and the IFPMA code were created primarily to protect public health, there are a few differences in the key provisions. For instance, while WHO's ethical criteria address advertisements and communications to the public and pharmaceutical sales representative conduct, these are not addressed by IFPMA. Also, while the IFPMA code was drafted by an industry-selected task force, the WHO ethical criteria were created pursuant to a consensus of drug regulatory agencies, consumers and the pharmaceutical industry. While the IFPMA code essentially is limited to pharmaceutical companies that are members of IFPMA, WHO's ethical criteria are intended to be applied more broadly.[22]

What is Advertising?

Advertising should be clearly distinguished from labeling and medical information contained in product data sheets. The following usually are considered to be advertising:

- provision of information to the general public or healthcare professionals (i.e., persons qualified to prescribe or supply medicinal products)
- sales representatives' visits to healthcare professionals
- supplying product samples
- gifts, offers or promises in the form of benefits or a bonus as inducements to prescribe or supply medicinal products

- sponsorship of promotional meetings for healthcare professionals
- sponsorship of scientific congresses attended by healthcare professionals and/or their spouses or partners[23]

The following activities usually are not considered to be advertising:

- health authority-approved package labeling and patient information leaflets
- nonpromotional correspondence and material in response to a query about a medicinal product
- factual, informative announcements and reference material including packaging changes, adverse-reaction warnings, trade catalogs and price lists (not containing product claims)
- general human health or disease information without direct or indirect reference to medicinal products[24]

Although labeling, such as accompanying package leaflets and medical information (e.g., product data sheets) are not considered advertising, they are the basis for advertising materials. The promotion of a drug prior to marketing authorization is prohibited.

WHO recommends that direct-to-consumer (DTC) advertising of prescription drugs not be allowed.[25] A limited number of countries, e.g., the US and New Zealand, permit the advertising of prescription drugs directly to consumers. Any advertising that makes deceptive claims, fails to reveal material information, is unfair or makes objective claims that are not based on clinical and/or scientific evidence should not be permitted.[26]

Advertising laws are enacted at the national level; hence, what is permitted in one country or jurisdiction may be prohibited in another. In general, advertising prescription drugs to the general public, especially those containing psychotropic or narcotic substances, is prohibited, while advertising OTC or nonprescription drugs is allowed.

Advertising Over-the-Counter (OTC) Products to the General Public

Even though advertising OTC products (also known as nonprescription drugs) to the general public is allowed in most jurisdictions, it is still a highly regulated process. Generally, advertisements can include only information from the registration that is supported by scientific and clinical evidence.

Following are items to consider in advertisements for the general public:

- The product's trade or brand name should be clearly visible.
- The name(s) of the active ingredient(s) must be included, using either international nonproprietary names (INN) or the drug's approved generic name.
- Information needed to ensure the correct use of the product, e.g., name, indications for use and any warnings, contraindications and precautions, must be included.
- There must be a clear reference to the instructions for use on the package leaflet or outer packaging.
- The manufacturer or distributor's name and address must be included.[27,28]

There also should be a listing of any known potential adverse reactions.

The following should not be included in advertisements made to the general public:

- comparison to other medicines of a similar nature
- statements addressed to children
- any recommendations by scientists, doctors, etc.
- a suggested diagnosis or treatment
- information that could lead to erroneous self-diagnosis
- improper claims of recovery
- improper pictorials of changes to the human body or action of the medicinal product
- suggestions that medical consultation and/or surgery are unnecessary
- any guarantee of the effect of taking the medicinal product
- any impression that the health of the subject can be enhanced or worsened by taking/not taking the medicine
- statement that the product belongs to another category such as a food, cosmetic or other product type
- any other false or misleading claims[29]

The main purpose of advertising to the general public is to help people make rational decisions on the use of drugs. According to the WHO resolution, advertising should, in general, be restricted to nonprescription drugs, although as noted above, the US and New Zealand allow DTC advertising of prescription drugs. Special care must be taken to combat drug misuse, addiction and dependency, especially related to narcotic and/or psychotropic drugs, and their advertising should be prohibited.[30] As noted above, drug advertisements should not be directed at children; however, health education information is acceptable. When using lay language in advertisements, any information provided must be consistent with the approved scientific data.

Advertising to Healthcare Professionals

Advertisements directed to physicians and other healthcare professionals should be based on scientific, clinical data and should be fully legible.[31] Advertisements that include promotional claims should include, at a minimum, summary scientific information. The following information (taken from the WHO Technical Report Series[32]) should be included in any advertisements:

- name(s) of the active ingredient(s) using either INN or the drug's approved generic name
- brand name
- content of active ingredient(s) per dosage form or regimen
- names of other ingredients known to cause problems
- approved therapeutic uses
- dosage form or regimen
- side effects and major adverse drug reactions
- precautions, contraindications and warnings
- major interactions
- manufacturer or distributor's name and address
- reference to scientific literature, as appropriate[33]

Reminder advertisements without claims normally are permitted; these advertisements should include at least the brand name, the INN or product's approved generic name, the name of each active ingredient and the name and address of the manufacturer or distributor.

Medical Representatives and Promotion

Medical representatives play a major role in the promotion of drugs and should have appropriate educational backgrounds. They should be adequately trained about appropriate ethical conduct, taking the WHO criteria into consideration, and have sufficient medical and technical knowledge to present product information. Medical representatives also must possess integrity to ensure they carry out their activities responsibly and avoid making false or misleading statements. The final responsibility for the statements and activities of medical representatives lies with their employers, who must ensure that their representatives do not offer inducements to healthcare professionals, prescribers and dispensers.[34] Medical representatives also should be trained to report any adverse reactions associated with the medicinal products they promote to the responsible department in their companies.[35]

Free Samples

Free samples of legally available prescription drugs should only be provided in modest quantities and only to prescribers, generally upon request.[36] In some jurisdictions, the provision of samples is clearly defined as advertising and is strictly controlled. Possible restrictions related to the supply of free samples are:

- The number of free samples for each prescribing agent is restricted; the exact number or samples permitted is determined at the local level.
- Free samples can only be supplied in response to a signed and dated written request.
- The company that supplies free samples must ensure traceability by implementing an adequate control and accountability system.
- There are restrictions on the sample size. For example, in the EU, samples may not be larger than the smallest presentation (package size) on the market.
- Each sample should bear a label and be clearly marked "free sample—not for sale."
- Free samples should be accompanied by appropriate scientific information.[37]

This list is not exhaustive; the exact restrictions on free samples are determined at the national level and are laid down in local laws and regulations. Practices in individual countries vary, especially regarding the provision of free samples of nonprescription drugs to the general public. In some jurisdictions, free samples to members of the general public are permitted; in others, they are not. In either case, free samples of nonprescription drugs distributed to the general public for promotional purposes should be used with great restraint.[38]

Gifts, Benefits

Events, gifts, pecuniary advantages, benefits or inducements provided to individuals qualified to supply medicinal products should not be expensive and should be related to their work. These may include symposia, which are useful for disseminating information. At such events, entertainment or other hospitality, and any gifts offered to healthcare professionals and allied fields should be modest. It is also important that the participation of individual healthcare practitioners in any domestic or international symposia be unconditional and unrelated to promoting any specific medicinal product(s).[39]

Impact of Social Media and the Internet

Since the inception of the WHO ethical criteria and the IFPMA codes, pharmaceutical promotion has changed considerably. With the advent of the Internet and social media, pharmaceutical advertising and promotion can be accessed throughout the world by inordinately large audiences. However, it is important to note that even with the evolution of the Internet, the approach to the regulation of advertising and promotion has not changed; the basic principles remain the same.[40]

Notably, different regions have varying regulations with respect to DTC advertising, which have implications for advertising and promotion on the Internet. For example, the EU does not permit advertisements of prescription-only or psychotropic or narcotic medicines to consumers.

Therefore, there is a need for clear distinctions and signals on pharmaceutical advertising and promotion to ensure that advertising and promotion are appropriately directed based on country-specific regulations. Also, it may behoove pharmaceutical manufacturers to consider technological methods to prevent access by consumer in regions where advertising and promotion are not allowed.

Few regions have attempted to provide guidance specific to the advertising and promotion of pharmaceuticals on the Internet. In 2011, the UK's Prescription Medicines Code of Practice Authority (PMCPA) issued an informal social media guidance on the use of digital communications by pharmaceutical manufacturers. In the US, FDA's Office of Prescription Drug Promotion (OPDP) has issued some enforcement on this topic, but has yet to issue an official guidance.[41,42]

Monitoring

To enable effective monitoring, companies must be in control of any information disseminated about their medicinal products. Postmarket surveillance can involve one or more of the following:

- keeping a sample of all advertising materials and a list of all addresses where these materials were disseminated, the method of dissemination and the date of first dissemination
- regulatory approval of all advertising materials to ensure compliance with local laws and regulations
- proper training and monitoring of medical sales representatives
- cooperation with governmental health authorities, especially in cases related to noncompliance[43]
- postmarketing clinical trials
- reporting substantiated information on hazards associated with medicinal drugs or adverse events to the appropriate national health authority immediately, and disseminating information internationally in very severe cases leading to corrective actions and/or batch recalls[44]

Medicinal product manufacturers are responsible for adhering to advertising laws in the countries or regions where their products are marketed. National governmental health authorities must have monitoring systems in place to ensure companies comply with legal requirements.

Conclusion

IFPMA and WHO set the stage for the development of industry codes, laws and regulations governing medicinal drug advertising and promotion. However, advertising is still a national issue within the purview of local governmental authorities. Since many countries do not have the resources to adequately monitor and regulate pharmaceutical advertising and promotion, they rely heavily on industry self-regulation. Also, in most jurisdictions, advertising and promotion of drugs and biologics for human use are controlled not by preapproval of advertising or promotional materials but by postmarket monitoring and surveillance.

The global overarching principles of advertising and promotion are that they should not be misleading or deceptive in nature, hide material information or be unfair. Also, they should be consistent with health authority-approved product labeling.

Although determined at the national level, generally, advertising prescription drugs to the general public, especially those containing psychotropic or narcotic substances, is prohibited, while advertising OTC/nonprescription drugs is allowed in most but not all jurisdictions. Companies selling medicinal products at the global level need to ensure they are familiar with local advertising laws and requirements and should maintain effective monitoring systems to avoid noncompliance.

Lastly, proper monitoring is paramount to ensuring that companies adhere to laws and codes to adequately protect public health.

References

1. World Health Organization. *Ethical Criteria for Medicinal Drug Promotion.* Geneva, Switzerland: World Health Organization; 1988. WHO website. http://apps.who.int/medicinedocs/en/d/Js16520e/16.1.html. Accessed 18 July 2013.
2. International Federation of Pharmaceutical Manufacturers Association (IFPMA), *Code of Pharmaceutical Marketing Practices*, Updated 2012. IFPMA website. http://www.ifpma.org/ethics/ifpma-code-of-practice/ifpma-code-of-practice.html. Accessed 18 July 2013.
3. The European Federation of Pharmaceutical Industries and Associations (EFPIA); *European Code of Practice on the Promotion of Medicines*, Updated 2011. EFPIA website. http://www.efpia.eu/documents/24/61/EFPIA-Code-of-Practice-on-the-promotion-of-prescription-only-medicines-to-and-interactions-with-healthcare-professionals-Amended-following-Statutory-General-Assembly-approval-of-14-June-2011. Accessed 18 July 2013.
4. Regulatory Affairs Professionals Society. Chapter 6, Advertising and Promotion. In: *Fundamentals of EU Regulatory Affairs Sixth Edition.* Rockville, MD; 2012:49–54.
5. Friese B, Jentges B and Muazzam U. Part A: Chapter 13, Advertising law. In: *Guide to Drug Regulatory Affairs.* Editio Cantor Verlag, Aulendorf, Germany.2007: 312.
6. Ibid.
7. WHO. *Ethical Criteria for Medicinal Drug Promotion* (1998).
8. Ziganshina L and Lexchin J. Chapter 7, Regulation of Pharmaceutical Promotion: Why Does Regulation Matter? In: *Understanding and Responding to Pharmaceutical Promotion.*
9. Ibid.
10. Dennis A., et al. Marketing, E-Commerce and Advertising in the Pharmaceutical Industry: France, the UK, and the US. Life Sciences. http://www.practicallaw.com/0-379-0848. Accessed 20 January 2013.
11. Op cit 8.
12. Op cit 4.
13. Global Legal Group Ltd. Chapter 16, France. In: *The International Comparative Legal Guide to Pharmaceutical Advertising 2009.* London; 2009.

14. Regulatory Affairs Professionals Society. Chapter 16, Prescription Drug Labeling, Advertising and Promotion. In: *Fundamentals of US Regulatory Affairs, Eighth Edition.*. Rockville, MD; 2013:199–210.
15. IFPMA website. http://www.ifpma.org/about-ifpma/welcome.html. Accessed 18 July 2013.
16. Op cit 8.
17. Op cit 7.
18. Resolution WHA41.17 adopted by the Forty-first World Health Assembly, 13 May 1988. WHO website. http://apps.who.int/medicinedocs/fr/d/Js2273e/13.8.1.html. Accessed 18 July 2013.
19. Op cit 7.
20. Op cot 8.
21. Op cit 4.
22. Op cit 8.
23. Directive 2004/27/EC of the European Parliament and of the Council of 31 March 2004 amending Directive 2001/83/EC on the Community code relating to medicinal products for human use, article 86(2). Eur-Lex website. http://eur-lex.europa.eu/Notice.do?val=343604:cs&lang=en&list=343604:cs,&pos=1&page=1&nbl=1&pgs=10&hwords=. Accessed 18 July 2013.
24. Ibid, article 86(1).
25. Op cit 8.
26. Op cit 17.
27. Op cit 13.
28. Op cit 18, (b) Advertisements in all forms to the general public (14–16).
29. Op cit 13.
30. Op cit 1.
31. Op cit 18, (a) Advertisements in all forms to physicians and health-related professionals, (10).
32. WHO Technical Report Series, No. 722, 1985, p. 43.
33. Ibid, p. 17.
34. Op cit 18, Medical representatives (17-19).
35. Ibid 5, p 317.
36. Op cit 18, Free samples of prescription drugs for promotional purposes (20).
37. Op cit 1.
38. Op cit 18, Free samples of non-prescription drugs to the general public for promotional purposes (21)
39. Op cit 18, Symposia and other scientific meetings (22–24).
40. Op cit 8.
41. Ibid.
42. Worden T and Furness A. Chapter 4. Social Media and Pharma in the UK: A Review of the Pitfalls and the Latest Guidance. The International Comparative Legal Guide to: Pharmaceutical Advertising 2011.
43. Op cit 5.
44. Op cit 18, Post-marketing scientific studies, surveillance and dissemination of information (25–27).

Chapter 7

Compliance and Enforcement

Updated by Siegfried Schmitt, PhD

OBJECTIVES

- ❑ Understand the basic principles of regulatory compliance
- ❑ Examine examples of some enforcement actions in practice
- ❑ Review the role of Competent Authorities
- ❑ Understand regulatory compliance of pharmaceuticals
- ❑ Understand regulatory compliance of medical devices

REGULATIONS AND GUIDELINES COVERED IN THIS CHAPTER

ICH

- ❑ *Good Manufacturing Practice Guide for Active Pharmaceutical Ingredients Q7*
- ❑ *Quality Risk Management Q9*
- ❑ *Pharmaceutical Quality System Q10*
- ❑ *Pharmacovigilance Planning E2E*
- ❑ *Guideline for Good Clinical Practice E6(R1)*

IMDRF

- ❑ GHTF/SG4/N28R4:2008 *Guidelines for Regulatory Auditing of Quality Management Systems of Medical Device Manufacturers—Part 1: General Requirements* (August 2008)
- ❑ GHTF/SG3/N17:2008 *Quality Management System—Medical Devices—Guidance on the Control of Products and Services Obtained from Suppliers* (December 2008)
- ❑ GHTF/SG3/N15R8:2005 *Implementation of Risk Management Principles and Activities Within a Quality Management System* (May 2005)
- ❑ GHTF/SG3/N99-10:2004 *Quality Management Systems—Process Validation Guidance* (January 2004)

EU

- ❑ Compilation of community procedures in inspections and exchange of information of 5 July 2011, EMA/INS/GMP/459921/2010 Rev 13
- ❑ Directive 2011/62/EU of the European Parliament and of the Council of 8 June 2011 amending Directive 2001/83/EC on the Community code relating to medicinal products for human use, as regards the prevention of the entry into the legal supply chain of falsified medicinal products

- ❑ Regulation (EC) 726/2004 of the European Parliament and of the Council of 31 March 2004 laying down Community procedures for the authorisation and supervision of medicinal products for human and veterinary use and establishing a European Medicines Agency

- ❑ Directive 2001/20/EC of the European Parliament and of the Council of 4 April 2001 on the approximation of the laws, regulations and administrative provisions of the Member States relating to the implementation of good clinical practices in the conduct of clinical trials for medicinal products for human use

- ❑ Commission Directive 2005/28/EC of 8 April 2005 laying down principles and guidelines for good clinical practice as regards investigational medicinal products for human use, as well as the requirements for authorisation of the manufacturing or importation of such products

- ❑ Commission Directive 2003/94/EC of 8 October 2003 laying down the principles and guidelines of good manufacturing practice in respect of medicinal products for human use and investigational medicinal products for human use

- ❑ Commission Directive 91/412/EEC of 23 July 1991 laying down the principles and guidelines of good manufacturing practice for veterinary medicinal products

- ❑ Council Directive 92/25/EEC of 31 March 1992 on the wholesale distribution of medicinal products for human use

- ❑ Directive 2004/10/EC of the European Parliament and of the Council of 11 February 2004 on the harmonization of laws, regulations and administrative provisions relating to the application of the principles of good laboratory practice and the verification of their applications for tests on chemical substances

- ❑ Directive 2004/9/EC of the European Parliament and of the Council of 11 February 2004 on the inspection and verification of good laboratory practice

- ❑ Council Directive 90/385/EEC of 20 June 1990 on the approximation of the laws of the Member States relating to active implantable medical devices

- ❑ Council Directive 93/42/EEC of 14 June 1993 concerning medical devices

- ❑ Directive 98/79/EC of the European Parliament and of the Council of 27 October 1998 on in vitro diagnostic medical devices

US

- ❑ *Federal Food, Drug, and Cosmetic Act* of 1938

- ❑ *Public Health Service Act* of 1944

- ❑ 21 CFR 210 Current Good Manufacturing Practice in Manufacturing, Processing, Packing, or Holding of Drugs; General

- ❑ 21 CFR 211 Current Good Manufacturing Practice for Finished Pharmaceuticals

- ❑ 21 CFR 807 Establishment Registration and Device Listing for Manufacturers and Initial Importers of Devices

- ❑ 21 CFR 820 Quality System Regulation

- ❑ 21 CFR 803 Medical Device Reporting

Introduction

Competent Authorities exercise a legal right to control product transport (e.g., transit or import), use or sale within their jurisdictions by ensuring compliance with laws, regulations, standards and any postmarketing commitments.[1] Marketing authorization holders (MAHs) must comply with both pre- and post-registration requirements. A number of postapproval regulatory activities, such as change management, may impact the manufacturing, labeling and compliance status of marketed new drug or biologic products.[2] License holders are obliged to notify the responsible Competent Authorities of any such changes. MAHs also must have pharmacovigilance and postmarketing surveillance systems in place, and maintain their quality systems to comply with Good Practice quality guidelines and regulations (GxPs) and/or requirements of the International Organization for Standardization (ISO) (depending upon the quality system and product type). National laws addressing compliance and enforcement are updated or amended periodically to reflect advances in technology and/or in response to public health crises. This chapter covers the basic principles of compliance and enforcement.

Pharmaceuticals and Biological Products

Regulatory compliance for pharmaceuticals and biologic products is enforced by inspections and monitoring. National legislation provides statutory powers to Competent Authorities to ensure compliance via such sanctions as monetary fines and/or imprisonment for noncompliance.[3] Activities subject to enforcement may include manufacture and quality control (including Good Manufacturing Practice (GMP)), preclinical and clinical testing (including Good Laboratory Practice (GLP) and Good Clinical Practice (GCP)), storage and distribution (including Good Distribution Practice (GDP)), advertising and promotion and pharmacovigilance. This list is not exhaustive; other issues may include combating fraud, counterfeiting and gross negligence.

Enforcement normally is carried out at the national level. In the US, it is implemented by regulations promulgated following enactment of a law, for example the *Federal Food, Drug, and Cosmetic Act* (*FD&C Act*)[4] and the *Public Health Service Act* (*PHS Act*).[5] In the EU, inspections are covered by various regulations and guidelines, among them: Regulation (EC) 726/2004 of the European Parliament and of the Council of 31 March 2004 laying down Community procedures for the authorisation and supervision of medicinal products for human and veterinary use and establishing a European Medicines Agency,[6] the *Clinical Trials Directive* (Directive 2001/20/EC),[7] the *GCP Directive* (Commission Directive 2005/28/EC),[8] the *GLP Directive* (Directive 2004/10/EC),[9] the *GMP Directives* (Commission Directive 2003/94/EC and Commission Directive 91/412/EC)[10] and the *GDP Directive* (Council Directive 92/25/EEC).[11] Article 3 of Commission Directive 2003/94/EC covers Member States' authorities' repeated inspections to ensure GMP compliance for human medicinal products and investigational medicinal products. Despite the fact that enforcement is a national issue, several Mutual Recognition Agreements (MRAs) exist across jurisdictions on conformity assessment, GxPs and inspections.[12] Generally, MRAs and other forms of international cooperation are intended to promote trade at the global level by facilitating market access and to ease the inspection burden of the respective authorities.

The International Conference on Harmonisation (ICH) has published guidelines outlining harmonized quality standards on several topics, such as GMP for active pharmaceutical ingredients (API) (Q7),[13] quality risk management (Q9),[14] pharmaceutical quality systems (Q10),[15] pharmacovigilance (E2E)[16] and GCP (E6).[17] Compliance with these basic standards is expected in the ICH countries. Inspections will verify that these requirements, plus any national regulatory requirements, are met.

Competent Authorities have established several means of exchanging information on critical issues, such as corrective actions, recalls, rejected import consignments and other product regulatory and enforcement problems.[18] For example, in September 2010, the European Medicines Agency (EMA) and the US Food and Drug Administration (FDA) extended confidentiality agreements indefinitely. EudraGMP is the name for the Community database on manufacturing and import authorizations and Good Manufacturing Practice (GMP) certificates. EMA launched the first release in April 2007, and future releases will include planning of inspections in third countries, alerts for quality defects and, in addition, also are expected to include information on Wholesale Distributors as a result of new Community legislation on anti-falsification.[19]

Inspections

Before medicinal products can be placed on the market, MAHs, manufacturers, distributors or wholesalers, dealers and/or marketers must undergo several preapproval inspections by Competent Authorities. These cover all areas of GxPs related to the product's development, testing, manufacture and distribution:

- GLP
- GCP
- GMP
- GDP
- Good Pharmacovigilance Practice (GPvP)

Other areas subject to inspection include quality system management and advertising and promotion. Following a successful inspection, a certificate of compliance such as a manufacturing authorization and/or GMP certificate usually is issued, which also specifies the terms and conditions of its issuance. This compliance certificate normally is part of the official marketing authorization application.

Postapproval inspections primarily involve monitoring activities to ensure that manufacturers maintain their quality systems and track any postmarketing changes to their products and processes by implementing rigorous change control systems. Certificates, such as manufacturing authorizations, need to be renewed regularly, requiring repeat inspections.

Figure 7-1 is an overview of the inspection and approval process.

Inspections are performed by the national Competent Authorities. This is part of the Member States' remit:

- licensing and control of manufacturers
- granting manufacturer's authorizations
- inspections of manufacturing sites

Most Members States have separate agencies for human and veterinary drugs, and listings of these are available on the Internet.[20]

EMA coordinates inspections, but does not conduct them.[21] The agency is responsible for coordinating any inspection requested by the Committee for Medicinal

Figure 7-1. The Inspection Process Related to Marketing Authorization Applications

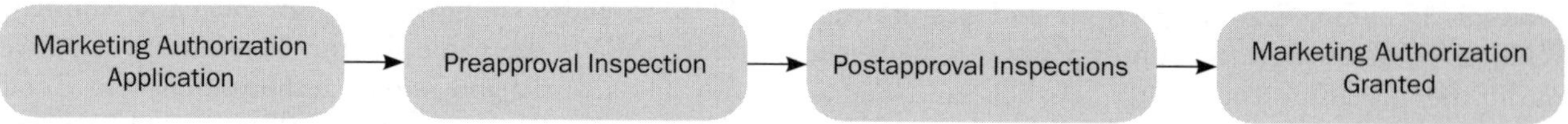

Products for Human Use (CHMP) or the Committee for Medicinal Products for Veterinary Use (CVMP) in connection with the assessment of marketing authorization applications or matters referred to these committees.

The need for harmonization led to the creation of the Inspectorates Association—the Pharmaceutical Inspection Cooperation (PIC) Scheme, a collaboration between authorities. The Pharmaceutical Inspection Convention and PIC Scheme (jointly referred to as PIC/S) are two international instruments involving countries and pharmaceutical inspection authorities that provide active and constructive cooperation in the field of GMP.[22] A total of 41 authorities currently participate in PIC/S.

GxP Activities: GMP, GLP, GCP, GPvP

GxP is a general term used mostly in the life science industry. The "G" stand for Good, the "P" for Practice and the "x" is a variable. Sometimes a "C" is added to indicate "current," i.e., CGMP (current Good Manufacturing Practice). Following are the most relevant GxP guidelines. **Figure 7-2** provides an overview of the applicability of these practices along the drug lifecycle.

GLP

GLP principles define a set of rules and criteria for a quality system concerned with the organizational process and the conditions under which nonclinical health and environmental safety studies are planned, performed, monitored, recorded, reported and archived. In the EU, procedures for requesting and reporting GLP inspections for centralized applications have been finalized. The procedure describes the coordination of GLP inspections of the nonclinical safety, toxicological and pharmacological studies proposed in human and veterinary applications for marketing authorizations under the Centralised Procedure. It took effect 16 May 2007.[23]

Nonclinical safety, toxicological and pharmacological studies proposed in human and veterinary marketing authorization applications normally are inspected by the national Competent Authority.

GCP

GCP is an international ethical and scientific quality standard for designing, recording and reporting trials that involve the participation of human subjects.[24] Compliance with this standard provides public assurance that the trial subjects' rights, safety and well-being are protected, trial conduct is consistent with ethical principles and the clinical trial data are credible.[25]

The exact requirements for the conduct of clinical trials are specified in national or regional laws and regulations. GCP compliance is ensured by inspections that entail an official review of documents, facilities, records, quality assurance arrangements and any other resources deemed by the Competent Authority to be related to the clinical trial. These inspections may take place at the trial site, the sponsor's facilities or those of the contract research organization, or any other sites the Competent Authority sees fit to inspect.[26] Good Clinical Data Management Practice (GCDMP) may also be inspected.

GMP

GMP can be defined as "that part of Quality Assurance which ensures that products are consistently produced and controlled to the quality standards appropriate to their intended use." The Guide to Good Manufacturing Practice is a series of detailed guidelines that interpret GMP principles, which in turn are supplemented by a series of annexes that modify or augment the detailed guidelines for certain types of products, or provide more-specific guidance on a particular topic.

PIC/S has published a series of GMP guidance documents that can be found on the PIC website.[27] These documents are nearly identical with *The Rules Governing Medicinal Products in the European Union* (EudraLex) Volume 4 (except for the sections referring to the Qualified Person, which is unique to the EU).[28] The equivalent regulations in the US are promulgated in the *Code of Federal Regulations* as predicate rules, namely 21 CFR Parts 210 and 211.[29]

The primary goal of these guidelines is to facilitate the removal of trade barriers to medicinal products, promote uniformity in licensing decisions and ensure that high quality assurance standards are maintained in the development, manufacture and control of such products.

Inspections usually evaluate the entire production facility, a specific product or an element of a product process or system and may include:

- quality functions
- production and processes
- qualification and validation activities
- (nonconforming) raw materials or active ingredients

- complaint handling
- equipment and facilities
- testing and inspection
- purchasing and materials handling
- records and documents
- labeling
- management controls
- other regulatory requirements
- pharmacovigilance/adverse event reporting system
- registration and listing[30]

Documents typically reviewed include:

- Site Master File
- quality manual
- job descriptions
- standard operating procedures (SOPs)
- validation reports
- manufacturing formulae, records and instructions
- specifications
- batch release procedure and the role of the Qualified Person(s) or person(s) releasing product

GDP

GDP covers quality issues throughout the distribution and supply chain network. Authorized medicinal products must be transported, stored and distributed under controlled conditions to ensure they reach the end user without any alteration of their properties. To this end, the entire distribution and supply chain must be inspected to ensure that wholesalers and other authorized supply chain parties comply with GDP principles and guidelines.

GDP should be implemented through a quality system operated by the medicinal product distributor, wholesaler and/or manufacturer to ensure:

- products are distributed legally
- products are stored under controlled conditions to meet the specified requirements (especially important for heat-sensitive products or those that should be stored below the freezing point)
- contamination is avoided
- products are stored in appropriately safe and secure areas
- products do not exceed shelf life or expiration dates
- products are delivered to the correct address
- traceability is ensured throughout the chain

The revised European Commission guideline on GDP was published for consultation in 2011 and is expected to come into force no later than 2013, with inspections based on this guide to begin no later than 2014.[31]

GPvP

GPvP requires compliance with legislative requirements and guidelines on monitoring the safety of medicines used in clinical practice and postmarketing. Pharmacovigilance inspections should be conducted to provide assurance that MAHs are complying with their regulatory obligations and to facilitate compliance. The legal requirements for pharmacovigilance systems are specified in national or regional laws and regulations. ICH has published guidance intended as an aid in planning pharmacovigilance activities (*Pharmacovigilance Planning E2E*).[32] Local regulations may contain additional requirements.[33]

The rapid and effective identification and assessment of drug safety issues are fundamental to the ability of Competent Authorities and MAHs to protect public or animal health by taking swift, appropriate action. This requires a properly functioning pharmacovigilance system. Competent Authorities have an obligation to enforce medicines legislation and to conduct inspections to detect noncompliance. Noncompliance with pharmacovigilance obligations could have a potentially serious human or animal health impact. Pharmacovigilance is the most likely area for an inspection of the regulatory affairs department.

Pharmacovigilance

In July 2012, new pharmacovigilance legislation came into effect across the EU as a result of changes set out in Regulation (EU) No1235/2010 and Directive 2010/84/EU. Transitional arrangements exist from July 2012 to 2015. The purpose of this new legislation is to:

- provide clear roles and responsibilities for key responsible parties
- strengthen transparency and communication on issues relating to safety of medicines
    - o particularly to patients and prescribers
- strengthen pharmaceutical industry pharmacovigilance systems
    - o reduce administrative burden
- improve risk management planning and non-interventional safety studies
- strengthen (and simplify) the reporting system for adverse event reactions
- ensure proactive and proportionate collection of high quality data
- simplify requirements and reduce duplication and administrative burden

The guidelines on GPvP[34] are published in a series of Modules. Module III covers pharmacovigilance inspections.

Advertising and Promotion

As noted in Chapter 6, the advertising and promotion of drugs and biologics for human use usually are not controlled in most jurisdictions by preapproval of advertising or promotional materials. The relevant authorities issue guidance on advertising for pharmaceutical products, which can differ greatly among jurisdictions. For example, the UK agency MHRA published a guide ("Blue Guide") on "Advertising and Promotion of Medicines in the UK" in August 2012.[35] Manufacturers use such guidelines as self-regulatory mechanisms in conjunction with postmarketing monitoring by Competent Authorities. Nonetheless, Competent Authorities are responsible for ensuring there are adequate and effective methods to monitor medicinal product advertising, which may be based on a system of prior evaluation. In many instances, even though preclearance of promotional labeling and advertising is not mandatory, manufacturers and/or license holders may still be required to submit a copy of all advertising materials to the Competent Authorities before or immediately after they are released.

The World Health Organization (WHO) recommends that prescription drug products only be advertised to healthcare professionals, while over-the-counter (OTC) products also may be advertised to the general public. In some jurisdictions, e.g., the US and New Zealand, direct-to-consumer (DTC) advertising of prescription drugs is permitted.

It is important to realize that sales representatives' visits to healthcare professionals and the supply of samples, gifts, offers or promises in the form of benefits or bonuses as inducements to prescribe or supply medicinal products are subject to advertising and promotion laws and regulations, as is the sponsorship of promotional/scientific meetings for healthcare professionals. Many noncompliance cases in the postmarketing phase arise from labeling or advertising issues. This situation is especially important since labeling and/or advertising texts are part of the product with which end users have direct contact and are a form of direct communication with them. Any information presented or claims made must comply with a product's registered details.

Medicinal product manufacturers must abide by national and international laws on advertising in the jurisdiction where the product is being sold. National Competent Authorities must have adequate monitoring systems in place to ensure companies comply with legal requirements.

Postmarketing Change Control

Marketed drugs may undergo labeling or manufacturing changes. Change control is handled differently by various countries and regions. Generally, however, minor changes often can be introduced without prior evaluation if they do not affect the product's approved quality, safety or efficacy.[36] Major changes normally must undergo an evaluation and can only be implemented after approval by the responsible Competent Authority. The exact classification of variations or changes and accompanying documentation that must be submitted are detailed in national and regional laws and regulations. Companies must have a functioning change control system to track all post-authorization changes and must apply for any changes to their products or make appropriate notification to the national Competent Authority after market entry. Inspections often focus on (even slight) changes that may affect the validity of the marketing authorization.

Especially in the developed world, companies under increasing regulatory and competitive pressure are adopting software solutions in areas such as document management, the electronic Common Technical Document (eCTD), change control, pharmacovigilance reporting and labeling. Such solutions have the functionality to help track any changes to products, allow timely submission to health authorities and keep companies in compliance. However, unless electronic reporting is mandated, the real issue is for companies to meet their legal reporting obligations regarding any changes to their products in the post-authorization phase.

Enforcement

Enforcement in the pharmaceutical sector can be defined as any action taken by a Competent Authority to protect the public from products of suspect quality, safety or efficacy, or to ensure that products are manufactured in compliance with appropriate laws, regulations and standards, as well as manufacturer commitments made as part of the product marketing approval. Competent Authorities must ensure that medicinal products are manufactured in compliance with appropriate laws, regulations, standards and commitments made as part of the product marketing approval.[37] To do this, a Competent Authority must have the legal right or mandate to control products entering, manufactured or put onto the market within its jurisdiction. Compliance can be confirmed by conducting GxP inspections of manufacturers', distributors', wholesalers' and MAHs' premises. Enforcement action, which may be administrative or judicial in nature, may be taken if violative acts or conditions are discovered. Examples of administrative measures, which usually do not require judiciary action, include inspections, voluntary correction programs, recalls and license suspension or revocation, public alerts or an importation ban. If after taking administrative measures, manufacturer compliance is not forthcoming, the Competent Authority may use judicial tools such as seizure, injunction, civil monetary penalties or prosecution.[38] Some common offenses that could result in criminal sanctions include:

- placing a product on the market in a way that is not in accordance with the marketing authorization
- manufacturing, distributing or marketing a product without a valid marketing authorization
- failing to adapt to technical and scientific advances
- failure to have a Qualified Person responsible for Pharmacovigilance (QPPV) or a Qualified Person (QP) for batch release
- failure to report a suspected adverse event

Figure 7-2. GxP Guidances Applicable to the Drug Lifecycle

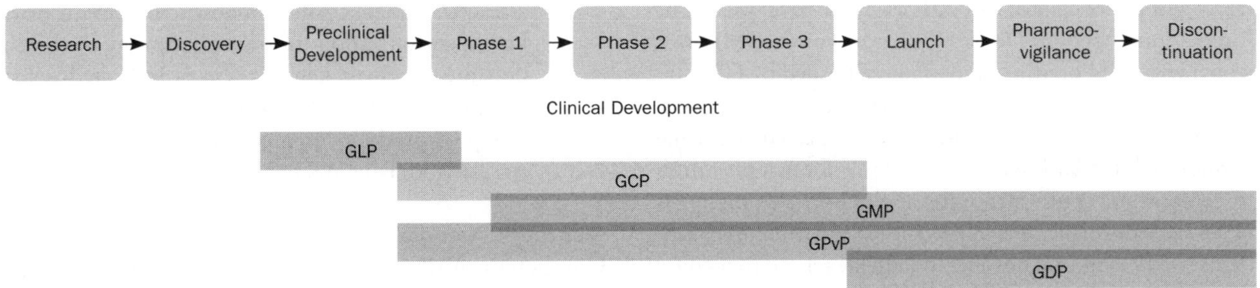

- marketing a product with noncompliant labeling or a noncompliant package leaflet
- making false advertising claims[39]

Competent Authorities sometimes face the difficult choice of either asking for the recall of a medicinal product or medical device from the market or leaving a defective product on the market to avoid causing a shortage, which could result in even more serious conditions than the noncompliant product or device. This is a particularly difficult decision in the case of orphan drugs. At the heart of the matter is always the patient.

Medical Devices and In Vitro Diagnostic Devices

Like pharmaceutical products, medical devices must comply with national and regional laws and regulations enforced by monitoring and inspections. The innovative nature of the medical device industry creates unique legal and enforcement risks, compliance rules and industry codes of conduct. The areas to be inspected at the pre- and postmarketing phases for drugs and devices are similar and cover preclinical and clinical testing, the manufacturing process and controls, vigilance reporting, change control, quality systems and labeling and advertising activities. As is the case for pharmaceutical products, national and regional laws and regulations form the legal basis of medical device compliance. In the EU, for example, medical device compliance is based on three directives: the *Active Implantable Medical Devices Directive* (*AIMDD*) (Council Directive 90/385/EEC)[40] and *Medical Devices Directive* (*MDD*) (Council Directive 93/42/EEC)[41]—both now supplemented by Directive 2007/47/EC—and the *In Vitro Diagnostic Medical Devices Directive* (*IVDD*) (Directive 98/79/EC).[42] Although these directives form the basis for enforcement, compliance with published guidance and harmonized standards, although not legally binding, is also a major part of inspection programs.

Unlike medicinal products, the authority granting market access (CE marking) in the EU is a Notified Body, acting on behalf of a regulatory authority. Market surveillance, i.e., pharmacovigilance, is, however, the remit of a national authority. This process is not harmonized within the EU. The EU maintains relevant information in the European Databank on Medical Devices (Eudamed).[43] Depending on the applicable directive, Eudamed contains data on:

- registration of manufacturers, Authorized Representatives and devices
- data relating to certificates issued, modified, supplemented, suspended, withdrawn or refused
- data obtained in accordance with the vigilance procedure
- data on clinical investigations

Eudamed is not publicly accessible, and it became obligatory in May 2011.

In the US, amendments to the *FD&C Act* passed in 1976 form the basis for establishment registration and device listing requirements (21 CFR 807).[44] In addition, the amendments addressed the issue of GMP for medical devices (21 CFR 820),[45] medical device reporting (MDR) and guidelines on policies, procedures and industry responsibilities for field corrections and removals (21 CFR 803).[46] Numerous changes to device laws and regulations have resulted from amendments to the *FD&C Act* over the years.[47] For example, the *Safe Medical Devices Act* of 1990 (*SMDA*) and the *Medical Device Amendments* of 1992 led to promulgation of the Quality System Regulation (21 CFR 820),[48] and the *Medical Device User Fee and Modernization Act* of 2002 (*MDUFMA*) resulted in changes to some compliance regulations relating to inspections, labeling and validation.[49]

The Global Harmonization Task Force was conceived in 1992 in an effort to achieve greater uniformity between national medical device regulatory systems to enhance patient safety and increase access to safe, effective and clinically beneficial medical technologies around the world. A partnership between regulatory authorities and regulated industry, GHTF was comprised of five Founding Members: EU, US, Canada, Australia and Japan. GHTF published numerous guidance documents related to device quality and compliance for premarket evaluation, postmarketing surveillance and vigilance, quality systems, auditing and clinical safety and performance.[50] In 2012, GHTF gave way to the International Medical Device Regulators Forum (IMDRF), which will build on the foundation established by GHTF.

In many regions, the use of international and/or regional standards, although not mandatory, is expected. Utilizing harmonized standards is a convenient way for manufacturers to demonstrate conformance to the Essential Requirements of device performance and safety. The list of harmonized standards is very long, and not all standards are related to medical devices. Common standards used to demonstrate compliance with the legal requirements of medical devices include:

- preclinical testing: the ISO 10993 series for biocompatibility testing
- clinical testing: ISO 14155-1 and 2
- risk analysis: ISO 14971
- quality systems: ISO 9001 and ISO 13485
- packaging: ISO 11607 (for terminally sterilized medical devices)
- labeling: ISO 15233, EN 980
- sterilization: ISO 11130 series

The above list is not exhaustive. In the absence of international standards, regional and/or national standards can be used. Reference to a regional, e.g., an EN standard, or a national standard usually is accepted in other regions that have no standards of their own, but this is determined on a case-by-case basis at the national level.

Inspections

Inspections form part of both the pre- and postmarketing phases of medical device manufacture. The objective of a government (Regulatory Authority) inspection is to assure that companies manufacture and supply products that are safe, effective and of the quality and purity the companies purport they possess and are supplied in accordance with the license particulars. Inspections are the ultimate test of a company's ability to demonstrate in a very short period of time and under stressful conditions how well it is adhering to its regulatory submissions, quality system and GxPs. There are three types of inspections:

- General GMP inspections (also termed regular, periodic, planned or routine) should be carried out before a manufacturing authorization is granted. This kind of inspection also may be necessary for a significant variation to the manufacturing authorization and if there is a history of noncompliance.
- Re-inspections (also termed follow-up or reassessment) may be indicated to monitor the corrective actions required as the result of the previous inspection.
- Product- or process-related inspections (also termed special or problem-oriented) may be indicated to assess the adherence of the manufacturer to the marketing authorization dossier and the way the batch documentation is kept. It also is indicated when complaints and recalls may concern one product or group of products or processing procedures (e.g., sterilization, labeling, etc.).

Inspection standards are available from the national Competent Authority, EMA, FDA and others (e.g., PIC/S).[51] The elements of an inspection are:

- planning
- notification
- conduct
- definition of deficiencies
- post-inspection letter
- company responses
- inspection report

Companies must always be inspection ready (in theory). National Competent Authorities do not have to give prior notification of an inspection; however they normally do (from days to months), except FDA for inspections within the US. Several joint inspection programs by the agencies have been announced and conducted.[52]

Active pharmaceutical ingredient (API) manufacturers can apply for a Certificate of Suitability (CEP) from the European Directorate for the Quality of Medicines & HealthCare (EDQM). The CEP does not replace a certificate of analysis and it is not a GMP certificate. Directive 2001/83/EC as amended (Article 111) and Directive 2001/82/EC as amended (Article 80) mandate EDQM to establish an annual program for inspections of manufacturing sites and brokers and distributors holding CEPs. The EDQM inspection program:

- is an integral part of the Certification Procedure
- may be performed before or after the CEP is granted: risk-based decision whether to inspect
- aims to verify compliance with the submitted dossier and GMP
- is carried out mainly outside Europe, involving sites holding or applying for CEP(s)
- permits only APIs produced in compliance with EU GMP to be used for the manufacture of medicinal products
- makes the MAH responsible for ensuring EU GMP compliance of the API manufacturer
- requires a declaration from the QP in the marketing authorization application and any relevant variation application

The EDQM inspection process:

- inspections are always product-related

- one EU/EEA inspector plus one EDQM inspector
- local inspector invited in non-European Pharmacopoeia countries
- inspection lasts about three days
- inspection includes facilities, production and quality unit documents
- reference documentation: ICH Q7 and CEP Application
- costs: fee for an inspection is €5,000 plus inspectors' travel expenses

For medical devices, in many instances, inspections are carried out by third parties accredited by Competent Authorities, e.g., Notified Bodies (NBs) in the EU or accredited firms in the US. In such cases, Competent Authorities must maintain lists on their websites of firms accredited to conduct inspections. Normally, the Notified Body[53] inspects, but the Competent Authority is equally empowered to inspect.[54]

Before placing medical devices on the market, manufacturers must undergo an inspection or self-certification in the form of an audit. An audit is a systematic, independent, documented process for obtaining records, statements of fact or other relevant information and assessing that information objectively to determine the extent to which specified requirements are fulfilled.[55]

Some areas that would normally be covered in an audit include:

- quality management systems
- resources
- staff training (training records)
- upper management involvement
- vigilance and postmarketing surveillance
- organizational charts, roles and responsibilities
- clinical trial material manufacture, storage and distribution logistics
- supply chain of any material or service (e.g., quality agreements, supplier audits)
- manufacture, storage and packaging
- utilities (e.g., water; heating, ventilation and air conditioning (HVAC))
- currently valid marketing authorization
- computerized systems (tools)
- validation and qualification

A typical audit process is shown in **Figure 7-3**.

Quality Systems

Most jurisdictions require medical device manufacturers to implement a quality management system. GHTF published three guidance documents on the topic:

- GHTF/SG3/N17:2008 *Quality Management System—Medical Devices—Guidance on the Control of Products and Services Obtained from Suppliers*[56]
- GHTF/SG3/N15R8:2005 *Implementation of Risk Management Principles and Activities Within a Quality Management System*[57]
- GHTF/SG3/N99-10:2004 *Quality Management Systems—Process Validation Guidance*[58]

These guidance documents are based in part on ISO standards, including:

- ISO 9000:2005 *Quality management systems—fundamentals and vocabulary*
- ISO 13485:2003 Medical devices—*Quality management systems—requirements for regulatory purposes*
- ISO 14971:2007 *Medical devices—Application of risk management to medical devices*

ISO 13485 specifies requirements for a quality management system for an organization that needs to demonstrate its ability to provide medical devices consistently meeting customer and regulatory requirements. ISO 14971 establishes risk management requirements for medical devices.

Some countries may specify risk and quality management requirements within their national legislation. In many cases, however, those requirements are based on the ISO and GHTF standards and guidelines. Most medical device manufacturers will become certified to ISO 13485 during a preapproval inspection before they place medical devices on the market. Inspections for ISO 13485 compliance normally cover areas such as:

- management responsibility
- design control
- corrective and preventive action (CAPA)
- production and process controls (P&PC)
- records/document change controls
- material controls
- facility and equipment controls (F&EC)[59]

The requirements for a pharmaceutical quality system are summarized in the ICH Q10 guideline,[60] which has been transposed or adopted by the ICH regions, including the US and Japan. In the EU, this is included in *EudraLex*[61] Volume 4 Part III under the title of "Q10 Note for Guidance on Pharmaceutical Quality System" and it has led to the revision of Chapter 1 of *EudraLex* Volume 4 Part I, which has been renamed "Pharmaceutical Quality System" and came into force 31 January 2013.

The introduction to Part III states:

> "ICH Q10 provides an example of a pharmaceutical quality system designed for the entire product lifecycle and therefore goes beyond current GMP requirements, which with the exception of the manufacture of investigational medicinal products for human use, do not apply to the development part of the lifecycle. At the time of the EU implementation of ICH Q10 it was also recognised that Chapters 1, 2 and 7 of the GMP Guide

Figure 7-3. Flow Chart – Overview of Typical Audit Process

Initiate the audit
(10)

- define audit objectives, scope and criteria
- establish initial contact with the manufacturer and/or auditee
- appoint the lead auditor
- determine the feasibility of the audit
- select the audit team

↓

Conduct document review
(10.6.2.1)

- review relevant management system documentation and determine its adequacy with respect to audit criteria

↓

Prepare for on-site audit activities
(10.6.2.2-5)

- prepare the audit plan, if appropriate, as part of an audit program
- assign work to the audit team
- prepare work documents

↓

Conduct on-site audit activities
(10.6.3)

- conduct opening meeting
- communicate during the audit
- define roles and responsibilities of guides and observers
- collect and verify information
- generate audit findings
- prepare audit conclusions
- conduct closing meeting

↓

Prepare, approve and distribute the audit report
(10.6.4)

- prepare the audit report
- approve and distribute the audit report

↓

Complete the audit
(10.6.5)

↓

Conduct audit follow-up
(10.8)

Source: GHTF: SG4/N28R4:2008

should be updated to align with the terminology and concepts utilised in ICH Q10.

The content of ICH Q10 that is additional to the scope of GMP is optional. Its use should facilitate innovation, continual improvement and strengthen the link between pharmaceutical development and manufacturing activities."

It is clear that the revisions have not yet been concluded and will be ongoing well into 2013 or beyond. What is not at all clear is the "optional" clause in this document, as it is generally acknowledged that all parts of *EudraLex* are enforceable. EMA still has to provide clarification on this subject.

Vigilance and Postmarketing Surveillance and Compliance

As noted in Chapter 22, manufacturers placing medical devices on the market must have a vigilance system for collecting and evaluating reported incidents and taking any needed corrective action to prevent the recurrence of such incidents. In addition, for certain classes of products, such as diagnostic devices where false positives and/or false negatives may occur, long-term implantable devices and devices for home use where the evaluation of the performance from adverse event reports alone would not be sufficient, postmarketing surveillance (PMS) should be used. The manufacturer must implement systematic procedures to monitor and review device experience once the product is placed on the market.

Competent Authorities need to check whether manufacturers comply with their legal obligations in implementing vigilance and PMS systems. Although these systems are normally checked in the premarket phase as part of the initial inspection(s), Competent Authorities need to ensure that manufacturers maintain their systems by performing periodic routine inspections (surveillance audits). Inspections, which can be conducted by accredited third parties and performed during regular audits, may check the following:

- relevant standard operating procedures (SOPs) on vigilance, handling of complaints and PMS
- training records
- curriculum vitae and location in the organogram of the person responsible for reporting incidents
- recordkeeping
- history of any recalls and or corrective actions

Advertising and Compliance

As noted in Chapter 22, medical device advertising should not include false, misleading or deceptive information about the device that could lead to an erroneous impression regarding its design, construction, performance, intended use, quantity, character, value, composition, merit or safety. Any claims should be supported by appropriate clinical and/

or scientific information. In many instances, cases of noncompliance may be reported to the Competent Authorities by competitors. Competent Authorities need to monitor advertising activities to ensure compliance with national or regional laws, imposing sanctions if necessary.

Postmarketing Change Control

Manufacturers are required to have functioning change control systems in place to continuously update their technical information in the postmarketing phase. Competent Authorities or other accredited institutions must be notified of any changes that affect the quality system before they are implemented. In addition, for higher-risk devices, all changes to the technical file must be submitted for approval before they can be implemented.

This process must be monitored during surveillance inspections. Ineffective change control of documents and processes could result in an audit finding of noncompliance.

Conclusion

Authorities are expected to carry out their public health mandates by facilitating the timely introduction of new medical products and medical devices to meet society's requirements. At the same time, national Competent Authorities are responsible for protecting the public from products of suspect quality, safety and efficacy and should be granted sufficient power to enforce laws and regulations and impose sanctions.

MAHs must comply with both pre- and post-registration requirements. Competent Authorities must ensure that these obligations are met. Enforcement generally is enacted at the national level, based on applicable laws and regulations in a particular jurisdiction. Inspections in both the pre- and postmarketing phases, surveillance and monitoring are used to identify noncompliance, which is punishable by such criminal sanctions as monetary fines and/or imprisonment. Competent Authorities also have established several means of exchanging information at the global level on critical issues such as corrective actions, recalls, rejected import consignments and other regulatory and enforcement problems.[62]

References

1. Regulatory Affairs Professionals Society. "Chapter 7 Enforcement and National Authorities," *Fundamentals of EU Regulatory Affairs Sixth Edition.* Rockville, MD. 2012:58.
2. Regulatory Affairs Professionals Society. "Chapter 16 Postmarketing and Other Activities," *Fundamentals of Canadian Regulatory Affairs Third Edition.* Rockville, MD. 2011:111.
3. Regulatory Affairs Professionals Society. "Chapter 7 Enforcement and National Authorities," *Fundamentals of EU Regulatory Affairs Sixth Edition.* Rockville, MD. 2012:59.
4. *Federal Food, Drug, and Cosmetic Act* of 1938, Public Law 75-717, 52 Statute 1040, Prohibited Acts Chapter 5. Drugs and Devices, 1938. FDA website. www.fda.gov/RegulatoryInformation/Legislation/FederalFoodDrugandCosmeticActFDCAct/FDCActChapterVDrugsandDevices/default.htm. Accessed 9 January 2013.
5. *Public Health Service Act* (*PHS Act*) of 1944. FDA website. www.fda.gov/regulatoryinformation/legislation/ucm148717.htm. Accessed 9 January 2013.
6. Regulation (EC) 726/2004 of the European Parliament and of the Council of 31 March 2004 laying down Community procedures for the authorisation and supervision of medicinal products for human and veterinary use and establishing a European Medicines Agency. EUR-Lex website. http://eur-lex.europa.eu/LexUriServ/LexUriServ.do?uri=OJ:L:2004:136:0001:0033:en:PDF. Accessed 9 January 2013.
7. Directive 2001/20/EC of the European Parliament and of the Council of 4 April 2001 on the approximation of the laws, regulations and administrative provisions of the Member States relating to the implementation of good clinical practices in the conduct of clinical trials for medicinal products for human use (*Clinical Trials Directive*). EUR-Lex website. http://eur-lex.europa.eu/LexUriServ/LexUriServ.do?uri=OJ:L:2001:121:0034:0044:en:PDF. Accessed 9 January 2013.
8. Commission Directive 2005/28/EC of 8 April 2005 laying down principles and guidelines for good clinical practice as regards investigational medicinal products for human use, as well as the requirements for authorisation of the manufacturing or importation of such products (*Good Clinical Practice Directive*). EUR-Lex website. http://eur-lex.europa.eu/LexUriServ/LexUriServ.do?uri=OJ:L:2005:091:0013:0019:en:PDF. Accessed 9 January 2013.
9. a) Directive 2004/10/EC of the European Parliament and of the Council of 11 February 2004 on the harmonisation of laws, regulations and administrative provisions relating to the application of the principles of good laboratory practice and the verification of their applications for tests on chemical substances. EUR-Lex website. http://eur-lex.europa.eu/LexUriServ/LexUriServ.do?uri=OJ:L:2004:050:0044:0044:EN:PDF. Accessed 9 January 2013. b) Directive 2004/9/EC of the European Parliament and of the Council of 11 February 2004 on the inspection and verification of good laboratory practice (GLP). EUR-Lex website. http://eur-lex.europa.eu/LexUriServ/LexUriServ.do?uri=OJ:L:2004:050:0028:0043:EN:PDF. Accessed 9 January 2013.
10. a) Commission Directive 2003/94/EC of 8 October 2003 laying down the principles and guidelines of good manufacturing practice in respect of medicinal products for human use and investigational medicinal products for human use (*Human GMP Directive*). EUR-Lex website. http://ec.europa.eu/health/files/eudralex/vol-1/dir_2003_94/dir_2003_94_en.pdf. Accessed 9 January 2013. b) Commission Directive 91/412/EEC of 23 July 1991 laying down the principles and guidelines of good manufacturing practice for veterinary medicinal products (*Veterinary GMP Directive*). EC website. http://ec.europa.eu/health/files/eudralex/vol-5/dir_1991_412/dir_1991_412_en.pdf. Accessed 9 January 2013.
11. Council Directive 92/25/EEC of 31 March 1992 on the wholesale distribution of medicinal products for human use (*GDP Directive*). EUR-Lex website. http://eur-lex.europa.eu/LexUriServ/LexUriServ.do?uri=OJ:L:1992:113:0001:0004:EN:PDF. Accessed 9 January 2013.
12 Mutual Recognition Agreements. European Medicines Agency website. www.ema.europa.eu/ema/index.jsp?curl=pages/regulation/document_listing/document_listing_000248.jsp&mid=WC0b01ac058005f8ac. Accessed 9 January 2013.
13. ICH, *Good Manufacturing Practice Guide for Active Pharmaceutical Ingredients Q7* (Current Step 4 version, November 2000). ICH website. www.ich.org/fileadmin/Public_Web_Site/ICH_Products/Guidelines/Quality/Q7/Step4/Q7_Guideline.pdf. Accessed 9 January 2013.
14. ICH, *Quality Risk Management Q9* (Current Step 4 version, November 2005). ICH website. www.ich.org/fileadmin/Public_Web_Site/ICH_Products/Guidelines/Quality/Q9/Step4/Q9_Guideline.pdf. Accessed 9 January 2013.

15. ICH, *Pharmaceutical Quality System Q10* (Current Step 4 version, June 2008). ICH website. www.ich.org/fileadmin/Public_Web_Site/ICH_Products/Guidelines/Quality/Q10/Step4/Q10_Guideline.pdf. Accessed 9 January 2013.
16. ICH, *Pharmacovigilance Planning E2E* (Current Step 4 version, November 2004). ICH website. www.ich.org/fileadmin/Public_Web_Site/ICH_Products/Guidelines/Efficacy/E2E/Step4/E2E_Guideline.pdf. Accessed 9 January 2013.
17. ICH, *Guideline for Good Clinical Practice E6(R1)* (Current Step 4 version, June 1996). ICH website. www.ich.org/fileadmin/Public_Web_Site/ICH_Products/Guidelines/Efficacy/E6_R1/Step4/E6_R1__Guideline.pdf. Accessed 9 January 2013.
18. Op cit 3.
19. EudraGMP database. EMA website. http://eudragmp.ema.europa.eu/inspections/displayWelcome.do;jsessionid=wTtbQnVM2kwxX9CvMVkTpFCqy5J0v0MBv8DQQzH00fBgLkhZhyh0!-244671738. Accessed 10 January 2013.
20. a) National competent authorities (human). EMA website. www.ema.europa.eu/ema/index.jsp?curl=pages/medicines/general/general_content_000155.jsp&murl=menus/partners_and_networks/partners_and_networks.jsp&mid=WC0b01ac0580036d63. Accessed 10 January 2013., b) National competent authorities (veterinary). EMA website. www.ema.europa.eu/ema/index.jsp?curl=pages/medicines/general/general_content_000167.jsp&murl=menus/partners_and_networks/partners_and_networks.jsp&mid=WC0b01ac0580036d65, accessed 15 October 2012.
21. Inspections. EMA website. www.ema.europa.eu/ema/index.jsp?curl=pages/regulation/general/general_content_000161.jsp&mid=WC0b01ac0580024592. Accessed 10 January 2013.
22. Pharmaceutical Inspection Co-operation Scheme. PIC website. www.picscheme.org/. Accessed 10 January 2013.
23. Good laboratory practice compliance. EMA website. www.emea.europa.eu/ema/index.jsp?curl=pages/regulation/general/general_content_000158.jsp&mid=WC0b01ac05800268ae. Accessed 10 January 2013.
24. Ibid.
25. Good-clinical-practice compliance. EMA website. www.emea.europa.eu/ema/index.jsp?curl=pages/regulation/general/general_content_000072.jsp&mid=WC0b01ac05800268ad. Accessed 10 January 2013.
26. GCP Inspections procedure. EMA website. www.emea.europa.eu/ema/index.jsp?curl=pages/regulation/document_listing/document_listing_000140.jsp&mid=WC0b01ac05800296c6. Accessed 10 January 2013.
27. PIC Publications. PIC website. www.picscheme.org/publication.php. Accessed 10 January 2013.
28. EudraLex—Volume 4 Good manufacturing practice guidelines. EC website. http://ec.europa.eu/health/documents/eudralex/vol-4/index_en.htm. Accessed 10 January 2013.
29. CFR—Code of Federal Regulations Title 21. FDA website. www.accessdata.fda.gov/scripts/cdrh/cfdocs/cfcfr/cfrsearch.cfm. Accessed 10 January 2013.
30. Regulatory Affairs Professionals Society. "Chapter 7 FDA Inspections and Enforcement." *Fundamentals of US Regulatory Affairs Fifth Edition.* Rockville, MD. 2007:55.
31. Commission Guidelines on Good Distribution Practice of Medicinal Products for Human Use. EC website, http://ec.europa.eu/health/files/eudralex/vol-4/2011-07_gdpguidline_publicconsultation.pdf. Accessed 10 January 2013.
32. Op cit 16
33. Good Pharmacovigilance Practice. MHRA website. www.mhra.gov.uk/Howweregulate/Medicines/Inspectionandstandards/GoodPharmacovigilancePractice/index.htm. Accessed 10 January 2013.
34. Good pharmacovigilance practices. EMA website. www.ema.europa.eu/ema/index.jsp?curl=pages/regulation/document_listing/document_listing_000345.jsp&mid=WC0b01ac058058f32c. Accessed 10 January 2013.
35. The Blue Guide. MHRA website. http://www.mhra.gov.uk/home/groups/pl-a/documents/publication/con2022589.pdf. Accessed 10 January 2013.
36. Michor S. "Product Lifecycle Management: A European Perspective," *Regulatory Affairs Focus*, Vol. 13, No. 8, pp. 18–27.
37. Regulatory Affairs Professionals Society. "Chapter 21 Enforcement and National Authorities." *Fundamentals of EU Regulatory Affairs Fourth Edition.* Rockville, MD. 2008:236.
38. Regulatory Affairs Professionals Society. "Chapter 5 Medical Device Premarket Requirements." *Fundamentals of EU Regulatory Affairs Fourth Edition.* Rockville, MD. 2009:48.
39. Regulatory Affairs Professionals Society. "Chapter 7 Enforcement and National Authorities." *Fundamentals of EU Regulatory Affairs Sixth Edition.* Rockville, MD. 2012:61.
40. Council Directive 90/385/EEC of 20 June 1990 on the approximation of the laws of the Member States relating to active implantable medical devices (*AIMD Directive*). EUR-Lex website. http://eur-lex.europa.eu/LexUriServ/LexUriServ.do?uri=CONSLEG:1990L0385:20071011:en:PDF. Accessed 10 January 2013.
41. Council Directive 93/42/EEC of 14 June 1993 concerning medical devices (*Medical Devices Directive* (*MDD*). EUR-Lex website. http://eur-lex.europa.eu/LexUriServ/LexUriServ.do?uri=CONSLEG:1993L0042:20071011:en:PDF. Accessed 10 January 2013.
42. Directive 98/79/EC of the European Parliament and of the Council of 27 October 1998 on in vitro diagnostic medical devices (*IVD Directive*). EUR-Lex website. http://eur-lex.europa.eu/LexUriServ/LexUriServ.do?uri=CONSLEG:1998L0079:20031120:en:PDF. Accessed 10 January 2013.
43. European Databank on Medical Devices—EUDAMED. EC website. http://ec.europa.eu/consumers/sectors/medical-devices/market-surveillance-vigilance/eudamed/. Accessed 10 January 2013.
44. 21 CFR 807, Establishment Registration and Device Listing for Manufacturers and Initial Importers of Devices. FDA website. www.accessdata.fda.gov/scripts/cdrh/cfdocs/cfcfr/CFRsearch.cfm?CFRPart=807. Accessed 10 January 2013.
45. 21 CFR 820, Quality System Regulation. FDA website. www.accessdata.fda.gov/scripts/cdrh/cfdocs/cfcfr/cfrsearch.cfm?cfrpart=820. Accessed 10 January 2013.
46. 21 CFR 803, Medical Device Reporting. FDA website. www.accessdata.fda.gov/scripts/cdrh/cfdocs/cfcfr/CFRSearch.cfm?CFRPart=803. Accessed 10 January 2013.
47. Regulatory Affairs Professionals Society. "Chapter 15 Medical Device Submissions." *Fundamentals of US Regulatory Affairs Seventh Edition.* Rockville, MD. 2011:189.
48. Op cit 44.
49. Op cit 46.
50. GHTF Documents. IMDRF website. www.imdrf.org/documents/documents.asp#ghtf. Accessed 10 January 2013.
51. See, for example, Inspection and standards. MHRA website. www.mhra.gov.uk/Howweregulate/Medicines/Inspectionandstandards/index.htm. Accessed 10 January 2013.
52. a) Programme to rationalise international GMP inspections of active pharmaceutical ingredients/active substances manufacturers. EMA website. www.ema.europa.eu/docs/en_GB/document_library/Other/2012/02/WC500123489.pdf. Accessed 10 January 2013. b) European Medicines Agency and United States Food and Drug Administration to share manufacturing site inspections. EMA website. http://www.ema.europa.eu/ema/index.jsp?curl=pages/news_and_events/news/2011/12/news_detail_001399.jsp&mid=WC0b01ac058004d5c1. Accessed 10 January 2013.
53. MHRA. Safeguarding public health, EC Medical Devices Directives, 6, Requirements for UK Notified Bodies. MHRA website. www.mhra.gov.uk/home/groups/es-era/documents/publication/con007510.pdf. Accessed 28 January 2013.

54. See, for example, Enforcement policy—Compliance inspection and action—Your rights. MHRA website. www.mhra.gov.uk/Howweregulate/Devices/Enforcementpolicy-Complianceinspectionandaction-Yourrights/index.htm. Accessed 10 January 2013.
55. GHTF/SG4/N28R4:2008 *Guidelines for Regulatory Auditing of Quality Management Systems of Medical Device Manufacturers—Part 1: General Requirements* (24 October 2008). IMDRF website. www.imdrf.org/docs/ghtf/final/sg4/technical-docs/ghtf-sg4-guidelines-auditing-qms-part-1-general-requirements-080827.pdf. Accessed 10 January 2013.
56. GHTF/SG3/N17:2008 *Quality Management System—Medical Devices—Guidance on the Control of Products and Services Obtained from Suppliers* (5 February 2009). IMDRF website. www.imdrf.org/docs/ghtf/final/sg3/technical-docs/ghtf-sg3-n17-guidance-on-quality-management-system-081211.pdf. Accessed 10 January 2012.
57. GHTF/SG3/N15R8:2005 *Implementation of Risk Management Principles and Activities Within a Quality Management System* (21 July 2005). IMDRF website. www.imdrf.org/docs/ghtf/final/sg3/technical-docs/ghtf-sg3-n15r8-risk-management-principles-qms-050520.pdf. Accessed 10 January 2013.
58. GHTF/SG3/N99-10:2004 *Quality Management Systems—Process Validation Guidance* (22 January 2004). IMDRF website. www.imdrf.org/docs/ghtf/final/sg3/technical-docs/ghtf-sg3-n99-10-2004-qms-process-guidance-04010.pdf. Accessed 10 January 2013.
59. Regulatory Affairs Professionals Society. "Chapter 31 FDA Inspection and Enforcement." *Fundamentals of US Regulatory Affairs Seventh Edition*. Rockville, MD. 2011:371.
60. ICH. *Pharmaceutical Quality System Q10*, 4 June 2008. ICH website. www.ich.org/fileadmin/Public_Web_Site/ICH_Products/Guidelines/Quality/Q10/Step4/Q10_Guideline.pdf. Accessed 10 January 2013.
61. Op cit 28.
62. Op cit 3.

Chapter 8

Counterfeit Deterrence

By Philipp Novales-Li, DMedSc, PhD, DPhil (Oxford), RAC

OBJECTIVES

- ❑ Understand the role of the World Health Organization's IMPACT

LIST OF STANDARDS AND GUIDELINES

- ❑ IMPACT (International Medical Products Anti-Counterfeiting Taskforce). *The Handbook. (Facts, Activities, Documents developed by the assembly and the working groups of IMPACT).* January 2011.

Introduction

Drug counterfeiting is an insidious worldwide problem. Adverse events—including serious injury and death—have been linked to the use of counterfeit drugs. According to the Center for Medicine in the Public Interest, it is estimated that the global trade of counterfeit drugs reached $75 billion (US) in one year alone. Most counterfeit drugs have been shown to be substandard, ineffective, unsafe and potentially harmful to patients. They also undermine consumer trust in the drug industry, regulators and healthcare professionals at large. Finally, the availability of these products impacts pharmaceutical manufacturers financially.

Vigilance has increased at all levels in the medical products distribution chain, and worldwide efforts, mainly by the World Health Organization's (WHO) International Medicinal Products Anti-Counterfeiting Taskforce (IMPACT), is widely credited with improving collaboration among concerned stakeholders at local, regional and international levels. This chapter focuses on the various initiatives that have been undertaken by IMPACT since it was launched in February 2006. IMPACT's goal is to build coordinated networks across and between countries in order to halt the production, trade and sale of counterfeit medical products around the world.

Factors Precipitating Drug Counterfeiting

The number of counterfeit drug cases has increased dramatically in recent years. According to WHO, several factors are driving this increase.

- Supply and demand—when supply is short and erratic, especially in developing countries, patients resort to alternative sources of drugs, e.g., smuggled or unlicensed drug products.
- Drug affordability—given the high price of proprietary drugs and price differentials among similar drugs, consumers tend to buy the cheaper versions, thus creating a market for counterfeit drugs.
- Drugs as high-profit-margin products—if a counterfeiter does not have to invest in research and development, intellectual property protection or sales and marketing efforts, the difference between the cost of manufacturing a drug and the proprietary list price is huge. A counterfeiter selling an adulterated drug below a legal manufacturer's list price will still net a huge profit since the costs of substitute ingredients are very low and active ingredients are sometimes omitted entirely.
- Lax customs controls—many developing countries have lax customs enforcement or officials who can be bribed. This facilitates the entry of counterfeit drugs through smuggling or even such legitimate routes as the postal service or courier express systems.
- Penetrable gaps in intermediaries—drug sales involve many middlemen or intermediaries, such as brokers, agents and trading houses. The absence

Table 8-1. Government Responsibilities

- establish an adequate legal basis (comprising criminal, administrative and civil frameworks), for imposing and supervising compliance with and enforcement of obligations by all concerned parties;
- ensure that this legal basis can be applied to all medical products, including counterfeit medical products, in transit/transshipment, bonded warehouses, free zones and all situations of the international trade;
- establish adequately resourced authorities charged with combating counterfeiting of medical products with appropriate investigative and enforcement powers delineated in legislation;
- in case a third-party assessment body is established, ensure that the body is adequately designated and regular oversight established;
- establish liability for Internet Service Providers and other operators who facilitate advertisement of or trade in counterfeit medical products;
- regularly review and amend legislation as required;
- regulate the manufacture, importation, exportation, distribution, supply, donation, offer for sale and sale of medical products, thereby ensuring that those who manufacture, import, export, distribute, supply and perform any transaction related to medical products, are in the possession of a specific license, as applicable;
- establish regulations aimed at fostering a safe, transparent and secure distribution system including the establishment of measures for traceability of medical products, as applicable, throughout the distribution channels from the manufacturer/importer to the retailer;
- regulate the manufacture of active substances and of certain excipients entailing possible public health risks;
- establish specific import (and export) procedures; this may include designation of a limited number of points of entry for imported medical products, as applicable
- ensure that all medical products in the national distribution channels are licensed/authorized as required by national legislation;
- establish and enforce compliance with documented procedures for the appropriate destruction of counterfeit products; this includes the identification of operational and financial responsibilities;
- revoke licenses/authorizations for poor or illegal performance according to established laws and regulations;
- issue and renew licenses on the basis of documented satisfactory compliance with existing laws and regulations;
- require that medical products are suitably labeled and packaged according to their required specifications and licenses/authorizations;
- ensure that the conditions for importation of medical products are clearly specified and importation is undertaken only with the appropriate import licenses/authorizations issued by the national Competent Authority;
- ensure that imported medical products are licensed/authorized in the country of manufacture or, if not, there are acceptable reasons for such non-authorization;
- adequately fund medical product licensing and authorization activities including related assessments and inspections;
- provide adequate initial and in-service training for medical products control, customs and law enforcement personnel;
- establish legal mechanisms to allow/improve coordination and information exchange among health, regulatory, police, customs and other enforcement officers/authorities at a national, regional and international level including the ability to use the information exchanged in legal/regulatory/investigative actions;
- ensure that imported medical products are subject of inspection at points of entry and that samples are collected and analyzed as required by a national strategic plan;
- permit investigators, per appropriate guidelines, to conduct effective investigations, including undercover operations, in which samples can be obtained anonymously;
- perform effective controls and tests on medical products authorized for marketing in order to ascertain their quality and authenticity;
- ensure that noncompliance with anti-counterfeiting laws and regulations results in prosecution and severe penal sanctions including the confiscation, forfeiture and destruction of counterfeit medical products as well as equipment and other materials used in conjunction with their manufacture;
- foster international cooperation in the regulation of medical products by entering into bilateral and multilateral agreements with other governments and with regional and international organizations such as WHO, Interpol, World Customs Organization, Council of Europe;
- ensure that policies/regulations concerning exported medical products address the following issues:
    - same standards for exported as for domestic products (e.g., WHO Certification Scheme for pharmaceuticals, other official certification as applicable, marketing authorization, compliance with manufacturing practices requirements, appropriate product information, etc.);

- allowing importing countries to obtain products that satisfy their requirements in cases where such products might not have marketing authorization in the exporting country;
- exported products must have a remaining shelf life allowing exportation providing a reasonable timeframe for use (e.g., residual shelf life should be at least 2/3 of shelf life at lot release or six months if 2/3 of shelf life is shorter than six months);
- regulating international trade of labels and packaging materials for medical products;

- communicate information on counterfeit medical products and product recalls to manufacturers, operators of the distribution chain, retailers, other operators and health professionals in a timely manner, according to established policies, standards and risk assessment;
- conduct awareness initiatives and ensure that appropriate information is provided to the public on counterfeit medical products in order to minimize the risk of exposure to such products;
- establish contact mechanisms, such as phone number/website, to allow health professionals and the general public to report suspected cases of counterfeit medical products.

of a pedigree system to trace a drug product from manufacturer to pharmacy provides opportunities for counterfeiters to introduce adulterated drugs into the distribution system.

- Ineffective legislation and/or weak enforcement—only a handful of nations have enacted legislation or regulations to curb drug counterfeiting. Ineffective or weak drug regulation opens the door to illegal activities, such as drug smuggling or counterfeiting. Counterfeiting is most pervasive in countries where regulatory and legal oversight is weakest.
- Increased misuse of drugs—drug addiction and inappropriate use of drugs, such as the use of pain killers and antibiotics, are tied to the growing counterfeiting problem.

Legislation

Clearly, there is a need for governments and regulatory agencies to develop stronger legislation to effectively combat the proliferation of counterfeit medical products. IMPACT has developed a draft "Principles and Elements for National Legislation Against Counterfeit Medical Products" that lays out its current thinking on the obligations and responsibilities of stakeholders that can be implemented through legislation. The principles should be viewed within the context of a broader regulatory framework, and are intended to complement or bolster, rather than replace current legislation.

Tables 8-1–8-6 present the stakeholder responsibilities from IMPACT's draft principles. In general, all stakeholders such as governmental institutions, manufacturers, operators of the distribution chain, retailers and other operators should endeavor to fulfill their obligations to ensure success in the battle against counterfeit medical products.[1,2]

Communication Efforts

To effectively carry out its vision to eradicate all counterfeit medicines, IMPACT has laid out a communications strategy, with the aim of creating risk awareness, supporting program policy remedies and increasing commitment from stakeholders. Such a strategy seeks to ensure consistent and regular information sharing so timely and accurate information can be disseminated to an international audience. Since counterfeit medical products are a worldwide threat to public health, communication efforts can be effective only if the audience understands the hazards and dangers of this risk and the mitigation strategies needed to ensure public health safety. To this end, specific key messages have been developed and tailored for target audiences, such as patients, the general public, the media, healthcare professionals, pharmaceutical supply chains, enforcement officers and governments.[3–5]

The following key messages were developed by IMPACT's communications working group:

- Only get medicines from known reliable sources. (target: patients and the general public)
- Counterfeit medicines are a threat to personal and public health worldwide. (target: media)
- When treatment fails, consider counterfeits as possible suspects. (target: healthcare professionals)
- The road to success: the joint combat against counterfeits of all stakeholders in the supply chain. (target: pharmaceutical supply chains)
- Medicines should not be treated as a commodity. (target: pharmaceutical supply chains and governments)
- When existing laws are not adequate and rigorously enforced, crimes such as counterfeiting tend to perpetrate. (target: enforcement officers and governments)

To effectively disseminate these key messages, IMPACT's goal is to gain media exposure at the global level, using print and broadcast television and radio compaigns, media events and the Internet.

Anti-counterfeiting Technologies

Innovations in authentication and electronic track and trace technologies provide promising means of establishing pedigree, thus bolstering the integrity of the medical product supply chain. Common features of these anti-counterfeiting technologies are: difficult to forge or simulate; easy visual judgment, without the need for special equipment (or if required, verification with a simple tool); and ability to detect tampering of an anti-counterfeit solution. Examples include the following:[6]

Overt Features

Overt technologies are designed to be easily recognizable by the naked eye but difficult for counterfeiters to copy. These features generally are authenticated visually, without the need for any special device or high-level training.

- Holograms—these are three-dimensional images reproduced from patterns of interference, produced by beams of radiation (such as a laser). Holograms are one of the most popular anti-counterfeiting solutions on the market. Tamper-proof hologram stickers are designed with advanced laser technology; logos are imprinted on holographic paper and laminated with a laser. The process of manufacturing tamper-proof hologram labels and stickers is too complex to be forged by counterfeiters.
- Optically variable devices (OVDs)—OVDs can be created through a combination of printing and embossing and are based on diffractive optical structures. The iridescent image that is created can exhibit various optical effects such as movement or color changes. The image has different patterns, colors and designs depending on the amount of light striking the OVD and the angle at which it is viewed. (Note: OVDs are similar to holograms, but without any 3D component.)
- Color-shifting security inks and films—for items that do not have a flat surface or do not have enough area on which to affix a label, security ink can be a good solution. Security inks contain covert security elements that require some sort of basic tool for authentication. The inks could be used to print a serial or model number. These inks can be laid down in a thick opaque film to achieve the desired optical effect. Security ink can have a normal "trigger" temperature of 88°F, which will either disappear or change colors when the ink is rubbed, usually by the fingertips.
- Security graphics—a number of technical methods are used in the security printing industry. Intaglio is a printing technique in which the image is incised into a surface. This involves the use of extremely small text, generally indiscernible to the naked eye. A guilloché, an ornamental pattern formed of two or more curved bands that interlace to repeat a circular design, is another security measure. The use of color also can greatly assist the prevention of forgeries. By including a color on a drug package insert, a color photocopier must be used in the attempt to make a copy; however, the use of these machines also tends to enhance the effectiveness of other technologies such as void pantographs and verification grids.
- Sequential product numbering—unique serial numbers are not difficult to forge, but make legitimate documents easier to track and audit, since they can be authenticated easily by using a database to check for duplicates or invalid numbers.
- On-product markings—pills, capsules or tablets can be marked with special images or codes, which offer an added level of security, especially when products are separated from their original packaging material.

Covert Features

Covert authentication technologies contain hidden features that can be detected only by commercially available microscopes or specialized readers. These sophisticated technologies can either be incorporated into overt authentication solutions or can function on a standalone basis to protect against counterfeiting and diversion. Current technology features a broad spectrum of covert authentication solutions that vary from machine-readable technology, micro-text, nano-text, imbedded images in holographic images and a mix of machine-readable technology and holographic imagery.

- Invisible printing—invisible ink, also known as security ink, is a substance used for printing that is invisible either on application or soon thereafter, and which can be made visible by some means at a later time. The ink substance changes color when mixed with an acid or base. Some inks glow faintly (fluoresce) when placed under an ultraviolet lamp.
- Embedded image—carefully created images can be hidden in the background or in a picture. These images cannot be seen without the help of an inexpensive lens with a specific line screening. When placed over the image and rotated, the image becomes visible. If the document is photocopied, the "halo" (image) is lost.
- Digital watermarks—like traditional watermarks, digital watermarks are only perceptible under certain conditions, i.e., after using an algorithm, and are otherwise imperceptible. Traditional watermarks may be applied to visible media (like images), whereas in digital watermarking, the signal may be audio, pictures, video, texts or 3D models. A signal may carry several different watermarks at the same time.

Table 8-2. Manufacturer Responsibilities

- comply with applicable laws and regulations;
- comply with official Good Practice Guidelines (e.g., Good Manufacturing Practices for medicinal products, Good Distribution Practices);
- comply with applicable Quality Management Systems requirement for medical devices;
- ensure suppliers of raw, starting and packaging materials are legitimate and finished medical products are delivered to legitimate operators of the distribution chain; this may include conducting audits or verifying the legitimacy of business partners;
- establish policies and maintain copies of records of transactions (including written contracts, where applicable) with suppliers, subcontractors and operators of the distribution chain;
- document the origin of all materials used in the manufacture of authorized products in accordance with applicable GMP requirements;
- institute a process to ensure that each batch received and shipped is accompanied by control reports (e.g., a Certificate of Analysis), as required by applicable legislation;
- establish a quality assurance system that addresses (a) the manufacturer's response to reports of possible counterfeit medical products, (b) mandatory reporting of information to Competent Authorities and (c) handling of product recalls, all in compliance with applicable legislation;
- document the appropriate disposal of expired or otherwise unusable products in a manufacturer's possession to prevent such products from re-entering the distribution chain;
- cooperate with health, customs, police, other enforcement authorities and other stakeholders in the detection of counterfeit medical products, investigation of cases and the prosecution of those responsible for their manufacture or distribution.

- Hidden marks and printing—void pantographs are essentially invisible to the untrained, naked eye on an original, but when scanned or copied, the layout of lines, dots and dashes will reveal a word (frequently "VOID," hence the name) or symbol that clearly allows the copy to be identified.
- Anti-copy or anti-scan design—advances in printer technology have made it possible to easily make photocopies. Printer software and hardware have filtering capabilities that sense inherent anti-copy or anti-scan features, which lock out the reproduction of any material with these marks.
- Laser coding—surface engraving by laser offers an effective solution for permanently applying codes or marks using a low-energy laser to engrave data matrix codes directly onto glass containers.
- Substrates—an example is a security thread, which is a thin aluminum (coated and partly demetalized polyester film thread) with embedded microprinting. These can be incorporated within a substrate, such as carton board or paper.
- Odor—unique scents can be micro-encapsulated, a process in which tiny particles or droplets are surrounded by a coating to give microcapsules many useful properties. This can be applied to special inks or coatings.

Forensic Markers

Forensic markers are special materials that are invisible to the naked eye, and their unique properties require that they be taken to a laboratory for verification. For example, taggants can provide a unique code or fingerprint to authenticate originality.

- Chemical-biological-DNA-micro taggants—these are microscopic or nano materials that are uniquely encoded and virtually impossible to duplicate—like a fingerprint. They can be incorporated into or applied to a wide variety of materials, surfaces, products and solutions.

  A single taggant can be used for an application, or multiple taggant technologies can work together to create a higher level of security. An invisible taggant is embedded into a carrier that permanently marks the product. The taggant generates a unique chemical, biological, DNA or nano signature.
- Isotope ratios—this measures naturally-occurring isotopic ratios using explorative chemometric techniques (such as laser fluorescence or magnetic resonance) to distinguish compounds originating from different countries and manufacturers.

Track and Trace Technologies

The purpose of tracking is to ensure that manufacturers are able to quickly locate their medical products in the supply

Table 8-3. Operators of the Distribution Chain Responsibilities

- comply with applicable laws and regulations;
- comply with official Good Practice Guidelines (e.g., GDP) for medicinal products and applicable guidelines for active pharmaceutical ingredients (APIs) and excipients;
- ensure suppliers of products are legitimate manufacturers or operators of the distribution chain and ensure delivery to legitimate operators of the distribution chain or retailers; this may include performing audits or verifying the legitimacy of business partners;
- establish and maintain copies of records of transactions (including written contracts) with suppliers, subcontractors and operators of the distribution chain;
- accurately document the purchase and supply of all medical products, including returns from retailers;
- ensure that each batch received and shipped is accompanied by appropriate documentation as required by national legislation;
- establish a quality assurance system that addresses (a) the operator's response to suspected or confirmed counterfeit medical products, (b) mandatory reporting of information to Competent Authorities and (c) handling of product recalls, all in compliance with applicable legislation;
- cooperate with health, customs, police, other enforcement authorities and other stakeholders in the detection of counterfeit medical products, investigation of cases and the prosecution of those responsible for their manufacture or distribution;
- document the appropriate disposal of expired or otherwise unusable products in the operator's possession to prevent such products from re-entering the distribution chain.

chain. This is complemented by traceability, which establishes and maintains procedures for identifying finished medical products (via a control number for each unit, lot or batch) and their components, as appropriate. Tracking information may be used to facilitate notifications and recalls, while traceability provides a history of the items. Track and trace technologies also enable authentication, which allows better checking on pedigree by purchasers.

- Serialization—encodes a unique identification number, which when linked to a database, can provide identification and verification that a medical product has not been copied, is not expired, has not been recalled and is legally available for sale.
- Barcodes—machine-readable graphic representations (with bars and spaces of varying widths).
- Radio Frequency Identification (RFID)—tagging with a chip that contains identifying information that can be read by a radio-frequency (RF) reader. Radio waves transmit signals via electromagnetic or electrostatic coupling. "ID" refers to several identification methods that can be stored on a tag or transponder.
- Unique surface marking or topography—an example is optical character recognition (OCR) in which images of printed characters are converted into ASCII code read by a scanner.

Regulatory Enforcement

The trade in counterfeit medical products is a growing threat facing the international community. IMPACT serves as a global platform that allows enforcement officers to set communication initiatives with Competent Authorities, manufacturers and healthcare providers to combat this illegal activity. IMPACT considers counterfeiting an illegal activity, which should be deemed a criminal offence, regardless of the value or volume involved and whether or not it was committed by negligence.[7]

The following are deemed as illegal acts:

- manufacture of a counterfeit medical product
- ownership, possession or control of counterfeit medical products in transit, transshipment, etc. or likely to enter the distribution chain
- introduction of counterfeit medical products into the distribution chain
- design, production, printing, sale, delivery, distribution, importation, exportation, donation or supply of packaging material intended for a counterfeit medical product
- manufacture, transportation or distribution of any equipment, materials, components or documentation used for a counterfeit medical product
- provision of online services, electronic sale platforms, electronic payments or transport in relation to counterfeit medical products
- conspiracy or attempt to commit, aid and abet, counsel or facilitate or incite to commit any of the above offences

IMPACT recommends severe criminal sanctions for those who commit illegal acts associated with the trade in counterfeit medical products, regardless of evidence of actual harm caused to others. The sanctions considered by IMPACT comprise:

- custodial sentences
- fines
- confiscation and forfeitures
- total or partial closure of establishment/operation/related activities
- permanent or temporary prohibition
- destruction of counterfeit goods and recovery of costs
- ban on access to public assistance or subsidies
- judicial supervision of the errant operator
- indemnification of affected/impacted parties
- publication of judicial decisions
- withdrawal of licenses

Through joint efforts with international agencies, such as INTERPOL and the World Customs Organization, as well as a network of enforcement officers (e.g., the Permanent Forum on International Pharmaceutical Crime), notable (high-profile) operations were coordinated at a global level to combat the trade and sale of counterfeit and illicit medical products. Examples of joint activities include:[8]

- PANGEA II involved customs officers, police and regulatory authorities from 25 countries, focusing on the online trade of illegal and counterfeit medicines, particularly Internet service providers (ISPs), electronic payment systems and mail delivery service. More than 1,200 websites were monitored and over 21,200 shipped packages were inspected. A total of 153 websites were shut down and 2,356 mailed packages were seized.
- PANGEA III had participation by 45 countries that resulted in detainment of packages, seizure of tablets, execution of warrants, shut down websites and individual arrests.
- OPERATION MAMBA III was conducted across East Africa, resulting in some 300 premises being checked or raided and the seizure of vaccines, antimalarial drugs and antibiotics.

Country-specific Regulations

The following are highlights of salient regulatory oversight related to counterfeit medical products, from the founding member countries of the Global Harmonization Task Force (since supplanted by the International Medical Device Regulators Forum (IMDRF)):

- Australia—The Therapeutic Goods Administration (TGA) recognizes that counterfeit medicines and medical devices pose a serious threat to public health. Under the *Therapeutic Goods Act* of 1989, the importation, manufacture and supply of counterfeit therapeutic goods are subject to criminal and civil penalties, notwithstanding the fact that producing counterfeit therapeutic goods is also a breach of intellectual property. TGA's Regulatory Compliance Unit (RCU) is responsible for investigating such matters, with a view to initiating civil or criminal legal actions. Judgment can include imprisonment (up to seven years) and/or heavy fines.
- Canada—Health Canada's Health Products and Food Branch Inspectorate has issued a Policy on Counterfeit Health Products (POL-0048) that provides guiding principles for identifying, assessing and managing health and safety risks posed by counterfeit health products. Provisions of the policy include: educating stakeholders on the risks of counterfeit health products; compliance verification to identify suspect counterfeits; identifying counterfeiters and taking appropriate action; notifying federal, provincial or municipal law enforcement and regulatory bodies and international regulators, as appropriate; examining and conducting lab analysis to authenticate suspected counterfeited products;

Table 8-4. Retailers' Responsibilities

- comply with applicable laws and regulations;
- comply with official Good Practice Guidelines (e.g., GDP, GPP);
- ensure products are sourced from legitimate operators of the distribution chain;
- establish policies and maintain records of written contracts with suppliers, subcontractors and operators of the distribution chain;
- document the purchase and return of all medical products;
- establish a quality assurance system that addresses (a) the retailer's response to suspected or confirmed counterfeit medical products, (b) mandatory reporting of information to Competent Authorities and (c), handling of product recalls, all in compliance with applicable legislation;
- cooperate with health, customs, police, other enforcement authorities and other stakeholders in the detection of counterfeit medical products, investigation of cases and the prosecution of those responsible for their manufacture or distribution;
- document the disposal of expired or otherwise unusable products to prevent them from entering into the distribution chain.

Table 8-5. Responsibilities of Other Operators

- maintain awareness of legal requirements regarding medical products and comply with applicable legislation;
- exert due diligence for ensuring business with legitimate business partners;
- cooperate with health, customs, police, other enforcement authorities and other stakeholders in the detection of counterfeit medical products, investigation of cases and the prosecution of those responsible for their manufacture or distribution;
- document any activity related to medical products;
- take necessary actions if there are reasons to suspect or if the appropriate authorities have cited that the services are being exploited for the trade/advertisement of counterfeit medical products.

removing counterfeit health products from the supply chain; collaborating with other international regulators; and publishing public advisories and warnings. Under Canada's *Food and Drugs Act*, the inspectorate has the authority to take enforcement action on the manufacture, importation and sale of counterfeited health products.

- EU—The European Commission uses the term "falsified medicines" to distinguish the use of the term "counterfeits," which is more commonly used in intellectual property infringement matters. The European Commission implemented Directive 2011/62/EU, the Community code relating to medicinal products for human use, as regards the prevention of the entry into the legal supply chain of falsified medicinal products, and introduced tougher rules to improve protection of public health. New measures include: obligatory authenticity feature on the outer packaging of medicines; a common EU-wide logo to identify legal online pharmacies; tougher rules on the controls and inspections of producers of active pharmaceutical ingredients; and strengthened record-keeping requirements for wholesalers.
- Japan—Article 55 of Japan's *Pharmaceutical Affairs Law* prohibits the sale, grant, storage and exhibit of counterfeit medicines. Violators can be sentenced to imprisonment (less than three years) and/or subject to penalties less than three million yen (US$25,000).
- US—The US Food and Drug Administration (FDA) has a Counterfeit Drug Task Force that continues to leverage regulatory actions and use new technologies to strengthen existing protections against the growing problem of counterfeit drugs. In fact, FDA scientists have developed a handheld device (Counterfeit Detection Device Number 3 (CD3)) that can be used to rapidly screen and detect counterfeit products and packaging. CD3 provides real-time findings in the field by comparing differences between images of a suspect product and an authentic product. The device emits 10 wavelengths of light over products and can alert inspectors to potential issues and likely forgeries. FDA also has issued guidance on the use of physical-chemical identifiers (PCID), which are substances that can be incorporated into the drug (or packaging/labeling) to uniquely identify and authenticate a drug product or dosage form.

Conclusion

Where do we go from here? High-tech companies, utilizing venture capital, are developing new technologies to improve the global prevention, tracking and detection of drug counterfeiting. Regulatory agencies are becoming more vigilant regarding this public health threat, with

Table 8-6. Regional/International Obligations

- regional/international information exchange among health, regulatory, police, customs and other enforcement officers/authorities (including the ability to provide and use the information exchanged in legal/regulatory actions); this includes all areas within member states as well as free trade zones;
- cross-border joint coordinated activities among health, regulatory, police, customs and other enforcement officers/authorities; this includes all areas within member states as well as free trade zones;
- effective regional/international cooperation in criminal matters for the purpose of investigating, collecting evidence or proceedings concerning criminal offences related to counterfeit medical products;
- criminal offences directly related to counterfeit medical products to be considered extraditable offences;
- the ability to prosecute criminal offences directly related to counterfeit medical products by a country affected by such criminal offences, even if committed abroad by, or against, a citizen of that country.

more nations drafting tougher legislation or strengthening existing enforcement schemes to curb counterfeit drug trafficking. In the US, FDA's Counterfeit Drug Task Force developed a multilayer approach to this problem, taking measures to secure products and packing, heighten vigilance and awareness, enhance international cooperation and ensure appropriate regulatory oversight and enforcement. Globally, WHO established IMPACT to investigate innovative technological solutions for detecting counterfeit drugs.

Technology can help resolve this problem, but it is not the ultimate solution since any technology can be reverse engineered, and its implementation can be prohibitive, depending on levels of mass production and infrastructure requirements. Successfully combating drug counterfeiting requires a combination of innovative technologies and old-fashioned vigilance by all stakeholders, including manufacturers, wholesalers, healthcare professionals, pharmacists and patients.

References

1. Directive 2011/62/EU of the European Parliament and of the Council of 8 June 2011 amending Directive 2001/83/EC on the Community code relating to medicinal products for human use, as regards the prevention of the entry into the legal supply chain of falsified medicinal products. EC website. http://ec.europa.eu/health/files/eudralex/vol-1/dir_2011_62/dir_2011_62_en.pdf. Accessed 18 March 2013.
2. IMPACT (2008) Draft Principles and Elements for National Legislation Against Counterfeit Medical Products. WHO website. www.who.int/impact/events/FinalPrinciplesforLegislation.pdf. Accessed 18 March 2013.
3. Op cit 1.
4. Op cit 2.
5. IMPACT (2011). *The Handbook.* (Facts, Activities, Documents developed by the assembly and the working groups of IMPACT). WHO website. www.who.int/impact/resources/handobook/en/index.html. Accessed 18 March 2013.
6. Novales-Li P. (2007) Combating Counterfeit Drugs. *Regulatory Affairs Focus.* 12(11), 26–29.
7. Op cit 5.
8. Ibid.

Chapter 9

Premarket Requirements/ Dossier Requirements

Updated by Shekhar Natarajan, MSc, MRSC, MTOPRA

OBJECTIVES

- Gain an understanding of the premarket requirements for medicinal products
- Learn about aspects to consider in compiling an application
- Get to know individual modules of a marketing authorization application dossier
- Learn about the different types of applications

LAWS, REGULATIONS AND GUIDELINES COVERED IN THIS CHAPTER

- ICH, *Organization of the CTD for the Registration of Pharmaceuticals for Human Use M4(R3)*
- ICH, *The Common Technical Document for the Registration of Pharmaceuticals for Human Use: Quality—M4Q(R1), Quality Overall Summary of Module 2, Module 3: Quality)*
- ICH, *The Common Technical Document for the Registration of Pharmaceuticals for Human Use: Safety—M4S(R2), Nonclinical Overview and Nonclinical Summaries of Module 2, Organisation of Module 4*
- ICH, *The Common Technical Document for the Registration of Pharmaceuticals for Human Use: Efficacy—M4E(R1), Clinical Overview and Clinical Summary of Module 2, Module 5: Clinical Study Reports* (Current Step 4 version, September 2002)
- ICH, *Impurities in New Drug Substances Q3A(R2)*
- ICH, *Specifications: Test Procedures and Acceptance Criteria for New Drug Substances and New Drug Products: Chemical Substances Q6A (including Decision Trees)*
- ICH, *Specifications: Test Procedures and Acceptance Criteria for Biotechnological/ Biological Products Q6B*
- ICH, *Pharmaceutical Development Q8(R2)*
- ICH, *Safety Pharmacology Studies for Human Pharmaceuticals S7A*

Introduction

To understand the regulatory procedures that govern granting a marketing license for a medicinal product, it is necessary to understand the different types of registration applications that exist. Before gaining market access, pharmaceutical products must undergo a rigorous evaluation by Competent Authorities. To this end, prospective Marketing Authorization Holders (MAHs) must carry out intensive formulation development, analytical testing and preclinical and clinical studies on new molecular entities (NMEs) to ensure their products are safe and efficacious. Only entities that demonstrate a favorable benefit:risk profile following the successful completion of the above mentioned activities are considered for market access.

Market access is achieved after an official application is made to a Competent Authority. Although the application procedure differs from region to region, in all cases, market access is granted only after rigorous evaluation by the Competent Authority.

The Competent Authority evaluates the dossier or technical file that contains information on quality (manufacturing and testing), the nonclinical and clinical testing results and the manufacturing process.

This chapter is divided into two parts. The first part covers the Common Technical Document (CTD) and the type of information to be included in the dossier. The second part covers different application types and corresponding data requirements based on the CTD.

Common Technical Document (CTD)

The exact information to be provided for evaluation may differ by country and/or region. However, the International Conference on Harmonisation (ICH) has developed the CTD, which helps harmonize dossier requirements.

The CTD for marketing applications for drugs and biologics was finalized by ICH[1] in 2003. Today, the CTD format is highly recommended for marketing applications in the US, and is mandatory in other regions, including Canada, Japan and Europe.

Not only has the dossier structure been harmonized but, to a large extent, so has the content. With globalization, planning global regulatory strategies for drug development programs has become commonplace and the idea of a "core dossier" has become a reality.[2] For international market access, companies must ensure that the nonclinical, clinical , manufacturing and analytical data that have been generated will satisfy the requirements for all regions. Certain specific requirements for tests may still differ, and prospective MAHs or sponsors should consult with the local Competent Authorities in the countries or regions where they intend to market their products.

A number of guidelines for industry have been adopted by the ICH steering committee in the following areas:

- periodic safety updates
- photostability testing
- stability testing for new drug substances and products
- in-use shelf life
- dosage form impurities
- validation of analytical procedures
- dose selection for carcinogenicity studies
- repeated-dose tissue distribution studies
- extent of population exposure to assess clinical safety
- geriatric population clinical trials

Information about ICH guidelines can be found at www.ich.org.[3] Various ICH expert working groups are responsible for creating guidelines and defining standards for different dossier sections. Initially, the topics selected for harmonization were divided into "Safety," "Quality" and "Efficacy" to reflect the three criteria that are the basis for approving and authorizing new medicinal products.

- M4Q—The Quality Working Group is responsible for the application section covering chemical and pharmaceutical data, including data for biological/biotechnological products.
- M4E—The Efficacy Working Group is responsible for the application's clinical section.
- M4S—The Safety Working Group is responsible for the application's nonclinical section.[4]

A guideline on the agreed-upon common format for an application made to Competent Authorities is outlined in the ICH guidance, *Organisation of the Common Technical Document M4*.[5]

In fact, the agencies now have moved toward the electronic Common Technical Document (eCTD) format, which has become mandatory in key markets for electronic submissions. Since January 2010, the European Medicines Agency (EMA) has required all applications in the Centralised Procedure to use the eCTD format. Since January 2008, the US Food and Drug Administration's (FDA) Center for Drug Evaluation and Research (CDER) has required all electronic submissions be in the eCTD format. FDA's Center for Biologics Evaluation and Research (CBER) requires the eCTD format for priority review and rolling submissions.

Organization of the Common Technical Document (CTD)

The CTD is organized into five modules (**See Figure 2-1**).

Module 1

This module contains region-specific information that cannot be harmonized, such as application forms in the local language and labeling text. Module 1 also could contain the curricula vitae of the experts signing the summary information in Module 2. Other regional information also may be required. For example, in the EU, Module 1 contains a Risk Management Plan (RMP), a Pharmacovigilance (PV) Plan as part of the RMP, an Environmental Risk Assessment (ERA) and the results of user testing of the Patient Information Leaflet (PIL). In the US, Module 1 contains FDA Form 356h (first document in Module 1), prescribing information and Risk Evaluation and Mitigation Strategy (REMS), if applicable, etc.

Module 2

Module 2 contains high-level summaries and overviews (the quality overall summary, nonclinical overview and

Figure 9-1. CTD Organization

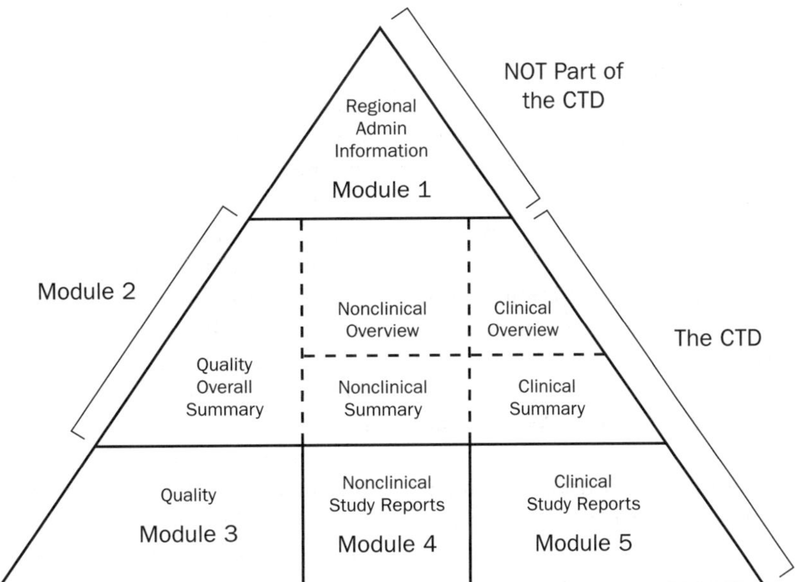

summary, and clinical overview and summary), which must be prepared by suitably qualified and experienced people (i.e., experts).[6]

Module 2 consists of seven sections:

- 2.1 CTD table of contents
- 2.2 CTD introduction
- 2.3 Quality overall summary (QOS)
- 2.4 Nonclinical overview
- 2.5 Clinical overview
- 2.6 Nonclinical written and tabulated summaries
- 2.7 Clinical written and tabulated summaries

Guidance for the content is provided in the ICH guidelines: *Quality, Module 2: Quality Overall Summary (QOS), Module 3: Quality M4Q(R1);*[7] *Safety, Nonclinical Summaries and Organisation of Module 4 M4S(R2);*[8] and *Efficacy, Module 2: Clinical Overview and Clinical Summary, Module 5: Clinical Study Reports M4E(R1).*[9]

2.3 Quality Overall Summary (QOS)

The quality overall summary follows the scope and outline of data in Module 3.[10] There should be sufficient information in the QOS to enable the Competent Authority reviewer to gain an overview of the module.

This section should highlight any critical issues or key parameters and the justification for any instances where, for example, guidelines are not followed.[11] The length and scope of the QOS depend on the type of product, ranging from 20 to 40 pages for simple to complex biotech products, respectively.

The quality section of the CTD (M4Q) also includes information and guidance on the structure and content of Module 3. M4Q provides a harmonized structure and format for presenting chemistry, manufacturing and controls (CMC) information in a registration dossier.

The different regions have implemented M4Q as follows:

- EU—adopted by the Committee for Proprietary Medicinal Products (CPMP, now Committee for Medicinal Products for Human Use (CHMP)), March 2003, issued as CPMP/ICH/2887/99 rev.1 Quality
- Japan Ministry of Health, Labour and Welfare (MHLW)—adopted 1 July 2003, PFSB/ELD Notification No. 0701004
- US FDA—final guidance issued by FDA in August 2001; subsequently, Quality Questions and Answers/Location Issues, issued in June 2004.

2.4 Nonclinical Overview and 2.6 Nonclinical Written and Tabulated Summaries

The CTD safety guideline (M4S) delineates the structure and format of the nonclinical summaries in Module 2 and provides the organization of Module 4, the nonclinical study reports.[12]

A critical assessment of the pharmacologic, pharmacokinetic and toxicologic evaluation of the drug in question should be presented in the nonclinical overview (2.4). The length and scope depend on the pharmaceutical product's complexity but, in general, should be about 30 pages. More-extensive summaries and discussion of the nonclinical information on pharmacology, pharmacokinetics and toxicology should be given in 2.6, the nonclinical written summaries (100–150 pages).

The organization of CTD Module 4, comprising the nonclinical study reports, is also described in M4S.

The different regions have implemented M4S as follows:

- EU—adopted by CPMP, March 2003, issued as CPMP/ICH/2887/99 rev.1 Safety
- MHLW—adopted 1 July 2003, PFSB/ELD Notification No. 0701004
- US FDA—final guidance issued by FDA in August 2001; subsequently, Safety Questions and Answers issued in February 2003

2.5 Clinical Overview and 2.7 Clinical Written and Tabulated Summaries

The structure and format of the clinical data in an application, including summaries and detailed study reports, are described in the ICH CTD efficacy guidance (M4E). Similar to the nonclinical section, the clinical overview (2.5), includes a critical assessment of the clinical data, and a clinical summary (2.6), a longer document that focuses on data summarization and integration.

Module 5 of the CTD includes clinical study reports and raw data, where applicable.

The different regions have implemented M4E as follows:

- EU—adopted by CPMP, March 2003, issued as CPMP/ICH/2887/99 rev.1 Efficacy
- MHLW—adopted 1 July 2003, PFSB/ELD Notification No. 0701004
- US FDA—final guidance issued by FDA in August 2001; subsequently, Efficacy Questions and Answers issued in December 2004

Companies applying for approval in a specific region may want to take regional documents into consideration when compiling their dossiers.

Module 3

The structure and format of Module 3 are described in M4Q. The quality section of the CTD provides a harmonized structure and format for presenting CMC information in a registration dossier.[13]

Not all sections of Module 3 have been harmonized due to the fact that, to date, specific CMC topics have not been the subject of ICH guidelines. These nonharmonized topics include drug substance synthesis, drug product manufacture and container closure.[14] For example, a dossier prepared for submission in the US may test according to the US Pharmacopeia, whereas in the EU, compliance with the European Pharmacopoeia (PhEu) is required and in Japan, companies must comply with the Japanese Pharmacopoeia. This is important since it implies, for example, that some sections of the dossier of a product intended for the US market may have to be modified for an EU submission.

It also is important to ensure the section regarding impurities complies with regional requirements. The ICH guideline on impurities, *Impurities in New Drug Substances Q3A(R2)*,[15] gives some guidance on the rationale for reporting and the control of organic and inorganic impurities and solvents for new drug substances. This guidance includes analytical methods, how to report batch impurity content and listing impurities in specifications.

Analytical results for all new drug substance batches used for clinical, safety and stability testing should be provided in an application. The guidance document[16] provides a decision tree to help manufacturers identify and qualify impurities.

Companies acting globally may want to give careful consideration to impurity testing during the development of their product(s). Using the standards with higher levels of control may ensure wider acceptance. This is part of regulatory strategic planning that could significantly impact financial and human resources.

ICH M4Q has a specific section, 3.2.R, for regional information.

Module 3 consists of three sections:

- 3.1 Module 3 table of contents
- 3.2 Body of data (drug substance and drug product)
- 3.3 Literature references[17]

The body of data in 3.2 consists of two parts:

3.2.S Drug Substance

This section covers the following information, which may be slightly different for NCEs[18] as opposed to biotech products.[19] In addition, this section may differ depending on the intended route of administration.

- 3.2.S.1 General information pertaining to the active pharmaceutical ingredient
- 3.2.S.1 Information about the manufacturer
    - o Name and address
    - o Manufacturing process and controls
    - o Control of materials and critical steps
    - o Process validation
    - o Manufacturing process development
- 3.2.S.3 Characterization
- 3.2.S.4 Control of drug substance
- 3.2.S.5 Reference standards
- 3.2.S.6 Container closure system
- 3.2.S.7 Stability information including a stability summary and conclusion, postapproval stability protocol and commitments and stability data.

Manufacturers can also use a Certificate of Suitability to a monograph of the European Pharmacopoeia (CEP[20]) to register and supply drug substance, starting materials and excipients in the EU and other international countries where CEPs are accepted.

CEP
Where an active substance, a starting material or an excipient is the subject of a PhEu monograph, the applicant can apply for a CEP. CEPs are issued by the European Directorate for the Quality of Medicines and Healthcare (EDQM) once compliance with the PhEu monograph is shown and following successful inspection of the manufacturing site (if applicable).

Legal Framework
Several legal texts describe the certification procedure:

- Resolution AP-CSP (07) 1 on the 'Certification of Suitability to the Monographs of the European Pharmacopoeia (Revised Version) (Adopted by the Public Health Committee (CD-P-SP) 21 February 2007)
- Directive 2001/82/EC of the European Council and of the Parliament of 6 November 2001 on the Community code relating to veterinary medicinal products, as amended
- Directive 2001/83/EC of the European Council and of the Parliament of 6 November 2001 on the Community code relating to medicinal products for human use, as amended

CEPs are recognized by the 37 signatory parties of the Convention on the Elaboration of a European Pharmacopoeia, including all EU Member States. They also are recognized by other countries, e.g., Canada, Australia, New Zealand, Tunisia and Morocco.

3.2.P Drug Product
Similar information is required for the drug product, including:

- 3.2.P.1 Description and composition of the drug product
- 3.2.P.2 Pharmaceutical development: This section should include the product name, components, dosage form formulation, overages and excipients. In addition, information about the manufacturing process, container closure system, microbiological attributes and compatibility is required. More information can be obtained from ICH guideline *Pharmaceutical Development Q8(R2)*.[21] Additional useful information is listed in the annex. The product should be developed in such a way as to meet patients' needs and achieve the intended performance.

  Strategies for product development vary from company to company and from product to product. The approach to, and extent of, development also can vary and should be outlined in the submission. In any case, evidence must be given that any approach used is based on sound scientific principles.[22]

  The use of overages to compensate for degradation during manufacture or shelf life is not recommended. If used, overages must be justified and included in the information listed in the batch formula.[23]
- 3.2.P.3 Manufacturer: This includes manufacturer name and address, information about the batch formula, description of the manufacturing process, control of critical steps and intermediates and process validation.
- 3.2.P.4 Control of excipients: This section should include specifications, analytical procedures, validation, justification of specifications and any information pertaining to excipients of human or animal origin or novel excipients.
- 3.2.P.5 Control of drug product: This section should include specifications, analytical procedures, validation, batch analyses, characterization of impurities and justification of specifications.
- 3.2.P.6 Reference standards or materials
- 3.2.P.7 Container closure system
- 3.2.P.8 Stability data: This section should include a stability summary and conclusion, postapproval stability protocol and commitments and stability data

It should be noted that if a product is wholly or partially manufactured by a third party, the manufacturer may not wish to disclose certain confidential information to the sponsor. To this end, a Drug Master File could have an open and closed part. The applicant's (open) part should be included in section 3.2.S of the quality documentation presented in the CTD format.

This international format applies to all drug and medicinal product categories (including such products as NCEs, radiopharmaceuticals, vaccines and herbals) and all application types (standalone and generic/abridged[24]). In addition, ICH foresees technical specifications such as font size, borders, etc., to facilitate the reviewer's assessment.

Module 4

The structure and format of Module 4 are described in M4S.

Module 4 consists of three sections:

- 4.1 Module 4 table of contents
- 4.2 Study reports
- 4.3 Literature references[25]

The body of the data in 4.2 is organized into the following sections:

- 4.2.1 Pharmacology: This includes primary and secondary pharmacodynamics, safety pharmacology and pharmacodynamic drug interactions.

- 4.2.2 Pharmacokinetics: Analytical methods and validation reports should be presented in this section. The information sought is data about absorption, distribution, metabolism, excretion, pharmacokinetic drug interactions (nonclinical) and any other pharmacokinetic studies.
- 4.2.3 Toxicology: The results of single-dose and repeat-dose toxicity and genotoxicity (*in vitro* and *in vivo*) are the topic of this section. In addition, results of short-, medium- and long-term carcinogenicity studies plus any other studies should be provided. Reproductive and developmental toxicity, including fertility, embryo and early embryonic development, embryo-fetal development and prenatal and postnatal development, also should be covered.

  The results of local tolerance and other toxicity studies such as antigenicity, immunotoxicity, mechanistic studies, dependence, metabolites and impurities also should be presented if available.

ICH also has published the guideline, *Safety Pharmacology Studies for Human Pharmaceuticals S7A*.[26] This guideline was developed for NCEs and products derived from biotechnology. The guideline indicates that supplemental safety pharmacology studies can be performed to evaluate potential adverse pharmacodynamic effects on organ system functions not addressed by the core battery or repeat-dose toxicity studies when there is a cause for concern.[27]

Module 5

The structure and format of Module 5 are described in M4E.

Module 5 consists of four sections:

- 5.1 Module 5 table of contents
- 5.2 Tabular listing of all clinical studies
- 5.3 Clinical study reports
- 5.4 Literature references[28]

The body of the data in 5.3 is organized into the following sections:

- 5.3.1 Reports of Biopharmaceutic Studies: This includes bioavailability (BA) study reports, comparative BA and bioequivalence (BE) study reports, *in vitro-in vivo* correlation study reports and reports of bioanalytical and analytical methods for human studies.
- 5.3.2 Reports of Studies Pertinent to Pharmacokinetics using Human Biomaterials: Study reports covering plasma protein binding, hepatic metabolism and drug interactions and use of human biomaterial should be presented in this section.
- 5.3.3 Reports of Human Pharmacokinetic (PK) Studies: This section should include study reports of healthy subject PK and initial tolerability tests, patient PK and initial tolerability tests, intrinsic factor PK tests, extrinsic factor PK tests and population PK tests.
- 5.3.4 Reports of Human Pharmacodynamic (PD) Studies: Healthy subject PD and PK/PD study reports and patient PD and PK/PD study reports should be presented in this section.
- 5.3.5 Reports of Efficacy and Safety Studies: This section covers the results of controlled clinical studies pertinent to the claimed indication, the results of uncontrolled clinical studies, analyses of data from more than one study and other clinical study reports.
- 5.3.6 Reports of Postmarketing Experience: All postmarketing experience, including Periodic Safety Update Reports for approved products, is presented in this section.
- 5.3.7 Case Report Forms and Individual Patient Listings: In this section, individual case report forms and individual patient listings should be presented.

Types of Applications

Complete/Full and Independent Applications

A full (standalone) Marketing Authorization Application (MAA) must include the results of:

- physicochemical, biological or microbiological tests
- pharmacological and toxicological tests
- clinical trials

In general, full applications are mandatory for NCEs and New Biological Entities (NBEs) including:[29]

- a chemical, biological or radiopharmaceutical active substance not previously authorized
- an isomer, a mixture of isomers, a complex or a derivative or salt of a chemical substance previously authorized in the country where an application is made but differing from the authorized substance in safety and efficacy properties
- a biological substance previously authorized that differs from the authorized substance in molecular structure, nature of the source material or manufacturing
- new radiopharmaceuticals
- new fixed combinations

The exact requirements for specific products and what is mandatory may differ from region to region; however, sponsors should realize that any NCE or other high-risk product needs to undergo the full range of preclinical and clinical testing.

Mixed Data Applications

For certain products about which there is significant published scientific literature, sponsors may skip some tests if sufficient information is available in the public domain to cover specific aspects of the application. In such cases, sponsors can carry out a limited number of tests to gather any information not covered in the scientific literature. Such an application is still considered to be a full, complete application. This can save considerable time and money and avoid unnecessary animal and human testing.

Bibliographic References/Applications

For various reasons, prospective MAHs may consider reintroducing old chemical entities as new products. Where the chemical entity is very old (usually on the market for more than 10 years) and there is no original or reference medicinal product to which essential similarity can be claimed, it is possible to replace pharmacological and toxicological tests or clinical trial results entirely with detailed references to published scientific literature. This is also recommended to avoid unnecessary testing if a medicinal product's constituent(s) has a well-established medicinal use with recognized efficacy and an acceptable safety profile.

If, however, the known chemical entity is to be registered for a new therapeutic use, extra tests and trials would need to be conducted. These are also full applications since no cross-referencing takes place.

Generic or Abridged Applications

Generic or abridged applications are those for which the applicant is not required to provide pharmacological and toxicological testing or clinical trial results. This is the case for generics where the product is essentially similar or comparable to the innovator product (i.e., product already authorized in the country of application).

The concept of essential similarity implies the following criteria are met:

- the same qualitative and quantitative composition in terms of active principles
- the same pharmaceutical form
- demonstrated bioequivalence[30]

The applicant is required to provide only Modules 1, 2, 3 and 5. Module 5 contains the results of BE studies. BE information is required to ensure therapeutic equivalence between a pharmaceutically equivalent product and a Reference Product (EU) or Reference Listed Drug (US). In some cases, a biowaiver can be applied for drug products that are in solution form, based on the assumption that release of the drug substance from the drug product is self-evident and that solutions do not contain any excipients that significantly affect drug absorption.

The original product dossier must be at the disposal of the Competent Authority that is reviewing the abridged application. This usually happens after patent expiry but, in certain instances, could also occur beforehand if the originator company grants the generic manufacturer permission to use information contained in its dossier. In such a case, a written confirmation from the innovator company is required.

Abridged applications for biotech products are not accepted in all regions. For example, in the EU, biosimilars are allowed for first-generation molecules. In other regions, numerous biosimilars already have been registered, especially in China and India.

Annex 9-1 shows the organization of an ASEAN Common Technical Document (ACTD) dossier for the Registration of Pharmaceuticals for Human Use.

Herbal Medicinal Products

For certain classes of products, such as herbal medicines, simplified registration procedures are in place in most countries.

Conclusion

It is important to understand data and dossier structure requirements for regulatory submissions. Although data requirements may differ significantly from region to region, ICH has made significant progress in defining a CTD. Not all sections of the CTD requirements have been harmonized at the global level; however, significant progress has been made. This greatly helps international companies by enabling them to use the same dossier with slight modifications for registration in various geographic regions.

The amount of data required for evaluation depends on the product type. Simple or low-risk molecules may not need the same amount of detail as complex or high-risk products. For a well-established medicinal product with a favorable benefit:risk profile, Modules 4 and 5 could be presented as bibliographic references; this can save significant time and money. Abridged applications do not need to provide pharmacological and toxicological testing or clinical trial results; rather, references are made to the data for an original reference product.

Understanding national and/or regional differences in data requirements is important in formulating appropriate and effective regulatory strategies for submissions across the globe.

References

1. ICH website. www.ich.org. Accessed 16 September 2012.
2. *Fundamentals of US Regulatory Affairs*, Fifth Edition. "Chapter 4 History of US Regulatory Affairs." Copyright 2007 by the Regulatory Affairs Professionals Society, pp 1–8.
3. Op cit 1.
4. Ibid.

5. ICH, *Organization of the CTD for the Registration of Pharmaceuticals for Human Use M4(R3)* (Current Step 4 version, January 2004). ICH website. www.ich.org/fileadmin/Public_Web_Site/ICH_Products/CTD/M4_R3_Organisation/M4_R3__organisation.pdf. Accessed 9 October 2012.
6. *Fundamentals of EU Regulatory Affairs*, Fourth Edition. "Chapter 2 Overview of Authorization Procedures for Medicinal Products and Medical Devices." Copyright 2008 by the Regulatory Affairs Professionals Society, pp 15-26.
7. ICH, *The Common Technical Document for the Registration of Pharmaceuticals for Human Use: Quality—M4Q(R1), Quality Overall Summary of Module 2 Module 3: Quality* (Current Step 4 version, September 2002). ICH website. www.ich.org/fileadmin/Public_Web_Site/ICH_Products/CTD/M4_R1_Quality/M4Q__R1_.pdf. Accessed 8 October 2012.
8. ICH, *The Common Technical Document for the Registration of Pharmaceuticals for Human Use: Safety—M4S(R2), Nonclinical overview and Nonclinical Summaries of Module 2, Organisation of Module 4* (Current Step 4 version, December 2002). ICH website. www.ich.org/fileadmin/Public_Web_Site/ICH_Products/CTD/M4__R2__Safety/M4S_R2_.pdf. Accessed 8 October 2012.
9. ICH, *The Common Technical Document for the Registration of Pharmaceuticals for Human Use: Efficacy—M4E(R1), Clinical Overview and Clinical Summaries of Module 2, Module 5 Clinical Study Reports* (Current Step 4 version, September 2002). ICH website. www.ich.org/fileadmin/Public_Web_Site/ICH_Products/CTD/M4__R1__Efficacy/M4E__R1_.pdf. Accessed 8 October 2012.
10. Op cit 7.
11. Ibid.
12. Op cit 8.
13. Op cit 1.
14. Ibid.
15. ICH, *Impurities in New Drug Substances Q3A(R2)* (Current Step 4 version, October 2006). ICH website. www.ich.org/fileadmin/Public_Web_Site/ICH_Products/Guidelines/Quality/Q3A_R2/Step4/Q3A_R2__Guideline.pdf. Accessed 8 October 2012.
16 Op cit 8.
17. Op cit 5.
18. ICH, *Specifications: Test Procedures and Acceptance Criteria for New Drug Substances and New Drug Products: Chemical Substances Q6A (including Decision Trees)* (Current Step 4 version, October 1999). ICH website. www.ich.org/fileadmin/Public_Web_Site/ICH_Products/Guidelines/Quality/Q6A/Step4/Q6Astep4.pdf. Accessed 8 October 2012.
19. ICH, *Specification: Test Procedures and Acceptance Criteria for Biotechnological/Biological Products Q6B* (Current Step 4 version, March 1999). ICH website. www.ich.org/fileadmin/Public_Web_Site/ICH_Products/Guidelines/Quality/Q6B/Step4/Q6B_Guideline.pdf. Accessed 8 October 2012.
20. CEP, Certification of Suitability to the Monograph of European Pharmacopoeia. EDQM website. www.edqm.eu/en/certification-background-77.html. Accessed 16 September 2012.
21. ICH, *Pharmaceutical Development Q8(R2)* (Current Step 4 version, August 2009). ICH website. www.ich.org/fileadmin/Public_Web_Site/ICH_Products/Guidelines/Quality/Q8_R1/Step4/Q8_R2_Guideline.pdf. Accessed 8 October 2012.
22 Op cit 15.
23. Ibid.
24. Op cit 6.
25. Op cit 5.
26. ICH, *Safety Pharmacology Studies for Human Pharmaceuticals S7A* (Current Step 4 version, November 2000). ICH website. www.ich.org/fileadmin/Public_Web_Site/ICH_Products/Guidelines/Safety/S7A/Step4/S7A_Guideline.pdf. Accessed 8 October 2012.
27. Ibid.
28. Op cit 5.
29. Op cit 6.
30. Ibid.
31. ASEAN Common Technical Document (ACTD), Organization of the Dossier. ASEAN website. www.aseansec.org/18215.htm. Accessed 31 October 2012.

Annex 9-1. The ASEAN Common Technical Dossier (ACTD) for the Registration of Pharmaceuticals for Human Use

Organization of the Dossier

Preamble

This ASEAN Common Technical Dossier (ACTD) is a guideline of the agreed upon common format for the preparation of a well-structured Common Technical Dossier (CTD) applications that will be submitted to ASEAN regulatory authorities for the registration of pharmaceuticals for human use. This guideline describes a CTD format that will significantly reduce the time and resources needed to compile applications for registration and in the future, will ease the preparation of electronic documental submissions. Regulatory reviews and communication with the applicant will be facilitated by a standard document of common elements.

This guideline merely demonstrates an appropriate write-up format for acquired data. However, applicants can modify, if needed, to provide the best possible presentation of the technical information, in order to facilitate the understanding and evaluation of the results upon pharmaceutical registration.

Throughout the ACTD, the display of information should be unambiguous and transparent, in order to facilitate the review of the basic data and to help a reviewer become quickly oriented to the application contents. Text and tables should be prepared using margins that allow the document to be printed on either A4 or 8.5 x 11 paper. The left-hand margin should be sufficiently large that information is not obscured by the method of binding. Font and size, (Times New Roman, 12-point font), for text and tables should be of a style and size that are large enough to be easily legible, even after photocopying. Every page should be numbered, with the first page of each part designated as page 1. For a paper, Common Technical Acronyms and abbreviations should be defined the first time they are used in each part. References should be cited in accordance with the 1979 Vancouver Declaration on Uniform requirements for Manuscripts Submitted to Biomedical Journals.

The Common Technical Document is organized into four parts as follows:

Part I. Table of Contents, Administrative Data and Product Information

Part I contains initially the overall Table of Contents of the whole ACTD to provide basicaly the informations that could be looked through respectively. Secondly, the next content is the Administrative Data where required specific documentation in details is put together such as application forms, label, package insert etc. The last section of this part is Product Information where necessary information includes prescribed information, mode of action, side effects etc.

A general introduction to the pharmaceutical, including its pharmacologic class and mode of action should be included.

Part II. Quality Document

Part II should provide the Overall Summary followed by the Study Reports. The quality control document should be described in details as much as possible.

Part III. Nonclinicall Document

Part III should provide the **Nonclinical** Overview, followed by the Nonclinical Written Summaries and the Nonclinical Tabulated Summaries. The document of this part is not required for Generic Products, Minor Variation Products and some Major Variation Products. For ASEAN member countries, the Study Reports of this part may not be required for NCE, Biotechnological Products and other Major Variation Products if the Original Products are already registered and approved for market authorization in Reference Countries. Therefore, the authority who requires specific Study Reports should ask for the necessary documents.

Part IV. Clinical Document

Part IV should provide the Clinical Overview and the Clinical Summary. The document of this part is not required for Generic Products, Minor Variation Products and some Major Variation Products. For ASEAN member countries, the Study Reports of this part may not be required for NCE, Biotechnological Products and other Major Variation Products if the Original Products are already registered and approved for market authorization in Reference Countries. Therefore, the authority who requires specific Study Reports should ask for the necessary documents.

The overall organisation of the Common Technical Dossier is presented on the following in parts:

Part I. Table of Content Administrative Information and Prescribing Information

Section A: Introduction
Section B: Overall ASEAN Common Technical Dossier Table of Contents
Section C: Documents required for registration (for example, application forms, labelling, Product Data Sheet, prescribing information)

Part II. Quality Document

Section A: Table of Contents
Section B: Quality Overall Summary
Section C: Body of Data

Part III. Nonclinical Document

Section A: Table of Contents
Section B: Nonclinical Overview
Section C: Nonclinical Written and Tabulated Summaries
1. Table of Contents
2. Pharmacology
3. Pharmacokinetics
4. Toxicology

Section D: Nonclinical Study Reports
1. Table of Contents
2. Pharmacology
3. Pharmacokinetics
4. Toxicology

Part IV. Clinical Document

Section A: Table of Contents
Section B: Clinical Overview
Section C: Clinical Summary
1. Summary of Biopharmaceutics and Associated Analytical Methods
2. Summary of Clinical Pharmacology Studies
3. Summary of Clinical Efficacy
4. Summary of Clinical Safety
5. Synopses of Individual Studies

Section D: Tabular Listing of All Clinical Studies
Section E: Clinical Study Reports
Section F: List of Key Literature References

Reference

1. The word "Nonclinical" replaces "Pre-clinical."

Chapter 10

Authorization Procedures for Pharmaceutical Products

Updated by Jasmina Savic, MSc, RAC

OBJECTIVES

- ❑ Gain an understanding of the regulatory procedures necessary to grant a medicinal product access to the marketplace
- ❑ Understand primary development considerations for successful authorization
- ❑ Get to know legislation, individual steps of the procedures and the Competent Authorities involved

LAWS, REGULATION AND GUIDELINES COVERED IN THIS CHAPTER

ICH

- ❑ ICH, *Guidance on Nonclinical Safety Studies for the Conduct of Human Clinical Trials and Marketing Authorisation for Pharmaceuticals M3(R2)*
- ❑ ICH, *Detection of Toxicity to Reproduction for Medicinal Products & Toxicity to Male Fertility S5(R2)*
- ❑ ICH, *Guidance on Genotoxicity Testing and Data Interpretation for Pharmaceuticals Intended for Human Use S2(R1)*
- ❑ ICH, *Guideline on the Need for Carcinogenicity Studies of Pharmaceuticals S1A*
- ❑ ICH, *Testing for Carcinogenicity of Pharmaceuticals S1B*
- ❑ ICH, *Concept Paper: Rodent Carcinogenicity Studies for Human Pharmaceuticals, S1*
- ❑ ICH, *Safety Pharmacology Studies for Human Pharmaceuticals* S7A
- ❑ ICH, *Note for Guidance on Toxicokinetics: The Assessment of Systemic Exposure in Toxicity Studies S3A*
- ❑ ICH, *Pharmacokinetics: Guidance for Repeated Dose Tissue Distribution Studies S3B*
- ❑ ICH, *Structure and Content of Clinical Study Reports E3*
- ❑ ICH, *Guideline for Good Clinical Practice E6(R1)*
- ❑ ICH, *Good Manufacturing Practice Guide for Active Pharmaceutical Ingredients Q7*

OECD

- ❑ OECD, Series on Principles of Good Laboratory Practice and Compliance Monitoring (ENV/MC/CHEM(98)17, 1997)

WHO

- ❑ WHO, *Guidelines on pre-approval inspections, WHO Technical Report Series*, No. 902, 2002

EU

- ❑ Regulation (EC) No 726/2004 of the European Parliament and of the Council of 31 March 2004 laying down Community procedures for the authorisation and supervision of medicinal products for human and veterinary use and establishing a European Medicines Agency
- ❑ Directive 2004/27/EC of the European Parliament and of the Council of 31 March 2004 amending Directive 2001/83/EC on the Community code relating to medicinal products for human use
- ❑ Directive 2004/10/EC of the European Parliament and of the Council of 11 February 2004 on the harmonisation of laws, regulations and administrative provisions relating to the application of the principles of good laboratory practice and the verification of their applications for tests on chemical substances
- ❑ Directive 2004/9/EC of the European Parliament and of the Council of 11 February 2004 on the inspection and verification of good laboratory practice (GLP)
- ❑ Regulation (EC) No 1901/2006 of the European Parliament and of the Council of 12 December 2006 on medicinal products for paediatric use and amending Regulation (EEC) No 1768/92, Directive 2001/20/EC, Directive 2001/83/EC and Regulation (EC) No 726/2004

US

- ❑ 21 CFR 58 Good Laboratory Practice for Nonclinical Laboratory Studies
- ❑ 21 CFR 314 Applications for FDA Approval to Market a New Drug
- ❑ *Federal Food, Drug, and Cosmetic Act* of 1938, Part II
- ❑ *US Food and Drug Administration Safety and Innovation Act (FDASIA)* of 2012

Introduction

In most regions of the world, national legislation is enacted to regulate medicinal products for human use, stipulating that a medicinal product may be placed on the local market only after a Marketing Authorization (MA) has been granted by the local Competent Authority.

In general, the term medicinal product includes prescription and nonprescription pharmaceuticals, as well as biologically derived products such as vaccines and sera and blood-derived products. In addition, less critical products such as natural health products (food supplements and herbal products), for which therapeutic claims are made, also are regulated as drugs.

As noted in Chapter 9, the evaluation by Competent Authorities is based on information provided by the prospective Marketing Authorization Holder (MAH). The data provided should include at least the results of the preclinical and clinical testing and manufacturing information.

In certain regions, one issued license could cover many countries or states. For transnational commerce, special agreements and regulations must be in place to cover the whole territory. For example, in the EU, for products registered via the Centralised Procedure, administered through the European Medicines Agency (EMA), an authorization is granted for the entire Community (Community authorization).[1] Another example is the Central Drug Registration process in the Middle East, approved on 15 May 1999, which includes Bahrain, Kuwait, Oman, Qatar, Saudi Arabia and the United Arab Emirates.[2]

Legislation in all regions is developing rapidly and brings new requirements that should be followed diligently and to which applicants must adjust quickly. One example is the introduction of pediatric legislation in the US (1997)[3] and the EU (2007),[4] which aims to improve medical product research in children and the availability of high quality, safe and effective treatments for children. As a result, each MAH needs to have a pediatric plan in place when applying for an MA in these regions.

MAH Legal Responsibilities

An MAH is a person holding a marketing authorization for a product and responsible for placing that product on the market. MAHs have certain legal responsibilities, which although determined by individual nations, are similar from region to region. The following list, although not exhaustive, includes the most important MAH responsibilities.

- The MAH is responsible for taking any technical and scientific progress into consideration and updating manufacturing and control operations. Normally, these changes must be communicated to the Competent Authority that issued the MA. For critical changes, the Competent Authority will carry out an evaluation and approve or reject the proposed changes before the variations can be implemented.
- When an MAH is not the manufacturer, especially when utilizing a contract manufacturer, the MAH must ensure that a written agreement with the manufacturer is in place, to guarantee that manufacturing

operations comply with dossier rules, conditions and Good Manufacturing Practice (GMP) standards and oblige the manufacturer to inform the MAH of any changes before implementation.
- If any information is brought to the attention of the MAH, including safety issues that could lead to modification of the marketing authorization dossier or Summary of Product Characteristics (SmPC), the Competent Authorities must be informed immediately.
- In most countries, MAs are issued for a limited time. The MAH is responsible for renewing the license before the MA's expiration date. The rules governing this vary from region to region.
- In certain regions, the MAH is required to have a qualified person (QP) for batch release. This includes, among others, the EU (usually head of the quality department), Canada, Switzerland, Australia, Japan, New Zealand and the US (head of the quality unit).
- The MAH must have a QP in charge of pharmacovigilance.
- The MAH must take full responsibility for medicinal product advertising.
- The MAH must ensure that all medicinal product documentation, including clinical trial information, is retained and archived.
- The MAH must have a scientific service in charge of information about the product on the market.
- Special requirements may apply to high-risk products such as immunological medicinal products and medicinal products derived from human blood or human plasma.

The MAH assumes full responsibility for products it places on the market. It must ensure that drugs are prepared, preserved, packaged or stored under sanitary conditions and are unadulterated. If any defects are noticed that could result in a recall or abnormal restrictions on the supply, the MAH is obliged to inform the Competent Authorities. In addition, the MAH must ensure that the information presented in the labeling, on packaging and in advertising material is correct and not misleading or deceptive.

Authorization Procedures

Authorization procedures are still very much a national issue. As mentioned above, certain territories may accept licenses for whole regions, e.g., the EU, some Middle Eastern countries or all 50 US states. In contrast to the mutual recognition of GMP and other batch release agreements between countries where Mutual Recognition Agreements (MRAs) are in place (see Chapter 12), drug licenses are not mutually recognized between regions. Consequently, a drug with a valid license in the US cannot be sold elsewhere, e.g., the EU, Asia or the Middle East, without obtaining appropriate licenses in those regions. This section covers various regional authorization procedures and looks at some specific cases of mutual recognition.

General Procedures

Although the exact requirements and processes involved are country-specific, in almost all regions new drug applications require at least:
- nonclinical testing
- application to begin clinical trials and proper finalization of trials
- new drug application, including results of nonclinical and clinical testing plus manufacturing information
- pricing and reimbursement information
- postmarketing activities

Throughout this process, applicants are in frequent contact with the Competent Authorities. Presubmission meetings can be arranged to discuss any critical issues, especially during the development phase. In some countries, meetings are arranged to introduce the new drug application to prospective Competent Authority reviewers.

The complexity of the registration process and the data requirements depend upon whether an application is for a new drug application, a generic, a new combination or an herbal product.

Some regions, e.g., the US and the EU, require special consideration regarding pediatric product development that should be part of the overall product development plan and also require adequate pediatric plans to be submitted at the time of new drug application.

Nonclinical Testing

Nonclinical testing can take from one to four years and provides the basic toxicologic and pharmacologic information required to evaluate a new drug's safety before commencing human clinical trials. The tests normally consist of *in vitro* and *in vivo* animal toxicology and pharmacology tests. Nonclinical safety studies to support the various stages of clinical development differ among the EU, US and Japan. ICH has published *Guidance on Nonclinical Safety Studies for the Conduct of Human Clinical Trials and Marketing Authorization for Pharmaceuticals M3(R2)*,[5] recommending international standards for and promoting harmonization of the nonclinical safety studies needed to support human clinical trials of a given scope and duration.

Test results can be used to:
- assess activity and mechanism of action
- detect overt toxicity and identify toxic effects and principal target organs

- assess drug absorption, distribution to organ systems and tissues, metabolism and elimination pathways (ADME)
- assess pharmacokinetics
- assess carcinogenicity
- assess reproductive toxicity and teratogenic potential
- estimate dose-response relationships of pharmacological and toxicological effects
- estimate a safe starting dose for study in humans
- suggest clinical safety assessments[6]

Nonclinical safety studies usually include:

- single and repeated dose toxicity studies
- reproduction toxicity studies
- genotoxicity studies
- local tolerance toxicity studies
- carcinogenicity studies for drugs intended for chronic use
- pharmacology studies (including safety pharmacology studies)
- pharmacokinetic studies (ADME)[7]

Single and Repeated Dose Toxicity Studies
Single dose (acute) toxicity should be evaluated in two mammalian species prior to the first human exposure.[8]

The duration of the repeated dose toxicity studies, as recommended by the ICH M3(R2) guideline, should be related to the duration, therapeutic indication and scale of the proposed clinical trial. The results of these tests can be used to support prospective clinical trials.

Reproduction Toxicity Studies
Reproduction toxicity studies are covered by the ICH guideline, *Detection of Toxicity to Reproduction for Medicinal Products and Toxicity to Male Fertility S5(R2)*.[9] The aim of these studies is to test for any effect one or more active substance(s) may have on mammalian reproduction.

Genotoxicity Tests
Genotoxicity tests can be defined as *in vitro* and *in vivo* tests designed to detect compounds that induce genetic damage directly or indirectly by various mechanisms (ICH, *Guidance on Genotoxicity Testing and Data Interpretation for Pharmaceuticals Intended for Human Use S2(R1)*).[10] These tests should enable hazard identification with respect to DNA and its fixation in the form of gene mutations, larger scale chromosomal damage, recombination and numerical chromosome changes. Registration of pharmaceuticals requires a comprehensive assessment of their genotoxic potential.

When conducting dose range-finding studies in the preclinical phase, the shape of the toxicity dose-response curve shows whether the test compound exhibits toxicity. In addition, the tests should include highly toxic concentrations and quantification of mutants in the cytotoxic range. In either case, mutants should be quantified.[11]

Local Tolerance Toxicity Studies
The assessment of local tolerance may be part of other toxicity studies using routes relevant to the proposed clinical tests and should be done prior to testing on humans.

Carcinogenicity Tests
When considering the necessity for carcinogenicity tests, ICH's *Guideline on the Need for Carcinogenicity Studies of Pharmaceuticals S1A*,[12] should be taken into consideration. The guideline states that carcinogenicity studies should be performed for any pharmaceutical product whose expected clinical use is continuous for at least six months. Carcinogenicity testing also can be conducted if there is cause for concern about carcinogenic potential or in the presence of genotoxic compounds. The experimental approaches intended to assess the carcinogenic potential are described in ICH's *Testing for Carcinogenicity of Pharmaceuticals S1B*.[13] For pharmaceutical products developed to treat certain serious diseases, carcinogenicity testing need not be conducted before marketing approval, although these studies should be conducted postapproval.[14] The route of exposure in animals should be the same as the intended use in humans. In addition, carcinogenicity studies also may be required for topical pharmaceutical products. ICH recently (April 2012) published a concept paper, *Rodent Carcinogenicity Studies for Human Pharmaceuticals S1*,[15] with the intent of strengthening the testing strategy for predicting human carcinogens and reducing the number of two-year rodent bioassays. Once finalized in June 2017, this concept paper will impact both the S1A and S1B guidelines.

Safety Pharmacology Studies
Safety pharmacology studies have been performed worldwide for many years as part of the nonclinical evaluation of pharmaceuticals for human use.[16] The objectives of safety pharmacology studies are to:

- identify undesirable pharmacodynamic properties of a substance that may have relevance to its human safety
- evaluate adverse pharmacodynamic and/or pathophysiological effects of a substance observed in toxicology and/or clinical studies
- investigate the mechanism of the adverse pharmacodynamic effects observed and/or suspected

The investigational plan to meet these objectives should be clearly identified and delineated (ICH guideline, *Safety Pharmacology Studies for Human Pharmaceuticals S7A*).

Supplemental studies to evaluate potential adverse pharmacodynamic effects on organ system functions not addressed by the core battery or repeated dose toxicity studies may be necessary when there is a cause for concern.[17] The effect of the test substance on the following organs could be tested: renal/urinary system, autonomic nervous system, gastrointestinal system or other organ systems.

Pharmacokinetic Studies

Toxicokinetic studies are carried out mainly to describe the systemic exposure achieved in animals and its relationship to dose level and the time course of the toxicity study.[18] In addition, pharmacokinetic studies provide information on a compound's ADME, important for interpreting pharmacology and toxicology studies.[19]

All nonclinical studies should be carried out in conformity with Good Laboratory Practice (GLP) provisions. GLP is a quality system concerned with the organizational process and conditions under which nonclinical health and environmental safety studies are planned, performed, monitored, recorded, reported and archived.[20]

GLP is outlined in the Organization for Economic Co-operation and Development (OECD) *Principles of GLP*[21] and national regulations. For example, in the US, rules relating to GLP are outlined in 21 CFR 58[22] and in the EU, in Directive 2004/10/EC of the European Parliament and of the Council of 11 February 2004 on the harmonisation of laws, regulations and administrative provisions relating to the application of the principles of good laboratory practice and the verification of their applications for tests on chemical substances[23] and Directive 2004/9/EC of the European Parliament and of the Council of 11 February 2004 on the inspection and verification of good laboratory practice (GLP).[24] By harmonizing testing procedures for the Mutual Acceptance of Data (MAD), tests carried out according to GLP are accepted by both OECD members and some nonmember states.

GLP Covers

- organization and personnel
- facilities
- equipment
- testing facilities operation
- test and control articles
- protocol(s) and conduct of nonclinical studies
- records and reports of nonclinical study results
- disqualification of testing facilities[25]

The processes used must be properly documented in standard operating procedures (SOPs) and the staff adequately trained. Each study must have an approved written protocol, and any protocol changes or revisions must be signed by a qualified person, usually the study director.

Safety pharmacology studies may be omitted in the case of locally applied agents where the pharmacology of the test substance is well characterized, and where it has been demonstrated that systemic exposure or distribution to other organs or tissues is low.[26]

Application for Clinical Trials

Clinical trials are pivotal to successful drug development. Clinical trials generally are regulated under each national authority's laws, regulations and administrative provisions. As a consequence, companies involved in multicenter and multinational clinical trials find themselves facing a wide array of national application and approval processes, combined with a lack of standardization in applying Good Clinical Practices (GCPs) and GMPs across the globe.

The *Helsinki Declaration*, originally adopted in June 1964, in Helsinki, Finland, set forth for the first time ethical standards for the conduct of clinical trials in humans, and has since undergone six revisions. Physicians are legally bound by this declaration, which sets out the principles of respect for individuals and their right to self-determination. This includes their right to make informed decisions regarding participating in medical research.

Details of the clinical trials principles and procedures are explained in more detail in Chapter 4.

ICH has published a number of guidelines pertaining to clinical testing and expedited reporting under "Efficacy."[27]

Each clinical trial can only commence once proper Ethics Committee and Competent Authority approvals are received. Time needed to obtain the positive opinions varies among countries and regions (from 60 days in the EU to up to a few months in China).

Applications for New Marketing Authorization—Manufacturing Information

If the results of the nonclinical and clinical trials are positive, sponsors can proceed to the manufacturing phase for registration and market purposes. This section of the application dossier is also known as chemistry, manufacturing and controls (CMC). All ICH countries and some countries outside this group accept these data as a part of the Common Technical Document (CTD). According to ICH's guidance on the structure of the CTD, the quality and manufacturing information are presented in Module 3. Module 3 should contain information on the:

- drug substance—including manufacturing information, characterization, controls, validation and stability information
- drug product—including description and composition, pharmaceutical development, manufacturing information, excipient and drug product control and stability information

For a more detailed description, see "Module 3" in Chapter 9.

The exact processes and administrative requirements are determined by the national Competent Authorities;

however, in general terms, drug registration requires certain key documents:

- cover letter
- application form
- letters of authorizations (Powers of Attorney)
- information on experts signing the quality, nonclinical and clinical information
- product information (SmPC, Patient Information leaflet (PIL) and label texts), mock-ups and/or specimens
- specific information pertaining to the type of application, e.g., generic, bibliographic, etc.
- pharmacovigilance information
- technical file/dossier, consisting of the results of the nonclinical and clinical trials and manufacturing information
- certificates: including GMPs, Manufacturing Authorisations and Certificate of Pharmaceutical Products (CPP)

Other specific requirements may include environmental risk assessment, a risk management system, copies of approved licenses and SmPCs worldwide, etc. In many regions, such as the Middle East, Russia and the CIS, Africa and others, a copy of the CPP is always requested from the country of origin. The CPP should conform to the format recommended by the World Health Organization.[28]

In many regions, such as the Middle East and India, foreign companies must first register their company/manufacturer before the drug registration process can begin. This is important because the application and review can be time-consuming, lasting anywhere from six months to two years.

Certificate of Pharmaceutical Product (CPP)
The CPP should contain at least:

- certificate number
- exporting country
- importing country
- product name and dosage form
- active ingredient and amount per unit dose (plus excipients)
- marketing information
- product information
- applicant name and address
- information pertaining to inspections
- GMP status

Country-specific requirements may mandate that all certificates be notarized and sealed with an apostille from the local embassy.

When making an application, a prospective MAH should make sure the product's intended name is covered by a valid trademark. This can be done via the international procedural mechanism or the Madrid system, which offers a trademark owner the possibility to have the trademark protected in several countries by filing one application directly with its own national or regional trademark office. Alternatively, an applicant can make an application or register the same mark directly in each of the countries concerned.[29]

Good Manufacturing Practice (GMP)
GMP applies not only to the manufacturer of the finished product but also to the manufacturer of the active pharmaceutical ingredient (API). ICH has published *Good Manufacturing Practice Guide for Active Pharmaceutical Ingredients Q7*[30] on this topic. The classification of materials as APIs may vary from region to region. Any material classified as an API in the country where it is manufactured or where it is used in a drug product should, in principle, be manufactured to GMP standards. Regular quality reviews of APIs should be conducted with the objective of verifying the process consistency, including reviewing critical steps, batches that failed to meet specifications, nonconformances, change control, stability monitoring, quality complaints and adequacy of corrective actions.[31]

A formal change control system should be in place to capture all changes that may affect the production and control of the intermediate or API.[32]

Preapproval Inspections (PAI)
A number of global and regional/national regulations and guidelines state that the MAH is responsible for complying with GMPs and GCPs.

As a part of the assessment procedure, Competent Authorities might decide to conduct a GMP or GCP inspection as a prerequisite for granting an MA in their territories.

Since these add significantly to authorities' workloads, these inspections are not conducted routinely, but are likely to be conducted in the following instances:

- New Chemical Entities (NCEs)
- drugs of narrow therapeutic range and drugs for serious conditions
- products previously associated with serious adverse effects, complaints or recalls
- products that are difficult to manufacture or test or that are of doubtful stability
- new applicants or manufacturers
- applications from manufacturers who have previously failed to comply with GMP or official quality specifications[33]

Marketing Authorization Procedures
The exact steps involved in obtaining a license to market pharmaceuticals differ among countries and/or regions;

Figure 10-1. Procedure for EU Drug Registration

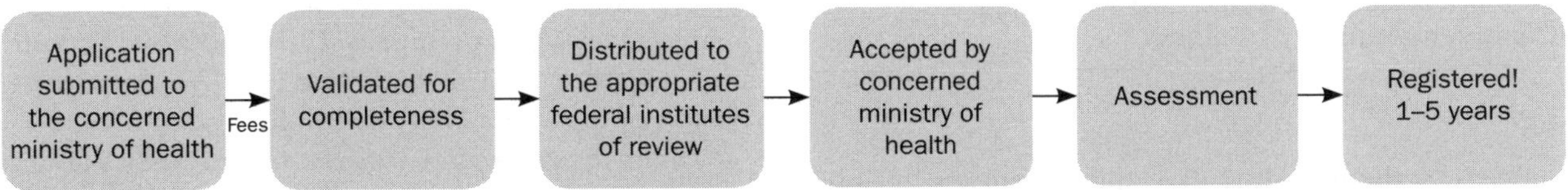

however, the basic steps are quite similar. In the EU, an MA is granted in the following sequence:

- submission to the Competent Authority(ies)
- validation for completeness
- if validation is successful, the dossier is sent to the corresponding institutes for evaluation
- evaluation (can take anywhere from one to five years)
- approval
- issuing of an MA (see **Figure 10-1**)

The exact process and timelines vary considerably from region to region.

Pricing and Reimbursement

Once a license has been issued, the sponsor may wish to launch the product immediately. However, the sale of very expensive medicines often will rely heavily on reimbursement by a particular country's local governing and reimbursement bodies. Applicants should be aware that national reimbursement bodies may be independent of the Competent Authority that evaluated and approved the product.

In many countries, reimbursement may delay product launch by one to two years. Making a reimbursement application can be time- and resource-intensive. Sponsors should plan ahead and ensure close cooperation among the regulatory, marketing and medical departments to ensure the submission of timely reimbursement applications.

In addition to reimbursement, pricing is another major issue that affects product launch. For example, in the EU, pricing is set based on the lowest possible price in the Union. Hence, applicants may want to launch their products in markets with better pricing first, before launching the product at a lower price in another Member State that may have lower pricing policies.

Postmarketing Activities

Postmarketing activities include lifecycle management and pharmacovigilance. When a medicinal product has been authorized and placed on the market, its risk:benefit profile continues to evolve with use; hence, the need for postmarketing activities.

Lifecycle Management

Product Lifecycle Management (PLM) can be defined as the process of managing the entire lifecycle of a product from its conception, through design and manufacture, to service and disposal.[34] MAHs are obliged to keep track of any changes in the manufacturing processes and to inform the Competent Authorities of such changes. Some postapproval changes, if major, may entail evaluation and approval by the Competent Authority before they can be implemented. Each country has its own system of classifying postapproval changes depending on the impact on the medicine's quality, safety and efficacy.

Pharmacovigilance

"Pharmacovigilance" can be defined as the science and activities relating to the detection, assessment, understanding and prevention of adverse effects or any other medicine-related problem.[35] Both the MAH and the Competent Authority have clearly defined responsibilities for pharmacovigilance activities for each approved product.

Country-specific Information

The above mentioned processes apply to global drug registrations; however, it is important to note that the actual registration procedure, the documentation and certificates needed and preregistration activities can differ from region to region. Companies working at the global level must familiarize themselves with applicable local procedures and conditions.

Many multinational companies have local affiliates in countries that are responsible for carrying out local registration procedures. If a local affiliate does not exist, companies must employ the services of local consultants and agents to carry out the registration process and act as the local MAH. In many cases, the local agent also will perform the registration process.

In many regions in the Far and Middle East, company registration is a prerequisite for drugs to be registered and placed on the market. This is a separate process from the drug registration process and may take anywhere from six months to two years to complete. Companies utilizing local agents need to ensure they have contracts in place that clearly specify each partner's responsibilities.

The following is a brief description of regulatory highlights in some selected countries worldwide. A good starting point to look for information is by visiting the local Competent Authority's website.

US

In the US, the new drug development process includes several distinct stages:

- nonclinical testing
- clinical testing—Investigational New Drug (IND) submission and US Food and Drug Administration (FDA), Institutional Review Boards (IRB) or Independent Ethics Committee (IEC) review
- preparation of pediatric plan
- New Drug Application (NDA) preparation and submission
- FDA NDA review and approval or disapproval

A "new drug" is defined in section 201(p)(1) of the *Federal Food, Drug and Cosmetic Act* (*FD&C Act*) as any drug with a composition that is not generally recognized as safe and effective (GRASE) for a use for which it is labeled, and in section 201(p)(2) as any drug with a composition that is not generally used to a material extend or for a material time under its conditions of use, except in the investigations to examine its safety and effectiveness.[36] The exact definition of a new drug may differ slightly from country to country in different regions, but in general is very similar.

For clinical trial applications, if FDA does not put the proposed clinical trial on hold within 30 days, the clinical trial can start once IRB or IEC approval is obtained. During development, the IND must be updated continually as new information emerges.

The NDA data requirements follow the ICH M4 guidelines and the CTD structure. Today, FDA encourages regulatory submissions in the electronic CTD (eCTD) format, and the number of eCTD submissions is growing steadily.

Sponsors can request meetings with the agency at different stages of product development. There are three meeting types: A, B and C:

- Type A meetings are reserved for those immediately necessary (e.g., dispute resolution, clinical holds, special protocol assessment).
- Type B meetings are pivotal development meetings that occur prior to progression to the next registration stage (e.g., Pre-IND, End-of-Phase 1, End-of-Phase 2/Pre-Phase 3, Pre-NDA).
- Type C meetings include any other meetings other than Type A and B (e.g., discussions on modification of the pediatric development plan).[37]

Regulations regarding NDAs are codified in 21 CFR 314 and can be found on the FDA website. Information on the NDA process can be found at www.fda.gov/Drugs/DevelopmentApprovalProcess/HowDrugsareDevelopedandApproved/ApprovalApplications/NewDrugApplicationNDA/default.htm.

Under the *Prescription User Fee Act* (*PDUFA*), FDA has committed to review approximately 90% of NDAs within 10 months (standard review). In addition to the standard review, there is also a priority review process under which FDA has committed to review 90% of submissions within six months.[38]

As mentioned earlier, at the time of the NDA submission, it is mandatory to also submit the pediatric plan for assessment. This assessment runs in parallel to the NDA review.[39]

The CDER website lists all regulatory and scientific guidance: www.fda.gov/Drugs/GuidanceCompliance RegulatoryInformation/Guidances/default.htm.[40]

Canada

In Canada, the *Food and Drugs Act (F&DA)* applies to all foods, drugs, cosmetics and medical devices and clearly outlines safety, composition, efficacy, purity and labeling requirements.[41]

The act is divided into sections and coded by division number. Schedules attached to the act include:

- Schedule C—drugs, other than radionuclides sold and represented for use in preparing radiopharmaceuticals
- Schedule D—biologics and related drugs
- Schedule F—drugs that require a prescription

Health Canada's Therapeutic Products Directorate (TPD) is the federal authority that regulates drugs and medical devices.[42] TPD is responsible for setting standards, conducting submission reviews and granting authorizations for initiating clinical trials and marketing new and generic drugs.

Schedule B of the *F&DA* lists the publications of standards that are recognized in Canada. These include the *United States Pharmacopoeia* (*USP*), the US *National Formulary* (*NF*) and the *European Pharmacopoeia* (*PhEur*). Although Canada is only a participant, many of the directorate's guidelines—especially regarding the Common Technical Document—are derived from those of ICH.[43]

Presubmission

Before filing a New Drug Submission (NDS), Supplementary New Drug Submission (SNDS), Abbreviated New Drug Submission (ANDS) or Clinical Trial Application (CTA), sponsors may wish to make a brief resubmission presentation to the appropriate directorate within Health Canada (TPD for drugs and the Biologics and Genetic Therapies Directorate (BGTD) for biologics).[44] Such meetings may be initiated if the sponsor/applicant wishes to discuss data to be presented in the dossier, introduce the dossier to the evaluators, discuss any potential issues and/or discuss submission details.

Filing

All submissions, including NDS, SNDS, PSUR-C, ANDS, SANDS, etc., must be sent to the Submission and Information Policy Division (SIPD), which will acknowledge submission receipt by mail and send the submission to the reviewing bureau within 10 calendar days. Clinical trial applications must be sent to the appropriate bureau (TPD for drugs and BGTD for biologics).[45]

Information on the NDS process can be found at www.hc-sc.gc.ca/ahc-asc/pubs/hpfb-dgpsa/access-therapeutic_acces-therapeutique-eng.php#6.2.

International Cooperation

Health Canada is engaged in several cooperation schemes with international counterparts and organizations.[46] These include information exchanges and multilateral harmonization initiatives to leverage resources and knowledge, ensure sound regulatory practice and standards and strengthen and facilitate mutual cooperation with international jurisdictions in scientific and regulatory areas.

Cooperation with the EU includes the exchange of information on legislation under development and draft regulatory guidance documents. This applies to nonpublic information related to ensuring the quality, safety and efficacy of medicinal or therapeutic products for human and veterinary use, including pharmaceuticals, radiopharmaceuticals and human biologics that are authorized or under review both in Canada and the EU.

Additionally, there is a trilateral cooperation between Canada, the US and Mexico, the main purpose of which is to increase communication, collaboration and the exchange of information among the three countries in the areas of drugs, biologics, medical devices, food safety and nutrition to protect and promote human health.[47]

Australia

The regulating body for drug applications in Australia is the Therapeutic Goods Administration (TGA). TGA carries out a range of assessment and monitoring activities to ensure therapeutic goods available nationally are of an acceptable standard, with the aim of ensuring that the Australian community has access, within a reasonable time, to therapeutic advances.[48]

The regulatory framework is based on a risk management approach and is designed to ensure public health and safety, while also aiming to free industry from any unnecessary regulatory burden. Medicines must be licensed under Part 4 of the *Therapeutic Goods Act* of 1989 and must comply with GMP principles.[49] Medicines are evaluated for quality, safety and efficacy and, depending on their level of risk, also registered on the Australian Register of Therapeutic Goods (ARTG).

Submissions must be in CTD format.[50]

After the decision is reached, TGA publishes its decision in an Australian Public Assessment Report (AusPAR). For applications with a positive outcome, the AusPAR generally will be published no more than a month after the product has been registered on the ARTG.[51]

More information on the submission process can be found at www.tga.gov.au/industry/pm-argpm.htm.

India

The Central Drugs Standard Control Organization (CDSCO) is the regulating body in India. With the introduction of Gazette Notification, GSR no. 604 (E) dated 24.08.2001,[52] the *Drugs and Cosmetics (5th Amendment) Rules, 2001*, foreign manufacturers have to apply for a registration certificate for their manufacturing premises before individual drugs can be imported. Applications for drug registrations need to be made by authorized agents of foreign firms in India.

The regulations under *Drugs and Cosmetics Rules* 122A, 122B and 122D and further Appendix I, IA and VI of Schedule Y, describe the information required for approval of an application to import or manufacture a new drug for marketing.

Registration certificates are issued for three years, after which they must be renewed. Currently, company registration costs the equivalent of $1,500 (US) and the registration of individual drugs the equivalent of $1,000 (US). Extra costs occur if the manufacturing premises are inspected.

After the company/manufacturer and drug product are registered successfully, an import license must be obtained before drugs can be shipped into the country. The drug registration process follows the same requirements as in other regions, namely an application must be made to the Competent Authority, including a dossier, certificates and samples. Evaluation is carried out by the Competent Authority based on information provided by the manufacturer.

Under the *Drug and Cosmetics Act*, Competent Authority duties are divided between the central government and state authorities. The responsibilities of the former are related mostly to regulations and setting standards for the approval of new drugs and clinical trials in the country, while the latter is concerned with regulation of drug manufacture, sale and distribution.

CDSCO also decided to adopt CTD format for technical requirements for registration of pharmaceutical products for human use.[53]

Figure 10-2. Mutual Recognition Procedure in the EU

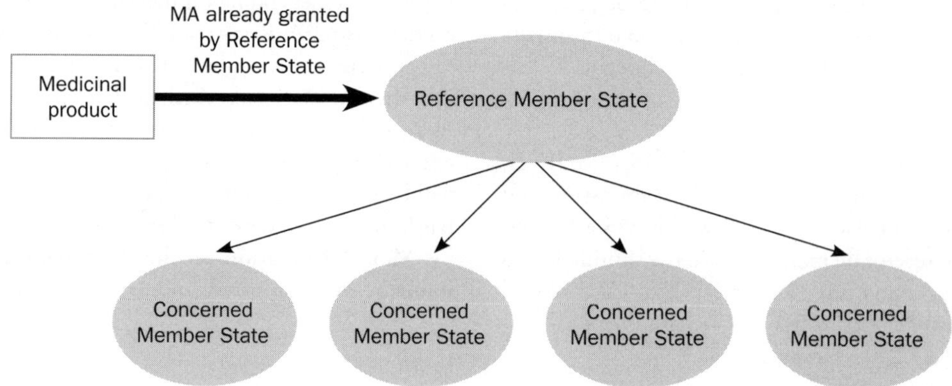

Japan

In Japan, the regulating body is the Pharmaceuticals and Medical Devices Agency (PMDA), which requires foreign manufacturers to be accredited. A company that has a local partner with a valid importing license can be considered to be temporarily accredited.[54] Foreign companies should either have a local operating affiliate in Japan or appoint a local agent (Article 19-2 of the *Pharmaceutical Affairs Law* (*PAL*); PFSB Notification No.0709004, dated 9 July 2004).

It is possible to obtain exceptional foreign approval by appointing, at the time of application, a drug MAH according to the drug type. The appointed MAH takes the necessary measures to prevent health and sanitation problems related to the approved drug in Japan.

The drug MAH appointed by the exceptional foreign approval holder (Designated MAH) is authorized to market the drug in Japan.

Japan follows a Master File System for drug substances, allowing manufacturers to voluntarily register manufacturing and quality data of their drug substances. API and finished product manufacturers must comply with GMP requirements.

The review of the NDA is done by PMDA, but approval is granted by the Ministry of Health, Labour and Welfare (MHLW).

PMDA does not accept applications in languages other than Japanese. This implies that forms related to the marketing application must be submitted in Japanese.[55]

China

China is interesting as a market due to its sheer size, and is the third largest pharmaceutical market in the world.[56] The China Food and Drug Administration (CFDA) is in the process of streamlining the country's pharmaceutical regulations to bring them more in line with international standards.

One of the main obstacles to drug registration in China is the lengthy approval process, which, in some cases, can take up to five years. On-site inspection for drug registration was introduced in May 2008, and new regulations, the "Special Drug Review Approval Process" and re-registration of imported drugs, were introduced in 2009.

There are four categories of drug registration application, including

1. New Drug Application
2. Application for the Drug Standardized by the State (generics/abbreviated applications)
3. Import Drug Application
4. Supplementary Application[57]

Areas With Mutual Recognition Agreements for Specific Territories

European Union

In the EU, two types of licenses can be issued: a national licence, issued by a Member State Competent Authority for its own territory, or a community authorization, issued by the European Commission for the whole community.[58] The former is granted for purely national authorizations or for authorizations obtained by one of the European procedures known as the Mutual Recognition Procedure or the Decentralised Procedure. The latter is granted for centrally registered products.

In either case, the MAH must have its official place of business established either in the Member State where the application is made for purely national licenses or in the European Economic Area (EEA), which comprises the 28 Member States plus Norway, Iceland and Liechtenstein.

With recent legislative developments (Regulation (EC) No 1901/2006) it became mandatory to have a Paediatric Investigation Plan (PIP) agreed with EMA's Paediatric Committee (PDCO) at the time of application submission through all registration routes.[59]

Figure 10-3. Decentralised Procedure in the EU

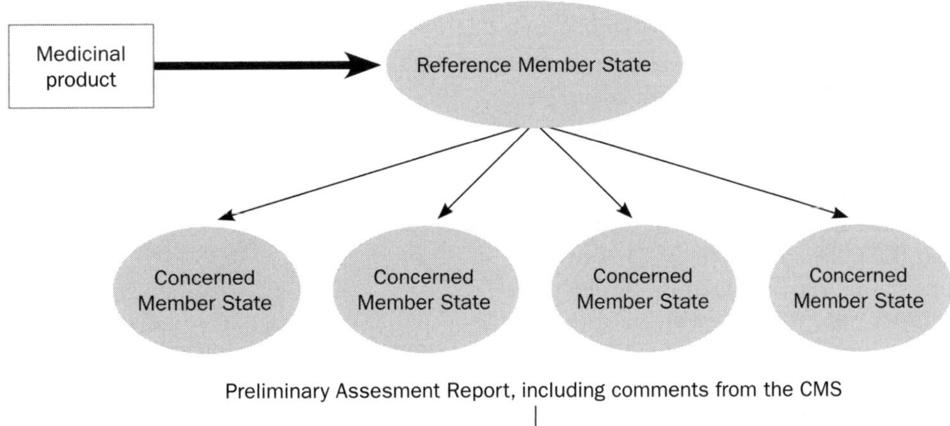

Preliminary Assesment Report, including comments from the CMS

MA granted and mutually recognized by CMS. This procedure avoids facing arbitration (refusal by one Member State) at a later date.

Types of Procedures

Basically, there are three types of procedures that can be used to register medicinal products:

1. National Procedure
2. Mutual Recognition Procedure/Decentralised Procedure
3. Centralised Procedure

National Authorizations

Here, the national Competent Authorities are responsible for granting marketing authorization for products placed on their markets. For obtaining national authorizations in more than one Member State, the applicant must use either the Mutual Recognition or Decentralised Procedure.

A national application is based on certain principles:

- An application is made to the national Competent Authority.
- Since 1998, this procedure has been limited to the initial stages of Mutual Recognition Procedure or for those medicines not intended to be authorized in more than one Member State.
- It can still be used for products with well-established use (Bibliographic Applications) and for line extensions of existing licenses.

After approval, an application for price approval can be submitted to the section of the federal ministry that is responsible for approving prices.

Mutual Recognition Procedure/Decentralised Procedure

In these procedures, the marketing authorization in one state, known as the Reference Member State, is mutually recognized by the Competent Authorities in other countries, known as the Concerned Member States.

Under the new legislation,[60,61] the Mutual Recognition Procedure can only be used when a marketing authorization in at least one Member State already exists (see **Figure 10-2**). For new products, where no marketing authorization in the community exists, the Decentralised Procedure (see **Figure 10-3**) must be utilized unless the Centralised Procedure is mandated for that product.

Principles of the Mutual Recognition and Decentralised Procedure

- The marketing authorization in one Member State (Reference Member State) is recognized by the regulatory authorities of other Member States (Concerned Member States), unless there are grounds to believe that the marketing authorization may present a risk to public health.
- The procedure may be triggered by the applicant or by a Member State.
- Procedures consist of European phase and national phase.
- European phase of both procedures have set timelines: Mutual Recognition Procedure lasts 90 days and Decentralised Procedure 210 (excluding "clock off" periods when the applicant prepares responses to the questions received and validation phase).
- Member States should issue national approvals within 30 days after the end of European phase.
- In case of a disagreement between the Member States on topics of potential serious risks to public health, a scientific evaluation is carried out first by the Co-ordination Group for Mutual Recognition

and Decentralised Procedures—Human (CMDh). The process is called a referral. If agreement is not reached on this level, the issues are discussed by the Committee for Medicinal Products for Human Use (CHMP). This process is known as arbitration. The result of the CHMP decision in the area of disagreement leads to a single decision that is binding on all Member States.

- All postapproval variations (including changes falling under the scope of Annex I of Commission Regulation (EC) No. 1234/2008 of 24 November 2008 concerning the examination of variations to the terms of an MA for medicinal products for human use and veterinary medicinal products granted by a Competent Authority of a Member State, i.e., those leading to an extension application) to these medicinal products must use the Mutual Recognition Procedure or Decentralised Procedure.

Centralised Procedure

In the Centralised Procedure, the evaluation is carried out by EMA. The license is issued by the European Commission (EC) based on EMA recommendations.[62]

The Centralised Procedure is mandated for products falling into one of the following categories:

- those developed by means of the following biotechnological processes:
  - recombinant DNA technology
  - controlled expression of genes coding for biologically active proteins in prokaryotes and eukaryotes, including transformed mammalian cells
  - hybridoma and monoclonal antibody methods
  - any medicinal product containing a proteinaceous constituent obtained by recombinant DNA technology
- veterinary medicinal products, including those not derived from biotechnology, intended primarily for use as performance enhancers to promote the growth of treated animals or increase yields from treated animals
- orphan medicinal products
- medicinal products intended for administration to human beings that contain a new active substance for the treatment of acquired immune deficiency syndrome (AIDS), cancer, neurodegenerative disorders or diabetes
- medicinal products used to treat autoimmune diseases, other immune dysfunctions and viral diseases

If the applicant believes and can provide sufficient evidence that its product shows significant therapeutic, scientific or technical innovation or that being accessible in the whole Community is in the interest of patients or animal health, it also might use the Centralised Procedure.

Figure 10-4. Centralised Procedure in the EU

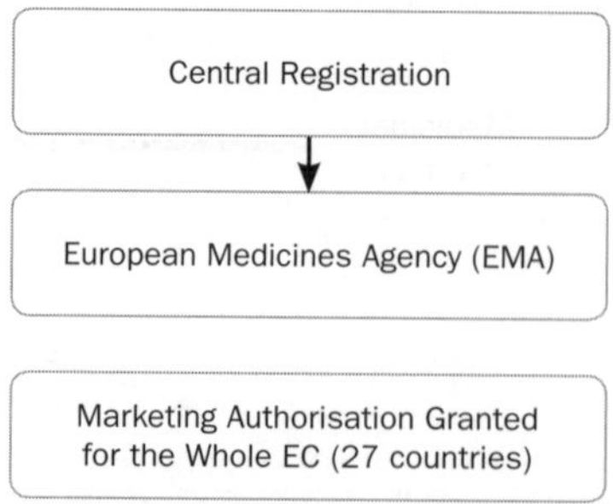

The Centralised Procedure lasts 210 days, and once the positive opinion is granted, the product can be marketed in the whole EU (**Figure 10-4**), and there is no need for national phase.

The mandatory dossier format when using the Centralised Procedure is the eCTD.

Middle East

In the Middle East, company registration must be completed before the drug registration process can begin. Although this process is quite time consuming, once company registration has been achieved, the drug registration process is usually relatively short. This is especially the case if it can be shown that the drug is already registered in either the US or the EU.

Central Registration

To facilitate the granting of marketing authorization by several countries in the Middle East, a central registration process was approved on 15 May 1999 among the following countries: Bahrain, Kuwait, Oman, Qatar, Saudi Arabia and the United Arab Emirates. The Gulf Central Committee for Drug Registration (GCC-DR) Executive Office for Health Ministers is located in Riyadh, Saudi Arabia and consists of a committee of two members nominated by each state. GCC-DR's responsibilities are:

- registration of pharmaceutical companies
- registration of pharmaceutical products
- inspection of pharmaceutical companies for GMP compliance
- approval of quality control laboratories
- review of technical and postmarketing surveillance reports
- implementing the Program of Bioequivalence study as part of quality assurance[63]

Drugs registered centrally allow consolidated purchasing. All countries involved must sanction and approve the export price that the committee approves upon completion of the registration procedures in the country. Any analysis should be carried out in a reference laboratory accredited by a council country.

Procedural Steps

- Eight completed copies of the registration files must be forwarded by the company to the Executive Office along with 17 samples. Each member country's Competent Authority will receive at least two samples.
- The registration fee must be paid to the Executive Office.
- Evaluation is carried out by each member country, which issues its recommendations to the committee.
- The company is obliged to provide standard materials, analytical methods, etc.
- If consensus is reached and a recommendation of approval is made by the member countries, the committee shall dispatch the samples of chemical entities presented for registration to the accredited reference laboratories for analysis.
- At least four member countries need to be present at the consensus meeting for it to be deemed legal.
- The committee's resolutions shall be adopted by the majority vote of the attendant members.
- After approving the registration of the company or drug—centrally—authentication and documentation procedures and fees shall be finalized in every country per its prescribed and established policies.
- The Executive Office shall issue the companies registration certificates and their chemical entities in accordance with the decision of the committee.[64]
- The committee may demand GMP inspections if deemed necessary, the costs of which must be borne by the company.

Conclusion

Drug registration is a complex process that can take several years. Therefore, it is imperative that companies comply with agreed upon standards and follow published guidelines as closely as possible to ensure a smooth and timely approval. Drug registration must be planned many years in advance, starting with the initial nonclinical and clinical testing, to ensure safety and efficacy but also to support any claimed indications.

Legislative changes can impact the overall product development planning significantly (e.g., pediatric regulations in the EU and US) and therefore must be closely monitored.

The quality and manufacturing processes must comply with international standards. This is especially important in today's global economy.

Since the registration of pharmaceutical products is still very much a national issue, companies operating at the global level need to have reliable and easy access to regulatory information. Although the basic principles for drug registration regarding efficacy, safety and quality have been fairly well harmonized globally, it is important to take into account local requirements to avoid delaying the registration process and to ensure global compliance.

References

1. Regulation (EC) No 726/2004 of the European Parliament and of the Council of 31 March 2004 laying down Community procedures for the authorisation and supervision of medicinal products for human and veterinary use and establishing a European Medicines Agency. EUR-Lex website. http://eur-lex.europa.eu/LexUriServ/LexUriServ.do?uri=OJ:L:2004:136:0001:0033:en:PDF. Accessed 17 January 2013.
2. Gulf Central Committee for Drug Registration. SGH website. www.sgh.org.sa. Accessed 17 January 2013.
3. *Food and Drug Administration Safety and Innovation Act* (*FDASIA*) of 2012. US Government Printing Office website. www.gpo.gov/fdsys/pkg/PLAW-112publ144/pdf/PLAW-112publ144.pdf. Accessed 17 January 2013.
4. Regulation (EC) No 1901/2006 of the European Parliament and of the Council od 12 December 2006 on medicinal products for paediatric use and amending Regulation (EEC) No 1768/92, Directive 2001/20/EC, Directive 2001/83/EC and Regulation (EC) No 726/2004. EUR-Lex website. http://eur-lex.europa.eu/LexUriServ/LexUriServ.do?uri=OJ:L:2006:378:0001:0019:en:PDF. Accessed 17 January 2013.
5. ICH, *Guidance on Nonclinical Safety Studies for the Conduct of Human Clinical Trials and Marketing Authorization for Pharmaceuticals M3(R2)* (Current Step 4 version, June 2009). ICH website. www.ich.org/fileadmin/Public_Web_Site/ICH_Products/Guidelines/Multidisciplinary/M3_R2/Step4/M3_R2__Guideline.pdf. Accessed 17 January 2013.
6. US Food and Drug Administration (FDA), *21 CFR 58* Good Laboratory Practice Regulations. FDA website. www.accessdata.fda.gov/scripts/cdrh/cfdocs/cfcfr/cfrsearch.cfm?cfrpart=58. Accessed 17 January 2013.
7. Friese B, Jentges B and Muazzam U. *Guide to Drug Regulatory Affairs*, Europe, Editio Cantor Verlag, Copyright ECV 2007. Part A, Chapter 8, pp 233-238.
8. Op cit 5.
9. ICH, *Detection of Toxicity to Reproduction for Medicinal Products & Toxicity to Male Fertility S5(R2)* (Current Step 4 version, Parent Guideline dated 24 June 1993; Addendum dated 9 November 2000 incorporated in November 2005). ICH website. www.ich.org/fileadmin/Public_Web_Site/ICH_Products/Guidelines/Safety/S5_R2/Step4/S5_R2__Guideline.pdf. Accessed 17 January 2013.
10. ICH, *Guidance on Genotoxicity Testing and Data Interpretation for Pharmaceuticals Intended for Human Use S2(R1)* (Current Step 4 version, November 2011). ICH website. www.ich.org/fileadmin/Public_Web_Site/ICH_Products/Guidelines/Safety/S5_R2/Step4/S5_R2__Guideline.pdf. Accessed 17 January 2013.
11. Op cit 7.
12. ICH, *Guideline on the Need for Carcinogenicity Studies of Pharmaceuticals S1A* (Current Step 4 version, November 1995). ICH website. www.ich.org/fileadmin/Public_Web_Site/ICH_Products/Guidelines/Safety/S5_R2/Step4/S5_R2__Guideline.pdf. Accessed 17 January 2013.
13. ICH, *Testing of Carcinogenicity of Pharmaceuticals S1B* (Current Step 4 version, July 1997). ICH website. www.ich.org/fileadmin/Public_Web_Site/ICH_Products/Guidelines/Safety/S1B/Step4/S1B_Guideline.pdf. Accessed 17 January 2013.
14. Op cit 5.
15. ICH, *Concept Paper: Rodent Carcinogenicity Studies for Human Pharmaceuticals, S1* (Current Step 1 version, April 2012). ICH website. www.ich.org/fileadmin/Public_Web_Site/ICH_Products/

Guidelines/Safety/S1/S1_Concept_Paper_14_November_2012.pdf. Accessed 17 January 2013.
16. ICH, *Safety Pharmacology Studies for Human Pharmaceuticals S7A* (Current Step 4 version, November 2000). ICH website. www.ich.org/fileadmin/Public_Web_Site/ICH_Products/Guidelines/Safety/S7A/Step4/S7A_Guideline.pdf. Accessed 17 January 2013.
17. Op cit 9.
18. ICH, *Note for Guidance on Toxicokinetics: The Assessment of Systemic Exposure in Toxicity Studies S3A* (Current Step 4 version, October 1994). ICH website. www.ich.org/fileadmin/Public_Web_Site/ICH_Products/Guidelines/Safety/S3A/Step4/S3A_Guideline.pdf. Accessed 17 January 2013.
19. ICH, *Pharmacokinetics: Guidance for Repeated Dose Tissue Distribution Studies S3B* (Current Step 4 version, October 1994). ICH website. www.ich.org/fileadmin/Public_Web_Site/ICH_Products/Guidelines/Safety/S3B/Step4/S3B_Guideline.pdf. Accessed 17 January 2013.
20. OECD series on principles of GLP and compliance monitoring, EVV/MC/CHEM(98)17, 1997, pp. 1-41.
21. Ibid.
22. Op cit 4.
23. Directive 2004/10/EC of the European Parliament and of the Council of 11 February 2004 on the harmonisation of laws, regulations and administrative provisions relating to the application of the principles of good laboratory practice and the verification of their applications for tests on chemical substances. EUR-Lex website. http://eur-lex.europa.eu/LexUriServ/LexUriServ.do?uri=OJ:L:2004:050:0044:0044:EN:PDF. Accessed 17 January 2013..
24. Directive 2004/9/EC of the European Parliament and of the Council of 11 February 2004 on the inspection and verification of good laboratory practice (GLP). EUR-Lex website. http://eur-lex.europa.eu/LexUriServ/LexUriServ.do?uri=OJ:L:2004:050:0044:0044:EN:PDF. Accessed 17 January 2013.
25. *Fundamentals of US Regulatory Affairs, Seventh Edition*, Chapter 6, Good Laboratory Practice for Nonclinical Laboratory Studies. Copyright 2011 by Regulatory Affairs Professionals Society, pp. 66-69.
26. Op cit 9.
27. International Conference on Harmonisation Efficacy guidelines. ICH website. www.ich.org/products/guidelines/efficacy/article/efficacy-guidelines.html. Accessed 17 January 2013.
28. World Health Organization, Model Certificate of a Pharmaceutical Product. WHO website. www.who.int/medicines/areas/quality_safety/regulation_legislation/certification/modelcertificate/en/. Accessed 17 January 2013.
29. World Intellectual Property Organization, Madrid System for the International Registration of Marks. WIPO website. www.wipo.int/madrid/en/. Accessed 17 January 2013.
30. ICH, *Good Manufacturing Practice Guide for Active Pharmaceutical Ingredients Q7* (Current Step 4 version, November 2000. ICH website. www.ich.org/fileadmin/Public_Web_Site/ICH_Products/Guidelines/Quality/Q7/Step4/Q7_Guideline.pdf. Accessed 17 January 2013.
31. Ibid.
32. Ibid.
33. WHO, *Guidelines on pre-approval inspections, WHO Technical Report Series*, No. 902, 2002. WHO website. http://whqlibdoc.who.int/trs/who_trs_902.pdf. Accessed 17 January 2013.
34. Michor S. "Product Lifecycle Management: A European Perspective." *Regulatory Focus*, Vol. 13, No. 8, August 2008, pp. 18-27.
35. World Health Organization, *Pharmacovigilance: Ensuring the Safe Use of Medicines—WHO Policy Perspectives on Medicines*, No. 009, October 2004. WHO website. http://apps.who.int/medicinedocs/en/d/Js6164e/. Accessed 17 January 2013.
36. US Food and Drug Administration (FDA), *Federal Food, Drug and Cosmetic Act (FD&C Act)*, Subchapter II, section 201. FDA website. www.fda.gov/RegulatoryInformation/Legislation/FederalFoodDrugandCosmeticActFDCAct/FDCActChaptersIandIIShortTitleandDefinitions/default.htm. Accessed 17 January 2013.
37. *Fundamentals of US Regulatory Affairs, Seventh Edition*, Chapter 9 Prescription Drug Submissions, Copyright 2011 by Regulatory Affairs Professionals Society, pp. 105-118.
38. Ibid.
39. Op cit 3.
40. *Fundamentals of Canadian Regulatory Affairs, Third Edition,* Chapter 12 Management of Health Canada Drug Submissions, Copyright 2011 by Regulatory Affairs Professionals Society, pp. 85-94..
41. *Fundamentals of Canadian Regulatory Affairs, Third Edition,* Chapter 9 New Drug Submissions—General Overview of Drugs and Biologics, Copyright 2011 by Regulatory Affairs Professionals Society, pp. 61-70.
42. About Health Canada, Therapeutic Products Directorate. Health Canada website. www.hc-sc.gc.ca/ahc-asc/branch-dirgen/hpfb-dgpsa/tpd-dpt/index-eng.php. Accessed 17 January 2013.
43. Ibid.
44. Op cit 40.
45. Ibid.
46. Health Canada, International Activities. Health Canada website. www.hc-sc.gc.ca/ahc-asc/intactiv/index-eng.php. Accessed 17 January 2013.
47. Health Canada, Trilateral cooperation. Health Canada website. www.hc-sc.gc.ca/fn-an/intactivit/trilateral-coop/charter_charte-eng.php. Accessed 17 January 2013.
48. Therapeutic Goods Administration website. www.tga.gov.au/index.htm. Accessed 17 January 2013.
49. Ibid.
50. Therapeutic Goods Administration website. TGA website. www.tga.gov.au/industry/pm-ctd.htm. Accessed 17 January 2013.
51. Therapeutic Goods Administration website. TGA website. www.tga.gov.au/industry/pm-basics-regulation.htm. Accessed 17 January 2013.
52. Ministry of Health and Family Welfare, G.S.R. 604(E). MOHFW website. http://mohfw.nic.in/WriteReadData/l892s/gsr604-74698469.pdf. Accessed 17 January 2013.
53. CDSCO, *Guidance for industry on preparation of Common Technical Document (CTD) for import/manufacture and marketing approval of drugs for human use (New Drug Application- NDA),* 2010. CDSCO website. http://cdsco.nic.in/ctd_guidance%20-final.pdf. Accessed 17 January 2013.
54. Pharmaceuticals and Medical Devices Agency website. www.pmda.go.jp/english/service/regulation.html. Accessed 17 January 2013.
55. Ibid.
56. Industry Insight: Global Pharmaceutical Market. Businessvibes blog. www.businessvibes.com/blog/industry-insight-global-pharmaceutical-industry. Accessed 17 January 2013.
57. Zhen LH. "Drug Registration Application in China," *J Pharm Pharmaceut Sci*, June 2003. Univsity of Alberta website. www.ualberta.ca/~csps/JPPS6(2)/Lihuizhen/registration.htm. Accessed 17 January 2013.
58. *Fundamentals of EU Regulatory Affairs, Fifth Edition*, Chapter 13 Overview of Authorization Procedures for Medicinal Products and Medical Devices. Copyright 2011 by Regulatory Affairs Professionals Society, pp. 111-128.
59. Op cit 4.
60. Op cit 1.
61. Directive 2004/27/EC of the European Parliament and of the Council of 31 March 2004 amending Directive 2001/83/EC on the Community code relating to medicinal products for human use (*Official Journal L 136, 30/4/2004 p. 34–57*). EUR-Lex website. http://eur-lex.europa.eu/LexUriServ/LexUriServ.do?uri=OJ:L:2004:136:0034:0057:EN:PDF. Accessed 17 January 2013.
62. Op cit 1.
63. Op cit 2.
64. Ibid.

Chapter 11

Stability Test Requirements

By Nicole Beard, MSc, PhD

OBJECTIVES

- ❑ Understand the regulations for stability testing, including International Conference on Harmonisation (ICH) guidelines and regional guidance from around the world
- ❑ Understand the development of stability indicating methods
- ❑ Understand establishment of drug substance and drug product shelf life
- ❑ Understand matrixing and bracketing to support reduced stability testing
- ❑ Understand postapproval considerations

REGULATIONS AND GUIDELINES COVERED IN THIS CHAPTER

- ❑ ICH, *Stability testing of new drug substances and products Q1A(R2)*
- ❑ ICH, *Photostability testing of new drug substances and products Q1B*
- ❑ ICH, *Stability testing of new dosage forms Q1C*
- ❑ ICH, *Bracketing and matrixing designs for stability testing of new drug substances and products Q1D*
- ❑ ICH,*Evaluation for stability data Q1E*
- ❑ ICH, Explanatory note on the withdrawal of ICH Q1F from the ICH website
- ❑ ICH, *Validation of analytical procedures: text and methodology Q2(R1)*
- ❑ ICH, *Impurities in new drug substances Q3A*
- ❑ ICH, *Impurities in new drug products Q3B*
- ❑ ICH, *Quality of Biotechnological Products: Stability Testing of Biotechnological/Biological Products Q5C*
- ❑ ICH, *Specifications: Test procedures and acceptance criteria for new drug substances and new drug products: Chemical substances Q6A*
- ❑ ICH, *Specifications: Test procedures and acceptance criteria for biotechnological/ biological products Q6B*

Introduction

Stability is a critical quality attribute of medicinal products that depends on several factors; therefore, stability testing is crucial in the drug development process.

The purpose of stability testing is to provide evidence of how the quality of a drug substance or drug product varies with time not only under the influence of a variety of environmental factors, such as temperature, humidity and light, but also on product-related factors. These factors include the drug substance's physical and chemical properties and its interaction with the excipients, the dosage form and its composition, the manufacturing process, the nature of the container closure system and the properties of the packaging materials. In fixed-dose combinations, the interaction between two or more drug substances also has to be considered.

Stability testing also is used to establish a re-test period or shelf life for the drug substance and to determine the drug product's shelf life and recommendations for storage conditions.[1] Therefore, the submission of data generated during the stability testing program is an important requirement for regulatory approval of a medicinal product.

In 1988, work on the stability of medicinal products was initiated by the World Health Organization (WHO) with the adoption of *Guidelines on stability testing for well-established drug substance in conventional dosage forms*.

In 2000, WHO and the International Conference on Harmonisation (ICH) initiated a program to harmonize stability testing and conditions worldwide. Stability testing conditions were based on climatic conditions in the three ICH regions: the EU, US and Japan. A new guidance document, ICH Q1F *Stability Data Package for Registration Applications in Climatic Zones III and IV,* defined storage conditions for stability testing in countries not located in the ICH regions, with the objective of reducing the number of recommendations for different storage conditions. In the course of the discussions that led to the development of the guideline, WHO conducted a survey to find consensus on 30°C/65% RH as the long-term storage conditions for hot and humid regions. As no significant objections were raised in this survey, 30°C/65% RH were defined as the long-term storage conditions for Climatic Zone III/IV countries in ICH Q1F, which was adopted by ICH in February 2002.

However, based on new discussions, some countries in Climatic Zone IV have requested a larger safety margin for medicinal products to be marketed in their countries than was outlined in ICH Q1F. Therefore, several countries have revised their own stability testing guidelines, defining up to 30°C/75% RH as the long-term storage conditions for hot and humid regions. Due to this divergence in global stability testing requirements, ICH Q1F was withdrawn[2] and the definition of storage conditions in Climatic Zones III and IV was assessed by the respective regions and WHO.[3]

In assessing the impact of the withdrawal of ICH Q1F on intermediate testing conditions defined in ICH Q1A(R2), the decision was reached to retain 30°C/65% RH. However, regulatory authorities in the ICH regions have agreed that the use of more stringent humidity conditions, such as 30°C/75% RH, will be acceptable should the applicant decide to use them.

The world is divided into four climatic zones as presented in **Table 11-1**.

ICH Regions (EU, US, Japan)

ICH has issued a range of guidelines pertaining to the stability of drug substances and drug products, which are applicable in the EU, US and Japan and other countries that recognize ICH (e.g., Canada, Switzerland, Australia, New Zealand).

The established principle is that stability data generated in any one of the three ICH regions would be mutually acceptable to the other two regions. Unless otherwise specified, ICH guidelines address Climatic Zones I and II.

General Considerations

Obtaining data on drug substance (DS) stability is an integral part of the systematic approach to stability evaluation.

Stability study design for the drug product (DP) should be based on the characteristics and stability results of the DS and on experience gained from clinical formulation studies.

Stability Batches: Choice and Characteristics

Stability study data should be provided on at least three primary DS batches and three primary DP batches. The manufacturing process for these batches should simulate the final process applied to production batches and should provide a DS and a DP that meet the same quality standards and specifications as those intended for marketing.

Stability studies should include validated analytical procedures on the DS and DP characteristics that are susceptible to change during storage and are likely to influence quality, safety and/or efficacy.[4–6] These stability-indicating parameters with proposed acceptance criteria should cover, as appropriate, physical, chemical, biological and microbiological attributes of the DS and the DP, but also preservative content (e.g., antioxidant or antimicrobial preservative) and functionality tests (e.g., for a dose delivery system) that are more specific to the DP.

Stability testing should be performed at batch release and at the end of the proposed DP shelf life. It may be appropriate to have justifiable differences between release and shelf life acceptance criteria based on evaluation of stability data and changes observed during storage.

Stability testing should be conducted on the DS in the packaged container closure system proposed for storage and distribution. The DP batches should be of the same formulation and packaged in the same container closure system as proposed for marketing. Stability studies should be performed on each individual strength, dosage form and container type and size unless bracketing or matrixing is applied.

Storage Conditions

In general, DS and DP should be evaluated under monitored and recorded storage conditions with specified tolerances defined as acceptable variations in temperature and relative humidity (RH). The storage conditions are presented in **Table 11-2.** The lengths of studies chosen should

Table 11-1. Climatic Zones

Climatic Zone	Definition	Criteria Mean annual temperature measured in the open air/ mean annual partial water vapor pressure.	Long-term Testing Conditions
I	Temperate climate	≤15°C/≤11 hPa	21°C/45% RH
II	Subtropical and Mediterranean climate	>15 to 22°C/>11 to 18 hPa	25°C/60% RH
III	Hot and dry climate	>22°C/≤15 hPa	30°C/35% RH
IVa	Hot and humid climate	>22°C/>15 to 27 hPa	30°C/65% RH
IVb	Hot and very humid climate	>22°C/>27 hPa	30°C/75% RH

be sufficient to cover storage, shipment and subsequent use of the DS or the DP and to climatic conditions in which the DP is intended to be marketed. Alternative storage conditions can be used if justified.

Long-term testing should cover a minimum of 12 months for the DS and a minimum of 12 months for the DP at the time of submission and should continue for a period of time sufficient to cover the proposed shelf life of the DS or the DP.

Frequency of testing should be sufficient to establish the stability profile of the DS and DP. For long-term studies, testing frequency normally should be every three months over the first year, every six months over the second year and annually thereafter throughout the proposed DS re-test period or the proposed DP shelf life.

If justified, reduced designs can be applied to stability studies of most DP types; testing frequency is reduced or certain factor combinations are not tested at all. Bracketing and matrixing[7] are reduced designs based on different principles, e.g., strength, container size and/or fill. Therefore, careful consideration and scientific justification should precede the use of bracketing and matrixing together in one design.

If long-term studies are conducted on the DS or DP at 25°C ± 2°C/60% RH ± 5% RH and "significant change" occurs at any time during six months of testing at the accelerated storage condition, additional testing at the intermediate storage condition should be conducted and evaluated against significant change criteria. In this case, for the DS, testing at the intermediate storage condition should include all tests on the DS, unless otherwise justified. The initial application should include, respectively on the DS or the DP, a minimum of six months' data from a 12- month study at the intermediate storage condition.

In general "significant change" for a DS or a DP is defined as failure to meet its specifications.[8,9]

Accelerated and intermediate storage conditions, where appropriate, can be used to evaluate the effect of short-term excursions outside the label storage conditions.

For accelerated storage conditions, frequency testing with a minimum of three time points, including the initial and final time points (e.g., zero, three and six months) from a six-month study is recommended. A fourth time point may be included where significant changes are expected based on development experience. When intermediate storage conditions are included in the stability program as a result of significant changes at the accelerated storage conditions, a minimum of four time points, including the initial and final time points (e.g., zero, six, nine, 12 months) from a 12-month study is recommended.

Stress testing conditions used on DS can help to identify the likely degradation products and to elucidate the intrinsic stability of the DS. Such testing is part of the development strategy and normally is carried out on one batch of DS to analyze the effect of temperatures in 10°C increments above that for accelerated testing and humidity levels (e.g., 75% RH or higher).

Photostability testing,[10] which is an integral part of stress testing, should be conducted on at least one primary batch of the DS and DP if appropriate. It is used to demonstrate that light exposure does not result in unacceptable changes.

Specific Intended Storage Conditions

For DS or DP intended for storage in a refrigerator, recommended storage conditions are:

- accelerated—25°C ± 2°C/60% RH ± 5% RH for a minimum of six months
- long term—5°C ± 3°C for a minimum of 12 months of stability data at submission

For DS or DP intended for storage in a freezer, recommended long-term storage conditions are -20°C ± 5°C for a minimum of 12 months at time of submission. The DS re-test period or the DP shelf life should be based on the long-term data obtained at the long-term storage condition. In the absence of an accelerated storage condition for DS or DP intended to be stored in a freezer, testing on a single batch at an elevated temperature (e.g., 5°C ± 3°C or 25°C ± 2°C) for an appropriate time period should be conducted to address the effect of short-term excursions outside the proposed label storage condition, e.g., during shipping or handling.

Table 11-2. Stability Testing Conditions for Drug Substance and Drug Product for ICH Countries

Study	Storage Condition	Minimum Time Period Covered by Data at Submission
Long-term	25°C ± 2°C/60% RH ± 5% RH or 30°C ± 2°C/65% RH ± 5% RH	12 months
Intermediate[a]	30°C ± 2°C/65% RH ± 5% RH	6 months
Accelerated	40°C ± 2°C/75% RH ± 5% RH	6 months

a. If 30°C ± 2°C/65% RH ± 5% RH is the long-term condition, there is no intermediate storage condition.

DS or DP intended for storage below -20°C should be treated on a case-by-case basis.

Impermeable or semi-impermeable containers may have an influence on the design of the DP stability conditions. Packaging materials are classified as permeable or impermeable depending on their characteristics, such as thickness and permeability coefficient. The suitability of the packaging material used for a particular product is determined by its product characteristics.

Containers generally considered to be impermeable to moisture include glass ampoules. Sensitivity to moisture or potential for solvent loss is not a concern for DP packaged in impermeable containers that provide a permanent barrier to passage of moisture or solvent. Thus stability studies for products stored in impermeable containers can be conducted under any controlled or ambient relative humidity condition.

Aqueous-based products packaged in semi-permeable containers should be evaluated for potential water loss in addition to physical, chemical, biological and microbiological stability. This evaluation can be carried out under conditions of low relative humidity. An alternative approach to studies at low relative humidity is to perform the stability studies under higher relative humidity and derive the water loss at the low relative humidity through calculation.[11]

Stability Commitment

When the available long-term stability data on primary batches do not cover the proposed shelf life granted at the time of approval, a commitment should be made to continue the stability studies postapproval to firmly establish the DS re-test period or to establish the DP shelf life.

Where the submission includes long-term stability data from the production batches covering the proposed re-test period or shelf life, a postapproval commitment is considered unnecessary.

The stability protocol used for studies on commitment batches should be the same as that for the primary batches, unless otherwise scientifically justified.

Stability Evaluation

The purpose of a stability study is to establish, based on testing a minimum of three batches of DS or DP, a re-test period or shelf life and label storage instructions applicable to all future batches manufactured under similar processes. The degree of variability of individual batches affects the confidence that a future production batch will remain within specification throughout its re-test period or shelf life.[12]

Where stability data show so little degradation and variability that it is apparent from looking at the data that the requested re-test period or shelf life will be granted, it normally is unnecessary to go through a statistical analysis, if appropriately justified. However, statistical analysis can be useful in supporting the extrapolation of the re-test period or shelf life in certain situations and can be used to verify the proposed re-test period or shelf life in other cases.

An approach for analyzing data on a quantitative attribute that is expected to change with time is to determine the time at which the 95% one-sided confidence limit for the mean curve intersects the acceptance criterion. If analysis shows that the batch-to-batch variability is small, it is advantageous to combine the data into one overall estimate. If it is inappropriate to combine data from several batches, the overall shelf life should be based on the minimum time a batch can be expected to remain within acceptance criteria.

The nature of any degradation relationship will determine whether the data should be transformed for linear regression analysis. Usually, the relationship can be represented by a linear, quadratic or cubic function on an arithmetic or logarithmic scale. As far as possible, the choice of model should be justified by a physical and/or chemical rationale and should also take into account the amount of available data.

Statistical methods should be employed to test the goodness of fit of the data on all batches and combined batches to the assumed degradation line or curve.

Limited extrapolation of the long-term data from the long-term storage condition beyond the observed range to extend the shelf life can be undertaken, if justified. This justification should be based on what is known about the mechanism of degradation, the results of testing under accelerated conditions, the goodness of fit of any mathematical model, batch size and the existence of supporting stability data. However, this extrapolation assumes that the same degradation relationship will continue to apply beyond the observed data.

Any evaluation should cover not only the assay but also the levels of degradation products and other appropriate attributes. Where appropriate, attention should be paid to reviewing the adequacy of evaluation linked to DP stability and degradation "behavior" during the testing.

Statements and Labeling

Results from stability studies, presented at the time of submission, should serve as guidance, and there should be a direct link between the label statements and the demonstrated DS and DP stability characteristics. However, a storage statement cannot be used to compensate for insufficient stability data, e.g., omission of stability studies at accelerated or intermediate testing conditions. In addition, an expiry date should be displayed on the container label.

Declaration of storage conditions in the Product Information (e.g., European Summary of Product Characteristics (SmPC), labeling and Patient Leaflet) of medicinal products is country-specific.[13] Recommended labeling statements should be supported by appropriate stability studies.

In-use StabilityTesting

The purpose of in-use stability testing is to provide information for the DP labeling, storage conditions and utilization period of multi-dose products after first opening and for the reconstitution of a powder or dilution of a solution.

The DP physical, chemical and microbial properties susceptible to change during storage should be determined over the period of the proposed in-use shelf life. If possible, testing should be performed at intermediate time points and at the end of the proposed in-use shelf life on the final amount of the DP remaining in the container.

This testing should be performed on the reconstituted or diluted DP throughout the proposed in-use period on primary batches as part of the stability studies at the initial and final time points and, if full shelf life, long-term data are not available before submission, at 12 months or the last time point at which data will be available.

In general, this testing need not be repeated on commitment batches.

Stability Data for Variations

Once the medicinal product has been registered, additional stability studies may be required if changes occur in the DS or DP manufacturing process, in the DP composition, including a new dosage form[14] or changes that affect primary packaging. In all cases, it is important to investigate whether the intended change will have an impact on the quality parameters of the DS and/or the DP and consequently on their stability characteristics.

The scope and design of the stability studies for changes are based on the knowledge and experience acquired on the DS and DP. The results of these stability studies should be part of the variation application.

Asia Pacific

The Association of Southeast Asian Nations (ASEAN) was established in 1967 in Bangkok, Thailand, with the signing of the Bangkok Declaration by the founding nations of ASEAN: Indonesia, Malaysia, Philippines, Singapore and Thailand. Brunei Darussalam joined in1984, Viet Nam in 1995, Laos and Myanmar in 1997, and Cambodia in 1999, making up what are today the ten ASEAN member states.

While no common regulatory procedures exist in Asia, there are ongoing efforts toward harmonizing the regulatory framework in ASEAN member states. Harmonization focuses on technical requirements for marketing authorization for medicinal products and has resulted in special stability requirements.[16]

All the criteria under the ICH Q1A(R2) guideline have been adopted except the conditions for humidity. The ASEAN stability requirements for long-term studies should be at 30°C/75% RH ± 5% RH due to the differences of the climatic conditions in ASEAN countries classified as hot and humid Climatic Zone IV. ICH and ASEAN currently are collaborating on this issue. **Table 11-3** presents a comparison between ICH, WHO and ASEAN stability requirements.

China is located in Climatic Zone II. Recommended conditions for stability testing are as follows:

- long term—25°C ± 2°C, 60% RH ±10% RH
- accelerated—40°C ± 2°C/75% RH ± 5% RH
- intermediate—30°C ± 2°C/65% RH ± 5% RH

As part of the registration process, sample testing is a specific requirement performed by the National Institute for the Control of Pharmaceutical and Biological Products (NICPBP). Full stability studies are required to accept samples for testing. The manufacturing process used for these sample batches should be identical to the final process applied to production batches and should provide a DS and a DP that meet the same quality standards and specifications as intended for marketing. In addition, site-specific stability testing is required in China.

Hong Kong is governed as an autonomous region of China but its regulatory requirements are to a large extent still influenced by its British heritage. Therefore, there is no guideline on stability studies. The Hong Kong Drug Office recommends using ICH Q1A(R2) as a reference

Table 11-3. Comparisons Between ICH, WHO and ASEAN Stability Requirements

Parameter	ICH	WHO	ASEAN
Storage conditions for drug substance	**General case:** Long term: 12 m data 25°C ± 2°C/60% RH ± 5% RH or 30°C ± 2°C/65% RH ± 5% RH Intermediate: 6 m data 30°C ± 2°C/65% RH ± 5% RH Accelerated: 6 m data 40°C ± 2°C/75% RH ± 5% RH **Refrigerator** Long term: 12 m data 5°C ± 3°C Accelerated: 6 m data 25°C ± 2°C/60% RH ± 5% RH **Freezer:** Long term: 12 m data -20°C ± 5°C	**General case:** Long term: 12 m data 25°C ± 2°C/60% RH ± 5% RH or 30°C ± 2°C/65% RH ± 5% RH 30°C ± 2°C/75% RH ± 5% RH Intermediate: 6 m data 30°C ± 2°C/65% RH ± 5% RH Accelerated: 6 m data 40°C ± 2°C/75% RH ± 5% RH **Refrigerator:** Long term: 12 m data 5°C ± 3°C Accelerated: 6 m data 25°C ± 2°C/60% RH ± 5% RH 30°C ± 2°C/65% RH ± 5% RH 30°C ± 2°C/75% RH ± 5% RH **Freezer:** Long term: 12 m data -20°C ± 5°C	ASEAN stability guideline is given for drug product only
Storage conditions for drug product	**General case:** Long term: 12 m data 25°C ± 2°C/60% RH ± 5% RH or 30°C ± 2°C/65% RH ± 5% RH Intermediate: 6 m data 30°C ± 2°C/65% RH ± 5% RH Accelerated: 6 m data 40°C ± 2°C/75% RH ± 5% RH **Refrigerator:** Long term: 12 m data 5°C ± 3°C Accelerated: 6 m data 25°C ± 2°C/60% RH ± 5% RH **Freezer:** Long term: 12 m data -20°C ± 5°C **Semi permeable Containers:** Long Term: 12 m data 25°C ± 2°C/40% RH ± 5% RH or 30°C ± 2°C/35% RH ± 5% RH Intermediate: 6 m data 30°C ± 2°C/65% RH ± 5% RH Accelerated: 6 m data 40°C ± 2°C/NMT 25% RH	**General case:** Long term: 6 or 12 m data 25°C ± 2°C/60% RH ± 5% RH or 30°C ± 2°C/65% RH ± 5% RH 30°C ± 2°C/75% RH ± 5% RH Intermediate: 6 m data 30°C ± 2°C/65% RH ± 5% RH Accelerated: 6 m data 40°C ± 2°C/75% RH ± 5% RH **Refrigerator:** Long term: 12 m data 5°C ± 3°C Accelerated: 6 m data 25°C ± 2°C/60% RH ± 5% RH 30°C ± 2°C/65% RH ± 5% RH 30°C ± 2°C/75% RH ± 5% RH **Freezer:** Long term: 12 m data -20°C ± 5°C **Semi permeable Containers:** Long term: 12 m data 25°C ± 2°C/40% RH ± 5% RH or 30°C ± 2°C/35% RH ± 5% RH Intermediate: 6 m data 30°C ± 2°C/65% RH ± 5% RH Accelerated: 6 m data 40°C ± 2°C/ NMT 25% RH	**General case:** Long term: 12 m data 30°C ± 2°C/ 75% ± 5 % RH Accelerated: 6 m data 40°C ± 2°C/75% ± 5 % RH **Refrigerator:** Long term: 12 m data 5°C ± 3°C Accelerated: 6 m data 25°C ± 2°C/60% RH ± 5% RH **Freezer:** Long term: 12 m data -20°C ± 5°C **Containers permeable to water vapor:** Long term: 30°C ± 2°C/75% RH ± 5% RH **Containers impermeable to water vapor:** Long term: 30°C ± 2°C
Stress testing	– Stress studies at temperatures (in 10°C increments (e.g., 50°C, 60°C, etc.) above that for accelerated testing, humidity (e.g., 75% RH or greater) Photostability testing as per ICH Q1B	Same as ICH	– Stress studies at : 40°C ± 2°C/75% RH ± 5% RH – Photostability testing as per ICH Q1B

Batch selection	Three primary batches of Drug Substance and Drug Product	Three primary batches of drug substance and drug product. For drug products made from stable drug substances, at least two primary batches should be sufficient.	Stability data should be provided on at least three primary batches of the drug product.
Container closure system	Same as marketed containers	Same as marketed containers	Same as marketed containers proposed for the drug product
Specifications	Stability studies should include testing of those attributes of the drug substance or drug product that are susceptible to change during storage and are likely to influence quality, safety and/or efficacy	Same as ICH	Stability studies should include testing of those attributes of the drug product that are susceptible to change during storage and are likely to influence quality, safety and/or efficacy.
Testing frequency	Long term: 0,3,6,9,12,18,24,36, 48 and 60 m Accelerated: 0,1,2,3 and 6 m	Same as ICH	Same as ICH

for performing stability studies. Stability data should be provided at one of the following conditions:

- long term—25°C ± 2°C, 60% RH ± 5% RH or —30°C ± 2°C/65% RH ± 5% RH or —30°C ± 2°C/75% RH ± 5% RH
- accelerated—40°C ± 2°C/75% RH ± 5% RH

At least three months of long-term stability data must be made available at the time of submission.

Bracketing according to ICH guidelines is acceptable. Stability data from one single batch are required except when ICH bracketing is used. In that case, stability data on three batches are required for each extreme.

Other temperature and/or RH conditions can be used, if justified. Appropriate labeling of storage conditions in English and Chinese must be provided on the packaging intended for marketing.

India is located in Climatic Zone IV. For stability studies carried out in India, local guidelines recommend using 30°C/65%RH as testing conditions. However, if stability studies are performed outside of India, WHO guidelines should be followed. In addition, no specific stability testing sites are required in India.

Taiwan is located in Climatic Zone IV. Local guidelines on stability testing requirements are based on the ICH guidelines as follows:

- long term—25°C ± 2°C, 60% RH ± 5% RH or —30°C ± 2°C/65% RH ± 5% RH or
- accelerated—40°C ± 2°C/75% RH ± 5% RH
- intermediate—30° C ± 2° C/65% RH ± 5% RH if not used in long-term.

Site-specific stability data are not required for product registration in Taiwan.

Latin America

Argentina is located in Climatic Zone II, and recommended conditions for stability testing for long-term study are 25°C ± 2°C/60% RH ± 5% RH. Stability data must support the DP shelf life. Disposition 3555/96 internalized the Technical MERCOSUR Regulation for Pharmaceutical Products Stability. Annex III of Disposition 3555/96 includes several aspects about stability testing and describes, in detail, the procedures and conditions to comply with stability testing requirements in Argentina.

Mexico also is located in Climatic Zone II and therefore the official Mexican Norm NOM-073-SSA1-2005 on stability studies is based on ICH guidelines.

Brazil is located in Climatic Zone IV. The guidelines for the implementation of the stability studies of medicinal products are established by Resolution RE 01 published in July 2005 and follow the ICH guidelines. The Brazilian Health Surveillance Agency (ANVISA) accepts reduced stability testing requirements based on bracketing and matrixing as recommended by ICH.

Southern/Eastern Europe (SEE)

The Southern/Eastern Europe region is also called Adriatic and includes Croatia, Serbia, Bosnia-Herzegovina, Kosovo, Macedonia, Montenegro and Albania.

Croatia is located in Climatic Zone II. Croatia was a member of the Collaboration Agreement between Drug Regulatory Authorities in EU Associated Countries (CADREAC), and acceded to the EU in July 2013. Therefore, stability requirements follow ICH and EU recommendations.

The other countries in this region are also classified as Climatic Zone II and follow ICH stability testing recommendations.

Africa/Middle East

South Africa is located in Climatic Zone II. Guidelines on DS and DP stability testing are based on ICH recommendations.

Algeria, Morocco and Tunisia are located in Climatic Zone II. These countries accept EU files, and their stability testing requirements are based on ICH guidelines.

The Gulf States are located in Climatic Zone III and IVa. Stability guidelines[17] were implemented in May 2011 in Gulf Cooperation Council (GCC) countries, including Saudi Arabia, Kuwait, United Arab Emirates, Qatar, Oman and Bahrain, as well as Yemen. These guidelines are adapted from WHO guidelines and, where needed and justified, ICH recommendations also can be considered, i.e., photostability testing.

Stability data should be provided at the following conditions:

- long term—30°C ± 2°C/65% RH ± 5% RH
- accelerated—40°C ± 2°C/75% RH ± 5% RH

For DS intended for storage in a refrigerator:

- long term—5°C ± 3°C
- accelerated—30°C ± 2°C/65% RH ± 5% RH

For DS intended for storage in a freezer:

- long term— -20°C ± 5°C

Bracketing according to ICH guidelines is acceptable, if justified. Stability data from one single batch are required except when ICH bracketing is used. In that case, stability data on three batches are required for each extreme.

Other temperature and/or RH conditions can be used, if justified. Appropriate labeling of storage conditions in English and Arabic must be provided on the packaging intended for marketing.

Russia is classified under Climatic Zones I and II. Accelerated and intermediate testing conditions are not required, and there are no formal requirements for long-term testing. In general, it is recommended that stability studies be conducted with samples in the container closure system intended for market, according to the conditions (i.e., temperature, type of package, volume of package, humidity, etc.) described in the instructions for use. Product from three batches should be used for testing. Testing frequency is the same as proposed in ICH guidelines. Results of stability studies for all presented packages should be provided, and it is recommended that two years of stability data are presented at the time of submission. There is no clear requirement for site-specific stability studies.

The Russian file generally is used as a reference in the Confederation of Independent States (CIS), including Armenia, Azerbaijan, Belarus, Georgia, Kazakhstan, Kyrgyzstan, Moldova, Russia, Tajikistan, Turkmenistan, Ukraine and Uzbekistan.

Conclusion

Stability testing is a crucial element in a medicinal product's development program. The objectives of these studies are to establish adequate storage conditions and shelf life for display on the labeling and to ensure the medicinal product's quality, safety and efficacy throughout its shelf life.

Various analyses have been conducted on the current international and regional or country-specific stability requirements to achieve these objectives in all climatic zones under all possible temperatures and relative humidity levels during the medicinal product's entire shelflife.

References

1. ICH. *Stability Testing of New Drug Substances and Products Q1A(R2).* ICH website. www.ich.org/fileadmin/Public_Web_Site/ICH_Products/Guidelines/Quality/Q1A_R2/Step4/Q1A_R2__Guideline.pdf. Accessed 11 March 2013.
2. ICH. Explanatory note on the withdrawal of ICH Q1F from the ICH website. ICH website. www.ich.org/fileadmin/Public_Web_Site/ICH_Products/Guidelines/Quality/Q1F/Q1F_Explanatory_Note.pdf. Accessed 11 March 2013.
3. WHO. *Guidelines on stability testing for well-established drug substance in conventional dosage forms.*
4. ICH. *Specifications: Test Procedures and Acceptance Criteria forNew Drug Substances and New DrugProducts: Chemical SubstancesQ6A.* ICH website. www.ich.org/fileadmin/Public_Web_Site/ICH_Products/Guidelines/Quality/Q6A/Step4/Q6Astep4.pdf. Accessed 11 March 2013.
5. ICH. *Specifications: Test Procedures and Acceptance Criteria for Biotechnological/Biological Products Q6B.* ICH website. www.ich.org/fileadmin/Public_Web_Site/ICH_Products/Guidelines/Quality/Q6B/Step4/Q6B_Guideline.pdf. Accessed 11 March 2013.
6. ICH. *Validation of Analytical Procedures: Text and Methodology Q2(R1).* ICH website. www.ich.org/fileadmin/Public_Web_Site/ICH_Products/Guidelines/Quality/Q2_R1/Step4/Q2_R1__Guideline.pdf. Accessed 11 March 2013.
7. ICH. *Bracketing and MatrixingDesigns for Stability Testing of New Drug Substances and Products Q1D.* ICH website. www.ich.org/fileadmin/Public_Web_Site/ICH_Products/Guidelines/Quality/Q1D/Step4/Q1D_Guideline.pdf. Accessed 11 March 2013.
8. ICH. *Impurities in New Drug SubstancesQ3A(R2).* ICH website. www.ich.org/fileadmin/Public_Web_Site/ICH_Products/Guidelines/Quality/Q3A_R2/Step4/Q3A_R2__Guideline.pdf. Accessed 11 March 2013.
9. ICH. *Impurities in New Drug ProductsQ3B(R2).* ICH website. www.ich.org/fileadmin/Public_Web_Site/ICH_Products/Guidelines/Quality/Q3B_R2/Step4/Q3B_R2__Guideline.pdf. Accessed 11 March 2013.
10. ICH. *PhotostabilityTesting of New Drug Substances and Products Q1B.* ICH website. www.ich.org/fileadmin/Public_Web_Site/

ICH_Products/Guidelines/Quality/Q1B/Step4/Q1B_Guideline.pdf. Accessed 11 March 2013.
11. Op cit1
12. ICH. *Evaluation for Stability Data Q1E.* ICH website. www.ich.org/fileadmin/Public_Web_Site/ICH_Products/Guidelines/Quality/Q1E/Step4/Q1E_Guideline.pdf. Accessed 11 March 2013.
13. EMA. CPMP/QWP/609/96/Rev 2. Guideline on declaration of storage conditions: A: in the product information of medicinal products. B: for active substances. EMA website. www.ema.europa.eu/docs/en_GB/document_library/Scientific_guideline/2009/09/WC500003468.pdf. Accessed 11 March 2013.
14. ICH. *Stability Testing of New Dosage Forms Q1C.* ICH website. www.ich.org/fileadmin/Public_Web_Site/ICH_Products/Guidelines/Quality/Q1C/Step4/Q1C_Guideline.pdf. Accessed 11 March 2013.
15. ICH. *Quality of Biotechnological Products: Stability Testing of Biotechnological/Biological Products Q5C.* ICH website. www.ich.org/fileadmin/Public_Web_Site/ICH_Products/Guidelines/Quality/Q5C/Step4/Q5C_Guideline.pdf. Accessed 11 March 2013.
16. ASEAN Guideline on stability study of drug product. 9th ACCSQ-PPWG Meeting, Philippines, 21–24 February 2005. Update revision 22 February 2005. Singapore Health Sciences Authority website. www.hsa.gov.sg/publish/etc/medialib/hsa_library/health_products_regulation/western_medicines/files_guidelines.Par.61592.File.dat/ACTR_GuidelineforDrugProductStabilityStudy_Apr05.pdf. Accessed 11 March 2013.
17. The GCC guidelines for stability testing of active pharmaceutical ingredients and finished pharmaceutical products. Executive Board of the Health Ministers' Council for GCC States, May 2011, Version 3.0 Saudi Food and Drug Authority website. www.sfda.gov.sa/en/drug/drug_reg/Pages/drug_reg.aspx. Accessed 28 March 2013.

Chapter 12

Quality Systems and Inspection Processes—Pharmaceuticals

Updated by Siegfried Schmitt, PhD

OBJECTIVES

- ❑ Understand global quality systems legislation
- ❑ Understand the *Guide to Good Manufacturing Practice* for finished products and active pharmaceutical ingredients, and Mutual Recognition Agreements
- ❑ Learn about inspection systems and the Pharmaceutical Inspection Convention (PIC)
- ❑ Learn about treaties and programs within different regions
- ❑ Understand the applicability of guidances from the International Conference on Harmonisation (ICH)

LAWS, REGULATIONS AND GUIDELINES COVERED IN THIS CHAPTER

ICH

- ❑ ICH, *The Common Technical Document for the Registration of Pharmaceuticals for Human Use—M4Q(R1), Quality Overall Summary of Module 2, Module 3: Quality* (Step 5)
- ❑ ICH, *Quality Risk Management Q9* (Step 5)
- ❑ ICH, *Pharmaceutical Development Q8(R2)* (Step 5)
- ❑ ICH, *Good Manufacturing Practice Guide for Active Pharmaceutical Ingredients Q7* (Step 5)
- ❑ ICH, *Pharmaceutical Quality System Q10* (Step 5)

World Health Organization (WHO)

- ❑ WHO, *Quality Assurance of Pharmaceuticals, A compendium of guidelines and related materials, Volume 2, second updated edition, Good Manufacturing Practices and Inspection*

Europe

- ❑ Commission Directive 2003/94/EC of 8 October 2003 laying down the principles and guidelines of good manufacturing practice in respect of medicinal products for human use and investigational medicinal products for human use
- ❑ Commission Directive 91/412/EEC of 23 July 1991 laying down the principles and guidelines of good manufacturing practice for veterinary medicinal products
- ❑ *The Rules Governing Medicinal Products in the European Union, Volume 4, EU Guidelines to Good Manufacturing Practices for Medicinal Products for Human and Veterinary Use*
- ❑ Directive 2001/83/EC of the European Parliament and of the Council of 6 November 2001 on the Community code related to medicinal products for human use as amended by Directive 2004/27/EC of the European Parliament and of the Council of 31 March 2004 and Regulation (EC) No 1901/2006 of

the European Parliament and of the Council of 12 December 2006 on medicinal products for paediatric use

- Directive 2001/82/EC of the European Parliament and of the Council of 6 November 2001 on the Community code relating to veterinary medicinal products, as amended by Directive 2004/28/EC of the European Parliament and the Council of 31 March 2004

US

- *Federal Food, Drug, and Cosmetic Act (FD&C Act)*, Section 501(a)(2)(b)
- 21 CFR 210 CGMP in Manufacturing, Processing, Packaging or Holding of Drugs; General
- 21 CFR 211 CGMP for Finished Pharmaceuticals
- 21 CFR 606 CGMP for Blood and Blood Components

Canada

- *Food and Drug Regulations*, Division 2 Good Manufacturing Practices
- *Good Manufacturing Practices (GMP) Guidelines*, 2009 Edition, Version 2 (4 March 2011)

Introduction

As noted in Chapter 1, countries worldwide introduced drug regulations at different points in time. Human and veterinary drugs must meet minimum requirements regarding quality, efficacy and safety. In most industrialized countries, the second half of the 20th century saw a rapid increase in directives, regulations and guidelines for evaluating safety, quality and efficacy data of new medicinal products.[1] Even though the different regulatory systems were historically based on the same fundamental obligations, their detailed technical requirements evolved differently over time. These differences resulted in duplicate, time-consuming and expensive testing and inspection procedures for international registrations.

Concerns over the rising costs of healthcare and the escalation of research and development costs, coupled with the need to meet public expectations of safe and fast availability of new treatments, paved the way to rationalization and harmonization of international healthcare regulations.

The establishment of Good Manufacturing Practice (GMP) principles is one of several "good" practices, which are the focus of international harmonization efforts.[2] The need for harmonization has led to the emergence of the Pharmaceutical Inspection Cooperation Scheme (PIC/S) and the International Conference on Harmonisation (ICH), and the signing of Mutual Recognition Agreements (MRAs) or Memoranda of Understanding (MOUs).

ICH is an initiative among three regions—the EU, the US and Japan—with the objective of achieving greater harmonization in the interpretation and application of technical guidelines and requirements for pharmaceutical product registration, thereby reducing or obviating duplication of testing during the research and development of new human medicines. Recent emphasis on global cooperation has, however, made apparent the importance of disseminating information and providing input beyond the ICH regions via international organizations such as the World Health Organization (WHO). Topics initially selected for harmonization included safety, quality and efficacy to reflect the three basic criteria for approving and authorizing new medicinal products.

ICH has published a series of quality guidelines relating to chemical and pharmaceutical quality assurance (stability testing, impurity testing, etc.), known as the "Q" series. It is important to realize, however, that although many regions, especially in the developing world, may accept ICH standards and guidelines, local requirements may differ.

GMP Overview

GMP is that part of quality assurance that ensures medicinal products are consistently produced and controlled to the quality standards appropriate to their intended use and as required by the marketing authorization (MA) or product specification. GMP is concerned with both production and quality control.[3] For drugs, the primary goal of GMP regulations is to ensure they are safe and meet quality and purity requirements by the introduction of appropriate controls. GMP aims to diminish the risks inherent in any pharmaceutical production process, including cross-contamination/mix-ups and false labeling.[4]

The currently accepted adage is that quality cannot be tested into a product, meaning that product quality is assured through a validated process that repeatedly yields a product meeting its predetermined specifications. It is thus not sufficient to test the finished product; it is equally essential to prove that the established process has been followed.

Drug GMP principles are incorporated into local regulations where compliance at the local level is mandatory. Drug GMP regulations establish minimum requirements for drug product manufacturing, processing, packing or holding methods, facilities and controls.[5] The marketing authorization holder (MAH) assures the regulatory agencies that it complies with GMP through its application detailing the process, the controls and the specifications. To verify compliance with the regulations, including GMP, manufacturers must accept being inspected by regulatory authorities.

Figure 12-1. The GMP Lifecycle

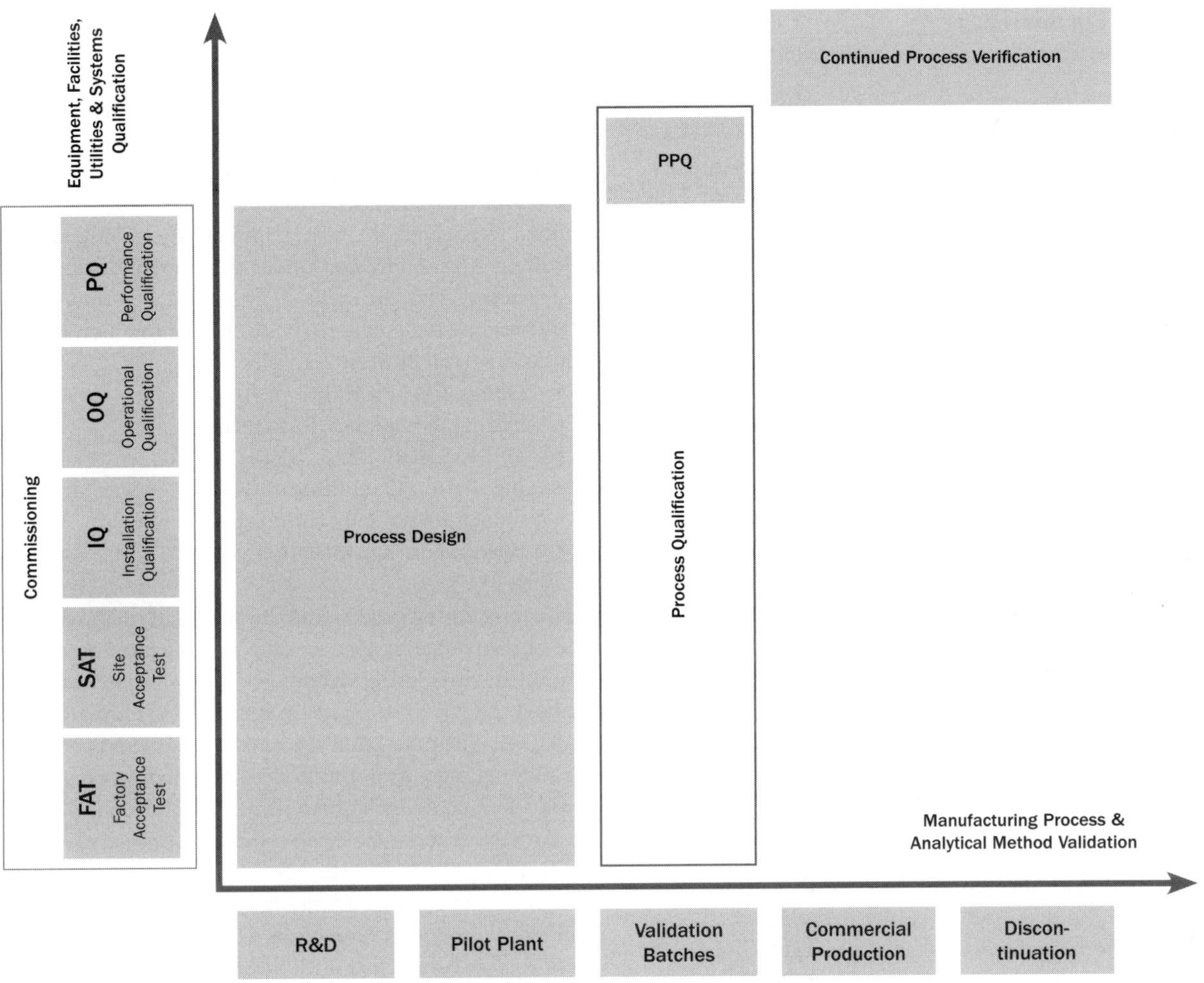

GMP requires that all steps involved in the manufacturing process be documented to allow traceability. This is especially important if problems arise that lead to (possible) adverse effects in patients, potentially resulting in a recall of the drug from the market. Other aspects of GMP include qualification and validation of all manufacturing and testing equipment and processes.

The WHO version of GMP is used by a many countries worldwide, especially developing countries. Some regions, such as the EU, the US and Japan, follow and abide by the ICH guidelines and add additional, specific compliance requirements. Other countries or regions have established or developed similarly stringent requirements, e.g., Brazil and ASEAN countries.[6]

GMP for active pharmaceutical ingredients also applies in countries that are signatories to ICH (the EU, Japan and the US) and in others that have adopted ICH guidelines, including Australia, Canada, Switzerland and Singapore.[7]

Main GMP Principles

GMP assumes that licensed pharmaceutical products are manufactured by licensed manufacturers. To ensure compliance, manufacturers should be regularly inspected by Competent Authorities.[8]

A commonly accepted GMP compliance approach is a "systems approach."[9] The systems concept involves the interrelationships among equipment (e.g., containers, machinery, etc.), materials (raw materials, in-process and finished products, etc.), processes, procedures and people.

The fundamental concept is that the manufacturer has to have verified that the correct equipment is in working order, the process is adequately developed and robust, the appropriate analytical methods have been established and tested and staff is suitably trained and experienced. **Figure 12-1** "The GMP Lifecycle" illustrates this interrelationship over time. The expressions used in **Figure 12-1** are explained later in this chapter.

GMP is based on the following main principles:

Quality Unit (QA and QC)

An independent quality unit must be in charge of the quality management system (QMS). The quality unit is often split into quality assurance (QA) and quality control (QC). QA establishes, owns and maintains the QMS, and assures compliance with the applicable laws and regulations. QC establishes the analytical controls to ensure that pharmaceutical products are of the required quality for their intended use. Drug manufacturers must have an appropriate QMS in place. The system should ensure that pharmaceutical products are designed and developed in a way that takes GMP requirements, as well as Good Laboratory Practice (GLP) or Good Clinical Practice (GCP) provisions, into account. The QMS must cover Good Documentation Practice (GDP) and ensure that managerial responsibilities are clearly defined. The QMS is a company's interpretation of the healthcare regulations for its specific circumstances. The QMS also addresses issues related to batch release, storage, self-inspection, deviation reporting, change control and process improvement, among others.

GMP

The goal of GMP is to manage and control risks associated with pharmaceutical production. GMP requires that all manufacturing processes be clearly defined and able to consistently produce pharmaceutical products of the desired quality that comply with approved product specifications. Under GMP, appropriate equipment qualification and process and method validation are required.

Manufacturers must ensure they have the appropriate resources at their disposal, including: appropriate number of qualified personnel, premises, equipment, materials and containers; standard operating procedures (SOPs) and instructions; suitable storage and transportation; and adequate controls. Any written procedures must be in clear and unambiguous language, and all relevant personnel must be trained on the procedures.[10]

Records must be maintained to allow inspection and traceability. GMP also requires a system for batch recall and recording complaints.

Sanitation and Hygiene

At every stage of the drug manufacturing process, sanitation and hygiene play a major role. They encompass personnel, equipment, premises, apparatus, containers, disinfection and cleaning materials and any other possible source of contamination.

Qualification and Validation

The terminology for qualification and validation is not harmonized. The terminology used here (see **Figure 12-1**) is understood by industry and regulators globally, regardless of terminology used in the respective laws and regulations.

Equipment, facilities, utilities and systems must be qualified to establish they are fit for use. These activities are typically performed by and under the control of the engineering/technical department. They commission these items before handing them over to the users. Commissioning can include any or all of these activities:

- Design Qualification (DQ)
- Factory Acceptance Test (FAT)
- Site Acceptance Test (SAT)
- Installation Qualification (IQ)
- Operational Qualification (OQ)
- Performance Qualification (PQ)

The manufacturing process and the analytical methods need to be validated. Validation can only be performed on equipment, in facilities, using systems and utilities that have been qualified. DQ is performed by Research & Development (R&D) and the pilot plant. Process Qualification confirms that the manufacturing process, as designed, is capable of reproducible commercial manufacturing and that the analytical methods are suitable and robust. Process performance qualification (PPQ), i.e., the manufacture of the validation batches of the drug product, must be successful before commercial production can begin. Continued process verification ensures compliance with the marketing authorization and the regulations throughout the product lifecycle.

Qualification and validation must be repeated if there are major changes to equipment, process or legislation.[11] Such changes must be captured in an appropriate change control system.

Complaints

Manufacturers must continuously collect and assess complaints about quality and other issues reported in the clinical and postmarketing periods. Written procedures to collect and assess incoming complaints must be in place. Systematic review of complaints enables product and process improvement.[12]

Product Recalls

Manufacturers must have a system in place to carry out recalls promptly and effectively. This system should allow immediate recall to the desired level in the distribution chain. A person should be designated to handle product recalls. Recalled products should be segregated from other products.

Contract Production and Analysis

If activities such as production are outsourced, there must be written quality and technical agreements that clearly outline each party's role and responsibilities. The MAH should be allowed to audit the contractor's facilities to ensure compliance with GMP and with its own corporate standards.

Self-inspection and Quality Audits

Companies need to conduct self-inspections (i.e., internal audits) to ensure adherence to the QMS, and thus GMP, and detect and rectify any deviations. The frequency of self-inspections is not specifically defined, but ideally, a self-inspection should take place at least once per year. All outsourced activities need to be part of the audit program. Written instructions for self-inspections should cover at a minimum and as applicable:

- personnel
- premises, including personnel facilities
- building and equipment maintenance
- starting material and finished product storage, handling and transport
- equipment
- production and in-process controls
- QC
- stability samples management
- documentation
- sanitation and hygiene
- qualification and requalification programs
- validation and revalidation programs
- deviation management, corrective and preventive actions (CAPA)
- calibration of instruments or measurement systems
- recall procedures
- complaint management
- label control
- results from regulatory intelligence
- results of previous self-inspections and any corrective steps taken[13]

Personnel and Training

Compliance with GMP is dependent on the availability of adequately qualified, educated and trained staff in the right numbers. Staff members should have written job descriptions and the authority to carry out their tasks.

All staff, especially new recruits, should be trained on appropriate processes and procedures.

Personnel must undergo health examinations related to their job functions. For example, staff involved in visual inspection should have regular eye examinations. Staff should be trained in matters of hygiene, e.g., washing hands before entering the production area.

Management must be aware of its responsibilities under the regulations and be suitably educated and trained.

Premises, Equipment and Materials

The premises and equipment must be located, designed, constructed and adapted to fulfill the requirements of the intended operations.

Materials should be strictly controlled. For example, cleaning and disinfection materials should not come into contact with the final product.

Documentation

All documentation should follow GDP rules, which ensure trustworthiness and traceability. All controlled documents must be approved, signed and dated. Documents must be reviewed regularly and updated if necessary.

All controlled electronic records must be backed up on magnetic tape, microfilm, paper print-outs or other suitable means.[14]

GMP in Production

GMP stipulates that all production operations follow clearly defined procedures, which should be in accordance with manufacturing and marketing authorizations. Materials and product handling, including receipt and cleaning, quarantine, sampling, storage, labeling, dispensing, processing, packaging and distribution, should be conducted in accordance with SOPs and appropriately recorded.[15]

SOPs should be strictly followed; any deviation from an approved SOP should be done in accordance with an approved procedure and properly documented. All such deviations from SOPs should be approved by a designated person, usually from the quality department. Access to production premises should be restricted to authorized personnel only.

GMP in production requires steps to be taken to prevent cross-contamination and microbial contamination during production. These steps can include such technical or organizational measures as carrying out production in dedicated, self-contained areas; providing appropriately designed airlocks, pressure differentials and air supply and extraction systems; and wearing protective clothing where products or materials are handled.[16] Such measures should be reviewed periodically.

To comply with GMP requirements, processing operations and any in-process and environmental controls should be appropriately executed and recorded. Any failures should be captured and recorded, including failure of equipment and/or services (e.g., water, gas) supplied to equipment. Equipment should be properly cleaned according to a

Table 12-1. Application of This Guide to API Manufacturing (From ICH Q7)

Type of manufacturing	Application of this guide to steps (shown in gray) used in this type of manufacturing				
Chemical manufacturing	Production of API starting material	Introduction of API starting material into process	Production of intermediate(s)	Isolation and purification	Physical processing and packaging
API derived from animal sources	Collection of organ, fluid or tissue	Cutting, mixing and/or initial processing	Introduction of API starting material into process	Isolation and purification	Physical processing and packaging
API extracted from plant sources	Collection of plants	Cutting and initial extraction(s)	Introduction of API starting material into process	Isolation and purification	Physical processing and packaging
Herbal extracts used as API	Collection of plants	Cutting and initial extraction		Further extraction	Physical processing and packaging
API consisting of comminuted or powdered herbs	Collection of plants and/or cultivation and harvesting	Cutting/ comminuting			Physical processing and packaging
Biotechnology: fermentation/ cell culture	Establishment of master cell bank and working cell bank	Maintenance of working cell bank	Cell culture and/or fermentation	Isolation and purification	Physical processing and packaging
"Classical" fermentation to produce an API	Establishment of cell bank	Maintenance of cell bank	Introduction of cells into fermentation	Isolation and purification	Physical processing and packaging

Increasing GMP requirements →

schedule. Any deviation from the expected yield range should be recorded and investigated.

The risk of cross-contamination and/or mix-ups or substitutions is especially high during packaging operations. Physical segregation of products can help avoid contamination during packaging.[17]

GMP in QC and QA

According to WHO Technical Report (961), QC can be considered the part of GMP concerned with sampling, specifications and testing. It includes the organization, documentation and release procedures to ensure necessary and relevant tests actually are conducted and materials are not released for use, or products released for sale or supply, until their quality has been judged to be satisfactory.[18]

Fundamental to the concept of QC is the independent operation of the production and QC units. The QC unit also should be independent of other departments and should be under the supervision of a person with adequate qualifications, experience, resources and authority to carry out the department's functions. Manufacturers and/or MAHs must ensure they have a QC function within their operations.

Basic QC requirements include adequate facilities, trained personnel and approved procedures for sampling, inspecting and testing starting materials, packaging materials and intermediate, bulk and finished products. All processes should undergo qualification and validation and be properly documented.

The purpose of QC is to ensure the finished product contains ingredients complying with the qualitative and quantitative composition described in its marketing authorization. All starting materials and intermediate, bulk and finished products should be subject to QC. All in-process control records should be maintained and included in the batch records.

Central to the concept of QA is batch release. Production and QC records should be reviewed as part of the batch release approval process. No batch of product should be released for sale or supply prior to certification by the authorized person(s) who should ensure that products to be released are in accordance with the requirements of the marketing authorization. QA review of finished products should include production conditions, the results of in-process testing, the manufacturing (including packaging) documentation, compliance with the specification for the finished product and an examination of the finished package.[19]

The requirements and legal responsibilities of the person responsible for batch release are specified in national laws and regulations and may vary in different jurisdictions.

GMP for Active Substances Used as Starting Materials

Early in the ICH process, it was decided that adequate international agreement existed on the technical aspects of GMP for pharmaceutical products and that further harmonization action through ICH was not needed.[20] However, in February 1998, the ICH steering committee adopted GMP for active pharmaceutical ingredients (APIs) as an ICH topic.

Based on the work already in progress by the Pharmaceutical Inspection Cooperation Scheme (PIC/S), US Food and Drug Administration (FDA) and other parties, the steering committee started work on this topic. It was apparent that GMP for APIs would have wide-reaching implications, hence a much extended expert working group (EWG) was established including, in addition to the six ICH parties and observers, experts representing the International Generic Pharmaceutical Alliance (IGPA), the World Self-Medication Industry (WSMI) and PIC/S (with representatives from Australia).[21]

On 10 November 2000, ICH published *Good Manufacturing Practice Guide for Active Pharmaceutical Ingredients Q7*.[22] The guide applies to the manufacture of APIs for use in drugs manufactured for human use and to the manufacture of sterile APIs only up to the point immediately prior to the APIs being rendered sterile (see **Table 12-1**). The sterilization and aseptic processing of sterile APIs are defined by local authorities.

The scope of the guidance includes APIs that are manufactured by chemical synthesis, extraction, cell culture/fermentation, recovery from natural sources or any combination of these processes. It also includes APIs that are produced using blood or plasma as raw materials; however, it excludes all vaccines, whole cells, whole blood and plasma, blood and plasma derivatives (plasma fractionation) and gene therapy APIs.

APIs used in the manufacture of investigational medicinal products (IMPs), i.e., clinical trial materials, do not have to be manufactured in accordance with GMPs. In January 2012, the European Commission published the concept paper "Delegated Act on the Principles and Guidelines of Good Manufacturing Practice for Active Substances in Medicinal Products for Human Use," which would mean an extension of Directive 2003/94/EC to GMP for APIs. This document has received strong criticism from industry.[23]

The guidance addresses the same areas as GMP for finished products including:

Quality Management

Quality is not limited to the quality department but should be the responsibility of everyone involved in manufacturing. Manufacturers are responsible for establishing, documenting and implementing an effective QMS, which should involve the active participation of management and appropriate manufacturing personnel.

The quality unit's responsibilities should be described in writing and should include, but not necessarily be limited to, releasing or rejecting all APIs and intermediates and establishing a system to release or reject raw materials, intermediates, packaging and labeling materials. In addition, the quality unit should review batch records and approve all specifications and procedures impacting quality. Internal audits to ensure compliance are also the quality unit's responsibility. A detailed list of the quality unit's responsibilities is given in the ICH Q7 guidance document.[24]

Production activities should be clearly described in writing. APIs and intermediates should be produced according to preapproved instructions. Batch records should be reviewed and any deviations reported. The production unit is also responsible for ensuring that all facilities are clean, calibrated and maintained.

To verify compliance with GMP principles for APIs, the quality unit should perform regular internal audits in accordance with an approved schedule. Regular quality reviews of APIs should be conducted and the results evaluated to assess whether corrective action or any revalidation is required.[25]

Personnel

GMP requires an adequate number of personnel, qualified by appropriate education, training and/or experience, to perform and supervise the manufacture of intermediates and APIs. Personnel also should practice good sanitation and health habits. These same criteria apply to consultants advising on the manufacture and control of intermediates or APIs.

Buildings and Facilities

All buildings and facilities used in the manufacture of intermediates and APIs should be located, designed and constructed to facilitate cleaning, maintenance and operations appropriate to the type and stage of manufacture. All utilities that could impact product quality (e.g., steam, gases, compressed air and heating, ventilation and air conditioning) should be qualified and appropriately monitored. Water used in the manufacturing process should be carefully controlled. Sewage, refuse and other waste should be disposed of appropriately.

Process Equipment

All equipment used in the manufacture of intermediates and APIs should be appropriately designed and suitably located for its intended use, cleaning, sanitization and maintenance. Schedules should be established for adequate equipment maintenance. Equipment used for testing should be calibrated according to written procedures and an established schedule. All GMP-related computerized systems should be validated.

Documentation

There should be written procedures for the preparation, review, approval and distribution of all documents related to the manufacture of intermediates or APIs. Such documents can be in paper or electronic form. The issuance, revision, supersession and withdrawal of all documents should be controlled by maintaining revision histories (ICH Q7).[26] Records of all major equipment use, cleaning, sanitization and/or sterilization and maintenance should include at least the date, time, product and batch number of each batch processed in the equipment. In addition, the name of the individual who performed the cleaning and maintenance should be documented. Records of raw materials, intermediates and API labeling and packaging materials also should be maintained.

To ensure batch-to-batch uniformity, master production instructions and batch production records—including controls for each intermediate and API—should be prepared and maintained. Laboratory control records also should be prepared and maintained. All production and control records should be reviewed regularly.

Materials and Management

Manufacturers must have written procedures describing the receipt, identification, quarantine, storage, transport, handling, sampling, testing and approval or rejection of materials used in the production of pharmaceuticals. A rigid system for evaluating suppliers of critical materials should be in place. Incoming materials should be held under quarantine until they have been sampled, examined or tested, as appropriate, before being released for use.

Production and In-process Controls

Production and in-process controls and their acceptance criteria should be defined based on information gained during the development stage or historic data. All weighing and measuring devices should be of suitable accuracy for the intended use.

Packaging and Identification Labeling of APIs and Intermediates

Written procedures that describe the receipt, identification, quarantine, sampling, examination and/or testing and release and handling of packaging and labeling materials should be in place. Labeling operations should be designed to prevent mix-ups. Manufacturers should ensure there is physical or spatial separation from operations involving other intermediates or APIs.

Storage and Distribution

Manufacturers must ensure there are adequate storage and distribution facilities. Records of the operating storage conditions, such as temperature, humidity, etc., should be retained if they are critical for the maintenance of material characteristics. All APIs and intermediates should be kept under quarantine until they have been released by the quality unit(s).

Laboratory Controls

Manufacturers must have appropriate laboratory and testing facilities. Documented procedures describing materials sampling, testing, approval or rejection, and laboratory data recording and storage should be maintained.

Manufacturers must ensure that all specifications, sampling plans and test procedures are scientifically sound and appropriate to ensure that raw materials, intermediates, APIs and labels and packaging materials conform to established standards of quality and/or purity. In addition, specifications and test procedures should be consistent with those included in the registration/filing.[27] All tests should be validated.

Validation

GMP requires validation of production processes, cleaning procedures, analytical methods, in-process control test procedures and computerized systems. All parameters critical to the API's quality and purity should be identified and validated. Prior to process validation, appropriate qualification of critical equipment and ancillary systems should be completed, including DQ, IQ, OQ and PQ (see **Figure 12-1**). The production process, cleaning methods and analytical methods all should be validated.

Change Control

A formal change control system should be established and maintained to evaluate all changes that may affect the intermediate or API's production and control. Written procedures should define the change control process and all personnel should be trained in the procedures. All GMP-relevant changes should be reviewed and approved by the appropriate organizational units, including regulatory and medical, and reviewed and approved by the quality unit(s).

Rejections and Reuse of Materials

Any intermediates and APIs failing to meet established specifications should be identified and put under quarantine. The materials can either be reprocessed to meet specifications or rejected.

Complaints and Recalls

There should be a written procedure for recording and investigating all quality-related complaints. This enables prompt action in case of a recall. Complaint records should be retained to enable trends to be evaluated and to detect the frequency and severity of product-related incidents with a view to taking additional and, if appropriate, immediate corrective action.[28] Written SOPs on recalls should clearly define the steps and actions to be taken in case of an intermediate or API recall.

Outsourced Activities

All outsourced activities, such as contract manufacturers and laboratories, should comply with GMP and GLP principles, with special emphasis on avoiding cross-contamination. Appropriate documentation should be maintained to ensure traceability of all operations being carried out at the contract manufacturer's site. The responsibilities and expectations of both the MAH and the contract acceptor should be set out in written technical and quality agreements that should permit the MAH to audit the contract acceptor's facilities for GMP or GLP compliance.

Records also should be maintained to ensure traceability of agents, brokers, traders, distributors, repackers, etc.

Inspections by Competent Authorities

Inspections can be considered part of the overall drug QA system.[29] Inspections can be general or product-related, routine or for cause. The objective of inspecting pharmaceutical manufacturing facilities is to assess the degree of conformity to prescribed GMP standards and to assess compliance with the relevant regulatory requirements, for example, license or marketing authorization provisions.[30] Inspections also are designed to monitor the quality of pharmaceutical products in distribution channels, e.g., inspections of licensed wholesale dealers, to eliminate the hazard posed by the infiltration of counterfeit or falsified drugs.

GMP is established at the national level. Before a medicinal product can be manufactured and released onto the market, a manufacturing authorization based on GMP compliance must be granted. GMP noncompliance is one of the conditions under which a Competent Authority may suspend or revoke a manufacturing authorization. If a marketed product is thought to pose a risk to public health, the local authorities can require a company to recall the product, which can be very costly. In some countries, manufacturers of APIs also require a manufacturing authorization. Inspection of API facilities is not harmonized and is dependent on country-specific legislation.

To ensure GMP compliance, Competent Authorities periodically inspect manufacturers, distributors, wholesalers and laboratories. The frequency of inspections depends on the type of products being manufactured, the compliance history and the Competent Authorities' resources.

Mutual Recognition Agreements (MRAs)

MRAs on GMP and acceptance of inspections and quality systems among countries improve the pace of global trade. For most MRAs, each party evaluates the other during a transitional assessment period, which has a predefined timeframe. The assessment may include an appraisal of the other party's pharmaceutical legislation, guidances and systems; the findings usually are confirmed during compliance visits and joint inspections. If each party can confirm that the other's systems are equivalent to its own, an operational phase can begin.

For example, in the EU, imported batches manufactured in a country outside the European Economic Area (EEA) that has an MRA with the EU are no longer required to be retested in the EU before release by a Qualified Person. Batch release is then based on a certificate of analysis from the manufacturer giving the batch test results and stating compliance with GMPs and the marketing authorization. Standard batch certificate formats have been negotiated by the parties.[31]

Following are MRAs existing between the EU and other countries and their status:

- Australia—fully operational
- Canada—in operation, with the exception of preapproval inspections and medicinal products derived from blood or blood plasma
- Japan—operational on 29 May 2004, with limited scope
- New Zealand—fully operational
- Switzerland—fully operational
- US—not in operation[32]

Canada is also a signatory to several MRAs for drug and medicinal product GMP compliance programs. The MRAs do not include harmonization of standards and drug regulations, but they do provide opportunities to develop closer and stronger relationships with other regulatory authorities.[33] Canada has MRAs with the EU/EEA, Australia and Switzerland. In addition, as noted in Chapter 10, a trilateral cooperation agreement exists among Canada, the US and Mexico that covers regulatory issues pertaining to drugs, biologics, medical devices, food safety and nutrition.

Australia is a signatory to MRAs with the EU, the US, Canada, Switzerland and Singapore. On 16 March 2004, the governments of Australia and Canada signed an MRA on conformity assessment in relation to medicines, GMP inspection and certification.[34] The MRA on standards and conformity assessment between Australia and the European Community (EC) was signed on 24 June 1998 and took effect on 1 January 1999. This agreement covers eight industry sectors, including medicinal product GMP inspection and batch certification and medical device conformity assessment.

In the US, FDA's Harmonization and Multilateral Relations Office is responsible for coordinating activities and collaborating with other governments and various international organizations such as the World Health Organization (WHO), ICH, International Cooperation on Harmonisation of Technical Requirements on Registration of Veterinary Medicinal Products (VICH), International Cooperation on Cosmetics Regulation (ICCR) and the International Medical Device Regulators Forum (IMDRF), among others.[35]

To obtain specific information about MRAs for a particular region or country, consult local websites. The FDA website, www.fda.gov/InternationalPrograms/default.htm, is also a good source of information.

The reason for the low number of MRAs is because of their legal status, i.e., these are legal contracts between governments, not merely between agencies, which have much lower legal hurdles.

Pharmaceutical Inspection Convention

The Pharmaceutical Inspection Convention and Pharmaceutical Inspection Co-operation Scheme (jointly referred to as PIC/S) are two international instruments among countries and pharmaceutical inspection authorities, which together provide an active and constructive co-operation in the field of GMP.[36]

PIC was founded in October 1970 by the European Free Trade Association (EFTA) under "The Convention for the Mutual Recognition of Inspections in Respect of the Manufacture of Pharmaceutical Products."[37]

The purpose of the PIC Scheme, with regard to public health, is:

- to pursue and strengthen the cooperation established among the participating authorities in the field of inspection and related areas with a view to maintaining the mutual confidence and promoting quality assurance of inspections
- to provide the framework for all necessary exchange of information and experience
- to coordinate mutual training for inspectors and other technical experts in related fields
- to continue common efforts toward the improvement and harmonization of technical standards and procedures regarding the inspection of the manufacture of medicinal products and the testing of medicinal products by official control laboratories
- to continue common efforts for the development, harmonization and maintenance of GMP
- to extend cooperation to other Competent Authorities having the necessary national arrangements to apply equivalent standards and procedures with a view to contributing to global harmonization

PIC/S currently has 43 participating authorities.

The European Directorate for the Quality of Medicines and HealthCare (EDQM), the European Medicines Agency (EMA), WHO and the United Nations International Children's Emergency Fund (UNICEF) act as partners to PIC/S.

Legal Implementation of GMP Requirements

The first modern good manufacturing regulations, also known as the QUAD regulations, were issued in 1957 by the Canadian Specifications Board of the Supply and Services Department.[38] These regulations served to ensure that drugs supplied to the Canadian military met quality specifications. Following the success of these regulations, GMPs began to be issued by other regulatory agencies around the world at a rapid pace; FDA issued its first version of GMPs in 1963, while British GMPs were issued in 1973.

By the early 1980s, distinct GMP codes had been issued by more than 25 countries, albeit with local differences. With the exception of the US (which has not substantially changed its GMP regulations since 1976), most countries revise and update their GMPs about every five years to keep up with changes in the industry, manufacturing and testing technology.

In the EU, GMP requirements are encoded in directives, which must be transposed into national law by the Member States. Though the European Commission provides dates at which time the legislation comes into force, the transposition into national law is dependent on the respective authorities' agenda. The interpretation of the directives by the Member States is by no means harmonized. For example, Italy has a requirement that a Qualified Person (QP) must be employed by the company for which the QP acts, whereas in the UK this can be an outsourced activity.

Regional Information

EU

In the EU, the history of GMP guidance dates back more than a quarter of a century. Several early directives for human drugs (including Council Directive 65/65/EEC of 26 January 1965 on the approximation of provisions laid down by law, regulation or administrative action related to medicinal products and Council Directive 75/319/EEC of 20 May 1975 on the approximation of provisions laid down by law, regulation or administrative action relating to medicinal products) and for veterinary products (Council Directive 81/851/EEC of 28 September 1981 on the approximation of the laws of Member States relating to veterinary medicinal products and Council Directive 81/852/EEC of 28 September 1981 on the approximation of laws of Member States relating to analytical, pharmaco-toxicological and clinical standards and protocols in respect of the testing of veterinary medicinal products) provided a framework for current manufacturing authorization harmonization.[39] The directives outlined authorized manufacturers' responsibilities and inspection arrangements and established requirements for batch release and accountability.

In addition, clear arrangements for communicating manufacturing information among regulatory authorities were outlined. Directive 75/319/EEC (updated by directive 2001/83/EC, which was amended by 2004/27/EC) was especially important since it introduced the role of the QP in the EC, defining the legal responsibility for individual batch release.[40]

Current GMP directives include Commission Directive 2003/94/EC of 8 October 2003 laying down the principles and guidelines of good manufacturing practice in respect of medicinal products for human use and investigational medicinal products for human use and Commission Directive 91/412/EEC of 23 July 1991 laying down the principles and guidelines of good manufacturing practice for veterinary medicinal products. More information and consensus regarding the interpretation of GMP principles can be found in *Volume 4* of *The Rules Governing Medicinal Products in the European Union* (*EudraLex*), published by the European Commission.[41]

Originally, the primary European documents pertaining to active substances were the *Pharmaceutical Inspection Convention Guide*[42] (published in 1997) and the *European Federation of Pharmaceutical Industry Association's Guide*[43] (published in 1996). The International Pharmaceutical Excipients Council (IPEC) also has developed industry-level guidances. The ICH *Good Manufacturing Practice Guide for Active Pharmaceutical Ingredients Q7* was published in November 2000 as Annex 18 to *Volume 4 Good manufacturing practice guidelines of the Notice to Applicants,* reflecting EU agreement with the ICH guidance, and has been used by manufacturers and GMP inspectorates on a voluntary basis. On 3 February 2010, Annex 18 was moved to become Part II: Basic Requirements for Active Substances used as Starting Materials of *EudraLex Volume 4 Good manufacturing practice (GMP) Guidelines*. Article 46f of Directive 2001/83/EC of the European Parliament and of the Council of 6 November 2001 on the Community code relating to medicinal products for human use, as amended by Directive 2004/27/EC of the European Parliament and of the Council of 31 March 2004 and Regulation (EC) No 1901/2006 of the European Parliament and of the Council of 12 December 2006 on medicinal products for paediatric use, and Article 50f of Directive 2001/82/EC of the European Parliament and of the Council of 6 November 2001 on the Community code relating to veterinary medicinal products, as amended by Directive 2004/28/EC of the European Parliament and of the Council of 31 March 2004, place new obligations on marketing authorization holders to use only active substances manufactured in accordance with GMP for starting materials.

In the EU, finished product batches may be released only once the batch has been certified by a QP. The QP may need to rely in part upon the advice and decisions of others and should ensure that such reliance is well founded, either from personal knowledge or from confirmation by other QPs about a quality system (including agreements) that he or she has accepted.[44]

Products imported into the EU must be retested and certified by an EU-based QP unless an MRA is in operation between the EU and a third country (see section on MRAs). This requirement also applies to investigational medicinal products used in clinical trials.

US

In the US, Section 501(s)(2)(b) of the *Federal Food, Drug, and Cosmetic Act* of 1938 (*FD&C Act*) specifically declares that a drug or device is deemed to be adulterated unless it is manufactured in accordance with "current Good Manufacturing Practice."[45] The first drug GMP regulations were promulgated in 1963 and underwent a major revision in 1978. Several minor revisions have been introduced since that time.

GMP regulations in 21 CFR 210 and 211 pertain to drugs and most biologics; GMPs for certain biological products (including blood and blood components) are covered in 21 CFR 600–680.

On 21 August 2002, FDA initiated a new approach to drug product quality regulation based on advances in science and risk, which incorporates an integrated quality system.[46] The new approach was adopted to ensure compliance and to encourage adoption of new technological advances.

In the US, the drug GMP regulation, 21 CFR 211, specifically applies to "finished pharmaceuticals"[47] including clinical supply dosage forms, placebos and commercially marketed final dosage forms. Although APIs are subject to the general GMP legal concept via the law itself, FDA has never promulgated specific GMP regulations for APIs. FDA has worked with the API industry to publish non-mandatory guidelines that describe agency expectations for API facility compliance with GMP.[48] The requirements are based on ICH Q7.

Canada

Canadian manufacturing quality standards were introduced in 1961 in Standard 74-GP-1. This program established a standard with which companies bidding on federal government contracts had to comply but was voluntary for companies not seeking government contracts. In the early 1970s, the *Manufacturing Facilities Control Regulations* were published along with two guidance documents, the *Guide for Drug Manufacturers* and the *Guide for the Preparation of Plant Master Files and Imported Drug Submissions*, to assist companies in complying with this standard.[49]

In 1981, Health Canada introduced Division 2, Part C of the *Food and Drug Regulations*, which forms the basis of current GMP regulations and has remained essentially unchanged since. Current regulations apply to all product classes, including radiopharmaceuticals and biologics.

Like the US, Canada has no specific GMP regulations relating to APIs. The ICH Q7A guidance has been adopted, however, with the intent of amending the *Food and Drug Regulations* to incorporate an API GMP framework and extend GMPs to veterinary products as well.[50] In addition, natural health products, regulated under the *Natural Health Product Regulations*, have separate GMP guidelines.

Australia

The Australian Code of Good Manufacturing Practice for Medicinal Products was published 16 August 2002. This replaced the Australian Code of Good Manufacturing Practice for Therapeutic Goods–Medicinal Products (August 1990) and Australian Code of Good Manufacturing Practice–Medicinal Gases (July 1992). It also replaced the Investigational Medicinal Products Code of GMP (Annex 13, EC GMP Guide, 1997). The new code was based on the international standard, *Guide to Good Manufacturing Practices for Medicinal Products*, version PH 1/97 (Rev. 3), 15 January 2002, published by the PIC/S.[51]

On 29 July 2009, the Therapeutic Goods Agency adopted the *Guide to Good Manufacturing Practice* as issued by PIC/S to become the new Code of Good Manufacturing Practice for Medicinal Products (New GMP): Therapeutic Goods (Manufacturing Principles) Determination No. 1 of 2009. The New GMP became mandatory from 1 July 2010. The New GMP replaces the previous Australian Code of Good Manufacturing Practice for Medicinal Products (2002) and the Australian Code of Good Manufacturing Practice for sunscreen products (1994). Australian manufacturers of medicinal products must comply with GMP requirements.

Japan

Originally, the style and content of GMPs issued in Japan were unlike those of any other country. While addressing the same issues as other GMP codes, the Japanese style resembled detailed job descriptions, describing the duties and responsibilities of various members of key management staff such as the manufacturing control manager, the quality control manager and the product security pharmacist, etc., within the pharmaceutical company.[52] The role of the security pharmacist was very similar to that of the QP in the EU. Although the Japanese approach was initially different from conventional GMP, the quality systems were extremely good, with comprehensive handling of quality complaints and product improvement processes. Today, GMPs in Japan follow a similar approach to other regions.

On 9 March 2012, Japan's Ministry of Health, Labour and Welfare (MHLW) applied in its name as well as on behalf of the Pharmaceuticals and Medical Devices Agency (PMDA) and the Japanese Prefectures for PIC/S membership. As a result of this application, it is expected that Japan's regulatory framework will be revised to become aligned with the PIC/S GMP guide.

Developing Countries

WHO issued its own set of GMPs as part of the scheme, Certification Of The Movement Of Pharmaceutical Products In International Commerce. Although initially not very demanding, these first GMPs issued by WHO were an attempt to provide a basic outline of the minimum steps required to establish a pharmaceutical manufacturing facility meeting acceptable standards. One of the main constraints of developing countries is the lack of economic resources to meet GMP requirements; hence, GMPs issued in or for developing countries may not meet the same standards as those issued in developed countries. Nonetheless, WHO guidelines support and enforce the same guiding principles of the good practices as implemented in the leading industrial nations.

Conclusion

In setting quality standards, harmonization at the regional and international level has played a major role. The globalization of industry necessitates harmonized GMPs on the one hand and inspection systems on the other. GMP legally codifies sound quality principles that have been used by the life sciences industry for more than 50 years.[53]

In the history of GMPs, Europe provided the greatest impetus for implementation and in elaborating and expanding the concepts involved with GMPs. With such treaties and cooperation agreements as MRAs, ICH and PIC/S, GMPs take on a worldwide dimension. GMPs are in effect in more than 100 countries worldwide, and GMP compliance is a prerequisite to exporting pharmaceuticals to most countries.[54]

The latest developments in the areas of GMP enforcement are in the prevention of falsified medicines entering the supply chain. These requirements will further encourage harmonization of the regulations.

References

1. Patel KT and Chotai NP. "Documentation and Records: Harmonized GMP Requirements." *J Young Pharm.* 2011 Apr-Jun; 3(2): 138–150. National Library of Medicine website. www.ncbi.nlm.nih.gov/pmc/articles/PMC3122044. Accessed 30 December 2012.
2. Quality Guidelines. www.ich.org/products/guidelines/quality/article/quality-guidelines.html. Accessed 30 December 2012.
3. Good Manufacturing Practice: Background, MHRA website. www.mhra.gov.uk/Howweregulate/Medicines/Inspectionandstandards/GoodManufacturingPractice/Background/index.htm#l2. Accessed 30 December 2012.
4. Good Manufacturing Practices. World Health Organization website. www.who.int/medicines/areas/quality_safety/quality_assurance/production/en/. Accessed 30 December 2012.
5. Chapter 8: Current Good Manufacturing Practice and Quality System Design. In: *Fundamentals of US Regulatory Affairs, Seventh ed.*, Rockville, MD, Regulatory Affairs Professionals Society, 2011:92.
6. GMP Question and Answers. World Health Organization website. www.who.int/medicines/areas/quality_safety/quality_assurance/gmp/en/index.html. Accessed 30 December 2012.
7. ICH website. www.ich.org. Accessed 29 January 2013.
8. Quality Assurance of Pharmaceuticals, A compendium of guidelines and related materials, Updated 2011. World Health Organization website. http://apps.who.int/bookorders/anglais/detart1.jsp?codlan=1&codcol=99&codcch=51. Accessed 30 December 2012.
9. Op cit 5.
10. Op cit 8.
11. Ibid.
12. Ibid.
13. Ibid.
14. Ibid.
15. WHO Technical Report Series, No. 961, 2011. WHO Expert Committee on Specifications for Pharmaceutical Preparations. WHO website. http://whqlibdoc.who.int/trs/WHO_TRS_961_eng.pdf. Accessed 30 December 2012.
16. Ibid.
17. Ibid.
18. Ibid.
19. Ibid.
20. Op cit 1.
21. Ibid.
22. ICH, *Good Manufacturing Practice Guide for Active Pharmaceutical Ingredients Q7* (Step 5, November 2000). ICH website. www.ich.org/fileadmin/Public_Web_Site/ICH_Products/Guidelines/Quality/Q7/Step4/Q7_Guideline.pdf. Accessed 29 January 2013.
23 Delegated act on the principles and guidelines of good manufacturing practice for active substances in medicinal products for human use; Concept paper submitted for public consultation. EC website. http://ec.europa.eu/health/files/gmp/2012_01_20_gmp_cp_en.pdf. Accessed 30 December 2012.
24. Op cit 22.
25. Ibid.
26. Ibid.
27. Ibid.
28. Ibid.
29. Inspection and standard. MHRA website. www.mhra.gov.uk/Howweregulate/Medicines/Inspectionandstandards/index.htm. Accessed 30 December 2012.
30. Ibid.
31. Mutual Recognition Agreements. EMA website. www.emea.europa.eu/ema/index.jsp?curl=pages/regulation/document_listing/document_listing_000248.jsp&mid=WC0b01ac058005f8ac. Accessed 30 December 2012.
32. Ibid.
33. Drugs and Health Products. Health Canada website. www.hc-sc.gc.ca/dhp-mps/compli-conform/int/mra-arm/backgroun-generalite_tc-tm-eng.php. Accessed 30 December 2012.
34. Updates—Mutual Recognition Agreements. www.hc-sc.gc.ca/dhp-mps/compli-conform/int/mra-arm/update-miseajour/index-eng.php. Accessed 30 December 2012.
35. Harmonization and Multilateral Relations Office. US Food and Drug Administration website. www.fda.gov/AboutFDA/CentersOffices/OfficeofGlobalRegulatoryOperationsandPolicy/OfficeofInternationalPrograms/ucm243679.htm. Accessed 30 December 2012.
36. PIC/S website. www.picscheme.org. Accessed 30 December 2012.
37. Ibid.
38. International GMPs. Globepharm website. www.globepharm.org/what-is-gmp/international-GMPs/gmp-implementation.html. Accessed 30 December 2012.
39. Chapter 20: Quality Systems and Inspectorate Process—Medicinal Products. In: *Fundamentals of EU Regulatory Affairs*, Sixth ed. Rockville, MD, Regulatory Affairs Professionals Society, 2012:198.
40. Annex 16 Certification by a Qualified Person and Batch Release. http://ec.europa.eu/health/documents/eudralex/vol-4/index_en.htm. Accessed 30 December 2012.
41. Ibid.
42. Op cit 4.
43. Op cit 5.
44. Op cit 39.
45. Op cit 5.
46. Ibid.
47. Ibid.
48. Ibid.
49. Rägo L and Santoso B. Drug Regulation: History, Present and Future. WHO website. www.who.int/entity/medicines/technical_briefing/tbs/Drug_Regulation_History_Present_Future.pdf. Accessed 30 December 2012.
50. Ibid.
51. TGA website. www.tga.gov.au. Accessed 30 December 2012.
52. Op cit 38.
53. Ibid.
54. Ibid.

Chapter 13

Generic Drug Products

By Sofina M. Jain, MS, RAC

OBJECTIVES

- ❑ Review and understand the basic concept of generics around the world
- ❑ Obtain a good understanding of the current scenario of generics in developed and emerging countries
- ❑ Understand the business of generics

REGULATIONS AND GUIDELINES COVERED IN THIS CHAPTER

EU

- ❑ Regulation (EC) No 726/2004 of the European Parliament and of the Council of 31 March 2004 laying down Community procedures for the authorisation and supervision of medicinal products for human and veterinary use and establishing a European Medicines Agency
- ❑ Directive 2001/83/EC of the European Parliament and of the Council of 6 November 2001 on the Community code relating to medicinal products for human use
- ❑ Council Regulation No. (EEC) 1768/92 of 18 June 1992 concerning the creation of a supplementary protection certificate for medicinal products
- ❑ COM(2012) 84 final, 2012/0035 (COD), Proposal for a Directive of the European Parliament and of the Council relating to the transparency of measures regulating the prices of medicinal products for human use and their inclusion in the scope of public health insurance systems

Japan

- ❑ *Guideline for Bioequivalence Studies of Generic Products*
- ❑ *Guideline for Bioequivalence Studies of Generic Products for Topical Use*
- ❑ Pharmaceutical Administration and Regulations in Japan 2012

Brazil

- ❑ Resolution - RDC n° 135 of 29 May 2003
- ❑ Resolution - RE n° 896 of 29 May 2003

What Is a Generic Drug?

The World Health Organization (WHO) defines a generic drug as a pharmaceutical product, usually intended to be interchangeable with an innovator product that is manufactured without a license from the innovator company and marketed after the expiry date of the patent or other exclusive rights.[1]

EU guidelines define a generic medicinal product as a medicinal product that has:

- the same qualitative and quantitative composition in active substance(s) as the reference product

- the same pharmaceutical form as the reference medicinal product
- and whose bioequivalence with the reference medicinal product has been demonstrated by appropriate bioavailability studies[2,3]

Generic drugs are known by their nonproprietary names. For more than 50 years, the International Nonproprietary Names (INN) program has provided names for substances that allow their identification worldwide. WHO established and maintains the International Pharmacopoeia. The tests and analysis conducted on drugs by WHO are centered on:

- drugs that are on the Model List of Essential Drugs
- drug products and drug substances used for priority diseases such as malaria, tuberculosis and HIV/AIDS

Global Scenario

The global generic market is expanding, and with major blockbuster drugs coming off patent, the revenue generated by generic companies is predicted to skyrocket. All major countries (US, UK, Germany, France, China, Japan, etc.) are educating their patients about the advantage of taking generic drugs as an alternative to available brand-name drugs. Many have created action plans to spread the message that generic drugs are as safe and effective as brand-name drugs. Substituting generic drugs for brand-name ones drives down the healthcare costs in these countries, which is a driving force behind the practice.

The global generic market is divided into two segments:

- developed markets—US, UK, Japan, Germany, France, Italy and Spain
- developing or emerging markets—Brazil, Russia, India, China, Turkey, South Korea and Mexico

Sales of over $290 billion (US) are at risk due to patent expirations between 2012 and 2018,[4] and the estimated value of the global generics markets is forecast to hit $127.8 billion by the end of 2013 alone.[5] Increase in the demand for prescription drugs, increase in the acceptance of generic drugs and insurance companies favoring generics are a few of the many reasons why the expansion of the generic industry is expected to be unprecedented. The top players in the world by market share are Teva (14.5%), Novartis (13.2%), Mylan (8.6%), Watson (5.1%) and Sanofi (3.7%).[6]

Patent Protection No More

The pharmaceutical industry is experiencing a major change in terms of a lack of blockbuster drugs by pharmaceutical giants. There have been situations in the past where a blockbuster drug has gone off-patent, but this is the first time when a list of major revenue-generating patented drugs will lose patents. This loss is not being offset by a good pipeline of new drugs. This has led to a number of specialty generic companies entering the competition. Along with drugs going off-patent, the additional push by governments is helping change people's outlook toward generic drugs. This has led to the prediction that generic manufacturers will play a big, direct role in the future of the pharmaceutical industry.

In these tough economic times, cheaper generic products help the patients' wallets and help drive public health. This is one of the primary reasons so much emphasis is being placed on the acceptability of generic products by patients worldwide. The average price of a generic is 80% cheaper than that of a brand-name product. Even though generic products are prescribed much more often than brand-name products, they make up a very small portion of drug spending.[6] With the patent expiration phenomena, the use of generics is only going to increase.

To compensate for the patent expirations and foreseeing the loss in revenue, the brand-name manufacturers have been merging or acquiring other companies to increase their research and development pipelines. These mergers lead to less generic competition but bigger and stronger generic companies. These companies are committed to selling drugs at the cheapest possible price; finding innovative methods to work around formulations and, in some cases, work around patents.

As an example of the current trend, Watson purchased Actavis in April 2012. Acquiring and expanding will allow Watson to compete with other large generic companies such as Teva and Mylan. Teva, on the other hand, has acquired Ratiopharm and Cephalon in the last two years; becoming one of the largest generic pharmaceutical companies in the world.[8] The brand-name manufacturers initially were involved in acquisitions to add drugs to their diminishing pipelines in an effort to overcome the expiration of their blockbuster drugs.

While major generic firms are pursuing acquisitions, there are some key points they must consider while deciding on their products:

- product segments they should target
- time of launch
- regulations are becoming more stringent
- government measures to control prices
- challenging formulations that require significant technology to duplicate
- targeting formulations with limited availability of actives so as to exhaust the market
- specialty products

Leading generic companies also are targeting biosimilars or follow-on biologics due to their huge profit margins. Since biologics are more complex and difficult to duplicate, manufacturing and marketing generic versions of them at a cheaper price is a tough challenge. More information on biosimilars is available in Chapter 24.

International Markets

EU

In the EU, generic medicines are marketed in compliance with international patent law. They are used in EU countries as a part of programs to make cheaper medicines available to patients and save healthcare costs. Generic drugs are 20%–90% cheaper than their brand-name alternatives.[9] This difference in pricing saves EU patients and the healthcare system about 35 billion euros each year. The rate of generic substitution in France in June 2011 was 71%, according to a report from the Caisse Nationale de l'Assurance Maladie (CNAM), which oversees healthcare policy. This compares with Germany, where generics substitution is 96%. The French government's goal is to reach 85% generics substitution by the end of 2012.[10]

One has to submit a Marketing Authorisation Application (MAA) to the European Medicines Agency (EMA) if seeking approval. The MAA is submitted in the Common Technical Document (CTD) format.[11] There are four routes of approval, and a company can submit via any of them depending on which market it wants to target. A company can go through the Centralised Procedure, wherein it submits a single application to EMA. A single evaluation is conducted, and a single authorization gives them direct access to the EU market for five years. Regulation (EC) No 726/2004 and directive 2001/83/EC created the Centralised Procedure for the authorization of medicinal products.[12]

If a company wishes to submit a dossier (application) to EMA, the intent to submit should be conveyed to the agency six to 18 months before the submission. A presubmission meeting also is essential at least six months prior to submission.[13] In cases where there are safety concerns regarding the reference medicinal product (originator/brand-name drug), an EU Risk Management Plan is required that mirrors the US Risk Evaluation and Mitigation Strategies (REMS) practice.[14]

The second route is the Decentralised Procedure, wherein an application is submitted to Competent Authorities in each Member State where a marketing authorization is sought. To obtain marketing authorizations in several Member States, the Decentralised Procedure is mandatory. One Member State acts as the Reference Member State (RMS) and drafts the summary and other reports. The RMS also communicates with the applicant if issues arise.

The third is the Mutual Recognition Procedure, which is only a little different from the Decentralised Procedure. The Mutual Recognition Procedure is applicable to products that have already been approved in one Member State, whereas the Decentralised Procedure is applicable to products that have never received any marketing authorization in the EU.

Another procedure is the National Procedure. This involves approval on a country-by-country basis. If the product is approved in one Member State, it can only be sold in that state and none of the other Member States.

To submit a new application, a generic company seeking an approval has to make sure the patent protection period has expired. An MAA can be submitted only after a brand-name product is off patent. Standard patent protection in the EU lasts for 20 years, although this protection can be extended by a Supplementary Protection Certificate (SPC). This extension is granted to compensate for the period of patent protection that is lost between the filing of the patent and the authorization to place the product on the market. An SPC is granted for a maximum of five years. Generic medicines can be made available to patients in the EU only after the relevant patents and SPCs on the originator product have expired. Prior to 2004, generic companies could not even conduct experiments required to demonstrate bioequivalence to an originator drug before patent on that drug had expired. This essentially meant added dominance of the originator drug in the market even after expiration of its product's patent as the generic companies would require time to submit bioequivalence data to the authorities. In March 2004, the EU introduced the Bolar provision to assist generic competition. Per this provision, generic companies now can test and experiment with the patented drug prior to its patent expiration. Legally, this would not infringe on the drug's patent. The introduction of the "Bolar provision" in the EU has enabled European manufacturers to develop generic medicines within Europe prior to patent expiry.[15,16]

Another limitation to the entry of generics is the data exclusivity period, during which regulators cannot accept applications by generic companies.

Generic medicines account for more than 80% of all applications made under the Mutual Recognition Procedure and Decentralised Procedure.[17]

According to Article 10(1) of Directive 2001/83/EC, as amended, the applicant is not required to provide the results of preclinical tests and clinical trials if it can demonstrate that the medicinal product is a generic version of a reference medicinal product that is or has been authorized under Article 6 of Directive 2001/83/EC, as amended, for not less than eight years in a Member State.[18,19] This involves proving the bioequivalence of the generic product with the reference medicinal product.

The brand-name pharmaceutical companies use a set of instruments to delay the entry of affordable generic drugs into the market.[20] The delay averages seven months; without it, if generic products were available immediately upon patent expiry, savings could be 20% higher.[21,22] Evergreening, the process of patenting minor changes to the original product to delay competition, is one of the tactics used to delay generic product market access.

To overcome this hurdle, a proposal for a Transparency Directive (2012/0035(COD)) was drafted and introduced in 2012. When implemented, this directive will help patients save on their medical expenses as it takes initiative on generic pricing and reimbursement policies.

Japan

Japan is the world's second largest pharmaceutical market after the US. With a $52 billion (US) drug market, it represents 11% of global sales.[23] Forecasts say that Japan will see more than 12% growth, to exceed $9.5 billion in 2014.

The generic industry finds itself struggling to get a market share in this country, as opposed to other countries. Sales from generics account for a mere 10% in Japan compared to 50% in other countries.[24] The use of generics is still not that common in Japan. The Ministry of Health, Labour and Welfare (MHLW) is the regulatory body responsible for the evaluation and subsequent approval of drugs in Japan. In the last few years, the agency has taken all measures required to increase generic sales in Japan. Not only will it be cost effective for patients, but since 30% of medical expenses in Japan are covered by the government,[25] this change would ease the healthcare budget.

Within MHLW, the Pharmaceutical and Medical Devices Agency (PMDA) reviews and approves generic drugs. PMDA reviews the generic applications required for the approval, export certification and quality reevaluations of generic prescription drugs, nonprescription drugs, quasi-drugs and cosmetics.

The generic industry faces two main obstacles in Japan. The first, as in the EU, involves brand-name product patents and the inability to file a generic application until the patents have expired. Japanese brand-name products are covered by patents for 20 years, during which time they are protected from generics. In the past, if some brand-name product indications or dosage and administration were patented, partial approvals were not granted because of patent protection. However, since Notification No. 0605014 of the Evaluation and Licensing Division, PFSB dated 5 June 2009 took effect, partial approvals of indications or dosage and administration not covered by the patent are permitted.[26]

The second obstacle, even though Japan is a member of the International Conference on Harmonization (ICH), is that the Japanese regulatory environment and structure has kept many foreign manufacturers from entering the market. This barrier stems from the lack of harmonization with international standards. By comparison, the US and EU have successfully adopted international standards into their regulatory frameworks.[27]

It is rather difficult for an international company to gain approval of its drug product in Japan. The majority of generics in Japan are manufactured locally. But, doctors and pharmacists in Japan are brand-name product oriented, [28] and prefer prescribing drugs from established companies. Therefore, the Japanese government is making prescription of generic drugs a national policy.

To increase the use of generic medicines in Japan, the government has initiated the "Action Program for the Promotion of the Safe Use of Generic Drugs" to educate patients about the safety and reliability of cheaper alternatives to brand-name drugs, i.e., generics.[29]

National Health Insurance Drug Price List of Japan

The National Health Insurance (NHI) Drug Price List is a list of drugs for which medical providers can be reimbursed under the health insurance programs as specified in the regulations for hospitals and nursing homes covered by health insurance.[30] The prices to be invoiced for drugs used in hospitals are set by the Minister of Health, Labour and Welfare and included in the NHI Drug Price List.

Generic Drugs in the NHI Drug Price List

In the past, generic drugs were added to the NHI drug price list every two years, but since 2008 they have been added twice a year (May and November).[31] These prices are calculated based on drug pricing formulas that were last updated in March 2000. The reimbursement prices of these drugs are based on the following principles:

- When a brand-name drug is on the list, and a generic identical to the brand-name product is entered for the first time, its price is obtained by multiplying the drug price of the brand by a factor of 0.7.
- If both brand-name and generic drugs are already on the list, the price of a new generic will be the same as that of the lowest-priced generic.
- When many products, i.e., more than 20, are on the list, the price of the new generic will be obtained by multiplying the cost of the lowest-priced generic by 0.9.

Brazil

Brazil has the largest generic market in Latin America, and Pró Genéricos estimates it will achieve a 35% market share, in units, by 2015 while it already enjoys a 20.5% share of the market in terms of revenue.[32] The Brazilian regulatory body governing medical products is the National Health Surveillance Agency, ANVISA. Brazilian regulations require the generic drug to be at least 35% less expensive than the originator drug.[33]

The majority of Latin American countries are pharmaceutical importers, especially of active ingredients. They produce finished materials from imported raw materials. Brazil, for example, imports approximately 85% of the raw materials used in the production of generic drugs. But

Brazil, through its trade agreements, has participated in technology transfers that have led to increased manufacturing in the country. Brazil uses three drug classifications: branded, generic and similar.[34]

- Branded—the innovator or reference drug is the branded drug with patent protection.
- Generics—drugs sold under their INN or local nonproprietary name.
- Similars—drugs with the same active ingredient, same pharmaceutical dosage form, same concentration and administered in the same way as the branded drugs. They also have the same therapeutic result as the reference drug but do not have the same bioequivalency as the reference drug. They are sold as separate brand names.

Brazil is unique in that it mandates the use of generics in the public sector, while substitution can be carried out by doctors and pharmacists in other sectors only between reference and generic drugs, but not similar drugs. Some of the developed countries that have implemented policies to decrease the cost of medicines have mandated that pharmacists substitute cheaper generic products for prescriptions for brand-name drugs. This is an effective strategy but is difficult to implement in Brazil and other Latin American countries because, in most instances, pharmacy clerks with little or no knowledge of pharmacology dispense the majority of drugs. In addition, prescription-only drugs are often accessible over-the-counter in Latin America. This makes it even more difficult to assure the substitution of generic drugs for branded drugs.

ANVISA has been taking steps toward increasing the local generic market. It provides incentives to companies filing for generic products, shortens review times and discounts the registration fee for generic products. The generic companies must be registered with ANVISA to conduct the processes that are a part of the product application.

Of the 2,792 generics registered in Brazil, 90% are made locally, with the rest imported along with brand-name drugs.[35]

According to a study by the IMS Health Consulting Institute, generics currently represent 20.6% of Brazilian pharmaceutical industry sales.[36] Based on patent expiration of many blockbuster drugs within the next few years, certain therapy segments will open up and will become key investment areas for Brazil's generics industry.

Compulsory Licensing—India, China and Rest of the World

Compulsory licensing is when a government allows a manufacturer to produce a patented product or process without the consent of the patent owner, but under strict terms. It is one of the flexibilities on patent protection under the World Trade Organization Agreement on Trade-Related Aspects of Intellectual Property Rights (TRIPS). In the past 12 years, 24 Compulsory Licenses (CLs) have been issued worldwide.[37] Most of these resulted in a price reduction of the drug in question. The majority of these were issued for communicable diseases like HIV/AIDS, until India recently issued a CL for an anti-cancer drug. Previously, in early 2007, Thailand became the most active issuer of CLs for drugs targeting non-communicable diseases (NCDs) like cardiovascular diseases and cancer.

Major pharmaceutical companies launch drugs for NCDs like cancer at prices not affordable to the local population. India has a big and growing generic drug market that generates a lot of revenue from manufacturing active ingredients and drug products. Issuing CLs to them would be the first step toward making these medicines available at affordable prices.

In March 2012, India granted approval of an application by a local generic drug manufacturer to manufacture and sell a patented cancer drug under this compulsory license. The generic company, Natco Pharma Ltd., has developed a manufacturing process of its own and will be selling the drug at a much lower price. But under the terms of the license, Natco has to provide 6% royalty of the net sales quarterly to Bayer.[38]

This royalty (6%) is aligned with the United Nations Development Programme recommendation of a 4% royalty, which can be adjusted upward as much as 2% for products of particular therapeutic value, or reduced as much as 2% if development of the drug involved public funds. Under this license, the generic company cannot outsource product manufacturing.

This is an initiative by the Indian government to provide cancer drugs to patients at more-affordable prices. In another initiative, the Indian government approved Cipla's (a generic drug manufacturer) appeal to launch another cancer drug patented by Bayer. Only recently, Cipla slashed the price of the cancer drug by 76% on humanitarian grounds.[39]

These developments have influenced other developing countries like China to issue CLs.[40] China is facing a major epidemic of NCDs that accounts for more than 85% of the total deaths in the country. To make matters worse, it doesn't have the research and development capability to successfully handle this issue.[41] Hence it relies on imports of expensive drugs. After the TRIPS agreement, China was one of the first countries to start procedures to bring CL into effect. At this point, no CLs have been issued by China.

Brazil, Canada, Australia and Korea also have issued CLs in the past to local generic manufacturers. Generic drug manufacturers will be key players in countries like India, Brazil, Turkey and China, as these are volume-driven markets. Hence, generic companies investing in these places will profit not by higher selling prices but lower profit on drugs with high volume.

This WTO initiative is based on interest in public health. But, this overriding of patents of major pharmaceutical companies might just drive direct foreign investments away from these countries. In the face of such hurdles, the larger pharmaceutical companies have acquired local generic manufacturers to secure a foothold in the local markets (e.g., Pfizer bought 40% of Brazilian generic pharmaceutical firm Laboratorio Teuto Brasileiro and Amgen has invested in another Brazilian local generic manufacturer, Bergamo).

Conclusion

The growth of the generic industry in markets worldwide is here to stay. Aging populations, high rates of chronic diseases, skyrocketing healthcare costs and a bad economy are all drivers of the expansion of generic medicines, so these markets will only increase in the coming years.

Some factors that will play key roles are stringent regulations in different parts of the world, authorized and branded generics, patent expiry, mandated generic drug prescribing linked to national budgets, growing consumer acceptance of generic medicines and government initiatives.

References

1. World Health Organization. Generic Drugs. WHO website. www.who.int/trade/glossary/story03`/en/index.html. Accessed 7 March 2013.
2. EMA. EMEA/CHMP/225411/2006, *EMA Procedural advice for users of the centralized procedure for generic/hybrid applications.* EMA website. www.ema.europa.eu/docs/en_GB/document_library/Regulatory_and_procedural_guideline/2009/10/WC500004018.pdf. Accessed 7 March 2013.
3. Generics and Biosimilars Initiative (GaBI). "EU guidelines for generics." GaBIonline website. http://gabionline.net/Guidelines/EU-guidelines-for-generics. Accessed 7 March 2013.
4. Evaluatepharma World Preview 2013. Evaluate website. www.evaluatepharma.com/worldpreview2018.aspx. Accessed 19 April 2013. Subscription required.
5. Global generic drugs market driven by the expansion of healthcare coverage. Companies and Markets.com website. www.companiesandmarkets.com/News/Healthcare-and-Medical/Global-generic-drugs-market-driven-by-the-expansion-of-healthcare-coverage/NI6659. Accessed 19 April 2013.
6. Op cit 4.
7. Op cit 5.
8. Ibid.
9. European Generics Association. "Introduction." EGA website. www.egagenerics.com/index.php/generic-medicines/introduction. Accessed 7 March 2013.
10. GaBI. "French Government pushing generics." GaBI website. http://gabionline.net/Generics/General/French-Government-pushing-generics. Accessed 7 March 2013.
11. Op cit 5.
12. Ibid.
13. Ibid.
14. Ibid.
15. Sheppard A. Generic Medicines: Essential contributors to the long-term health of society. EGA website. www.egagenerics.com/images/publication/PDF/IMS.pdf. Accessed 7 March 2013.
16. Bolar Provision and Regulatory Data Exclusivity in Europe. CMS websote. www.cms-cmck.com/Hubbard.FileSystem/files/Publication/3ed51f5e-7615-44dc-a399-076a7ccc3745/Presentation/PublicationAttachment/2a4563f5-b970-4fa2-9d61-0bac21c0b232/BolarProvisioninEU.pdf. Accessed 19 April 2013.
17. Ibid.
18. Op cit 2.
19. Op cit 3.
20. EGA. EGA FACT SHEET on generic medicines. www.egagenerics.com/images/factsheet/EGA_factsheet_05.pdf. Accessed 7 March 2013.
21. Op cit 15.
22. Op cit 19.
23. Ramesh T, Saravanan D and Khullar P. "Regulatory Perspective for Entering Global Pharma Markets. Indian Pharmaceutical Association website. www.ipapharma.org/pt/Sep2011/15-20.pdf. Accessed 7 March 2013.
24. Israeli Embassy, Tokyo. *Overview of Pharmaceutical and Health Care in Japan.* Israel Ministry of Industry, Trade & Labor website. www.moital.gov.il/NR/rdonlyres/061BE5FC-DA0A-4A84-B90F-0778E7A53301/0/PharmaceuticalandMedicalCareReport.pdf. Accessed 7 March 2013.
25. Ibid.
26. Japan Pharmaceutical Manufacturers Association. *Pharmaceutical Administration and Regulations in Japan.* National Institute of Health Sciences website. www.nihs.go.jp/mhlw/yakuji/yakuji-e_20110502-02.pdf. Accessed 7 March 2013.
27. Brunschier R. "Generic Submissions in Japan from a Global Generic Player's Perspective." Japan Generic Drug Society website. www.ge-academy.org/img/academic_jounal_sample/vol2-1/GE_V2_No1_p15.pdf. Accessed 7 March 2013.
28. Nikkei Business. "Foreign Firms Target Japan's "Newly Emerging" Generics Market." 3 September 2012. Nikkei Business website. http://business.nikkeibp.co.jp/article/eng/20120831/236222/. Accessed 7 March 2013.
29. MHLW. Policy Report: Promotion of the Use of Generic Drugs. MHLW website. www.mhlw.go.jp/english/policy_report/2012/09/120921.html. Accessed 7 March 2013.
30. Op cit 25.
31. Ibid.
32. Pró Genericos—Brazilian Association of Generic Drug Manufacturers. Healthcare Global website. www.healthcareglobal.com/reports/2progenericos2. Accessed 19 April 2013.
33. Mello J. "The Brazilian Market for Generic Drugs. February 2012. The Brazil Business website. http://thebrazilbusiness.com/article/the-brazilian-market-for-generic-drugs. Accessed 7 March 2013.
34. Homedes N, Linares RL and Ugalde A. HNP Discussion Paper, "Generic Drug Policies in Latin America. World Bank website. http://siteresources.worldbank.org/HEALTHNUTRITIONANDPOPULATION/Resources/281627-1095698140167/HomedesGenericDrugFinal.pdf. Accessed 7 March 2013.
35. Op cit 30.
36. Op cit 31.
37. Huang Y. "The Compulsory Licensing of Pharmaceuticals: Will China Follow in India's Footsteps?" Council on Foreign Relations website. http://blogs.cfr.org/asia/2012/10/01/the-compulsory-licensing-of-pharmaceuticals-will-china-follow-in-indias-footsteps/. Accessed 7 March 2013.
38. Estavillo M. "India Grants First Compulsory License, For Bayer Cancer Drug. Intellectual Property Watch website. www.ip-watch.org/2012/03/12/india-grants-first-compulsory-licence-for-bayer-cancer-drug/. Accessed 7 March 2013.
39. Ibid.
40. Op cit 5.
41. Op cit 34.

Chapter 14

Over-the-Counter Products (OTCs)

Updated by Evelyn Steele, MTOPRA

OBJECTIVES

- ❑ Gain an understanding of nonprescription/over-the-counter (OTC) drugs
- ❑ Understand safety implications for OTCs
- ❑ Learn about OTC switching procedures
- ❑ Learn about labeling and advertising requirements

REGULATIONS AND GUIDELINES COVERED IN THIS CHAPTER

- ❑ Australia, *Australian Regulatory Guidelines for Over-The-Counter Medicines (ARGOM)*
- ❑ Canada, *Food and Drugs Act* and *Food and Drug Regulations*, Part C
- ❑ EU, Directive 2001/83/EC, as amended on the Community code relating to medicinal products for human use
- ❑ EU, *Guideline on changing the classification for the supply of a medicinal product for human use, The Rules Governing Medicinal Products in the European Community Volume 2C: Guidelines* (January 2006)
- ❑ Japan, *Pharmaceutical Affairs Act,* Act No. 145 of 1960, as amended
- ❑ US, *Durham-Humphrey Amendment* to the *Federal Food, Drug, and Cosmetic Act*, Public Law 82-215 (1951)

Introduction

In the most general terms, an over-the-counter (OTC) product can be described as a medicine available without prescription for the purposes of self-medication. The World Self-Medication Industry has defined self-medication as "… the treatment of common health problems with medicines especially designed and labeled for use without medical supervision and approved as safe and effective for such use."[1] However, the understanding of what constitutes an OTC drug and the mode of dispensing can differ widely between regions and countries.

In the US, the *Durham-Humphrey Amendment* to the *Federal Food, Drug, and Cosmetic Act* (*FD&C Act*) in 1951[2] established the statutory basis for distinguishing between nonprescription and prescription drugs, where the sale of nonprescription drugs is not limited to pharmacies.[3] There is, however, a distinction between unrestricted OTCs that can be obtained in convenience or grocery stores and restricted OTCs that typically are sold in pharmacies only, stored behind the counter and dispensed by registered pharmacists.

In some EU countries, many classes of drugs, although available without prescription, can only be obtained in a pharmacy. The classification and mode of dispensing differ from country to country. For example, in the UK, there are three product categories: Prescription Only Medicines (POM); Pharmacy (P) Medicines, which are sold under the supervision of a pharmacist; and General Sales List (GSL) medicines, which can be purchased without advice from a physician or pharmacist. To compound matters, some drugs fall into more than one category, depending on, for example, the dose or pack size. In Japan, nonprescription drugs previously could only be sold behind the counter in a pharmacy employing a qualified pharmacist. Under the revised *Pharmaceutical Affairs Law*[4] (put into force in June 2009), stores are no longer required to be staffed by a pharmacist to sell most nonprescription drugs; this can now be done by a drug sales clerk registered with the prefectural government.

Use of OTCs

OTC medicines give the end user the responsibility for diagnosing his or her condition and for purchasing and administering the medicine to treat that condition. Examples of minor ailments for which self-medication usually is used include colds and flu, cough, sore throat, hay fever and mild to moderate pains such as headaches and muscular pain, among others. OTC medicines now generally are accepted as an important part of healthcare.[5] The responsible use of self-medication can considerably reduce social security system and healthcare costs at the national level. As such, self-care and self-medication are expected to play an even more important part in the framework of public health policy, especially in countries where a large part of the national healthcare system is publicly financed. This trend is due in part to an aging population but also due to rising healthcare expectations. Another factor contributing to the growing popularity of self-medication is that people are increasingly interested in playing a more active role in managing their own health.[6] However, self-medication is not without risks; drug abuse is of particular concern. For drugs to be granted OTC status, certain conditions should be fulfilled:

1. Indications are self-recognizable, relatively minor ailments.
2. Since the patient bears full responsibility for his or her own treatment, the patient information (labeling) must be clearly understandable (at a consumer reading level), regarding directions of use, self-selection (and de-selection when contraindicated/inappropriate) and when to consult a doctor if undesirable effects occur.
3. The duration of use reflects the condition that is being treated. This will be shorter for the self-medication of minor acute conditions (e.g., cold symptoms with acetaminophen) compared to more chronic conditions (e.g., allergy symptoms with non-sedating antihistamines).
4. The possibility of masking underlying serious illness is manageable (through labeling or duration of use).

Safety

The fact that a drug is OTC rather than prescription does not mean it is risk free. It is especially important that patients understand that all drugs, including OTCs, can have side effects. OTC drugs can interact with prescription and other OTC drugs,[7] which can cause one of the drugs to work less effectively, or could have more serious, even deadly, results and/or aggravate certain medical conditions. Therefore, when considering product safety, the same rules tend to apply to prescription and OTC drugs. For example, regular reports on product safety (e.g., adverse events) are required for all medicinal products approved in the EU and US.

Including clear, legible patient information is also important to minimize the potential for misuse of medicinal products. This is especially pertinent for OTC drugs where the consumer assumes full responsibility for taking the drug. It is the responsibility of the manufacturer and the relevant authority to ensure that the information on the package is easy to understand, legible and clearly outlines any side effects.

Switching From Prescription to OTC

Prescription medicines can move to nonprescription status (Rx-to-OTC) using what is known as a "switching" procedure. The commercialization of self-medication historically has been accompanied by strong political support.[8] National variations on self-medication and switching procedures arise primarily due to differences in tradition, reasons for initiating a switch, consumer information and education and the degree to which political support is translated into national legislation.[9]

From a political viewpoint, switching from prescription to OTC status can reduce healthcare expenditures by cutting the number of medical consultations. However, any move toward self-medication has to be accompanied by an increased familiarity with the product and clearly understandable information. It is important that patients be made aware that they should seek medical advice if symptoms persist or they are uncertain about the problem. The World Health Organization (WHO) published *Guideline for Developing National Drug Policies* in 1995, which supports self-medication.

The Rx-to-OTC switch is handled differently by each nation or region. In many regions, OTC drugs are not reimbursed, which may be a major factor for a company in deciding whether to make a switch. Also, depending on the data submitted to support the switch application, a period of data exclusivity may be available to the applicant. However, regardless of potential commercial benefits for the applicant, a switch decision is based on an assessment of the benefit:risk ratio for consumers.

To decide whether to switch a product from Rx to OTC status, there must be a clear definition of what constitutes a prescription medicine. Issues to consider include the direct or indirect danger or safety profile, benefit:risk analysis, including the consequences of incorrect use, and the quality and clarity of available patient information. Experience with the drug and the route of administration also must be examined. Recently, researchers proposed a values tree-based framework to define domains relevant to benefit risk assessment in a nonprescription setting. [10] This framework concept has been considered by several regulatory authorities and is included as part of the new Medicines and Healthcare products Regulatory Agency (MHRA) guidance, *How to Change the Legal Classification of a Medicine in the UK.*

In most jurisdictions, a legal application for a switch must be made to the relevant authority with accompanying information. This normally would include information on safety and efficacy, packaging, the product's history of use and side effects and a list of other countries where the product already has OTC status, including the switch dates.

Occasionally, an OTC product will be switched to prescription status if postmarket data show the possibility of harmful abuse.[11]

Labeling and Advertising

Since OTC drugs are available without prescription, it is important that they be accompanied by adequate directions for use and warnings, to provide a high degree of consumer protection. The information required on the label and package leaflet is clearly specified in national laws. In addition, some countries mandate user testing of patient information leaflets.

Certain statements, such as the following, may also be required:

- "Keep out of reach of children."
- "In case of overdose, get medical help or contact a Poison Control Center right away."
- Warning statements for particular ingredients, e.g., "May cause allergic reactions."

Most countries allow advertising of nonprescription medicines, although restrictions still can apply in some markets. For example, in Australia, Schedule 3 OTC drugs can be purchased in pharmacies without a prescription, but not all Schedule 3 drugs can be advertised to consumers. When advertising is permitted, any claims in advertising materials must be substantiated by information contained in the product details, Patient Information Leaflet (PIL) or the final OTC monograph (depending upon national laws). Advertising includes any form of door-to-door information gathering activity or inducement designed to promote the prescription, supply, sale or consumption of medicinal products. Examples include:

- advertising medicinal products to the general public
- advertising medicinal products to medical practitioners or people qualified to prescribe or supply them
- visits by medical sales representatives to medical practitioners or people qualified to prescribe medicinal products
- supplying product samples
- promising any benefits or bonuses, in money or in kind, except when their intrinsic value is minimal
- sponsoring promotional meetings attended by people (and/or their families) qualified to prescribe or supply medicinal products
- sponsoring scientific congresses attended by people qualified to prescribe or supply medicinal products, including payment of traveling and accommodation expenses in connection with those congresses[12]

Generally, advertising should not encourage injudicious use of the medicinal product. Advertising should present the product objectively and should not be misleading. National Competent Authorities should ensure there are adequate and effective methods to monitor medicinal product advertising and take legal action against noncompliant companies.

Postmarket Reporting of Adverse Drug Experiences/Pharmacovigilance

Postmarket reporting of adverse events, known as adverse drug experiences in the US or pharmacovigilance in the EU, is the process by which the safety of approved drugs is monitored on an ongoing basis. The increasing number of OTC drugs has created a growing need for systems that carefully monitor both their safety and their interactions with other drugs.[13] For prescription drugs, the prescribing physician can collect information about interactions and adverse reactions relatively easily during subsequent patient visits. However, it is more difficult to compile information about self-medication products. Therefore, novel means of pharmacovigilance, e.g., data collection via community pharmacies, are required.[14]

In the EU, pharmacovigilance is required for all approved medicinal products. In the US, OTC products that have received marketing approval via a New Drug Application (NDA) must comply with applicable postmarketing reporting requirements. However, reporting is not mandated for OTC monograph products that are classified as Generally Recognized as Safe and Effective (GRASE).[15] In general, the US Food and Drug Administration (FDA) collects less postmarket surveillance information and conducts fewer product performance analyses for OTC drugs than for prescription products.

Country-specific Information

EU

In the EU, Directive 2001/83/EC of the European Parliament and of the Council of 6 November 2001 on the Community code relating to medicinal products for human use, as amended, lays down the rules for the classification of medicinal products.

Articles 70–75 deal with "Classification of Medicinal Products," with Article 71 addressing classification criteria.

In general, products are classified as prescription or nonprescription. The main criteria for medical prescription status in Article 71 are:

- the danger the drug poses (directly or indirectly) even when used correctly, if used without a medical prescription
- the product is frequently and to a large extent used incorrectly, thus presenting a direct or indirect danger to human health
- the product contains substances with unknown adverse reactions that require further investigation
- they normally are prescribed by a doctor to be used parenterally

According to Article 72, medicines that do not meet the criteria listed in Article 71 are considered nonprescription. In addition, the directive states that the Competent Authorities are required to draw up a list of products on the market in their territories subject to medical prescription that should be reviewed in light of new facts that could affect the classification status; the list should be updated annually.

Prescription status and switching procedures are not fully harmonized across the EU. For example, in Germany, an active ingredient (or combination of active ingredients) is switched, thereby impacting all products containing the ingredients, while in Italy the switch is based on a product.[16] These disparities are largely due to previous national evaluations, national reimbursement policies and cultural differences. To harmonize basic medicinal product assessment and classification principles in the Community, the EC adopted a detailed guidance[17] in September 1998 (last revised in January 2006), to increase the number of EU OTC switches. In some markets, e.g., Ireland, the same product marketed for prescription use and for nonprescription use must have different names.[18]

US

In the US, the primary criteria for determining drug status (prescription or nonprescription) are:

- the margin of safety
- the method of use and collateral measures necessary to use the drug
- the benefit:risk ratio
- the adequacy of labeling for nonprescription drugs

Originally, under the *FD&C Act*, only those products that had been on the market for a "significant period of time" and "to a material extent" could be considered for OTC status as GRASE. In 1972, the OTC Drug Products Review established the use of monographs to determine the GRASE status of OTC drugs.[19]

Ingredients are placed in one of three categories:

- Category I—GRASE for the claimed medical indication
- Category II—not generally recognized as safe or effective (NGRASE)
- Category III—insufficient data available to permit a final classification

Products classified as Category II must be withdrawn from the market within 60 days following the publication of a final monograph. Category III products can remain on the market, but safety and efficacy testing must be conducted and FDA notified of any such testing within 60 days of the final monograph publication.[20] After successful testing, an ingredient can be moved to Category I. In the US, drugs with Category I monograph status do not need FDA clearance.

Switching Procedures

The "switch regulation" in the US was promulgated by FDA in 1956. If public health is not at risk, FDA can exempt an NDA from prescription status. Switches also can be made via an NDA or a supplemental New Drug Application (sNDA) submitted to FDA's Center for Drug Evaluation and Research (CDER) to be reviewed conjointly with the OTC drug division. For this to be possible, the product should have been on the market for at least three years with a relatively high usage rate to enable a fair assessment of any adverse effects. The frequency of any such adverse reactions should not increase during the assessment period. Alternatively, switches can be made before publication of the final monograph by using the "rush-to-market" regulation, provided the product is recommended for Category I and there is no objection from the FDA commissioner.

Canada

In Canada, nonprescription drugs are regulated by Health Canada's Therapeutic Products Directorate (TPD) and must comply with the *Food and Drugs Act* and the *Food and Drug Regulations, Part C*.[21] Nonprescription drugs are subject to Division 1 (old drugs with established ingredients or indications) or Division 8 (new drugs with new ingredients or novel indications), where they are issued a drug identification number (DIN) and Notice of Compliance (NOC) (in the case of Division 8 drugs). A DIN indicates that the product has undergone and passed a review of its formulation, labeling and instructions for use. A drug product sold in Canada without a DIN is not in compliance with Canadian law. A DIN identifies the following product characteristics:

- manufacturer
- brand name
- medicinal ingredient(s)
- strength of medicinal ingredient(s)
- pharmaceutical form
- route of administration[22]

Additionally, in 2004, the *Natural Health Products (NHP) Regulations* came into effect, which regulate vitamins and minerals, herbal remedies, homeopathic medicines, traditional medicines, probiotics, amino acids and essential fatty acids. Many health products that were once considered drug products were reclassified as NHPs, such as fluoride-containing toothpastes and antacids. Manufacturers must submit formulation information, labeling, safety and efficacy information for NHPs to be reviewed by Health Canada's Natural Health Products Directorate. Approved products receive a natural health product number (NPN).

Switching Procedures

Rx-to-OTC switching of a drug product in Canada includes a three-part process. The first two parts remove the ingredient from the prescription listing of medicinal ingredients (Schedule F to the *Food and Drug Regulations*). Part 1: A supplemental New Drug Submission (NDS) is submitted to Health Canada's Therapeutic Products Directorate in one of two types of switch submissions:

- A Type I submission proposes nonprescription marketing of a prescription product with no change to the indication, strength, dose, duration of use, dosage form, route of administration and target population.
- A Type II submission is a proposal for nonprescription marketing of a prescription drug with changes to the approved drug's parameters and conditions. In such a case, additional data must be filed to demonstrate that the proposed changes do not compromise the drug's safety and efficacy and are compatible with nonprescription conditions of use.[23]

When TPD has assessed the switch submission and found it does not meet the factors to maintain it in the listing of Schedule F, Part 2 is a Parliamentary review of the switch proposal and publication in *Canada Gazette* to change the Canadian regulations. Part 3 is a Provincial review of the ingredient to determine its placement for sale as either prescription, behind-the-counter, pharmacy only or mass market.

There is a proposal to streamline the Rx-to-OTC switch process in Canada to remove the Parliamentary Review and Gazetteing step.

Australia

In Australia, OTC products are available in pharmacies, with selected products also available in supermarkets, health food stores and other retailers.[24] Examples of the latter include cough and cold remedies, anti-fungal treatments, sunscreens and nonprescription analgesics such as aspirin and paracetamol. The current *Australian Regulatory Guidelines for Over-the-counter Medicines (ARGOM)* is undergoing a process of review and update by the Therapeutic Goods Administration (TGA). Selected chapters have been removed and replaced with references to appendices related to the quality, safety, efficacy and new substance aspects of OTC registrations.[25]

Medicines are evaluated by one of three regulatory units:

1. OTC medicines are evaluated by the OTC Medicines Section (OTCMES) of the Office of Medicines Authorization (OMA).
2. Complementary medicines are evaluated by the Office of Complementary Medicines (OCM).
3. Prescription and other specified medicines are evaluated by the Office of Medicines Authorization (OMA).

Products containing new active substances usually are evaluated by OMA. The decision whether to evaluate via the OTC or OCM route is based on several factors including:

- active substance safety
- need for professional counseling before use
- nature of ailments or symptoms to be treated
- abuse potential of the product or substance
- incidence of adverse effects and contraindications
- risk of masking serious disease
- product's benefit:risk profile (Australian regulatory guidelines for OTC medicines)

Other factors include the product form (different pack size, strength, indications, etc.) and the prescription status in other countries.

Switching Procedures

Scheduling is a national classification system that controls how medicines and poisons are made available to the public in Australia. Medicines and poisons are classified into schedules according to the level of regulatory control over the availability of the medicine or poison, required to protect public health and safety. The schedules are categorized by ingredient name or drug class in the Poisons Standard (the SUSMP).[26]

Medicines are grouped into the following schedules according to the appropriate level of regulatory control over their availability to consumers:

- pharmacy medicines (included in Schedule 2 to the Poisons Standard)
- pharmacist-only medicines (included in Schedule 3 to the Poisons Standard)
- general sales medicines that are not included in any of the schedules to the Poisons Standard

Switch applications intended to amend the current SUSMP can be made to the TGA.[27] This application can be independent of a product registration application.

Other Countries

India

In India, OTC drugs fall into two main classes, Schedule K "Household Remedies" and pharmacy sale OTC drugs. The major piece of drug control legislation is termed the *Drug and Cosmetics Rules*, and an up-to-date consolidated version, which contains the drug schedules, is available under "Rules and Regulations."[28] A definitive OTC list is under development; the present rules permit any drug not mentioned in the prescription schedules to be sold directly to the patient through pharmacies.

Household Remedies (which include simple analgesics such as paracetamol) may be sold as general sale items in villages with a population of less than 1,000 and by licensed non-pharmacy retailers in larger towns and cities. All other OTC products may be sold only via pharmacies. Generic versions of OTC products already on sale in India are subject to a rapid licensing process at the state level, whereas OTC formulations new to the Indian market require Central Registration via the Central Drugs Standard Control Organization (CDSCO).

There is also a class of traditional (Ayurvedic) medicines in India that may be sold over the counter as General Sale Items. Advertising to the public is permitted for all nonprescription items, but not for prescription medicines.

China

In China, OTC drugs are available through pharmacies (List A Products) and as General Sale items (List B products). The registration process for OTC drugs follows the same path as for prescription products, usually requiring application for a clinical trial permission, followed by a mandatory local clinical trial (or bioequivalence study for generic OTC products) followed by a full registration application. Bioequivalence studies can be waived for generic oral solutions and topical products if locally manufactured. The full registration process typically takes five years or more. Equivalent classifications and registration procedures (List A OTC, List B OTC and prescription) exist for traditional Chinese medicines.

An English translation of some of the complex drug registration regulations is available.[29] At the time of writing, the State Food and Drug Administration (SFDA) is unwilling to accept applications for copies of OTC formulations already available in China, and also has imposed restrictions on branding of OTC products. An improvement in the regulatory environment for OTC medicines is under consideration for the next revision of the *Drug Administration Law*, but this may be some years away.

Japan

Pharmaceutical administration in Japan is based on various laws and regulations, the main one being the *Pharmaceutical Affairs Law* (Law No. 145). For the enforcement and management of these laws, detailed regulations are prepared by the government in the form of ministerial ordinances and notices, such as the *Enforcement Ordinance* and the *Enforcement Regulations of the Pharmaceutical Affairs Law*, and notifications issued by the director general of the bureaus or the directors of the divisions in charge in the Ministry of Health, Labour and Welfare.

Drugs (medicinal products) are classified as follows based on the regulatory provisions in the *Pharmaceutical Affairs Law*:

1. Prescription drugs—drugs intended for use by a physician or dentist or under the prescription or instructions of a physician or a dentist.
2. Nonprescription (OTC) drugs—drugs other than prescription drugs that are intended for use at the discretion of general consumers by direct purchase in a pharmacy or drug store under guidance by pharmacist or by registered drug sales clerk. These are defined as the drugs not having very strong intended actions (indications) in humans and those to be selected by users based on information provided by pharmacists or other medical personnel.

In Japan, nonprescription drugs originally could be handled only by pharmacies and dispensed by qualified and registered pharmacists. With the revision of the *Pharmaceutical Affairs Law*, which took effect in June 2009, it is now possible to sell some nonprescription drugs, depending on their risk levels, under registered drug sales clerk consultation.

The *Law for Partial Amendment of the Pharmaceutical Affairs Law* (Law No. 69), revising the OTC drug selling system, was issued on 14 June 2006 and entered into force on 1 June 2009. In the amendment, nonprescription drugs (OTC) were classified according to their potential risks:

- Type 1—especially high risk
- Type 2—relatively high risk
- Type 3—relatively low risk

In addition, a requirement for consultation for OTC drugs of each classification when sold was implemented. A notification also was issued to allow drug sales clerks (registered with the prefectural government) to sell Type 2 and/or Type 3 drugs (Notification No. 0808001 of the General Affairs Division, dated 8 August 2007) went into force on 1 April 2008.

Very low-risk products were re-classified from OTC to new designated quasi-drug (six categories such as antimicrobial for external use) by Notification No. 280 PBA, dated 12 March 1999. In 2004, 15 categories (such as mouthwash) were re-classified from OTC to new range quasi-drug by Notification No. 0716002 PBA, dated 16 July 2004. Very low-risk products can now be sold in supermarkets and convenience stores.

Summary

OTC drugs are gaining in importance, especially in industrialized societies. Governments want to reduce national social security system expenses and healthcare costs, while patients' healthcare expectations and interest in becoming more active in managing their own health is growing. OTC drug use must be accompanied by consumer education and awareness. Only informed and educated consumers will be able to make better choices in controlling their own healthcare. It is the responsibility of both the pharmaceutical industry and regulatory authorities to raise public awareness of both the benefits and risks involved in self-medication so patients can use medicines correctly and reduce the risk of drug abuse.

References

1. World Self-Medication Industry, www.wsmi.org. Accessed 11 March 2013.
2. *Durham-Humphrey Amendment* of 1951 to the *Federal Food, Drug, and Cosmetic Act (FD&C Act)*. Public Law 82-215.
3. Michor S. "OTC Opportunities in an Emerging Market." *Regulatory Affairs Focus*. January 2006.
4. Matsuo D. "Effect of Amendment to Japan's Pharmaceutical Affairs Law. Nomura Research Institute (NRI) papers, No. 149, 1 December 2009. NRI website. www.nri.co.jp/english/opinion/papers/2009/pdf/np2009149.pdf. Accessed 12 March 2013.
5. Association of the European Self-Medication Industry. HEALTH is the most precious thing we have and we are all interested in staying healthy. AESGP website. www.aesgp.eu/self-care/about-self-care/en/. Accessed 12 March 2013.
6. WSMI. About self-medication. WSMI website. www.wsmi.org/aboutsm.htm. Accessed 12 March 2013.
7. faqs.org. Over-the-Counter Drugs. Faqs.org website. www.faqs.org/health/Healthy-Living-V2/Over-the-Counter-Drugs.html. Accessed 12 March 2013.
8. Eberwein B. "Rx-to-OTC switch: a global perspective." The World Self-Medication Industry (WSMI) 13th General Assembly, The Association of the European Self-Medication Industry (AESGP) 35th Annual Meeting, Self-care—a vital element of health policy in the information age. Berlin, 9-12 June 1999. WSMI website. www.self-medication.org/Berlin1999/15Eberweinformat.pdf. Accessed 12 March 2013.
9. Op cit 2.
10. Brass EP, Lofstedt R, Renn O. Improving the Decision-Making Process for Nonprescription Drugs: A Framework for Benefit–Risk Assessment. *Clinical Pharmacology & Therapeutics* (2011); 90 6, 791–803.
11. Regulatory Affairs Professionals Society. Chapter 14, Over-the-Counter Drugs. In: *Fundamentals of US Regulatory Affairs Fifth Edition.* Rockville, MD; 2007:132.
12. Regulatory Affairs Professionals Society. Chapter 19, Over-the-Counter Products. In: *Fundamentals of EU Regulatory Affairs Fourth Edition.* Rockville, MD; 2008: 224.
13. Wade AG. "Monitoring safety of over the counter drugs." BMJ, 2002 February 16; 324(7334):424. NLM website. http://www.ncbi.nlm.nih.gov/pmc/articles/PMC1122344/ Accessed 12 March 2013.
14. Layton D, Sinclair HK, Bond CM, Hannaford PC and Shakir SAW. "Pharmacovigilance of over-the-counter products based in community pharmacy: methodological issues from pilot work conducted in Hampshire and Grampian, UK." *Pharmacoepidemiology and Drug Safety,* September 2002; 11(6): 503–513. Wiley Online Library website. http://www3.interscience.wiley.com/journal/98518547/abstract. Accessed 12 March 2013.
15. Regulatory Affairs Professionals Society. Chapter 14, Over-the-Counter (OTC) Drugs. In: *Fundamentals of US Regulatory Affairs Fifth Edition.* Rockville, MD; 2007:134.
16. Regulatory Affairs Professionals Society. Chapter 19, Over-the-Counter Products. In: *Fundamentals of EU Regulatory Affairs Fourth Edition.* Rockville, MD; 2008:218.
17. EMA, *Guideline on changing the classification for the supply of a medicinal product for human use* (January 2006). EC website. ec.europa.eu/health/files/eudralex/vol-2/c/switchguide_160106_en.pdf. Accessed 12 March 2013.
18. Irish Medicines Board Guide to Invented Names of Human Medicines. IMB website. http://www.imb.ie/images/uploaded/documents/AUT-G0022%20Guide%20to%20Invented%20Names%20of%20Human%20Medicines%20v5_clean.pdf. Accessed 12 March 2013.
19. Regulatory Affairs Professionals Society. Chapter 14, Over-the-Counter (OTC) Drugs. In: *Fundamentals of US Regulatory Affairs Fifth Edition.* Rockville, MD; 2007:130.
20. Op cit 14.
21. Regulatory Affairs Professionals Society. Chapter 22 Nonprescription Drugs. In: *Fundamentals of Canadian Regulatory Affairs.* Rockville, MD; 2006:185.
22. Op cit 17.
23. Ibid.
24. TGA. Australian regulation of over-the-counter medicines. TGA website. www.tga.gov.au/industry/otc-basics-regulation.htm. Accessed 12 March 2013.
25. TGA. Australian regulatory guidelines for OTC medicines (ARGOM). TGA website. www.tga.gov.au/industry/otc-argom.htm. Accessed 12 March 2013.
26. TGA. Scheduling of medicines and poisons. TGA website. www.tga.gov.au/industry/scheduling.htm. Accessed 12 March 2013.
27. TGA. Application to amend the Poisons Standard. TGA website. www.tga.gov.au/industry/scheduling-forms-poisons-standard-amend.htm. Accessed 12 March 2013.
28. Central Drugs Standard Control Organization homepage. www.cdsco.nic.in/. Accessed 12 March 2013.
29. SFDA website (English). http://eng.sfda.gov.cn/. Accessed 12 March 2013.

Chapter 15

Pharmaceutical Postmarketing and Compliance

Updated by Jasmina Savic, MSc, RAC

OBJECTIVES

- ❑ Understand postmarketing requirements and commitments
- ❑ Understand the variations/amendments to marketing authorization applications
- ❑ Understand pharmacovigilance requirements

REGULATIONS AND GUIDELINES COVERED IN THIS CHAPTER

ICH & WHO

- ❑ ICH, *Pharmaceutical Quality System Q10*
- ❑ ICH, *Pharmaceutical Development Q8(R2)*
- ❑ ICH, *Quality Risk Management Q9*
- ❑ ICH, *Post-Approval Safety Data Management: Definitions and Standards for Expedited Reporting E2D)*
- ❑ ICH, *Clinical Data Safety Management: Definitions and Standards for Expedited Reporting E2A*
- ❑ ICH, *Clinical Data Safety Management: Periodic Safety Update Reports for Marketed Drugs E2C(R1)*
- ❑ ICH, *Pharmacovigilance Planning E2E*
- ❑ ICH, *Periodic Benefit-Risk Evaluation Report (PBRER) E2C (R2)*

EU

- ❑ Regulation (EC) No 726/2004 of the European Parliament and of the Council of 31 March 2004 laying down Community procedures for the authorisation and supervision of medicinal products for human and veterinary use and establishing a European Medicines Agency
- ❑ Directive 2001/83/EC of the European Parliament and of the Council of 6 November 2001 on the Community code relating to medicinal products for human use, as amended
- ❑ Commission Regulation (EC) No. 1084/2003 of 3 June 2003 concerning the examination of variations to the terms of a marketing authorisation for medicinal products for human use and veterinary medicinal products granted by a competent authority of a Member State
- ❑ Commission Regulation (EC) No. 1085/2003 of 3 June 2003 concerning the examination of variations to the terms of a marketing authorisation for medicinal products for human use and veterinary medicinal products falling within the scope of Council Regulation (EEC) No. 2309/93
- ❑ Commission Regulation (EC) No. 1234/2008 of 24 November 2008 concerning the examination of variations to the terms of marketing authorisations for medicinal products for human use and veterinary medicinal products

- *Guideline on dossier requirements for Type IA and Type IB notifications*, Revision 1 (July 2006)
- Regulation (EU) No 1235/2010 of the European Parliament and of the Council of 15 December 2010 amending, as regards pharmacovigilance of medicinal products for human use, Regulation (EC) No 726/2004 laying down Community procedures for the authorisation and supervision of medicinal products for human and veterinary use and establishing a European Medicines Agency, and Regulation (EC) No 1394/2007 on advanced therapy medicinal products, L 348/1, December 2010
- Directive 2010/84/EU of the European Parliament and of the Council of 15 December 2010 amending, as regards pharmacovigilance, Directive 2001/83/EC on the Community code relating to medicinal products for human use, L 348/74, December 2010
- Commission Implementing Regulation (EU) No. 520/2012 of 19 June 2012 on the performance of pharmacovigilance activities provided for in Regulation (EC) No 726/2004 of the European Parliament and of the Council and Directive 2001/83/EC of the European Parliament and of the Council, L 159/5, June 2012

US

- 21 CFR 314.70 Supplements and other changes to an approved application
- 21 CFR 314.81 Other postmarketing reports
- 21 CFR 314.80 Postmarketing reporting of adverse drug experiences
- *Guidance for Industry: SUPAC-IR: Immediate Release Solid Oral Dosage Forms, Scale-Up and Post-approval Changes: Chemistry, Manufacturing and Controls, In Vitro Dissolution Testing and In Vivo Bioequivalence Documentation*, US Food and Drug Administration, Center for Drug Evaluation and Research (CDER) (November 1995)
- *Guidance for Industry: SUPAC-MR: Modified Release Solid Oral Dosage Forms: Scale-Up and Post-Approval Changes: Chemistry, Manufacturing and Controls, In Vitro Dissolution Testing and In Vivo Bioequivalence Documentation*, CDER (October 1997)
- *Guidance for Industry: SUPAC-SS: Nonsterile Semisolid Dosage Forms; Scale-Up and Post-Approval Changes: Chemistry, Manufacturing and Controls, In Vitro Release Testing and In Vivo Bioequivalence Documentation*, CDER (May 1997)
- *Guidance for Industry: Changes to an Approved (A)NDA*, CDER (April 2004)
- *Food and Drug Administration Amendments Act of 2007, Title IV Pediatric Research Equity Act of 2007*
- *Food and Drug Administration Amendments Act of 2007, Title V Best Pharmaceuticals for Children Act of 2007*
- *Food and Drug Administration Safety and Innovation Act (FDASIA)* of 2012

Canada

- *Guidance for Industry: Changes in Product-Specific Facility Information*, Health Canada, Biologics and Genetic Therapies Directorate (BGTD) (July 2004)
- *Canadian Adverse Drug Reaction Monitoring Program: Guidelines for the Voluntary Reporting of Suspected Adverse Reactions by Health Professionals*
- Guidelines for Reporting Adverse Reactions to Marketed Drugs, *Guidelines for the Canadian Pharmaceutical Industry on Reporting Adverse Reactions to Marketed Drugs*, Therapeutic Products Directorate (August 2009)
- *Guidelines for Reporting Adverse Events Associated with Vaccine Products. Supplementary Guidelines for the Canadian Pharmaceutical Industry*, Laboratory Centre for Disease Control (February 2000)
- *Annual Drug Notification 2008 Guidance*, Therapeutic Products Directorate

Australia

- *Australian guideline for pharmacovigilance responsibilities of sponsors of medicines* (2011)
- *Australian regulatory guidelines for prescription medicines (ARGPM)*, appendices 12 and 13, TGA

Introduction

Marketed pharmaceutical products change over time, and these changes must be managed as they move through successive stages. The changes involved may be minor or major, affecting manufacturing, labeling, quality or other product characteristics that could impact the compliance status of marketed new drugs or biologics. Throughout the postmarket phase, the medicinal product must be manufactured in accordance with the marketing authorization application. Although changes may be handled differently from region to region, in general, most countries enforce reporting requirements for labeling and manufacturing changes and adverse drug reactions (ADRs) for approved products.

Other postapproval issues include maintaining Good Manufacturing Practices (GMPs) and labeling compliance, and adhering to national regulations on pricing, reimbursement, promotion and advertising, among others.[1] Postmarket changes may take the form of variations, which are notified or filed to the authorities immediately and where prior approval is needed, or amendments that are communicated to the authorities on an annual basis.

After a product is marketed, most authorities will reassess the product's risks and benefits to assure that the real-life data confirm the evaluated benefit:risk ratio. In certain regions, this is known as a marketing authorization renewal and is considered an important postmarketing activity.

Under postmarket commitments, marketing authorization holders (MAHs) are required to implement a functioning pharmacovigilance system that is designed to collect and evaluate safety data from all available international sources. This information also is shared with the authorities on a regular basis.

Variations and Changes

Among the drivers of change are innovation, continual improvement, the results of process performance and product quality monitoring, and corrective and preventive action (CAPA).[2] To evaluate, approve and implement these changes properly, companies must have an effective change management system. In most territories, postapproval changes must be recorded and notified to the Competent Authorities. As previously noted, change management is handled differently in the pre- and postsubmission phases, and filing and submission requirements to the Competent Authorities are determined locally and differ significantly from region to region (for more information, refer to the regional information section at the end of this chapter). In all instances, the implemented change management system must ensure continuous improvement is undertaken in a timely and effective manner with minimum risk.

A change management system should be based on sound principles. A good reference is the International Conference on Harmonisation (ICH) guideline, *Pharmaceutical Quality System Q10*,[3] which describes a comprehensive model for an effective pharmaceutical quality system based on International Organization for Standardization (ISO) quality concepts, and includes applicable GMP regulations. This publication complements ICH's *Pharmaceutical Development Q8(R2)*[4] and *Quality Risk Management Q9*.[5] Q10 provides a harmonized model for a pharmaceutical quality system throughout the product lifecycle and is intended to be used with regional GMP requirements.

Pharmaceutical Quality System Elements

Some Q10 elements already may be included in regional GMP regulations; however, the Q10 model's intent is to enhance these elements to promote the lifecycle approach to product quality.

The four basic elements are:

- process performance and product quality monitoring system
- CAPA system
- change management system
- management review of process performance and product quality[6]

Table 15-1. Application of Process Performance and Product Quality Monitoring System Throughout the Product Lifecycle*

Pharmaceutical Development	Technology Transfer	Commercial Manufacturing	Product Discontinuation
Process and product knowledge generated, and process and product monitoring conducted throughout development can be used to establish a control strategy for manufacturing.	Monitoring during scale-up activities can provide a preliminary indication of process performance and successful integration into manufacturing. Knowledge obtained during transfer and scale-up activities can be useful in further developing the control strategy.	A well-defined system for process performance and product quality monitoring should be applied to ensure performance within a state of control and to identify improvement areas.	Once manufacturing ceases, monitoring such as stability testing should continue to completion of the studies. Appropriate action on marketed products should continue to be executed according to regional regulations.

**From ICH Pharmaceutical Quality System Q10*

Table 15-2. Application of CAPA System Throughout the Product Lifecycle*

Pharmaceutical Development	Technology Transfer	Commercial Manufacturing	Product Discontinuation
Product or process variability is explored. CAPA methodology is useful where corrective actions and preventive actions are incorporated into the iterative design and development process.	CAPA can be used as an effective system for feedback, feedforward and continuous improvement.	CAPA should be used and the effectiveness of the actions should be evaluated.	CAPA should continue after the product is discontinued. The impact on product remaining on the market should be considered as well as other products that might be impacted.

**From ICH Pharmaceutical Quality System Q10*

Process Performance and Product Quality Monitoring System

Pharmaceutical companies should plan and implement a risk-based system for monitoring process performance and product quality to ensure a state of control is maintained. The primary aim of continuous monitoring is to provide assurance that the processes and controls will continue to produce a product of desired quality and to identify areas for improvement.[7] Monitoring applies in both the pre- and postmarket phases. **Table 15-1** shows the application of process performance and product quality monitoring throughout the product lifecycle.

Corrective Action and Preventive Action System

One of the MAH's postmarketing obligations is the implementation and maintenance of a complaint handling system. Pharmaceutical companies should have a system for implementing CAPAs resulting from the investigation of complaints, product rejections, nonconformances, recalls, deviations, audits, regulatory inspections and findings and trends from process performance and product quality monitoring among others.[8]

Table 15-2 shows the application of a CAPA system throughout the product lifecycle.

Change Management System

A robust change management system should address, at a minimum, the following:

- Any proposed change(s) should be assessed for risk, based on a quality risk management system. The level of effort and formality of the evaluation should be commensurate with the level of risk.[9]
- Proposed change(s) should be evaluated relative to the marketing authorization, including design space (where established) and/or current product and process changes (ICH Q10).[10] Before implementation, changes should be assessed to determine whether a change to the regulatory filing is required under regional requirements. Although changes in the design phase (ICH Q8[11]) are not considered to be changes from a regulatory filing perspective, all changes should be evaluated by a company's change management system.
- Before implementation, proposed changes should be evaluated by a team of experts who can contribute the appropriate expertise and knowledge from relevant areas (e.g., pharmaceutical development, manufacturing, quality, regulatory and medical) to ensure the change is technically justified. Evaluation criteria should be established for each prospective change.
- Post-implementation follow-up should include an evaluation of the change to confirm that its objectives were achieved with no deleterious impact on product quality.[12]

Table 15-3 shows the application of a change management system throughout the product lifecycle.

Management Review of Process Performance and Product Quality

Process performance and product quality should be managed throughout the product lifecycle by appropriate management review. The management review system should include the results of regulatory inspections and findings, audits and other assessments and commitments made to regulatory authorities. It also should include periodic quality reviews and any follow-up actions from previous reviews.

Table 15-4 shows the application of management review of process performance and product quality throughout the product lifecycle.

Regional GMPs do not explicitly address all product lifecycle stages (e.g., development); ICH Q10 encourages the use of science- and risk-based approaches at each stage of the product lifecycle.

Pharmacovigilance

MAHs must implement a pharmacovigilance system to ensure all information relevant to a medicinal product's balance of benefits and risks is fully and promptly reported to the Competent Authorities. In addition, the MAH generally is required to have a qualified person responsible for pharmacovigilance (QPPV) available at all times.

Periodic safety update reports (PSURs) at defined times—also known as periodic adverse drug experience reports—are required in most regions. Adverse reaction report sources include spontaneous reports from healthcare professionals, data from postauthorization studies and the published literature. Reports should reflect a medicinal product's worldwide safety experience and normally should be made available immediately upon request or at predefined reporting intervals. More-frequent reporting is required in the period immediately following authorization, especially for new active ingredients. After sufficient experience has been gained with the product, reporting timelines can be extended.

ICH's *Postapproval Safety Data Management: Definitions and Standards for Expedited Reporting E2D*[13] provides a standardized procedure for managing postapproval safety data, including expedited reporting to the relevant authority.

As a result of the evolving pharmacovigilance environment, the ICH regions saw the need o enhance the usefulness of the MAH's periodic reports. As mentioned above, the primary objective of the PSUR is to provide a comprehensive picture of approved medicinal products' safety. It was recognized that the assessment of a medicinal product's risk is most meaningful when considered in light of its benefits, therefore ICH published the draft consensus guideline *Periodic Benefit-Risk Evaluation Report (PBRER) E2C (R2).*[14] The proposal is to prepare the PBRER based on an evaluation of new information relevant to the medicinal product that becomes available to the MAH during the reporting interval. A PBRER should be concise and provide sufficient information to assure regulatory authorities that the MAH is adequately monitoring and evaluating the medicinal product's evolving risk profile.[15]

Other relevant guidelines pertaining to postapproval safety data management can be found on the ICH website under the E series, e.g., *Pharmacovigilance Planning E2E*[16] among others.

Sources of Individual Case Safety Reports (ICSRs)

ICSRs can have different sources including: unsolicited sources, solicited sources, information from contractual agreements and regulatory authority sources.[17]

Unsolicited Sources

Spontaneous Reports

A spontaneous report is an unsolicited communication by a healthcare professional or consumer to a company, regulatory authority or other organization (e.g., WHO, regional center, poison control center).[18] The spontaneous report usually describes an adverse drug reaction resulting from a patient taking one or more medicinal products. Spontaneous reports do not include information from organized data collection systems, e.g., clinical trials.

Regulatory authorities require medical confirmation for the purpose of expedited reporting; however, consumer adverse reaction reports should be handled as spontaneous reports even if there is no "medical confirmation."

Literature

MAHs are obliged to regularly screen the worldwide scientific literature by accessing widely used systematic literature reviews or reference databases.[19] The frequency of screening depends on local requirements, but should not exceed every two weeks.

As with actual events, the regulatory reporting time clock starts as soon as the MAH has knowledge that the case meets minimum criteria for reportability.[20]

Internet

Company websites should be regularly screened for potential ADR case reports. Internal websites should, as far as possible, be utilized to facilitate ADR data collection, e.g., by providing ADR reporting forms or by providing appropriate contact details for direct communication.[21]

Table 15-3. Application of Change Management System Throughout the Product Lifecycle*

Pharmaceutical Development	Technology Transfer	Commercial Manufacturing	Product Discontinuation
Change is an inherent part of the development process and should be documented; the formality of the change management process should be consistent with the stage of pharmaceutical development.	The change management system should provide documentation of adjustments made to the process during technology transfer activities.	A formal change management system should be in place for commercial manufacturing. Oversight by the quality unit should provide assurance of appropriate science- and risk-based assessments.	Any changes after product discontinuation should go through an appropriate change management system.

**From ICH Pharmaceutical Quality System Q10*

Table 15-4. Application of Management Review of Process Performance and Product Quality Throughout the Product Lifecycle*

Pharmaceutical Development	Technology Transfer	Commercial Manufacturing	Product Discontinuation
Aspects of management review can be performed to ensure adequacy of product and process design.	Aspects of management review should be performed to ensure the developed product can be manufactured at commercial scale.	Management review should be a structured system and should support continual improvement.	Management review should include such items as product stability and product quality complaints.

**From ICH Pharmaceutical Quality System Q10*

Other Sources

If an MAH becomes aware of a case report from non-medical sources, it should be handled as a spontaneous report (ICH- E2D).

Solicited Sources

Solicited reports are nonspontaneous reports derived from organized data collection systems, e.g., clinical trials, registries, postapproval named patient use programs, other patient support and disease management programs, surveys of patients or healthcare providers, or information-gathering on efficacy or patient compliance[22] (more information on study-related issues can be found in the ICH's *Clinical Data Safety Management: Definitions and Standards for Expedited Reporting E2A*[23]).

Contractual Agreements

Explicit licensing or contractual agreements should specify the processes for exchange of safety information, including timelines and regulatory reporting responsibilities.[24]

Duplicate reporting to the regulatory authority should especially be avoided. It should be clear, however, that the MAH carries the actual reporting responsibility, regardless of whether the method is actual reporting or contractual agreements.

Regulatory Authority Sources

The MAH also is responsible for reporting individual serious unexpected adverse drug reaction reports originating from regulatory authorities in other countries.

Standards for Expedited Reporting

What Should Be Reported

Serious ADRs

All cases of adverse drug reactions that are both serious and unexpected should be subject to expedited reporting. The reporting of serious expected reactions in an expedited manner varies from region to region. Expected or unexpected non-serious adverse reactions normally are not subject to expedited reporting.[25]

Other Observations

Apart from single case reports, any safety information from other observations that could change a product's benefit:risk ratio should be communicated as soon as possible to the regulatory authorities in accordance with local requirements. Except for medicinal products used to treat life-threatening or serious diseases, vaccines and contraceptives, information related to lack of efficacy normally should be reported or discussed in the relevant PSUR. Reports of overdose with no associated adverse outcome should not be reported as adverse reactions. Exact reporting requirements are determined locally.

Minimum Criteria for Reporting

For the purpose of regulatory reporting, the minimum data elements for an ADR case are:

- an identifiable reporter
- an identifiable patient
- an adverse reaction
- a suspect product

MAHs are obligated to make every possible effort to collect any missing data.

Reporting Timeframes

According to ICH E2D, expedited reporting of serious and unexpected ADRs is required as soon as possible, but no later than 15 calendar days after initial receipt of the information by the MAH. The exact reporting timelines for other serious reports vary among countries. In general, the regulatory reporting time clock start date is considered to be when the MAH first receives a case report that fulfills minimum reporting criteria as well as the criteria for expedited reporting.

To this end, companies must ensure that all personnel are adequately trained and that incoming reports are transferred immediately to the relevant department for further processing.

Non-serious ADRs

According to ICH's *Clinical Data Safety Management: Periodic Safety Update Reports for Marketed Drugs E2C(R2)*,[26] expected or unexpected non-serious ADRs do not require expedited reporting but should be included in the PSUR. When submitting PSURs, MAHs are expected to provide summary information together with a critical evaluation of the product's benefit:risk balance in light of new or changing post-authorization information.[27] MAHs are expected to submit one PSUR to cover all of a given drug substance's dosage forms, formulations and indications. However, it may make sense to present separate sections for different dosage forms, indications or populations (e.g., children versus adults).

Urgent Safety Restrictions

Once a medicinal product is granted marketing authorization, safety issues may arise that may have a serious impact on public health. Depending on the nature of the risk and the impact on public health, a range of regulatory actions can be taken.[28]

The decision to trigger this kind of action can be made by the MAH or the authorities. If this kind of situation occurs, the Competent Authority should be contacted immediately.

Changes to the Labels

Another frequent postmarketing change is a revision to the labels. Labeling changes can be the result of new postapproval safety data, new clinical data or new quality data.

It is common for MAHs to prepare their own Company Core Data Sheet (CCDS), which includes product information relating to safety, indications, dosing, pharmacology and other information.[29] A part of the CCDS is the so-called Company Core Safety Information (CCSI), which contains the core safety data about the product that is required to be on the product's label in each country. This safety information is obtained from worldwide case reporting and screening of all product safety information.

The CCDS presents the reference safety information that is included in periodic reports, such as PSURs or Development Update Safety Reports (DSURs).

The CCDS should be updated regularly based on the availability of new information. Once the CCDS is updated, these changes must be implemented globally.

How labeling changes are classified is determined nationally, but in general, most Competent Authorities differentiate safety changes from other changes. Safety changes usually are reviewed more carefully and usually are placed in the higher variation/change category.

It is important to note that local labels can contain more information (that is not contradictory to the CCDS) but must contain the basic CCDS information.

SOPs

All postmarket activities for products manufactured in a GMP environment require relevant standard operating procedures (SOPs). The SOPs must be implemented, i.e., procedures written and signed off and personnel trained. Records must be kept of all staff trained on the procedures. Staff need to be re-trained if SOPs undergo major changes. Postmarket areas for which SOPs are needed include but are not limited to:

- production
- change control and lifecycle management
- labeling and packaging
- pharmacovigilance
- quality complaints and batch recalls
- supply chain and logistics

Inspections

As noted in Chapter 12, inspections form part of the overall drug quality assurance system. The purpose of routine and quality systems inspections is to assess GMP compliance and postmarket compliance.

Inspections can be performed to verify compliance with the principles of GMP, Good Clinical Practice (GCP), Good Laboratory Practice (GLP), verification of compliance with pharmacovigilance obligations and inspections of blood establishments under the Plasma Master File (PMF) certification system. Focus areas may include checking whether products are being manufactured according to the registered details or checking that the label texts comply with the approved texts.

Inspectors may check the availability and status of SOPs, including training records. The handling of variations and change control is a typical area to be targeted during routine inspections. Inspectors also will check whether software in use has been properly validated.

Some typical postmarket compliance issues are listed below:

- changes implemented in the plant before notification of the Competent Authority
- wrong manufacturer address on the label
- label claims not corresponding to the registered details
- software used to manage change not validated
- staff not trained on applicable procedures
- change control system not allowing proper traceability

Legal requirements and enforcement are covered in detail in Chapter 7.

Postapproval Commitments

During the marketing authorization process, the MAH may commit to postapproval activities. The purpose of these obligations is to provide additional information to the Competent Authority on real-time use of the product in a wider population and under uncontrolled circumstances compared to those of clinical trials. Authorities usually are concerned with the local population and, therefore, often require postapproval studies to be conducted locally.

In addition, postapproval commitments usually include providing stability data to support the product's proposed and approved shelf life.

Deadlines are provided for each commitment, and if these commitments cannot be met within this timeframe, the Competent Authority should be notified.

Portfolio Extension

After the product has been registered, companies may start thinking of portfolio extension in terms of possible new strengths, formulations, routes of administration, indications, etc.

These are normal lifecycle activities and require careful planning and a stable business environment. They usually are developed based on the product characteristics and market requirements.

Each country has its own rules about how to address these changes. In some regions or countries, these changes might be treated as completely new registrations and not as variations or changes to existing marketing authorizations.

Pricing and Reimbursement

Market access is a complex phase in product development.

The pricing and reimbursement process is nationally driven since it is tightly related to the national health systems and their power to support innovation. Because today's national health systems are under pressure to provide high quality health protection to their citizens while at the same time saving money, new drugs are critically analyzed for cost-effectiveness. These authorities are usually separated from regulatory authorities and perform their own analyses relying on initial regulatory approvals.

As a result of high demand from the pricing and reimbursement authorities, an increasing number of companies are developing their Phase 3 clinical programs to meet the requirement to provide a "reimbursable package."

Launching a Product

After the product has passed the pricing and reimbursement authorities and the price is set, a company has a certain timeframe in which to launch the product on the market. If the product is not put on the market within the nationally set timeframe, the marketing authorization will be invalidated.

This process is regulated by each country but the principle is similar—if the product is not put on the market within the nationally set timeframe after the marketing authorization is granted (e.g., three years) or if the marketed product becomes unavailable for a period of time equal to the nationally set timeframe (e.g., three years), the marketing authorization will be invalidated. To maintain their marketing authorizations, companies should carefully plan their supply activities.

Pediatric Development

As mentioned in Chapter 4, new legislation has led to new requirements concerning pediatric development. As a result, in the US and EU, each MAH must have a pediatric plan in place when applying for marketing authorization.

The pediatric plan outlines the upcoming clinical development activities for the product in question in the pediatric population. This means that pediatric development will be active during the product's postapproval phase.

Once data from the pediatric program become available, MAHs are requested to introduce the information obtained (both positive and negative) in the labels.

Based on this action and compliance with the agreed pediatric plan and set timelines, MAHs could be entitled to receive the six-month Supplementary Protection Certificate extension that governs the protection of active substances.

Scientific Advice/Protocol Assistance

Scientific advice or protocol assistance can be requested from the authorities before the marketing authorization is granted but also after the product is placed on the market.

Postapproval scientific advice or protocol assistance usually is requested in the following situations:

- development of a new formulation or dosage form
- planning an indication extension
- pediatric development planning
- a new or changed manufacturing process

Scientific advice or protocol assistance also can be requested to discuss any aspect of postapproval commitments made during the authorization process.

Each country has its own process for offering advice.

Parallel Distribution

In some regions (e.g., the EU), there is an established practice of parallel distribution of a registered product.

Parallel distribution involves the transfer of genuine, original branded products, authorized in accordance with regional legislation, marketed in one country (the source country) at a lower price to another country (the country of destination) by a parallel distributor, and placed on the market in competition with a therapeutically identical product already marketed there at a higher price by or under license from the owner of the brand's intellectual property (the directly distributed product).

The process allows third-party payers and consumers to realize savings that are both:

- direct (from the lower cost of parallel-distributed products) and
- indirect (from price competition entered into with the parallel product by the directly distributed version)[30]

Withdrawal of Approved Authorization

In most regions, it is possible to withdraw an approved authorization. This can be done voluntarily by the MAH or it can be done involuntarily, based on a recommendation by the Competent Authority.

If there are no product safety or quality issues, the Competent Authority will withdraw the approved authorization per the MAH's request. If the Competent Authority recognizes there are some serious problems associated with the product, it will ask the MAH to remove the product from the market.

Voluntary withdrawals are performed in accordance with national procedures and are similar in all countries. Withdrawal requests are sent to the Competent Authority with proper justification for the withdrawal. Specific timelines may differ between countries.

Change in Product Ownership

Frequently, ownership of the product changes in the postmarketing phase as a result of business mergers or acquisitions where the previous MAH is taken over by another company and the original MAH no longer exists as a separate legal entity. In addition, a change in ownership can be the result of a simple portfolio sale to another company.

Each Competent Authority sets its own rules on how this change should be notified.

Regulatory Variation Information in Selected Markets

EU

In the EU, Commission Regulations (EC) No. 1084/2003[31] and (EC) No. 1085/2003[32] formed the legal basis of variations and postregistration changes for products licensed via the Mutual Recognition Procedure or Decentralised Procedure and Centralised Procedure, respectively. These regulations were replaced by Regulation (EC) No. 1234/2008[33] of 24 November 2008, which was published in the *Official Journal of the European Union* on 12 December 2008 and entered into force on the 20th day following its publication. This regulation was binding in its entirety and directly applicable in all Member States from 1 January 2010.

The new regulation's main objective was to establish a simpler, clearer and more flexible legal framework, while keeping the same level of health protection.[34] The classification of variations remains the same; however, under the new legislation, the variations to be assessed are reduced to those that impact product quality, safety and/or efficacy. Certain minor variations that would have fallen under the previous notification system now can be bundled and notified annually.

Types of variations:

- Type IA Variation—any well-defined minor change, to be notified within 12 months following implementation
- Type IA_{IN} Variation—to be notified immediately after the change has been implemented
- Type IB Variation—minor change; this procedure is also considered a notification, but a Competent Authority assessment is made within 30 days; Type IB needs to be approved prior to implementation
- Type II Variation—any major change to the MAH's proposed documentation; a Type II variation is a product change that does not meet Type IA and Type IB classifications or criteria, but is not so extensive as to require a line extension or new application procedure; Type II needs to be approved prior to implementation
- Line Extension Application—a major change that requires a full assessment in accordance with Article 17 of Directive 2001/83/EEC, as amended (i.e., 210 days); categories are listed in Annex II of regulations 1084/2003 and 1085/2003

Annex II of Regulation (EC) No. 1234/2008 lists variations that should be classified as Type IA or Type II.[35] Variations that are neither minor variations of Type IA nor major variations of Type II nor an extension are classified as Type IB variations by default. In some cases, the Competent Authorities may classify such changes as Type II variations during validation if there is a significant impact on the medicinal product's quality, safety or efficacy.

More-detailed guidance on the usual variation categories and their classifications is provided in the *Communication from the Commission—Guideline on the details of the various categories of variations to the terms of marketing authorisations for medicinal products for human use and veterinary medicinal products.*[36]

If the proposed change cannot be found in the abovementioned document, additional guidance is provided in the *CMDh recommendation for classification of unforeseen variations according to Article 5 of Commission Regulation (EC) No. 1234/2008.*[37] This document is updated continually to reflect newly classified variations that were not previously in the classification guideline. If the change cannot be found in either document, the MAH should contact the Reference Member State to discuss the classification or to initiate an official request for classification.

A separate application is required for each Type II variation; consequential changes can be bundled with an

Table 15-5. Differences Between Old and New EU Variations Regulations

Type of Variation	Type of Filing	Regulations (EC) No1084/2003 and (EC) No 1085/2003	Regulation (EC) No 1234/2008
IA	Notification	Notification immediately to RMS and CMS.* Immediate implementation possible after waiting 14 days.	To be submitted to RMS and CMS within 12 months following implementation of the variation, or to be submitted immediately after the implementation of the variation in the case of minor variations requiring immediate notification for the continuous supervision of the medicinal product concerned.**
IA_{IN}	Notification	N/A	Immediate notification to RMS and CMS after the changes have been implemented.***
IB	Notification (30-day assessment)	Notification immediately to RMS and CMS.* Immediate implementation possible after waiting 30 days.	If the RMS has not sent the holder an unfavorable opinion within 30 days from the application date, the notification shall be deemed accepted by all relevant authorities (RMS and CMS).
II	Approval necessary	Regulatory filing immediately to RMS and CMS.* Implementation possible after approval—60-day assessment (+ clock stop) plus 30-day mutual recognition foreseen. Extension of the assessment period can apply.	Regulatory filing immediately to RMS and CMS.* Implementation possible after approval—60-day assessment (+ clock stop) plus 30-day mutual recognition foreseen. Extension of the assessment period can apply.
Line Extension	New application	New application	New application

**RMS = Reference Member State, CMS = Concerned Member State*
*** COMMISSION REGULATION (EC) No 1234/2008, article 8(1) second sub-paragraph.*
****Public Consultation Paper for the preparation of guidelines on the details of the various categories of variations, Article 4(1)(a) of Commission Regulation (EC) No. 1234/2008 of 24 November 2008 concerning the examination of variations to the terms of marketing authorizations for medicinal products for human use and veterinary medicinal products*

explanation of the relationship between them. Where a variation requires consequential revision of the Summary of Product Characteristics (SmPC), labeling or package leaflet or insert, this is considered part of the variation.

Table 15-5 highlights some of the differences between the old and new regulations.

In the EU, pharmacovigilance for medicinal products for human use authorized through the National, Mutual Recognition or Centralised Procedure is governed by Directive 2001/83/EC, as amended,[38] and Regulation (EC) No. 726/2004.[39] These are complemented by a series of guidelines published in *Eudralex, Volume 9 Pharmacovigilance*, based on ICH requirements.

In 2012, the new pharmacovigilance legislation came into force[40,41] with the introduction of the Good Pharmacovigilance Practice guidelines (GVP) released by the European Medicines Agency (EMA).

GVPs are a set of measures to facilitate the performance of pharmacovigilance in the EU. The GVP guideline is divided into 16 modules, each covering one major pharmacovigilance process. Each module was developed by a team consisting of experts from EMA and EU Member States. The GVP modules refer to the implementing regulation, a legally binding act published by the European Commission in June 2012.[42]

The main focuses of the new legislation are:

- proactive and proportionate risk management
- higher quality safety data
- stronger link between safety assessments and regulatory action
- strengthened transparency, communication and patient involvement
- clear tasks and responsibilities for all parties (MAHs, Competent Authorities, EMA)
- improved EU decision-making procedures (harmonized decisions and efficient use of resources)
- establishment of a new scientific committee at EMA: the Pharmacovigilance Risk Assessment Committee (PRAC)[43]

While the new pharmacovigilance legislation became applicable in July 2012, some of its new features will be subject to a phased implementation (the 16 modules mentioned above were developed over a period of years (with some finalized in 2013). To facilitate the transition, the Commission has published a Question and Answer document,[44] which outlines the main transitional provisions until the new legislation is fully operative.

Although the process itself is not considered a typical postmarketing activity, pediatric development requirements

Table 15-6. FDA Postapproval Change Reporting

Change Category	Reporting Category
Major change	Must be submitted as a Prior Approval Supplement (PAS). Approval is required before implementation.
Moderate change	Changes Being Effected in 30 days (CBE-30). Submission of a supplement to FDA is required at least 30 days before distributing the product manufactured using the implemented change.
	Changes Being Effected (CBE) supplement. This change can be implemented immediately after notification.
Minor change	Reportable in Annual Report.

must continue to be met after the product has received marketing authorization. Based on the new EU *Paediatric Regulation*,[45] a Pediatric Investigation Plan (PIP) must be submitted with the marketing authorization. The PIP can contain waivers for certain pediatric subpopulations or deferrals for certain trials if the Pediatric Committee (PDCO) and MAH agree that adult data should be obtained first to ensure the product is safe before testing in children. The EU *Pediatric Regulation* drastically changed the regulatory landscape with this additional product development requirement.

More information on the pediatric development and requirements in the EU can be found at www.ema.europa.eu/ema/index.jsp?curl=pages/regulation/general/general_content_000023.jsp.

US

Under the *Federal Food, Drug, and Cosmetic Act* (*FD&C Act*), Section 506A, changes to an approved New Drug Application (NDA) or Abbreviated New Drug Application (ANDA) that have a potential effect on the product's safety and quality are required to be reported to the US Food and Drug Administration (FDA).[46] These may include changes to the approved drug substance or drug product chemistry, manufacturing and control, product labeling revisions, the addition of new indications, etc. Changes are classified as major, moderate or minor (§314.70)[47] depending on their degree or potential to adversely affect the drug product's identity, strength, purity or potency.

FDA has published several guidance documents to help define changes to an approved application and clarify documentation and submission requirements. *Guidance for Industry: Changes to an Approved NDA or ANDA*, was first published in November 1999 and revised in April 2004. It includes recommendations and requirements pertaining to postapproval changes.

Among other guidance documents addressing postapproval change are the "Scale-Up and Post-Approval Changes" (SUPAC) guidance documents:

- SUPAC-IR[48] guidance for immediate-release, solid oral dosage forms
- SUPAC-MR[49] guidance for modified-release, solid oral dosage forms
- SUPAC-SS[50] guidance for nonsterile, semisolid dosage forms (see **Table 15-6**)

More information can be found on FDA's Center for Drug Evaluation and Research (CDER) guidance website at www.fda.gov/Drugs/GuidanceComplianceRegulatoryInformation/Guidances/default.htm under the Chemistry, Manufacturing and Controls section.

Other Postapproval Requirements (21 CFR §314.80 and §314.81)

Regulations governing adverse drug experience reporting (21 CFR §314.80[51]) require the holder of an approved NDA to review all adverse drug experience information obtained from any source, foreign or domestic, including information derived from commercial marketing experience, postmarket clinical investigations, postmarket epidemiological or surveillance studies, and reports in the scientific literature and unpublished scientific papers.[52] The regulations specifically require the manufacturer to develop written SOPs for postmarket adverse drug experience surveillance information receipt, evaluation and reporting to FDA.

Postmarket responsibilities include postmarket 15-day "Alert reports" and "Periodic adverse drug experience reports" (at quarterly intervals for three years from the application's approval date, and annually thereafter). In addition, the holder of an approved NDA is required to file a "Field Alert Report" (§314.81(b)(1)) within three working days on:

- incidents that cause the drug product or its labeling to be mistaken for or applied to another article
- any bacteriological contamination, or significant chemical, physical or other change or deterioration in the distributed drug product, or any failure of one or more distributed drug product batches to meet the specifications the application established for it

Manufacturers, user facilities and distributors use MedWatch Form 3500A for mandatory reporting of both adverse events and problems with human drugs and other

FDA-regulated products. The MedWatch website is www.fda.gov/medwatch/index.html.

The holder of an approved NDA also is required to submit an Annual Report (§314.81(b)(2)) within 60 days of the approval's anniversary date. The reporting period is defined as one full year from the anniversary date of the preceding year.

As in the EU, the *Pediatric Research Equity Act (PREA)* of 2007 (Title IV of *Food and Drug Administration Amendments Act* of 2007)[53] and the *Best Pharmaceuticals for Children Act (BPCA)* of 2007[54] (Title V of *Food and Drug Administration Amendments Act* of 2007) require the sponsor to submit assessments related to the use of the product in all pediatric subpopulations at the time of submission for marketing authorization or earlier.

These acts have been made permanent (and are no longer subject to review every five years) with the newly signed *Food and Drug Administration Safety and Innovation Act* (*FDASIA*).[55] More information on pediatric development requirements in the US can be found at www.fda.gov/ScienceResearch/SpecialTopics/PediatricTherapeuticsResearch/default.htm.

Canada

In Canada, new drugs and biologics are assigned a drug identification number (DIN). MAHs must submit an annual DIN notification to Health Canada before October of each year to confirm that all information previously supplied is still correct and current. If changes occur, these may have to be reported, depending on the level of risk involved.

Types of Changes

- Level 1 changes—high-risk changes with the potential to affect a product's safety and effectiveness. In such a case, a supplemental New Drug Submission (sNDS) must be filed and a Notice of Compliance (NOC) issued before the change is implemented.
- Level 2 changes—changes that pose less risk than Level 1 changes. A notifiable change (NC) or notice of intent to change should be filed before implementation.
- Level 3 changes—less-risky changes that do not need prior approval before implementation. These types of changes are filed annually before October in the annual DIN update.
- Level 4 changes—changes that pose the least risk and can be made without notification.

FDA has published a series of guidance documents intended to help manufacturers manage postapproval manufacturing changes.[56] These include:

- Scale-up and Postapproval Changes (SUPAC)
- Postapproval Changes—Analytical Testing Laboratory Sites (PAC-ATLS)
- Bulk Actives Postapproval Changes (BACPAC)

These are in line with the risk-based approach adopted by Health Canada and can be used as guides in the change control decision-making process.

Specific product-related facility change criteria apply to approved biologics.[57] An sNDS, NC, notice of change or record of change is required for facility changes that have substantial, moderate, minimal and no potential, respectively, to adversely affect a product's safety, purity, potency or effectiveness. As with other product types, only the sNDS and NC require prior approval before the change can be implemented for biologics.

Since 1996, Canada has attempted to harmonize ADR definitions pertaining to pharmacovigilance reporting with those of the World Health Organization, Council for International Organizations of Medical Sciences, ICH and FDA.[58]

In Canada, ADR reporting can be either voluntary or mandatory. Voluntary reports are collected by regional ADR centers in five provinces across Canada, as well as by Health Canada's national office in Ottawa. Voluntary reports of suspected ADRs are submitted by healthcare professionals or consumers. Healthcare professionals and consumers also may report an ADR to a manufacturer.

Mandatory ADR reporting is statutorily imposed on manufacturers. The law stipulates that manufacturers must send a report to the appropriate Health Canada directorate on any serious ADR (including a literature report) that has occurred in Canada, or any serious unexpected ADR (including literature reports) that has occurred outside Canada, within 15 calendar days of receiving the information. Annual reporting and critical analysis are also required. Special measures are in place for vaccine-associated adverse events.

Australia

Appendices 12 and 13 of the *Australian Regulatory Guidelines for Prescription Medicines (ARGPM)* address how changes to the quality information of registered medicines and self-assessable changes for biological products should be handled.[59]

Changes to the quality information of registered products are classified as:

- changes that only require notification to the Therapeutic Goods Administration (TGA) on implementation or no notification at all
- changes that are self-assessable by the sponsor and do not require approval before implementation
- changes that require approval before implementation

Table 15-7. Summary of Australian Guidelines on Drug Sponsor Reporting of Adverse Drug Reactions

Drug status	Format	Timeframe
REGISTERED (PRESCRIPTION) DRUGS		
Spontaneous report		
Serious	Blue card	< 15 days
Other	Line listing	in PSUR
Company-sponsored postmarketing surveillance study		
Serious	Blue card	< 15 days
Other	Tabulation	At end of study
REGISTERED (OTC) OR LISTED DRUGS		
Spontaneous report		
Serious/ unexpected	Blue card	< 72 hours
Other	Blue card	Regularly

Pharmacovigilance reporting requirements are similar to those in the EU. An MAH must have an appropriate pharmacovigilance system in place to ensure responsibility and liability for its products on the market and to ensure that appropriate action can be taken, when necessary.[60]

As in the EU, a sponsor in Australia should have a qualified person responsible for pharmacovigilance permanently and continuously at its disposal. This person must be experienced in all aspects of pharmacovigilance and, if not medically qualified, should report to or have access to a medically qualified person (see **Table 15-7**).

Conclusion

In the pharmaceutical industry, the postmarketing phase is the most resource-intensive phase of the entire product lifecycle. Postmarketing activities include managing the product lifecycle from conception, through design and manufacture, to service/use and disposal. Following a product's commercialization, a company must employ an appropriate change control system to ensure that information on actual manufacturing and other processes is reflected in the product's documentation. In addition, MAHs must ensure that marketed products are in line with scientific and technical advances.

Change management is handled differently from region to region. However, in general, changes that impact product quality, safety and/or efficacy should be tracked and appropriately communicated to the Competent Authorities. Each Competent Authority might treat the same change differently, and this should be known for planning purposes to avoid possible stock-out or noncompliance.

MAHs are required to have a functioning pharmacovigilance system to ensure all information relevant to a medicinal product's balance of benefits and risks is fully and promptly reported to the Competent Authorities. To ensure compliance with postmarket obligations, MAHs and manufacturing plants are periodically inspected by the authorities. As noted in Chapter 12, GMP noncompliance is one of the conditions under which a Competent Authority may suspend or revoke a marketing authorization. Likewise, if local authorities believe noncompliance with one of the postmarket obligations poses a risk to public health, they could require a company to recall the product from the market.

References

1. Regulatory Affairs Professionals Society. Chapter 16: Postmarketing and other activities, *Fundamentals of Canadian Regulatory Affairs, Third Edition.* 2011:111-118.
2. ICH, *Pharmaceutical Quality System Q10* (Current Step 4 version, June 2008). ICH website. www.ich.org/fileadmin/Public_Web_Site/ICH_Products/Guidelines/Quality/Q10/Step4/Q10_Guideline.pdf. Accessed 15 March 2013.
3. Ibid.
4. ICH, *Pharmaceutical Development Q8(R1)* (Current Step 4 version, November 2008). ICH website. www.ich.org/fileadmin/Public_Web_Site/ICH_Products/Guidelines/Quality/Q8_R1/Step4/Q8_R2_Guideline.pdf. Accessed 15 March 2013.
5. ICH, *Quality Risk Management Q9* (Current Step 4 version, November 2005). ICH website. www.ich.org/fileadmin/Public_Web_Site/ICH_Products/Guidelines/Quality/Q9/Step4/Q9_Guideline.pdf. Accessed 15 March 2013.
6. Op cit. 4.
7. Op cit. 2.
8. Ibid.
9. Ibid.
10. Ibid.
11. Op cit. 4.
12. Op cit. 2.
13. ICH, *Post-Approval Safety Data Management: Definitions and Standards for Expedited Reporting E2D* (Current Step 4 version, November 2003). ICH website. www.ich.org/fileadmin/Public_Web_Site/ICH_Products/Guidelines/Efficacy/E2D/Step4/E2D_Guideline.pdf. Accessed 15 March 2013.
14. ICH, *Periodic Benefit-Risk Evaluation Report (PBRER) E2C(R2)* (Current Step 2 version, February 2012). ICH website. www.ich.org/fileadmin/Public_Web_Site/ICH_Products/Guidelines/Efficacy/E2C/E2C_R2_Step4.pdf. Accessed 15 March 2013.
15. Ibid.
16. ICH, *Pharmacovigilance Planning E2E* (Current Step 4 Version, November 2004). ICH website. www.ich.org/fileadmin/Public_Web_Site/ICH_Products/Guidelines/Efficacy/E2E/Step4/E2E_Guideline.pdf. Accessed 15 March 2013.
17. Op cit. 13.
18. Ibid.
19. Ibid.
20. Ibid.
21. Ibid.
22. Ibid.
23. ICH, *Clinical Safety Data Management: Definitions and Standards for Expedited Reporting E2A* (Current Step 4 version, October 1994). ICH website. www.ich.org/fileadmin/Public_Web_Site/ICH_Products/Guidelines/Efficacy/E2A/Step4/E2A_Guideline.pdf. Accessed 15 March 2013.
24. Op cit. 13.
25. Ibid.
26. ICH, *Clinical Data Safety Management: Periodic Safety Update Reports for Marketed Drugs E2C(R2)* (Current Step 4 version, December 2012). ICH website. www.ich.org/fileadmin/Public_Web_Site/

ICH_Products/Guidelines/Efficacy/E2C/E2C_R2_Step4.pdf. Accessed 26 March 2013.

27. *Eudralex, The Rules Governing Medicinal Products in the European Union, Volume 9, Pharmacovigilance: Medicinal Products for Human Use*, 2001. Available at http://ec.europa.eu/health/files/eudralex/vol-9/pdf/vol9a_09-2008_en.pdf.
28. European Medicines Agency, Standard Operation Procedure for Urgent Safety Restrictions (USRs), 2008. EMA website. www.ema.europa.eu/docs/en_GB/document_library/Standard_Operating_Procedure_-_SOP/2009/09/WC500002956.pdf. Accessed 15 March 2013.
29. Op cit 26.
30. European Association of Euro-Pharmaceutical Companies (EAEPC). *Good Parallel Distribution Practice Guidelines for Medicinal Products*, September 2005. EAEPC website. www.eaepc.org/admin/files/eaepc_good_parallel_distribution_practice_guidelines.pdf.
31. Commission Regulation (EC) No. 1084/2003 concerning the examination of variations to the terms of a marketing authorisation for medicinal products for human use and veterinary medicinal products granted by a competent authority of a Member State. EC website. http://ec.europa.eu/health/files/eudralex/vol-1/reg_2003_1084/reg_2003_1084_en.pdf. Accessed 15 March 2013.
32. Commission Regulation (EC) No. 1085/2003 concerning the examination of variations to the terms of a marketing authorisation for medicinal products for human use and veterinary medicinal products falling within the scope of Council Regulation (EEC) No. 2309/93. EC website. http://ec.europa.eu/health/files/eudralex/vol-1/reg_2003_1085/reg_2003_1085_en.pdf. Accessed 15 March 2013.
33. Commission Regulation (EC) No. 1234/2008 of 24 November 2008 concerning the examination of variations to the terms of marketing authorisations for medicinal products for human use and veterinary medicinal products. EUR-Lex website. http://eur-lex.europa.eu/LexUriServ/LexUriServ.do?uri=OJ:L:2008:334:0007:0024:en:PDF. Accessed 15 March 2013.
34. Michor S. "Product Lifecycle Management: A European Perspective," *Regulatory Focus*. 2008; 13(8):18–22, 27.
35. Op cit. 21.
36. Communication from the Commission—Guideline on the details of the various categories of variations to the terms of marketing authorisations for medicinal products for human use and veterinary medicinal products, February 2010. EC website. http://ec.europa.eu/health/files/betterreg/pharmacos/classification_guideline_adopted.pdf. Accessed 15 March 2013.
37. Heads of Medicines Agencies. CMDh recommendation for classification of unforeseen variations according to Article 5 of Commission Regulation (EC) No. 1234/2008. Available on HMA website, http://www.hma.eu/293.html. Accessed 15 March 2013.
38. Directive 2001/83/EC of the European Parliament and of the Council of 6 November 2001 on the Community code relating to medicinal products for human use, as amended. EMA website. www.emea.europa.eu/docs/en_GB/document_library/Regulatory_and_procedural_guideline/2009/10/WC500004481.pdf. Accessed 15 March 2013.
39. Regulation (EC) No 726/2004 of the European Parliament and of the Council of 31 March 2004 laying down Community procedures for the authorisation and supervision of medicinal products for human and veterinary use and establishing a European Medicines Agency. EUR-Lex website. http://eur-lex.europa.eu/LexUriServ/LexUriServ.do?uri=OJ:L:2004:136:0001:0033:en:PDF. Accessed 15 March 2013.
40. Regulation (EU) No 1235/2010 of the European Parliament and of the Council of 15 December 2010 amending, as regards pharmacovigilance of medicinal products for human use, Regulation (EC) No 726/2004 laying down Community procedures for the authorisation and supervision of medicinal products for human and veterinary use and establishing a European Medicines Agency, and Regulation (EC) No 1394/2007 on advanced therapy medicinal products. EUR-Lex website. http://eur-lex.europa.eu/LexUriServ/LexUriServ.do?uri=OJ:L:2010:348:0001:0016:EN:PDF. Accessed 15 March 2013.
41. Directive 2010/84/EU of the European Parliament and of the Council of 15 December 2010 amending, as regards pharmacovigilance, Directive 2001/83/EC on the Community code relating to medicinal products for human use. EUR-Lex website. http://eur-lex.europa.eu/LexUriServ/LexUriServ.do?uri=OJ:L:2010:348:0074:0099:EN:PDF. Accessed 15 March 2013.
42. Commission Implementing Regulation (EU) No. 520/2012 of 19 June 2012 on the performance of pharmacovigilance activities provided for in Regulation (EC) No 726/2004 of the European Parliament and of the Council and Directive 2001/83/EC of the European Parliament and of the Council. EUR-Lex website, http://eur-lex.europa.eu/LexUriServ/LexUriServ.do?uri=OJ:L:2012:159:0005:0025:EN:PDF. Accessed 15 March 2013.
43. European Commission, The EU pharmacovigilance system. EC website. http://ec.europa.eu/health/human-use/pharmacovigilance/index_en.htm. Accessed 15 March 2013.
44. European Commission, Question and Answers on transitional agreements concerning the entering into force of the new pharmacovigilance rules provided by Directive 2010/84/EU amending Directive 2001/83/EC and Regulation (EU) No 1235/2010 amending Regulation (EC) 726/2004, version 2.0, July 2012. EC website. http://ec.europa.eu/health/files/pharmacovigilance/2012-07_qa_transitional_en.pdf. Accessed 15 March 2013.
45. Regulation (EC) No 1901/2006 of the European Parliament and of the Council od 12December 2006 on medicinal products for paediatric use and amending Regulation (EEC) No 1768/92, Directive 2001/20/EC, Directive 2001/83/EC and Regulation (EC) No 726/2004. EUR-Lex website. http://eur-lex.europa.eu/LexUriServ/LexUriServ.do?uri=OJ:L:2006:378:0001:0019:en:PDF. Accessed 15 March 2013.
46. Regulatory Affairs Professionals Society. Chapter 10, Postapproval Prescription Drug Submissions and Compliance. *Fundamentals of US Regulatory Affairs, Seventh Edition*. 2011: 119–132.
47. 21 CFR 314.70: Supplements and other changes to an approved application. FDA website. www.accessdata.fda.gov/scripts/cdrh/cfdocs/cfcfr/CFRSearch.cfm?fr=314.70. Accessed 15 March 2013.
48. FDA. *Guidance for Industry—SUPAC-IR: Immediate Release Solid Oral Dosage Forms, Scale-Up and Post-approval Changes: Chemistry, Manufacturing and Controls, In Vitro Dissolution Testing and In Vivo Bioequivalence Documentation*, Center for Drug Evaluation and Research (CDER), November 1995. FDA website. www.fda.gov/downloads/Drugs/Guidances/UCM070636.pdf. Accessed 15 March 2013.
49. FDA. *Guidance for Industry—SUPAC-MR: Modified Release Solid Oral Dosage Forms: Scale-Up and Post-Approval Changes: Chemistry, Manufacturing and Controls, In Vitro Dissolution Testing and In Vivo Bioequivalence Documentation*, CDER, October 1997. FDA website. www.fda.gov/downloads/Drugs/Guidances/UCM070640.pdf. Accessed 15 March 2013.
50. FDA. *Guidance for Industry: SUPAC-SS—Nonsterile Semisolid Dosage Forms; Scale-Up and Post-Approval Changes: Chemistry, Manufacturing and Controls, In Vitro Release Testing and In Vivo Bioequivalence Documentation*, CDER, May 1997. FDA website. www.fda.gov/downloads/Drugs/Guidances/UCM070930.pdf. Accessed 15 March 2013.
51. 21 CFR 314.80: Postmarketing reporting of adverse drug experiences. FDA website. www.accessdata.fda.gov/scripts/cdrh/cfdocs/cfcfr/cfrsearch.cfm?fr=314.80. Accessed 15 March 2013.
52. Op cit 39.
53. FDA, *Food and Drug Administration Amendments Act* of 2007, *Title IV Pediatric Research Equity Act* of 2007.
54. FDA, *Food and Drug Administration Amendments Act* of 2007, *Title V Best Pharmaceuticals for Children Act* of 2007.
55. *Food and Drug Administration Safety and Innovation Act* (FDASIA), 2012

56. Op cit. 1.
57. *Guidance for Industry: Changes in Product-Specific Facility Information,* Biologics and Genetic Therapies Directorate (BGTD), Health Canada, 2004.
58. Op cit. 1.
59. *Australian regulatory guidelines for prescription medicines* (ARGPM), appendices 12 and 13. TGA website. www.tga.gov.au/industry/pm-argpm.htm. Accessed 15 March 2013.
60. *Australian guideline for pharmacovigilance responsibilities of sponsors of medicines* (2013). TGA website. www.tga.gov.au/safety/australian-pharmacovigilance-sponsors-00.htm. Accessed 15 March 2013.

Chapter 16

Medical Device Premarket Requirements

Updated by Sharad Mi. Shukla, MSc, RAC (US, EU) and Rajaram Balasubramanian, PGDOM, RAC (US, EU)

OBJECTIVES

- ❑ Gain insight into regulatory premarket requirements for medical devices
- ❑ Understand the *Essential Principles of Safety & Performance of Medical Devices*
- ❑ Understand the *Principles of Conformity Assessment for Medical Devices*
- ❑ Learn *Principles of Medical Devices Classification*
- ❑ Understand the role of standards in the assessment of medical devices

REGULATIONS AND GUIDELINES COVERED IN THIS CHAPTER

IMDRF

- ❑ GHTF/SG1/N071:2012 (revision of GHTF/SG1/N29:2005) *Definition of the Terms 'Medical Device' and 'In Vitro Diagnostic (IVD) Medical Device'*
- ❑ GHTF/SG1/N055:2009 *Definitions of the Terms Manufacturer, Authorised Representative, Distributor and Importer*
- ❑ GHTF/SG1/N41R9:2005 *Essential Principles of Safety and Performance of Medical Devices*
- ❑ GHTF/SG1/N70:2011 *Label and Instructions for Use for Medical Devices*
- ❑ GHTF/SG1/N40:2006 *Principles of Conformity Assessment for Medical Devices*
- ❑ GHTF/SG1/N15:2006 *Principles of Medical Devices Classification*
- ❑ GHTF/SG1/N011:2008 *Summary Technical Documentation for Demonstrating Conformity to the Essential Principles of Safety and Performance of Medical Devices (STED)*
- ❑ GHTF/SG1/N044:2008 *Role of Standards in the Assessment of Medical Devices*

ISO

- ❑ ISO/TR 16142:2004 *Medical Devices–Guidance on the Selection of Standards in Support of the Recognized Essential Principles of Safety and Performance of Medical*

Introduction

Premarket regulatory approval is a process of scientific and regulatory review to evaluate the safety and effectiveness of medical devices, performed by regulatory authorities and Conformity Assessment Bodies (CABs). The way medical devices are regulated at the national level may vary from jurisdiction to jurisdiction.

The Global Harmonization Task Force (GHTF) was conceived in 1992 in an effort to achieve greater uniformity between national medical device regulatory systems. In 2012, the International Medical Device Regulators Forum (IMDRF) succeeded GHTF. It will continue GHTF's goals: enhancing patient safety and increasing access to safe, effective and clinically beneficial medical technologies around the world. GHTF's guidance documents now are available on the IMDRF website.

Definition of Medical Device

GHTF published a document intended to provide harmonized definitions of the terms "medical device" and "in vitro diagnostic (IVD) medical device."[1]

"'Medical device' means any instrument, apparatus, implement, machine, appliance, implant, reagent for in vitro use, software, material or other similar or related article, intended by the manufacturer to be used, alone or in combination, for human beings, for one or more of the specific medical purpose(s) of:

- diagnosis, prevention, monitoring, treatment or alleviation of disease,
- diagnosis, monitoring, treatment, alleviation of or compensation for an injury,
- investigation, replacement, modification, or support of the anatomy or of a physiological process,
- supporting or sustaining life,
- control of conception,
- disinfection of medical devices,
- providing information by means of in vitro examination of specimens derived from the human body; and does not achieve its primary intended action by pharmacological, immunological or metabolic means, in or on the human body, but which may be assisted in its intended function by such means."

In general, accessories are considered to be medical devices in their own right. GHTF also has provided insight into the definition of accessories:

> "Accessory to a medical device: means an article intended specifically by its manufacturer to be used together with a particular medical device to enable or assist that device to be used in accordance with its intended use."

Essential Principles of Safety & Performance of Medical Devices

GHTF published *Essential Principles of Safety & Performance of Medical Devices*, to assist in harmonization.[2] This document helps manufacturers design and manufacture a device and demonstrate its suitability for its intended use while reducing costs by eliminating differences between jurisdictions.

The document is based on six general safety and performance requirements that apply to all medical devices.

1. Medical devices should be designed and manufactured in such a way that, when used under the conditions and for the purposes intended and, taking into account the technical knowledge, experience, education or training of intended users, they will not compromise the clinical condition or the safety of patients, of users or, where applicable, other persons. This should be considered in the context of the risk:benefit ratio.
2. The solutions adopted by the manufacturer for the design and manufacture of the devices should conform to the most current safety principles and should address the issue of residual risk and risk reduction. The manufacturer is obliged to:
   - identify known or foreseeable hazards and estimate the associated risks arising from intended use or misuse
   - eliminate risks as much as possible
   - reduce remaining risks as far as is reasonably practicable
   - inform users of any residual risks
3. Devices should achieve the performance intended by the manufacturer.
4. Device characteristics and performance should not be adversely affected to such a degree that the health or safety of the patient or the user is compromised during the device's lifetime, under normal conditions of use.
5. The devices should be designed, manufactured and packed in such a way that their characteristics and performances are not affected under transport and storage conditions.
6. The benefits must be determined to outweigh any undesirable side effects for the performance intended.[3]

Design and Manufacturing Requirements

Chemical, Physical and Biological Properties

The choice of materials used in the manufacture of medical devices is very important, and special attention should be paid to toxicity and flammability. In addition, compatibility of the materials used with biological tissues, cells, body fluids and specimens is of significance. Devices should be designed, manufactured and packed in such a way as to minimize the risk posed by contaminants and residues.

Special attention needs to be paid to devices that incorporate, as an integral part, a substance which, if used separately, may be considered to be a medicinal product or drug as defined in the relevant legislation.

Infection and Microbial Contamination

Devices and manufacturing processes should be designed to eliminate or reduce risk of infection to patients, users and,

Table 16-1. Class A Device

	Conformity Assessment Element	Manufacturer Responsibility	Regulatory Authority/ Conformity Assessment Body Responsibility
Conformity assessment of the QMS	QMS	Establish and maintain a full QMS **or** a QMS without design and development controls	Regulatory audit normally not required except in special cases, e.g., assurance of sterility and of measuring function(s)
	Postmarket surveillance	Establish and maintain an adverse event reporting procedure according to GHTF SG2 guidance	May audit postmarket to investigate specific safety or regulatory concerns
Conformity assessment of device safety and performance	Technical documentation	Prepare STED and have available for review by regulatory authority upon request	Premarket submission of STED normally not requested
	Declaration of Conformity	Prepare, sign and maintain	Submission normally not requested
Registration	Registration of manufacturers and their devices	Perform according to regulatory requirements	Maintain and verify as appropriate

Source: GHTF/SG1/N15:2006 Principles of Medical Devices Classification

where applicable, other people. Especially for devices that incorporate substances of biological origin, the risk of infection must be reduced as much as is reasonably practicable and appropriate. This goal can be achieved by careful selection of donors and substances and validated inactivation coupled with strict controls.

In some jurisdictions, products incorporating tissues, cells and substances of non-human origin may be considered medical devices, while in others they are subject to drug laws. In either case, all claims made on the labels—such as "sterilized"—must be validated.

In particular, safety with regard to viruses and other transmissible agents should be addressed by implementation of validated methods of elimination or inactivation during the course of the manufacturing process.

Devices intended to be sterilized should be manufactured in appropriately controlled (e.g., environmental) conditions.

Manufacturing and Environmental Properties

If the device is intended for use in combination with other devices or equipment, the whole combination, including the connection system, should be safe. Devices should be designed and manufactured in such a way as to remove or reduce the risk of injury due to fire, explosion or any other environmental condition.

Devices With a Diagnostic or Measuring Function

Devices with a measuring function, where inaccuracy could have a significant adverse effect on the patient, should ensure sufficient accuracy, precision and stability for their intended purpose, and the limits of accuracy should be indicated by the manufacturer. Values expressed numerically should be in commonly accepted standardized units and understood by device users. Diagnostic devices should be designed and manufactured to provide sufficient accuracy, precision and stability for their intended use, based on appropriate scientific and technical methods. Among other things, the design should address sensitivity, specificity, trueness, repeatability, reproducibility, control of known relevant interference and limits of detection, as appropriate.

Protection Against Radiation

Devices should be designed, manufactured and packaged in such a way as to minimize exposure of patients, users and other persons to any emitted radiation as far as practicable and appropriate.

Requirements for Medical Devices Connected to or Equipped With an Energy Source

Devices incorporating electronic programmable systems, including software, should be designed to ensure these systems' repeatability, reliability and performance according to their intended use. Such systems also should be properly validated.

Protection Against Mechanical Risks

Devices should be designed and manufactured in such a way as to protect the patient and user against mechanical risks such as resistance to movement, instability and moving parts.

Protection Against the Risks Posed by Supplied Energy or Substances

Devices for supplying the patient with energy or substances should be designed and constructed so the delivered amount

Table 16-2. Class B Device

	Conformity Assessment Element	Manufacturer Responsibility	Regulatory Authority/ Conformity Assessment Body Responsibility
Conformity assessment of the QMS	QMS	Establish and maintain a full QMS **or** a QMS without design and development controls	Be satisfied that a current and appropriate QMS is in place or otherwise conduct a QMS audit prior to marketing authorization
	Postmarket surveillance	Establish and maintain an adverse event reporting procedure according to GHTF SG2 guidance	Be satisfied that a current and appropriate adverse event reporting procedure is in place as part of the QMS
Conformity assessment of device safety and performance	Technical documentation	Prepare STED and have available for review upon request	Not normally reviewed premarket; if submission is requested, receive and conduct a premarket review of the STED sufficient to determine conformity to Essential Principles
	Declaration of Conformity	Prepare, sign and make available for review	Review and verify compliance with requirements
Registration	Registration of manufacturers and their devices	Perform according to regulatory requirements	Maintain and verify as appropriate

Source: GHTF/SG1/N15:2006 Principles of Medical Devices Classification

Table 16-3. Class C Device

	Conformity Assessment Element	Manufacturer Responsibility	Regulatory Authority/ Conformity Assessment Body Responsibility
Conformity assessment of the QMS	QMS	Establish and maintain a full QMS	Be satisfied that a current and appropriate QMS is in place or otherwise conduct a QMS audit prior to marketing authorization
	Postmarket surveillance	Establish and maintain an adverse event reporting procedure according to GHTF SG2 guidance	Be satisfied that a current and appropriate adverse event reporting procedure is in place as part of the QMS
Conformity assessment of device safety and performance	Technical documentation	Prepare and submit a STED for review	Conduct a review, normally premarket, of the STED sufficient to determine conformity to Essential Principles
	Declaration of Conformity	Prepare, sign and submit	Review and verify compliance with requirements
Registration	Registration of manufacturers and their devices	Perform according to regulatory requirements	Maintain and verify as appropriate

Source: GHTF/SG1/N15:2006 Principles of Medical Devices Classification

Table 16-4. Class D Device

	Conformity Assessment Element	Manufacturer Responsibility	Regulatory Authority/ Conformity Assessment Body Responsibility
Conformity assessment of the QMS	QMS	Establish and maintain a full QMS	Be satisfied that a current and appropriate QMS is in place or otherwise conduct a QMS audit prior to marketing authorization
	Postmarket surveillance	Establish and maintain an adverse event reporting procedure according to GHTF SG2 guidance	Be satisfied that a current and appropriate adverse event reporting procedure is in place as part of the QMS
Conformity assessment of device safety and performance	Technical documentation	Prepare and submit a STED for review	Receive and conduct an in-depth premarket review of the STED to determine conformity to Essential Principles
	Declaration of Conformity	Prepare, sign and submit	Review and verify compliance with requirements
Registration	Registration of manufacturers and their devices	Perform according to regulatory requirements	Maintain and verify as appropriate

Source: GHTF/SG1/N15:2006 Principles of Medical Devices Classification

Table 16-5. Noninvasive Devices

RULE	EXAMPLES
Rule 1. All noninvasive devices that come into contact with injured skin (Note: Devices covered by this rule are extremely claim sensitive):	
are in Class A if they are intended to be used as a mechanical barrier, for compression or for absorption of exudates only, i.e., they heal by primary intent	simple wound dressings; cotton wool
are in Class B if they are intended to be used principally with wounds that have breached the dermis, including devices principally intended to manage the microenvironment of a wound	nonmedicated impregnated gauze dressings
unless they are intended to be used principally with wounds that have breached the dermis and can only heal by secondary intent, in which case they are in Class C	dressings for chronic ulcerated wounds; dressings for severe burns
Rule 2. All noninvasive devices intended for channeling or storing body liquids or tissues, liquids or gases for the purpose of eventual infusion, administration or introduction into the body (Note: Such devices are 'indirectly invasive' in that they channel or store liquids that will eventually be delivered into the body):	
are in Class A	administration sets for gravity infusion; syringes without needles
unless they may be connected to an active medical device in Class B or a higher class, in which case they are in Class B	syringes and administration sets for infusion pumps; anesthesia breathing circuits
unless they are intended for use of • channeling blood or • storing or channeling other body liquids or • for storing organs, parts of organs or body tissues in which case they are in Class B.	tubes used for blood transfusion, organ storage containers
unless they are blood bags, in which case they are in Class C	blood bags that do not incorporate an anti-coagulant
Rule 3. All noninvasive devices intended for modifying the biological or chemical composition of blood, other body liquids or other liquids intended for infusion into the body (Note: Such devices are indirectly invasive in that they treat or modify substances that will eventually be delivered into the body):	
are in Class C	hemodializers; devices to remove white blood cells from whole blood
unless the treatment consists of filtration, centrifuging or exchanges of gas or of heat, in which case they are in Class B	devices to remove carbon dioxide; particulate filters in an extracorporial circulation system
Rule 4. All other noninvasive devices (Note: These devices either do not touch the patient or contact intact skin only):	
are in Class A	urine collection bottles; compression hosiery; noninvasive electrodes, hospital beds

Source: GHTF/SG1/N15:2006 Principles of Medical Devices Classification

can be accurately set and maintained to ensure the safety of the patient and the user.

Protection Against the Risks Posed by Devices for Self-testing or Self Administration

Devices for self-testing should be designed and manufactured to perform appropriately for their intended purpose, taking into account the skills and the means available to users. The information provided by the manufacturer for such devices is very critical and should be easy for the user to understand and apply.

Information Supplied by the Manufacturer

Users should be provided with clear instructions that can be easily understood. The instructions should include information needed to use the device safely and to ensure the intended performance, taking users' training and knowledge into account. To this end, GHTF published GHTF/SG1/N009 *Labelling for Medical Devices* in February 2000. That document was superseded by GHTF/SG1/N70[4] *Label and Instructions for use for Medical Devices* (revised), which added guidance on the labeling of in vitro devices.

According to this guidance,[5] device labeling must clearly inform the user of:

- the device's identity and intended use/purpose
- how the device should be used, maintained and stored
- any residual risks, warnings or contraindications

Manufacturers are encouraged to take intended users' technical knowledge, experience, education or training into consideration and to use symbols where possible. Harmonization is encouraged and the use of country-specific requirements should be avoided.

Table 16-6. Invasive Devices

RULE	EXAMPLES
Rule 5. All invasive devices with respect to body orifices (other than those that are surgically invasive) and that are not intended for connection to an active medical device, or are intended for connection to a Class A medical device only:	
are in Class A if they are intended for transient use	examination gloves; enema devices
are in Class B if they are intended for short-term use	urinary catheters, tracheal tubes
unless they are intended for short-term use in the oral cavity as far as the pharynx, in an ear canal up to the ear drum or in a nasal cavity, in which case they are in Class A	dentures intended to be removed by the patient; dressings for nose bleeds
are in Class C if they are intended for long-term use	urethral stent; contact lenses for long-term continuous use (for this device, removal of the lens for cleaning or maintenance is considered as part of the continuous use)
unless they are intended for long-term use in the oral cavity as far as the pharynx, in an ear canal up to the ear-drum or in a nasal cavity and are not liable to be absorbed by the mucous membrane, in which case they are in Class B	orthodontic wire, fixed dental prosthesis
All invasive devices with respect to body orifices (other than those that are surgically invasive) that are intended to be connected to an active medical device in Class B or a higher class, are in Class B	tracheal tubes connected to a ventilator; suction catheters for stomach drainage; dental aspirator tips
Rule 6. All surgically invasive devices intended for transient use are:	
are in Class B	a majority of such devices fall into several major groups: those that create a conduit through the skin (e.g., syringe needles; lancets), surgical instruments (e.g., single-use scalpels; surgical staplers; single-use aortic punch); surgical gloves; and various types of catheter/sucker, etc.
unless they are reusable surgical instruments, in which case they are in Class A	manually operated surgical drill bits and saws
unless intended to supply energy in the form of ionizing radiation, in which case they are in Class C	catheter incorporating/containing sealed radioisotopes
unless intended to have a biological effect or be wholly or mainly absorbed, in which case they are in Class C	insufflation gases for the abdominal cavity
unless intended to administer medicinal products by means of a delivery system, if this is done in a manner that is potentially hazardous taking account of the mode of application, in which they are in Class C	insulin pen for self-administration
unless they are intended specifically for use in direct contact with the central nervous system, in which case they are in Class D	
unless intended specifically to diagnose, monitor or correct a defect of the heart or of the central circulatory system through direct contact with these parts of the body, in which case they are in Class D	angioplasty balloon catheters and related guide wires; dedicated disposable cardiovascular surgical instruments
Rule 7. All surgically invasive devices intended for short-term use (Note: such devices are mostly used in the context of surgery or postoperative care, or are infusion devices or are catheters of various types):	
are in Class B	infusion cannulae; temporary filling materials; nonabsorbable skin closure devices; tissue stabilizers used in cardiac surgery
unless they are intended to administer medicinal products, in which case they are in Class C	
unless they are intended to undergo chemical change in the body (except if the devices are placed in the teeth), in which case they are in Class C	surgical adhesive
unless they are intended to supply energy in the form of ionizing radiation, in which case they are in Class C	brachytherapy device
unless they are intended to have a biological effect or to be wholly or mainly absorbed, in which case they are in Class D	absorbable suture; biological adhesive **NOTE**: the "biological effect" referred to is an intended one rather than unintentional; the term "absorption" refers to the degradation of a material within the body and the metabolic elimination of the resulting degradation products from the body
unless they are intended specifically for use in direct contact with the central nervous system, in which case they are in Class D	neurological catheter
unless they are intended specifically to diagnose, monitor or correct a defect of the heart or of the central circulatory system through direct contact with these parts of the body, in which case they are in Class D	cardiovascular catheters; temporary pacemaker leads; carotid artery shunts

RULE	EXAMPLES
Rule 8. All implantable devices, and long-term surgically invasive devices (Note: most of the devices covered by this rule are implants used in the orthopedic, dental, ophthalmic and cardiovascular fields):	
are in Class C	maxilla-facial implants; prosthetic joint replacements; bone cement; nonabsorbable internal sutures; posts to secure teeth to the mandibula bone (without a bioactive coating)
unless they are intended to be placed into the teeth, in which case they are in Class B	bridges; crowns; dental filling materials
unless they are intended to be used in direct contact with the heart, the central circulatory system or the central nervous system, in which case they are in Class D	prosthetic heart valves; spinal and vascular stents
unless they are intended to be life-supporting or life-sustaining, in which case they are in Class D	
unless they are intended to be active implantable medical devices, in which case they are in Class D	pacemakers, their electrodes and their leads; implantable defibrillators
unless they are intended to have a biological effect or to be wholly or mainly absorbed, in which case they are in Class D	implants claimed to be bioactive
unless they are intended to administer medicinal products, in which case they are in Class D	rechargeable nonactive drug delivery system
unless they are intended to undergo chemical change in the body (except if the devices are placed in the teeth), in which case they are in Class D	
unless they are breast implants, in which case they are in Class D	

Source: GHTF/SG1/N15:2006 Principles of Medical Devices Classification

Performance Evaluation Including, Where Appropriate, Clinical Evaluation

Performance and clinical evaluations are still very much national issues. All data generated should be obtained in accordance with the relevant requirements applicable in each jurisdiction, and clinical investigations on human subjects should be carried out in accordance with the spirit of the *Helsinki Declaration*.[6]

Principles of Conformity Assessment for Medical Devices

Regulatory systems are intended to ensure a high level of protection of public health and safety. Conformity assessments, conducted before and after a medical device is placed on the market, and postmarket surveillance of devices in actual use are intended to provide the objective evidence of safety, performance and benefits and risks to maintain public confidence.

Conformity assessment is primarily the responsibility of the medical device manufacturer. However, it is done in the context of the established regulatory requirements, and both the process and conclusions are subject to further review by the regulatory authority and/or Conformity Assessment Body (CAB) in the countries and regions where the device is sold.

In general, the degree of involvement of the regulatory authority or CAB in such reviews is proportional to the risks associated with a particular device category.

The inter-relationship between device class and conformity assessment is critical in establishing a consistent approach across all countries/regions adopting the harmonized principles, so the premarket approval process and evidence requirements for a particular medical device are acceptable globally.

To place medical devices on the market, manufacturers must demonstrate conformity to the minimum requirements for device safety and functionality. Conformity assessment elements include:[7]

- a quality management system (QMS)
- a system for postmarket surveillance
- summary of technical documentation
- a declaration of conformity
- the registration of manufacturers and their medical devices with the regulatory authority

These five elements are required for all device classes.

QMS

Manufacturers are obliged to have a QMS that meets internationally recognized standards to ensure that medical devices will be safe and perform as the manufacturer intends. Internationally recognized standards are those deemed to offer the presumption of conformity to specific Essential Principles of safety and performance. Further, medical devices must be manufactured in such a way as to consistently meet both customer and regulatory requirements. The scope and complexity of the QMS varies depending on

Table 16-7. Active Devices

RULE	EXAMPLES
Rule 9(i). All active therapeutic devices intended to administer or exchange energy (Note: such devices are mostly electrically powered equipment used in surgery; devices for specialized treatment and some stimulators):	
are in Class B	muscle stimulators; TENS devices; powered dental hand pieces; hearing aids; neonatal phototherapy equipment; ultrasound equipment for physiotherapy
unless their characteristics are such that they may administer or exchange energy to or from the human body in a potentially hazardous way, including ionizing radiation, taking account of the nature, the density and site of application of the energy, in which case they are in Class C	lung ventilators; baby incubators; electrosurgical generators; external pacemakers and defibrillators; surgical lasers; lithotripters; therapeutic X-ray and other sources of ionizing radiation
Rule 9(ii). All active devices intended to control or monitor the performance of active therapeutic devices in Class C, or intended directly to influence the performance of such devices:	
are in Class C	external feedback systems for active therapeutic devices
Rule 10(i). Active devices intended for diagnosis:	
are in Class B	equipment for ultrasonic diagnosis/imaging, capture of physiological signals, interventional radiology and diagnostic radiology)
if they are intended to supply energy that will be absorbed by the human body (except for devices used solely to illuminate the patient's body, with light in the visible or near infra-red spectrum, in which case they are Class A)	magnetic resonance equipment; diagnostic ultrasound in noncritical applications; evoked response stimulators
if they are intended to image *in vivo* distribution of radiopharmaceuticals	gamma/nuclear cameras
if they are intended to allow direct diagnosis or monitoring of vital physiological processes	electronic thermometers, stethoscopes and blood pressure monitors; electrocardiographs
unless they are specifically intended for: a) monitoring of vital physiological parameters, where the nature of variations is such that it could result in immediate danger to the patient, for instance variations in cardiac performance, respiration, activity of central nervous system or b) diagnosing in clinical situations where the patient is in immediate danger, in which case they are in Class C	monitors/alarms for intensive care; biological sensors; oxygen saturation monitors; apnea monitors Ultrasound equipment for use in interventional cardiac procedures
Rule 10(ii). Active devices intended to emit ionizing radiation and intended for diagnostic and/or interventional radiology, including devices that control or monitor such devices, or those that directly influence their performance:	
are in Class C	devices for the control, monitoring or influencing of the emission of ionizing radiation
Rule 11. All active devices intended to administer and/or remove medicinal products, body liquids or other substances to or from the body (Note: Such devices are mostly drug delivery systems or anesthesia equipment):	
are in Class B	suction equipment; feeding pumps; jet injectors for vaccination; nebulizer to be used on conscious and spontaneously breathing patients where failure to deliver the appropriate dosage characteristics is not potentially hazardous
unless this is done in a manner that is potentially hazardous, taking account of the nature of the substances involved, of the part of the body concerned and of the mode and route of administration, in which case they are in Class C	infusion pumps; anesthesia equipment; dialysis equipment; hyperbaric chambers; nebulizer where the failure to deliver the appropriate dosage characteristics could be hazardous
Rule 12. All other active devices:	
are in Class A	examination lamps; surgical microscopes; powered hospital beds and wheelchairs; powered equipment for the recording, processing, viewing of diagnostic images; dental curing lights

Source: GHTF/SG1/N15:2006 Principles of Medical Devices Classification

the type of device being manufactured, the organization's size and structure and specific regulatory requirements.

Activities carried out by third parties remain the manufacturer's responsibility and are subject to control under the manufacturer's QMS. The adequacy of this control will be assessed by CABs and regulatory authorities during inspections.

In some jurisdictions, design and development activities may be excluded from the scope of the manufacturer's QMS. For example, some regional or country regulations may allow manufacturers to choose an alternate examination type to

Table 16-8. Additional Rules

RULE	EXAMPLES
Rule 13. All devices incorporating, as an integral part, a substance that, if used separately, can be considered to be a medicinal product, and that is liable to act on the human body with action ancillary to that of the devices (Note: these medical devices incorporate medicinal substances in an ancillary role):	
are in Class D	antibiotic bone cements; heparin-coated catheters; wound dressings incorporating antimicrobial agents to provide ancillary action on the wound; blood bags incorporating an anticoagulant
Rule 14. All devices manufactured from or incorporating animal or human cells/tissues/derivatives thereof, whether viable or nonviable (Note: in some jurisdictions, such products are considered to be outside the scope of the medical device definition and may be subject to different controls):	
are in Class D	porcine heart valves; catgut sutures
unless such devices are manufactured from or incorporate nonviable animal tissues or their derivatives that come in contact with intact skin only, where they are in Class A	leather components of orthopaedic appliances
Rule 15. All devices intended specifically to be used for sterilizing medical devices, or disinfecting as the end point of processing (**NOTE:** this rule does not apply to products that are intended to clean medical devices by means of physical action, e.g., washing machines):	
are in Class C	devices for disinfecting or sterilizing endoscopes; disinfectants intended to be used with medical devices
unless they are intended for disinfecting medical devices prior to end point sterilization or higher level disinfection, in which case they are in Class B	washer disinfectors
unless they are intended specifically to be used for disinfecting, cleaning, rinsing or, when appropriate, hydrating contact lenses, in which case they are in Class C	in some jurisdictions, solutions for use with contact lenses: · are considered to be outside the scope of the medical devices definition · may be subject to different controls
Rule 16. All devices used for contraception or the prevention of the transmission of sexually transmitted diseases:	
are in Class C	condoms; contraceptive diaphragms
unless they are implantable or long-term invasive devices, in which case they are in Class D	intrauterine contraceptive device

Source: GHTF/SG1/N15:2006 Principles of Medical Devices Classification

demonstrate conformity with the essential requirements of safety and performance. A full QMS is the preferred approach because it implements a full cycle of design and development controls that ensure medical devices comply with the relevant Essential Principles.[8]

Postmarket Surveillance (PMS)

As part of the QMS, prior to placing products on the market, manufacturers must have a functioning postmarket surveillance (PMS) system in place. This allows assessment of the device's continued conformity to the Essential Principles through the postmarketing phase. This system comprises complaint handling, postmarket vigilance reporting and corrective and preventive actions (CAPA).[9]

Summary Technical Documentation

The technical documentation provides the evidence used in the conformity assessment process. Manufacturers are required to prepare and keep detailed technical documentation that shows how each medical device was developed, designed and manufactured and the descriptions and explanations necessary to understand how the manufacturer ensures the device's conformity to the Essential Principles (GHTF/SG1/N011:2008 *Summary Technical Documentation for Demonstrating Conformity to the Essential Principles of Safety and Performance of Medical Devices (STED)*). The technical file provides the evidence used in the conformity assessment process. Part of the technical documentation generated, comprising summary information on selected topics, detailed information on certain specific topics (controlled documents sufficient to communicate key relevant information) and an Essential Principles checklist (EP checklist), is submitted to either the regulatory authority or CAB or kept on the manufacturer's premises ready for inspection. Not all documents relating to a device form part of the STED; many controlled documents are referenced in the EP checklist but only some are contained within the STED. The EP checklist is created as part of the manufacturer's technical documentation. This is a controlled document within the manufacturer's QMS and provides a tabular overview of the Essential Principles and identifies those that are applicable to the device, while showing the chosen method of demonstrating that the device conforms to each relevant Essential Principle. The EP checklist references controlled documents that allow regulatory and/or Competent Authorities to request additional information as appropriate.

Figure 16-1. Decision Tree for Noninvasive Device Classification

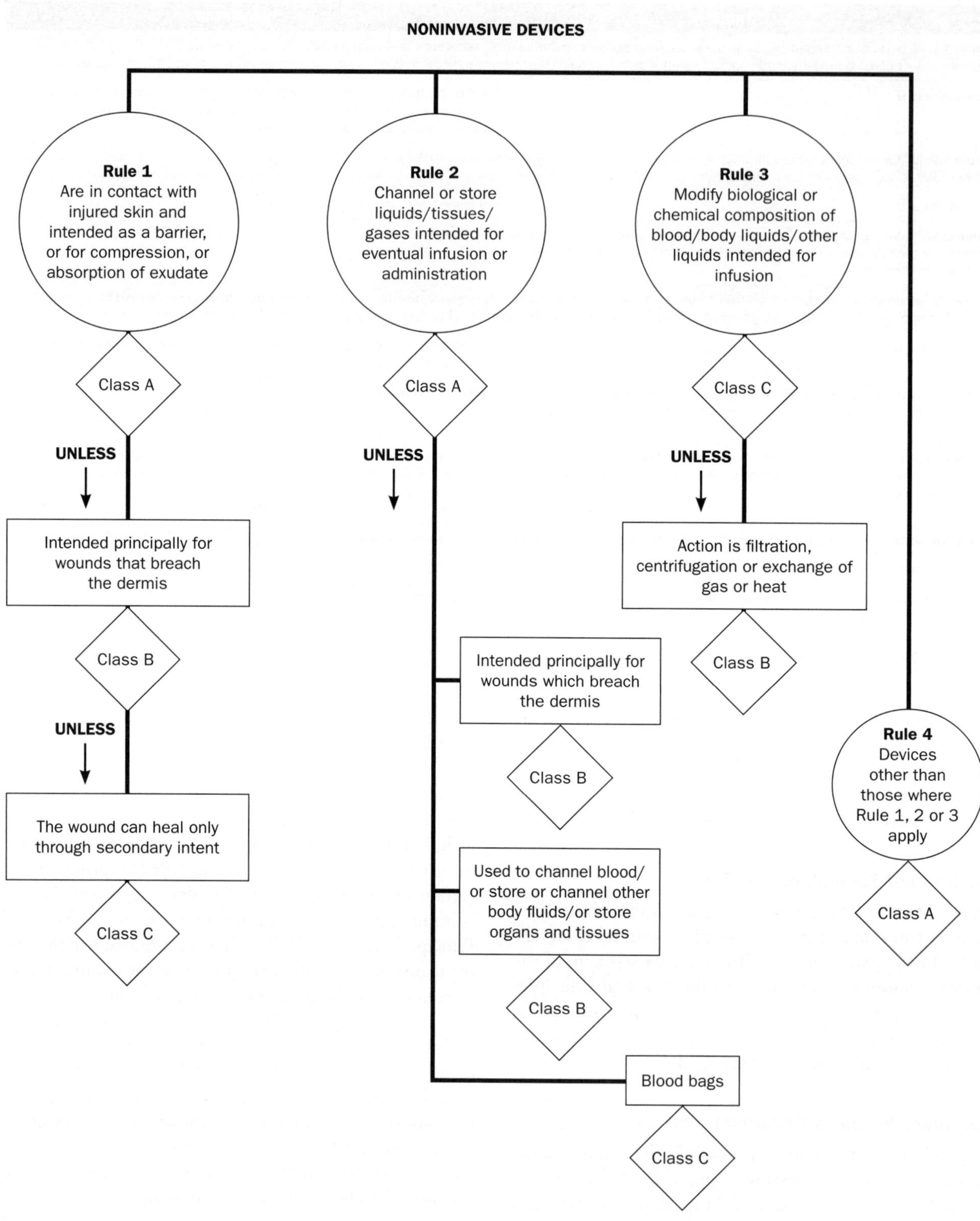

Source: SG1-N15:2006 Principles of Medical Devices Classification

Figure 16-2. Decision Trees for Invasive Device Classification

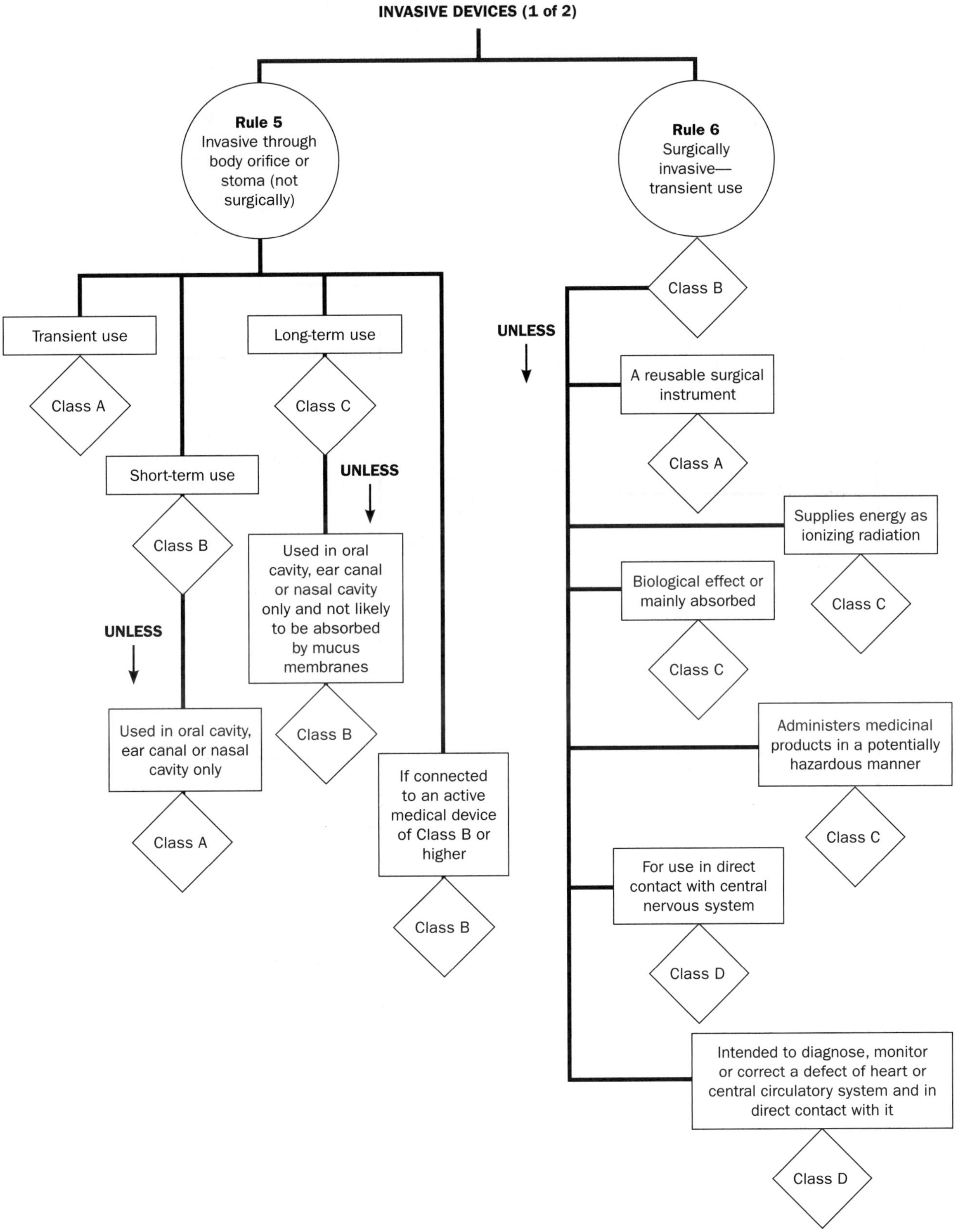

Source: SG1-N15:2006 Principles of Medical Devices Classification

Figure 16-3. Decision Tree 2 for Invasive Devices

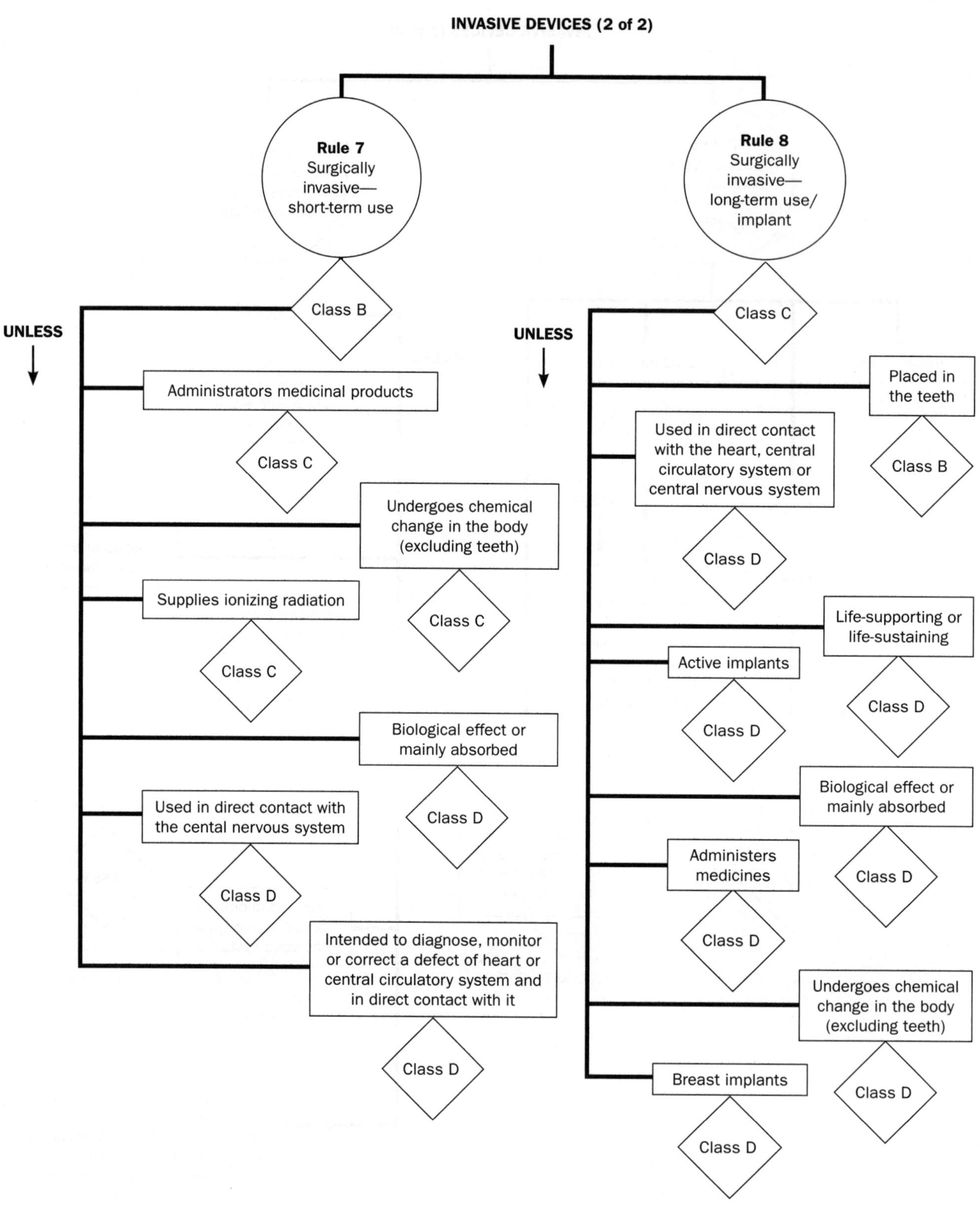

Source: SG1-N15:2006 Principles of Medical Devices Classification

Figure 16-4. Decision Tree 1 for Active Device Classification

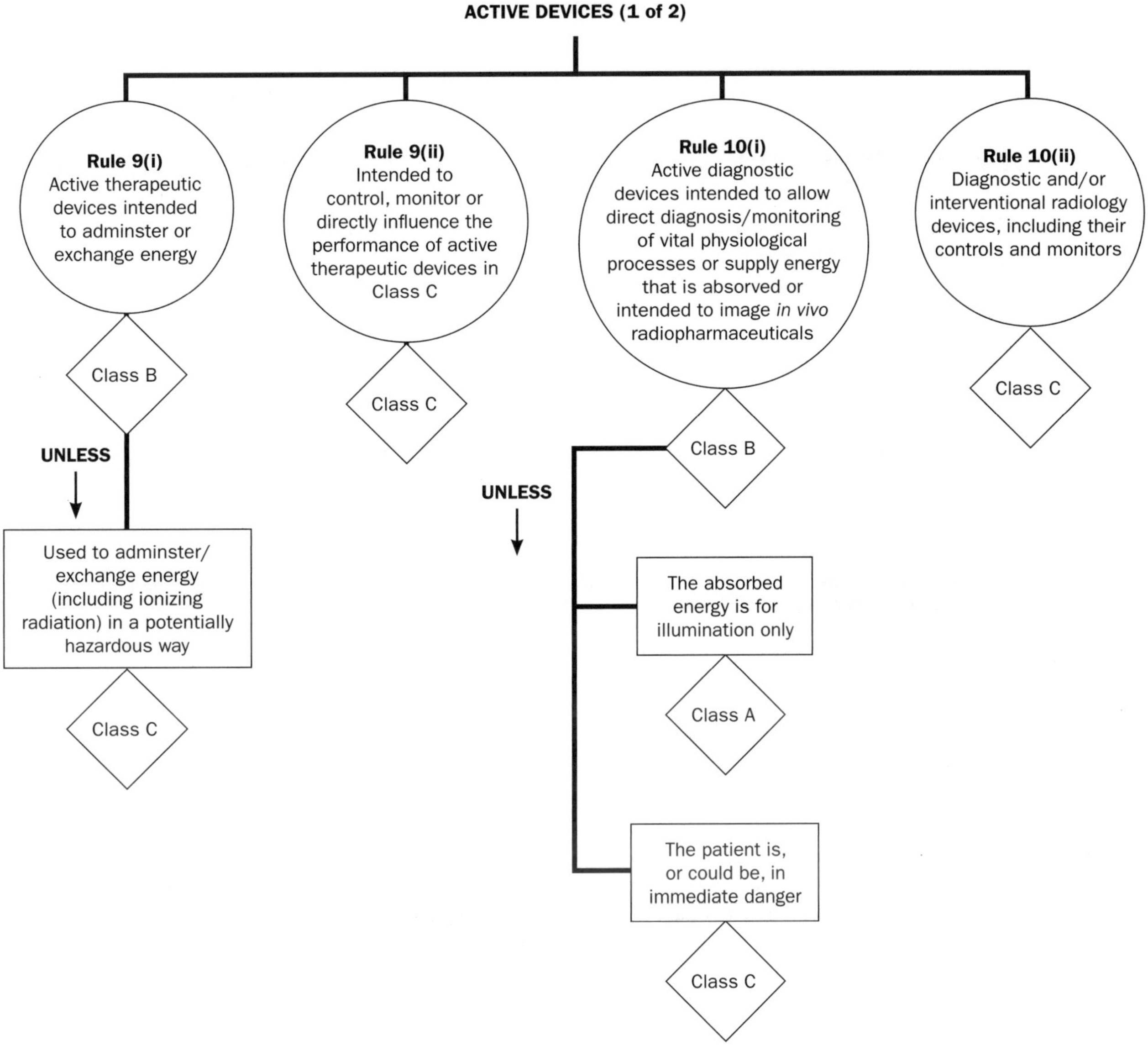

Source: SG1-N15:2006 Principles of Medical Devices Classification

The depth and detail of the information contained in the STED will depend on the classification of the device in question and its complexity. *Summary Technical Documentation for Demonstrating Conformity to the Essential Principles of Safety and Performance of Medical Devices (STED)* is discussed in more detail in Chapter 17.

Declaration of Conformity

A common approach to placing medical devices on the market involves the issuance of a Declaration of Conformity. This is a statement drawn up by the manufacturer attesting that the medical device placed on the market under its name fully complies with all applicable Essential Principles.

At minimum, the declaration should contain information attesting that each device subject to the declaration complies with the applicable Essential Principles, has been classified according to the classification rules and meets all applicable conformity assessment elements. In addition, both the manufacturer and the medical devices subject to the declaration must be clearly identifiable.

Other particulars include:

- information on device identification
- Global Medical Device Nomenclature (GMDN) code and term for the device

Figure 16-5. Decision Tree 2 for Active Device Classification

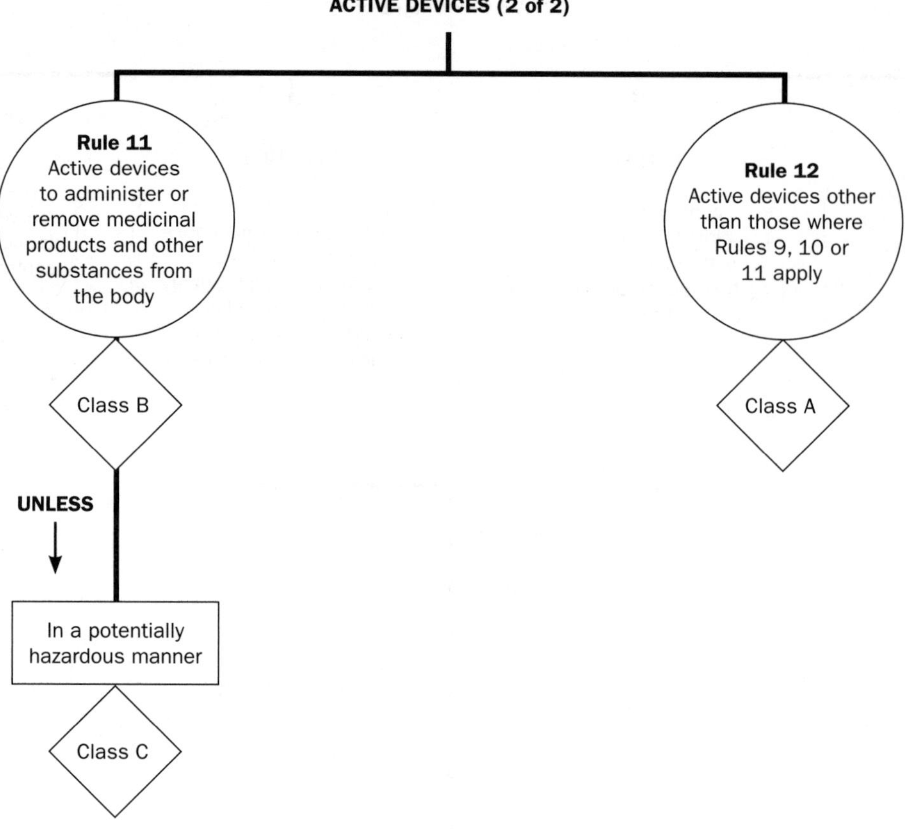

Source: SG1-N15:2006 Principles of Medical Devices Classification

- risk class to which the device is allocated
- which conformity assessment elements have been applied
- manufacturer name and address
- date from which the Declaration of Conformity is valid
- name, position and signature of the responsible person authorized to complete the Declaration of Conformity on the manufacturer's behalf

Registration of Manufacturers and Devices by the Regulatory Authority

Registration of manufacturers and their medical devices with the regulatory authority is the first step in exercising control over devices in the market. The registration system should be able to identify the device and the party responsible for the device within the particular jurisdiction, expediting any regulatory activity. The information must be filed with the regulatory authority by the manufacturer, its local distributor or its Authorized Representative before products are placed on the market.

Harmonized Conformity Assessment Procedures

GHTF recommended that each medical device be allocated to one of four risk classes, based on a set of rules (see below, classification rules):

- lowest risk: Class A devices (examples—surgical retractors, tongue depressors)
- moderate to medium risk: Class B (examples—hypodermic needles, suction equipment)
- moderate to high risk: Class C (examples—lung ventilator, bone fixation plate)
- highest risk: Class D devices (Examples—heart valves, implantable defibrillator)

Tables 16-1–16-4[10] identify available conformity assessment elements and possible combinations of those elements. These elements may be applied to different classes of medical devices to construct a harmonized conformity assessment system that may be adopted as part of a global medical device regulatory model.[11]

Figure 16-6. Decision Tree for Device Classification With Additional Rules

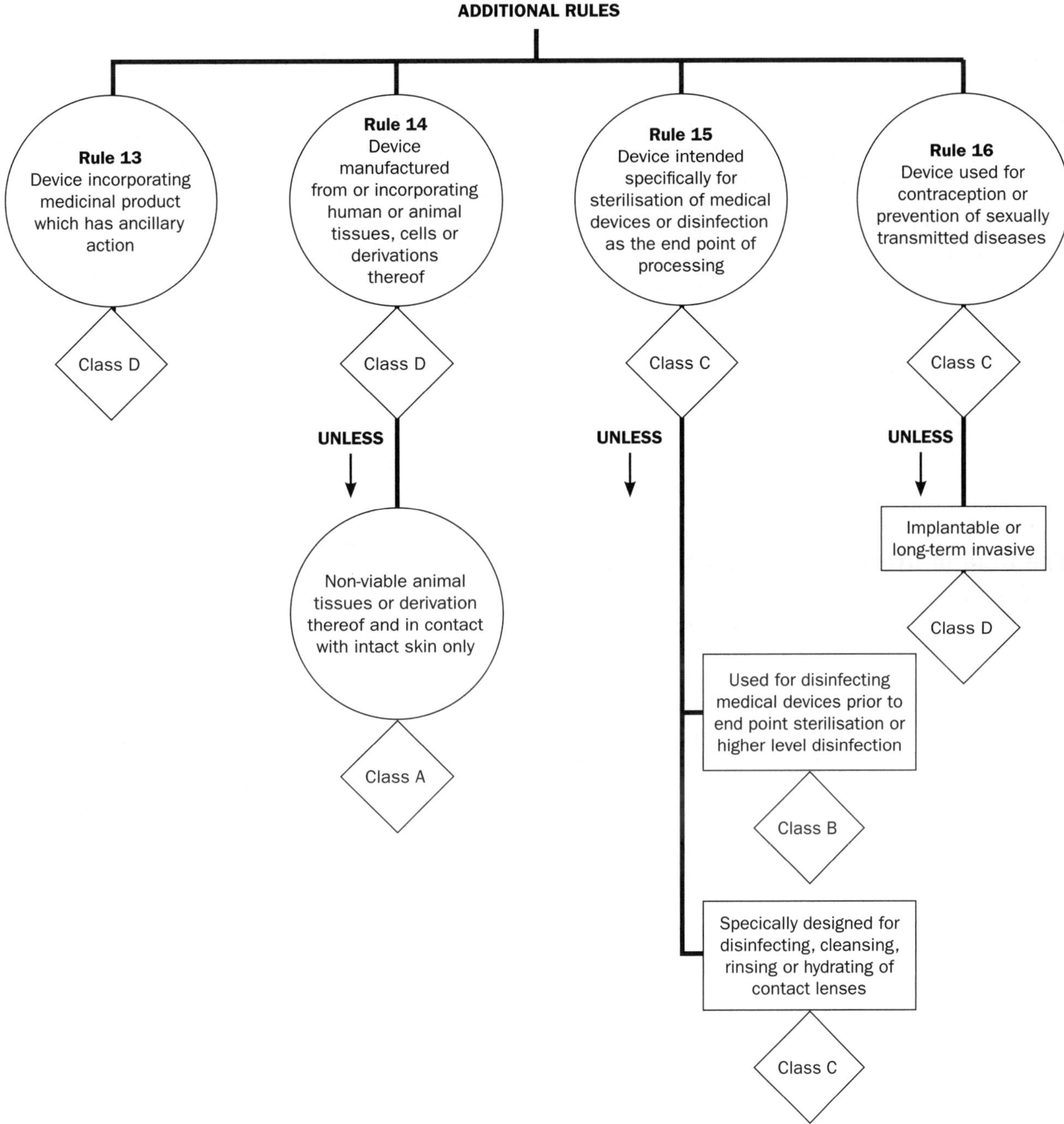

Source: SG1-N15:2006 Principles of Medical Devices Classification

Principles of Medical Devices Classification

GHTF recommended the establishment of a global classification system based on four risk classes.[12] This in turn should be based on a set of rules related to device risk as explained below under classification rules. It is important that any classification system also be capable of accommodating future technological developments. Device classification depends on a number of factors, including the duration of device contact with the body, the degree of invasiveness, whether the device delivers medicinal products or energy to the patient, whether it is intended to have a biological affect on the patient and local versus systemic effects.[13]

Where one medical device is intended to be used together with another (from one or more manufacturers), the classification rules should be applied separately to each device.

Classification Rules

The actual classification of each device depends on the manufacturer's claims and the device's intended use.[14]

To properly classify a device, the manufacturer should decide whether the product falls under the definition of a medical device and determine its intended use. The classification should be made based on the set of rules shown in Tables **16-5–16-8**. In addition to the proposed 16 rules, manufacturers should determine whether the device also is subject to special national rules that apply within a particular jurisdiction.

Decision trees (**Figures 16-1–16-6**) often are used to demonstrate how the rules may be used to classify specific devices.[15] The determination of a risk class for a particular device should, however, be made by referring to the rules themselves and not the decision trees (see **Tables 16-5–16-8**).

The Role of Standards in the Assessment of Medical Devices

Standards also play an important role in harmonizing regulatory processes to assure the safety, quality and performance of medical devices. Standards represent the opinions of experts from all interested parties and stakeholders on a particular topic. Standards exist at different levels: international, such as the International Organization for Standardization (ISO) standards; regional, e.g., the European EN series; and national standards written and promoted by national standardization bodies, e.g., the American National Standards Institute (ANSI).

Standards are reviewed and updated on a regular and ongoing basis. The use of recognized standards is encouraged when designing and manufacturing medical devices.

The use of standards is voluntary. Manufacturers have the option of selecting alternative methods to demonstrate that their medical devices meet the relevant Essential Principles. In such cases, the manufacturer must demonstrate that the "in-house" or other methods used are at least equivalent to established standards in achieving conformity.

Conclusion

The premarket regulatory approval process and requirements vary from country to country. GHTF was established to achieve greater uniformity between national medical device regulatory systems with the aim of enhancing patient safety and increasing access to safe, effective and clinically beneficial medical technologies around the world. As of 2012, those efforts have been assumed by IMDRF.

The *Essential Principles of Safety & Performance of Medical Devices* help manufacturers design and manufacture a device and demonstrate its suitability for its intended use while reducing costs by eliminating differences between jurisdictions. Conformity assessment, conducted before and after a medical device is placed on the market, and postmarket surveillance of devices in actual use are intended to provide the objective evidence of safety, performance and benefits and risks to maintain public confidence. The interrelationship between device class and conformity assessment is critical in establishing a consistent approach across all countries/regions adopting the harmonized principles, so the premarket approval process and evidence requirements for a particular medical device are acceptable globally.

The basic concepts of medical device classification and conformity assessment have been accepted in many jurisdictions globally; however, regional differences still exist. For example, in the US, devices are classified based on risk, subject to the following different levels of controls:

Classes and Requirements:[16]

- Class I: General Controls
- Class II: General Controls and Special Controls
- Class III: General Controls, Special Controls and Premarket Approval

In the EU,[17] devices are classified based on risk:

- Class I (nonsterile/no measuring function)—low risk
- Class I (sterile or with measuring function)—low risk
- Class IIa—medium risk
- Class IIb—high risk
- Class III—highest risk level

In Canada,[18] devices are classified as Classes I, II, III or IV, based on risk, essentially following the same principles as the EU.

Conformity to the Essential Requirements is a prerequisite in most regions. The requirements for design and manufacturing requirements, conformity assessment and medical device classification apply universally, and standards are widely used around the globe.

References

1. GHTF/SG1/N071:2012, *Definition of the Terms 'Medical Device' and 'In Vitro Diagnostic (IVD) Medical Device'* (May 2012). IMDRF website. www.imdrf.org/docs/ghtf/final/sg1/technical-docs/ghtf-sg1-n071-2012-definition-of-terms-120516.pdf. Accessed 23 January 2013.
2. GHTF/SG1/N41R9:2005, *Essential Principles of Safety and Performance of Medical Devices* (May 2005). IMDRF website. www.imdrf.org/docs/ghtf/final/sg1/technical-docs/ghtf-sg1-n41r9-2008-principles-safety-performance-050520.pdf. Accessed 23 Janjuary 2013.
3. Ibid.
4. GHTF/SG1/N70:2011, *Label and Instructions for Use for Medical Devices* (Sept 2011). IMDRF website. www.imdrf.org/docs/ghtf/final/sg1/technical-docs/ghtf-sg1-n70-2011-label-instruction-use-medical-devices-110916.pdf. Accessed 23 January 2013.

5. Ibid.
6. Op cit 2.
7. GHTF/SG1/N40:2006, *Principles of Conformity Assessment for Medical Devices* (June 2006). IMDRF website. www.imdrf.org/docs/ghtf/final/sg1/technical-docs/ghtf-sg1-n40-2006-guidance-ca-principles-060626.pdf. Accessed 23 January 2013.
8. Ibid.
9. Ibid.
10. Ibid.
11. Ibid.
12. GHTF/SG1/N15:2006, *Principles of Medical Devices Classification* (June 2006). IMDRF website. www.imdrf.org/docs/ghtf/final/sg1/technical-docs/ghtf-sg1-n15-2006-guidance-classification-060627.pdf. Accessed 23 Januar 2013.
13. Ibid.
14. Ibid.
15. Ibid.
16. Regulatory Affairs Professionals Society. "Chapter 15 Medical Device Submissions," *Fundamentals of US Regulatory Affairs Seventh Edition*. 2011:189–202.
17. Regulatory Affairs Professionals Society. "Chapter 9 Overview of Authorisation Procedures for Medical Devices," *Fundamentals of EU Regulatory Affairs Sixth Edition*. 2012:87–92..
18. Regulatory Affairs Professionals Society. "Chapter 23 Medical Device Classification and Submissions," *Fundamentals of Canadian Regulatory Affairs Third Edition*. 2011:167–178.
19. GHTF/SG1/N044:2008, *Role of Standards in the Assessment of Medical Devices*. IMDRF website. www.imdrf.org/docs/ghtf/final/sg1/procedural-docs/ghtf-sg1-n044-2008-standards-in-assessment-of-medical-devices-080305.pdf. Accessed 7 October 2012.
20. GHTF/SG1/N011:2008, *Summary Technical Documentation for Demonstrating Conformity to the Essential Principles of Safety and Performance of Medical Devices (STED)*. IMDRF website. http://www.imdrf.org/docs/ghtf/final/sg1/technical-docs/ghtf-sg1-n011-2008-principles-safety-performance-medical-devices-080221.pdf. Accessed 23 January 2013.

Chapter 17

Technical and Regulatory Requirements

Updated by Rajaram Balasubramanian, PGDOM, RAC (US, EU) and Sharad Mi Shukla, MSc, RAC (US, EU)

OBJECTIVES

- Understand the technical requirements that need to be met in order to demonstrate conformity with the Essential Requirements
- Review the elements of a technical file (STED)
- Understand documentation requirements
- Understand the role of recognized standards in the conformity assessment process
- Understand how risk management principles and processes are fundamental to conformity assessment

REGULATIONS AND GUIDELINES COVERED IN THIS CHAPTER

IMDRF

- GHTF/SG1/N011:2008 *Summary Technical Documentation for Demonstrating Conformity to the Essential Principles of Safety and Performance of Medical Devices (STED)* (February 2008)
- GHTF/SG1/N044:2008 *Role of Standards in the Assessment of Medical Device* (February 2008)
- GHTF/SG5 Guidance documents
- GHTF/SG1/N40:2006 *Principles of Conformity Assessment for Medical Devices* (June 2006)
- GHTF/SG1/N55:2009 *Definition of the Terms Manufacturer, Authorised Representative, Distributor and Importer* (March 2009)
- GHTF/SG3/N99-10 (Edition 2) *Quality Management Systems—Process Validation Guidance* (January 2004)
- GHTF/SG3/N15R8:2005 *Implementation of Risk Management Principles and Activities Within a Quality Management System* (May 2005)
- GHTF/SG3/N17R9:2008 *Quality Management System—Medical Devices—Guidance on the Control of Products and Services Obtained from Suppliers* (December 2008)

ISO

- ISO 14971: 2007 Application of risk management to medical devices
- ISO 10993 -1: 2009 Biological Evaluation of Medical Devices

Introduction

Legal requirements for the registration and marketing of medical devices differ from region to region. However, in most cases, manufacturers are expected to prepare and keep on their premises technical documentation that shows how each medical device was designed, developed and

Figure 17-1. Premarket Use of the STED

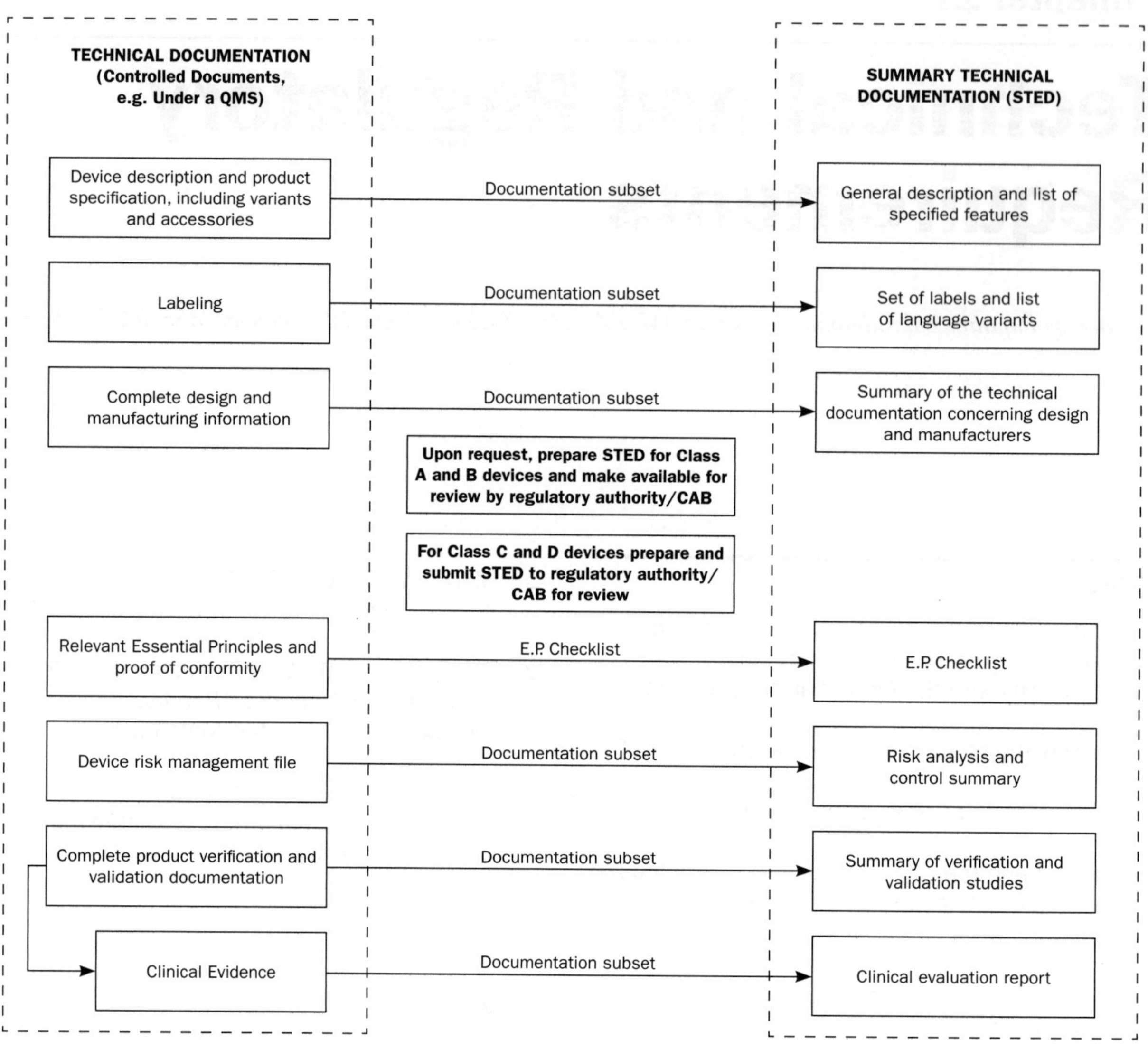

Source SG1-N11:2008

manufactured. For certain device classes, a design dossier must be submitted to the authorities for assessment before market entry. In either case, the manufacturer must ensure timely access to the technical documentation either for assessment or during an audit, when the authorities carrying out the inspection may request access to certain documents.[1]

This technical documentation, typically controlled in the manufacturer's quality management system (QMS), is often extensive, and sections may be held in different locations.[2] Usually, a subset of the technical documentation is prepared in the form of a technical file to be presented to the authorities responsible for assessing and inspecting the data. The availability of the Summary Technical Documentation (STED) should help eliminate differences in documentation requirements between jurisdictions, decrease the cost of achieving regulatory compliance and allow patients earlier access to new technologies and treatments.[3]

Essential Technical File Elements

The technical file is a means for manufacturers of all device classes to demonstrate a product's conformity to the Essential Principles of safety and performance of medical devices. The technical documentation should show how each medical device was developed, designed and manufactured, and should include descriptions and explanations necessary to understand the manufacturer's determination regarding conformity to the Essential Requirements. This technical documentation is a living document that must

Figure 17-2. Postmarket Use of the STED

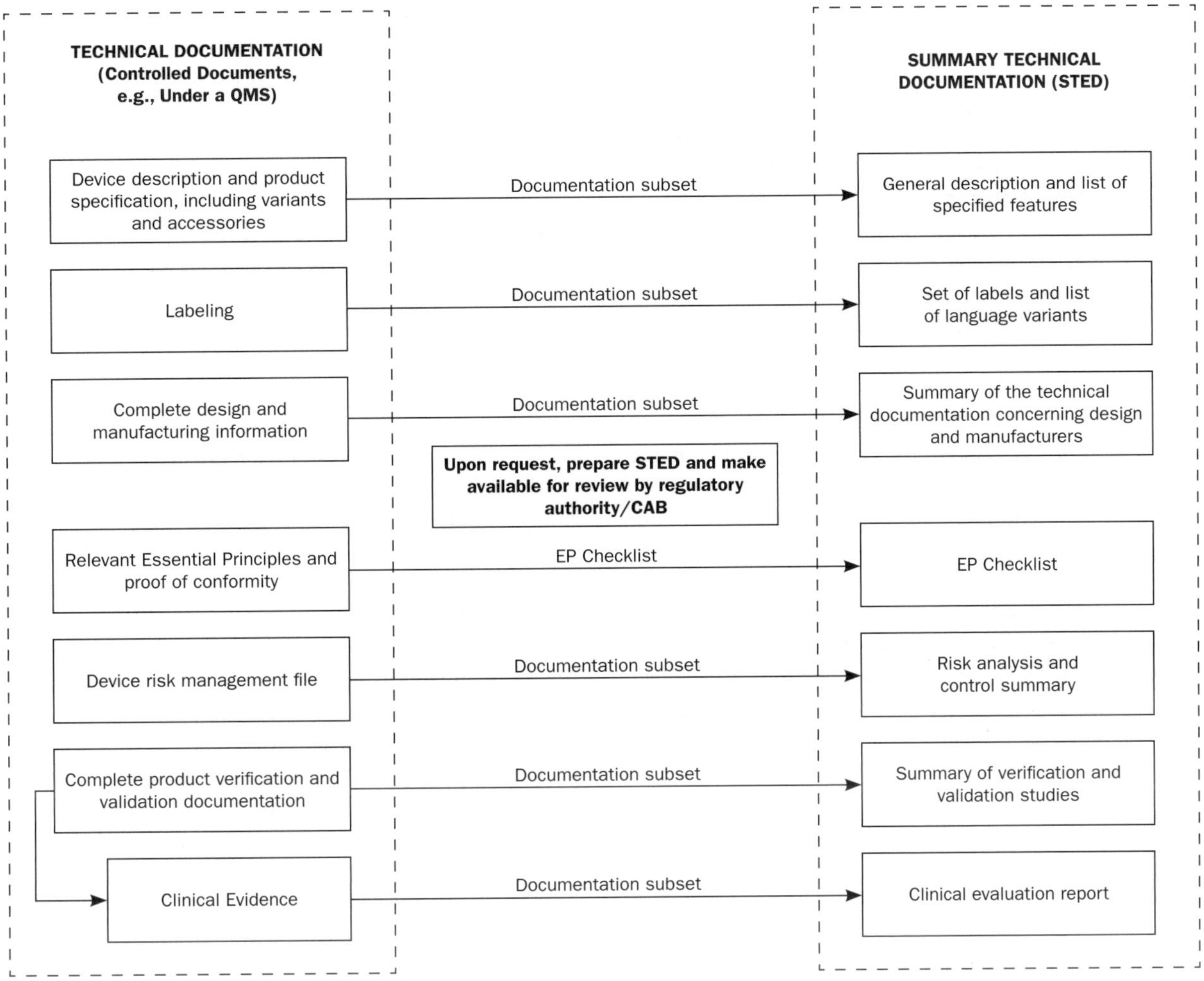

Source SG1-N11:2008

be updated regularly to reflect the device's current status, specifications and configuration.[4]

Premarket Phase

As noted above, the technical file for critical devices must be submitted to the regulatory authority for evaluation, while it is sufficient to have a copy of the files for less-critical devices readily available for inspection. The Global Harmonization Task Force (GHTF) published the submission guidance shown in **Figure 17-1** for devices classified as A or B (lower risk) and C or D (critical devices). Note that in 2012, GHTF was succeeded by the International Medical Device Regulators Forum (IMDRF), and all GHTF guidances now may be found on the IMDRF website.

Postmarket Phase

The regulatory authority may, at any time, request a copy of the technical file for Class A and B (lower risk) devices. The technical file must follow the lifecycle management (LCM) process in the postmarket phase. Changes that affect the quality system must be reported to the regulatory authority. At the same time, the technical file must be updated to reflect any changes. GHTF published the submission guidance shown in **Figure 17-2** for the postmarket phase.

Summary Technical Documentation (STED) Content

The exact content of the technical file can differ from region to region. The STED provides guidance on which general information should be included to aid in an evaluation of the device and its intended use. Following is a brief overview of a technical file's contents using the STED format.

Device Description

The STED should contain the following descriptive information for the device:

a) general description of the device, including its intended use/purpose
b) intended patient population and medical condition to be diagnosed and/or treated and other considerations such as patient selection criteria
c) principles of operation
d) risk class and the applicable classification rule (see Chapter 16 on device classification)
e) explanation of any novel features
f) description of any accessories, other medical devices and other products intended to be used with the device
g) description or complete list of the various configurations/variants of the device that will be made available
h) general description of the device's key functional elements, including any parts, components, software, formulation, composition and functionality (may be presented via labeled pictorial representations)
i) description of the materials incorporated into key functional elements and those making either direct contact with a human body or indirect contact with the body, e.g., during extracorporeal circulation of body fluids[5]

Product Specification

Any product specifications made available to the end user in the form of brochures, catalogs, etc., should be included in the STED. Specifically, the STED should contain a list of the features, dimensions and performance attributes of the medical device and its variants and accessories.

Reference to Similar and Previous Generations of the Device

Information about the manufacturer's previous generation(s) of the device, if any, and/or any similar devices should be included in the technical file if it is relevant to demonstrating conformity to the Essential Principles.

Labeling

The STED should contain a complete set of all labeling associated with the device. If the device is available on multiple markets, a list of language variants should be included. Labeling includes labels on the device and its packaging, instructions for use and promotional material. The labeling set should be in a language acceptable to the reviewing regulatory authorities or Conformity Assessment Body (CAB).

Design and Manufacturing Information

This section of the file should include information to allow the reviewer to evaluate and understand the design stages applied to the device. In addition, the STED should contain sufficient information to allow the reviewer to obtain a general understanding of the manufacturing processes involved in the the form of a process flow chart. The STED also should identify the sites where the design and manufacturing activities are performed. If there are any QMS certificates or the equivalent for these sites, they should be annexed to the STED.

Essential Principles (EP) Checklist

It is customary for the STED to contain an EP checklist that identifies:

a) the Essential Principles
b) whether each Essential Principle applies to the device and if not, why not
c) method(s) used to demonstrate conformity with each applicable Essential Principle
d) reference for the method(s) employed (e.g., standard)
e) precise identity of the controlled document(s) that offers evidence of conformity with each method used[6]

The way in which conformity is achieved may differ. Commonly used methods include: conformity with recognized or other standards;[7] conformity with a commonly accepted industry test method(s); conformity with an in-house test method(s); evaluation of preclinical and clinical evidence;[8] and comparison to a similar device already available on the market.

The EP checklist should incorporate a cross reference to the location of such evidence within both the full technical documentation held by the manufacturer and the STED.

A template for a checklist was published by GHTF and is in Appendix A of GHTF/SG1/N011:2008.

Risk Analysis and Control Summary

The STED should contain a summary of the risks identified during the risk analysis process and how these risks have been controlled to an acceptable level. Preferably, this risk analysis should be based on recognized standards and be part of the manufacturer's risk management plan.

Product Verification and Validation

The STED should contain product verification and validation documentation. In general, the STED should summarize results of verification and validation studies undertaken to demonstrate the device's conformity with the applicable Essential Principles. These results include outcomes of engineering tests, laboratory tests, simulated use testing, animal tests for demonstrating feasibility or proof of concept of the finished device and any published literature regarding the device or substantially similar devices.

In addition, where applicable to the device, the STED should contain detailed information on biocompatibility;

any medicinal substances incorporated into the device; biological safety of devices incorporating animal or human cells, tissues or their derivatives; sterilization; and software verification and validation. Animal studies that provide evidence of the device's safety and performance, especially when no clinical investigation of the device was conducted, and any clinical evidence also should be included.

Biocompatibility

The STED should contain a list of all materials in direct or indirect contact with the patient or user.

Where biocompatibility testing has been conducted to characterize a material's physical, chemical, toxicological and biological response, detailed information should be included on the tests conducted, standards applied, test protocols, the analysis of data and the summary of results. At a minimum, tests should be conducted on samples from the finished, sterilised (when supplied sterile) device.

Medicinal Substances

Where the medical device incorporates a medicinal substance(s), the STED should provide detailed information concerning that medicinal substance, its identity and source, the intended reason for its presence and its safety and performance in the intended application.

Biological Safety

The STED should contain a list of all materials of animal or human origin used in the device. For these materials, detailed information should be provided concerning the selection of sources/donors; the harvesting, processing, preservation, testing and handling of tissues, cells and substances of such origin also should be provided.

Process validation results should be included to substantiate that manufacturing procedures are in place to minimize biological risks, particularly with regard to viruses and other transmissible agents. The system for recordkeeping to allow traceability from sources to the finished device should be fully described.

Sterilisation

Where the device is supplied sterile, the STED should contain detailed information on the initial sterilization validation including bioburden testing, pyrogen testing, testing for sterilant residues (if applicable) and packaging validation.

Typically, the detailed validation information should include the method used, sterility assurance level attained, standards applied, the sterilization protocol developed in accordance with those standards, and a summary of results.

Evidence of ongoing process revalidation also should be provided. Typically, this would consist of arrangements for, or evidence of, revalidation of the packaging and sterilization processes.

Software Verification and Validation

The STED should contain information on the software design and development process and evidence of the validation of the software, as used in the finished device. This information typically should include the summary results of all verification, validation and testing performed both in-house and in a simulated or actual user environment prior to final release. It also should address all the different hardware configurations and, where applicable, operating systems identified in the labeling.

Animal Studies

Where studies in an animal model have been conducted to provide evidence of conformity with the Essential Principles related to functional safety and performance, detailed information should be contained in the STED.

The STED should describe the study objectives, methodology, results, analysis and conclusions, and document conformity with Good Laboratory Practices. The rationale (and limitations) of selecting the particular animal model should be discussed.

Clinical Evidence

The STED should contain clinical evidence that demonstrates the device's conformity to the applicable Essential Principles. It needs to address the elements contained in the Clinical Evaluation Report described in the GHTF/SG5/N2:2012 guidance.

STED Format

The technical file format is not specified, but following the STED guidance's general outline makes it easier for regulatory reviewers to analyze the file and locate information.

Declaration of Conformity

The Declaration of Conformity is not part of the STED. However, it may be annexed to the STED once the manufacturer has completed the Conformity Assessment Procedure.[9] The content of the Declaration of Conformity is described in GHTF/SG1/N40:2006 *Principles of Conformity Assessment for Medical Devices.*

Use of Standards

A standard is a consensus document. GHTF sees international consensus standards as tools for harmonizing regulatory processes to ensure medical devices' safety, quality and performance. The International Organization for Standardization (ISO) defines a "standard" as a document, established by consensus and approved by a recognized body, that provides, for common and repeated use, rules, guidelines or characteristics for activities or their results, aimed at achieving the optimum degree of order in a given context. It further notes that standards should be based on the consolidated results of science, technology and experience and aimed at the promotion of optimum community benefits.

The consensus described in the standard was reached by the members of the committee that wrote it, influenced by the comments of those who participated in the consultation phases. The way standards' writing bodies are constituted and execute their tasks, therefore, affects a standard's quality, which should be an important factor in the extent to which a particular standard is used. It is good practice to consider objectively the extent to which the use of a standard ensures compliance with the Essential Requirements and identify any aspects of conformity assessment that need to be addressed by other means. This chapter, therefore, presents some general observations about the nature of standards and the way they are generated.

International standards, such as basic standards, group standards and product standards, are a tool for harmonizing regulatory processes to ensure medical devices' safety, quality and performance. Standards represent the opinion of experts from all interested parties, including industry, regulators, users and others.

The manufacturer may use conformity with recognized standards to demonstrate conformity with the relevant Essential Principles and/or specific pre- or postmarket requirements. When used, the manufacturer should identify the version and date of the relevant recognized standard(s) in its technical documentation.

However, the use of standards by the manufacturer is voluntary.[7] The term "recognized standard" does not imply that such a standard is mandatory. When a standard is not applied, or is not applied in full, the manufacturer should retain, and submit where appropriate, data or information to demonstrate that:

- conformity with the Essential Principles has been achieved by other means

and/or

- the parts of the standard that were not applied were not pertinent to the particular device in question

Risk Management Principles

The manufacture of medical devices requires the evaluation and control of risks. Risk management activities normally are recorded and referenced in various files such as the risk management file, design history file, technical file/technical documentation, design dossier, device master record, device history record and process validation files. Integrating risk management procedures, documents and records directly into the QMS is a good approach and makes the quality management process more manageable.[10] Care should be taken to ensure that all risk management aspects are covered.

Management should ensure that risk is properly assessed and controlled. Risk management activities may include:

- establishment of risk acceptability criteria
- risk analysis
- risk evaluation
- risk control and monitoring[11]

Management is responsible for ensuring that the company has sufficient resources to carry out risk management activities.

Outsourcing

A manufacturer may outsource one or several parts of the production process—e.g., sterilization, coating or design—or an entire product. However, the manufacturer is responsible for monitoring any outsourced activities and incorporating appropriate risk management activities to ensure product quality. After a device has been placed on the market, risk management activities should be linked to quality management processes, such as production and process controls, corrective and preventive actions (CAPA), servicing and customer feedback, etc.

Risk management activities also should cover any outsourced activities or potential risks introduced by suppliers.

Design and Development and Planning

The objective of risk management is to reduce a device's risk to an acceptable level while maintaining the product's feasibility and functionality.[12] Risk-associated activities must be planned early in the development process and should cover the entire product lifecycle. Risk control measures are part of the design output and should be evaluated during design verification.

Risks in the development phase can be grouped by those arising during the design input phase and those occurring during the design output phase. Different risk assessment tools—e.g., failure modes and effects analysis (FMEA)—may be used to assess and reduce risks. The main principles of risk analysis and control are described in ISO 14971:2007, *Application of risk management to medical devices*.[13]

Design and development activities also should be verified and validated. Any changes occurring after the device is placed on the market should be monitored and captured using an appropriate change control system. Traceability forms an important part of any serious risk management system.

Corrective and Preventive Actions (CAPAs)

Corrective actions are planned in retrospect, whereas preventive actions can be planned before an incident occurs. CAPA reviews should reveal any previously unrecognized risks and the effectiveness of risk control measures.[14]

Conclusion

Although the registration procedures for medical devices differ from region to region, GHTF proposed a common technical file (STED) to comply with the requirements in most regions. This important document provides a way for manufacturers of all device classes to demonstrate the conformity of their devices with the Essential Principles of safety and performance of medical devices. Manufacturers are required to present the results of preclinical and clinical testing as well as manufacturing information to gain market access. Technical documentation must be updated using a lifecycle management approach.

Quality and risk management play a vital role in medical device development and manufacture. Medical device manufacturers ensure that risks are reduced to an acceptable level by initiating risk minimization activities, as necessary. Risk management can be integrated into the overall quality management system to allow a comprehensive approach and simplify the control of documents.

References

1. GHTF/SG1/N011:2008: *Summary Technical Documentation for Demonstrating Conformity to the Essential Principles of Safety and Performance of Medical Devices (STED)* (February 2008). IMDRF website. www.imdrf.org/docs/ghtf/final/sg1/technical-docs/ghtf-sg1-n011-2008-principles-safety-performance-medical-devices-080221.pdf. Accessed 24 January 2013.
2. Ibid.
3. Ibid.
4. Ibid.
5. Ibid.
6. Ibid
7. GHTF/SG1/N044:2008 *Role of Standards in the Assessment of Medical Devices* (February 2008). IMDRF website. www.imdrf.org/docs/ghtf/final/sg1/procedural-docs/ghtf-sg1-n044-2008-standards-in-assessment-of-medical-devices-080305.pdf. Accessed 24 January 2013.
8. GHTF/SG5 guidance documents. IMDRF website. www.imdrf.org/documents/doc-ghtf-sg5.asp. Accessed 24 January 2013.
9. GHTF/SG1/N40:2006 *Principles of Conformity Assessment for Medical Devices* (June 2006). IMDRF website. www.imdrf.org/docs/ghtf/final/sg1/technical-docs/ghtf-sg1-n40-2006-guidance-ca-principles-060626.pdf. Accessed 24 January 2013.
10. GHTF/SG3/N15R8:2005 *Implementation of Risk Management Principles and Activities Within a Quality Management System* (May 2005). IMDRF website. www.imdrf.org/docs/ghtf/final/sg3/technical-docs/ghtf-sg3-n15r8-risk-management-principles-qms-050520.pdf. Accessed 24 January 2013.
11. Ibid.
12. Ibid.
13. ISO 14971:2007 *Application of risk management to medical devices.*
14. Ibid.

Chapter 18

Device Quality Systems

By Marcelo de Moraes Antunes, RAC (Global)

OBJECTIVES

- ❑ Provide an overview of international quality management systems requirements for medical devices
- ❑ Review the essential requirements of ISO 13485
- ❑ Explain how ISO 13485 is used in the most important regulatory systems in the world
- ❑ Explain specific topics in medical device quality systems such as process validation

STANDARDS AND GUIDELINES COVERED IN THIS CHAPTER

- ❑ ISO 13485:2003—*Medical devices—Quality management systems—Requirements for regulatory purposes*
- ❑ ISO 13485:2003/Cor 1:2009
- ❑ ISO/TR 14969:2004—*Medical devices—Quality management systems—Guidance on the application of ISO 13485: 2003*
- ❑ World Health Organization, *Medical Device Regulations: Global Overview and Guiding Principles, 2003*
- ❑ GHTF/SG3/N19:2012 *Quality management system—Medical devices—Nonconformity Grading System for Regulatory Purposes and Information Exchange*
- ❑ GHTF/SG3/N18:2010 *Quality management system—Medical Devices—Guidance on corrective action and preventive action and related QMS processes* (November 2010)
- ❑ GHTF/SG3/N17:2008 *Quality Management System—Medical Devices—Guidance on the Control of Products and Services Obtained from Suppliers*
- ❑ GHTF/SG3/N15R8 *Risk Management Principles and Activities within a QMS* (May 2005)
- ❑ GHTF/SG3/N99-10:2004 *QMS—Process Validation Guidance* (January 2004)

Introduction

A quality management system (QMS) is one of the five conformity assessment elements for medical devices.[1]

A manufacturer is expected to implement, document and maintain a QMS that "ensures the medical devices it designs, manufactures and supplies to the market are safe, perform as intended and comply with the relevant provisions of the regulations."[2]

Today, a QMS is seen as a set of interrelated or interacting processes to establish policy and objectives and to achieve those objectives in regard to quality.[3]

The recognized international standard for medical device quality management systems is ISO 13485:2003 *Medical devices—Quality management systems—Requirements for regulatory purposes.* As this standard is the basis for QMS requirements in the regulations of several countries, and also for guidelines developed by the Global Harmonization Task Force (GHTF), the rest of this chapter will focus on this standard and related documentation.

QMS Versus Good Manufacturing Practice (GMP)

It is important to understand that a QMS (and the QMS requirements in regulations and standards) can relate to several, if not all, processes within an organization that can impact all phases of the medical device lifecycle.[4]

When applied to the manufacturing process, QMS requirements impose strict controls as a way to create a controlled manufacturing system, also known as GMP. The objective is to reduce the likelihood of a nonconforming product and thus ensure the safety and effectiveness of products manufactured by this process.[5]

QMS Requirements and Conformity Assessment

As with other aspects of medical device conformity assessment, QMS requirements usually are dependent on the device's risk class; they also are dependent on the regulatory system in the related country or region. For example, requirements for design controls usually are not required for low- to medium-risk devices.

Historical Perspective on ISO 13485

In the past, the only means to ensure that satisfactory products were manufactured was for manufacturers to inspect the finished products. This reactive approach was modified after World War II when a more proactive approach was used to control the manufacturing process. Out of this new approach and the work of Walter A. Shewhart on statistical methods, quality control was born. Another development, the use of a management system that enabled the fulfillment of requirements, was based on the work of William Edwards Deming and is now known as quality assurance.

For decades, major manufacturers and purchasers (with a strong emphasis on government and military purchasers) used their own sets of requirements to manage quality. In England, it was noted that standards could be used by different manufacturers and purchasers to help the commercial exchange of goods and thus British Standard (BS) 5750 on quality systems was created.

An international series of standards on quality system requirements, the ISO 9000 series, was created in 1987, based on BS 5750 and other quality systems documents of the time. This series has been updated several times, but for this chapter, the 1994 and 2000 updates are the most important.

In Europe, in the late 1980s and early 1990s, new regulations (called directives) were introduced (revised regulations to be applied by all Member States to solve the problem of each country having its own—sometimes conflicting—regulations). As part of the conformity assessment under these regulatory requirements, it was imperative for manufacturers to use quality systems and the European counterpart to ISO 9001, EN 29000. However, for medical devices, it was decided that the use of ISO 9001 requirements alone were not enough. Therefore, a new standard was created, based on the 1994 version of ISO 9001/EN but with several additions and changes —EN 46000.

In 1996, ISO created an international version, which was the first version of ISO 13485, based on EN 46000. This version was revised in 2003 to keep the standard current with the 2000 version of ISO 9001. ISO 13485 also has a corrigendum from 2009, which was developed mainly to correct references to ISO 9001:2000.

A guidance document on ISO 13485 was created in 1999, ISO 14969 *Medical devices—Quality management systems—Guidance on the application of ISO 13485*. This document was revised in 2004 to align with the revised version of ISO 13485.

ISO 13485 currently is being revised, with an estimated publication date of late 2014 or early 2015. This revised standard is expected to be different than ISO 9001 and will address current medical device regulatory requirements more appropriately.

Overview of ISO 13485:2003 Requirements

Since ISO 13485 was based on ISO 9001, the requirements of both are similar. ISO 13485 includes requirements from ISO 9001, some of which were modified or added based on medical device regulatory requirements.

The requirements from the standard, as in ISO 9001, are divided into clauses. An overview of each clause follows:

- Clause 4—Quality management system requirements is divided into two parts: general requirements and documentation requirements.

  The general requirements in 4.1 outline the manufacturer's responsibility to establish, document, implement and maintain an effective QMS and to identify all the processes related to the design, manufacture and distribution of products (including lifecycle activities). These processes form the QMS and shall be monitored and measured for their efficacy.

  The documentation requirements in 4.1 outline the organization's responsibility to develop the quality policy and objectives, the quality manual and all documents and records necessary for the QMS to be effective. Documents shall conform to several requirements related to approval and controlled use, including change control.

Figure 18-1. Influence of Design Controls on the Design Process

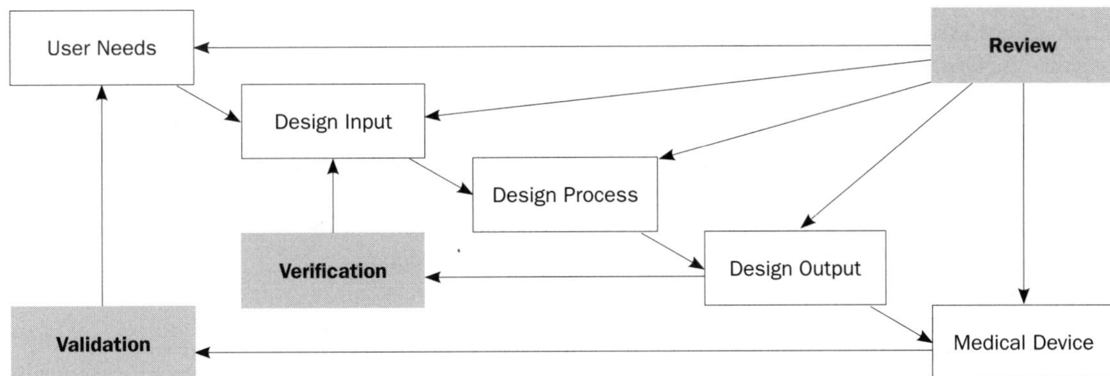

The standard also requires that the organization create a file containing the technical specifications and QMS requirements for each medical device type or model. This was created as a generic requirement because an international standard, such as ISO 13485, should not use definitions from specific regulations (such as the technical file requirement for CE marking).

- Clause 5—The organization's top management is responsible for specific requirements.

  This includes requirements for management commitment, the definition of a management representative and the very important management review, where the effectiveness of the QMS is evaluated and accepted (or actions needed to maintain effectiveness are defined).

  Top management also has to define the quality policy and define quality objectives based on the quality policy and the purpose of the organization; plan the implementation of the QMS and define responsibility and authority to those involved; and create clear and effective communication channels.
- Clause 6 on resource management requires the determination of the resources the QMS needs to operate effectively.

  Human resource requirements are related to the competency needed to perform defined activities, including any training needed to achieve the required competency.

  Infrastructure requirements are related to the physical components of the system, such as buildings. Work environment requirements are related to health, cleanliness and clothing of personnel, work environment conditions and contaminated product.
- Clause 7—Product realization

Clauses 4, 5, 6 and 8 (on measurement, analysis and improvement) can be thought of as clauses related to supporting processes.

Clause 7 is related to the process of designing, manufacturing and distributing the medical device.

Product realization shall be planned, including the customer interaction and processes that will input the requirements for the product.

Design and development shall be controlled, beginning with a planning requirement. Other steps in the control of design and development are the definition of design inputs and the provision of design output after the product has been created and verification and validation activities have been conducted. A change control process shall be active throughout the device's lifecycle. **Figure 18-1** shows the steps in flowchart form.

Purchasing controls are needed to ensure purchased products or services conform to the requirements; this includes the verification process for purchased products and services.

The manufacturing process shall have controls related to product cleanliness and contamination control, installation and service activities, including specific requirements particular to sterile medical devices, such as records of sterilization parameters.

Processes where the resulting output cannot be verified (called "special processes" in some regulations) shall be validated.

The products must be identified during manufacturing and shall fulfill traceability requirements to ensure they can be traced after distribution (however, traceability requirements might not be applicable to all products, depending on risk classes and specific regulation requirements).

Measuring and monitoring devices must be defined and maintained to enable correct measuring and monitoring, including, calibration and safeguarding from adjustments, as appropriate.

- Clause 8 on measurement, monitoring and improvement define the requirements for processes to verify whether the QMS is performing as intended, and if not, the actions to be taken.

  Monitoring and measurement include obtaining feedback on meeting customer requirements, internal audits, process monitoring and measurement and product monitoring and measurement.

  Nonconforming product shall be identified and controlled to prevent unintended use or delivery.

  Data from the measuring and monitoring processes shall be analyzed.

  Improvement includes, among other requirements, corrective and preventive actions resulting from analysis that will enable the system to maintain its efficacy.

ISO 13485 in Regulatory Systems

Although ISO 13485 is the recognized international standard for medical device quality systems, it is not accepted globally because:

- It is a standard, and standards are voluntary in nature. A standard only becomes mandatory if required by regulation.
- Some regulatory systems have their own versions of quality management system requirements (e.g., the US Food and Drug Administration (FDA) has its own set of QMS requirements—Quality System Regulation (QSR)).

However, many, if not most, countries in the world use and accept ISO 13485 in some form or another.

Another recent development within the International Medical Device Regulators Forum (IMDRF), which is the successor organization to GHTF, is the Medical Device Single Audit Program (MDSAP). The objective of the MDSAP is to "develop a standard set of requirements for auditing organizations performing regulatory audits of medical device manufacturers' quality management systems."[6] This "standard set of requirements" will be based on the revised version of ISO 13485, which will be published at in late 2014 or early 2015.

ISO 13485 in the US

FDA does not accept ISO 13485 in its regulatory framework because it has its own set of QMS requirements. They are defined in the Code of Federal Regulations (CFR) Title 21 Part 820 and are called the QSR.[7] The QSR was created in 1996 based on the 1994 version of ISO 9001 and the 1996 version of ISO 13485.

However, even if FDA does not accept ISO 13485 directly, it is developing some activities that might lead to future recognition and acceptance.

The first is the Medical Device ISO 13485:2003 Voluntary Audit Report Submission Pilot Program,[8] which aims to reduce FDA's workload (by removing the manufacturer for one year from the FDA audit plan) if an ISO 13485 compliance audit trail evaluation by the regulatory agencies of Canada, Japan, EU or Australia is evidenced.

The second is the implementation of the IMDRF MDSAP program.

ISO 13485 in Canada

Health Canada has formal requirements for a quality management system for medical device manufacturers,[9] and they rely directly on compliance with ISO 13485 (Canadian version of the international standard).

The requirement only applies to Class II, III and IV devices. Manufacturers of Class I devices face no regulatory requirements for a QMS in Canada.

Certificates for the QMS will only be accepted by Health Canada if they are issued by a special type of third-party auditing organization, called Canadian Medical Devices Conformity Assessment System (CMDCAS) recognized registrars.

ISO 13485 in the EU

The EU version of ISO 13485 (currently EN ISO 13485:2012) is a harmonized standard, which means that, although its implementation is voluntary, it provides an easy way to comply with the medical device regulations because applying a harmonized standard presumes conformity with the related regulation requirements.

It is important to understand that a QMS is not required by the Essential Principles of the medical devices regulations in the EU, but there are QMS requirements in the various possible routes to obtain the CE Mark (e.g., the most complex and complete route, Annex II, is called the "Full Quality Assurance" route).[10]

It also is important to understand that although ISO 13485 certification is not required, it usually is better for manufacturers to become certified so they can use this certification in other countries where it is accepted.

ISO 13485 in Brazil

Brazil's National Health Surveillance Agency (ANVISA) does not accept ISO 13485 in its regulatory framework because it has its own set of QMS requirements. They are defined in RDC 16:2013.[11] RDC 16 revises the old regulation, RDC 59:2000, parts of which were based on the 1996 and 1978 versions of FDA's QSR.

Figure 18-2. Process Validation Decision Tree

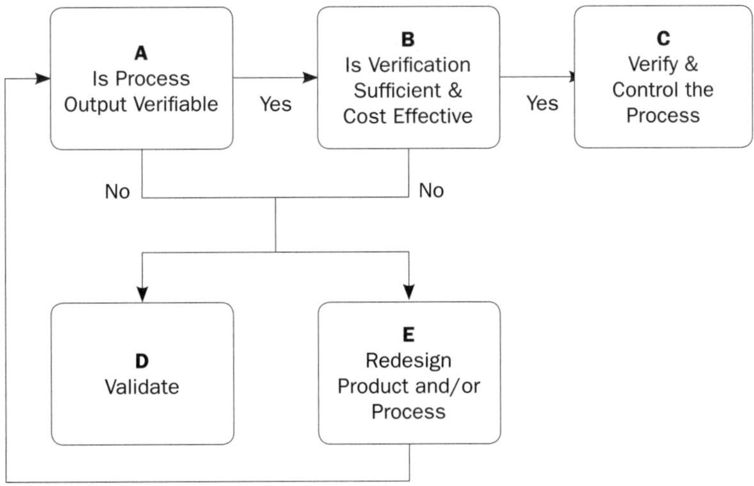

Source SG3/N99-10 (Ed 2)

ISO 13485, however, is used in the certification processes performed by the National Institute of Metrology, Quality and Technology (INMETRO) and required by ANVISA to provide registration to some devices (e.g., medical electrical equipment). [12]

ANVISA also is involved in the IMDRF MDSAP program.

ISO 13485 in Other Countries

As mentioned previously, several, if not most, countries in the world use and accept some form of ISO 13485.

For example, countries without formally developed medical device regulations require or accept CE marking as a way to enter the country; in this instance, ISO 13485 is accepted as a way to comply with EU regulations.

Other countries may accept certificates of compliance with ISO 13485 for compliance with general quality systems requirements from their regulations.

QMS—Process Validation

GHTF published a guidance document to assist manufacturers in understanding QMS requirements for process validation.[13] Qualification and validation processes go hand in hand. Qualification involves design qualification (DQ), installation qualification (IQ), operational qualification (OQ) and performance qualification (PQ).

Process validation uses objective evidence to prove that a process consistently produces a result or product meeting its predetermined requirements.[1]4 This evidence must be documented in a protocol explaining the different validation steps and test parameters. Process validation is only one element of validation and includes facility and equipment validation (DQ, IQ, OQ and PQ), in addition to cleaning validation, analytical validation and computer validation. All of these activities are generally defined in a validation master plan.

Product development and manufacture involve diverse and complex steps. Adequate controls must be in place to ensure that products meet their declared specifications and that processes produce consistent results.

Inadequate process validation could result in critical process deviations at a later stage that may require corrective actions and revalidation and could raise compliance issues.

Figure 18-2 shows a process validation decision tree.

Such decision trees can help manufacturers determine whether a process needs to be validated, which is especially important for very complex processes. Software, even when used in verifiable processes, also should be validated.[15] Annex A of GHTF/SG3/N99-10 (Edition 2) *Quality Management Systems—Process Validation Guidance* provides statistical methods and tools for process validation.

Practical steps involved in a validation process include:

- creating a validation master plan
- choosing team members from quality assurance, engineering, manufacturing, etc.
- developing a protocol to define which processes and devices need to be validated
- selecting statistical methods for data collection and analysis
- creating a maintenance plan and repair criteria
- developing criteria for revalidation

IQ, OQ and PQ

Facility and equipment validation relates to IQ, OQ and PQ and may include calibration and computer validation.

- IQ determines: Is the equipment installed correctly?

Figure 18-3. Key Activities for Supplier Control

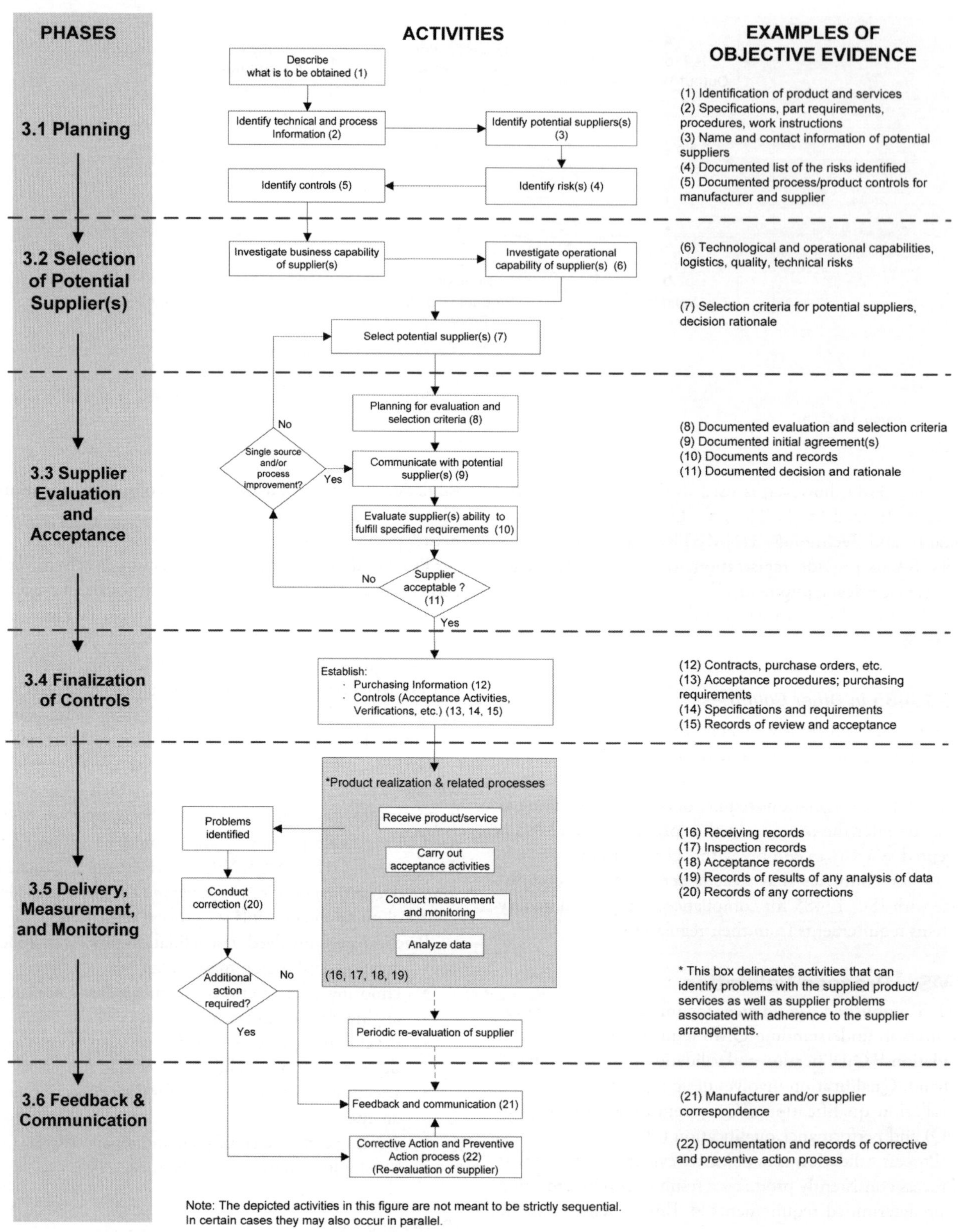

Source SG3/N17/2008 pg 10

- OQ determines: Will the end product meet all defined requirements under all anticipated conditions of manufacturing, i.e., worst case testing?
- PQ determines: Will the process consistently produce acceptable product under normal operating conditions?

All validation activities should be recorded in a final report. The validated state should be maintained by continuous monitoring and control. If major changes are implemented, the process must be revalidated.

Validation Master Plan (VMP)

A Validation Master Plan (VMP), although not mandatory, is useful; it is a document that outlines the principles involved in the qualification of a facility, defining the areas and systems to be validated.[16] The VMP, if available, forms the foundation for the validation program and should include process validation, facility and utility qualification and validation, equipment qualification, cleaning and computer validation. It provides a written program for achieving and maintaining a qualified facility with validated processes. The specific qualification and validation procedures and activities should be defined in specific standard operating procedures (SOPs) covering both equipment and processes.

Examples of equipment-related SOPs:

- IQ
- OQ
- PQ
- calibration
- computer validation

Examples of process-related SOPs:

- process validation
- cleaning validation
- validation of analytical methods[17]

QMS—Medical Devices—Guidance on the Control of Products and Services Obtained from Suppliers

In today's complex manufacturing environment, medical device manufacturers rely heavily on suppliers for chemicals, parts, etc.

Typical services offered by suppliers include:

- off-the-shelf products
- parts and components made to a manufacturer's specifications
- services (e.g., sterilization, design, document archiving, transport)
- finished medical device

Although the term "manufacturer" may be defined differently in various jurisdictions, regulatory authorities ultimately hold one medical device "manufacturer" or entity primarily responsible for meeting regulatory QMS requirements.[17] If parts of the manufacturing process are outsourced, the responsibility for complying with the QMS requirements lies with the manufacturer and cannot be delegated to any supplier of products and services.

Although some suppliers may undergo some form of oversight by either a regulatory authority or a third party operating on behalf of a regulatory authority, this does not relinquish the manufacturer's responsibility to establish controls and provide evidence for products and services obtained from suppliers. This control typically comprises six phases:

- planning
- selection of potential supplier(s)
- supplier evaluation and acceptance
- finalizing controls
- delivery, measurement and monitoring
- feedback and communication, including the corrective and preventive action (CAPA) process[18]

Figure 18-3 shows key activities that a manufacturer should perform to help demonstrate its control over suppliers.

All products and services received from a supplier should be strictly controlled to ensure they meet the manufacturer's standards to enable the manufacturer to fulfill its legal obligations. Manufacturers should have a formal evaluation and selection procedure to verify suppliers' capabilities. This may be a formal audit or, for less-important suppliers, verification of ISO certification. Once selected, suppliers and contract manufacturers should be inspected and reassessed at least once a year. Evidence of control over products and services from suppliers (on site or readily available) normally will be subject to inspection by regulatory authorities and/or third parties. Failure to demonstrate evidence of the controls associated with products and services from suppliers could result in the manufacturer's QMS being deemed noncompliant.[19]

Conclusion

An effective QMS enables an organization to control the design, manufacturing and supply processes to ensure that its devices perform in a safe and effective way and conform to the required regulations and expectations of medical device regulatory agencies around the world.

References

1. GHTF/SG1/N78:2012 *Principles of Conformity Assessment for Medical Devices* (November 2012). IMDRF website. http://www.imdrf.org/docs/ghtf/final/sg1/technical-docs/ghtf-sg1-n78-2012-conformity-assessment-medical-devices-121102.pdf. Accessed 17 July 2013.
2. Ibid.
3. ISO 9000:2005 *Quality management systems—Fundamentals and vocabulary.*
4. Higson GR. *The Regulation of Medical Devices for Public Health and Safety.* Institute of Physics Publishing, London, 2002.

5. WHO. *Medical Device Regulations—Global overview and guiding principles* (2003) WHO website. http://www.who.int/medical_devices/publications/en/MD_Regulations.pdf. Accessed 17 July 2013..
6. Medical device single audit program (MDSAP). IMDRF website. http://www.imdrf.org/workitems/wi-mdsap.asp. Accessed 29 April 2013.
7. Code of Federal Regulations Title 21—Food and Drugs—Chapter I—Food and Drug Administration—Department of Health and Human Services—Subchapter H—Medical Devices—Part 820—Qualiity System Regulation. FDA website. http://www.accessdata.fda.gov/scripts/cdrh/cfdocs/cfcfr/CFRsearch.cfm?CFRPart=820. Accessed 17 July 2013.
8. *Guidance for Industry, Third Parties and Food and Drug Administration Staff—Medical Device ISO 13485:2003 Voluntary Audit Report Submission Pilot Program* (2012). FDA website. http://www.fda.gov/MedicalDevices/DeviceRegulationandGuidance/GuidanceDocuments/ucm212795.htm. Accessed 17 July 2013.
9. Medical Devices Regulations—SOR/98-282—*Food and Drugs Act*—Canada—1998, amended in 2011. Justice Laws Website. http://laws-lois.justice.gc.ca/eng/regulations/SOR-98-282/. Accessed 17 July.2013.
10. Council Directive 93/42/EEC of 14 June 1993 concerning medical devices, Council of the European Communities (1994), last amended in 2011. Eur-Lex website. http://eur-lex.europa.eu/LexUriServ/LexUriServ.do?uri=CONSLEG:1993L0042:20071011:en:PDF. Accessed 17 July 2013.
11. RESOLUÇÃO DA DIRETORIA COLEGIADA - RDC N°16, DE 28 DE MARÇO DE 2013 - Aprova o Regulamento Técnico de Boas Práticas de Fabricação de Produtos Médicos e Produtos para Diagnóstico de Uso In Vitro e dá outras providências.
12. Portaria INMETRO n.º 350, de 06 de setembro de 2010 - Requisitos de Avaliação da Conformidade - RAC para Equipamentos Elétricos sob regime de Vigilância Sanitária.
13. GHTF/SG3/N99-10 (Edition 2) *Quality Management Systems—Process Validation Guidance* (January 2004). IMDRF website. http://www.imdrf.org/docs/ghtf/final/sg3/technical-docs/ghtf-sg3-n99-10-2004-qms-process-guidance-04010.pdf. Accessed 17 July 2013.
14. Ibid.
15. Ibid.
16. Validation Online Documentation Centre. Validation-Online.net. http://www.validation-online.net/index.html. Accessed 29 January 2013.
17. Sofer S and Zabriskie DW (eds.). *Biopharmaceutical Process Validation.* Marcel Dekker Inc., New York: 2000.
18. GHTF/SG3/N17:2008 *Quality Management System—Medical Devices—Guidance on the Control of Products and Services Obtained from Suppliers.* IMDRF website. http://www.imdrf.org/docs/ghtf/final/sg3/technical-docs/ghtf-sg3-n17-guidance-on-quality-management-system-081211.pdf. Accessed 17 July 2013.
19. Ibid.

Chapter 19

In Vitro Diagnostic Medical Devices

Updated by Alexander Krieg, PhD, RAC

OBJECTIVES

- ❑ Understand the basic principles of in vitro diagnostic (IVD) medical devices
- ❑ Understand IVD classification
- ❑ Understand IVD classification rules
- ❑ Understand IVD conformity assessment procedures

REGULATIONS AND GUIDELINES COVERED IN THIS CHAPTER

GHTF

- ❑ GHTF/SG1/N045:2008 *Principles of In Vitro Diagnostic (IVD) Medical Devices Classification* (February 2008)
- ❑ GHTF/SG1/N046:2008 *Principles of Conformity Assessment for In Vitro Diagnostic (IVD) Medical Devices* (July 2008)
- ❑ GHTF/SG1/N41R9:2005 *Essential Principles of Safety and Performance of Medical Devices* (May 2005)
- ❑ GHTF/SG1/N044:2008 *Role of Standards in the Assessment of Medical Devices* (March 2008)
- ❑ MEDDEV 2.12-1 rev. 8 Vigilance Guidelines on a Medical Devices Vigilance System (January 2013)
- ❑ AHWEG-UDI/N2R3:*2011 Unique Device Identification System for Medical Devices* (September 2011)
- ❑ GHTF/SG1/N063: *Summary Technical Documentation (STED) for Demonstrating Conformity to the Essential Principles of Safety and Performance of In Vitro Diagnostic Medical Devices* (March 2011)

Introduction

An "in vitro diagnostic (IVD) medical device" is defined as a device that, whether used alone or in combination, is intended by the manufacturer for the *in vitro* examination of specimens derived from the human body solely or principally to provide information for diagnostic, monitoring or compatibility purposes.[1] Examples include:

- reagents
- calibrators
- control materials
- specimen receptacles
- software and related instruments
- apparatus or other articles

IVD medical devices for self testing are intended by the manufacturer for use by lay people. In some jurisdictions, some classes of IVD medical devices may be covered by separate national regulations.

Table 19-1. General GHTF Classification System for IVD Medical Devices

Class	Risk Level	Examples
A	Low Individual Risk and Low Public Health Risk	Clinical chemistry analyzer, prepared selective culture media
B	Moderate Individual Risk and/or Low Public Health Risk	Pregnancy self testing, anti-nuclear antibody, urine test strips
C	High Individual Risk and/or Moderate Public Health Risk	Blood glucose self testing, HLA typing, PSA screening, Rubella
D	High Individual Risk and High Public Health Risk	HIV blood donor screening, HIV blood diagnostic

Source: GHTF/SG1/N045:2008, p. 9.

Principles of IVD Medical Device Classification

The interrelationship between device class and conformity assessment is critical in establishing a consistent approach to premarket approval across all countries/regions.[2] In 2012, the International Medical Device Regulators Forum (IMDRF) succeeded the Global Harmonization Task Force (GHTF) in working toward the harmonization of medical device regulation. Previously, GHTF published *Principles of In Vitro Diagnostic (IVD) Medical Devices Classification* (GHTF/SG1/N045:2008) to help manufacturers assign in vitro diagnostic devices to the correct risk class based on their intended use. According to this guidance, the classification for IVDs depends upon the:

- intended use and indications for use as specified by the manufacturer
- technical, scientific and/or medical expertise of the intended user, including whether the user is a lay person or a healthcare professional
- importance of the information to the diagnosis, i.e., sole determinant or one of several
- impact the result (true or false) may have on the individual and/or on public health[3]

Figure 19-1. Regulatory Requirements Related to the Device Risk Class

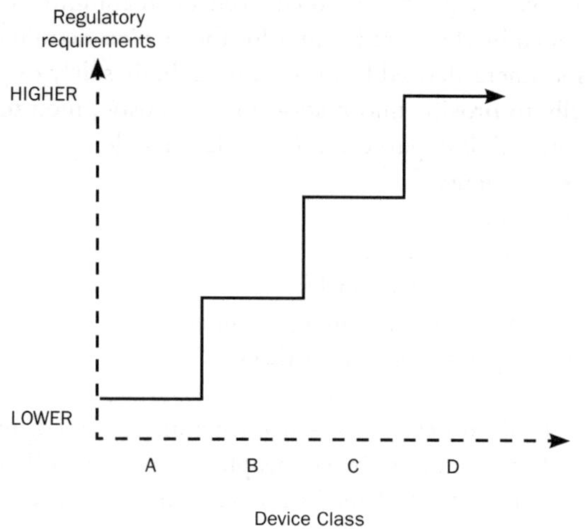

Source GHTF/SG1/N045:2008, p. 10

The exact rules for classification may differ slightly from one jurisdiction to another but are, in general, based on a device's associated risk.

GHTF Proposed General Principles of Classification

GHTF proposed a four-class system (see **Table 19-1**). As the risk level increases from A (low risk) to D (very high risk), so do the regulatory requirements. Increasing requirements may include an operational quality system, a larger amount of clinical data, greater detail in the technical file and external audits. This escalation of requirements can be shown using a stepwise approach, as in **Figure 19-1**.

Device Class and Classification Rules

Section 9 of GHTF/SG1/N045:2008 proposed seven rules to help manufacturers classify their IVD devices correctly. It should be noted, however, that the exact classification should be based on existing national laws and regulations. As a general rule, if more than one classification rule applies to the IVD medical device, or in borderline cases, the device should be assigned to the highest class indicated. The device class will have an effect on the conformity assessment procedure chosen. This, in turn, may affect the acceptability of such devices in various regions and countries. In such cases, the importing country may require the manufacturer to carry out additional tests to comply with local conformity assessment requirements. See **Tables 19-2** for the seven rules proposed by GHTF.

Principles of Conformity Assessment for In Vitro Diagnostic (IVD) Medical Devices

According to GHTF's *Principles of Conformity Assessment for In Vitro Diagnostic (IVD) Medical Devices* (GHTF/SG1/N046:2008), such assessment can be defined as[4]

> "the systematic examination of evidence generated and procedures undertaken by the manufacturer, under requirements established by the Regulatory Authority, to determine that a medical device is safe and performs

Table 19-2. Classification Rules for IVDs

Rule	IVD Medical Device Intended Purpose	Class	Example
1	1. Used to detect the presence of, or exposure to, a transmissible agent in blood, blood components, blood derivatives, cells, tissues or organs in order to assess their suitability for transfusion or transplantation 2. Devices intended to be used to detect the presence of, or exposure to, a transmissible agent that causes a life-threatening, often incurable, disease with a high risk of propagation	D	Examples include tests to detect infection by HIV, HCV, HBV, HTLV. The rule applies to first-line assays, confirmatory assays and supplemental assays.
2	1. Intended to be used for blood grouping or tissue typing to ensure the immunological compatibility of blood, blood components, cells, tissue or organs that are intended for transfusion or transplantation, are classified as Class C, except for ABO system (A (ABO1), B (ABO2), AB (ABO3)), rhesus system (RH1 (D), RH2 (C), RH3 (E), RH4 (c), RH5 (e)), Kell system (Kel1 (K)), Kidd system (JK1 (Jka), JK2 (Jkb)) and Duffy system (FY1 (Fya), FY2 (Fyb)) determinations, which are classified as Class D	C or D	Examples include HLA, Duffy system (other Duffy systems except those listed in the rule as Class D are in Class C)
3	1. To detect the presence of, or exposure to, a sexually transmitted agent 2. To detect the presence in cerebrospinal fluid or blood of an infectious agent with a risk of limited propagation 3. To detect the presence of an infectious agent where there is a significant risk that an erroneous result would cause death or severe disability to the individual or fetus being tested 4. Used in prenatal screening of women in order to determine their immune status towards transmissible agents 5. To determine infective disease status or immune status, and where there is a risk that an erroneous result will lead to a patient management decision resulting in an imminent life-threatening situation for the patient 6. Used in screening for selection of patients for selective therapy and management, or for disease staging, or in the diagnosis of cancer 7. Used in human genetic testing 8. Used to monitor levels of medicines, substances or biological components, when there is a risk that an erroneous result will lead to a patient management decision resulting in an immediate life-threatening situation for the patient 9. Used in the management of patients suffering from a life-threatening infectious disease 10. Used in screening for congenital disorders in the fetus		1. Sexually transmitted diseases, such as Chlamydia trachomatis, Neisseria gonorrhoeae 2. Neisseria meningitidis or Cryptococcus neoformans 3. Diagnostic assay for CMV, *Chlamydia pneumoniae*, Methycillin Resistant *Staphylococcus aureus* 4. Immune status tests for Rubella or Toxoplasmosis 5. Enteroviruses, CMV and HSV in transplant patients 6. Personalized medicine 7. Huntington's Disease, Cystic Fibrosis 8. Cardiac markers, Cyclosporin, Prothrombin time testing 9. HCV viral load, HIV Viral Load and HIV and HCV geno- and subtyping 10. Spina Bifida or Down Syndrome
4	1. IVD medical devices intended for self testing are classified as Class C, except those devices from which the result is not determining a medically critical status, or is preliminary and requires follow-up with the appropriate laboratory test, in which case they are Class B 2. IVD medical devices intended for blood gases and blood glucose determinations for near-patient testing would be Class C; other IVD medical devices that are intended for near-patient testing should be classified in their own right using the classification rules	C or B	1. Example for self testing Class C: blood glucose monitoring 2. Example for self testing Class B: pregnancy self test, fertility testing, urine test-strips
5	1. Reagents or other articles which possess specific characteristics, intended by the manufacturer to make them suitable for in vitro diagnostic procedures related to a specific examination 2. Instruments intended by the manufacturer specifically to be used for in vitro diagnostic procedures 3. Specimen receptacles	A	Selective/differential microbiological media (excluding the dehydrated powders which are considered not to be a finished IVD medical device), identification kits for cultured microorganisms, wash solutions, instruments and plain urine cup
6	IVD medical devices not covered in Rules 1 through 5 are classified as Class B	**B**	Blood gases, *H. pylori* and physiological markers such as hormones, vitamins, enzymes, metabolic markers, specific IgE assays and celiac disease markers
7	IVD medical devices that are controls without a quantitative or qualitative assigned value will be classified as Class B	**B**	

Source GHTF/SG1/N045:2008, Section 9.

Table 19-3. Class A Device

Conformity Assessment Element	Manufacturer Responsibility	Regulatory Authority/Conformity Assessment Body Responsibility
Quality Management System (QMS)	Establish and maintain a full QMS or a QMS without design and development controls	Premarket regulatory audit not required
Postmarket Surveillance	Establish and maintain an adverse event reporting procedure according to GHTF SG2 guidance	May audit postmarket to investigate specific safety or regulatory concerns
Technical Documentation	Upon request prepare STED	Premarket submission of STED not required; may be requested to investigate specific safety or regulatory concerns
Declaration of Conformity	Prepare, sign and maintain	On file with the manufacturer; available upon request
Registration of Manufacturers and Their Devices	Perform according to regulatory requirements	Maintain and verify as appropriate

Source GHTF/SG1/N046:2008, pp. 11–14.

Table 19-4. Class B Device

Conformity Assessment Element	Manufacturer Responsibility	Regulatory Authority/Conformity Assessment Body Responsibility
Quality Management System (QMS)	Establish and maintain a full QMS or a QMS without design and development controls	Be satisfied that a current and appropriate QMS is in place or otherwise conduct a QMS audit prior to marketing authorization
Postmarket Surveillance	Establish and maintain an adverse event reporting procedure according to GHTF SG2 guidance	Be satisfied that a current and appropriate adverse event reporting procedure is in place as part of the QMS
Technical Documentation	Upon request, prepare STED	Premarket submission normally not required but if requested, receive and conduct a review of the STED to determine conformity to Essential Principles
Declaration of Conformity	Prepare, sign and submit	Review and verify compliance with requirements
Registration of Manufacturers and Their Devices	Perform according to regulatory requirements	Maintain and verify as appropriate

Source GHTF/SG1/N046:2008, pp. 11–14.

Table 19-5. Class C Device

Conformity Assessment Element	Manufacturer Responsibility	Regulatory Authority/Conformity Assessment Body Responsibility
Quality Management System (QMS)	Establish and maintain a full QMS	Be satisfied that a current and appropriate QMS is in place or otherwise conduct a QMS audit prior to marketing authorization
Postmarket Surveillance	Establish and maintain an adverse event reporting procedure according to GHTF SG2 guidance	Be satisfied that a current and appropriate adverse event reporting procedure is in place as part of the QMS
Technical Documentation	Prepare and submit STED for review	Receive and conduct a premarket review of the STED to determine conformity to Essential Principles
Declaration of Conformity	Prepare, sign and submit	Review and verify compliance with requirements
Registration of Manufacturers and Their Devices	Perform according to regulatory requirements	Maintain and verify as appropriate

Source GHTF/SG1/N046:2008, pp. 11-14.

as intended by the manufacturer and, therefore, conforms to the *Essential Principles of Safety and Performance of Medical Devices (SG1/N041)*"[5]

Carrying out a conformity assessment is the sole responsibility of the IVD medical device manufacturer; however, it must be done according to established regulatory requirements. In addition, except for very low-risk devices, a conformity assessment conducted by the manufacturer is subject to further review by the regulatory authority and/or Conformity Assessment Body (CAB).

Conformity Assessment Elements

The main elements of a conformity assessment system are:

- a quality management system (QMS)
- a postmarket surveillance system (PMS)
- summary technical documentation
- a Declaration of Conformity
- registration of manufacturers and their IVD medical devices with the regulatory authority[6]

The amount of detail needed for each of these elements to prove conformity for IVD medical devices is directly proportional to the device's associated risk. This requirement applies primarily to the level of detail in the clinical and/or performance data and details of the manufacturer's quality control release program included in the technical documentation (for more information, please see Chapter 17 Technical and Regulatory Requirements).

QMS

As is the case with other medical device makers, IVD manufacturers must have a suitable QMS in place. The purpose of the QMS (in combination with other conformity assessment elements) is to ensure that IVD medical devices will be safe and perform as intended by the manufacturer. A QMS usually is based on internationally accepted standards.[7] The QMS ensures that the manufactured products consistently meet both customer and regulatory requirements.

The scope and complexity of the QMS needed depends upon the size of the organization and the type of products manufactured (i.e., high or low risk). Any outsourced processes must be properly controlled (for more information about QMS and outsourcing, please see Chapter 16 Medical Device Premarket Requirements).

Except for the lowest-risk devices (Class A), the QMS will be subject to inspections by the regulatory authority and/or CAB.

PMS System

Prior to placing IVD devices on the market, manufacturers must have a system in place to collect and assess incoming complaints, perform vigilance reporting to the Competent Authority and carry out any corrective and/or preventive action (CAPA). For more information about vigilance reporting and PMS, please see Chapter 22 Postmarket Requirements for Medical Devices. The PMS system will be inspected during the quality management inspections and periodically thereafter. The PMS system is of special significance for IVD device manufacturers since vigilance alone cannot capture all risks related to the use of these devices. Examples include false positive and/or false negative results and adverse events arising from use in the home, where it may be difficult or even impossible to evaluate the device's performance.[8]

Technical Documentation

To demonstrate conformity, manufacturers must provide evidence in the form of technical documentation that the IVD medical device meets the required Essential Principles. Normally, the manufacturer establishes a subset of technical documentation (Summary Technical Documentation (STED)), which should either be submitted for evaluation and review before market entry (high-risk devices) or kept on the premises of the manufacturer to be reviewed during routine inspections. (For more information about STED requirements, please see Chapter 17 Technical and Regulatory Requirements, and GHTF/SG1/N063: *Summary Technical Documentation (STED) for Demonstrating Conformity to the Essential Principles of Safety and Performance of In Vitro Diagnostic Medical Devices* (March 2011)).[9] The amount of detail required in the STED is directly related to the device's class and associated risk.

Declaration of Conformity

The manufacturer of an IVD, like makers of other medical devices, is responsible for issuing a written Declaration of Conformity (DOC) that attests to the compliance of the IVD medical device with all applicable Essential Principles of safety and performance of medical devices (GHTF/SG1/N41R9:2005). The DOC also confirms that that the device has been properly classified[10] and has met all applicable conformity assessment elements.

The DOC must contain sufficient information to identify the device(s) to which it applies and the device's associated risk class. In addition, the DOC should clearly show which conformity assessment procedures have been applied, and include other information such as the date from which the DOC is valid and the device manufacturer's name and address. The DOC must be signed by a responsible person who has been authorized to complete it on the manufacturer's behalf.[11]

Registration of Manufacturers and Their IVD Medical Devices With the Regulatory Authority

Prior to placing an IVD medical device on the market, the manufacturer, its local distributor or its authorized representative should register with the local regulatory authority. This helps the regulatory authority identify the IVD medical device and the party responsible for it within a particular jurisdiction, thereby facilitating any necessary regulatory activity. It is the regulatory authority's responsibility to maintain this register and to initiate enforcement in case of noncompliance.

The Relationship Between Conformity Assessment and Device Classification

Utilizing the GHTF guidance, IVD medical devices should be assigned to one of four classes (starting with lowest risk, A, to highest risk, D), using a set of rules as defined in *Principles of In Vitro Diagnostic (IVD) Medical Devices Classification.*[12] The level of manufacturer scrutiny from regulatory authorities and conformity assessment bodies is based on the device's associated risk. Although regulatory authorities and conformity assessment bodies have the same responsibilities for Class C and D IVD medical devices, the amount of detail in the STED related to clinical and/or performance data and details of the manufacturer's quality control release program will depend upon the risk level. **Tables 19-4–19-6**, excerpted from GHTF/SG1/N046:2008, illustrate this.

Unique Device Identification

Unique Device Identification System for Medical Devices (GHTF/AHWEG-UDI/N2R3:2011) lays out the advantages of a global Unique Device Identification (UDI) system:

> "A globally harmonized and consistent approach to UDI is expected to increase patient safety and help optimize patient care by facilitating the:
> 1. traceability of devices, especially for recalls and other field service corrective actions,
> 2. adequate identification of the device through its distribution and use,
> 3. identification of devices in adverse events,
> 4. reduction of medical errors, and
> 5. documentation and longitudinal capture of data on medical devices."[13]

A UDI system comprises three parts:

1. the development of the UDI using a globally accepted standard
2. the application of that UDI on the label or on the device itself and
3. the submission of appropriate information to the UDI Database (UDID)[14]

In addition, this guidance describes the required elements of a global UDI system. The US is already preparing to implement UDI requirements in its national laws, and UDI is part of the proposed revision of the EU *IVD Directive.*

Environmental Standards

Environmental regulations like the EU directives "Registration, Evaluation, Authorisation and Restriction of Chemicals (REACH)," 1907/2006/EC or "Restriction of the use of certain Hazardous Substances" 2011/65/EC, previously 2002/95/EC (RoHS), are not only in Europe; similar regulations are becoming applicable in other major markets ("China-RoHS"). These regulations demand increased effort, especially in the characterization of the materials used in or for the in vitro diagnosticum (instruments and reagents) as well as in the control of the supply chain.

The increased emphasis on environmental issues is also expressed in the new proposal of the European IVD regulation:

> "7.3 The devices shall be designed and manufactured in such a way as to reduce as far as possible the risks posed by substances that may leach or leak from the device. Special attention shall be given to substances which are carcinogenic, mutagenic or toxic to reproduction, in accordance with Part 3 of Annex VI to Regulation (EC) No 1272/2008 of the European Parliament and of the Council of 16 December 2008 on classification, labelling and packaging of substances and mixtures, amending and repealing Directives 67/548/EEC and 1999/45/EC, and amending Regulation (EC) No 1907/200640, and to substances having endocrine disrupting properties for which there is scientific evidence of probable serious effects to human health and which are identified in accordance with the procedure set out in Article 59 of Regulation (EC) No 1907/2006 of the European Parliament and of the Council of 18 December 2006 concerning the Registration, Evaluation, Authorisation and Restriction of Chemicals (REACH)."[15]

Conclusion

Incident reporting and vigilance may not be the most suitable way to monitor an IVD's performance after market entry. Therefore, for this class of devices, more emphasis is placed on an effective, functioning PMS system as compared with other device groups. In addition, clinical investigations generally are replaced by so-called "performance evaluations." However, for the most part, the regulatory requirements for IVD medical devices follow the same basic principles of performance and safety as those for other medical devices. GHTF proposed seven classification rules and four device classes from A (low risk) to D (high risk). The route to achieving conformity assessment depends upon the device class. The complexity of established quality management systems and the detail needed in the accompanying technical documentation are directly proportional to the risk associated with the IVD medical device. In most jurisdictions, the internationally accepted GHTF guidance(s) must be read in conjunction with local regulations and restrictions to ensure compliance with national requirements.

For example, the IVD device classifications in Australia, Canada and the proposed revision of the EU IVD regulations follow the suggested four device classification rules.

References

1. GHTF/SG1/N045:2008 *Principles of In Vitro Diagnostic (IVD) Medical Devices Classification* (February 2008), p. 5. IMDRF website. www.imdrf.org/docs/ghtf/final/sg1/procedural-docs/ghtf-sg1-n045-2008-principles-ivd-medical-devices-classification-080219.pdf. Accessed 22 January 2013.
2. Ibid.
3. Ibid, p 8.
4. GHTF/SG1/N046:2008 *Principles of Conformity Assessment for In Vitro Diagnostic (IVD) Medical Devices* (July 2008), p. 7. IMDRF website. www.imdrf.org/docs/ghtf/final/sg1/procedural-docs/ghtf-sg1-n046-2008-principles-of-ca-for-ivd-medical-devices-080731.pdf. Accessed 22 January 2013.
5. GHTF/SG1/N41R9:2005: *Essential Principles of Safety and Performance of Medical Devices* (May 2005). IMDRF website. www.imdrf.org/docs/ghtf/final/sg1/technical-docs/ghtf-sg1-n41r9-2008-principles-safety-performance-050520.pdf. Accessed 22 January 2013.
6. Ibid 4.
7. GHTF/SG1/N044:2008 *Role of Standards in the Assessment of Medical Devices* (March 2008). IMDRF website. www.imdrf.org/docs/ghtf/final/sg1/procedural-docs/ghtf-sg1-n044-2008-standards-in-assessment-of-medical-devices-080305.pdf. Accessed 22 January 2013.
8. MEDDEV 2 12-1 rev. 8 *Vigilance Guidelines on a Medical Devices Vigilance System.* http://ec.europa.eu/health/medical-devices/files/meddev/2_12_1_ol_en.pdf . European Comission website, Accessed 17 February 2013.
9. GHTF/SG1/N063:2011 *Summary Technical Documentation (STED) for Demonstrating Conformity to the Essential Principles of Safety and Performance of In Vitro Diagnostic Medical Devices* (March 2011). IMDRF website. www.imdrf.org/docs/ghtf/final/sg1/technical-docs/ghtf-sg1-n063-2011-summary-technical-documentation-ivd-safety-conformity-110317.pdf. Accessed 22 January 2013.
10. Ibid 1.
11. Op cit 4, pp. 9-10.
12. Ibid, pp. 10-14.
13. AHWEG-UDI/N2R3:*2011 Unique Device Identification System for Medical Devices* (September 2011), p. 4. IMDRF website. www.gs1.org/docs/healthcare/GHTF_The_UDI_System_for_Medical_Devices_AHWG-UDI-N2R3.pdf. Accessed 22 January 2013.
14. Ibid, p. 9.
15. COM(2012) 541 (26.9.2012)2012/0267 (COD): *Proposal for a Regulation of the European Parliament and of the Council on in vitro diagnostic medical devices, Annex 1, Chapter 7.3.* p. 87. EUR-Lex website. http://eur-lex.europa.eu/LexUriServ/LexUriServ.do?uri=COM:2012:0541:FIN:EN:PDF. Accessed 22 January 2013.

Chapter 20

Active Implantable Medical Devices

By Renee Hardley, RAC and Manuel Urena, RAC

OBJECTIVES

- ❑ Understand the main requirements for the development of active implantable medical devices
- ❑ Understand the unique country-specific requirements established by regulatory bodies around the world for the market authorization of these devices.

REGULATIONS AND GUIDELINES COVERED IN THIS CHAPTER

- ❑ ISO 13485:2003 *Medical Devices—Quality Management Systems—Requirements for regulatory purposes*
- ❑ ISO 14971:2007 *Medical Devices—Application of Risk Management to Medical Devices*
- ❑ EN 45502-1:1997 *Active implantable medical devices—Part 1: General requirements for safety, marking and information to be provided by the manufacturer*
- ❑ EN 45502-2-1:2003 *Active implantable medical devices—Part 2-1: Particular requirements for active implantable medical devices intended to treat bradyarrhythmia (cardiac pacemakers)*
- ❑ EN 45502-2-2:2008 *Active implantable medical devices—Part 2-2: Particular requirements for active implantable medical devices intended to treat tachyarrhythmia (includes implantable defibrillators)*
- ❑ EN 45502-2-3:2010 *Active implantable medical devices—Part 2-3: Particular requirements for cochlear and auditory brainstem implant systems*
- ❑ ISO 14708-1:2000 *Implants for surgery—Active implantable medical devices—Part 1: General requirements for safety, marking and for information to be provided by the manufacturer*
- ❑ ISO 14708-5:2010 *Implants for surgery—Active implantable medical devices—Part 5: Circulatory support devices*
- ❑ ISO 14708-3:2008 *Implants for surgery—Active implantable medical devices—Part 3: Implantable neurostimulators*
- ❑ ISO 10993-1:2009 *Biological evaluation of medical devices—Part 1: Evaluation and testing*
- ❑ ISO 14937:2009 *General requirements for characterisation of a sterilising agent and the development, validation and routine control of a sterilisation process for medical devices*
- ❑ ISO 11135-1:2007 *Sterilisation of health care products—Ethylene oxide—Part 1: Requirements for development, validation and*

routine control of a sterilisation process for medical devices

- ISO 11137-1:2006 *Sterilisation of health care products—Radiation—Part 1: Requirements for development, validation and routine control of a sterilisation process for medical devices*
- ISO 17996-1:2006 *Sterilisation of health care products—Moist heat—Part 1: Requirements for development, validation and routine control of a sterilisation process for medical devices*
- ISO 11607-1:2006 *Packaging for terminally sterilised medical devices—Part 1: Requirements for materials, sterile barrier systems and packaging systems*
- ISO/TS 10974:2012 *Assessment of the safety of MRI for patients with an active implantable medical device*
- IEC 60601:2005 *Medical electrical equipment: General requirements for basic safety and essential performance*
- FDA *Draft Guidance for Industry and FDA Staff: Radio-Frequency Wireless Technology in Medical Devices* (2007)
- EN 980:2008 *Symbols for use in the labelling of medical devices*
- GHTF final document on STED *(Summary Technical Documentation for Demonstrating Conformity to the Essential Principles of Safety and Performance for Medical Devices)*
- ASEAN CSDT (Common Submission Dossier Template)
- Directive 90/385/EEC (Council Directive of 20 June 1990 on the approximation of the laws of the Member States relating to active implantable medical devices)
- Australia *Therapeutic Goods Act* 1989
- Australia *Therapeutic Goods (Medical Device) Regulations* 2002
- US *Federal Food, Drug, and Cosmetic Act*
- Canada *Food and Drugs Act*
- Canada *Medical Devices Regulations*
- Brazil Resolution RDC No. 185 of October 22, 2012
- Singapore *Health Products Act* 2007
- Singapore *Health Products (Medical Device) Regulations* 2010
- GHTF *Final Document for Clinical Evaluation*

Introduction

Active implantable medical devices (AIMDs) comprise a category of medical devices, specifically recognized as such in certain jurisdictions, such as Australia and the EU. In other countries, although there is no specific classification category for AIMDs, they fall into the highest risk class within the classification scheme. Therefore, there are common expectations and regulatory practices for AIMDs in most countries, regardless of how they are classified. High-risk medical devices require more-detailed evidence to demonstrate their safety and effectiveness and a more in-depth assessment by the regulatory authorities compared to lower-risk medical devices.

This chapter covers the general requirements and considerations for AIMDs, given the inherent risks with these types of devices. It also provides generic guidance on the structure and information required for an application for regulatory approval of an AIMD. Finally, the regulatory requirements for AIMDs in representative countries or regions are discussed. Some Asian countries like Japan, China and Korea are not included in this chapter, as their fundamental regulatory framework for market authorization of an AIMD is similar to that of the EU and US. While there are similarities in their regulatory requirements, total harmonization has not been achieved, resulting in some countries still having their own unique regulatory paths, such as the Type Testing process in China.

Definition

Classification rules in some regulated jurisdictions have provisions to classify AIMDs. Once the conditions have been met to be considered a medical device, a device must meet two additional factors to be classified as an AIMD:

- Active—This indicates that the device relies on electrical energy or some other power source other than that directly generated by the human body or gravity. The definition implies that the function of the device involves using the source of power to perform useful clinical work.
- Implantable—This means that the device is totally or partly introduced, surgically or medically, into

the human body or by medical intervention into a natural orifice, and is intended to remain in place after the procedure for a certain period, typically longer than 30 days.

Examples of AIMDs are implantable pulse generators, implantable stimulators and implantable drug administration devices, such as:

- implantable cardiac pacemakers and their leads and adaptors
- implantable defibrillators and their leads and adaptors
- implantable nerve stimulators
- implantable brain stimulators
- implantable ventricular assist devices
- bladder stimulators
- sphincter stimulators
- diaphragm stimulators
- cochlear implants
- auditory brainstem implants
- retinal implants
- implantable active drug administration device
- implantable active monitoring devices

Special Considerations for AIMDs

General Standards

AIMDs may present particular hazards, e.g., with regard to the impossibility of maintenance, calibration or control and problems relating to the aging of materials. Therefore, consideration and analysis should be conducted to ensure the patient's safety, but also to ensure that the device does not sustain damage through its implanted life. There are multiple guidelines and standards addressing those risks.

The two main horizontal standards applicable to AIMDs in general, developed by the International Organization for Standardization (ISO), are ISO 13485-1 *Medical devices—Quality management systems—Requirements for regulatory purposes* and ISO 14971-1 *Medical devices—Application of risk management to medical devices.* These two standards are widely used in the medical device industry.

In the EU, a joint working group from CEN (European Committee for Standardisation) and CENELEC (European Committee for Electrotechnical Standardisation) developed the European Standard, EN 45502-1 *Active implantable medical devices—Part 1: General requirements for safety, marking and information to be provided by the manufacturer.* This standard provides a comprehensive set of requirements to consider for the development and manufacturing of AIMDs and also provides references to other recommended standards. EN 45502-1 is a harmonized standard in the EU, hence complying with this standard presumes compliance to the Essential Requirements of Council Directive 90/385/EEC of 20 June 1990 on the approximation of laws of the Member States relating to active implantable medical devices (*Active Medical Devices Directive* or *AIMDD*). There are three harmonised collateral standards: EN 45502-2-1 for cardiac pacemakers, EN 45502-2-2 for implantable defibrillators and EN 45502-2-3 for cochlear and auditory brainstem implants, which provide additional requirements to EN 45502-1 for these specific types of devices.

ISO also has developed a series of standards specific to AIMDs, based on ISO 14708-1. EN 45502-1:1997 and ISO 14708-1:2000 are similar, but one of the main differences of the ISO standards is they have a more extensive series of collateral standards for specific types of devices, including implantable neurostimulators and implantable infusion pumps. ISO 14708-1 and its collateral standards are not harmonized in the EU, but the US Food and Drug Administration (FDA) has recognized two of its collateral standards: ISO 14708-5:2010 for circulatory support devices and ISO 14708-3:2008 for implantable neurostimulators.

In addition to the technical usefulness of applying a standard issued by a recognized agency like CEN or ISO, a practical advantage is derived from the concept of state of the art, expected by other regulatory authorities. It is possible that another regulatory authority outside the US or EU, for example the Australian Therapeutic Goods Agency (TGA), will have the expectation of compliance to EN 45502-1 or ISO 14708-1, and their applicable collateral standards, even though the standards would not be officially recognized by that authority.

Finally, at the time of publication, several initiatives are underway to update or create standards relevant to AIMDs. For example, both EN 45502-1 and ISO 14708-1 are being reviewed, and in the US, the Association for the Advancement of Medical Instrumentation (AAMI) is coordinating the development of a standard for cochlear implants.

Biological Safety

Protecting patients from potential biological risks arising from the use of medical devices is the primary aim of the ISO 10993 standard series. These standards are globally recognized and intended to be used as guidance for the biological evaluation of medical devices within a risk management process using a combination of existing data assessment and testing where necessary.

ISO 10993-1 is the primary standard of the series and provides a classification system for medical devices according to the nature and duration of their anticipated contact with human tissue when in use. The classification indicates the biological data sets that are considered relevant for each specific category.

ISO 10993 is not intended to provide a rigid set of test methods, including pass/fail criteria, as this might result in either an unnecessary constraint on the development and use of novel medical devices, or a false sense of security in the general use of medical devices. Therefore, it is the manufacturer's responsibility to determine the specific applications for device assessment, within the risk management process.

Naturally, long-term implanted devices are considered in the classification scheme, and the recommended testing varies according to the type of contact: blood or tissue/bone. There are 18 additional standards and technical specifications in the ISO 10993 series, which define specific requirements and guidance for analysis or testing, most of them relevant to implantable devices.

The level of recognition of the ISO 10993 standards varies among regulatory authorities. For example, FDA's recognition of ISO 10993-1:2009 excludes the risk management approach for not conducting biological testing based on existing data. Also, certain regulatory authorities, such as the Pharmaceutical and Medical Devices Agency (PMDA) in Japan or the China Food and Drug Administration (CFDA), require specific tests or acceptance criteria for biological testing. Specifically, China requires a certain level of testing to be performed by authorized test centers in China.

Sterilization and Packaging

As AIMDs are intended for implantation, it is essential they remain free of viable microorganisms until they are surgically implanted. Medical device sterilization is a complex process, with multiple requirements, standards and guidelines at the international and national levels. This discussion is beyond the scope of this chapter; therefore, only a brief overview of the most relevant information is provided.

Sterilization processes for AIMDs typically use radiation, steam or ethylene oxide (EtO). When selecting the correct sterilization process, manufacturers should consider the available technology and the medical device's specific characteristics. For example, an AIMD typically will have some kind of electronic assembly that may not be able to withstand some of the temperatures required for an effective steam sterilization process; therefore, an alternative, such as EtO sterilization may be more appropriate.

Some of the high-level standards and guidance documents applicable to the sterilization process are ISO 14937 (*General requirements for characterization of a sterilizing agent and the development, validation and routine control of a sterilization process for medical devices*), ISO 11135 for EtO sterilization, ISO 11137 for radiation sterilization and ISO 17665 for steam sterilization.

Once the sterilization process is established and validated, it is critical that the packaging configuration of the device maintains the achieved sterility level. ISO 11607 provides appropriate guidance on the requirements for the materials, sterile barriers and packaging systems, and its process validation.

Magnetic Resonance Imaging (MRI) and Other Medical Treatments

When considering risks posed to patients from AIMDs, it is important to take into account future medical treatments the patient may undergo that could adversely affect the functioning of the AIMD.

One such risk is the use of Magnetic Resonance Imaging (MRI), which exposes the patient, and potentially the AIMD, to a strong magnetic field. ISO/TS 10974 *Assessment of the safety of MRI for patients with an active implantable medical device* is a recently developed standard that provides guidance on the testing and marking required to ensure patients are protected from radio frequency (RF)-induced heating, mechanical movement, implant malfunction and effect on the MRI image.

Other medical procedures to consider as part of the risk management process are those that may expose the patient to ultrasound, high-power electrical fields and electric shock. When there is residual risk from these cases, clear information and marking should be provided to ensure both the patient and the healthcare professional are aware and can take appropriate measures.

Electrical and Electromagnetic Safety

Except for their intended function, AIMDs shall be electrically neutral when in contact with the body. Electrostatic discharge before and after implantation is a risk that should be considered and tested to ensure that the AIMD's functionality is not affected when exposed to an electrostatic discharge.

AIMDs should be immune to electrical influences from external electromagnetic fields, avoiding unacceptable risks from malfunction, damage, heating or increase of induced electrical current density.

Although AIMDs are outside the scope of IEC 60601 (*Medical electrical equipment: General requirements for basic safety and essential performance*) standard series, their requirements and collateral standards can provide guidance during the risk management process, e.g., on electrostatic discharge or electromagnetic immunity.

Heat

Under normal and single fault conditions, it is expected that an AIMD shall not have a surface temperature higher than the average body temperature, e.g., the limit of 2°C specified in EN 45502-1:1997. This consideration is especially important when the energy source of the device is part of the implant.

Mechanical Safety

An AIMD should be constructed to withstand the mechanical forces that may occur during normal use, including transportation. Vibration, impact, tensile stress, flexural stress, connector retention strength, mechanical shock, atmospheric pressure and mechanical fatigue should be assessed during the risk management process and verified as acceptable during the design control process. EN 45502-1 provides relevant references to testing standards for mechanical-related risks.

Radiofrequency Communication

It is not uncommon for some AIMDs to be able to communicate wirelessly with external devices for the purposes of programming, data logging or monitoring. When this technology is part of an AIMD, the inherent risks of this functionality should be assessed, such as immunity to interference, coexistence with other radio-frequency sources and protection from malware attacks. Regulatory authorities are updating guidelines to address these risks, and a current good source to consider for advice is the FDA draft *Guidance for Radio-Frequency Wireless Technology in Medical Devices.*

An additional regulatory consideration for AIMDs with radio-frequency communication is that in some countries, devices with this function require approval or registration from the government authority responsible for managing the radio-frequency spectrum for communication. For example, in Australia, an AIMD with this technology must comply with the Australian Communication and Media Authority (ACMA) radio spectrum licensing requirements and display a special approval mark, known as the C-Tick. The ACMA Radio Communications Class Licence (Low Interference Potential Devices) 2000 (also known as the LIPD Class Licence) makes specific allowances for some AIMDs with low-power radio communications, including those using Medical Implant Communications Systems (MICS) under specific conditions. Similar provisions and requirements exist in other countries, such as the US with the Federal Communications Commission (FCC) and Canada with Industry Canada.

Surgical

In addition to the clinical validation of the surgical technique recommended for an AIMD, which is provided to the medical professional through information accompanying the device or through training, there are other important considerations. First, the usability of the surgical instructions should also be validated to ensure they can be followed as intended and result in the expected efficacy of the device. To the extent possible, the AIMD and the surgical technique should be developed to minimize outcome variations from the operating medical professional.

Another consideration that can affect the device's design is the need for explantation, either because of malfunction, upgrade to new technology or because the device is no longer needed. The risks associated with the explant procedure should be considered and minimized and, if possible, should not affect the patient in such a way that the performance from a replacement device might be compromised.

Markings

In some regulatory jurisdictions such as the EU, there are special requirements for markings and symbols for AIMDs. EN 45502-1 requires a series of markings to be included on the package and labeling, and EN 980 provides standards for the applicable symbols to be used. In other jurisdictions, such as the US, symbols without text are not accepted, but nevertheless, markings are required.

Information such as sterilization expiry date, sterilization agent and "do not reuse" statements should be considered. Depending on the intended market of the device, this information can be displayed with text and/or symbols.

Basic Principles for Regulatory Approval of AIMD

With some specific variances in certain countries, the approval of AIMDs is mainly based on regulatory authorities' review and analysis of documentation provided by the manufacturer, also known as a design dossier. The key difference between a low-risk medical device submission and a submission for an AIMD is the level of detail provided in the information, rather than the type of information required.

The Global Harmonization Task Force (GHTF) final document on Summary Technical Documentation (STED) or the ASEAN *Common Submission Dossier Template (CSDT) for Demonstrating Conformity to the Essential Principles of Safety and Performance for Medical Devices* provide generally accepted guidance on the structure of a submission. The main types of information expected for the review of an AIMD application are listed below.

Although requirements and document structures differ among countries, the overall intent of any submission dossier is to demonstrate the device is safe and effective for the defined indications.

Device Description

Typically, this section will include the high-level design documents, including mechanical drawings and electrical schematics. In addition, the submission will contain a detailed description of the AIMD, covering the main technologies, functional principles and specifications.

If any external accessories, surgical tools or programming equipment are used with the AIMD, they also should be described in this section, and depending on the regulatory jurisdiction (like the EU or US), those components may be considered part of the AIMD system, and therefore, require the same types of supporting documentation.

Labeling

Instructions for use, surgical instructions, packaging labels and any other information accompanying the AIMD should be included in this section of the submission. This information includes the intended use statement, the indications for use and the contraindications.

Risk Analysis

If the manufacturer follows ISO 14971, this section will include the main documents from the Risk Management File, such as the Risk Management Plan, the Risk Management Summary and the lower-level risk analysis, hazard analysis and failure mode effects and analysis (FMEA).

Verification and Validation

A summary of the design verification and validation activities should be provided in the submission, together with the protocols and reports required by the relevant standards and testing identified during the risk management processes. This section also includes the clinical documentation to demonstrate the device's effectiveness.

The previous section of this chapter, covering the special considerations for AIMD, provides guidance on how to assess the main risks during the development stage. Most of those risks and any other identified risks for a particular AIMD eventually may be transposed into a verification or validation activity, for which the derived documentation will be included in this part of the submission.

There are different options for including clinical evidence in a submission, depending on the AIMD's novelty or the application for a certain indication and the type of data gathered. A clinical investigation involves patients using the device for a period of time to make an assessment with statistical significance of the AIMD's expected effectiveness for a given indication, which in common terms is known as a clinical trial. This kind of investigation requires regulatory approval or registration in most countries before it can be conducted, and should follow Good Clinical Practices.

The other option for clinical evidence is the development of a clinical evaluation, which assesses existing data from third-party sources, such as published scientific papers and any other available information related to the application of an AIMD for a specific indication. This clinical evaluation is a critical analysis of all the available data to draw a conclusion about the expected effectiveness of the AIMD.

Manufacturing

A description of the manufacturing process, the validation information on the critical processes, including sterilization, and a high-level manufacturing flow chart normally are included in this section. The objective is to provide enough information to the regulatory reviewer to permit a conclusion that the device's design specifications will not be affected negatively by the manufacturing process. If part of the manufacturing process is carried out by a supplier, the process validation documentation from the supplier is included in the submission.

Country-Specific Requirements

EU

The *AIMDD* covers placing AIMDs on the market and putting them into service. The definition of device within the *AIMDD* relates to a product intended by the manufacturer for a medical purpose whether used alone or in combination, together with any accessories or software for its proper functioning. The medical purpose may be achieved either by a standalone device or as a result of several devices acting each in combination with one another as part of a system. Where the medical purpose is achieved by a system, each element of the system may be regarded as a medical device; for the purposes of the *AIMDD*, each part belonging to such system is covered by the directive regardless of whether such part, on its own, is active, active implantable or not.

Accessories to an AIMD are by definition AIMDs and therefore are covered by the *AIMDD*. This does not presuppose that the attributes "active" and "implantable" necessarily must be met by a product called an "accessory." It is sufficient that a product is ancillary to the purpose of an AIMD in such a way that it enables the device to be used in accordance with the intended device purpose or that it enhances the purpose of a device as intended by the manufacturer. Therefore, a programmer or an external transmitter intended for activating or controlling the implantable part of the device is covered by the *AIMDD*.

The most common approach for the approval of AIMDs in Europe is following *AIMDD* Annex 2. This annex establishes three main requirements:

- a certified quality management system, which complies with ISO 13485, and is periodically reviewed on-site by a Notified Body
- examination of the product design, with evidence to demonstrate that the device meets the Essential Requirements specified in *AIMDD* Annex 1 (The examination of the documentation is conducted by a Notified Body.)
- a Declaration of Conformity, which is a document in which the manufacturer asserts compliance or the product under review to the applicable *AIMDD* provisions

The Essential Requirements specified in *AIMDD* Annex 1 provide useful guidance for the development of AIMDs, and can be included as part of the design input for new devices, as they specify safety and effectiveness requirements, which are considered critical for the regulatory approval of a device.

At the time of publication, there is an initiative in the EU to issue a new regulation for medical devices, which will merge the existing directives for AIMDs and those of medical devices into a single regulation. Although this new regulation proposes major changes, especially in areas such as Notified Body governance and postmarket surveillance, it is not expected to bring significant change to AIMDs, with the exception of reclassification as Class III devices. This reclassification would not significantly change conformity assessment procedures.

Australia

TGA regulates medical devices in Australia under the *Therapeutic Goods Act* of 1989 and its subsidiary legislation, the *Therapeutic Goods (Medical Device) Regulations* of 2002. The Australian medical device regulations are closely aligned with those of the EU; however, some variances still exist.

TGA is one of the few regulators globally to have a specific risk classification for AIMDs. In Australia, AIMDs are classified as Class AIMD in accordance with Schedule 2 Rule 5.7(1) of the regulations.

Accessories to AIMDs are classified in their own right, and accessories may be Class I, Class I sterile, Class I measuring, Class IIa, Class IIb or Class III, depending on the intended purpose. This is a key difference from the European system.

To introduce an AIMD onto the Australian market, a manufacturer must demonstrate that both the device and the manufacturing processes used to make the device conform to the requirements of the *Therapeutic Goods Regulations*.

The conformity assessment procedure specified for an AIMD in Australia is the implementation of a full quality management system encompassing design, production, packaging, labeling and final inspection of a medical device in accordance with ISO 13485. The quality management system must be audited by either TGA or an EU Notified Body.

In addition to obtaining certification of the quality management system, a full design examination of the device (design dossier) must be performed. The TGA requirements for the contents of the design dossier are aligned to the GHTF STED guidance document.

A manufacturer that has not implemented a full design control process or does not wish to implement one in the future may try alternate conformity assessment procedures; however, these procedures are rarely used as they are generally more expensive.

In accordance with the regulations, for devices manufactured outside Australia, TGA is able to accept conformity assessments from regulatory bodies that are considered to have the appropriate authority and expertise. As the Australian and the EU regulatory requirements are similar, TGA has determined that certificates issued by EU Notified Bodies may be accepted as conformity assessment evidence for the supply of devices in Australia, thereby omitting the need to apply for conformity assessment certification through TGA.

In accordance with the regulations, all foreign manufacturers of AIMDs (devices covered by EC Certificates) will undergo a mandatory application audit once the sponsor lodges an application for inclusion on the ARTG (Australian Register of Therapeutic Goods). The application audit is to confirm that the medical device manufacturer has carried out conformity assessment procedures appropriate to the classification of the medical device.

AIMD manufacturers that seek product approval in Australia must assign a UPI (Unique Product Identifier) to uniquely identify the device and any variants. Different manufacturers identify their products in different ways; therefore, the UPI can be a combination of words, numbers, symbols or letters.

A variant is a medical device, the design of which has been varied to accommodate different patient anatomical requirements or any other variation approved by TGA. AIMDs can have more than one variant that is aligned with the same intended purpose, and more than one variant can be associated with an ARTG, minimizing the number of entries required on the ARTG.

As a requirement for inclusion on the ARTG, AIMD manufacturers must supply three consecutive annual reports to TGA. The first report following the date of inclusion in the ARTG must be for a period of at least six months but no longer than 18 months. The following reports must be filed with TGA by 1 October each year. The annual reports require the collection of postmarket data relating to the device's performance on the market, including both local and global statistics on the number of devices supplied, complaints received, adverse events and rates of incidents.

US

The *Medical Device Amendments* of 1976 to the *Federal Food, Drug, and Cosmetic Act* (*FD&C Act*) established three regulatory classes for medical devices. The three classes are based on the degree of control necessary to ensure the various types of devices are safe and effective. The most regulated devices are in Class III, and although not specifically expressed, most AIMDs fall into that category.

Under Section 515 of the *FD&C Act*, all devices placed into Class III are subject to premarket approval (PMA) requirements. Premarket approval by FDA is the required process of scientific review to ensure the safety and effectiveness of the devices.

PMA is the most rigorous device marketing application required by FDA. The applicant must receive FDA approval of its PMA application prior to marketing the device. PMA approval is based on a determination by FDA that the submission contains sufficient valid scientific evidence to ensure the device is safe and effective for its intended use.

There are administrative elements of a PMA application, but good engineering documentation and clear writing are key elements for approval. The main content of a PMA application comprises:

- The technical sections containing data and information that allow FDA to determine whether to approve or disapprove the application. These sections usually are divided into nonclinical laboratory studies and clinical investigations.
    - o Nonclinical laboratory studies section—includes information on microbiology, toxicology, immunology, biocompatibility, stress, wear, shelf life and other laboratory or animal tests.
    - o Clinical investigations section—includes study protocols, safety and effectiveness data, adverse reactions and complications, device failures and replacements, patient information, patient complaints, tabulations of data from all individual subjects, results of statistical analyses and any other information from the clinical investigations.

After FDA has approved a PMA, an applicant must submit a PMA supplement for FDA review and approval before implementing any change affecting the device's safety or effectiveness. All changes must meet the requirements of the Quality System Regulation under 21 CFR Part 820. An applicant must submit a PMA supplement for such changes as:

- new indication for the device's use
- labeling revisions
- the use of a different facility or establishment to manufacture, process, sterilize or package the device
- changes in manufacturing facilities, methods or quality control procedures
- sterilization procedure changes
- packaging changes
- changes in the device's performance or design specifications, circuits, components, materials, principles of operation or physical layout
- extension of the expiration date of the device based on data obtained under a new or revised stability or sterility testing protocol

Depending on the type of change, a manufacturer could file a 180-day PMA supplement, a Special PMA supplement or a 30-day Manufacturing Change Notice. Minor changes that do not affect the device's safety or effectiveness and do not require a PMA supplement are notified to FDA through an annual report.

Canada

The *Food and Drugs Act* provides the legal framework for the regulation of medical devices in Canada, and the Therapeutic Products Directorate, a sub-branch within Health Canada, is the entity responsible for administering the application of the act and the attendant *Medical Devices Regulations*.

The risk classification rules for medical devices in Canada do not specify a special category for AIMDs. The highest risk classification is Class IV, which includes, among others, active devices intended to control the treatment of a patient's condition through a closed-loop system. A closed-loop system is a device that is capable of sensing, interpreting and treating the patient without a human interface at any point in the procedure. Most AIMDs are considered Class IV due to this classification rule.

The content of a license application for a Class IV medical device is very consistent with the GHTF STED format. Besides the specific administrative information, a license application also will include implant registration cards, marketing history including adverse events, materials identification and specifications and quality plan and quality control methods.

Brazil

Resolution RDC No. 185 (2001) is the primary regulation applicable to the approval and classification of all medical devices in Brazil, with the exception of in vitro diagnostic devices. This resolution describes the applicable device registration protocol and lists the documents required to legally register a medical device in Brazil. Annex II of RDC No. 185 describes the classification structure applicable to medical devices, assigning medical devices to one of four distinct risk classes according to 18 different rules. The classification structure for medical devices in Brazil corresponds to that used in the EU under Directive 93/42/EEC, and as expected, AIMDs fall into Class IV.

All medical devices imported into or distributed within Brazil must first be registered with the National Health Surveillance Agency (ANVISA). When applying for ANVISA registration, manufacturers of Class IV devices may be required to provide some or all of the following documentation with the application:

- free sales certificate
- Certificate of Good Manufacturing Practice (ISO 13485)
- instructions manual in Portuguese
- labeling and packaging samples
- letter from the device manufacturer, authorizing a Brazilian company to hold the registration and distribute the device
- clinical evidence
- list of all accessories
- Economic Information Report

- INMETRO (National Institute of Metrology, Quality and Technology) certificate, when applicable

Singapore

Medical devices are regulated in Singapore under the *Health Products Act* of 2007 and its subsidiary legislation, *Health Products (Medical Device) Regulations* of 2010, by the Health Science Authority (HSA).

Medical devices are classified into four risk categories: A, B, C and D, with Class D being high-risk medical devices. Although HSA does not have a specific AIMD classification, all AIMDs are placed in Class D, in accordance with Classification Rule 8 of the regulations.

Product registration applications in Singapore can take two routes: an abridged or full evaluation. The abridged evaluation route applies to those medical devices that have been evaluated and have gained marketing approval clearance in at least one of the GHTF founding member countries. This includes evaluations conducted by the EU under Annex II, Sections 3 and 4 of the *AIMDD*. The abridged evaluation route only requires select information to be submitted to HSA for evaluation.

A product registration application in Singapore must be prepared using the ASEAN CSDT format. The key difference between the requirements of a CSDT dossier for a Class B or C medical device and a Class D (including AIMDs) is the requirement for clinical evidence.

All Class D medical device applications must include a full clinical evaluation report including copies of all the studies referenced in the report. The clinical evaluation report must provide a comprehensive analysis of premarket and postmarket clinical data relevant to the device's intended purpose. HSA requirements for a clinical evaluation report are aligned with those in the GHTF Final Document for Clinical Evaluation.

Conclusion

AIMDs are considered by regulatory authorities to be devices in the highest risk category. Therefore, the required evidence for approval and the level of control during development and manufacturing are very rigorous.

Given the level of risks assigned to AIMDs, multiple information resources are available to support development and manufacturing activities in the form of standards, guidance documents and regulations. This chapter has presented a summary of some of that information and the specific approval requirements outlined by some of the major regulatory authorities in the world.

Readers are encouraged to use the information in this chapter as the basis for their own research, specific for the particular characteristics of their AIMDs and the countries where it is intended to be marketed.

Chapter 21

Software

By Erik Vollebregt

OBJECTIVES

- ❑ Learn to understand and apply the scope of different definitions of "medical device" to determine whether the software is regulated as a medical device
- ❑ Gain insight into specific regulatory issues associated with software
- ❑ Learn about the important national and international guidelines for software as a medical device, in particular US and EU law
- ❑ Learn about design and quality system requirements for software

STANDARDS AND GUIDELINES COVERED IN THIS CHAPTER

- ❑ IEC 62304
- ❑ GHTF definition of medical device
- ❑ EU MEDDEV 2.1/6
- ❑ US draft mobile medical apps guidelines

Introduction

Software is playing an increasingly important role in the medical field as more medical devices either run software or consist entirely of software. Software allows medical devices to perform complicated tasks and to acquire and process complex information about a patient's condition. Software enables medical devices to act more and more autonomously to provide support for clinical decisions and other therapeutic or diagnostic purposes. The autonomous character of software and the often critical processes managed by it require a thorough evaluation of its clinical use as physicians have come to rely on its performance. The vast majority of software problems are traceable to errors during the design and development process, making design controls on software very important. Indeed, malfunctioning software can cause patient injury and even death. This high-risk operation aspect is, however, not unique to the medical devices industry: software is flying airplanes and controlling nuclear plants. We have come to trust software to support mission-critical processes and have developed good methodologies for testing its safety and performance. These methodologies have been adopted by medical device regulators as well, to ensure medical device software performs according to the safety and performance expectations of regulators, patients and the market.

The medical device industry is on the verge of a true software boom with the development of a plethora of wearable and implantable sensors that theoretically can provide information about every physical parameter of a person. Also, software is used more and more to help personalize medicinal products for specific patients based on the application of evidence-based rules to large datasets. Software is at the heart of these developments. All information harvested from patient-monitoring devices can and will be shared via the "internet of things," consisting of potentially billions of devices and software modules interacting to store, transmit and interpret this information.[1] This development is welcomed by policymakers and payers as a possible means of controlling increasing healthcare spending. On the other

Figure 21-1. MDD Decision Tree

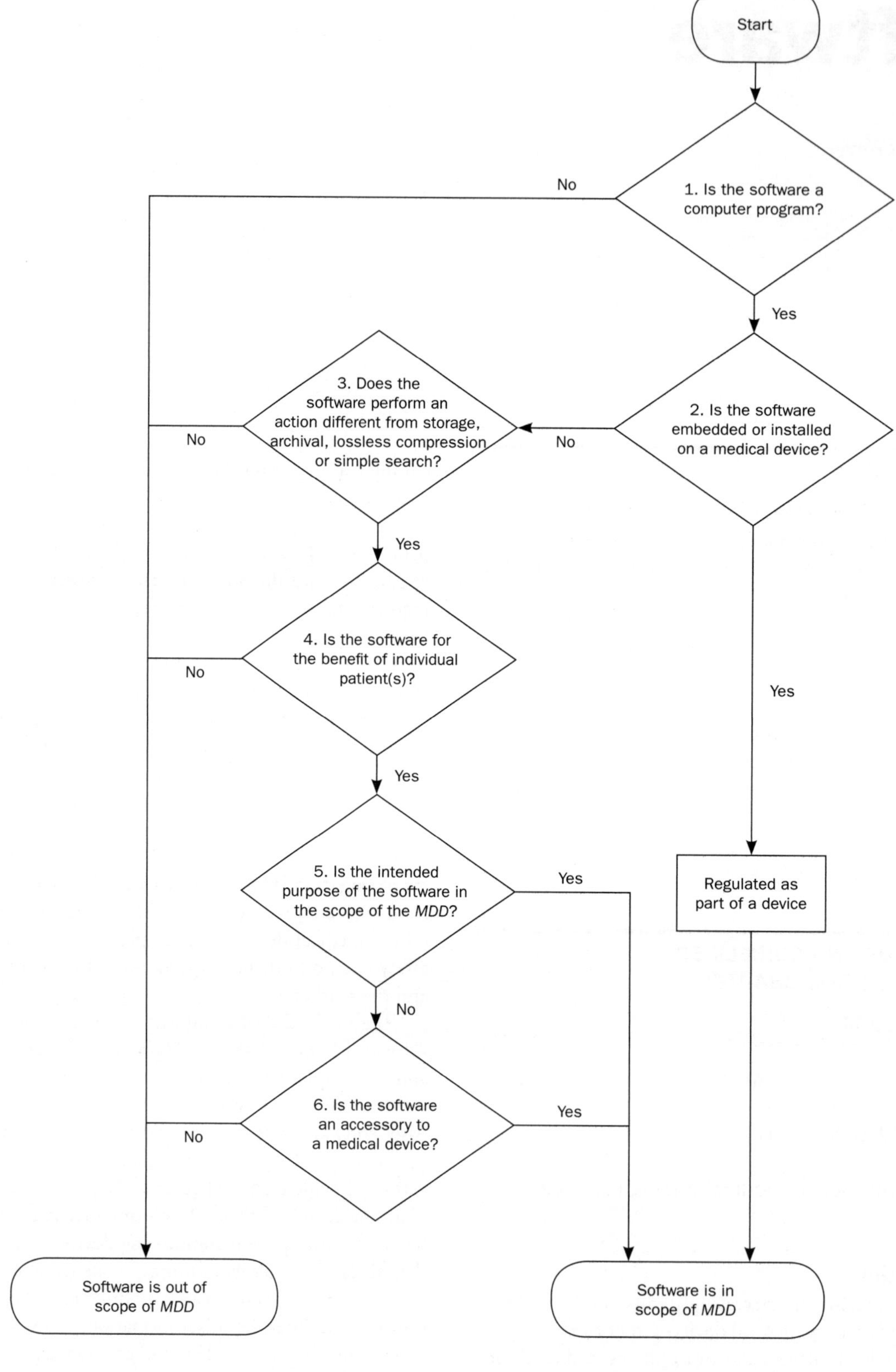

hand, society is sensitive to potential risks associated with this development. Mobile medical devices potentially can be hacked, and health data security may be compromised.

This chapter focuses on the regulation of medical device software in the US and the EU. However, much of the underlying theory, especially where this comes from the International Organization for Standardization (ISO) and other international standards or from the Global Harmonization Task Force (GHTF), will be applicable in other jurisdictions or may serve as a frame of reference.

Software as a Regulated Medical Device

The GHTF definition of a medical device explicitly includes software,[2] as do the EU[3] and US definitions.

In both the EU and the US, the same basic principles of interpretation apply to the qualification of software as a medical device:

- The legal definition is based on the intent of the product.
- The legal definition is not based on the engineering definition of software functionality. (For example, the term 'standalone software' used in the EU MEDDEV 2.1/6 guidance document has a very different meaning in software engineering terminology.)
- The legal definition does not contain any reference to any specific hardware, software or information technology.

Accordingly, there is no definitive or exhaustive list of regulated software. Since the intended use is the determining factor, the same software application may be regulated as a medical device or not depending on the manufacturer's intended use. If the intended use is, broadly speaking, therapeutic or diagnostic, the software and/or the device running it will constitute a medical device. In both the EU and the US, the intended use follows from the information that the manufacturer makes available about the software (e.g., labeling claims, advertising material or oral or written statements by the manufacturers or their representatives).

The delivery mechanism for getting the software to the end user does not make any difference in the question of whether software constitutes a medical device. For example, it is immaterial whether the software is pre-installed, delivered on a DVD or downloadable from the Internet.

Regulatory Status

Medical device software typically is regulated under one of the following three options:

1. Software that does not meet the legal definition of a medical device and is not regulated under the applicable medical devices legislation
2. software that does meet the legal definition of a device and can be self-certified before it may be placed on the market or put into service
3. software that does meet the definition of a device and needs to be approved by an external party like a Notified Body or a regulatory body like the US Food and Drug Administration (FDA) before it may be placed on the market or put into service

EU

Software that does not meet the legal definition of a device would be, for example, a system that would not serve any of the intended purposes set out in the definition of "device" in the EU *Medical Devices Directive* (*MDD*):[4]

- diagnosis, prevention, monitoring, treatment or alleviation of disease
- diagnosis, monitoring, treatment, alleviation of or compensation for an injury or handicap
- investigation, replacement or modification of the anatomy or of a physiological process control of conception

If the software falls within the scope of the *MDD*, the manufacturer must take another step to determine specifically how the software is regulated: as a "general" medical device or as an in vitro diagnostic device. The latter category is regulated under yet another EU directive, the *In Vitro Diagnostic Devices Directive* (*IVDD*).[5] Software is regulated under the *IVDD* if it qualifies as a medical device in the above definition and is, moreover, intended to be used *in vitro* for the examination of specimens, including blood and tissue donations, derived from the human body, solely or principally for the purpose of providing information:

- concerning a physiological or pathological state
- concerning a congenital abnormality
- to determine the safety and compatibility with potential recipients
- to monitor therapeutic measures

The EU MEDDEV 2.1/6 guidance document on standalone software as a medical device[6] contains two convenient decision trees for determining whether first, the software constitutes a medical device, and subsequently, whether the medical device is regulated under the general *MDD* (see **Figure 21-1**) or under the *IVDD* (see **Figure 21-2**). The MEDDEV contains detailed guidance on the application of the respective steps in each decision tree.

A good rule of thumb is, software that is intended to create or modify medical information might qualify as a medical device. If such alterations are made to facilitate the perceptual and/or interpretative tasks performed by the healthcare professionals when reviewing medical information (e.g., when searching a medical image for findings that

Figure 21-2. IVDD Decision Tree

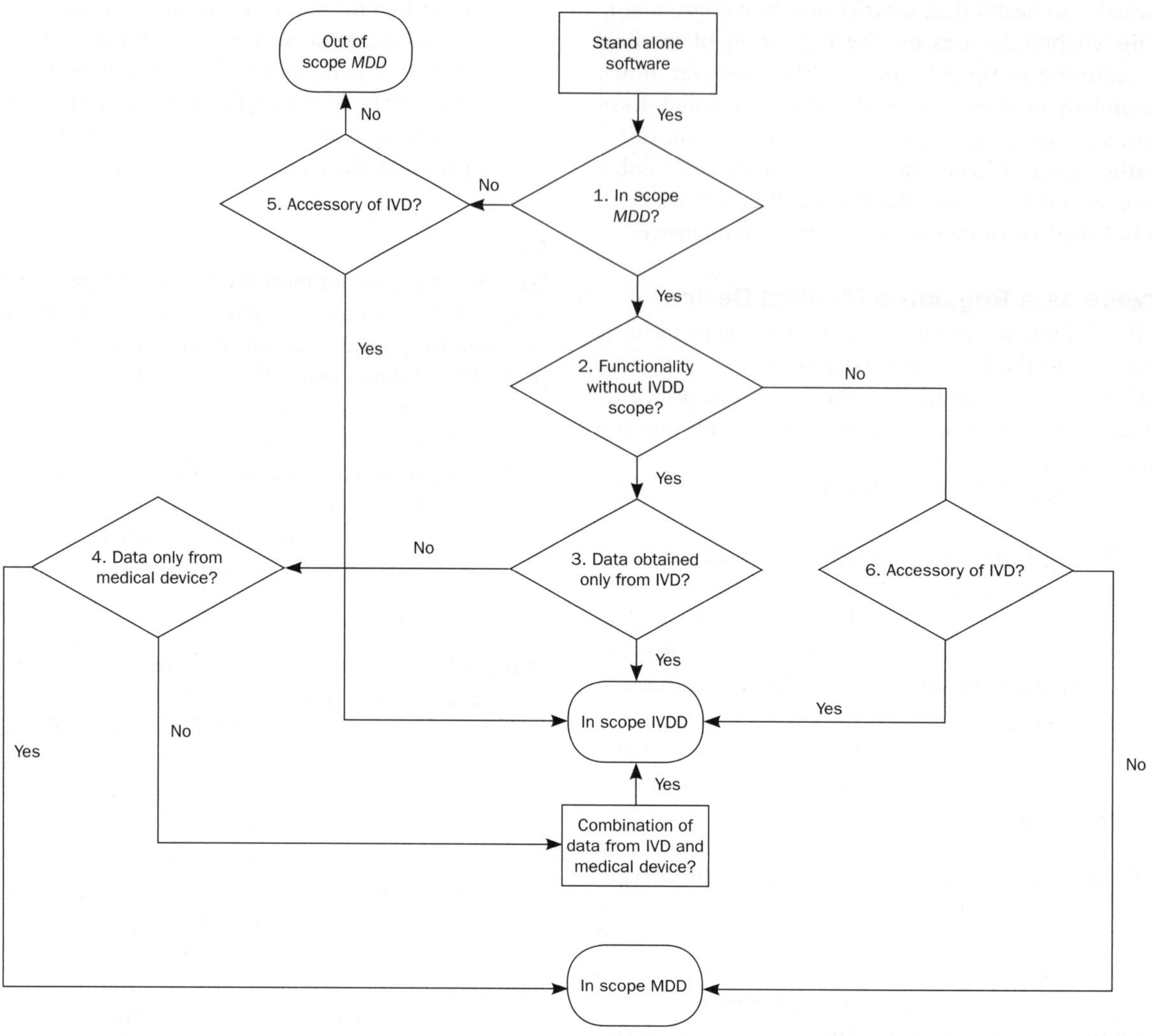

support a clinical hypothesis as to the diagnosis or evolution of therapy), the software could be a medical device.

US

Products that are built with or consist of computer and/or software components or applications are subject to regulation as devices when they meet the definition of a device in Section 201(h) of the *Federal Food, Drug, and Cosmetic Act* (*FD&C Act*). That provision defines a device as:

> "…an instrument, apparatus, implement, machine, contrivance, implant, in vitro reagent…" that is "…intended for use in the diagnosis of disease or other conditions, or in the cure, mitigation, treatment, or prevention of disease, in man…" or "…intended to affect the structure or any function of the body of man or other animals…"

Thus, software applications that run on a desktop computer, laptop computer, remotely on a website or "cloud" or on a handheld computer may be subject to device regulation if they are intended for use in the diagnosis, cure, mitigation, treatment or prevention of disease, or to affect the structure or any function of the human body.

FDA-regulated medical device applications include software that:[7]

- is a component, part or accessory of a medical device
- is, itself, a medical device, or
- is used in manufacturing, design and development, or any other part of the quality system

Unlike the EU, the US requires that computer systems used to create, modify and maintain electronic records and to manage electronic signatures are always subject to validation requirements.[8] Such computer systems must be validated to ensure accuracy, reliability, consistent intended performance and the ability to discern invalid or altered records.

The US has a longer history of specific regulation of medical device software than the EU. For example, FDA has had guidance on the use of off-the-shelf (OTS) software[9] and software validation[10] since 1997. The guidance on OTS software covers the use of such software in medical devices and specifies the documentation that should be provided in premarket submissions for medical devices using OTS software. The guidance on software validation discusses general validation principles FDA considers to be applicable to the validation of medical device software or the validation of software used to design, develop or manufacture medical devices.

FDA also has issued *Guidance for the Content of Premarket Submissions for Software Contained in Medical Devices*, the latest version of which is dated of May 2005.[11]

FDA created a new category of regulated medical device software with the 2011 Medical Device Data Systems (MDDS) rule, which served to reclassify MDDS from Class III (premarket approval) into Class I (general controls). MDDS devices are intended to transfer, store or convert data from one format to another according to preset specifications or to display medical device data. MDDS perform all intended functions without controlling or altering the function or parameters of any connected medical devices. An MDDS is not intended to be used in connection with active patient monitoring. FDA is exempting MDDS from premarket notification requirements.

In view of the ever-increasing use of mobile devices in clinical settings, FDA currently is working on guidance for mobile medical applications.[12] It issued draft guidance on the subject in late 2011, and currently is in the process of finalizing guidance incorporating the flood of feedback from the market.

The draft guidance is surprisingly synchronized with EU software regulations.[13] FDA defines a "mobile app" as a software application that can be executed on a mobile platform, or a web-based software application that is tailored to a mobile platform but is executed on a server. "Mobile platforms" are defined as commercial off-the-shelf (COTS) computing platforms, with or without wireless connectivity, that are handheld. Examples of these mobile platforms include mobile computers such as the iPhone®, BlackBerry® phones, Android® phones, tablet computers or other computers that are typically used as smart phones or personal digital assistants (PDAs). A "mobile medical app" is a mobile app that meets the definition of "device" in Section 201(h) of the *FD&C Act*; and either:

- is used as an accessory to a regulated medical device

or

- transforms a mobile platform into a regulated medical device

The intended use of a mobile app determines whether it meets the definition of a "device" as stated in 21 CFR 801.4.

A final version of the guidance has not yet been published.

According to FDA, this guidance will not, among other things, cause the following to be regulated:

- educational tools (e.g., apps that provide a list of questions to ask physicians)
- common, simple calculators (e.g., for apgar)
- BMI calculators
- drug-drug interaction formulae
- diabetes management guides (e.g., nutritional guides or pre-diabetes risk assessments)
- substance abuse behavior guides

Unregulated Software

Software that is outside the scope of the EU *MDD* is not regulated as a medical device. This typically concerns "software for general purposes when used in a healthcare setting."[14] However, all software "when specifically intended by the manufacturer to be used for one or more of the medical purposes set out in the definition of a medical device, is a medical device."[15] So, software that is not specifically intended by the manufacturer as a medical device is not covered (that would include general database software and spreadsheet software). Generally, if the software does not perform an action on data, or performs an action limited to storage, archival, communication, "simple search" or lossless compression (i.e., using a compression procedure that allows the exact reconstruction of the original data), it is not a medical device.[16]

In the US, the intended purpose of the software is the crucial demarcation criterion. When the intended use of the software is to diagnose disease or other conditions, or the cure, mitigation, treatment or prevention of disease, or to affect the structure or any function of the human body, the software is a device. One of the more recent articulations of the types of software FDA does not regulate was included in the agency's proposed MDDS classification, published in 2008. In that notice, FDA explained:

> "It is the FDA's long-standing practice to not regulate those manual office functions that are simply automated for the ease of the user (e.g., office automation).... For example, the report-writing functions of a computer system that allow for the manual (typewriter like) input of data by practitioners would not be... [regulated] because these systems are not directly connected to a medical device. In addition, software that merely performs library functions, such as storing, indexing, and retrieving information not specific to an individual patient, is not considered to be a medical device. Examples include medical texts or the Physician's Desk

Reference on CD-ROM that are indexed and cross-referenced for ease of use."

It further explained in the notice that the agency will not regulate "software that allows a doctor to enter or store a patient's health history in a computer file," presumably referring generally to electronic health records.

Beyond that passage, historically, there have been two key features for most unregulated software:[17]

1. The data are entered manually; they are not input directly from any machine that touches the patient or a patient specimen. That is important to avoid becoming an MDDS device or an accessory to a medical device.
2. Depending on how the data are entered, the output amounts simply providing the stored data back to the patient or professional. The system neither automatically guides the diagnosis or treatment, nor does it guide any medical instrument. In other words, the software does not contain any algorithms that provide clinical-like functions that go beyond what FDA often refers to as library functions. It merely displays the data for the user to read and interpret.

There is some difference of opinion about whether patient file database software (i.e., an electronic health record) is regulated or not. For example, Sweden (an EU Member State) requires all electronic patient file software to be certified. Standalone software normally would fall within Class I, as the default classification rule in the *MDD* places standalone software as an "active medical device."[18,19]

Categories and Classification

Categories

The US and EU medical device laws divide regulated software into two categories: (1) standalone software and (2) accessories. Software that comes pre-installed on the device when it is placed on the market is not regulated as a separate medical device, but is regulated as part of the device.

An accessory is software that is not intended to be standalone but, instead, is specifically intended by the manufacturer to be used together with another manufacturer's device (which can be standalone software). This combination enables the software to be used in accordance with the device's use (as intended by the device manufacturer).[20,21] A typical example would be software to be installed on a handheld computer that enables remote control of other devices, e.g., infusion pumps.

Understanding these distinctions is important because they determine the regulatory requirements that apply to a given piece of software. If the software is designed, for example, to analyze data downloaded from a blood glucose meter, the software is an accessory and will be regulated in the same manner as the blood glucose meter.

Classification

The classification and most of the regulatory requirements will be dictated by how the parent medical device is regulated. The regulation of standalone software, in contrast, is based on the software's own merits, without regard to another medical device.

Classification of the device also depends on its intended use.

Software That Does not Need Prior Authority Approval

The certification system for medical devices in the EU is set up so devices falling into Class I (the lowest risk class) are not subject to review by a third party but may be self-certified by the manufacturer. In the EU, all software is by default in Class I, on the basis of Annex IX classification rule 12, therefore, manufacturers can self-certify software, unless an exception applies.

In the EU, self-certification involves the composition of a technical file and design of a quality system under Annex VII of the *MDD*, for example, in conformity with ISO 13485, the standard for medical devices quality systems accepted by the EU as state of the art.

In the US, medical devices that do not require FDA prior approval via the 510(k) process or Premarket Approval (PMA) need to be registered and listed rather than self-certified as in the EU. In this case, however, there is no prior FDA intervention.

When does software need to be approved by a third party?

In the EU, all software by default falls into risk Class I, except if a classification rule applies that bumps it up to Class IIa, IIb or III. If the software has functionality that allows it to drive a device or influences the use of a device, it falls automatically into the same class as the device.[22] An example of this would be software that can implement the recommended action by exercising control over another device that is in Class IIa or higher (e.g., software that assists a cardiologist in interpreting data read from a patient's pacemaker at a distance via WiFi, which after obtaining the cardiologist's approval on a suggested reconfiguration, implements the reconfiguration of the patient's pacemaker at a distance).

Developing Compliant Medical Software

General

In both the EU and US, regulations impose rules on the development of software, as they do with medical device design and risk management in general. That means that the general rules for medical device design and risk management apply. FDA explicitly states that for a number of reasons, software engineering needs an even greater level of managerial scrutiny and control than hardware engineering.[23] For example, the quality of a software product is dependent primarily on design and development, with a minimum concern for software manufacture, because producing copies of software is far less complicated than developing an original that meets all specifications.

In addition, specific guidance or rules relating to software may apply. For example, the EU adopted a new Essential Requirement regarding software in 2007, Essential Requirement 12a, addressing the software lifecycle. Likewise, FDA has issued guidance setting out the general validation principles it considers to be applicable to the validation of medical device software or the validation of software used to design, develop or manufacture medical devices. The EU guidance issued in MEDDEV 2.1/6 does not enter into the same level of detail.

In both the US and EU, all software components must be under design control and/or purchasing control, including:

- design validation that includes software validation and risk analysis[24,25]
- evaluation and selection of potential suppliers, contractors and consultants on the basis of their ability to meet specified requirements, including quality requirements[26–28]

The International Electrotechnical Commision (IEC) 62304 standard, *Medical device software—Software life cycle processes*, is a standard that specifies lifecycle requirements for the development of medical software and software within medical devices. Like the FDA guidance mentioned above, it advocates an approach for integrating software lifecycle management and risk management activities.

This standard is harmonized by the EU and US and, therefore, can be used as a benchmark to comply with regulatory requirements for both markets. Designing to IEC 62304 ensures that software is produced by means of a defined and controlled software development process acceptable in both the EU and US. This standard provides a framework of lifecycle processes, with activities and tasks necessary for the safe design and maintenance of medical device software. This standard provides requirements for each lifecycle process, which is further divided into a set of activities, with most activities subdivided into a set of tasks. The activities and tasks to be performed depend on the software's risk profile, derived from a safety assessment applied to the software system as a whole. This classification is based on the potential to create a hazard that could result in an injury to the user, the patient or other people. The exact procedure is not prescribed; this is for the manufacturer to design and, where applicable, to obtain agreement from its Notified Body or Competent Authority. The risk classification also determines the burden for justification of software of unknown origin (SOUP) applied in the software system, e.g., open source modules. For example, the higher the risk class, the better the manufacturer must understand the SOUP and the more diversely it must be applied. Manufacturers that do not design their software entirely in-house should opt for software designers who have well-established risk management systems, as they already will have the foundations in place to meet IEC 62304. Preferably, the software designers can design IEC 62304 software from the start. In any event, this standard will have to be a requirement in any quality agreement between a medical device manufacturer and its outsourced software designer.

The EU MEDDEV on standalone software recognizes that standalone software may break down into a significant number of applications for the user, where each application is correlated with a module. Since some of the modules have a medical purpose and some do not, it is convenient to look at only the modules with a medical purpose for compliance under the medical device rules. It would, for example, not be necessary to regulate modules that provide invoicing and other accounting functions or provide a link to the social security system for reimbursement.[29]

Modules

Under the MEDDEV, modules that are subject to the medical devices directives must comply with the directives' requirements and must carry the European Conformity (CE) mark, while the non-medical device modules are not subject to the directives' requirements. It is the manufacturer's obligation to clearly identify different modules' boundaries and interfaces, using the intended use as a criterion. The MEDDEV goes on to state that if the regulated modules are intended for use in combination with other modules of the whole software structure, other devices or equipment, the whole combination, including the connection system, must be safe and must not impair the specified performances of the modules that are subject to the medical devices directives. This latter requirement follows directly from the current Essential Requirements for modular medical devices in *IVDD* Essential Requirement 3.1 and *MDD* Essential Requirement 9.1.

In contrast to the EU, the US has no methodology or guidance on modules. Manufacturers will have to obtain approval for their system as a whole.

Quality System, Postmarket Surveillance and Corrective Action

Software that constitutes a medical device and medical device software can take its place in the manufacturer's overall quality system. There are no quality system parts that would *a priori* not be applicable to software just because they do not specifically refer to it. There are, however, some practical considerations specific to the software.

The most critical quality system issues arise with outsourced software development. The general rule that the regulatory burden for the device lies with the manufacturer is even more pertinent in the field of software. With respect to outsourced software development, the developer's awareness of regulatory requirements usually is far lower than in the medical device parts industry. This needs to be taken into account in the quality system and be implemented in a sufficiently robust quality agreement with the developer.

Another important consideration is corrective and preventive action. In both the US and EU, implementing such action is the manufacturer's responsibility. This means the manufacturer must have sufficient software-specific instruments in the contractual arrangements with the outsourced developer to be able to execute corrective and preventive action.

Personal Health Data

An important consideration when developing medical software is compliance with rules governing the processing of patient health data. In practice, many companies overlook the implications of regulatory compliance in this field and consequently miss opportunities to design compliance into software at an early stage. Noncompliance with personal health data collection and processing rules also can have far-reaching consequences, like a prohibition on processing, class action lawsuits or other legal measures by patients resisting unlawful use of their data. These rules also vary quite substantially from jurisdiction to jurisdiction. For example, a company that is compliant in the US under both the *Health Insurance Portability & Accountability Act* (*HIPAA*) and the *Health Information Technology for Economic and Clinical Health Act* (*HITECH Act*) cannot assume it will be compliant under the EU *Protection of Personal Data Directive* and vice versa.

Other Factors to Take Into Account

The qualification of software as a medical device can have other regulatory consequences as well. For example, in the EU, standalone software, as opposed to the majority of other medical devices, may be e-labeled as of 1 March 2013.[30]

Future Developments

This chapter describes the current regulation of medical device software in the US and the EU, but this area is very much in regulatory flux, and the current regulatory frameworks are under revision.

On 26 September 2012, the European Commission launched a proposal for a regulation on medical devices (*MDR*) and a regulation on IVDs.[31] Software falls within the scope of the proposed *MDR* if it meets the criteria set out in Article 2(1) or (4). For software (incorporated and standalone), the proposed regulation lays down Essential Requirements in section 14. Software that is intended to be used in combination with mobile computing platforms "shall be designed and manufactured taking into account the specific features of the mobile platform and the external factors related to their use." The regulation does not, however, provide a definition of "mobile computing platform." Under the proposed regulation on IVDs, software is explicitly mentioned in the definition of IVDs. Software falls within the ambit of the regulation if it meets the criteria that are laid down in Article 2(1) or (2). In section 13 of the regulation, requirements for the design, development and manufacturing of both incorporated and standalone software are laid down, similar to those in the proposed *MDR*. Further, Annex II obliges the manufacturer to enclose a description of the software to be used in the device, including evidence of the validation of the software.

The definition of "accessory" potentially may be changed and may have far-reaching consequences. The proposed definition is "an article which, whilst not being a medical device, is intended by its manufacturer to be used together with one or several particular medical device(s) to specifically enable or assist the device(s) to be used in accordance with its/their intended purpose(s)." The addition of the term "assist" is expected to increase the scope considerably as it expands from "enable" to "enable or assist," with the term "assist" pointing to devices that are more remote and not a *conditio sine qua non* for the intended purpose of the parent device. In addition, the current MEDDEV 2.1/6 on standalone software is under revision, and a new version is expected to be released in 2013, which will include more guidance on networking, interconnectivity and mobile health applications.

On 9 July 2012, President Obama signed into law the *Food and Drug Administration Safety and Innovation Act* (*FDASIA*) that includes provisions designed to help FDA move forward with its plan to regulate mobile applications.[32] A report that describes the approach to the regulation of all health IT has not yet been published.

Conclusion

For regulatory purposes, software is either a component of a device or a device itself. In that sense, software can be treated as any component or device. However, as has been described in this chapter, the nature of software also necessitates specific controls on software of which manufacturers must be aware and must implement.

References

1. See for example Kurzweil R. *The Singularity Is Near: When Humans Transcend Biology*. Viking Press, New York (2005). Also see Topol E. *The Creative Destruction of Medicine*. Basic Books, New York (2012).
2. GHTF/SG1/N071:2012, Definition of the Terms "Medical Device" and "In Vitro Diagnostic (IVD) Medical Device." IMDRF

website. www.imdrf.org/docs/ghtf/final/sg1/technical-docs/ghtf-sg1-n071-2012-definition-of-terms-120516.pdf. Accessed 28 March 2013.

3. Council Directive 93/42/EEC of 14 June 1993 concerning medical devices (*Medical Devices Directive*), Article 1(2)(a). EUR-Lex website. http://eur-lex.europa.eu/LexUriServ/LexUriServ.do?uri=CELEX:31993L0042:en:HTML. Accessed 28 March 2013.
4. Ibid.
5. Directive 98/79/EC of the European Parliament and of the Council of 27 October 1998 on in vitro diagnostic medical devices. EUR-Lex website. http://eur-lex.europa.eu/LexUriServ/LexUriServ.do?uri=CONSLEG:1998L0079:20031120:en:PDF. Accessed 28 March 2013.
6. MEDDEV 2.1/6. *Guidelines on the Qualification and Classification of Stand Alone Software Used in Healthcare Within the Regulatory Framework of Medical Devices.* http://ec.europa.eu/health/medical-devices/files/meddev/2_1_6_ol_en.pdf. Accessed 18 March 2013.
7. FDA, *General Principles of Software Validation; Final Guidance for Industry and FDA Staff* (11 January 2002). FDA website. www.fda.gov/medicaldevices/deviceregulationandguidance/guidancedocuments/ucm085281.htm. Accessed 28 March 2013.
8. Ibid.
9. FDA, *Guidance for Industry, FDA Reviewers and Compliance on Off-The-Shelf Software Use in Medical Devices*, 9 September 1999. FDA website. www.fda.gov/medicaldevices/deviceregulationandguidance/guidancedocuments/ucm073778.htm. Accessed 28 March 2013.
10. Op cit. 10.
11. FDA, *Guidance for the Content of Premarket Submissions for Software Contained in Medical Devices*, May 11, 2005. FDA website. www.fda.gov/MedicalDevices/DeviceRegulationandGuidance/GuidanceDocuments/ucm089543.htm. Accessed 28 March 2013.
12. FDA. Mobile Medical Applications. FDA website. www.fda.gov/medicaldevices/productsandmedicalprocedures/ucm255978.htm. Accessed 18 March 2013.
13. Thompson B and Vollebregt E. "Mobile medical apps guidance: what's good for the US is good for the EU." *Scrip Regulatory Affairs*, October 2011, p. 10.
14. Directive 2007/47 of the European Parliament and of the Council of 5 September 2007 amending Council Directive 90/385/EEC on the approximation of the laws of the Member States relating to active implantable medical devices, Council Directive 93/42/EEC relating to medical devices and Directive 98/8/EC concerning the placing of biocidal products on the market, recital 6. EUR-Lex website. http://eur-lex.europa.eu/LexUriServ/LexUriServ.do?uri=OJ:L:2007:247:0021:0055:en:PDF. Accessed 28 March 2013.
15. Ibid.
16. MEDDEV 2.1/6 *Qualification and Classification of stand alone software, explanation of decision step 3 in respect of medical devices decision tree*, p. 12. EC website. http://ec.europa.eu/health/medical-devices/files/meddev/2_1_6_ol_en.pdf. Accessed 28 March 2013.
17. Thompson B and Brooke J. "The FDA's approach to clinical decision support software: A brief summary." FierceHealthIT. www.fiercehealthit.com/special-reports/fdas-approach-clinical-decision-support-software-brief-summary. Accessed 28 March 2013.
18. MEDDEV 2.4/1 Rev. 9 *Classification of Medical Devices*, p. 10. EC website. http://ec.europa.eu/health/medical-devices/files/meddev/2_4_1_rev_9_classification_en.pdf. Accessed 28 March 2013.
19. Op cit 3, point I.1.4.
20. Ibid, article 1 (2) (b).
21. *Federal Food, Drug, and Cosmetic Act*, section 201(h). US Senate website. http://epw.senate.gov/FDA_001.pdf. Accessed 28 March 2013.
22. Op cit 3, Annex IX, sub II, point 2.3.
23. Op cit 7, p. 8-9.
24. 21 CFR 820.30 (g) Design Controls. FDA website. www.accessdata.fda.gov/scripts/cdrh/cfdocs/cfcfr/cfrsearch.cfm?fr=820.30. Accessed 28 March 2013.
25. IEC 62304 *Medical device software—Software life cycle processes*. IEC website. http://webstore.iec.ch/preview/info_iec62304%7Bed1.0%7Den_d.pdf. Accessed 28 March 2013.
26. 21 CFR 820.50(a)(1) Purchasing Controls. FDA website. www.accessdata.fda.gov/scripts/cdrh/cfdocs/cfcfr/CFRSearch.cfm?fr=820.50. Accessed 28 March 2013.
27. Op cit 3, Annexes II, IV, V and VII.
28. EN 13485 Medical devices—Quality management systems—Requirements for regulatory purposes, 5.6 (management review) and 7.4 (purchasing controls). CENELEC website. www.cenelec.eu/dyn/www/f?p=104:110:4733143039283291::::FSP_ORG_ID,FSP_PROJECT,FSP_LANG_ID:10384,24011,25. Accessed 28 March 2013.
29. Op cit 6.
30. Commission Regulation (EU) No 207/2012 of 9 March 2012 on electronic instructions for use of medical devices, OJ 2012 L72/28, articles 3 (e) and 10. EUR-Lex website. http://eur-lex.europa.eu/LexUriServ/LexUriServ.do?uri=OJ:L:2012:072:0028:0031:en:PDF. Accessed 28 March 2013,
31. Revision of the medical device directives. EC website. http://ec.europa.eu/health/medical-devices/documents/revision/index_en.htm. Accessed 18 March 2013.
32. Statement by the Press Secretary on H.R. 33, H.R. 2297, and S. 3187. White House website. www.whitehouse.gov/the-press-office/2012/07/09/statement-press-secretary-hr-33-hr-2297-and-s-3187.

Recommended Reading

- Thompson B, Vollebregt E and Brooke J. "Stand-Alone Software Used in Healthcare Applications." *European Medical Device Technology*, March/April 2012, p. 30.
- Hall K. "Developing Medical Device Software to IEC 62304." *European Medical Device Technology*, June 2010, Volume 1, No. 6.
- Vollebregt E and Klümper M. "The Regulation of Software for Medical Devices in Europe." *Journal of Medical Device Law Regulation*, May 2010, p. 5.
- Vollebregt E and Klümper M. "Navigating the New EU Rules for Medical Device Software." *RAJ Devices*, Mar/Apr 2009, p. 83.

Chapter 22

Postmarket Requirements

Updated by C. David Lim, PhD, RAC, CQA

OBJECTIVES

- ❑ Understand postmarket requirements for medical devices
- ❑ Understand postmarket surveillance (PMS)
- ❑ Understand vigilance reporting
- ❑ Understand field safety corrective actions (FSCA)
- ❑ Understand field safety notices (FSN)
- ❑ Understand mandatory problem reporting in Canada
- ❑ Understand medical device reporting in the US
- ❑ Understand medical device advertising rules

REGULATIONS AND GUIDELINES COVERED IN THIS CHAPTER

European Commission

- ❑ MEDDEV 2.12/1 *Guidelines on a Medical Devices Vigilance System* (rev 8) (January 2013)

Canada

- ❑ *Canadian Medical Device Regulation* (CMDR)
- ❑ Mandatory Medical Device Problem Reporting Form for Industry (HC Pub.: 110180)

US

- ❑ US Medical Device Reporting Regulation
- ❑ 21 CFR Part 803
- ❑ Form FDA 3500A – Mandatory Reporting;

GHTF

- ❑ GHTF/SG2/N016R5 *Charge & Mission Statement* (June 29, 1999)
- ❑ GHTF/SG2/N008R4 *Guidance on How to Handle Information Concerning Vigilance Reporting Related to Medical Devices* (June 1999)
- ❑ GHTF/SG2/N79R11:2009 *Medical Devices: Post Market Surveillance: National Competent Authority Report Exchange Criteria and Report Form (*February 2009)
- ❑ GHTF/SG2/N54R8:2006 *Medical Devices Post Market Surveillance: Global Guidance for Adverse Event Reporting for Medical Devices* (November 2006)
- ❑ GHTF/SG2/N47R4: 2005 *Review of Current Requirements on Postmarket Surveillance* (May 2005)
- ❑ GHTF/SG2/N57R8:2006 *Medical Devices Post Market Surveillance: Content of Field Safety Notices* (June 2006)

- ❑ GHTF/SG2/N87:2012 *An XML Schema for the electronic transfer of adverse event data between manufacturers, authorised representatives and National Competent Authorities* (August 2012)

ISO

- ❑ EN ISO 13485:2012 *Medical devices—Quality management systems—Requirements for regulatory purposes*

- ❑ EN ISO 14971:2012 *Medical devices—Application of risk management to medical devices*

Introduction

A medical device manufacturer's obligations to meet regulatory requirements continue throughout the medical device's lifecycle including the post-production phase (postmarket). Medical device manufacturers are required to implement an effective postmarket surveillance system per the various applicable regulations. This chapter outlines the general requirements and background for implementing a postmarket surveillance program. Postmarket requirements include postmarket surveillance, vigilance reporting, the handling of customer complaints and recalls. Although national laws and regulations may differ, general postmarket requirements are similar at the global level. This chapter discusses some of the important postmarket requirements applicable to medical device manufacturers, including in vitro diagnostic medical device manufacturers (collectively called "manufacturers").

Postmarket Surveillance System (PMSS)

As set out in the EU directive annexes (II, IV, and V of the *Active Implantable Medical Devices Directive* (*AIMDD*); II, IV, V, VI and VII of the *Medical Devices Directive* (*MDD*); and III of the *In Vitro Diagnostic Medical Devices* (IVDD)), the postmarket surveillance system (PMSS) is a proactive, systematic procedure whereby manufacturers review various sources of information to gather data and detect infrequent complications or problems that become apparent only after widespread use of the device. This information is then used to monitor device performance and to implement appropriate corrective or preventive actions. Manufacturers of medical devices that are placed on the market with the CE Mark are required to develop and implement this system. There are many possible sources of information, including patient follow-up from clinical trials, scientific papers or articles, adverse events, customer complaints, service reports, user reports, changes to regulations or standards, communications from regulatory bodies and customer or user surveys.

Vigilance Reporting

The purpose of a vigilance and postmarket surveillance system is to better protect the health and safety of patients, users and others by reducing the likelihood of the same type of adverse incident being repeated in different places at different times.[1] The medical device vigilance system is an integral part of a PMSS.[2] Manufacturers placing medical devices on the EU market must have a vigilance system in place for collecting and evaluating reported incidents and taking corrective action, if needed, to prevent the recurrence of such incidents.[3]

Adverse Event Reportings at the National Level

Reporting medical device adverse events to the national Competent Authorities is an important element in a PMS. It is worth noting, however, that reporting requirements and scope differ among countries.[4] Reporting systems are compulsory in some regions and voluntary in others. The scope of the national or regional system also varies. The current trend in all systems is the obligatory reporting of incidents of which the manufacturer is made aware involving the manufacturer's device.

Manufacturers operating globally must ensure they meet local reporting requirements and have a system in place to gather all the necessary information on incidents to be reported in all regions. If third-party local distributors are part of the system, they should be trained on the relevant procedures to ensure they understand their reporting obligations regarding the manufacturer's requirements and to complement the overall reporting system.

A good national and worldwide reporting system can only be realized if all parties have confidence in one another.[5] The collected data, especially any patient-related information, should come from trusted sources and should be treated confidentially.

The following criteria should be considered when disseminating national information on adverse events:

- What is the benefit or use of disseminating device-related information (e.g., issues related to device safety, possible risks and information related to recalls)?
- Is the information relevant, and if so, to whom: other authorities, manufacturers, distributors, hospitals, users, etc.?
- What is the traceability of persons or institutions who should receive vigilance-related information?

Disseminating information is the responsibility of the manufacturer or its representative. Dissemination should be supervised by the national Competent Authority, which also can assist in the process if necessary. In critical cases, the national Competent Authority may wish to disseminate the information itself.[6] In either case, before information is released, the relevance and benefit of its dissemination should be considered. Some useful questions to ask include:

- Does the public need this information and do they have the right to know?
- Will releasing such information benefit public health?
- Could releasing the information frighten or harm the public?

Distribution Records for Traceability

If a critical event occurs, devices may have to be recalled from the market. Maintaining traceability of medical devices expedites their retrieval and removal during a product recall. Distribution records must contain sufficient information to permit devices to be recalled from the market completely and rapidly. Manufacturers of active implantable medical devices and implantable medical devices are required to maintain records of all device materials, components and work environment conditions. In addition, the manufacturer's agents or distributors shall maintain records of the distribution of medical devices, including the name and address of the shipping package consignee in the manufacturer's quality management system.[7]

National Competent Authority Report (NCAR) Exchange Criteria and Report Form[8]

In February 2009, the Global Harmonization Task Force (GHTF) published guidance entitled, *Medical Devices: Post Market Surveillance: National Competent Authority Report Exchange Criteria and Report Form.* This document provides guidance, forms and procedures for exchanging medical device safety reports among national Competent Authorities and other participants in the GHTF NCAR exchange program and provides guidance on the following:

- the criteria to be used for deciding when to exchange information with other Competent Authorities and NCAR participants
- procedures to follow when exchanging information
- forms to use for exchanging the information

The NCAR Secretariat is the organization that receives NCARs from reporting national Competent Authorities and distributes them to other NCAR participants.[9] "Active exchange" is the proactive exchange of information involving direct notification to nominated contact addresses via email and through the NCAR Secretariat. This form of exchange should be used for high-risk issues. For non-serious events, information should be entered into a database, website or other means for exchange participants to view at their discretion ("passive exchange").

An NCAR should be sent only if the issue is considered to be serious, in which case the information should be exchanged actively through the NCAR Secretariat. For example, an NCAR relating to an unexpected but non-serious event is unlikely to be exchanged actively. Whether the exchange is active or passive depends on the seriousness of the issue.

The following information should be disseminated among national Competent Authorities as an NCAR:[10]

A. when the manufacturer performs a Field Safety Correction Action (FSCA)
B. when the manufacturer is required by a national Competent Authority to perform an FSCA or to make changes in an ongoing FSCA
C. where there is a serious risk to the safety of patients or other users without corrective action being performed, although corrective measures are under consideration
D. when the manufacturer does not provide a final report in a timely manner

When a manufacturer has taken corrective action, national Competent Authorities should exercise their discretion to determine whether the corrective action is essential to protect the safety of patients or other users. If it is not considered to be essential, an NCAR may not be necessary. When in doubt, there should be a predisposition on the part of national Competent Authorities to disseminate the NCAR.

The national Competent Authority responsible for the manufacturer or the manufacturer's Authorized Representative should disseminate the NCAR concerning A above. The national Competent Authority requesting the FSCA or changes in the ongoing FSCA or identifying the serious risk and considering measures, or expecting the final report should disseminate the NCAR concerning B, C and D, respectively. The national Competent Authority should immediately (without any delay that could not be justified) distribute this NCAR, but not later than 14 calendar days after being informed by the manufacturer.

MEDDEV 2.12/1 Annex 8[11] is the same as the Criteria and Report Form provided in GHTF/SG2/N79,[12] with minor changes. Annex 8 contains the format for dissemination of information between national Competent Authorities and the Commission.

NCARs are intended for dissemination among national Competent Authorities and the Commission only. They are not distributed to users or other parties of interest unless otherwise subject to national requirements. Competent Authorities must consult the manufacturer, where appropriate, when preparing an NCAR, and must inform the manufacturer when one is issued.

Decision Criteria for Incidents to be Reported to Competent Authorities[13]

To be a reportable incident, an event must meet three basic criteria:

1. An event has occurred. Such events include, but are not limited to:
   - a malfunction or deterioration
   - false positive or false negative test results
   - unanticipated side effect or unanticipated adverse reaction
   - interactions with other products or substances
   - destruction or degradation of the device
   - inaccuracy in the labeling, Instructions for Use and/or promotional materials
   - inappropriate therapy
2. The manufacturer's device is suspected to be a contributory cause of the incident based on the following:
   - the available evidence-based opinion of healthcare professionals
   - the results of the manufacturer's own preliminary assessment of the incident
   - previous evidence of similar incidents
   - other information or evidence held by the manufacturer
3. The event led to the death, serious injury or serious deterioration in the state of health of a patient, user or other person. The incident also is reportable if no death or serious injury occurred but the event might lead to the death or serious injury of a patient, user or other person if it were to recur. A serious deterioration in state of health includes the following:
   - life-threatening illness
   - permanent impairment of a body function or permanent damage to a body structure
   - medical or surgical intervention (e.g., extended duration of a surgical procedure or hospitalization or significant prolongation of existing hospitalization)
   - any indirect harm as a result of an incorrect diagnostic or IVD test results
   - fetal death, fetal distress or any congenital abnormality or birth defects

When there is doubt about the reportability of an event—even if the manufacturer has incomplete information—there should be a predisposition to report rather than not report.

According to GHTF's *Medical Devices Post Market Surveillance: Global Guidance for Adverse Event Reporting for Medical Devices*,[14] events do not need to be reported if:

- the user found a deficiency in a device prior to patient use
- the adverse event was caused by patient conditions
- the event was caused by the device's service life or shelf life (i.e., when the only cause for the adverse event was that the device exceeded the service life or shelf life as specified by the manufacturer and the failure mode is not unusual, the adverse event does not need to be reported)
- malfunction protection operated correctly (i.e., adverse event did not lead to serious injury or death because a design feature protected against a malfunction's becoming a hazard)
- there is negligible likelihood of occurrence of death or serious injury
- the event is an expected and foreseeable side effect
- the adverse event is described in an Advisory Notice
- there are reporting exemptions granted by a national Competent Authority

To Whom to Report[15]

Adverse events must be reported to the national Competent Authority in the country in which the incident occurs.

When to Report

As soon as a medical device manufacturer becomes aware that an event has occurred and one of its devices may have caused or contributed to that event, it must determine whether it is an incident.

- An event that represents a serious public health threat must be reported immediately (without any delay that could not be justified) but not later than two calendar days after awareness.
- Any adverse event(s) that results in unanticipated death or unanticipated serious injury must be reported immediately (without any delay that could not be justified) by the manufacturer to the national Competent Authority but not later than 10 calendar days following the date of awareness.
- All other reportable events must be reported immediately, but no later than 30 calendar days after the date the manufacturer becomes aware of the event.

Postmarket Surveillance (PMS)

All regulatory systems recognize that adverse event reporting alone cannot capture all risks related to medical devices in the postmarket phase.[16] For certain classes of products, such as diagnostic devices, where false positives and/or false negatives may occur, long-term implantable devices and devices for home use, it is not sufficient to evaluate the device's performance from adverse event reports alone. To address this requirement, PMS activities are required in most countries. Currently, requirements, definitions and understanding of PMS activities are not harmonized.[17] GHTF actively investigated whether harmonizing some aspects of PMS activities might benefit regulatory authorities and industry.

While the exact definition varies from country to country, PMS generally can be understood to be proactive activities carried out (by either the regulator or the manufacturer) to gain information about the quality, safety or performance of medical devices that have been placed on the market. Surveillance activities by a Competent Authority may involve testing, product review, inspections and other controlling measures. Information relating to PMS also is given in ISO 13485*Medical Devices—Quality management systems—Requirements for regulatory purposes.*[18] This standard advises manufacturers to establish documented procedures for a feedback system to provide early warnings of quality problems and input to the corrective and preventive action (CAPA) processes. These processes are, in turn, intended to detect and minimize risk, per ISO 14971 *Medical Devices Application of risk management to medical devices.*[19]

The purpose of PMS is to implement and maintain a systematic procedure to review experience gained from devices in the post-production/postmarket phase and apply any necessary corrective action(s).[20]

Typical sources of information on device experience include:

- customer surveys
- user surveys
- adverse events (vigilance system)
- user reports
- user feedback
- customer complaints
- customer requirements, contract information and market needs
- patient follow-up after clinical trials or investigations
- service and evaluation reports
- scientific papers in peer-reviewed journals
- reports on similar products by competitors
- compliance-related communications from regulatory agencies
- changes to relevant standards and regulations

FSCA

Manufacturers placing medical devices on the market are obliged to put corrective and preventive action plans into place related to their products if those devices pose a risk to users or other individuals.[21] These plans include FSCAs taken by the manufacturer to reduce the risk of harm to patients, operators or others and/or to minimize chances the event will recur.

As defined in GHTF's *Medical Devices—Post Market Surveillance: Content of Field Safety Notices,*[22] an FSCA is an action taken by a manufacturer to reduce the risk of death or serious deterioration in the state of health associated with the use of a medical device. In assessing the need for the FSCA, the manufacturer should refer to the harmonized risk management standard ISO 14971, which describes the methodology. When in doubt, there should be a predisposition to report and to perform an FSCA. Among the reasons for issuing an FSCA are:

- the return of a medical device to the manufacturer
- device modification
- device exchange
- device destruction
- advice given by the manufacturer regarding the use of the device (especially in the case of implants)

An FSCA should be sent in the official language of the recipient, and per GHTF's guidance, should include:

- a clear title such as "Urgent Safety Notice" on the notice itself, on the envelope if sent by mail and in the subject line if sent by email or fax
- a clear statement about the intended audience for the notice
- a concise description of the subject device, including model, batch and/or serial number
- a factual statement explaining the reasons for the FSCA, including a description of the problem
- a clear description of the hazards associated with the device's specific failure and, where appropriate, the likelihood of occurrence, being mindful of the intended audience
- recommended action(s) to be taken by the recipient of the Field Safety Notice (FSN) including people who have previously used or been treated by affected devices
- where appropriate, timeframes during which the action(s) should be taken by the manufacturer and user
- designated contact point for the recipient of the FSN to obtain further information

FSN

The manufacturer must issue FSNs to the affected customers, patients or users and send copies to the Competent Authorities of all affected countries. Where a Notified Body was involved in the device's Conformity Assessment Procedure, the manufacturer should send it a copy of the FSN. The FSN should be communicated on company letterhead and in appropriate language accepted by the Competent Authority. The following information should be included:

- clearly titled with "Urgent Field Safety Notice"
- specific details to enable easy identification of the affected device including type, model number, batch/lot or serial numbers
- a factual statement explaining the reasons for the FSCA, including a description of the device malfunction, potential hazard and associated risks
- actions to be taken by the user, including identifying and quarantining the device; method of device recovery, disposal or modification; patient follow-up (for implants and IVDs); and timelines
- a request to pass the FSN to all those who need to be aware

- a request for the details of any affected devices that have been transferred to other organizations to be given to the manufacturer, and for a copy of the FSN to be passed on to the organization to which the device has been transferred (if relevant)
- a request to alert other organizations to which incorrect test results have been sent (for IVDs, if relevant)
- confirmation that the relevant national Competent Authorities have been advised of the FSCA
- contact point for customers, how and when to reach the designated person
- no comments that serve to play down the level of risk to advertise products or services

To ensure a more consistent process is followed, the MEDDEV Guidelines on a Medical Devices Vigilance System, should be consulted.[23]

Manufacturer's Periodic Summary Report and Trend Report

Periodic summary reports and trend reports should be agreed upon by the manufacturers and individual national Competent Authorities regarding the format and frequency of reports for certain types of devices and incidents. When a manufacturer has received the agreement of a national Competent Authority to switch to periodic summary reporting or trend reports, the manufacturer shall inform the other concerned Competent Authorities about the agreement and its modalities. The forms for periodic summary reporting and trend reports are provided in MEDDEV 2.12/1 Annex 6 and Annex 7, respectively.[24]

Technical File Lifecycle Management (LCM)

Postmarket Phase

The content and description of the technical file for medical devices are covered in Chapter 17. In the postmarket phase, it is important to realize that the regulatory authority may ask at any time for a copy of the technical file, even for lower-risk devices. Manufacturers of lower-risk medical devices are obliged to keep the technical file on their premises, while manufacturers of higher-risk devices must submit the technical file for review before placing the devices on the market. In the postmarket phase, manufacturers are obliged to have a functioning change control system in place that continuously updates the technical file. In general, changes that affect the quality system must be communicated to the authorities before implementation. For higher-risk devices, all changes that alter the information in the originally submitted technical file must be submitted for approval before implementation. In other words, the technical file must follow the lifecycle management process in the postmarket phase.

Advertising

Medical device advertising should not impart false, misleading or deceptive information about the device that could give an erroneous impression of its design, construction, performance, intended use, quantity, character, value, composition, merit or safety. Advertising can create expectations and have a powerful influence on users; therefore, regulation plays an important role in preventing fraudulent and/or misleading advertising.[25] From the user's perspective this may cause a delay in receiving appropriate treatment by the use of falsely advertised products making performance claims. To save patients from such situations, vendors must be properly controlled and regulated.

In addition, any claims made on product labeling should be supported by appropriate clinical evidence in the form of clinical investigations, performance evaluations or bibliographic literature.

Canada: Mandatory Problem Reporting[26]

Pursuant to the *Canadian Medical Device Regulation* (*CMDR*; Sections 59-61.1(2)), the manufacturer and the importer must each submit a preliminary and a final report to the minister concerning any incident that comes to their attention occurring inside or outside Canada and involving a device that is sold in Canada.

Typical events include a failure of the device or a deterioration in its effectiveness, or any inadequacy in its labeling or in its Instructions for Use that has led to the death or a serious deterioration in the state of health of a patient, user or other person, or could do so if were to recur.

For an incident outside Canada, manufacturers are not required to report unless they have indicated their intention to take corrective action to a foreign regulatory agency or unless the foreign regulatory agency has required the manufacturer to take corrective action. Manufacturers and importers are required to report incidents to the Bureau of Compliance and Enforcement within 10 calendar days for an incident or within 30 calendar days for a near incident.

For an incident occurring outside Canada, a preliminary report must be submitted as soon as possible (within 48 hours) after the manufacturer has informed the foreign regulatory agency of the intention to take corrective action, or as soon as possible after the foreign regulatory agency has required the manufacturer to take corrective action.

US: Medical Device Reporting

In the US, device manufacturers, user facilities and importers are subject to medical device reporting requirements under the Code of Federal Regulations (CFR). The definitions for the terms used below are set out in 21 CFR 803.3. The mandatory reporting form is Form FDA 3500A.[27] The applicable requirements for medical device adverse event reporting in the US are briefly summarized below.

User Facilities

Device user facilities are required to:

- report deaths to both the US Food and Drug Administration (FDA) and the manufacturer within no more than 10 workdays, if it is known that a device has or may have caused or contributed to the death
- report a serious injury to the manufacturer, if known, or to FDA within no more than 10 work days
- establish and maintain adverse event files
- submit summary Annual Reports

Importers

Device importers are required to:

- report deaths and serious injuries to FDA and copy the manufacturer if the manufacturer's device may have caused or contributed to deaths and serious injuries
- report within no more than 30 calendar days after becoming aware of the adverse event
- report certain device malfunction(s) to the manufacturer if one of its devices has malfunctioned and would be likely to cause or contribute to a death or serious injury if it were to recur
- establish and maintain adverse event files

Manufacturers

Device manufacturers and importers are required to:

- report deaths and serious injuries to FDA if a device may have caused or contributed to deaths and serious injuries within no more than 30 calendar days
- report that a device has malfunctioned and would be likely to cause or contribute to a death or serious injury if the malfunction were to recur.
- submit specified follow-up
- report remedial action within five working days to prevent an unreasonable risk of substantial harm to the public health or submit a five-day report when requested by FDA
- establish and maintain adverse event files

Conclusion

The postmarket surveillance system is important for better protection of the health and safety of patients, users and others by reducing the likelihood of recurrence of an incident. Manufacturers are required to implement a postmarket surveillance system to monitor postproduction performance in a proactive and systematic manner according to the applicable medical device laws and regulations. This is achieved by the evaluation of reported incidents and dissemination of information, as appropriate, to prevent repetition of similar incidents or to alleviate consequences of such an incident. Manufacturers must ensure they fulfill their responsibilities in the postmarket phase, including updating technical files regularly, reporting vigilance events, conducting any necessary FSCAs, including recalls or withdrawals related to patient safety or performance issues, maintaining a postmarket surveillance system and abiding by national or regional laws and regulations. An FSCA should be notified to customers and/or users via an FSN. Manufacturers also must update their quality systems, performing internal audits and ensuring that device safety and performance levels are maintained. Failure to meet postmarket obligations could result in noncompliance, which in turn, could lead to a batch recall or liability issues. It is worth noting that postmarket lifecycle management may well be the most resource-intensive phase for manufacturers placing medical devices on the market.

References

1. SG2-N16-R5 Charge & Mission Statement (29 June 1999). Blue Inspection website. www.blue-inspection.com/GxP/04_GHTF/SG2-N16-R5.pdf. Accessed 30 March 2013.
2. Ibid.
3. MEDDEV 2.12/1, Rev. 8: *Guidelines on a Medical Devices Vigilance System* (January 2013). EC website. http://ec.europa.eu/health/medical-devices/files/meddev/2_12_1_ol_en.pdf. Accessed 30 March 2013
4. GHTF-SG2-N008R4 *Guidance on How to Handle Information Concerning Vigilance Reporting Related to Medical Devices* (29 June 1999). IMDRF website. www.imdrf.org/docs/ghtf/final/sg2/technical-docs/ghtf-sg2-n008r4-reporting-guidance-990629.pdf. Accessed 30 March 2013.
5. Ibid.
6. Ibid.
7. EN ISO 13485:2012 *Medical devices—Quality management systems—Requirements for regulatory purposes.* CENELEC website. www.cenelec.eu/dyn/www/f?p=104:110:3317776796616989::::FSP_ORG_ID,FSP_PROJECT,FSP_LANG_ID:10384,24011,25. Accessed 30 March 2013.
8. GHTF/SG2/N79R11:2009 *Medical Devices: Post Market Surveillance: National Competent Authority Report Exchange Criteria and Report Form* (17 February 2009). IMDRF website. www.imdrf.org/docs/ghtf/final/sg2/technical-docs/ghtf-sg2-n79r11-medical-devices-post-market-surveillance-090217.pdf. Accessed 30 March 2013.
9. GHTF/SG2/N38R19:2009 *Application Requirements for Participation in the GHTF National Competent Authority Report Exchange Program* (July 2009). IMDRF website. www.imdrf.org/docs/ghtf/final/sg2/technical-docs/ghtf-sg2-n38r19-national-competent-authority-report-program-090701.pdf. Accessed 30 March 2013.
10. Op cit. 3.
11. Ibid.
12. Op cit. 8.
13. Op cit. 3.
14. GHTF/SG2/N54R8:2006 *Medical Devices Post Market Surveillance: Global Guidance for Adverse Event Reporting for Medical Devices* (November 2006). http://www.imdrf.org/docs/ghtf/final/sg2/technical-docs/ghtf-sg2-n54r8-guidance-adverse-events-061130.pdf. Accessed 5 April 2013
15. Op cit. 3.
16. GHTF/SG2/N47R4:2005 *Review of Current Requirements on Postmarket Surveillance* (May 2005). IMDRF website. www.imdrf.org/docs/ghtf/final/sg2/technical-docs/

ghtf-sg2-n47r4-2005-guidance-postmarket-surveillance.pdf. Accessed 30 March 2013.

17. Ibid.
18. Op cit 7.
19. International Organization for Standardization. EN ISO 14971:2012 *Medical devices—Application of risk management to medical devices.*
20. Op cit. 3.
21. GHTF/SG2/N57R8:2006 *Medical Devices Post Market Surveillance: Content of Field Safety Notices* (27 June 2006). IMDRF website. www.imdrf.org/docs/ghtf/final/sg2/technical-docs/ghtf-sg2-n57r8-2006-guidance-field-safety-060627.pdf. Accessed 30 March 2013.
22. Ibid.
23 Op cit. 3.
24. Ibid.
25. WHO, *Medical device regulations: global overview and guiding principles,* ISBN 92 4 154618 2, copyright, World Health Organization 2003. WHO website. www.who.int/medical_devices/publications/en/MD_Regulations.pdf. Accessed 30 March 2013.
26. HC Pub.: 110180 Mandatory Medical Device Problem Reporting Form for Industry (October 2011). Health Canada website. www.hc-sc.gc.ca/dhp-mps/alt_formats/pdf/medeff/report-declaration/md-mm_form-eng.pdf. Accessed 19 March 2013.
27. Medwatch Form FDA 3500A – Mandatory Reporting FDA website. www.fda.gov/downloads/Safety/MedWatch/HowToReport/DownloadForms/ucm082728.pdf. Accessed 30 March 2013.

Chapter 23

High-Risk Products: Products Derived from Biotechnology

Updated by Nicole Beard MSc, PhD

OBJECTIVES

- ❑ Understand the definition of a biotechnology product and regional differences
- ❑ Understand the special considerations involved in developing a biotechnology product
- ❑ Understand the registration principles in different regions of the world and special requirements pertaining to biotechnology and biologics
- ❑ Become familiar with International Conference on Harmonisation (ICH) documents

REGULATIONS AND GUIDELINES COVERED IN THIS CHAPTER

ICH

- ❑ *Viral Safety Evaluation of Biotechnology Products Derived from Cell Lines of Human or Animal Origin Q5A(R1)* (September 1999)
- ❑ *Quality of Biotechnological Products: Analysis of the Expression Construct in Cells Used for Production of r-DNA Derived Protein Products Q5B* (November 1995)
- ❑ *Quality of Biotechnological Products: Stability Testing of Biotechnological/Biological Products Q5C* (November 1995)
- ❑ *Derivation and Characterisation of Cell Substrates Used for Production of Biotechnological/Biological Products Q5D* (July 1997)
- ❑ *Comparability of Biotechnological/Biological Products Subject to Changes in Their Manufacturing Process Q5E* (November 2004)
- ❑ *Final Concept Paper Q5E: Comparability of Biotechnological/Biological Products Subject to Changes in Their Manufacturing Process* (February 2002)
- ❑ *Specifications: Test Procedures and Acceptance Criteria for Biotechnological/Biological Products Q6B* (March 1999)
- ❑ *Development and manufacture of drug substances (chemical entities and biotechnological/biological entities) Q11* (May 2012)
- ❑ *Preclinical Safety Evaluation of Biotechnology-Derived Pharmaceuticals S6(R1)* (Addendum June 2011)
- ❑ *M4: The Common Technical Document*

EU

- ❑ Regulation (EC) No. 726/2004 of the European Parliament and of the Council of 31 March 2004 laying down Community procedures for the authorisation and supervision of medicinal products for human and veterinary use and establishing a European Medicines Agency, as amended and consolidated (July 2012)

- *The Rules Governing Medicinal Products in the European Union, Volume 2A,* Procedures for Marketing Authorisation, Chapter 4: Centralised Procedure (April 2006)
- EMA/410/01 Rev.3, *Note for guidance on minimising the risk of transmitting animal spongiform encephalopathy agents via human and veterinary medicinal products*(March 2011)
- Regulation (EC) No 1394/2007 of the European Parliament and of the Council of 13 November 2007 on advanced therapy medicinal products and amending Directive 2001/83/EC and Regulation (EC) No 726/2004, as amended and consolidated (July 2012)
- Directive 2001/83/EC of the European Parliament and of the Council of 6 November 2001 on the Community code relating to medicinal products for human use, as amended and consolidated (January 2011)
- Guidance CHMP/QWP/227/02 Rev 3,*Guideline on Active Substance Master File Procedure* (October 2012)

US

- 21 CFR, Subchapter F Biologics, Part 600:Biological Products: General
- 21 CFR 312 Investigational New Drug Application
- *Guidance for Industry: Content and Format of Investigational New Drug Applications (INDs) for Phase 1 Studies of Drugs, Including Well-Characterized, Therapeutic, Biotechnology-derived Products* (November 1995)
- New Drug and Biological Drug Products; Evidence Needed to Demonstrate Effectiveness of New Drugs When Human Efficacy Studies Are Not Ethical or Feasible (Animal Efficacy Rule) (May 2002)

Introduction

Often, the terms "biotechnology" and "biological" are used synonymously or have overlapping definitions. Furthermore, the definitions for biological products and their regulatory requirements vary by region.

This chapter applies a broad definition of biotechnology products, including biologicals (products of biologic origin), vaccines, blood- and plasma-derived products, as well as products derived by biotechnological processes.

In most regions, biologicals are subject to the same or similar licensing procedures as other pharmaceutical products; however, evaluating them often requires specific expertise that goes beyond what is needed for conventional medicines. Thus, this class of products triggered or aided the move toward harmonization of scientific evaluation, leading to the establishment of the Centralised Procedure in the EU and the founding of the European Medicines Agency (EMA),[1]and in the US, evaluation by a specialized center (Center for Biologics Evaluation and Research (CBER[2])) within the Food and Drug Administration (FDA) using a specific evaluation process (Biologics License Application (BLA)). In addition, since the characterization and determination of biological active substances' quality attributes require not only a combination of physicochemical and biological testing, but also extensive knowledge of the production process and its control, certain limitations are imposed on this class of drugs. Examples are the non-eligibility of biologicals for the Active Substance Master File (ASMF) process in Europe and their exemption from "generics" or "similar biological medicinal products" or "biosimilars" provisions in many regions (see Chapter 13 Generic Drug Products and Chapter 24 Biosimilars).

However, as a result of increased scientific understanding and better characterization capabilities for biological molecules, as well as patent expiration of several blockbuster biologics, the concept of "follow-on biologics" (FOBs) or biosimilars is currently being discussed, and the first guidance documents are being developed in several regions. Outside the EU and US, some FOBs such as erythropoietin, insulin, human growth hormone and granulocyte-colony stimulating factor have been licensed already.

Scientific and technological progress in the field of biotechnology drugs, such as stem cell technology, tissue engineering, etc., has been addressed by new legislation and guidance, e.g., the *Advanced Therapy Medicinal Product Regulation* in Europe.[3] In the US, guidance regarding gene therapy and somatic cell therapy was first developed as early as 1991 and is still evolving.

For most countries, a product's licensure in a reference country or region (US, EU, Canada, Australia, etc.) or, in some cases, in the country of manufacture, must be demonstrated via a Certificate of a Pharmaceutical Product (CPP) also called Certificate of Medicinal Product (CMP).

To obtain more-detailed regulatory agreements with a specific country of interest, see the "Regulators outside the EU" page on the EMA website (www.ema.europa.eu/ema/index.jsp?curl=pages/partners_and_networks/general/general_content_000214.jsp&mid=WC0b01ac058003176d). This site provides links to the listed countries' ministry of health or organizations and the corresponding drug regulatory agency.

ICH Regions (EU, US, Japan)

International Conference on Harmonisation (ICH)

ICH has issued a range of guidelines pertaining to biologics, which are applicable in the EU, US and Japan, and other countries that recognize ICH (e.g., Canada, Switzerland, Australia, New Zealand).

In addition to the technical harmonization ICH has achieved in its three decades of existence, a major accomplishment is the development of a harmonized dossier structure, the Common Technical Document (CTD).[4] This format is applicable to both new chemical entities (NCEs) and biologics. Please refer to Chapter 9 for more information on ICH and CTD requirements.

EU

Introduction/History

In the EU, several separate regulatory procedures are in place for medicinal product registration. In addition to other criteria for selecting a registration process, one important determinant is whether licensure is sought for a conventional, chemically synthesized product or one derived from biotechnology or other innovative procedures.

In the early 1990s, EU authorities decided to institute a Centralised Procedure for registering NCEs and products derived from biotechnology. The intent was to have a single scientific evaluation utilizing the highest possible standard for these products' quality, safety and efficacy and to arrive at uniform decisions throughout the Community.

The Centralised Procedure involves a single application, a single evaluation and a single authorization allowing direct access to the whole Community market. In March 2004, the European Parliament and Council enacted Regulation (EC) No. 726/2004,[5] which consolidated the application and approval procedures and created a centralized medicines agency, EMA. It also established the Committee for Medicinal Products for Human Use (CHMP) as part of EMA. Following a positive CHMP opinion, the European Commission makes the final decision on whether to grant a marketing authorization. This regulation also reinforced the concept of a centralized approval process for products derived from biotechnology and for new active substances for certain therapeutics areas.

Description of Current Procedure and Guidance

Since a marketing authorization granted through the Centralised Procedure is valid for the entire Community market, the manufacturer has one EU license to market the product, rather than individual national licenses in specific EU Member States. Consequently, a medicinal product may be put on the market in all Member States; however, it is still necessary to negotiate pricing and reimbursement on a country-by-country basis because financial aspects of medicinal product supply are regulated by national laws.

The Centralised Procedure is described in detail in *The Rules Governing Medicinal Products in the European Union, Volume 2A*, Chapter 4.[6] For a more-detailed overview of the Centralised Procedure, please refer to Chapter 10, Authorization Procedures for Pharmaceutical Products. The Centralised Procedure has proven to be efficient and is mandatory for products developed using one of the following biotechnological processes:

- recombinant DNA technology
- controlled expression of gene coding for biologically active proteins in prokaryotes and eukaryotes, including transformed mammalian cells
- hybridoma and monoclonal antibody methods

Examples of new biotechnology products for which the Centralised Procedure is mandatory are products intended for gene therapy, vaccines from strains developed by means of recombinant DNA technology, any medicinal product for which a monoclonal antibody is used at any stage in the manufacturing process, orphan drugs and cell therapy products that are the result of any biotech process.

For medicinal products containing a new active substance intended for the treatment of acquired immune deficiency syndrome (AIDS), cancer, neurodegenerative disorders, diabetes, autoimmune diseases or other immune dysfunctions and viral diseases, the Centralised Procedure has been mandatory since 2008.

Other medicinal products can be authorized by the Centralised Procedure if the applicant shows that the product constitutes a significant therapeutic, scientific or technical innovation, or that granting authorization via the Centralised Procedure is in the interest of patients.

The procedure also has some disadvantages. One of the main drawbacks is the requirement that the product be made available in all 28 EU countries plus Norway and Iceland; selective filing or withdrawals are not possible, whether the manufacturer has a commercial interest in a particular country or not.

Among other things, this requirement involves preparing the Summary of Product Characteristics (SmPC), labeling and patient information leaflet (PIL)—and, subsequently, the mock-ups—in all 22 EU languages.

Following the marketing authorization, the European Public Assessment Report (EPAR) is made available via the EMA website. The company has the opportunity to delete commercially sensitive, confidential information from the EPAR before it is published.

A marketing authorization is valid for five years and then may be renewed on the basis of a reevaluation of the benefit:risk balance. Once renewed, the marketing authorization is valid for an unlimited period unless there are issues relating to pharmacovigilance, in which case the renewal would be for one additional five-year period.

The frequency of submitting Periodic Safety Update Reports (PSURs) has been increased to compensate for the reduced renewal requirements.

Dossier Requirements

Preclinical and Clinical

As is the case for conventional products, the product used in pivotal pharmacology and toxicology studies should be comparable to the product proposed for clinical studies. For *in vivo* safety evaluation, relevant animal species should be involved. Normally, such studies include two different species, although in some cases, one relevant species may suffice if the applicant presents adequate justification. The need for reproductive and developmental toxicity studies depends on the product and must be assessed on a case-by-case basis. Genotoxicity and carcinogenicity studies generally are not needed for biotechnology products.[7]

Clinical studies must be tailor-made for each product and should consider the route of administration, indication, intended treatment population, etc. Following a near-fatal incident involving a monoclonal antibody in a first in human Phase 1 study in the UK, safety requirements for early Phase 1 studies have been increased, involving staggered recruitment and independent Data Safety Monitoring Board reviews, to mitigate the risk to study subjects.

A marketing authorization for a medicinal product for human or veterinary use will be granted following assessment of its quality, safety and efficacy. Biotechnology products must fulfill the same basic quality, safety and efficacy criteria as any other pharmaceutical product.

In addition, all general requirements—such as Good Laboratory Practices (GLPs), Good Clinical Practices (GCPs), Good Manufacturing Practices (GMPs) and the need to have a manufacturing license—also apply equally to biotechnology and conventional products. Along with the standard regulatory requirements, however, a number of issues are specific to biotechnology products.

Quality and Manufacturing Information

A fair number of guidelines describe specific production and testing requirements for various biotechnology-derived product types. Many of these have been developed as ICH guidelines and are applicable in Europe, the US and Japan, and in any other countries that recognize ICH.

The drug substance and drug product development program requires special attention for biotechnology products (ICH Q5 guidelines).[8] Underlying physicochemical differences between biological/biotechnological products and chemically synthesized products may necessitate special pharmaceutical and biopharmaceutical considerations during the research and development program. Experimental processes that lead to a finalized manufacturing process and established product specifications usually require a more elaborate description than that required for a conventional product.

Production of biotechnological active ingredients requires rigorous processes and testing, including a detailed description of source material, production strain or cell line preparation, as well as genetic stability testing, cell bank system details, fermentation and harvesting information, purification details and a full product characterization. Analytical development of the special techniques involved, process validation and a detailed explanation of potential impurities, including batch results, also are required.

Biotechnology product quality is defined by the production and manufacturing process, and minor process changes can potentially affect the drug product's quality. Established details of the manufacturing process are, therefore, of paramount importance. To ensure consistency, the manufacturing parameters that can affect the drug substance's quality and stability in a formulated product (e.g., pH, heat, etc.) should be established. This is particularly important in relation to scaling up the manufacturing process. In contrast to traditional drugs, biotechnology products typically are complex and labile proteins. For authentic *in vivo* activity, the primary amino acid sequence is essential, as are the secondary linkages and tertiary folding of the molecule to reveal the appropriate functional sites. Small changes in structure can radically alter proteins' *in vivo* immunogenicity and pharmacokinetics.

Because of their physicochemical properties, it usually is not possible to terminally sterilize biotechnology products in the final container by autoclaving. In most instances, they are sterilized by membrane filtration before filling. Aseptic techniques are an absolute requirement. Compatibility with excipients and primary packaging components requires special attention.[9]

Transmissible Spongiform Encephalopathy

After many years of heated discussions and near bans on the use of ingredients of animal origin in medicinal products, the situation in the EU has stabilized. Concern about the use of animal ingredients is related to their potential for causing transmissible spongiform encephalopathy (TSE). Scrapie in sheep and goats, bovine spongiform encephalopathy (BSE) in cattle and Creutzfeldt-Jakob Disease (CJD) in humans all belong to the TSE family.

TSE is believed to be caused by prion proteins and no associated genetic material. TSE agents are difficult to destroy; such conventional sterilization methods as autoclaving at 121°C for 15 minutes, dry heat processes (e.g., 160°C for one hour) or irradiation at 25kGy do not inactivate the agents.

Because TSE-associated diseases, particularly CJD, are incurable and fatal, the policy has aimed at eliminating the use of tissues at particular risk for carrying BSE.

Unfortunately, the pharmaceutical industry depends on certain materials from bovine, ovine or caprine sources and their derivatives. Many organs, tissues and sera, such as heparin, glucagons, lactose, fetal calf serum and serum albumin, are used as raw material sources. Materials are extracted from hair and wool, and derivatives of materials of animal origin (in particular gelatin and tallow derivatives) are used in many pharmaceutical products. In addition, animal tissues are used to manufacture incubation media for the production of biotechnology products. Banning the use of bovine-derived materials in producing pharmaceuticals would have resulted in removal of a vast range of products from the EU market.

Instead, EU legislation has been amended to require the applicant to demonstrate that the medicinal product is manufactured in accordance with the *Note for Guidance on Minimising the Risk of TSE* (EMA/410/01 Rev.3).[10]

The ultimate goal still is to replace all ingredients of animal origin in human medicinal products with vegetable-derived or synthetic materials, using the appropriate variation procedures. Animal-derived materials may still be used, at least temporarily, provided compliance with the requirements is demonstrated as follows:

- submitting detailed information on animal materials used, including manufacturing procedure details, to the Competent Authorities
- submitting a European Pharmacopoeia (Ph. Eur.) certificate of TSE compliance (Certificate of Suitability); to obtain this certificate, manufacturers must submit full information to the European Directorate for the Quality of Medicines (EDQM)

The Certificate of Suitability can be used every time the particular ingredient is used in the production of any pharmaceutical product. In contrast, when the first route is followed, each Competent Authority must assess each animal-derived material separately for every final product application.

Viral Clearance/Extraneous Agents

When ingredients of animal or human origin are used in producing a pharmaceutical product, particularly when they are used as manufacturing fabric, the capacity of the production process to remove all viral contamination is vitally important. Testing and evaluating biotechnology products' viral safety is a standard requirement. The three complementary approaches for addressing viral safety are:

- selecting and testing cell lines and other raw materials, including media components, for the absence of undesirable viruses that may be infectious or pathogenic to humans
- assessing the capacity of the production process to clear infectious viruses by viral inactivation and viral removal
- testing the product at appropriate production steps for the absence of contaminating infectious viruses

All three approaches are necessary to establish a product's safety, and it is crucial to demonstrate that the purification regimen can remove and inactivate the viruses. Viral clearance requirements continue to become more stringent and—although there may be differences in implementing certain requirements—global regulatory requirements are comparable.[11]

Special Topics (Release Testing, etc.)

Release Testing in Europe

When a pharmaceutical product is manufactured outside the EU/EEA (European Economic Area) and imported into the market, release testing must be performed on every batch upon arrival in the EU/EEA. Therefore, a company should carefully consider which tests to list under release specifications and which could be considered in-process or final bulk product tests. The repeat testing requirement applies to all tests presented as final product release tests. Although this requirement is not specific to biotechnology products, the complexity of some release tests, the often small batch sizes and significant product cost may necessitate special attention to this issue.[12]

If a product is produced within the EU/EEA, it usually is not necessary for each batch to be released by an Official Medicines Control Laboratory (OMCL). However, for certain types of biological products, such as those derived from human blood or plasma as well as vaccines, special batch release requirements are in place mandating testing and release of each individual batch before it is placed on the market.

Advanced Therapy Medicinal Products (ATMPs)

Scientific and technological progress in the field of biotechnology led to the development of new legislation and guidance such as the *Advanced Therapy Regulation* (Regulation (EC) No. 1394/2007[13] amending Directive 2001/83/EC[14] and Regulation (EC) No. 726/2004.[15] ATMPs are new medicinal products based on genes (gene therapy), cells (cell therapy) and tissues (tissue engineering). These advanced therapies herald revolutionary treatments for a number of diseases or injuries, such as skin in burn victims, Alzheimer's, cancer and muscular dystrophy. These products seem to have huge potential for patients and industry.

Although ATMPs are regarded as medicinal products, they are considered to be separate from traditional pharmaceuticals, recognizing that they require different testing and control parameters.

The main elements of the regulation are:

- mandated use of the Centralised Procedure to benefit from the pooling of expertise at the European level and direct access to the EU market
- a new, multidisciplinary expert committee (Committee for Advanced Therapies (CAT)), within EMA, to assess advanced therapy products and follow scientific developments in the field
- technical requirements adapted to the particular characteristics of these products
- special incentives for small and medium-sized enterprises

This new regulation also recognizes that a number of ATMPs actually combine biological materials, such as tissues or cells, with chemical structures such as metal implants or polymer scaffolds. These combination products lie at the border of the traditional pharmaceutical area and other fields (e.g., medical devices). They therefore cannot be regulated as "conventional" drugs, and adapted requirements need to be developed for them. In addition, a significant number of firms involved in this field are not large pharmaceutical companies, but rather small and medium-sized enterprises or hospitals.

Active Substance Master File (ASMF)

The concept of the ASMF (previously known as European Drug Master File (EDMF)) is established in Directive 2001/83/EC as amended and described in EMA's *Guideline on Active Substance Master File Procedure.*[16] An ASMF consists of two parts: an open "applicant's" part and a closed "restricted" part. This allows an applicant to incorporate protected information from another manufacturer into its application, without needing to know the exact content. The evaluating authority, however, has access to both the open applicant's dossier and the closed part of the ASMF and can perform a full evaluation.

Marketing Authorisation Holders (MAHs) and applicants are advised that the concept of ASMF cannot be applied to biological medicinal products.

The characterization and determination of biological active substances' quality require not only a combination of physicochemical and biological testing, but also extensive knowledge of the production process and its control.

An MAH or applicant for a biological medicinal product, therefore, could not comply with the requirement to "take responsibility for the medicinal product" without having full and transparent access to these quality-related data. The use of an ASMF would prevent such access, and is therefore not allowed for biological active substances.

Likewise, the legislation does not provide for the use of open/closed parts in the Vaccine Antigen Master File (VAMF) or Plasma Master File (PMF). In fact, the legislation specifies that the VAMF holder cannot differ from the MAH or applicant for the concerned medicinal product.

For the PMF, the legislation specifies that where the MAH or applicant differs from the PMF holder, the PMF shall be made available to the MAH or applicant for submission to the Competent Authority.[17]

US

Introduction/History

Biologics are defined in 21 CFR, Subchapter F, Subpart A 600.3(h)[18] as medicinal products derived from or made with the aid of living organisms that are used to prevent, treat or cure diseases or injuries of man. These products are often complex substances or mixtures, and many are manufactured using biotechnology.

Initially, such products were confined to vaccines, antitoxins, sera, blood and blood products and allergenic extracts. Today, biologics also include therapeutic protein drugs derived from natural sources (e.g., factor IX, alglucerase, antithrombin III); therapeutic protein drugs derived through biotechnology (e.g., recombinant derived proteins, DNA/plasmid products and monoclonal antibodies); and gene, tissue and somatic cell therapies.

Biologics also are classified and regulated as drugs under the *Federal Food, Drug, and Cosmetic Act* (*FD&C Act*). All new pharmaceutical products must demonstrate safety and efficacy prior to receiving marketing approval. A proposed new biological product, whether a drug or vaccine, must follow the Investigational New Drug (IND) application process described in 21 CFR Part 312[19] and the BLA process described in 21 CFR Part 601.[20] Both FDA`s Center for Drug Evaluation and Research (CDER) and CBER[21] have responsibilities for regulating biological products. The assignment of products to either center is based on product classification.

For a more detailed overview of the procedures please see Chapter 10.

Description of Current Procedure and Guidance

FDA issues a variety of guidance documents to aid sponsors in complying with regulatory requirements while developing and marketing biological products. These guidelines represent the agency's current thinking on a particular topic and, when appropriate, are issued jointly by CBER, CDER and the Center for Devices and Radiological Health (CDRH). A list of current CBER guidelines is published quarterly in the *Federal Register*. Many of the documents are also available online at www.fda.gov/BiologicsBloodVaccines/GuidanceComplianceRegulatoryInformation/default.htm. The site also includes guidelines specific to biological products published by ICH. In 2006, FDA withdrew multiple chemistry, manufacturing and controls (CMC) guidances and recommended reference to ICH documents.

FDA accepts submissions in CTD format. However, CBER recommends consulting with the center prior to submitting a BLA, especially if an electronic submission is planned.

Dossier Requirements

Generally, similar requirements apply regarding description of the development work, raw material selection, the manufacturing process, extraneous agent removal and testing sections in the respective CTD modules, as described for the EU. In contrast to EMA, FDA puts more weight on facility description including equipment validation, monitoring schedules, etc., as the BLA incorporated the formerly separate establishment licensing application part into CTD Module 3.2.A.1.

A specific procedure to estimate the risk for vCJD in vaccines using bovine-derived materials is described by CBER, whereby the number of final product doses leading under worst case conditions to one theoretical case of vCJD is calculated (www.fda.gov/downloads/BiologicsBloodVaccines/SafetyAvailability/BloodSafety/UCM095104.pdf).

Clinical Trials

The regulatory requirements for the preparation and purpose of an Investigational New Drug application (IND) submitted to FDA are provided in 21 CFR 312.[19] The IND grants the sponsor permission to ship an investigational medicinal product (IMP) in interstate commerce for the purpose of conducting clinical studies. The IND submission should initially focus on the general investigational plan and specific human study protocols.

Each IND is reviewed by the appropriate CBER division: bacterial products, virology, cytokine biology, blood and blood products, biochemistry and biophysics, product quality control and certification. The IND may also be circulated to reviewers from the National Institutes of Health, CDER or outside experts.

FDA's *Guidance for Industry: Content and Format for Investigational New Drug Applications (INDs) for Phase 1 Studies of Drugs, Including Well-Characterized, Therapeutic, Biotechnology-derived Products*,[22] clarifies data requirements of 21 CFR Parts 312.22 and 312.23 related to initiation of human studies.

Following an IND review, if CBER has safety concerns, it may issue a clinical hold letter to a sponsor. IND amendments are required as clinical development progresses. New protocols, protocol amendments and manufacturing and safety data must be submitted to the IND periodically, and annual reports are required to be submitted within 60 days of the IND's anniversary date. Studies of new uses for previously approved biologics also can be conducted under an IND. Under 21 CFR 312.120, FDA may accept foreign clinical data.

Animal Rule

The final rule, *New Drug and Biological Drug Products; Evidence Needed to Demonstrate Effectiveness of New Drugs When Human Efficacy Studies Are Not Ethical or Feasible (Animal Rule)*,[23] allows FDA to approve a product for which evidence of safety and efficacy has been based on data obtained in adequate and well-controlled animal trials as further detailed in the concept paper, "Animal Models—Essential Elements to Address Efficacy Under the Animal Rule," published in 2009. This applies to products intended to reduce or prevent a serious illness due to exposure to a biological agent when human trials are not ethical or feasible. For example, vaccines for high-risk bioterrorism pathogens face difficulties in proceeding into Phase 3 efficacy clinical trials.

Under the *Animal Rule*, FDA will rely on animal efficacy data when:

- there is a well-understood pathophysiological mechanism of the substance's toxicity and its amelioration or prevention by the product
- the effect is demonstrated in more than one animal species expected to react with a response predictive for humans, unless the effect is demonstrated in a single animal species that represents a sufficiently well-characterized animal model for predicting the response in humans
- the endpoint is plainly related to the desired effect in humans
- data on the pharmacokinetics and pharmacodynamics of the product or other relevant data in animals allow the selection of an effective dose in humans
- the product's effect is reasonably likely to predict the effect in humans

Safety requirements for product approval remain the same, and it is believed that, in most cases, safety can be determined in humans. FDA recognizes that safety data regarding possible interactions between the product and the toxic substance (agent) may not be available. Postmarket studies, to be performed if feasible, will be required to verify product benefit, safety and distribution restrictions. FDA may withdraw product approval if postmarketing studies fail to demonstrate the benefit(s); the applicant fails to perform postmarket studies; postmarket restrictions fail to ensure safe use; the applicant fails to adhere to restrictions; promotion or advertising materials are false or misleading; or other data show the product to be unsafe or ineffective.

Manufacturing Arrangements

In most cases, the classic concept of a sole manufacturer completing every step of a complex manufacturing process is not feasible for start-up biotechnology companies with limited personnel and capital resources. Therefore, FDA issued *Guidance for Industry: Cooperative Manufacturing*

Arrangements for Licensed Biologics in November 2008, delineating four types of joint manufacturing arrangements:

1. short supply
2. shared
3. contract
4. divided

The short supply provisions have limited applicability. Licensed manufacturers may use these provisions to obtain source materials only.

Shared manufacturing involves multiple licensed manufacturers, each of which performs significant manufacturing steps in the production of one product.

Contract manufacturing involves a licensee contracting out one or more manufacturing steps.

Divided manufacturing involves the joint production of a biologic product by multiple manufacturers, each of which is licensed to manufacture the entire product.

A sponsor does not need to obtain a separate BLA for each contract manufacturer but can reference outside producers in its application by listing them and the production steps they perform. Unlike in the EU, in the US, a Drug Master File (DMF) may be utilized for biological products for referencing outside producers in the event of confidentiality concerns.

Lot Release

After a BLA is approved, the product also may be subject to official lot release. As part of the manufacturing process, the manufacturer is required to perform certain tests on each product lot before it is released for distribution. If the product is subject to official release by CBER, the manufacturer submits samples of each product lot to the center, together with a release protocol that summarizes the lot's manufacturing history and the results of all manufacturer tests on the lot. CBER also may perform certain confirmatory tests on lots of some products, such as viral vaccines, before releasing them for marketing distribution. In addition, CBER conducts laboratory research related to regulatory standards for biological products' safety, purity, potency and effectiveness.

In November 1995, President Bill Clinton and Vice President Al Gore signed *Reinventing the Regulation of Drugs Made from Biotechnology*, which—among other things—eliminated the lot release requirements for biotech drugs identified as "well-characterized." As more biologics categories achieve well-characterized or "specified" status, individual lot release is becoming more the exception than the rule. FDA also published guidelines prepared under the auspices of ICH in *Federal Register* notices on 21 September 1998 and 18 August 1999 that recommend appropriate standards for the production and release of biologics.

Inspections

CBER conducts inspections of the manufacturing plant before it approves a product. Following approval, facilities are inspected on a regular basis. The purpose of these inspections is to assess whether biological products are manufactured in compliance with appropriate laws and regulations. FDA has multiple types of manufacturing inspection programs to help ensure the quality and safety of drugs, biologics and devices. CBER also may inspect clinical study sites to determine whether trials are being carried out properly and to ensure accurate information is being submitted to the agency. A number of enforcement tools available to the center may be used when a manufacturer or clinical researcher is in violation of FDA laws and regulations.

Pharmacovigilance

A specific postmarket safety surveillance system, the Vaccine Adverse Event Reporting System (VAERS), has been implemented for vaccines. Although extensive studies are required for the licensure of new vaccines, postmarket research and surveillance are necessary to identify safety issues that may only be detected following vaccination in a much larger and more diverse population.

VAERS was created as a result of the *National Childhood Vaccine Injury Act* of 1986 (*NCVIA*) and is administered by FDA and the Centers for Disease Control and Prevention (CDC). VAERS accepts reports of adverse events from healthcare providers, manufacturers and the public that may be associated with US licensed vaccines. FDA continually monitors VAERS reports for any unexpected patterns or changes in rates of adverse events.

Japan

Introduction/History

In Japan, in addition to ICH guidance documents, other requirements, such as local clinical studies or quality requirements (testing according to the Japanese Pharmacopoeia (JP), specially designed stability studies) must be met. The Japanese biotechnology and biologics market is dominated by domestic manufacturers.

Due to a lengthy review process and the above-mentioned additional requirements, Japan experienced a "drug lag," where state-of-the-art drugs only became available several years after their approval in the EU or US. This triggered revision of the Japanese *Pharmaceutical Affairs Law* (*PAL*), which underwent major changes in 2004 and 2005, implementing a new evaluation body, the Pharmaceutical and Medical Devices Agency (PMDA) and more-stringent safety controls for biologics.

Description of Current Procedure and Guidance

Japan does not require a CPP or equivalent, but usually does require local clinical trials. Foreign manufacturers need to follow a designated procedure to obtain a Foreign Manufacturing Authorization (FMA). The FMA and the product dossier can be submitted in parallel; PMDA's evaluation process takes one year followed by an expert meeting and questions to the MAH. Responses are evaluated, and the evaluation process proceeds until approval is granted by the executive committee.

Local analytical testing of a sample is not required for marketing approval but is required for lot release. A site master file describing the production facility and an independent site inspection are required.

Dossier Requirements

Dossier requirements follow ICH guidance, thus the CTD format is used; modules 1 and 2 must be submitted in the Japanese language. Special requirements for biologics include raw material testing and a description for materials of biologic origin, cell and virus bank testing, etc.

Special attention must be paid to the clinical section, as clinical trials are required to bridge overseas trials to the Japanese population. Advice from PMDA should be sought on the design of such studies.

Canada

Introduction/History

Canada has both prescription and nonprescription pharmaceutical products, as well as biologically derived products such as vaccines, sera and blood-derived products.

A "biologic(al) drug" is a drug listed under *Food and Drugs Act (F&DA)* Schedule D. A New Drug Submission (NDS) is an application to Health Canada's Therapeutic Products Directorate (TPD)—the federal authority that regulates pharmaceutical drugs and medical devices for human use—requesting marketing approval for a new drug. To be granted market authorization, a manufacturer must present substantive scientific evidence of a product's safety, efficacy and quality (chemistry and manufacturing) as required by the act and regulations.

The Biologics and Genetic Therapies Directorate (BGTD) is the regulatory authority responsible for ensuring the safety, efficacy and quality of all biologics (Schedule D) and radiopharmaceuticals (Schedule C) for human use marketed in Canada. BGTD regulates blood and blood products, viral and bacterial vaccines, genetic therapeutic products, tissues, organs and xenografts manufactured in Canada or elsewhere.

Description of Current Procedure and Guidance

Biological products are defined by the organisms from which they are derived, and most impurities are host-driven rather than process-driven. This is the fundamental difference between biologic and synthetic pharmaceutical products; therefore, biologic submissions should focus on this area. BGTD has published several guidelines for sponsors filing a new biologic drug submission in CTD format, which can be found on the Health Canada homepage (http://www.hc-sc.gc.ca/index-eng.php). The directorate produced several Quality Information Summary—Biologicals (QIS-B) templates for particular biological product types in 2004. Specific facility information also is required, especially in terms of single-product versus multi-product facilities.

Two additional components are required for biologics—one preapproval and one postapproval. During the chemistry and manufacturing review, an on-site evaluation or inspection may be conducted before the NDS is approved. BGTD will request a production schedule during the review period, and the on-site evaluation must be completed before issuance of the Notice of Compliance (NOC). Secondly, the sponsor should provide test protocols and drug product consistency samples for evaluation. The specific sample components and numbers (e.g., drug substance, final drug product, reference samples, reagents, etc.) will be requested during the review.

Dossier Requirements

Many of the directorate's guidelines are derived from those of ICH. Canada is an ICH observer rather than a member, but has chosen to accept those guidelines that meet Canadian standards. Canadian submissions follow the CTD format.

Clinical Trials

Application for conducting clinical trials in Canada follows a process similar to the EU's. Sponsors must file a Clinical Trial Application (CTA) to conduct trials in Phases 1 through 3 of drug development. A CTA must be filed prior to the initiation of a clinical trial. The application is reviewed and the sponsor notified within 30 days if the application is found to be deficient; otherwise the sponsor may proceed. Further details can be found on the Health Canada website (www.hc-sc.gc.ca/dhp-mps/prodpharma/applic-demande/guide-ld/clini/ctdcta_ctddec-eng.php).

Lot Release

Lot release requirements for biologic products are different from those for synthetic pharmaceuticals. When a biologic product is issued an NOC, it is assigned to one of four evaluative groups. Based on the product's categorization, BGTD will review each lot before release and, in some cases, retest the product to confirm the certificate of analysis.

Asia Pacific

Introduction/History

Countries in Asia have for some time experienced a high overall economic growth rate. As a result, local populations have benefited from increased per capita spending power, which has led to demands for improved access to better healthcare and pharmaceuticals.

While no common regulatory procedures exist in Asia, there are ongoing efforts toward harmonization in the framework of the Association of Southeast Asian Nations (ASEAN). ASEAN harmonization focuses on technical requirements and has resulted in a special CTD format (ACTD).

A legislative framework regarding biological products is emerging.

Description of Current Procedure and Guidance

Most countries in Asia require foreign manufacturers to demonstrate licensure of their product in a reference country via a CPP. Some countries—e.g., Thailand, Philippines and Indonesia—require a CPP from the country of origin/manufacture.

Licensure timelines range from 1.5 to 2.5 years. In some countries (India, China), local Phase 3 clinical studies are required to bridge global studies to the specific population.

In China, marketing applications must be submitted in the Mandarin language. The English dossier can be attached for reference.

When available, marketing approval should be confirmed by a CPP. China established a New Biological Products division at the Center for Drug Evaluation and, as mentioned, requires local clinical trials. Another specific requirement is sample testing by the National Institute for the Control of Pharmaceutical and Biological Products (NICPBP). If the product is new to China, NICPBP will write a National Drug Standard for it after testing, which will be included in the Chinese Pharmacopoeia. Overall licensure timelines, including the clinical study and sample testing, etc. are quite lengthy, usually lasting several years.

In 2003, China established technical guidelines pertaining to biological and biotechnology products, e.g., DNA vaccines, monoclonal antibodies, biologics produced from bovine serum, etc. Biosimilar products currently are registered as new products, and there is no abridged approval procedure for them. Lack of efficient patent protection laws is considered an issue. State agencies began continuing efforts to improve the situation in 1993.

Hong Kong is governed as an autonomous region of China, but its regulatory requirements are to a large extent still influenced by its British heritage. English dossiers are acceptable and local clinical trials are not required.

For foreign companies, India's procedures are also simpler than those of China since the dossier is accepted in English. However, a domestic clinical trial is required. India separated biologics in the *Drug & Cosmetic Act* and implemented comprehensive special provisions for biologics in December 2008.

The other rapidly developing countries in Asia belong to ASEAN (Brunei, Cambodia, Indonesia, Laos, Malaysia, Myanmar, Philippines, Singapore, Thailand and Vietnam). Since 2009, they have shared a common dossier format, the ACTD. Each individual section of the ACTD may be mapped to a section in the standard ICH CTD dossier. However, as the ASEAN countries are located in a hot and humid climate zone, they have specific requirements for stability studies.

Korea and Taiwan are considered mature Asian markets. South Korea requires the dossier to be prepared largely in the Korean language, but accepts certain sections in English if a summary is provided in the local language. The requirements for local clinical trials and local analytical testing depend on the product type and the marketing experiences in the original and worldwide markets.

The Taiwanese authority accepts dossiers largely in English, with certain sections summarized in Standard Mandarin. A CPP, samples for local analytical testing and a local clinical trial are required for marketing approval. A unique Taiwanese plant master file (PMF) covering the production facility is required if the facility has not been registered previously in Taiwan.

A specific requirement impacting biologics is that no porcine material is allowed in drugs for some countries (Malaysia, Indonesia).

Clinical Trials

There is a requirement for one or more clinical trials in China (as well as in India), to include a minimum number of patients, depending on the trial phase and the nature of the drug. Companies new to China will need to hire a contract research organization (CRO) to conduct the trial. The applicant should submit detailed nonclinical, clinical and CMC information, plus a proposed clinical trial protocol and an application form, in Standard Mandarin, with the source documents in the original languages attached to the application.

India also requires a clinical study to bridge global studies to the local population, usually in a minimum of 100 subjects. Generally, approval of a clinical study is a lengthy process of more than six months. However, India implemented the so called "Schedule Y," which calls for drastically reduced timelines of only two to four weeks for clinical trial application approval if a global study to include sites in India is already approved in a reference country (US, EU, Switzerland, Australia, Canada, South Africa or Japan).

Latin America

Introduction/History

Regulatory procedures in Latin America are diverse, and no common drug licensing and evaluation procedure exists in the region. In most countries, licensure of the product in a reference country must be demonstrated via a CPP.

A legislative framework for biological products started to emerge in 2002 and this development continues, e.g., Venezuela drafted guidance on biological products in February 2008.

According to Federación Latino Americana de la Industria Farmacéutica (FIFARMA) survey results, approximately 180 registrations for insulin, erythropoeitin, human growth hormone, monoclonal antibodies and other biologic products were approved in Latin America between 1996 and 2005.

Other national legislation is evolving.

Previously, the same requirements were applicable to all drugs in Brazil. In 2002, RDC 80 was issued, which was the first legislation differentiating biological/biotechnology products from chemically derived drugs.

In Argentina, Disposition 705/2005 was implemented in 2005, establishing provisions for vaccine registration. The format and content of application for biotechnology medicinal products was introduced in October 2011 with the publication of Disposition 7075/2011. This new guideline applies to all products of biological origin for human use, including blood products, recombinant DNA biotech products, monoclonal antibodies and biological medicinal products manufactured from biological tissues or fluids. In June 2012, a new Disposition 3397/2012 provided guidance on registration of biological products and monoclonal antibodies.

In Mexico, products of biological origin are not well defined in legislation. However, products derived by biotechnological processes are regulated in RIS article 81. In November 2012, agreements establishing equivalence for the registration of biological products were signed with the health authorities from Europe, Switzerland, Canada, the US and Australia. These agreements facilitate the registration of biological products already marketed in the related countries.

In most countries, biologics—including immunotherapeutic products, human plasma and blood products—are excluded from generic or similar products approval provisions. Brazil, for instance, considers all biologics/biotech products new products for licensing purposes.

One of the drivers toward more fully harmonized requirements for biological and biotech products, particularly vaccines, is the Pan American Health Association (PAHO), which also serves as the Regional Office for the Americas of the World Health Organization.

Description of Current Procedure and Guidance

There is no common drug licensing and evaluation procedure in Latin America. Generally, the process comprises a pre-application phase, receipt and validation and queuing for review, followed by the actual review and questions/clarification process leading to authorization. Quality assessment is performed either in parallel with the safety and efficacy evaluation (e.g., Brazil) or in a stepwise subsequent fashion (e.g., Argentina and Mexico). Depending on the country and its health authority, internal or external reviewers are involved in the scientific evaluation.

Depending on available resources and expertise, different risk stratification strategies are pursued by the health authorities. Where sufficient resources (internal and external) are available, full dossier evaluation is carried out, with or without preregistration requirement (CPP) in the reference region (mostly US, EU).

Where there are limited resources, an abridged, independent assessment may be performed under local conditions (benefit:risk assessment in relation to local ethnic population, medical practice and culture, disease pattern, storage conditions, etc.) of a product registered in a reference region.

In other cases, licensure of a product in a reference region, as demonstrated by a CPP, is recognized without further technical evaluation of the dossier.

Timelines for approval vary from 12–18 months in Brazil to two to three months in Peru and Paraguay, with a tendency for longer procedure durations.

Dossier Requirements

The CTD format generally is mandatory or accepted. Depending on the pathway the respective health authority follows, the data requirements in the dossier differ. For biologics, special requirements regarding number of conformance lots for drug substance or drug product, etc., may apply.

English dossiers are not accepted in all Latin American countries—e.g., a dossier submitted in Brazil must be in Portuguese—however, scientific supporting documents are acceptable in Spanish or English.

Facility licensing requirements, including inspection provisions, vary from country to country. Limited harmonization via the Pharmaceutical Inspection Scheme (PIC/S) and mutual recognition agreements is taking place. Several Latin American national inspectorates frequently conduct inspections outside their borders, the most active being Brazil and Mexico (2006 EFPIA members survey). In most cases, GMP certificates from the country of manufacture are accepted from countries participating in PIC/S.

Clinical Trials

Generally, there are no requirements for local clinical studies in support of new product applications.

Southern/Eastern Europe (SEE)

This region, also called Adriatic, includes Serbia, Bosnia-Herzegovina, Kosovo, Macedonia, Montenegro and Albania.

All countries in this region have individual approval processes. With the exception of Albania, CTD files are accepted or required.

Africa/Middle East

South Africa

South Africa performs an independent dossier evaluation; however, a CPP is required for foreign manufacturers. A CTD in English is accepted, with some additional information for biologics such as suppliers of raw materials, etc. The registration procedure usually takes two to three years.

North French Africa

This region includes Algeria, Morocco and Tunisia, among others. Countries accept EU files in CTD format. Application forms and all official letters included in Module 1 usually are in French and a CPP typically is required.

Middle East

In most countries, facility registration documentation is required prior to product application submission. Countries usually require licenses from reference countries, demonstrated via a CPP. A specific requirement impacting biologics is that absolutely no porcine material is allowed in drugs for some countries.

For the Gulf States (Saudi Arabia, Kuwait, United Arab Emirates, Qatar, Oman, Bahrain and Yemen), a common Gulf Cooperation Council for Drug Registration (GCC-DR) procedure has been implemented in addition to national registration processes. Since December 2010, the company registration dossier and marketing authorization application can be submitted in parallel. However the company registration must be approved prior to the product registration. Following GCC-DR registration, a national implementation process including price negotiations takes place in each GCC country. Most companies reported that registration through the centralized procedure took longer than through the national procedure.

Regulations are similar to EU guidelines, and registration dossiers should be submitted under the CTD format.

Iran, Egypt, Libya and other countries each have individual requirements and procedures, e.g., the need for DMFs and Site Master Files.

Russia/CIS

The Confederation of Independent States (CIS) is comprised of Armenia, Azerbaijan, Belarus, Georgia, Kazakhstan, Kyrgyzstan, Moldova, Russia, Tajikistan, Turkmenistan, Ukraine and Uzbekistan.

Russia implemented a submission format based on the CTD format in 2007, with individual files for the drug substance and the drug product, which are registered separately. The file must be submitted in Russian.

Based on information submitted in the dossier, primarily Module 3, a Normative Documentation (ND) summarizing the product's requirements and labeling (based on the Russian Pharmacopeia and, if necessary, European Pharmacopoeia and US Pharmacopeia) needs to be provided. The ND forms the basis for local batch release of biological products, with each batch checked or retested against the ND.

Mandatory testing requirements for specific groups of biological products are found in industrial standards.

The other CIS countries generally use the Russian file as reference.

Conclusion

In most regions, products derived from biotechnology are subject to the same or similar licensing procedures as other pharmaceutical products; however, evaluating them often requires specific expertise that goes beyond what is needed for conventional medicines. Thus, in some regions, this class of products triggered or aided the move toward harmonization and/or specialization of scientific evaluation.

ICH has issued a range of guidelines pertaining to biologics, which are applicable in the EU, US and Japan, and other countries that recognize ICH (e.g., Switzerland, Canada, Australia, New Zealand).

Since the characterization and determination of biological active substances' quality attributes require not only a combination of physicochemical and biological testing, but also extensive knowledge of the production process and its control, certain limitations are imposed on this class of drugs.

For most non-ICH countries, a product's licensure in a reference country or region (the US, EU, Switzerland, Canada, Australia, etc.) or, in some cases, in the country of manufacture must be demonstrated via a CPP to enable or facilitate product licensure.

Generally, regulatory procedures in non-ICH countries are diverse, and no common drug licensing and evaluation procedures exist. Legislative frameworks for biological products have begun to emerge in recent years, and development continues.

References

1. Regulation (EC) No. 726/2004 of the European Parliament and of the Council of 31 March 2004 laying down Community procedures for the authorisation and supervision of medicinal products for human and veterinary use and establishing a European Medicines Agency, as amended and consolidated (July 2012). EUR-Lex website. http://eur-lex.europa.eu/LexUriServ/LexUriServ.do?uri=OJ:L:2004:136:0001:0033:en:PDF. Accessed 1 April 2013.
2. FDA. Vaccine, Blood & Biologics. FDA website. www.fda.gov/BiologicsBloodVaccines/default.htm. Accessed 1 April 2013.
3. Regulation (EC) No. 1394/2007 of the European Parliament and of the Council of 13 November 2007 on advanced therapy medicinal

products and amending Directive 2001/83/EC and Regulation (EC) No 726/2004, as amended and consolidated (July 2012). EUR-Lex website. http://eur-lex.europa.eu/LexUriServ/LexUriServ.do?uri=OJ:L:2007:324:0121:0137:en:PDF. Accessed 1 April 2013.

4. ICH, *Organization of the CTD for the registration of pharmaceuticals for human use M4*, Current Step 4 version, 13 January 2004. ICH website. www.ich.org/fileadmin/Public_Web_Site/ICH_Products/CTD/M4_R3_Organisation/M4_R3__organisation.pdf. Accessed 1 April 2013.
5. Op cit 1.
6. *EudraLex, The Rules Governing Medicinal Products in the European Union, Volume 2A, Procedures for Marketing Authorization*, Chapter 4: *Centralised Procedure*, April 2006. EC website. http://ec.europa.eu/health/files/eudralex/vol-2/a/chap4rev200604_en.pdf. Accessed 1 April 2013.
7. ICH, *Preclinical Safety Evaluation of Biotechnology-Derived PharmaceuticalsS6*, Current Step 4 version, 16 July 1997.ICH website. www.ich.org/fileadmin/Public_Web_Site/ICH_Products/Guidelines/Safety/S6_R1/Step4/S6_R1_Guideline.pdf. Accessed 1 April 2013.
8. ICH Q5 series:
   - *Viral Safety Evaluation of Biotechnology Products Derived from Cell Lines of Human or Animal Origin Q5A(R1)*, Current step 4 version, 23 September 1999. ICH website. www.ich.org/fileadmin/Public_Web_Site/ICH_Products/Guidelines/Quality/Q5A_R1/Step4/Q5A_R1__Guideline.pdf. Accessed 1 April 2013.
   - *Quality of Biotechnological Products: Analysis of the Expression Construct in Cells Used for Production of r-DNA Derived Protein Products Q5B*, Current Step 4 version, 30 November 1995. ICH website. www.ich.org/fileadmin/Public_Web_Site/ICH_Products/Guidelines/Quality/Q5B/Step4/Q5B_Guideline.pdf. Accessed 1 April 2013.
   - *Quality of Biotechnological Products: Stability Testing of Biotechnological/Biological Products Q5C*, Current Step 4 version, 30 November 1995. ICH website. www.ich.org/fileadmin/Public_Web_Site/ICH_Products/Guidelines/Quality/Q5C/Step4/Q5C_Guideline.pdf. Accessed 1 April 2013.
   - *Derivation and Characterisation of Cell Substrates Used for Production of Biotechnological/Biological Products Q5D*, Current Step 4 version, 16 July 1997. ICH website. www.ich.org/fileadmin/Public_Web_Site/ICH_Products/Guidelines/Quality/Q5D/Step4/Q5D_Guideline.pdf. Accessed 1 April 2013.
   - *Comparability of Biotechnological/Biological Products Subject to Changes in Their Manufacturing Process Q5E*, Current Step 4 version, 18 November 1994. ICH website. www.ich.org/fileadmin/Public_Web_Site/ICH_Products/Guidelines/Quality/Q5E/Step4/Q5E_Guideline.pdf. Accessed 1 April 2013.
9. Ibid.
10. EMA/410/01 Rev.3, *Note for guidance on minimising the risk of transmitting animal spongiform encephalopathy agents via human and veterinary medicinal products* (March 2011). EMA website. www.emea.europa.eu/docs/en_GB/document_library/Scientific_guideline/2009/09/WC500003700.pdf. Accessed 1 April 2013.
11. ICH, *Viral Safety Evaluation of Biotechnology Products Derived from Cell Lines of Human or Animal Origin Q5A(R1)*, Current step 4 version, 23 September 1999. ICH website. www.ich.org/fileadmin/Public_Web_Site/ICH_Products/Guidelines/Quality/Q5A_R1/Step4/Q5A_R1__Guideline.pdf. Accessed 1 April 2013.
12. ICH, *Specifications: Test Procedures and Acceptance Criteria for Biotechnological/Biological Products Q6B*, Current Step 4, 10 March 1999. ICH website. www.ich.org/fileadmin/Public_Web_Site/ICH_Products/Guidelines/Quality/Q6B/Step4/Q6B_Guideline.pdf. Accessed 1 April 2013.
13. Op cit 3.
14. Directive 2001/83/EC of the European Parliament and of the Council of 6 November 2001 on the Community code relating to medicinal products for human use, as amended and consolidated (January 2011). EMA website. www.emea.europa.eu/docs/en_GB/document_library/Regulatory_and_procedural_guideline/2009/10/WC500004481.pdf. Accessed 1 April 2013.
15. Op cit 1.
16. Guidance CHMP/QWP/227/02 Rev.3 *Guideline on Active Substance Master File Procedure* (October 2012). EMA website. www.ema.europa.eu/docs/en_GB/document_library/Scientific_guideline/2012/07/WC500129994.pdf. Accessed 1 April 2013.
17. Commission Directive 2003/63/EC of 25 June 2003 amending Directive 2001/83/EC of the European Parliament and of the Council on the Community code relating to medicinal products for human use. EUR-Lex website. http://eur-lex.europa.eu/LexUriServ/LexUriServ.do?uri=OJ:L:2003:159:0046:0094:en:PDF. Accessed 1 April 2013.
18. 21 CFR, Subchapter F—Biologics, Part 600Biological Products: General. FDA website. www.accessdata.fda.gov/scripts/cdrh/cfdocs/cfcfr/cfrsearch.cfm?cfrpart=600. Accessed 1 April 2013.
19. 21 CFR ,Subchapter D—Drugs for Human Use, Part 312 Investigational New Drug Application. FDA website. www.accessdata.fda.gov/scripts/cdrh/cfdocs/cfcfr/cfrsearch.cfm?cfrpart=312. Accessed 1 April 2013.
20. 21 CFR, Subchapter F—Biologics, Part 601 Licensing. FDA website. www.accessdata.fda.gov/scripts/cdrh/cfdocs/cfcfr/CFRsearch.cfm?CFRPart=601. Accessed 1 April 2013.
21. Op cit 2.
22. *Guidance for Industry: Content and Format of Investigational New Drug Applications (INDs) for Phase 1 Studies of Drugs, Including Well-Characterized, Therapeutic, Biotechnology-derived Products* (November 1995). FDA website. www.fda.gov/downloads/Drugs/GuidanceComplianceRegulatoryInformation/Guidances/UCM071597.pdf. Accessed 1 April 2013.
23. New Drug and Biological Drug Products; Evidence Needed to Demonstrate Effectiveness of New Drugs When Human Efficacy Studies Are Not Ethical or Feasible (Animal Efficacy Rule) (May 2002). FDA website. www.fda.gov/ohrms/dockets/98fr/053102a.htm. Accessed 1 April 2013.

Chapter 24

Advancement of Biosimilars Development

By Hoss A. Dowlat, PhD

OBJECTIVES

- ❑ Provide insight into what is meant by a biosimilar in medical practice based on EU experience 2006–present
- ❑ Describe the EU approval precedents of biosimilars and EMA's influence on the international WHO guidance and national guidances worldwide
- ❑ Describe the unfolding and adoption of biosimilar pathways of approval by agencies in the rest of the world
- ❑ Describe FDA's independent position laying down the basis of approval of biosimilars
- ❑ Describe the implications of biosimilars in medicinal therapy
- ❑ Describe the developing roles and influence of stakeholders

REGULATIONS AND GUIDELINES COVERED IN THIS CHAPTER

WHO

- ❑ *Guidelines on Evaluation of Similar Biotherapeutic Products* (SBPs) (22 April 2010)

EU

(For Product specific guidelines see Annex 1 to this chapter)

- ❑ Article 10(4) of Directive 2001/83/EC of the European Parliament and of the Council of 6 November 2001 on the Community code relating to medicinal products for human use, as amended by Directive 2004/27/EC
- ❑ *Draft Guideline on Similar Biological Medicinal Products*, 2 CHMP/437/04 Rev 1 (22 May 2013)
- ❑ Concept paper on the revision of the guideline on similar biological medicinal products containing biotechnology-derived proteins as active substance: non-clinical and clinical issues, EMA/CHMP/BMWP/572828/2011 (22 September 2011)
- ❑ *Guideline on similar biological medicinal products containing biotechnology-derived proteins as active substance: quality issues.* EMA/CHMP/BWP/247713/2012 (Final 2013)

US

- ❑ *Patient Protection and Affordable Care Act* (March 2010), including the *Biologics Price Competition and Innovation Act* of 2009 (*Biologics Act*)

- ❑ *Draft Guidance for Industry: Scientific Considerations in Demonstrating Biosimilarity to a Reference Product* (February 2012)
- ❑ *Draft Guidance for Industry: Quality Considerations in Demonstrating Biosimilarity to a Reference Protein Product* (February 2012)
- ❑ *Draft Guidance for Industry: Biosimilars: Questions and Answers Regarding Implementation of the Biologics Price Competition and Innovation Act of 2009* (February 2012)
- ❑ *Biosimilar User Fee Act* of 2012 (*BsUFA*) (Applies October 2012 through September 2017)
- ❑ *Formal Meetings Between the FDA and Biosimilar Biological Product Sponsors or Applicants* (March 2013)

Canada

- ❑ *Guidance for Sponsors: Information and Submission Requirements for Subsequent Entry Biologics (SEBs)* (March 5, 2010 10-10569-330
- ❑ *Questions & Answers to Accompany the Final Guidance for Sponsors: Information and Submission Requirements for Subsequent Entry Biologics (SEBs)* (Draft docs were 2009-03-27)

Brazil

Technical guidelines, Coordination of Biological Products (CPBIH) and ANVISA:

- ❑ *Guidelines for exercising comparability studies for registering biological products* (2011)
- ❑ *Guidelines for elaborating clinical study reports for registration purposes and/or for post-registration amendments of biological products* (2011)

Product-specific guidelines:

- ❑ *Guideline for registering Heparins using the comparability pathway* (2011)
- ❑ *Guidelines for registering Alpha Interferon using the comparability pathway* (2011)

(Coordination of Biological Products (CPBIH) and ANVISA)

India

- ❑ *Guideline on Similar Biologics Regulatory Requirements for Marketing Authorization in India*, Department Biotechnology/Central Drugs Standard Control Organisation (2012)

Saudi Arabia

- ❑ *Guidelines on Biosimilars Version 1.1*, Saudi Food & Drug Authority Kingdom of Saudi Arabia (sFDA) (2010)

Introduction

This chapter provides insight into the new paradigm of true biosimilar medicines (not "copy biologics") based on high standards of approval and medical experience postapproval internationally. It provides a framework for the understanding, development and acceptance of a new generation of biologic medicines—biosimilars—worldwide. Advances in biosimilars in the EU and US are presented, along with a discussion of how the principles of biosimilar development, approval and medical use have been established.

Currently, the knowledge gathered by regulators and industry, based on seven years of biosimilars pharmacovigilance in the EU, provides a degree of confidence and assurance in the regulatory approval process. The following discussions describe biosimilar development and regulatory approval criteria in the EU and the US and related safety and efficacy aspects.

Definition of Biosimilars

No single international definition of biosimilarity exists. Biosimilarity covers many facets of the properties of an approved biological product and is determined based on an abbreviated program of studies against a well-established originator reference biologic. The biosimilar can be used when switching from that reference product (RP) or when initiating treatment.

In Section 351(i) of the *US Public Health Service Act* (*PHS Act*), biosimilarity means "that the biological product is highly similar to the reference product notwithstanding minor differences in clinically inactive components" and that "there are no clinically meaningful differences between the biological product and the reference product in terms of the safety, purity, and potency of the product." The *Biologics Price Competition and Innovation Act* (*BPCI Act*) amended the definition of biological product to include "protein (except any chemically synthesized polypeptide)."

According to the EU definition, biosimilars evolve from generics, but the generic definition is insufficient:

Table 24-1. Terms Used in This Chapter

ADAs	Anti-drug antibodies
ADRs	Adverse drug reactions
Biosimilar	A biological medicine that is developed to be similar to an existing (originator) biological medicine (the 'reference medicine')
BMWP	Biosimilar Medicines Working Party
CDSCO	Central Drugs Standard Control Organization (India)
CHMP	Committee for Medicinal Products for Human Use
EC	European Commission
EEA	European Economic Area
EMA	European Medicines Agency
EPAR	European Public Assessment Report
EU	European Union
FD&C Act	Federal Food, Drug, and Cosmetic Act
KOLs	Key Opinion Leaders
G-CSF	granulocyte-colony stimulating factor
mAb	Monoclonal antibody
MAH	Marketing Authorization Holder
MD	Multiple dose
MHLW	Ministry of Health, Labour and Welfare (Japan)
NICE	National Institute for Health and Care Excellence (A UK reimbursement authority)
PD	Pharmacodynamics
PK	Pharmacokinetics
REMS	Risk Evaluation and Mitigation Strategy
RMP_{PV}	Risk Management Plan (PV Pharmacovigilance)
RMP	Reference Medicinal Product (biosimilar EU)
RP	Reference Product (biosimilar US); also used for all biosimilars generally
SAR	Serious adverse drug reaction
sFDA	Saudi Food and Drug Authority
SC	Subcutaneous (route of administration)
SmPCs	Summary of Product Characteristics (EU prescriber information)
PI	Package Insert (US prescriber information)
PMDA	Pharmaceuticals and Medical Devices Agency (Japan)
SBP	Similar biotherapeutic product (biosimilar WHO)
SEB	Subsequent Entry Biologic (biosimilar Canada)
US	United States

"The provisions of Article 10(1)(a)(iii) [i.e. for generic medicinal products] may not be sufficient in the case of biological medicinal products. If the information required in the case of essentially similar products (generics) does not permit the demonstration of the similar nature of two biological medicinal products, additional data, in particular, the toxicological and clinical profile shall be provided."

Article 10(4) of Directive 2001/83/EC) states:

> Where there are "differences (particularly) in raw materials or manufacturing processes of the biological medicinal product and the reference biological medicinal product, the results of appropriate pre-clinical tests or clinical trials relating to these conditions must be provided."[1]

Table 24-2. EU Biosimilar Landscape of Approvals (Marketing Authorisations (MAs))

(INN) of substance	MA holder	Date of EC approval	Brand name	Reference product
Somatropin	Sandoz GmbH	12 April 2006	Omnitrope®	Genotropin®
	BioPartners GmbH[1]	24 April 2006[2]	Valtropin®	Humatrope®
Epoetin alfa	Sandoz GmbH	28 August 2007	Binocrit®	Erypo® /Eprex®
	Hexal GmbH	28 August 2007	Epoetin alfa HEXAL®	Erypo® /Eprex®
	Medice Arzneimittel Pütter GmbH & Co. KG	28 August 2007	Abseamed®	Erypo® /Eprex®
Epoetin zeta	STADA Arzneimittel GmbH	18 December 2007	Silapo®	Erypo® /Eprex®
	Hospira UK Ltd.	18 December 2007	Retacrit®	Erypo® /Eprex®
Filgrastim	Ratiopharm GmbH[2]	15 September 2008[3]	Ratiograstim®	Neupogen®
	Teva Generics GmbH	15 September 2008	TevaGrastim®	Neupogen®
	CT Arzneimittel GmbH	15 September 2008	Biograstim®	Neupogen®
	Sandoz GmbH	6 February 2009	Zarzio®	Neupogen®
	Hexal GmbH	6 February 2009	Filgrastim HEXAL®	Neupogen®
	Hospira UK Ltd.	8 June 2010	Nivestim®	Neupogen®

1 BioPartners GmbH (an SME and virtual pharma company), source of drug substance was Korean LG Life Sciences.
2 BioPartners GmbH Valtropin® Withdrawn 30 May 2012 (Commercial reason.)
3 Ratiopharm Filgastrim Withdrawn 20 July 2011 (commercial reasons.)

Table 24-3. EU Biosimilar Landscape of Submissions Under Assessment or Withdrawn

(INN) of substance	MA holder	Date of EC action	Brand name	Reference product
Interferon alfa	BioPartners GmbH (German) [1,2]	June 2006, Negative CHMP Opinion	Alpheon®	Roferon A
Epoetin alfa	Reliance Genemedix (Irish)	15 March 2011	Epostim®	Erypo® /Eprex®
Insulins (3 products)	Marvel Life Sciences (British)	Withdrawn 16 January 2008	Short, Intermediate, Long	Humulin® Soluble, Isophane and Mix
Infliximab	Celltrion (Korean)	Positive CHMP/EMA Opinion (Public on 28 June 2013)[3]	Remsima	Remicade EU
Infliximab	Celltrion	Positive CHMP/EMA Opinion (Public on28 June 2013)[3]	Inflectra	Remicade EU
FSH	Finox Biotech AG (Swiss)	Under CHMP/EMA assessment (filed 30 October 2012)	Bemfola	Gonal-f
Insulins	Marvel	December 2012 withdrawn	Solumarv	Humulin S
Insulins	Marvel	December 2012 withdrawn	Isomarv	Humulin I
Insulins	Marvel	December 2012 withdrawn	Combimarv	Humulin M

[1] BioPartners GmbH (an SME and virtual pharmaceutical company), source of drug substance was Korean company LG Life Sciences.
[2] Interferon beta-1a was investigated as drug product Biferonex by BioPartners GmbH against RPs Avonex and Rebif, but not submitted as a biosimilar under Article 10 (4) of Directive 2004/27. There was a negative Opinion CHMP 19 Feb 2009; MAA was withdrawn 29 May 2009.
[3] EMA/CHMP/363689/2013 (Decision 27 June); parallel MAA, Hospira will market under licence.

Figure 24-1. Candidates for Biosimilar Medicines Approved or Under Development

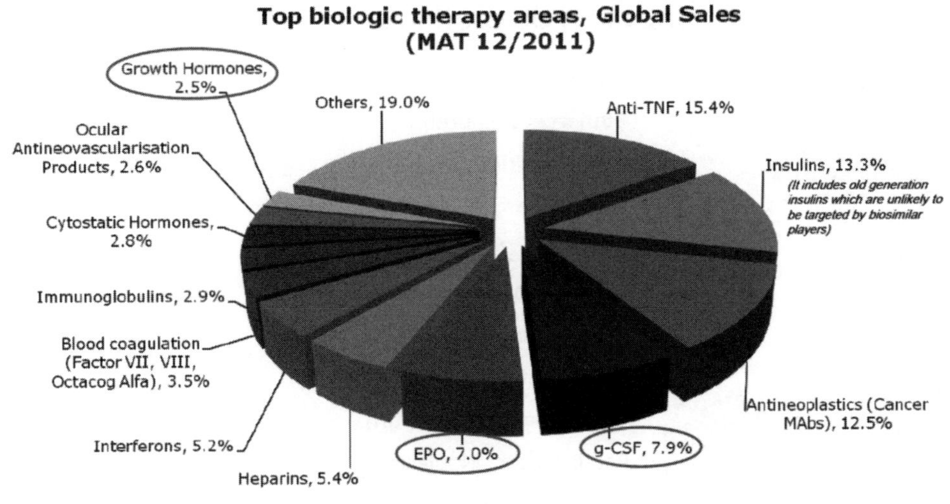

The CHMP/437/04 Rev 1 (2013) guideline recently defined a biosimilar as "a biological medicinal product that contains a version of the active substance of an already authorised original biological medicinal product (reference medicinal product). A biosimilar demonstrates similarity to the reference medicinal product in terms of quality characteristics, biological activity, safety and efficacy based on a comprehensive comparability exercise."

Current Status of Biosimilars

Biosimilars are a new paradigm in drug development, as were generic medicines in the 1980s. Not only do they fulfill an unmet need and reduce costs (for the biosimilar and originator product), but they also provide new insights about original biologics themselves as a result of new and sometimes unique comparability campaigns of studies.

To date, 13 biosimilar products out of 24 Marketing Authorisation Applications (MAAs) submitted have been approved in the EU under the highest burden of international regulatory standards. One of these approvals, Valtropin (somatropin), was withdrawn in 2012 for commercial reasons, and eight applications were withdrawn (see **Table 24-2**).[2] Currently, three new biosimilar candidates are under MAA review by the European Medicines Agency's (EMA) Committee for Medicinal Products for Human Use (CHMP): follitropin alfa (sex hormone) and two applications for the monoclonal antibody (mAb) infliximab (immunosuppressant).[3] The application for human insulin (three products that are used in the treatment of diabetes) was withdrawn in December 2012 (see **Table 24-3**),[4] but will be resubmitted after further clinical work.

The pivotal studies of Celltrion's infliximab are public knowledge and are described later. Celltrion has announced its plans to conduct clinical studies for the treatment of ankylosing spondylitis in 250 patients (monotherapy, pharmacokinetic (PK) part) and rheumatoid arthritis (RA) in 606 patients (in combination treatment with methotrexate and folic acid; safety studies include immunogenicity and efficacy).[5]

Other biosimilar candidates are in Phase 1 or Phase 3 development, including the recombinant mAbs trastuzumab, bevacizumab, adalimumab, rituximab, human insulins and insulin analogues, heparins, interferons alpha and beta, follicle-stimulating hormone and others (see **Figure 24-1**).

The World Health Organization (WHO) 2009 guidance,[6] which has been adopted worldwide, is based on practical experience in the EU and the extensive set of CHMP/EMA guidelines as well as regional legal requirements (specifics are described later).

Although not public, several therapeutic proteins and other biologicals are biosimilar candidates, including specific enzymes approved in the US under the *PHS Act's* Biologics License Application (BLA) process as orphan drugs for genetic enzymic diseases.

In India, biosimilar therapeutic proteins began receiving approval in 2006, including one mAb, rituximab, under regulatory prerequisites of approval prior to the current Indian 2012 guideline. The Korean Ministry of Food and Drug Safety (formerly, the Korean Food and Drug Administration (KFDA)) approved mAb infliximab Remsima (Celltrion), a biosimilar to Remicade, in October 2012; this same product received a positive opinion from CHMP/EMA on 28 June 2013 following an oral CHMP hearing, and is pending Marketing Authorisation by the EU Commission in August 2013.

Figure 24-2. Some targeted Biosimilars Under Development in the EU and US in 2011–13 and Onward

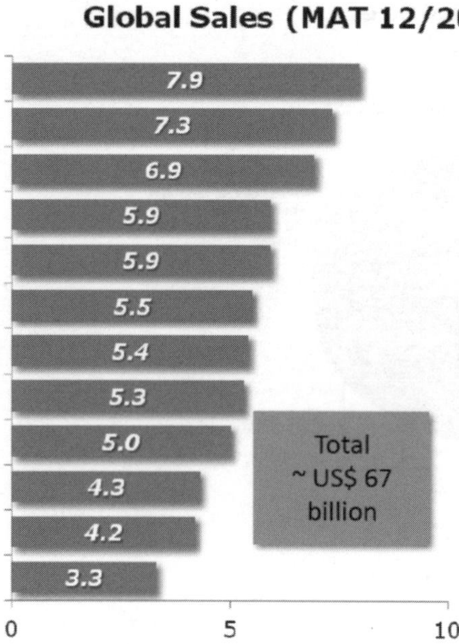

Global Sales (MAT 12/2011), US$, Billion

Global Sales (US$, Billion)	Product	EU expiry date	US expiry date
7.9	Adalimumab (Humira)	2018	2016
7.3	Etanercept (Enbrel)	2015	*2028 (extended)*
6.9	Infliximab (Remicade)	2014	2018
5.9	Insulin Glargine (Lantus)	2014	2014
5.9	Rituximab (MabThera)	2013	2016
5.5	Bevacizumb (Avastin)	2010	2017
5.4	Enoxaparin Sodium (Lovenox)	2012	Expired
5.3	Interf. Beta-1A (Rebif, Avonex)	2015	2015
5.0	Trastuzumab (Herceptin)	2014	2019
4.3	Pegfilgrastim (Neulasta)	2017	2015
4.2	Glatiramer Acetate (Copaxone)	2015	2014
3.3	Darbopoetin Alfa (Aranesp)	2016	2016

Total ~ US$ 67 billion

0 5 10

Not considered existing biosimilars such as Epoetin Alfa expired in EU, but still patent protected in US

Source: IMS MIDAS, 12/2011, IMS Patent focus

Remsima was approved in South Korea for the treatment of RA, ankylosing spondolytis, ulcerative colitis, Crohn's disease and psoriasis, based on data submitted in accordance with advanced regulatory standards requirements.[7]

Other products besides rituximab have been approved by the Indian Central Drugs Standard Control Organization (CDSCO) as stated in the guideline:

> "So far, these similar biologics were approved by RCGM and CDSCO using an abbreviated version of the pathway applicable to new drugs on a case by case basis."

It has not been possible for the author to obtain a list, but it is known that besides rituximab it includes rh-insulins and filgastrim.[8]

Incentives for Biosimilars

The regulatory burden of biosimilar approvals is substantial, both logistically and economically, but the reward is a portion of more than $100 billion (US) in sales, with more than $25 billion each in the areas of oncology and immunology and in the treatment of inflammation, and more than $15 billion in the treatment of diabetes.

Eleven products, mainly the mAbs and infusion therapeutic proteins, represent over $62 billion, as shown in **Figure 24-2** (Glatimer acetate is in fact erroneously included although it is not produced by a biologic process and also represents a synthetic peptide less than 100 aminoacid units by FDA definition.)[9]

The introduction of biosimilars across the healthcare industry in the US is expected to result in cost savings of $9–$12 billion by Medicare alone over the next 10 years.[10]

Monoclonal antibodies provide improved treatment options for patients with inflammatory bowel diseases, especially in Canada, which is one of the largest users of monoclonal antibodies in gastroenterology on a per capita basis.[11]

In Germany, biosimilar erythropoetin, granulocyte-colony stimulating factor (G-CSF) and somatropin have been adopted, taking a major percentage of the originators' markets. The IGES Institute, a large private and independent R&D institute for health and healthcare, based in Berlin, predicts that biosimilars will save €10 billion in sales by 2020.[12]

In the UK, the affordability of biosimilar G-CSF has meant that the National Institute for Health and Care Excellence (NICE) provides reimbursement, which in turn influences oncology treatment practice.[13]

Stakeholders

Stakeholders involved in the development of biosimilars include not only patients but the pharmaceutical industry, regulators and physicians (see **Figure 24-3**). In addition to the heavy regulatory burden, peer acceptance of biosimilars by medical key opinion leaders (KOLs) is a barrier to development. This resistance is evidenced by the slow penetration of biosimilars onto EU national markets, unfavorable survey results in the EU and US, critical articles and lectures by opinion leaders and a

Figure 24-3. Influence of Stakeholders as Drivers of Biosimilars

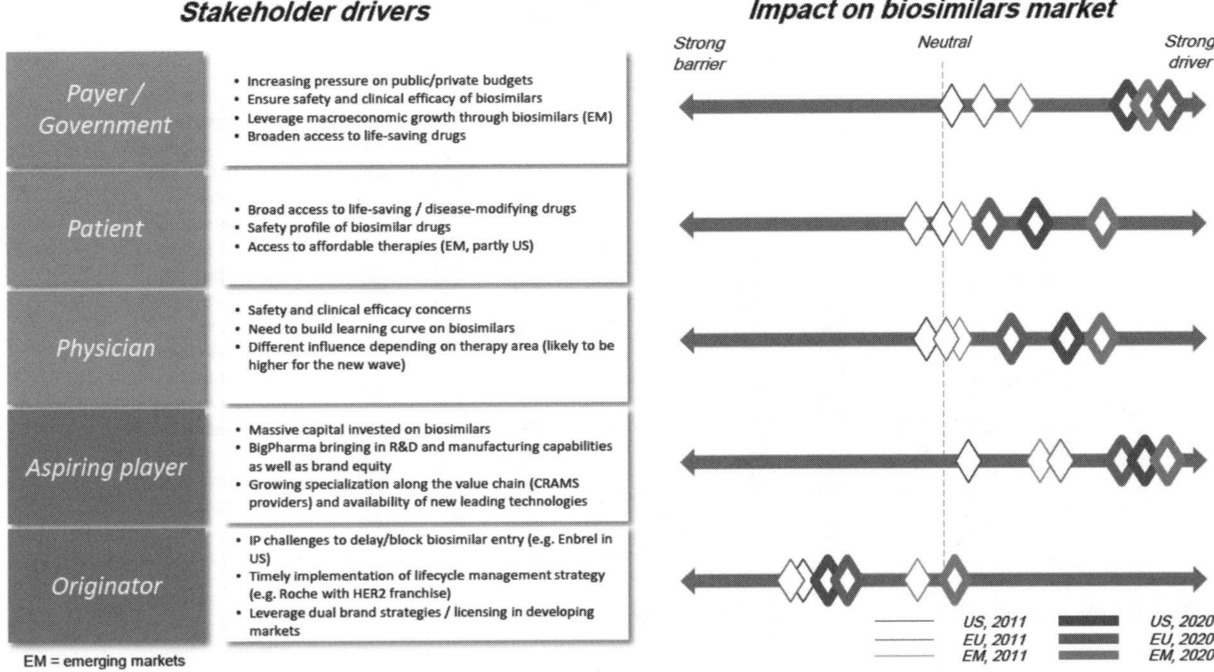

EM = emerging markets

lack of interest in promoting a deeper understanding of biosimilars by some medical journals and associations. However, this is gradually changing (**Figure 24-3**).

Acceptability of Biosimilars by Stakeholders

The fact that biosimilars are biological substances mostly endogenous to the human body, or analogs of the same, is perceived positively by the patient (i.e., they are considered "natural").[14] And yet, the regulator and the prescriber remain particularly cautious.

The regulator has concerns about unexpected risk (e.g., adverse drug reactions (ADRs) that may be immunogenically connected), while the prescriber aims for the best therapeutic outcome from an expensive treatment (as physicians tend to place more importance on effecting a cure than on ADRs, if the ADR can be managed). Patients rate side effects (the lay term for ADRs) as their main concern before electing to take any medicine.

Whereas an mAb may be unaffordable as an adjuvant in oncology in a healthcare system, a biosimilar might be accessible. Even the use of a G-CSF, filgrastim, as an adjuvant in oncology to reduce neutropenia, has increased greatly in some EU countries, such as the UK, due to cost savings and new reimbursement procedures (by NICE UK), offering a major advantage in treatment management and morbidity of patients.

Surveys have shown that the use of an mAb biosimilar might be perceived as less risky in palliative treatment, or in an adjuvant setting, compared to an acute life-saving scenario, or in a metastatic setting when compared to the cost of an originator product. It is hoped that this attitude regarding the perceived risks of biosimilars will be received more positively as these compounds are better understood.

In some poorer EU countries, biosimilars fulfill an unmet medical need. In developing countries worldwide, such as India or China, a biologic medicine might be affordable only after the introduction of the biosimilar; under these circumstances, the biosimilar would constitute a first entry into the market.

The EU Experience

The European Commission (EC), EMA and CHMP have established a legal and regulatory framework of directives, regulations and guidelines from 2003–present for the pharmaceutical industry that have permitted 13 biosimilar approvals in the EU (although these involved only seven original sponsors (all German with the exception of one Austrian), as some products are identical biosimilars with different invented (trade) names and duplicate or triplicate applications.) The first mAb, infliximab (Celltrion), is expected to be the 14th biosimilar to be approved.

Unlike unbranded generics, biosimilars face the challenge of market penetration in different EU countries; in particular, fierce promotion to physicians by originator companies that monopolize the market and further protect their interests with new generations of analogous molecules.

Figure 24-4. Middle Eastern Market Growth of Pharmaceuticals

Saudi, Algeria, Egypt and UAE represent ca.60% of MENA market

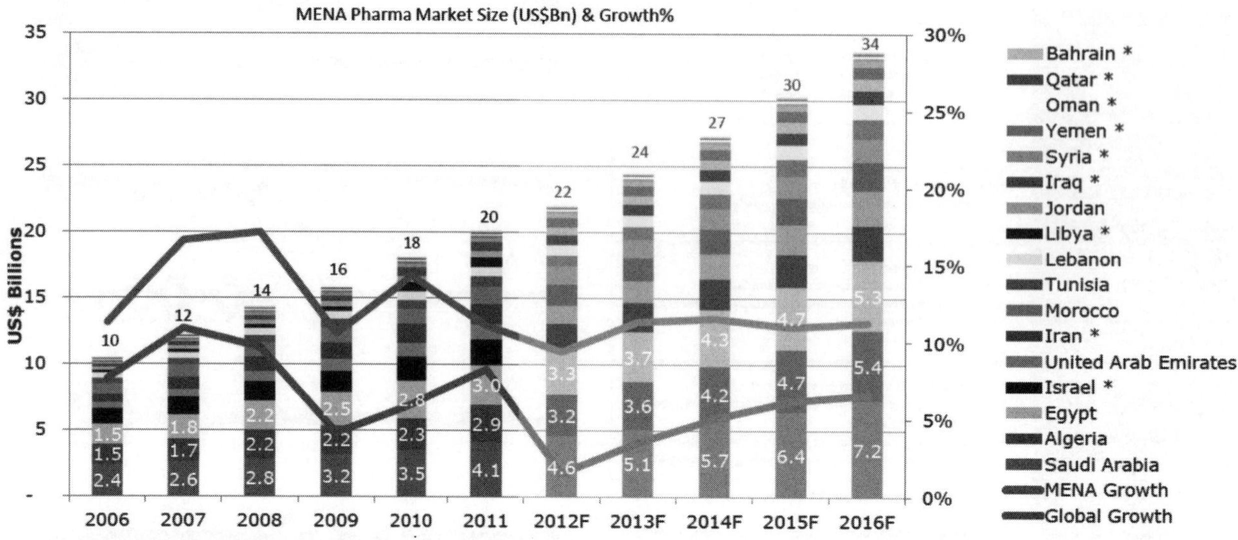

Source: IMS Global Market Prognosis, Forecasted updated Mar.2012

**Marked countries pharma market size is estimated, based on trade statistics to represent 23% of MENA total by 2016*

Pharmacy-level substitution of generic medicines is widely practiced, based on decisions made nationally or regionally by the payer and not by the EU Commission. For biosimilars, interchangeability is also decided at the national or regional level.

How biosimilars are perceived by EU physicians depends on the region where they practice (eastern or western Europe) and the type of disease they are treating.

The fourth EU stakeholder is the payer or Health Technology Assessment (HTA) body, which adds a layer of complexity because of the many national, regional or hospital controls and approvals needed to permit the listing of biosimilars and determine their pricing at the retail and hospital level across the EU. The approval process at the HTA level can take several months to more than a year. These same principles apply to biosimilars in the US and other regions.

FDA and US Expectations Compared with EU Experience

It remains to be seen how readily major regions other than the EU, such as the US, accept biosimilars. FDA has indicated that, for some drugs, it is possible to curtail the long European biosimilar development pathways, as exemplified by enoxaparin sodium,[15] a low molecular weight heparin (LMWH) classified as a biosimilar in the EU.[16] FDA approved enoxaparin sodium, a highly complex but well-characterized polysaccharide, through an Abbreviated New Drug Application (ANDA) pathway, deemed it an acceptable substitute for Lovenox and required a minimum of pharmacokinetic (PK) data.[17] In contrast, the EU published an LMWH guideline in 2009 that lists requirements for an extensive package of PK, pharmacodynamics (PD), clinical efficacy and immunogenicity studies, which are slightly relaxed as a result of the FDA decision, according to an EMA 2011 concept paper; FDA set a precedent that hugely surprised EMA and the Biosimilar Medicines Working Party (BMWP) and triggered this rapid response.[18]

FDA fingerprinted enoxaparin sodium by its five quality and pharmacology criteria, each of which captures different aspects of the substance's "sameness."

Immunogenicity also was resolved by FDA based on the decision on sameness, largely using quality comparability data. Even though enoxaparin was not a protein, its approval was used as an example of FDA's new principles, by senior FDA staffers in the August 2011 *New England Journal of Medicine* article, "Developing the Nation's Biosimilars Program," which may be viewed as an FDA policy paper on biosimilars.

The concept of "fingerprinting" is still uniquely American and, interestingly, was not adopted in the draft revision of the EU CHMP/EMA quality guideline finalized in May 2013.

FDA confirmed in its 2012 "Scientific Considerations" biosimilars guidance that it will consider "the totality of the evidence" in its evaluation.[19] This has been, in fact, the practice in the EU from 2006 to 2012 during the first biosimilars assessments by CHMP/EMA.

FDA also is expected to follow a "stepwise approach" in demonstrating biosimilarity, which can include "a comparison of the proposed product and the reference product with respect to structure, function, animal toxicity, human pharmacokinetics (PK) and pharmacodynamics (PD), clinical immunogenicity, and clinical safety and effectiveness."[20] Neither efficacy nor benefit is emphasized by FDA, as both are already implicit in the continued license of the originator medicine.[21,22,23]

These aspects are in line with the CHMP/EMA guideline on biosimilar mAb development,[24] which is, in effect, a retrospective and reflective position document illustrating the EU principles of biosimilars development in general, not only for mAbs. The EU mAb guideline describes an mAb development scenario in an oncology setting, but its principles can be applied more widely to immunomodulatory mAbs and other molecules. FDA has drawn parallels to it in the 2011 *NEJM* paper (but not by direct reference in the 2012 FDA guidelines themselves).

The three FDA February 2012 draft guidances are general and not product specific: *Draft Guidance for Industry: Scientific Considerations in Demonstrating Biosimilarity to a Reference Product; Draft Guidance for Industry: Quality Considerations in Demonstrating Biosimilarity to a Reference Protein Product*; and *Draft Guidance for Industry: Biosimilars: Questions and Answers Regarding Implementation of the Biologics Price Competition and Innovation Act of 2009* (regulatory aspects).

Detailed FDA data requirements will be ascertained through designated pre-Investigational New Drug application (IND) meetings.

Upon consultation with a therapeutic division, various FDA offices would be involved at the stages of advice, review and approval, and the associate director for biosimilars in the Office of New Drugs, Therapeutic Biologics would assist with the coordination and consistency of FDA guidance across the therapeutic divisions.

A biosimilars user fee program is in place to cover product development meetings, IND applications and scientific, regulatory, policy infrastructure and standards.[25]

FDA offers a biosimilar applicant at least five separate meetings within a one-year period. The agency does not charge for advice, and the user fee applies to biosimilars destined for a 351k, abbreviated BLA.

The director of the FDA Office of Pharmaceutical Science's Office of Biotechnology Products has indicated that since 8 February 2013, FDA had received 50 pre-IND meeting requests for biosimilars involving 11 RPs; 37 meetings have been held and 13 INDs have been received.[26]

Interchangeability of Biosimilars in the EU and US

There are different understandings of what interchangeability means.

From an EU perspective, EMA does not support automatic substitution of biosimilars (e.g., at the pharmacy level): "Since biosimilar and biological reference medicines are similar but not identical, the decision to treat a patient with a reference or a biosimilar medicine should be taken following the opinion of a qualified healthcare professional."[27]

From a US perspective, interchangeability means, in practical terms, automatic substitution similar to the AB rating of a generic version of the drug listed in the *Orange Book* and approved under the *FD&C Act*, allowing a substitution at the pharmacy level. It will afford the first successful applicant one year of marketing exclusivity.

The *BPCI Act* defines "interchangeable" or "interchangeability" as "a term that means that the biological product may be substituted for the reference product without the intervention of the healthcare provider who prescribed the reference product."

Some future FDA-approved "biosimilars" are foreseen by the FDA guidance as being interchangeable with the FDA-licensed biological RP, but surprisingly, the conditions are not laid down for industry in the current guidances. FDA's position is expressed in the Q&A guidance:

> "Additional considerations apply for a proposed interchangeable product. For example, in reviewing an application for a proposed interchangeable product, FDA may consider whether the differences from the reference product significantly alter critical design attributes, product performance, or operating principles, or would require additional instruction to healthcare providers or patients, for patients to be safely alternated or switched between the reference product and one or more interchangeable products without the intervention of the prescribing healthcare provider."
>
> "... and meet the other standards (concerning multiple switching between biosimilar and reference product-author) described in section 351(k)(4) of the PHS Act." And, "FDA is continuing to consider the type of information sufficient to enable FDA to determine that a biological product is interchangeable with the reference product." [28]

That is, the current FDA guidances cover general requirements for both non-interchangeable and interchangeable tiers of biosimilars, but, unfortunately, they lack any specifics of what would be needed to obtain industry's real objective of approval for the authorized interchangeable biosimilar.

The US package insert (PI) will state: "Labeling of a proposed product should include all the information necessary for a health professional to make prescribing decisions, including a clear statement advising that: This product is approved as biosimilar to a reference product for stated indication(s) and route of administration(s). This product (has or has not) been determined to be interchangeable with the reference product."[29]

Interchangeability by Other Stakeholders

The European Generics Association (EGA), which has several members with biosimilars medicine experience, takes the following position: "[Interchangeability] refers to the medicinal/pharmaceutical practice of switching one medicine for another that is equivalent, in a given clinical setting. A product is considered to be interchangeable if it can be administered or dispensed instead of another clinically approved product." Whereas, "substitution refers to the practice of dispensing ...at pharmacy level and without consultation of the prescriber."[30]

WHO defines interchangeability as "the medical practice of switching one medicine for another that is equivalent, in a given clinical setting."

Furthermore, WHO states that "The decision to allow automatic substitution of a Similar Biotherapeutic Product (SBP) for a Reference Biotherapeutic Product (RBP) should be made on a national level, taking into account potential safety issues with the product or class of products. Decisions on interchangeability should be based on appropriate scientific and clinical data and are beyond the scope of this document."[31]

What would be acceptable to the prescriber, the patient or the healthcare provider?

Interchangeability and Further Scientific and Regulatory Facts

FDA's viewpoint is that "slight differences in rates of occurrence of adverse events between the two products ordinarily would not be considered clinically meaningful differences." Further, the agency states that "lower immunogenic or other adverse events would not have implications for the effectiveness of a protein product."[32]

In a postmarketing scenario, FDA envisions spontaneous reports of "the identification of adverse events associated with the proposed product that have not been previously associated with the reference product."[33]

As the biosimilar usually has the same composition, with identical excipients as the originator, and in practically all cases the presentations are solution forms, the introduction of risk with the drug product is minimal. With the EU's approval of Valtropin in 2006,[34] CHMP/EMA also made a milestone decision to approve a yeast-based somatropin cell expression system, compared to an *E. coli*-based reference medicinal product (RMP) of Humatrope. Valtropin was produced in *Saccharomyces cerevisiae* (yeast) cells. The previously marketed somatropins were expressed in either *E. coli* (e.g., Humatrope, Genotropin, Nutropin) or in mammalian cells (Saizen), making the Valtropin yeast-cell process unique among growth hormones. Omnitrope's somatropin drug substance (also approved in April 2006) was produced in an *E. coli* (bacterial) host.[35]

This precedent of a new fermentation expression system was endorsed by CHMP/EMA six years later in the mAbs guideline.[36] FDA provides similar flexibility.[37]

Also, most interestingly, FDA shows considerable flexibility when it explicitly defines allowable differences in formulation or presentation when the dosage form (pharmaceutical form) of the biosimilar is the same as that of the RMP, according to its Q&A (regulatory) guidance.[38] For instance, albumin may be omitted as an excipient,[39] or the agency would allow a prefilled syringe or an autoinjector biosimilar instead of a solution for injection RMP, or a solution for injection for a powder instead of a solution for injection RMP.[40]

This new scope defined by FDA in pharmaceutical form and presentation of a biosimilar was adopted by EMA in 2013.[41]

Clinical Efficacy

A decrease in potency or lack of efficacy in a medicine on the market is a pharmacovigilance issue; to date, there is no evidence of this, based on six years of EU experience with marketed biosimilars.

The most sensitive, homogeneous patient population and clinical endpoint are chosen in the preapproval studies to detect any product-related differences. This minimizes any confounding patient- and disease-related factors to increase precision of analysis and maximize response. It also reduces the variability and sample size needed to prove equivalence and can simplify interpretation.

FDA places a high degree of importance on clinical pharmacology studies as evidence of comparative efficacy and does not consider it necessary to prove benefit; this is exactly the same opinion as EMA.

FDA also emphasizes the immunogenicity safety study, as does EMA, which is conducted for a minimum of 12 months. FDA requires an efficacy study only when necessary and describes some basic statistical criteria including the alternatives of equivalence and noninferiority designs.

An FDA hearing on 11 May 2012 was chaired by the director of the Office of Medical Policy at the agency's Center for Drug Research and Evaluation (CDER).[42]

Stakeholders raised the issues of the need for educational materials on biological and biosimilars for both patients and healthcare practitioners, more clarity on interchangeability and the need for traceability and manufacturer accountability, among others. Concern was expressed that US Congressional constraints on interchangeability being a "higher standard" than biosimilarity would create a public misconception that interchangeable products were "higher quality" than biosimilar products, reducing patient acceptance. Companies expressed their desire for

FDA to harmonize its requirements with EMA's biosimilars guidelines.

Equivalence versus Noninferiority as a Primary Design of Efficacy

Noninferiority as a primary design of efficacy has not been allowed in the EU as the basis for any biosimilar approval to date; EMA requires an equivalence study instead. Noninferiority is, however, acceptable for safety studies such as immunogenicity studies.

However, FDA will consider the alternatives. WHO explicitly allows noninferiority and compares its statistics with an equivalence approach (described in more detail later).

FDA recommends that sponsors consider the use of population pharmacokinetics (PPK) to explain observed differences in safety and effectiveness that may occur due to variability in PK.[43] According to the guidance, "PPK methods are an efficient way to quantitate the influence of covariates (e.g., age or renal function) on PK and, in some cases, PD."

Pediatric assessment under the US *Pediatric Research Equity Act* (*PREA*) will be triggered for non-interchangeable biosimilars at the time of an IND filing, although it may not be known to which of the two tiers of biosimilars the product will belong at that point in time.

> "Section 505B(n) of the FD&C Act, added by section 7002(d)(2) of the Affordable Care Act, provides that a biosimilar product that has not been determined to be interchangeable with the reference product is considered to have a 'new active ingredient' for purposes of PREA, and a pediatric assessment is required unless waived or deferred."

An interchangeable biosimilar product is not considered by FDA to have a "new active ingredient" for the purposes of *PREA*; therefore, a pediatric assessment of the product is required for the remaining biosimilars, which will make up the majority.[44]

General EU and US Pharmacovigilance Requirements

An EU risk management plan (RMP_{PV}), including a risk minimization and pharmacovigilance plan, is an essential part of a biologic MAA approval and is important throughout the lifecycles of both the biosimilar and the RP to predict, mitigate and contain risk.[45] Risk can be affected by exposure, route of administration, indication and severity.

The RMP_{PV} includes safety specifications consisting of a summary of important identified risks, including safety pharmacology and toxicology for potential risks and missing information obtained from clinical studies; immunogenicity testing and evidence of its symptomology; spontaneous adverse event reporting; and the scientific literature. In the EU, the new *PV Implementing Regulation* (Regulation (EU) No 520/2012 of 19 June 2012) has been introduced with a new influential regulatory body, the Pharmacovigilance Risk Assessment Committee (PRAC). This regulation requires implementing Good Pharmacovigilance Practices in 16 modules, and will involve much closer surveillance of new approvals.[46] This means EMA now requires that all biosimilar product information, i.e., the Summary of Product Characteristics (SmPC), Patient Information Leaflet (PIL) and package label, carry a black inverted triangle symbol. Medication errors and off-label use will be just two aspects of additional monitoring as safety signals.

It can be assumed an FDA Risk Evaluation and Mitigation Strategy (REMS)[47] would be relevant only to a biosimilar where the originator product already had a REMS.

A US biosimilar that does not qualify for interchangeability will be viewed as a "new active ingredient." As such, it would also be subject to FDA's pediatric requirements.

In fact, this would be triggered at the time of filing an IND application and would require preparation of a pediatric plan. In the EU, a biosimilar is exempt from a Pediatric Investigational Plan (PIP).

However, once approved, a biosimilar must follow changes in the approved RP summarized in the product information (the EU SmPC and the US PI). In the EU, it also can follow a separate lifecycle development pathway in principle, although this is not mentioned in the current regulations and was only introduced in the updated quality overarching draft guideline in 2012.[48] This could mean new pharmaceutical forms, new indications or new target populations. This postapproval principle is present in the Canadian biosimilars guideline,[49,50] but not in the US or EU guidelines prior to 2012.

Immunogenicity

The methodology used for immunogenicity testing is critical, and this is emphasized in particular by FDA, which provides background literature[51] and a dedicated guidance.[52] The EU has a general guideline covering quality, nonclinical and clinical aspects of immunogenicity[53] and a class-specific guidance for immunogenicity of mAbs.[54]

FDA, in its February 2012 guidance on scientific considerations, emphasizes the 2009 guidance on analytical validation methodology, which needs to be robust. The clinical requirements depend on "the severity of consequences and the incidence of immune responses" but it is "only important to demonstrate that the immunogenicity of the proposed product is not increased."

Clinical Safety Issues

Selection of Subjects

Like efficacy, patient homogeneity and sensitivity are important in immunogenicity.

The inclusion of patients from non-EU countries is generally acceptable for EU biosimilars, as long as there are no ethnicity or other concerns in connection with intrinsic (genetics, metabolism, etc.) and extrinsic (diet, habitat, etc.) factors. FDA allows non-US studies, but cites its guidances on foreign studies and ethnicity.[55] However, it is likely studies conducted in the EU or elsewhere in support of an EU biosimilar will be accepted. In the EU, knowledge of the RMP's efficacy and safety in a particular region may be necessary to prospectively define an equivalence margin. Stratification and appropriate subgroup analyses normally are expected in the EU if patients from different regions of the globe are included. Diagnostic and treatment strategies should be comparable to prevent the influence of extrinsic factors.

The EU has a postauthorization requirement for obtaining further indication-specific safety data for the RMP to capture data on safety across different licensed indications.

Reference Medicinal Product

The RP safety profile is defined by the comparator's SmPC (EU) or PI (US), the RP selected when more than one originator is marketed, which is the case with the r-somatropins or rhu-insulins, r-insulin analogues or LMWHs or r-interferons-alpha or r-interferons-beta, whereas for mAbs there is only one originator and one candidate.

Furthermore, the comprehensive battery of structural and analytical pharmaceutical comparability chemical, biophysical, biochemical and bioassay/bioidentity tests of the biosimilar versus the RP not only defines the identity, integrity and potency connected with the product's efficacy but also its impurity profile, stability, microbiology (sterility, endotoxins, preservative) and other safety aspects.

Selection of RP

FDA's decision to accept an RP from another major regulated region[56] to "scientifically justify the relevance of these data to an assessment of biosimilarity"[57] is far-reaching. A product approved in the EU generally would qualify as an FDA-acceptable RP as it complies with ICH regulatory standards.

FDA states in its Q&A guidance that one precondition is "as a scientific matter, analytical studies and at least one clinical pharmacokinetic (PK) study and, if appropriate, at least one pharmacodynamic (PD) study, intended to support a demonstration of biosimilarity must include an adequate comparison of the proposed biosimilar product directly with the US-licensed reference product."

FDA would need bridging scientific data (EU versus US RP) as proof of comparability, as well as all relevant information on manufacturing sites and license holders.

Accepting a foreign RP has only been possible in the EU since 2013, whereas from 2006-2012, the RP had to be purchased in the EU, according to the *acquis communautaire* legality, to render the studies pivotal. Otherwise, all the effort had been wasted, and the studies would be only supportive scientifically.

Canada also has had a provision since 2009 that allows a non-Canadian RP; this was implemented with the first biosimilar approval in 2011, which was Omnitrope.

In cases where the biosimilar has already been approved in the EU, bridging studies can be agreed on with FDA. Parallel FDA-EMA Scientific Advice can determine the priorities of studies and RPs for a new program, and the first such procedure for a biosimilar has been welcomed by both FDA and EMA (discussed at the February and April 2013 international conferences); and the first example (an mAb) is being submitted in the summer of 2013.

New 2013 EU Acceptance of the non-EEA Reference Medicinal Product and Global Development

EMA's major milestone decision to accept a non-EEA RP is stated in CHMP/437/04 Rev 1 (22 May 2013):

> "However, with the aim of facilitating the global development of biosimilars and to avoid unnecessary repetition of clinical trials, it may be possible for an Applicant to compare the biosimilar in certain clinical studies and in vivo non-clinical studies (where needed) with a non-EEA authorised comparator (i.e. a non-EEA authorised version of the reference medicinal product) which will need to be authorized by a regulatory authority with similar scientific and regulatory standards as EMA (i.e. ICH countries).
>
> If certain studies of the development programme are performed with only the non-EEA authorized comparator, the Applicant should provide adequate data or information to scientifically justify the relevance of these comparative data and establish an acceptable bridge to the EEA-authorised reference product. It will be the Applicant's responsibility to establish that the comparator authorised outside the EEA is representative of the reference product authorised in the EEA."

Pharmacovigilance Importance of Name to Ensure Informed Use and Tracing

One of the evolving issues within the US biosimilar regulatory landscape concerns whether 351(k) biosimilar products will have the same nonproprietary names as their 351(a) counterparts.

FDA believes that identical nonproprietary names may result in medication errors and confusion among

Table 24-4. Comparison of Clinical Models of Equivalence and Non-inferiority

Design	Advantages	Disadvantages
Equivalence	Demonstration of equivalence provides a strong rationale for the possibility of extrapolation of efficacy to other indications of the RBP Current experience for the licensing of SBPs is based on equivalence trials	An equivalence trial tends to need a larger sample size to achieve the same study power as a noninferiority trial A finding of superiority would lead to the failure of the equivalence trial. There would be no option to show that the superiority observed is not clinically relevant.
Noninferiority	A noninferiority trial requires a smaller sample size to achieve the same study power as an equivalence trial. A finding of superiority of the SBP compared to the RBP would not lead to failure of a noninferiority trial, provided it can be demonstrated that the superiority observed is not clinically relevant.	Post-hoc justification that a finding of statistically superior efficacy is not clinically relevant is difficult. Demonstration of noninferiority does not provide a strong rationale for the possibility of extrapolation to other indications of the RBP.

healthcare practitioners who may consider use of the same nonproprietary name to mean the biological products are indistinguishable. FDA further determined that identical nonproprietary names might result in "limitations in the ability to conduct appropriate pharmacovigilance."

WHO Leadership on Biosimilars

The WHO guideline applies to well-established and well-characterized biotherapeutic products such as recombinant DNA-derived therapeutic proteins.[58] Vaccines, plasma-derived products and their recombinant analogs are excluded from the scope of this document. Many agencies were involved in writing the 2009 guideline, including the deputy head of the European Biosimilars Working Party.

WHO's guideline largely followed the EU experience, although this has now expanded to incorporate knowledge gained from an additional four years of MAA assessment and approval experience and information from FDA's overarching guidances of February 2012.

Superseded by EU and US, for instance, is that WHO requires the dosage form and route of administration of the similar biotherapeutic product (SBP) to be the same as that of the reference biotherapeutic product (RBP).

However, WHO is taking an active role in monitoring the implementation of the guidelines, as well as collecting and sharing information and tools. A Q&A document is being developed for the WHO biological website. WHO recognizes that more work is needed to achieve global harmonization on the approval and regulation of SBPs, including the need for national regulatory authorities to build capacity in product testing and clinical trial review.

The WHO Reference Biotherapeutic Product

The RBP should have been marketed for a suitable duration and have a volume of marketed use such that a substantial body of acceptable data regarding its safety and efficacy has been generated.

Noninferiority Allowable by WHO but Equivalence Preferred by WHO

For an equivalence trial, both the lower and upper equivalence margins are required, while only one margin is required for a noninferiority trial (**Table 24-4**).

Although noninferiority designs may be justified according to WHO, in principle, equivalence designs, requiring lower and upper comparability margins, are clearly preferred for the comparison of the SBP's efficacy and safety with that of the RBP.

Equivalence trials ensure that the SBP is not clinically less or more effective than the RBP when used at the same dosage(s). However, for medicinal products with a wide safety margin, noninferiority trials also may be acceptable. A noninferior efficacy does not exclude the possibility of statistically and clinically superior efficacy of the SBP compared to the RBP that, if clinically relevant, would contradict the principle of similarity.

Superior efficacy could be associated with increased adverse events if the SBP is prescribed at the same dosage as the RBP. In an equivalence trial, clinically meaningful differences, including superior efficacy, between the SBP and the RBP, are excluded if the 95% confidence interval of the treatment difference is fully contained within the pre-specified two-sided (upper and lower) comparability margins.

The magnitude and variability of the effect size of the RBP derived from historic trials also should be taken into consideration in determining the comparability margin, both in terms of the endpoint chosen and the population to be studied. If a difference between the RBP and SBP exists, then the study is capable of showing that difference (this is referred to as "assay sensitivity").

Statistical analysis for both equivalence and noninferiority designs generally is based on the use of two-sided confidence intervals (typically at the 95% level) for the difference between treatments. Equivalence is demonstrated when the entire confidence interval falls within the lower and upper equivalence margins. Noninferiority evaluations are one-sided, and statistical inference is based only on the lower or upper confidence limit, whichever is appropriate for a given study. Analysis of noninferiority trials also can be based on a one-sided confidence interval at the 97.5% level.

Sample size calculations are slightly different between equivalence and noninferiority trials, and the two-sided equivalence trial tends to need a larger sample size than a one-sided noninferiority trial.

Naming the Biosimilar by WHO

The SBP should be clearly identifiable by a unique brand name. Where an INN is defined, this also should be stated. WHO policy on INNs should be followed (www.who.int/medicines/services/inn/innquidance/en/index.html).

Prescribing information of SmPC or PI

The prescribing information for the WHO SBP should be as similar as possible to that of the RBP except for product-specific aspects, such as different excipient(s).

However, if the SBP has fewer indications than the RBP when extrapolations are not allowed, the related text in various sections may be omitted "unless it is considered important to inform doctors and patients about certain risks; e.g. because of potential off-label use," according to WHO.

In some EU countries, such as Denmark, for even a classic generic not being granted all the indications (due to patents or exclusivities), there is an official statement that the drug may be prescribed by the physician for other uses.

International Experience

Most Latin American and Caribbean countries have regulations in place for biological products, but they often lack a clearly defined approval process.

Brazil, meanwhile, has a dual pathway for approval of biosimilar products, permitting product approval with abbreviated nonclinical and clinical data.

Korea and Singapore national regulatory authorities follow the principles for evaluation of biosimilars set out by EMA.

Guidelines in Cuba, Canada and Japan are similar to those of EMA and WHO. Malaysia and Thailand are committed to developing guidelines based on the WHO guidance, and India has based its 2012 final guidance on EMA and WHO guidance, while China is particularly lagging behind others in the development of appropriate regulations and guidelines, despite a fast-growing industry for producing 'copy biological' products, which are called "biosimilars."

Japan

The Japanese MHLW guideline is a 22-page document that only cites ICH guidelines.[59] The MHLW foresees possible substitution of the 'follow-on biologic:'

> "It is very important to assure the traceability of any adverse events arising during the respective surveillance period, and it is strongly recommended that if the originator biologics could be changed to the follow-on biologics with same indications, to practice of automatically substituting the originator biologics for the follow-on biologics should in principle be avoided throughout a certain period of treatment." (Guideline p19/22)

It was suggested in 2012 that it may be possible after "enough experiences accumulate after the approval."

The initial approval of Omnitrope in Japan (Sandoz, 2009) was for three out of six indications of growth hormone deficiency in children, Turner syndrome (in girls) and CRI deficiency; the second main indication of growth hormone deficiency in adults was given two years postapproval. A Japanese bridging study was required: a three-arm cross-over trial to compare Omnitrope solution (5mg/1.5mL), Omnitrope solution (10mg/1.5mL) vs Genotropin powder, in 54 Healthy volunteers (Japanese, Male).[60]

The next approval was that of Epoetin (Alfa BS"JCR" 2010) for renal anaemia (but not for the cancer indication). This required as the basis of approval four comparative Japanese studies: one double-blind trial to compare the safety and efficacy in 329 Hemodialysis (HD) patients, a two-arm cross-over trial to compare the safety and PK of a single IV dose in 24 HD patients and a two-arm cross-over trial to compare the safety and PK of a single subcutaneous (SC) dose in 32 healthy volunteers. These were of a smaller dimension relative to EU approved biosimilars Abseamed (Epoetin Alfa 403 vs 329 Alfa BS"JCR" patients, Phase 3), and Retacrit (Epoetin Zeta 541 + 239 vs 329 Alfa BS"JCR" patients, Phase 3).

PMDA has significant postmarketing surveillance requirements, for example:[61]

Somatropin BS s.c. "Sandoz"

All patient data (≧300) should be collected for two years as PMS.

- Clinical data about Turner syndrome (≧18) and Chronic renal insufficiency (≧3) also should be collected during PMS.
- The sponsor should analyze adverse effects possibly due to expression of antibodies against somatropin/HCP.

Epoetin Alfa BS Inj 750 "JCR"

Patient data (≧500) should be collected for five years as PMS.

- Clinical data about PD patients and anemia of prematurity also should be collected during PMS.
- The sponsor should analyze the lack of efficacy possibly due to expression of antibodies.

Canada

Health Canada considers Subsequent Entry Biologics (SEBs) to not be a new class of biologics.[62,63] They are considered second versions of biologics that already exist in the Canadian market and whose patents have expired. In Canada, qualifying as an SEB is not a declaration of pharmaceutical and/or therapeutic equivalence to the reference biologic drug.

No new regulations have been developed for SEBs; instead, Health Canada has adopted CHMP/EMA criteria used since 2006. Therefore, the Canadian draft guidance "Information and Submission Requirements for Subsequent Entry Biologics (SEBs)" was effective with the submission of a New Drug Submission (NDS) for Omnitrope on 13 April 2007, which was approved 20 April 2009 (Notice of Compliance) as the first SEB.

Health Canada will not make it mandatory for reference biologic drugs to be approved and marketed in Canada. There are alternative means of obtaining credible and valid information about a reference product for an SEB submission according to Health Canada.

Health Canada accepts that it may be possible to extrapolate clinical data for trastuzumab (Herceptin) in the setting of metastatic disease to its use as adjuvant therapy. However, the use of monotherapy or different combination therapies in these settings would be important considerations.[64]

Health Canada also considers that it may not be possible to extrapolate clinical data for an mAb in one rheumatologic indication to other rheumatologic indications because of differences in dose, duration of therapy, efficacy of monotherapy versus combination therapy, unless PK/PD data are available in the patient population of interest.

Efficacy data in patients with rheumatoid arthritis might not provide adequate justification for extrapolation to Crohn's disease.

In the EU, it is only since 2012 that the lifecycle of a biosimilar postapproval can be considered to be independent of the RP.

Additionally, for preapproval in Canada, clinical studies should be provided for each indication being sought and must have high enough statistical power to detect major differences in safety. In justified cases, a comparative PK/PD data package to bridge two or more indications may be sufficient.

The decision to allow substitution in Canada is in the hands of the provinces and territories influenced by the colleges of pharmacy that make reimbursement decisions.

The ICH guidance suggests the safety exposure required prior to approval of a product will be a minimum of 100 patients for one year. At present, EU approvals have involved from 200-1,000 patients preapproval with extensive post-approval pharmacovigilance surveillance; erythropoietin (EPO) is one example.

India

According to a report, approximately 20 Indian companies are already producing biosimilars. Dr. Reddy's Laboratories, Ranbaxy, Biocon, Shantha Biotech, Reliance Life Sciences, Panacea Biotec and Intas Biopharmaceuticals are among those that lead the way. Several other well-known companies have recently entered the field, including Glenmark, Cipla and Lupin Pharma.[65] The report claims that approximately 50 "biosimilars" (some of which actually may represent mainly 'copy biologics') already have reached the Indian market, and typically are sold at discounts of as much as 85%, fulfilling an unmet need. In 2009–10, domestic Indian sales of EPO rose to $22 million, while sales of c-GCSF rose to $11 million. Sales of interferons rose to $22 million and sales of streptokinase rose to $15 million.

The Indian Central Drugs Standard Control Organisation (CDSCO) biosimilars guideline was finalized in 2012. Based on EU and WHO guidelines, it is a thorough and comprehensive document.[66] The Indian CDSCO guideline cites ICH, EMA, Korean FDA (KFDA) (now replaced by the Ministry of Food and Drug Safety, MFDS) and WHO guidances, but does not include information from the recent FDA guidelines that were made public two years after its initial draft.

Some aspects of the Indian guideline are more specific and demanding than the US or EU overarching requirements. There is less information on clinical pharmacology or immunogenicity data, but more emphasis on toxicology and postapproval clinical data. India has adopted a "stepwise" approach to biosimilar approval, similar to the US and the EU, through a "sequential" approval process. The general requirements of CDSCO, FDA and EMA are aligned.

A new requirement is for data retention. Also unique to this guideline are examples of specifications and data criteria for different classes of biosimilars, with valuable checklists, including nucleic acid, therapeutic proteins, enzymes and antibodies.[67]

Major Latin American Markets

No product appears to have been approved in the major Latin American countries as a true biosimilar, but biosimilar copies[68] are available. Similar to advanced regulatory regions, only products that were approved based on a full dossier, including quality requirements and preclinical and clinical studies, are considered RMPs. Brazil, Mexico, Argentina and Peru have established new biologics regulations and guidance that include biosimilars. They all were influenced by WHO guidelines but are specific to each country.

Brazil

In Brazil, biologic products represent 41% of the Ministry of Health's total annual expenditure in medicines. Also, 1% of monoclonal antibodies represent 32% of the government expenditure on biologic products.

Resolution RDN N. 55 of 16 December 2010 concerns the current regulatory framework for registering biological products, both innovative new biological products (NBPs) and biosimilar biological products (follow-on) (BPs). Both require an immunogenicity study report and pharmacovigilance plan.

In 2011, the Coordination of Biological Products (CPBIH) and the regulatory agency ANVISA drafted relevant technical guidelines.

Mexico

Mexico introduced a biotech regulation 18 October 2011 and draft guidelines (Draft – Mexican Official Emergency Norm-NOM-EM-001-SSA1-2012 for Biotechnology drugs) that original and biocomparable medicine manufacturers must follow, which cover both innovative and biocomparable products.

Argentina

There are two registrations of biologic medicines possible with the Argentine agency ANMAT: Regulation N- 7075/2011—14 October 2011 and Regulation N-7729/2011—14 November 2011. Registration of biologic products through the comparability and complementary guidelines of 2012–13 are in progress. The scope of the requirements is the same as in the EU. ANMAT emphasizes that biologic products must be well-characterized.

Peru

The new regulation for the registration, control and pharmacovigilance of pharmaceutical products, medical devices and sanitarian products—Supreme Decree N- 016-2011-SA, published on 31 July 2011, Title III: About Pharmaceutical Products; Chapter V: About Biologic Products, Article 107: The similarity pathway—is based on WHO guidelines. There are just two codes for biologic products, BE0000: Foreign biologic product and BN0000: National biologic product.

MENA Countries (Middle East)

The most advanced of these countries in the implementation of biosimilars guidelines is Saudi Arabia.[69] The December 2010 guideline version 1.1 includes a comprehensive, systematic discussion of every aspect of biosimilars development in general terms, and also provides product-specific guidelines. This document is based on EMA's guidelines on insulins alpha interferons (IF), and beta-interferon, EPO, GCSF, pegylated IF, GCSF. It also contains formulations, a Saudi biosimilar Dossier (non-CTD section on clinical comparability against the RP studies, section 6 pharmacovigilance) and administration information.

Jordan currently is preparing a guideline, but it does depend on EU guidelines; it includes specific information on products such as insulin and hGH. Neither Saudi or Jordan have approved a biosimilar at the time of publication.

The MENA market size has grown by $10 billion from 2007 to 2012, doubling its size, and is forecast to grow another $14 billion by 2016 (Figure 4.)[70]

Korea

The (South) Korean Ministry of Food and Drug Safety (MFDS, formerly the Korean Food and Drug Administration) published a 2010 guideline that cites WHO, ICH and EMA overarching guidelines, EMA 2007 immunogenicity guidelines and various Korean drug development guidelines. It offers no new update in 2012–13 to maintain consistency with FDA or EMA guidelines. However, it should be noted that the South Korean industry has been an international pioneer in biosimilar development, with the first EU approval of Valtropin in April 2006 based on the supply of somatropin drug substance by Pharma company LG Life Sciences. Also, in 2012, the contract manufacturing organization (CMO) Celltrion was the applicant for the first mAb submission, infliximab.[71] A foreign RP is allowed by MFDS.

The Korean government has created industry incentives for biosimilars and has been supportive of major moves toward current Good Manufacturing Practice (CGMP), Good Clinical Praces (GCP) and other international standards over the last decade. MFDS encourages high international standards, stating "Further efforts should be focused on our capacity building, expertise, collaboration with other NRAs or WHO to promote global consensus on the regulation of biosimilar products."[72,73,74]

KFDA approved the mAb infliximab Remsima (Celltrion), a biosimilar to Remicade, in October 2012, while this same product is currently in the late stages of assessment by the CHMP/EMA.

Remsima was approved in South Korea for RA, ankolying spondolytis, ulcerative colitis, Crohn's disease and psoriasis, based on data submitted in accordance with advanced regulatory standards requirements.[75]

China

The China Food and Drug Administration (CFDA, formerly the State Food and Drug Administration (SFDA)) and its Center for Drug Evaluation (CDE) is determined to reach international standards regarding biologics and biosimilars.[76] Under current regulations issued in 2007, biological products are classified into two categories—prevention or treatment—and there is no clear classification for biosimilars. At present, there are no specific guidelines for biosimilars in China; therefore, they have to go through a new drug approval process, requiring Phase 3 trials for all 'copy biologicals.' Since there is no biosimilar approval pathway, all pharmaceuticals go through essentially the same CFDA drug registration process, with biologics being further reviewed by the Provincial Institute for the Control of Pharmaceutical and Biologic Products, which typically takes six years, or even longer, including both CTA/IND and NDA approval time. This protracted and complicated drug registration process increases regulatory approval timelines, with further delays for drugs not manufactured domestically.

Domestic claimed "biosimilars," actually 'copy biologics,' have been on the market in China for 20 years, representing 40% of China's $1.5 billion recombinant biologic product sales. The first recombinant human interferon 1-alpha was launched in 1989. Due to the relatively low entry barriers, there are now more than 100 biopharma companies producing approximately 50 biologics (excluding blood-derived products, whole bacterial products and vaccines). These include rhEPO, rhIFN, rhInsulin, rhIL-2, rhGCSF, rhGM-CSF and rhGH.

There are few mAbs in the domestic market due to technical hurdles. SFDA had approved mAbs Daclizumab and Etanercerpt, developed by Shanghai-based CP Guojian. Rituximab and Efalizumab are in late-stage (Phase 3) clinical development by CP Guojian, and Trastuzumab is under parallel development by Hayao Biotech,. Alemtuzumab is under development by a third pharmaceutical company, Zhangjiang Bio.

Conclusions

At the time of publication, the adoption of biosimilars in the EU is still relatively slow due to various postapproval hurdles, including Health Technology Assessment (HTA) body requirements, physician acceptance, patient acceptance and various lobby interest groups. However, this situation must change because of escalating drug costs and many novel biologic approvals, including therapeutic proteins fulfilling unique medical needs.

FDA guidance documents also describe the requirements for a very comprehensive package of data. However, FDA proposes a "step-wise" and risk-based "targeted" approach, based on its willingness to reduce the burden of nonclinical and clinical testing. According to FDA, "the scope and magnitude of clinical studies will depend on the extent of residual uncertainty about the biosimilarity of the two products after conducting structural and functional characterization and possible animal studies. The frequency and severity of safety risks and other safety and effectiveness concerns for the reference product may also affect the design of the clinical program."[77]

It is evident that the EU's rigorous regulatory assessment by 30 advanced national regulatory authorities, led by a harmonized CHMP (the scientific and regulatory assessment body) and based on EMA's perspective and oversight, is ensuring biosimilar safety and effectiveness, with a demanding data package requirement for approval. FDA's framework overlaps EMA requirements; at a minimum, the two approaches are aligned.

FDA might affect future biosimilar development in the EU by triggering a reconsideration of EMA's guidelines, as demonstrated by the regulatory pathway for anticoagulant, low molecular weight heparins (LMWHs), each a complex mixture of oligosaccharides (e.g., each product contains enoxaparin, dalteparin and tinzaparin). FDA surprisingly approved enoxaparin sodium in 2010 under an ANDA, a generic pathway.

WHO and many regulatory agencies worldwide have followed the high standards set by EMA. EMA itself has considered the FDA draft guidances in its revision of the EU overarching guidelines for quality in 2012, defining allowable differences in pharmaceutical form and presentation and in the planned 2013 update to the nonclinical and clinical guideline, allowing a non-EEA RP.

The assurance of a biosimilar's safety is fundamental to the CHMP/EMA review. Monitoring continues in parallel with the changes of the RP under an EU Risk Management Plan. The EU postauthorization requirement to capture safety data across different indications provides further assurance of safety. FDA has comparable demands for pharmacovigilance pre- and postapproval.

FDA and EMA's close cooperation and exchange in 2010–13 continues and covers MAA/NDA/BLA reviews, clinical safety, scientific advice, joint CGMP/GCP inspections and all facets of drug development and approval.[78] It will be most interesting to see how the so-called "biosimilars cluster" 2011 consultation forum between the two regulatory agencies will progress and affect international biosimilar development.

Certainly, the standards of international biosimilars development and approval, and even biologics development, are being raised as all national and regional regulatory authorities look to EMA, FDA and WHO for leadership on these issues.

References

1. Article 10(4) of Directive 2001/83/EC, as amended 2004/27/EC
2. European public assessment reports. EMA website. http://www.ema.europa.eu/ema/index.jsp?curl=pages/medicines/landing/epar_search.jsp&mid=WC0b01ac058001d125. Accessed 18 July 2013.
3. EMA. Applications for new human medicines under evaluation by the Committee for Medicinal Products for Human Use (1 June 2012),

EMA/362726/2012. EMA website. http://www.ema.europa.eu/docs/en_GB/document_library/Report/2012/06/WC500128151.pdf. Accessed 18 July 2013.

4. EMA/747975/2012, 27 November 2012, Marvel LifeSciences Ltd withdraws its marketing authorisation applications for Solumarv, Isomarv and Combimarv (human insulin) Q&A. EMA website. http://www.ema.europa.eu/docs/en_GB/document_library/Press_release/2012/11/WC500135156.pdf. Accessed 18 July 2013.
5. Yoo D (Celltrion), Miranda P, et al, Poster: A randomized, double blind, phase 3 study demonstrates clinical equivalence of CT-P13 to infliximab when co-administered with methotrexate in patients with active rheumatoid arthritis, European League Against Rheumatism (EULAR) in Berlin, Germany, 6-9 June 2012.
6. WHO. *Guidelines on evaluation of Similar Biotherapeutic Products (SBPs)*. WHO website.. http://www.who.int/biologicals/areas/biological_therapeutics/BIOTHERAPEUTICS_FOR_WEB_22APRIL2010.pdf. Accessed 18 July 2013.
7. World's first biosimilar antibody is approved in Korea. BioSimilar News, 23 July 2012. http://www.biosimilarnews.com/worlds-first-biosimilar-antibody-is-approved-in-korea. Accessed 18 July 2013.
8. *Guideline on Similar Biologics Regulatory Requirements for Marketing Authorization in India.* Department of Biotechnology, Ministry of Science & Technology, Central Drugs Standard Control Organisation (2012). Department of Biotechnology website. http://dbtbiosafety.nic.in/Files%5CCDSCO-DBTSimilarBiologicsfinal.pdf. Accessed 18 July 2013.
9. Shepphard A. IMS, Biosimilars: a tale of masquerade and intrigue? Second MENA Biosimilars Conference, 13–14 November 2012, Amman, Jordan.
10. Hackbarth GM, Crosson FJ, Miller ME. Report to the Congress: improving incentives in the Medicare program. Washington (DC): Medicare Payment Advisory Commission; 2009.
11. Kay J, Feagan BG, Guirguis MS,. Keystone EC, Klein AV, Lubiniecki AS, Mould DR, Nyarko KA, Ridgway AAG, Trudeau ME, Wang J. Biologicals 40 (2012) 517e527 Elsevier Health Canada/BIOTECanada Summit on regulatory and clinical topics related to subsequent entry biologics (biosimilars), Ottawa, Canada, 14 May 2012.
12. Häussler B. IGES Institut, Biosimilars in Germany, EGA International Symposium, Berlin Germany London, 19 April 2012.
13. Private communications and presentations by companies marketing biosimilars at European Generic Association Annual conferences 2009–2012.
14. Ibid.
15. Op cit 6.
16. Op cit 8.
17. FDA. Generic Enoxaparin Questions and Answers. FDA website. www.fda.gov/Drugs/DrugSafety/PostmarketDrugSafetyInformationforPatientsandProviders/ucm220037.htm. Accessed 18 July 2013.
18. EMA. Concept paper on the revision of the guideline on non-clinical and clinical development of similar biological medicinal products containing low-molecular-weight heparins (July 2011). EMA/CHMP/BMWP/522386/2011. EMA website. EMA/CHMP/BMWP/522386/2011. Accessed 18 July 2013.
19. FDA. *Draft Guidance for Industry: Scientific Considerations in Demonstrating Biosimilarity to a Reference Product* (February 2012). FDA website. http://www.fda.gov/downloads/Drugs/GuidanceComplianceRegulatoryInformation/Guidances/UCM291128.pdf. Accessed 18 July 2013.
20. Op cit 12.
21. Op cit 19.
22. FDA. *Draft Guidance for Industry: Quality Considerations in Demonstrating Biosimilarity to a Reference Protein Product* (February 2012). FDA website. http://www.fda.gov/downloads/Drugs/GuidanceComplianceRegulatoryInformation/Guidances/UCM291134.pdf . Accessed 18 Julky 2013.
23. FDA. *Draft Guidance for Industry, Biosimilars: Questions and Answers Regarding Implementation of the Biologics Price Competition and Innovation Act of 2009.*(February 2012). FDA website. http://www.fda.gov/downloads/Drugs/GuidanceComplianceRegulatoryInformation/Guidances/UCM273001.pdf. Accessed 18 July 2013.
24. EMA. *Guideline on similar biological medicinal products containing monoclonal antibodies—clinical and non-clinical issues* (May 2012). EMA/CHMP/BMWP/403543/2010. EMA website. http://www.ema.europa.eu/docs/en_GB/document_library/Scientific_guideline/2012/06/WC500128686.pdf. Accessed 18 July 2013.
25. FDA. *Biosimilars User Fee Act* of 2012. FDA website. http://www.fda.gov/ForIndustry/UserFees/BiosimilarUserFeeActBsUFA/default.htm. Accessed 18 July 2013.
26. Gingery D. "Biosimilar Pathway Not Smooth For Some Early Applicants," *The Pink Sheet* 22 October 2012, Vol. 74, No. 43.
27. European Medicines Agency. Q&A document EMEA/74562/2006 (Rev.1 22 October 2008).
28. Op cit 23.
29. Op cit 27.
30. European Generic Medicines Association. *EGA Biosimilars Handbook.* Sage Publications (2011).
31. Dowlat H. "The importance and impact of the EU RMP and US REMS to risk–benefit assessments." *Regulatory Rapporteur.* 2011:8(2) February 2011, 20-23.
32. EMA. *Draft Guideline on similar biological medicinal products containing biotechnology-derived proteins as active substance: quality issues (revision 1).* EMA/CHMP/BWP/247713/2012. EMA website. http://www.ema.europa.eu/docs/en_GB/document_library/Scientific_guideline/2012/05/WC500127960.pdf. Accessed 18 July 2013.
33. Health Canada. *Guidance for Sponsors: Information and Submission Requirements for Subsequent Entry Biologics (SEBs)* (5 March 2010) 10-10569-330. Health Canada website. http://www.hc-sc.gc.ca/dhp-mps/brgtherap/applic-demande/guides/seb-pbu/seb-pbu_2010-eng.php. Accessed 18 July 2013.
34. European Medicines Agency. EPARs: Valtropin H-C-602-en6; Scientific Discussion, non-inferiority, children as sensitive model, equivalence model: pp13, 15, 17, 19, 27.
35. European Medicines Agency. EPARs: Omnitrope H-C-607, 060706en6. Scientific Discussion.
36. Op cit 24.
37. Op cit 22.
38. Op cit 17.
39. Op cit 23.
40. European Medicines Agency. EPARS: Mabthera, Remicade, Enbrel.
41. Op cit 32.
42. FDA. Draft Guidances Related to the Development of Biosimilar Products; Public Hearing; Request for Comments (11 May 2012). FDA website. www.fda.gov/Drugs/NewsEvents/ucm265628.htm . Accessed 18 July 2013.
43. Op cit 22.
44. Op cit 23.
45. Op cit 31.
46. Directive 2010/84/EU of the European Parliament and of the Council of 15 December 2010 amending, as regards pharmacovigilance, Directive 2001/83/EC on the Community code relating to medicinal products for human use; Regulation (EU) 1235/2010 of the European Parliament and of the Council of 15 December 2010 amending, as regards pharmacovigilance of medicinal products for human use, Regulation (EC) No 726/2004 laying down Community procedures for the authorisation and supervision of medicinal products for human and veterinary use and establishing a European Medicines Agency and Regulation (EC) No 1394/2007 on advanced therapy medicinal products; and *The Rules Governing Medicinal Products in the European Union*, Volume 9 Pharmacovigilance Guidelines.
47. Op cit 12.
48. Op cit 32.
49. Op cit 33.

50,. Health Canada. *Questions & Answers To Accompany the Final Guidance for Sponsors: Information and Submission Requirements for Subsequent Entry Biologics (SEBs).* Health Canada website. http://www.hc-sc.gc.ca/dhp-mps/brgtherap/applic-demande/guides/seb-pbu/01-2010-seb-pbu-qa-qr-eng.php. Accessed 18 July 2013.

51. Mire-Sluis AR, et al. "Recommendations for the design and optimization of immunoassays used in the detection of host antibodies against biotechnology products." *Journal of Immunological Methods.* 2004:289(1-2); 1-16.

52. FDA. *Draft Guidance for Industry: Assay Development for Immunogenicity Testing of Therapeutic Proteins* (December 2009). FDA website. http://www.fda.gov/downloads/Drugs/.../Guidances/UCM192750.pdf. Accessed 18 July 2013.

53. EMA. *Guideline on immunogenicity assessment of biotechnology derived therapeutic proteins.* EMA/CHMP/BMWP/86289/2007.

54. EMA. *Guideline on immunogenicity assessment of monoclonal antibodies intended for in vivo clinical use* (May 2012). EMA/CHMP/BMWP/86289/2010. EMA website. http://www.ema.europa.eu/docs/en_GB/document_library/Scientific_guideline/2012/06/WC500128688.pdf. Accessed 18 July 2013.

55. Op cit 24.

56. EMA. Concept paper on the revision of the guideline on similar biological medicinal products containing biotechnology-derived proteins as active substance (February 2011). EMA/CHMP/BWP/617111/2010. EMA website. http://www.ema.europa.eu/docs/en_GB/document_library/Scientific_guideline/2011/02/WC500102285.pdf. Accessed 19 July 2013.

57. EMA. *Guideline on similar biological medicinal products containing biotechnology-derived proteins as active substance: non-clinical and clinical issues* (February 2006). EMEA/CHMP/BMWP/42832/2005. EMA website. http://www.ema.europa.eu/docs/en_GB/document_library/Scientific_guideline/2009/09/WC500003920.pdf. Accessed 19 July 2013.

58. Op cit 6.

59. *Guidelines for the Quality, Safety and Efficacy Assurance of Follow-on Biologics* (March 2009). Yakushoku shinsahatu 0304007 by MHLW.

60. PMDA. Yamaguchi T. Asian Pacific Economic Cooperation, Session 2 Biosimilar Regulation & Guideline Update: Regulator's Perspective, http://www.apec-ahc.org/images/training/20120412/[Presentation]%2011_Teruhide%20Yamaguchi.pdf. Accessed 19 July 2013.

61. PMDA. Arato T. Regulatory Guidelines for Biosimilars in Japan, Office of Regulatory Science, EGA, 2012.

62. Op cit 33.

63. Op cit 50.

64. Op cit 11.

65. ABLE-PriceWaterhouseCoopers, *A Bio Pharma Strategy for India, Vision 2020* (2010). ABLE India website. http://www.ableindia.in/admin/attachments/reports/reports17_Vision%202020%20Bio%20Pharma%20Strategy%20Report.pdf. Accessed 19 July 2013.

66. Op cit 8.

67. Op cit 8 Annexes 2-5

68. Scheinberg MA and Kay J. *Nat. Rev. Rheumatol.* Advance online publication 5 June 2012; doi:10.1038/nrrheum.2012.84 US/Brazilian.

69. Saudi Food & Drug Authority Kingdom of Saudi Arabia (sFDA) Guidelines and Regulations. sFDA website. http://www.sfda.gov.sa/en/drug/drug_reg/Pages/drug_reg.aspx. Accessed 19 July 2013.

70. Shepphard A. IMS, Biosimilars: a tale of masquerade and intrigue? Second MENA Biosimilars Conference, 13–14 November 2012, Amman, Jordan.

71. Op cit 5.

72. Suh SK and Park Y. *Regulatory guideline for biosimilar products in Korea.* Korea Food & Drug Administration, Republic of Korea, Biologicals 39 (2011)

73. Chang P. Celltrion Files For Korea Approval Of Herceptin Biosimilar, *Pharm Asia News* (Elsevier BI), 5 June 2013.

74. Wadhwa M, Kang HN, Knezevic I, Thorpe R, Griffiths E. WHO/KFDA joint workshop on implementing WHO guidelines on evaluating similar biotherapeutic products, Seoul, Republic of Korea, 24–26 August, 2010. Biologicals. 2011;39(5):349–57.

75. Op cit 7.

76. Generics and Biosimilars Initiative (GaBi) China to release biosimilars guidelines, Posted 23/11/2012, http://www.gabionline.net/Guidelines/China-to-release-biosimilars-guidelines ref Miller P. Wang F and Kubavat H, Deallus Group. Taming the Dragon: Reverting biosimilar threats into new opportunities for growth in China, http://www.deallusconsulting.com/wp-content/themes/Avada/pdf/Miller_thought_piece_2.pdf

77. Op cit. 19

78. EMA. Interactions between the European Medicines Agency and U.S. Food and Drug Administration September 2009 – September 2010 (June 2011). EMA/705027/2010. FDA website. http://www.fda.gov/downloads/InternationalPrograms/FDABeyondOurBordersForeignOffices/EuropeanUnion/EuropeanUnion/EuropeanCommission/UCM261565.pdf. Accessed 19 July 2013.

Annex 1. EU Product-specific Biosimilar Guidelines

Topic	Reference number	Effective date/Remarks
Similar biological medicinal products containing recombinant follicle stimulation hormone	CHMP/ BMWP/671292/2010	1 September 2013
Similar biological medicinal product containing recombinant interferon beta	CHMP/ BMWP/652000/20100	1 September 2013
Similar biological medicinal products containing monoclonal antibodies—non-clinical and clinical issues	EMA/CHMP/ BMWP/403543/2010	1 December 2012
Similar biological medicinal products containing recombinant erythropoietins	EMEA/CHMP/ BMWP/301636/08	Effective 30 September 2010
Guideline on non-clinical and clinical development of similar biological medicinal products containing low-molecular-weight-heparins	EMEA/CHMP/ BMWP/118264/2007 Rev. 1	Released for consultation, 17 January 2013 Deadline for comments 31 July 2013
Reflection Paper. Non-clinical and clinical development of similar medicinal products containing recombinant interferon alpha	EMEA/CHMP/ BMWP/102046/2006 (2009)	Adopted April 2009
Annex to guideline on similar biological medicinal products containing biotechnology-derived proteins as active substance: non-clinical and clinical Issues—Guidance on biosimilar medicinal products containing recombinant granulocyte-colony stimulating factor	EMEA/CHMP/ BMWP/31329/2005 (2006)	
Annex to guideline on similar biological medicinal products containing biotechnology-derived proteins as active substance: non-clinical and clinical issues—Guidance on similar medicinal products containing somatropin	EMEA/CHMP/ BMWP/94528/2005 (2006)	
Revision of the guideline on nonclinical and clinical development of similar biological medicinal products containing recombinant human insulin and insulin analogues	EMEA/CHMP/ BMWP/32775/2005	Released for consultation December 2012 Deadline for comments 30 June 2013
Annex to guideline on similar biological medicinal products containing biotechnology-derived proteins as active substance: non-clinical and clinical issues—Guidance on similar medicinal products containing recombinant human insulin	EMEA/CHMP/ BMWP/32775/2005 (2006)	

Chapter 25

Vaccines

By Shailesh S. Dewasthaly

OBJECTIVES

- ❑ Understand international development of vaccines
- ❑ Understand the role of WHO and ICH in vaccine regulations
- ❑ Understand regulations of vaccines in various territories
- ❑ Understand lot release requirements for vaccines
- ❑ Understand special topics in vaccines such as adjuvants and influenza vaccines, etc.

DIRECTIVES, REGULATIONS AND GUIDELINES COVERED IN THIS CHAPTER

WHO

- ❑ *Guidelines on the nonclinical evaluation of vaccine adjuvants and adjuvanted vaccines* (draft guideline, 2013)
- ❑ *Environmental Monitoring of Clean Rooms in Vaccine Manufacturing Facilities* (November 2012)
- ❑ *Guideline for independent lot release of vaccines by regulatory authorities*, TRS (in press), ECBS 2010
- ❑ *Guidelines for assuring the quality and nonclinical safety evaluation of DNA vaccines*, TRS 941 (2007)
- ❑ *Guidelines on non-clinical evaluation of Vaccines* (2005), TRS 927 Annex 1
- ❑ *Guidelines on clinical evaluation of vaccines: regulatory expectations*, TRS 924 (2004), Annex 1
- ❑ *Guidelines on regulatory expectations related to the elimination, reduction or replacement of thiomersal in vaccines*, TRS 926 (2004)
- ❑ *Good manufacturing practices for biological products*, TRS 822 (1992), Annex 1

ICH

- ❑ *Preclinical Safety Evaluation of Biotechnology-Derived Pharmaceuticals S6, 2011*
- ❑ *Comparability of Biotechnological/Biological Products Subject to Changes in Their Manufacturing Process Q5E, 2004*
- ❑ *Viral Safety Evaluation of Biotechnology Products Derived from Cell Lines of Human or Animal Origin Q5A(R1), 1999*
- ❑ *Specifications: Test Procedures and Acceptance Criteria for Biotechnological/Biological Products Q6B, 1999*

- *Derivation and Characterization of Cell Substrates Used for Production of Biotechnological/Biological Products Q5D, 1997*
- *Quality of Biotechnological Products: Analysis of the Expression Construct in Cells Used for Production of r-DNA Derived Protein Products Q5B, 1995*
- Quality of Biotechnological Products: Stability Testing of Biotechnological/*Biological Products Q5C, 1995*

EU

- *EudraLex, The Rules Governing Medicinal Products in the European Union, Volume 1, EU pharmaceutical legislation for medicinal products for human use*
- *Guideline on good pharmacovigilance practices (GVP): Product-or population-specific considerations I: Vaccines for prophylaxis against infectious diseases* (April *2013) EMA/488220/2012*
- *Draft Guideline on Influenza Vaccines – Quality Module (March 2013) EMA/CHMP/ BWP/310834/2012*
- *Procedural advice on the submission of variations for annual update of human influenza inactivated vaccines applications in the centralised procedure(March 2013) EMA/ CHMP/BWP/99698/2007 Rev. 2*
- *Guideline on quality, non-clinical and clinical aspects of live recombinant viral vectored vaccines* (January 2011), EMA/CHMP/ VWP/141697/2009
- *Concept paper on a revision of the guideline on pharmaceutical aspects of the product information for human vaccines* (July 2009), EMEA/CHMP/BWP/290688/09
- *Guideline on Virus Safety Evaluation of Biotechnological Investigational Medicinal Products* (February 2009), EMEA/CHMP/ BWP/398498/05
- Directive 2008/27/EC of the European Parliament and of the Council of 11 March 2008 amending Directive 2001/18/EC on the deliberate release into the environment of genetically modified organisms, as regards the implementing powers conferred on the Commission
- *Concept Paper on guidance for DNA vaccines* (October 2007), EMEA/CHMP/308136/2007
- *Guideline on Environmental Risk Assessments for Medicinal Products Consisting of, or Containing, Genetically Modified Organisms (GMOs)* (Module 1.6.2) (July 2007), EMEA/ CHMP/473191/06 Corr
- *Note for Guidance on the Clinical Evaluation of Vaccines* (February 2007), EMEA/CHMP/ VWP/164653/05
- *Guideline on Clinical Evaluation of New Vaccines Annex: SPC Requirements* (February 2007), EMEA/CHMP/VWP/382702/2006
- *CHMP Position Paper on Thiomersal: Implementation of the Warning Statement Relating to Sensitisation* (January 2007), EMEA/CHMP/VWP/19541/2007
- *Explanatory Note on Immunomodulators for the Guideline on Adjuvants in Vaccines for Human Use* (July 2006), CHMP/VWP/244894/2006
- *Guideline on Adjuvants in Vaccines for Human Use* (July 2005), CHMP/VEG/134716/04
- *EMEA Public Statement on Thiomersal in Vaccines for Human Use—Recent Evidence Supports Safety of Thiomersal-containing Vaccines* (March 2004), EMEA/CPMP/ VEG/1194/04
- *Guideline on the Scientific Data Requirements for a Vaccine Antigen Master File (VAMF)* (March 2004), CPMP/BWP/3734/03
- *Guideline on Requirements for Vaccine Antigen Master File (VAMF) Certification* (February 2004), CPMP/4548/03/Final/ Rev 1
- *Guideline on Pharmaceutical Aspects of the Product Information for Human Vaccines* (November 2003), CPMP/BWP/2758/02
- *CPMP Position Statement on the Quality of Water used in the production of Vaccines*

for parenteral use (October 2003), CPMP/BWP/1571/02 Rev 1

- *Note for Guidance on the Use of Bovine Serum in the Manufacture of Human Biological Medicinal Products* (October 2003), CPMP/BWP/1793/02
- *Note for Guidance on the Development of Vaccinia Virus Based Vaccines Against Smallpox* (July 2002), CPMP/1100/02
- *Testing for SV40 in poliovirus vaccines* (April 2002), CPMP/BWP/1412/02
- *Points to Consider on the Reduction, Elimination or Substitution of Thiomersal in Vaccines* (May 2001), CPMP/BWP/2517/00
- *Public Statement on the Evaluation of Bovine Spongiform Encephalopathies (BSE)—risk via the use of materials of bovine origin in or during the manufacture of vaccines* (February 2001), CPMP/BWP/476/01
- *Concept Paper on the Development of a Committee for Proprietary Medicinal Products (CPMP) Points to Consider on Stability and Traceability Requirements for Vaccine Intermediates* (2000), CPMP/BWP/4310/00
- *Development Pharmaceutics for Biotechnological and Biological Products—Annex to Note for Guidance on Development Pharmaceutics* (October 1999), CPMP/BWP/328/99
- *Note for Guidance on Pharmaceutical and Biological Aspects of Combined Vaccines* (January 1999), CPMP/BWP/477/97
- *Position Paper on Viral Safety of Oral Poliovirus Vaccine (OPV)* (May 1998), CPMP/BWP/972/98
- *Note for Guidance on Preclinical Pharmacological and Toxicological Testing of Vaccines* (December 1997), CPMP/SWP/465/95
- *Note for Guidance on Virus Validation Studies: The Design, Contribution and Interpretation of Studies Validating the Inactivation and Removal of Viruses* (1996), CPMP/BWP/268/95
- Council Directive 89/105/EEC of 21 December 1988 relating to the transparency of measures regulating the prices of medicinal products for human use and their inclusion in the scope of national health insurance systems

US

- 21 CFR part 600, part 601
- *Guidance for Industry: Immunogenicity Assessment for Therapeutic Protein Products*, 2013
- *Guidance for Industry: General Principles for the Development of Vaccines to Protect Against Global Infectious Diseases*, 2011
- *Guidance for Industry: Clinical Considerations for Therapeutic Cancer Vaccines*, 2011
- *Guidance for Industry: Characterization and Qualification of Cell Substrates and Other Biological Materials Used in the Production of Viral Vaccines for Infectious Disease Indications*, 2010
- *Guidance for Industry: Considerations for Plasmid DNA Vaccines for Infectious Disease Indications*, 2007
- *Guidance for Industry: Toxicity Grading Scale for Healthy Adult and Adolescent Volunteers Enrolled in Preventive Vaccine Clinical Trials*, 2007
- *Guidance for Industry: Clinical Data Needed to Support the Licensure of Pandemic Influenza Vaccines*, 2007
- *Guidance for Industry: Clinical Data Needed to Support the Licensure of Seasonal Inactivated Influenza Vaccines*, 2007
- *Guidance for Industry: Development of Preventive HIV Vaccines for Use in Pediatric Populations*, 2006
- *Guidance for Industry: Considerations for Developmental Toxicity Studies for Preventive and Therapeutic Vaccines for Infectious Disease Indications*, 2006

- ❑ *Guidance for Industry: FDA Review of Vaccine Labeling Requirements for Warnings, Use Instructions, and Precautionary Information,* 2004
- ❑ *Draft Guidance for Industry: Postmarketing Safety Reporting for Human Drug and Biological Products Including Vaccines*, 2001
- ❑ *Guidance for Reviewers: Potency Limits for Standardized Dust Mite and Grass Allergen Vaccines: A Revised Protocol*, 2000
- ❑ *Guidance for Industry: Content and Format of Chemistry, Manufacturing and Controls Information and Establishment Description Information for a Vaccine or Related Product,* 1999
- ❑ *Guidance for Industry: How to Complete the Vaccine Adverse Event Reporting System Form (VAERS-1),* 1998
- ❑ *Guidance for Industry for the Evaluation of Combination Vaccines for Preventable Diseases: Production, Testing and Clinical Studies,* 1997

Japan

- ❑ Nonclinical safety evaluation of prophylactic vaccines (Notification No. 0527-(1) of the Evaluation and Licensing Division (2010)
- ❑ Guidelines on prophylactic vaccines against infections (Notification no. 0525-(5) of evaluating and licensing division) (2010)

Note: The list of guidelines above is not exhaustive.

Introduction

Vaccines and vaccinations are considered one of the 10 great public health achievements of the 20th century.[1] Although vaccines are medicinal products, and therefore follow the same development pathways as drugs, they are different in many respects from other medicinal products. Vaccines are manufactured in biological systems that are more complex than "chemical reactions," and as a result, maintaining the purity, identity and general quality control (QC) of vaccines is a challenge. Additionally, vaccine "effects" are also unique, with short exposure and long-term response. They are given as a preventive (prophylactic) measure to healthy individuals, the majority of whom are children at a vulnerable age; hence, very high levels of safety are required during development. Additionally, as there is no immediate health benefit for an individual who is vaccinated, there is a limited acceptance for risks. Therefore, vaccines are assessed through a different risk:benefit profile than therapeutic drugs.

Vaccines are medicinal products; therefore, all regulations/guidelines applicable to medicinal products are automatically applicable to vaccines, unless otherwise specified by guidelines or regulations.

The development of vaccines has moved from the national arena to the international, multinational arena thanks to harmonized regulations, easy access to the global clinical trial market and difficulty in conducting large clinical trials in a single country. In principle, the development of vaccines throughout the world follows similar pathways for preclinical and clinical development. In spite of a reasonable effort to harmonize regulations, Competent Authorities continue to face complex issues surrounding the procedures and requirements for vaccine development. This chapter examines the regional requirements and various guidances issued by global bodies like ICH and WHO to harmonize regulations and help ensure high standards and quality vaccines.

International Institutions Involved With Vaccines

Broadly speaking, institutions (directly or indirectly) that are involved in regulating vaccines may be classified as international and national. National institutions include Competent Authorities, and international organizations include the International Conference on Harmonisation (ICH) and the World Health Organization (WHO), which are predominantly harmonization bodies that also help national Competent Authorities with national regulations.

ICH was established in 1990 to develop globally streamlined and harmonized pharmaceutical development guidelines. Six agencies are represented in the ICH: the European Commission (EC); the European Federation of Pharmaceutical Industries and Associations (EFPIA); the Ministry of Health, Labour and Welfare (MHLW); Japan Pharmaceutical Manufacturers Association (JPMA); US Food and Drug Administration (FDA); and the Pharmaceutical Research and Manufacturers of America (PhRMA). In addition to these six organizations, there are three observers: WHO, Health Canada and the European Free Trade Association (EFTA). More details on ICH can be found on its website (www.ich.org/).

WHO and WHO Guidelines

WHO serves as a nodal agency that facilitates discussions from a wide variety of experts from national regulatory agencies, industry, research institutions and public health bodies through the biological standardization program. Numerous guidelines have been developed as a result of these discussions and are published as WHO technical report series (TRS). These TRSs and various other position papers on vaccines serve as guidances for both vaccine developers and Competent Authorities. The position papers (www.who.int/immunization/documents/positionpapers/en/index.html) summarize essential background information on the respective diseases and vaccines and conclude with the current WHO position on their use in the global market. These position papers are published in the Weekly Epidemiological Record (WER).

One WHO committee that is relevant for vaccines is the Expert Committee on Biological Standardization (ECBS), established in 1947, which provides recommendations and guidelines on the manufacturing, licensing and control of biological products like vaccines, along with the establishment of biological reference materials. ECBS also distributes materials (reagents), which are standardized assays required for vaccine control and release, to various National Control Laboratories (NCLs).

The following WHO guidelines are important to vaccine development, and must be read along with other applicable guidelines issued by ICH and local Competent Authorities:

- *Quality assurance of pharmaceuticals: A compendium of guidelines and related materials Volume 2, second updated edition*—This quality assurance compendium includes GMP guidelines. The guidance is not specific to vaccines; however, a chapter is dedicated to biological products.
- Nonclinical evaluation of vaccines is discussed in the *WHO guideline on nonclinical evaluation of vaccines, WHO TRS 927 Annex 1*. This document provides guidance for vaccine developers and Competent Authorities on *in vivo* and *in vitro* testing during product development.
- *Guidelines on clinical evaluation of vaccines: regulatory expectations; TRS 924 Annex 1*—This guideline outlines the data needed for the evaluation of clinical trials and license applications, specifically addressing data requirements at different stages of development. It also provides guidance to govern protection of individual patients while safeguarding public health.

There are many guidelines regarding the manufacturing/quality of vaccines. An overarching guidance on pharmaceutical preparations was recently revised (*WHO expert committee on specifications for pharmaceutical preparations TRS 961, 2011*) and includes various updates to the quality guidances, including GMP guidance.

WHO also has issued guidelines for Competent Authorities and NCLs regarding lot release of vaccines (*Guidelines for independent lot release of vaccines by regulatory authorities. TRS* (in press)). This guideline is a useful resource for vaccine manufacturers in understanding NCL expectations on lot release. An important aspect in the development of a vaccine is stability and shelf life. Stability and shelf life are discussed in *Guidelines on stability evaluation of vaccines, TRS 962, Annex 3*. Other vaccine relevant topics discussed by the WHO include thiomersol in *Guidelines on regulatory expectations related to elimination, reduction or replacement of thiomersol in vaccines, TRS 926, Annex 4*, and safety testing for Transmissible Spongiform Encephalopathies in *WHO guidelines on Transmissible Spongiform Encephalopathies in relation to Biological and Pharmaceutical Products, ECBS 2003*.

Vaccine-specific guidelines have been issued by WHO , e.g., BCG, Hepatitis, Japanese encephalitis, Dengue fever, etc., which can be found on the WHO website. **Table 25-1** lists vaccine-specific WHO guidelines. Note that these guidelines discuss not only licensed vaccines but also may discuss vaccines under development, such as the Dengue vaccine.

WHO Prequalification of Vaccines

One important WHO regulatory activity in vaccines is prequalifying vaccines. Prequalification by WHO ensures an acceptable international standard for vaccines and also is a prerequisite for vaccine procurement by UN agencies. Prequalification ensures that only those vaccines that meet acceptable standards for quality, safety and efficacy can be procured for distribution through UN-sponsored immunization programs. The prequalification process begins with an invitation to manufacturers from the WHO Prequalification of Medicines Program (PQP) to submit an expression of interest (EOI) for a product. This is followed by a dossier submission (on quality, safety and efficacy) and an assessment. WHO has its own format for the dossier; however, the CTD format is accepted as long as there is adequate cross-referencing. The assessment is conducted by experts from WHO and national Competent Authorities. As a part of the prequalification assessment, the manufacturing site is inspected to ensure that the product is manufactured according to the current WHO GMP standards. If, after the assessment and inspection, the product is found to meet the required standards, it is added to the WHO list of prequalified medicinal products. Detailed guidance on prequalification can be found in *Procedure for assessing the acceptability, in principle, of vaccines for purchase by United Nations agencies, WHO 2010*.

WHO relies on the national Competent Authorities for prequalification; therefore WHO also has a process to assess eligible Competent Authorities. A streamlined option can be applied to vaccines that have been licensed by selected Competent Authorities that are willing to share review information. A streamlined option is also available for products that have received scientific opinion from the European Medicines Agency (EMA) through the "Article 58 procedure."

WHO has also developed a format for a Certification of Pharmaceutical Product (CPP). This certificate is issued by the country of origin's national regulatory agency/

Table 25-1. Vaccine specific guidelines published by WHO

Vaccine	Title	Year	Link
BCG	Recommendations to assure the quality, safety and efficacy of BCG vaccines	2011	http://www.who.int/biologicals/BCG_DB_HK_23_April_2012.pdf
Cholera	Guidelines for the production and control of inactivated oral cholera vaccines	2004	http://www.who.int/biologicals/publications/trs/areas/vaccines/cholera/129-149.pdf
Diptheria, Tetanus, Pertussis	Recommendations for diphtheria, tetanus, pertussis and combined vaccines (Amendments 2003)	2005	http://www.who.int/biologicals/publications/trs/areas/vaccines/dtp/ANNEX%205%20DTPP138-147.pdf
Haemophilus influenzae type b	Recommendations for the production and control of Haemophilus influenzae type b conjugate vaccines	2000	http://www.who.int/biologicals/publications/trs/areas/vaccines/influenza/WHO_TRS_897_A1.pdf
Hepatitis A	Requirements for a Hepatitis A vaccine (inactivated)	1995	http://www.who.int/biologicals/publications/trs/areas/vaccines/hepatitis/WHO_TRS_858_A2.pdf
Hepatitis B	Recommendations to Assure the Quality, Safety and Efficacy of Recombinant Hepatitis B Vaccines	2010	http://www.who.int/biologicals/HEP_B_Recomm_after_ECBS_endorsment_final.pdf
HPV	Guidelines to assure the quality, safety and efficacy of recombinant human papillomavirus virus-like particle vaccines	2006	http://www.who.int/biologicals/publications/trs/areas/vaccines/human_papillomavirus/HPVg%20Final%20BS%202050%20.pdf
Influenza	Recommendations for the production and control of influenza vaccine (inactivated)	2005	http://www.who.int/biologicals/publications/trs/areas/vaccines/influenza/ANNEX%203%20InfluenzaP99-134.pdf
	WHO recommendations to assure the quality, safety, and efficacy of influenza vaccines (human, live attenuated) for intranasal administration	2009	http://www.who.int/biologicals/areas/vaccines/influenza/Influenza_vaccines_final_14MAY_2010.pdf
	WHO biosafety risk assessment and guidelines for the production and quality control of human influenza pandemic vaccines	2007	http://www.who.int/biologicals/publications/trs/areas/vaccines/influenza/Annex%205%20human%20pandemic%20influenza.pdf
Japanese encephalitis	Guidelines for the production and control of Japanese encephalitis vaccine (live) for human use	2002	http://www.who.int/biologicals/areas/vaccines/jap_encephalitis/WHO_TRS_910_A3.pdf
	Recommendations for Japanese encephalitis vaccine (inactivated) for human use (Revised 2007)	2007	http://who.int/biologicals/vaccines/Annex_1_WHO_TRS_963.pdf
Dengue fever	Guidelines on the quality, safety and efficacy of dengue tetravalent vaccines (live, attenuated)	2011	http://www.who.int/biologicals/vaccines/Dengue_DB_5_April_2012_clean.pdf
Haemorrhagic fever with renal syndrome (HFRS)	Requirements for Haemorrhagic fever with renal syndrome (HFRS) vaccine (inactivated)	1994	http://www.who.int/biologicals/publications/trs/areas/vaccines/haem_fever/WHO_TRS_848_A2.pdf
Measles, Mumps, Rubella	Requirements for Measles, Mumps and Rubella vaccines and combined vaccine (live)	1994	http://who.int/biologicals/publications/trs/areas/vaccines/mmr/WHO_TRS_840_A3.pdf
Meningococcal Meningitis	(Various types of vaccines)		http://who.int/biologicals/vaccines/Meningococcal_Meningitis/en/index.html
Pertussis	Recommendations for whole-cell pertussis vaccine	2007	http://who.int/biologicals/publications/trs/areas/vaccines/whole_cell_pertussis/Annex%206%20whole%20cell%20pertussis.pdf
	Recommendations to Assure the Quality, Safety and Efficacy of Acellular Pertussis Vaccines	2011	http://who.int/biologicals/Acellular_pertussis_vaccines_DB_DL_June_2012.pdf
Pneumococcus	Recommendations to assure the quality, safety and efficacy of pneumococcal conjugate vaccines	2009	http://who.int/biologicals/vaccines/Pneumo_final_23APRIL_2010.pdf
Polio	Guidelines for the safe production and quality control of inactivated poliomyelitis vaccine manufactured from wild polioviruses (Addendum, 2003, to the Recommendations for the Production and Quality Control of Poliomyelitis Vaccine (Inactivated))	2004	http://who.int/biologicals/publications/trs/areas/vaccines/polio/Annex%202%20(65-89)TRS926Polio2003.pdf
	Recommendations for the production and control of poliomyelitis vaccine (oral) (Addendum 2000)	2002	http://who.int/biologicals/publications/trs/areas/vaccines/polio/WHOTRS910annex1polio%20opv.pdf

Rabies	Recommendations for inactivated rabies vaccine for human use produced in cell substrates and embryonated eggs	2007	http://who.int/biologicals/publications/trs/areas/vaccines/rabies/Annex%202%20inactivated%20rabies%20vaccine.pdf
Rift Valley fever	Proposed requirements for Rift valley fever vaccine (inactivated) for human use	1981	http://who.int/biologicals/publications/trs/areas/vaccines/rift_valley/WHO_TRS_673_A4.pdf
Rotavirus	Guidelines to assure the quality, safety and efficacy of live attenuated rotavirus vaccines (oral)	2007	http://who.int/biologicals/publications/trs/areas/vaccines/rotavirus/Annex%203%20rotavirus%20vaccines.pdf
Smallpox	Recommendations for the production and quality control of smallpox vaccine, revised 2003	2004	http://who.int/biologicals/publications/trs/areas/vaccines/smallpox/Annex%201%20(27-64)TRS926Smallpox2003.pdf
Tick borne encephalitis	Requirements for tick-borne encephalitis vaccine (inactivated)	1999	http://who.int/biologicals/publications/trs/areas/vaccines/tick_encephalitis/WHO_TRS_889_A2.pdf
Typhoid	Requirements for Vi polysaccharide typhoid vaccine	1994	http://who.int/biologicals/publications/trs/areas/vaccines/typhoid/WHO_TRS_840_A1.pdf
Varicella	Requirements for varicella vaccine (live)	1994	http://who.int/biologicals/publications/trs/areas/vaccines/varicella/WHO_TRS_848_A1.pdf
Yellow Fever	Recommendations to Assure the Quality, Safety and Efficacy of Live Attenuated Yellow Fever Vaccines	2010	http://who.int/biologicals/YF_Recommendations_post_ECBS_FINAL_rev_12_Nov_2010.pdf

Competent Authority on the status of the pharmaceutical product. This certificate is often required by the importing country of the medicinal product.

ICH Guidelines

ICH guidelines have been used to develop pharmaceuticals for the past 20 years. ICH guidelines are well accepted throughout the world and have been adopted into many national guidelines. Since vaccines generally are produced through biotechnological processes, most ICH guidelines appropriate to vaccines fall under the biotechnological/biological products category. Other relevant guidelines for medicinal products are also applicable to vaccines, e.g., the ICH stability guideline. In exceptional cases, it is specifically mentioned if a particular guideline is not applicable for a type of product, e.g., ICH's *Preclinical Safety Evaluation of Biotechnology-Derived Pharmaceuticals S6* is not applicable to vaccines. Other guidelines that have facilitated international development of vaccines and medicinal products include stability testing guidelines Q1A(R2), Q3 and Q5C; Good Manufacturing Practices (GMP) guideline Q7; virus safety evaluation Q5A(R1); comparability guideline Q5E; structure and content of clinical study report guideline E3; foreign clinical data E5(R1); and the GCP guideline E6(R1).

Local and Regional Institutions

Every country has a national Competent Authority that is responsible for regulating pharmaceuticals (e.g., FDA in the US). National authorities may have different centers or departments that are responsible for the regulatory oversight of vaccines. As vaccines are biological, they generally are regulated from centers that review biologics, e.g., FDA's Center for Biologics Evaluation and Research (CBER), PMDA's Office of Biologics and the Paul Erlich Institute in Germany.

In the EU, apart from the national Competent Authority, organizations also exist and operate at a pan-European level playing an important role in the regulation of pharmaceuticals, e.g., the European Commission (EC), EMA and the European Directorate of Quality of Medicines (EDQM). These agencies also help harmonize regulations in various countries across the EU. More detailed information about these institutions can found on their respective websites.

The EC, based in Brussels, is responsible for licenses for medicinal products authorized through the Centralised Procedure. The organization coordinates intergovernmental cooperation and also drafts proposals for harmonized legislation and new European laws.

EMA, based in London, is responsible for the scientific evaluation of applications (including license applications) through the Centralised Procedure. EMA's Committee for Medicinal Products for Human Use (CHMP) is responsible for regulating human medicines including vaccines. CHMP, in turn, has several working parties that help with topic-specific consultations. Permanent or standing working parties include the Biologics Working Party, the Patients and Consumers Working Party, the Quality Working Party, the Safety Working Party, and the Scientific Advice Working Party. The Vaccine Working Party (VWP) is one of the many temporary working parties. VWP's tasks include providing scientific advice on general and specific aspects of vaccines upon CHMP's request, supporting dossier evaluation for vaccines, issuing vaccine guidelines, working with other organizations like WHO on vaccine-related matters and completing other vaccine-related functions. Detailed descriptions of the various working parties' mandates are provided on the EMA website.

Figure 25-1. OCABR Flow Chart

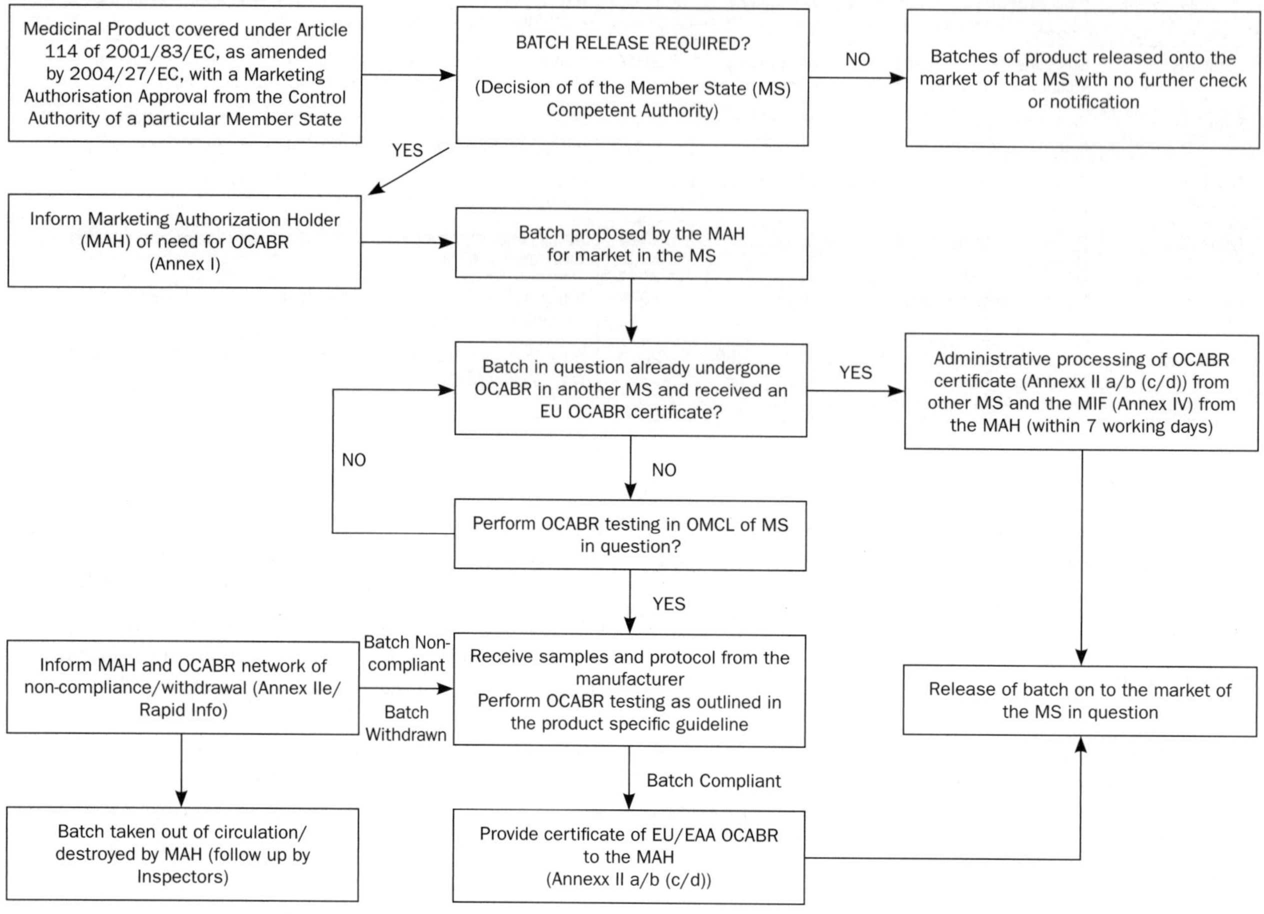

From http://www.edqm.eu accessed December 2012

EDQM is based in Strasbourg. The aim of EDQM is to ensure high quality medicines in the EU and also to provide expertise to the various national authorities regarding the quality of medicines. Under EDQM, a network of Official Medicinal Control Laboratories (OMCLs) is responsible for the testing and release of medicines, particularly vaccines. An OMCL release of every vaccine lot in the EU is required before the lot can be released into the market. The procedure for lot release of vaccines in the EU is briefly described later in the chapter.

Regulations and Guidelines from National/Regional Institutions

EU

In the EU, in addition to the respective national Competent Authorities, two organizations (the EC and EMA) work at the pan-European level to provide a "top down approach" into the guidance and regulations applicable to all EU Member States. EU directives and EMA guidelines for medicinal products provide the basic principles of vaccine production and control. It is important to note that in the EU, regulations are binding in their entirety and are directly applicable to all Member States. A directive, on the other hand, leaves the Member States to adapt the directive into national legislation or laws. As in many other countries, guidelines are not binding.

The nonclinical aspects of vaccine development are discussed in EMA's *Note for guidance on preclinical pharmacological and toxicological testing of vaccines* (CPMP/SWP/465/95). According to this guidance, many typical toxicological studies for "drugs" generally are not necessary for vaccines, e.g., genotoxicity, etc. The guidance also suggests that the omission of certain toxicology tests should be properly justified in the course of product development.

A recent industry initiative led to a reassessment of the need for a dedicated acute toxicology test, and as a result, the guideline was withdrawn. According to questions and answers on the withdrawal of the *Note for guidance on single dose toxicity* (EMA/CHMP/SWP/81714/2010), EMA recognized that traditional single-dose toxicity studies were of limited value and that eliminating them also would help reduce the number of animals used for testing. Data about acute toxicity can be obtained from other toxicology studies. Similar changes have been made to the ICH M3(R2) guideline.

Chemistry, manufacturing and control (CMC) requirements for investigational biological products, including vaccines, are discussed under *Requirements for quality documentation concerning biological investigational medicinal products in clinical trials* (EMEA/CHMP/BWP/534898/08). This guidance is specifically aimed at harmonizing requirements and assessing quality information for biological/biotechnological investigational medicinal products or clinical trial material throughout the EU. Similar guidance already exists that covers all investigational medicinal products (IMPs) in clinical trials (CHMP/QWP/185401/2004). In terms of quality documentation for clinical trials, manufacturers are required to submit an Investigational Medicinal Product Dossier (IMPD), which is unique to the EU. The IMPD follows CTD granularity, and the structure and content can be found in the *Guideline on requirements to the chemical and pharmaceutical quality documentation concerning investigational medicinal products in clinical trials* (CHMP/QWP/185401/2004 final).

Requirements for the clinical development of vaccines are described in *Guideline on clinical evaluation of new vaccines* (EMEA/CHMP/VWP/164653/2005). This guideline not only outlines requirements for vaccine clinical studies but also discusses situations where efficacy studies for vaccines are not possible. The annex to this main guidance (EMEA/CHMP/VWP/382702/2006) addresses the Summary of Product Characteristics (SmPC) requirements for vaccines and provides details on some sections (4 and 5, i.e., clinical particulars and pharmacological properties) of the standard SmPC template provided by the Quality Review of Documents (QRD) convention that is unique to vaccines.

Clinical trials performed in the EU are required to be conducted in accordance with the EU *Clinical Trials Directive* (Directive 2001/20/EC) and Good Clinical Practices (GCPs). Almost all of the elements in the EU directive have been incorporated into Member States' legislation. Although this has ensured similar standards and requirements across Member States, sometimes there may be additional local requirements. Similar to clinical trials for drugs, vaccine trials are regulated at the national level. Therefore, in addition to following the EU directives, trial sponsors should expect minor differences at the national level during the review of the clinical trial application. This can be especially true for such complex products as vaccines and biotechnological products. Based on feedback from stakeholders on the *Clinical Trials Directive*, a revised clinical directive has been suggested by the EC and is currently under consideration by Member States and stakeholders. More information can be found on the EC website (http://ec.europa.eu/health/human-use/clinical-trials/).

In the EU, vaccines, like other medicinal products, must be manufactured in compliance with GMP regulations, found in *The Rules Governing Medicinal Products in the European Union, Volume 4*, and Directive 2003/94/EC (the *GMP Directive*), for both clinical trial materials and approved products. In 2010, the EC released draft guidance for biologics' current GMPs (CGMPs), *Manufacture of Biological Medicinal Substances and Products for Human Use* (ENTR/C/8/SF D(2010) 380334) for public consultation. The guidance was revised to include advanced therapy medicinal products (ATMPs). Although the guidance has not been finalized, it does indicate the current thinking of EU experts on this topic.

A specific EU requirement for both drug and biological manufacturers is that a Qualified Person (QP) must certify that every lot/batch is in compliance with the approved product specifications and applicable regulations for use in clinical trials and on the market. The QP's role in lot certification throughout the development process became mandatory in the EU under Directive 2001/83/EC. The QP is bound by law to ensure the suitability of every lot before it is released for human use in any EU Member State. Details on the QP's role can be found in EMA's CGMP guidelines, which are applicable to all medicinal products, including vaccines and drugs. Lots manufactured outside the EU can be imported but are subject to QP certification and release.

There are other specific guidelines issued by the EU, e.g., the CHMP position paper on quality of water used for parenteral vaccines in the EU (CPMP/BWP/1571/02 Rev 1). This guideline clarifies that Water for Injection (WFI) must be used for final formulation of vaccines; lesser quality water may be used for other manufacturing steps.

In the EU, medicinal products that are intended exclusively for markets outside the Community are eligible for evaluation under 'Article 58.' This process is done with WHO and used for diseases that are not normally present in Europe. CHMP issues a scientific opinion on the benefit:risk conclusion ration of the product.

US

As vaccines fall under "biologics" criteria, they are regulated by FDA's CBER, and requirements for biologics can be found in 21 CFR Part 600. Vaccines also follow the Investigational New Drug (IND) process as described in 21 CFR Part 312. A Biologics License Application (BLA) is required for every vaccine and is regulated under 21 CFR 601.

Most of the pharmaceutical or drug guidances also are applicable to vaccines. However, FDA and CBER have issued many biologics guidances. Characterization, testing of cell substrates and biological materials used in viral vaccines are mentioned in *Characterization and Qualification of Cell Substrates and Other Biological Materials Used in the Production of Viral Vaccines for Infectious Disease Indications.* CMC information and establishment description for a license application are discussed under *Content and Format of Chemistry, Manufacturing and Controls Information and Establishment Description Information for a Vaccine or Related Product.*

For nonclinical aspects, vaccines also follow the IND regulation, 21 CFR 312.23(a)(8). FDA also was involved in the drafting process for WHO's guidance on the nonclinical evaluation of vaccines, hence these guidelines would be useful for vaccine development in the US. Considering the importance of developmental toxicology studies, FDA has issued guidance on this topic specifically for vaccines against infectious diseases, *Considerations for Developmental Toxicity Studies for Preventive and Therapeutic Vaccines for Infectious Disease Indications.*

Apart from the relevant clinical guidance, FDA has issued guidance on assessing safety in clinical trials with vaccines in *Toxicity Grading Scale for Healthy Adult and Adolescent Volunteers Enrolled in Preventive Vaccine Clinical Trials.* This guidance addresses both clinical and laboratory parameter abnormalities.

Currently, many companies are developing vaccines against diseases that generally are not prevalent in the US or EU. In 2011, FDA issued guidance on *General Principles for the Development of Vaccines to Protect Against Global Infectious Diseases*, which clarifies the US regulatory pathway for vaccines and the conditions for acceptance of data from clinical trials conducted outside the US. The guidance also contains a useful Q&A on this topic. It is interesting to note that under certain conditions, if efficacy studies are not possible in humans, FDA can license a biological product based on evidence of effectiveness from studies in animals under 21 CFR 601.90 & 91, popularly called the "Animal Rule." The Animal Rule is used under special circumstances where human trials are not ethical or feasible (e.g., against bioterrorism agents) and the effect of the product in the animal model is likely to predict the effect in humans.

Combination vaccines are being developed continuously for their convenience in administration and compliance. Hexavalent vaccine against diphtheria, tetanus, pertussis, polio, Hepatitis B and Hemophilus is one recent example. In order to help sponsors understand FDA's expectations on combination vaccines, FDA has issued the guidance, *Evaluation of combination vaccines for preventable diseases: production, testing and clinical studies.*

CBER has issued specific guidance on the content of vaccine labeling. Vaccine labeling review is discussed under *FDA Review of Vaccine Labeling Requirements for Warnings, Use Instructions, and Precautionary Information.*

There are also guidances for special vaccines in development, such as the HIV vaccine, *Development of Preventive HIV Vaccines for Use in Paediatric Populations*; plasmid vaccines, *Considerations for Plasmid DNA Vaccines for Infectious Disease Indications;* allergy vaccines, *Potency Limits for Standardized Dust Mite and Grass Allergen Vaccines: A Revised Protocol*; and *Clinical Considerations for Therapeutic Cancer Vaccines.*

Japan

In Japan, MHLW is responsible for regulating medicinal products. As mentioned earlier, Japan is a signatory to ICH; therefore, the ICH guidelines are also applicable in Japan. An independent organization came into force from 2004 that handles all scientific consultation concerning pharmaceutical products, PMDA. In addition to PMDA, the National Institute of Health Sciences (NIHS) also provides experts for consultation and scientific evaluation. NIHS is engaged in testing, evaluation and related research in maintaining quality, efficacy and safety of pharmaceuticals. In Japan, vaccine specifications, assays and tests are reviewed by NIHS or the Infectious Disease Surveillance Center prior to approval of the vaccine.

There are few vaccine-specific guidelines in Japan. PMDA has made the effort to translate certain important regulations into English. A general overarching description of pharmaceutical regulations in Japan is provided by the Japan Pharmaceutical Manufacturers Association (JPMA), www.jpma.or.jp/english/parj/1203.html. Product review reports also are translated into English to help understand PDMA's current thinking.

As long as companies develop vaccines following ICH guidelines, products can be adapted easily for development and/or licensure in Japan. Some guidances are available in English, e.g., *Nonclinical safety evaluation of prophylactic vaccines* (Notification No. 0527-(1) of the Evaluation and Licensing Division, 2010); *Guidelines on prophylactic vaccines against infections* (Notification no. 0525-(5) of evaluating and licensing division) in 2010. It must be noted that Japan has certain specific requirements, e.g., it generally is expected that vaccines also are tested for safety pharmacology, while this requirement usually is not strictly followed in the US or EU.

Due to the complexity of requirements in Japan specific to vaccines, it is always pragmatic to discuss the development strategy with PMDA. PMDA has published clear procedures on conducting face-to-face meetings with sponsors to discuss both clinical trials and licensure. An important publication is *Q& A on acceptability of foreign clinical data* based on the ICH E5 guideline, *Basic principles on global clinical trials* (www.pmda.go.jp/english/service/pdf/notifications/0928010-e.pdf).

Australia

In Australia, vaccines are regulated by the national Competent Authority, the Therapeutic Goods Administration (TGA). Data requirements for licensure are based largely on EU requirements. Many of the EU guidelines are applicable in Australia and have been officially adopted. However, there are many guidelines that have not been adopted. The TGA website has more information on these guidelines: www.tga.gov.au/industry/pm-euguidelines-adopted.htm and www.tga.gov.au/industry/pm-euguidelines-notadopted.htm. As in the US, TGA may refer the vaccine manufacturer to an advisory committee for its recommendation for licensure. For more information on the guidelines, please refer to Australian Regulatory Guidelines for Prescription Medicines.

Other Countries

A discussion of regulations for every country is not within the scope of this chapter. Vaccines that are developed according to US or EU standards or licensed in any of the main ICH countries have a better chance of receiving approval in other countries. However, many countries may have certain specific requirements for licensure, e.g., a small bridging clinical trial in the local population. Similarly, dossier requirements may vary even though the vaccines are already licensed in either the US, EU or Japan:

- Full dossier submitted for review, e.g., Australia and Canada for licensure in these countries.
- "Short" dossier submitted for review; however, in some countries, such as Singapore, this pathway is not applicable to biological/vaccines. For biologics/vaccines, a full dossier must be submitted for review.
- Very rarely, approvals will be provided purely on the basis of a CPP issued by the EU authorities.

Lot Release of Vaccines

Vaccines are subject to lot release by almost all authorities worldwide and lot release usually is included in vaccine regulations. Independent release of each lot by the NCL ensures suitable quality and consistency of an inherently complex product, like a vaccine. Some authorities may request lot testing even for investigational vaccines and those under product license review. It is therefore important to initiate discussions with the potential NCL as it may not have the expertise, resources and technical capabilities for a particular assay or product. Sometimes SOP transfer, reagent transfer or technology transfer may be required from the manufacturer to these laboratories for vaccine testing, which may be time consuming if special tests are required. Some guidelines on lot release of vaccine from different authorities are briefly discussed below.

WHO

WHO provides guidelines for independent lot release by national regulatory authorities, or in some cases, an NCL in the *Guidelines for independent lot release of vaccines by regulatory authorities,* TRS in press). This guideline is in the process of being published.

EU

In the EU, an OMCL in each Member State is responsible for testing and release of vaccine lots. Independent from manufacturers, OMCLs test products (or, at a minimum, check their release documentation) before they can be released into the market. A product certified by one OMCL is recognized by all other laboratories in the network. Within this OMCL organization, the Official Control Authority Batch Release (OCABR) network is responsible for human biologicals (vaccine) testing.

If the test results are satisfactory, the OMCL issues an "Official Control Authority Batch Release Certificate," which essentially confirms that the batch has been tested and found to be compliant with the OCABR-defined guidelines, specifications in the license/marketing authorization and relevant *European Pharmacopoeia* monographs. **Figure 25-1** describes the algorithm for OMCL lot release of medicinal products. A list of contacts for all OCABRs can be downloaded from www.edqm.eu/en/human-biologicals-611.html.

Under Article 58 of Regulation 726/2004, an OMCL can test an immunological medicinal product or a medicinal product derived from human blood or plasma for the purpose of batch release by a third country at the recommendation of EMA and in cooperation with WHO. The guideline, *Administrative Procedure for European Official Medicines Control Laboratory Certification of Compliance of Batches under Article 58*, regarding this procedure can be found on the EDQM website.

US

In the US, CBER is responsible for the lot or batch release of vaccines. The requirement for lot release is mentioned in 21 CFR Part 610.2. It is possible to submit the lot release documents electronically; guidance has been issued by the agency. The BLA review committee or team will decide on the test required for lot release. Manufacturers are encouraged to discuss the tests or assays with FDA during the pre-BLA meeting. For investigational vaccines, lot release is not required as long as a valid IND application is in place and the product is manufactured according to the IND.

Table 25-2. Adjuvants Licensed in the EU

Adjuvant	Contains Mainly	Manufacturer	Vaccines
Alum	Aluminum hydroxide/phosphate	*many*	Hep A,B, DTaP, Tdap, Hib, HPV, Anthrax, Rabies, Pneumococcal conjugate vaccine, etc.
MF59	Oil in water emulsion	Novartis	Influenza (Fluad/pandemic influenza)
AS03	Oil in water emulsion+tocopherol	GSK	Pandemic influenza
AS04	MPL+alum	GSK	HPV (Cervarix), HBV (Fendrix)
Liposomes	Oil in water emulsion	Crucell	HAV, Influenza

Modified from Mbow et al 2010 New Adjuvants for human vaccines. Curr Opinion Immunol. 22: 411-16

Other Countries

In almost all countries, lot release of vaccines is required. This could be in the form of actual testing or a release based on submission of documents. Based on the vaccine, the release is done following specific testing done by the authority; however, in some cases, lot release also can be done only based on the results (documentation) submitted by the sponsor without any sample testing by the authority. Therefore, vaccine manufacturers are encouraged to discuss lot release requirements with their local representatives/ local authorities and also to discuss the time required for lot release.

Specific Topics Unique to Vaccines

Vaccine Adjuvants

Charles Janeway, a well-known immunologist, called adjuvants "immunologists dirty secrets." Adjuvants are components that help enhance or modulate the immune response either by higher titres, long-lived titres or both, or by influencing the immune response in a particular direction (e.g., cellular rather than humoral). Although adjuvants have been used for a long time, their complete and precise mechanism of action still is unknown. Adjuvants are not licensed independently, but always licensed as a part of the vaccine. Universally, alum (either aluminum hydroxide or aluminum phosphate) is the most commonly used adjuvant in vaccines licensed for human use.

In the EU, the requirements for adjuvants are defined *in Guideline on adjuvants in vaccines for human use* (EMEA/ CHMP/VEG/134716/2004). This guidance discusses almost all aspects of adjuvant development, including manufacturing, characterization, etc. According to this guideline, all novel adjuvants are expected to be thoroughly characterized through both physicochemical and biological methods. In addition, microbiological and chemical purity should be ascertained. Studies to show adjuvant-antigen mechanism of action, stability and other routine studies generally are recommended. Both preclinical and clinical studies are required to show the benefit of the adjuvant. Preclinical studies for a novel adjuvant are determined based on the current guidance and the adjuvant-antigen combination and, in general, the strategy is decided on a case-by-case basis. If the adjuvant is intended to replace a licensed adjuvant-antigen (vaccine), immune response non-inferiority studies generally are expected. **Table 25-2** lists the adjuvants and their vaccines licensed in the EU.

Traditionally, the US has been more conservative about adjuvants. Until recently, alum was the only adjuvant in vaccines licensed in the US. Adjuvants are treated as biological products and therefore are regulated under 21 CFR 610. 21 CFR 610.15 specifically addresses "constituent materials" of biological products. Vaccine guidances discuss adjuvants, but currently no specific adjuvant guidelines have been issued by FDA.

The field of adjuvants has recently expanded with immunomodulators being included in certain products. In *Explanatory note on immunomodulators for the guideline on adjuvants in vaccines for human use* (EMEA/CHMP/ VWP/244894/2006), EMA clarifies that if compounds are given separately from the vaccine antigen, these will be considered immunomodulators, not adjuvants.

Although,there are no adjuvant guidances from WHO, the Global Advisory Committee on Vaccine Safety discusses vaccine adjuvant safety issues, e.g., *WER July 2012*. Recently, a draft guideline has been issued for public consultation by WHO on preclinical assessment of adjuvants and adjuvanted vaccines (*Draft Guidelines on the nonclinical evaluation of vaccine adjuvants and adjuvanted vaccines,* April 2013).

Vaccine Additives

Vaccines contain certain typical additives apart from the impurities resulting from the manufacturing process (e.g., host cell proteins). Thiomersal is one such additive (preservative) used historically in vaccines (especially in multidose vials). Due to the mercury content in thiomersal, its use has become a sensitive issue with almost all authorities. All Competent Authorities encourage manufacturers to develop vaccines without thiomersal. In 2004, EMA issued a public statement on the safety of vaccines containing thiomersal (EMEA/CPMP/VEG/1194/04). EMA also encourages vaccine manufacturers to produce vaccines with

Figure 25-2. Process for Production and Licensing of Seasonal Influenza Vaccines in Europe

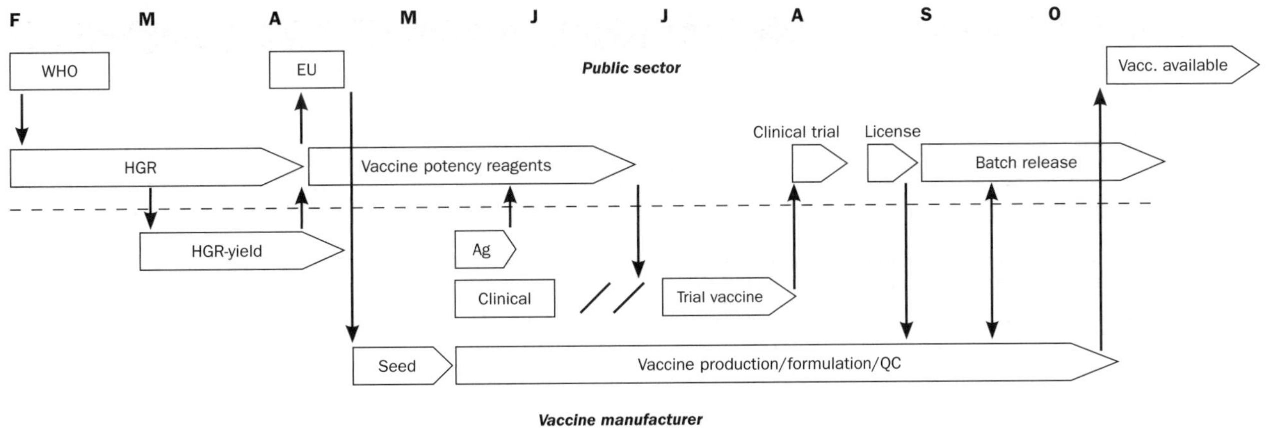

From Minor PD Clin Infect Dis. 2010;50:560-565

very low to no thiomersal. Specific guidance exists on how to implement the warning statement to sensitization in the SmPC (EMEA/CHMP/VWP/19541/2007).

WHO's position on thiomersol is outlined in the TRS 926 Annex 4, *Guidelines on regulatory expectations related to elimination, reduction or replacement of thiomersal from vaccines*. This guidance was a result of expert consultation from various regulatory authorities and industry representatives.

FDA has also published its position in *Thiomersal in Vaccines* (www.fda.gov/BiologicsBloodVaccines/SafetyAvailability/VaccineSafety/UCM096228). Other information on thiomersal is available in the form of Q&As and other related guidances from FDA.

Influenza Vaccines

Although influenza vaccines are like any other vaccines, from a regulatory perspective, they follow a unique pathway. Influenza viruses can be classified as seasonal and pandemic; therefore, the vaccines also can be classified as seasonal and pandemic. Seasonal vaccines are produced every year for the strains that are most predominant during the review period. Usually, there are three different strains in a seasonal influenza vaccine; however, some manufacturers have already moved to a quadrivalent influenza vaccine. Pandemic influenza vaccines, on the other hand, are produced only when there is an influenza pandemic, as in 2009, or a threat of pandemic.

Seasonal influenza vaccine manufacture and approval is a well-organized and standardized process for regulators and manufacturers at (**Figure 25-2**), starting with an expert review at WHO of the its epidemiology data in mid-February every year for the northern hemisphere.[4] This is followed by the recommendation on the use of reassortants or strains for influenza vaccine manufacture through the individual countries' advisory groups, e.g., the EU's Ad hoc Influenza Working Party and the US Vaccines and Related Biological Products Advisory Committee (VRBPAC). Following the recommendation, manufacturers start vaccine production and submit chemistry, manufacturing and controls (CMC) information. For seasonal influenza vaccines, the change of strain is usually done through a specific variation or supplement to the original license. EMA has published guidance on the specific variation procedure for the annual update of the influenza vaccines, *Procedural advice on the submission of variations for annual update of human influenza inactivated vaccine applications in the centralised procedure* (EMA/CHMP/BWP/99698/2007 Rev. 1).

For pandemic influenza vaccines, EMA and the EC have developed an innovative core pandemic dossier approach, where a company submits a license application with a "mock" strain of influenza. The strain used in the core pandemic dossier is a strain for which the population is naïve but could cause a pandemic. This way, the core dossier would mimic the future pandemic vaccine in quality, nonclinical and clinical aspects. Naturally, the safety and immunogenicity data in the core dossier are based on the premise that subjects will respond similarly to the actual pandemic strain. As soon as the pandemic starts or is an imminent threat, the strain is replaced, specific predefined development steps are performed and resulting data are submitted and evaluated as a variation to the marketing application. This process significantly accelerates the licensure and availability of such vaccines within a reduced pandemic response time.

In the EU, several guidelines are in place for influenza vaccines (**Table 25-3**). Due to pandemic scares and the lessons learned from them, the EU has decided to develop a single comprehensive influenza vaccine guideline that deals with quality, nonclinical and clinical requirements for all kinds of influenza vaccines. The *Concept paper on the revision of guidelines for influenza Vaccines* was published and released in September 2011, and consultation ended

Table 25-3. European Guidelines for Influenza Vaccines

Title	Date	Number
General		
Concept paper on the revision of guidelines for influenza vaccines	October 2011	EMA/CHMP/VWP/734330/2011
*Guideline on Influenza Vaccines – Quality Module (draft)**	March 2013	EMA/CHMP/BWP/310834/2012
Seasonal Vaccines		
Guideline on quality aspects on the isolation of candidate influenza vaccine viruses in cell culture	February 2012	CHMP/BWP/368186/2011
Procedural advice on the submission of variations for annual update of human influenza inactivated vaccines applications in the centralised procedure	March 2013	EMA/CHMP/BWP/99698/2007 Rev 2
Points to Consider on the Development of Live Attenuated Influenza Vaccines	August 2003	CPMP/BWP/2289/01
Cell Culture Inactivated Influenza Vaccines—Annex to Note for Guidance on Harmonisation of Requirements for Influenza Vaccines (CPMP/BWP/214/96)	August 2002	CPMP/BWP/2490/00
Annex I variation application(s) content for live attenuated influenza vaccines	October 2011	EMA/CHMP/BWP/577998/2010
Pandemic Vaccines		
Concept paper on the revision of guidelines for influenza vaccines	October 2011	EMA/CHMP/VWP/734330/2011
Core SPC for Pandemic Influenza Vaccines	July 2010	EMEA/CHMP/VWP/193031/2004 Rev- 1
Standard Paediatric Investigation Plan for non-adjuvanted or adjuvanted pandemic influenza vaccines during a pandemic	March 2010	EMA/185099/2010
CHMP Recommendations for the Pharmacovigilance Plan as part of the Risk Management Plan to be submitted with the Marketing Authorisation Application for a Pandemic Influenza Vaccine	September 2009	EMEA/359381/2009
Guideline on Dossier Structure and Content for Pandemic Influenza Vaccine Marketing Authorisation Application	January 2009	CHMP/VEG/4717/03 Rev 1
Guideline on Dossier Structure and Content of Marketing Authorisation Applications for Influenza Vaccines Derived from Strains with a Pandemic Potential for Use Outside the Core Dossier Context	January 2007	CHMP/VWP/263499/06
Guideline on Submission of Marketing Authorisation Applications for Pandemic Influenza Vaccines through the Centralised Procedure	April 2004	CPMP/4986/03

**Once finalised, this Quality Module will replace the guidelines that are 'shaded' in the table*

in December 2011. Since the consultation, two guidelines have been released,

- *Draft Guideline on Influenza Vaccines—Quality Module 2013. (EMA/CHMP/BWP/310834/2012)*
- *Procedural advice on the submission of variations for annual update of human influenza inactivated vaccines applications in the centralised procedure (EMA/CHMP/BWP/99698/2007 Rev. 2).*

FDA also has issued guidance on influenza vaccines for both seasonal and pandemic vaccines. For seasonal influenza vaccines, a guidance from May 2007, *Clinical Data Needed to Support the Licensure of Seasonal Inactivated Influenza Vaccines*, is widely used. Similarly, for pandemic influenza vaccines, FDA's position is discussed in *Clinical Data Needed to Support the Licensure of Pandemic Influenza Vaccines* (May 2007). In the US, the seasonal influenza vaccine process starts with the VRBPAC meeting in February, where the selection of reassortants or strains for the composition of the influenza vaccine are discussed for the upcoming flu season. During this meeting, the Advisory Committee reviews the surveillance data related to epidemiology and antigenic characteristics of recent influenza isolates, serological responses to previous influenza vaccines and notification from WHO.

In Australia, since the influenza season is different than the northern hemisphere, every September WHO issues recommendations on the strains. Following the recommendation, the Australian Influenza Vaccine Committee (AIVC) meets to discuss and recommend the composition of the vaccine strain for Australia.

Other Topics Related to Development of Vaccines

Vaccine development follows the same path as other drugs for human use. In general, during development there is a short- to medium-term goal of ensuring activities for clinical trial authorization and a long-term goal of fulfilling requirements for product licensure. Given the nature of vaccines (biologics, different risk versus benefit assessment, etc.), some aspects of the product require special attention even during early development, because the manufacturing process defines the product. It is always pragmatic to follow ICH and WHO guidelines even during early phases of development. A vaccine developed in line with ICH and WHO guidelines will face fewer regulatory hurdles in various countries around the world. If there are deviations from the guideline recommendation, they must be well justified. For global submissions, the use of the CTD format and eCTD is recommended. The CTD format is well accepted in many countries for license application, and the eCTD currently is accepted only in limited regions like Japan, Canada, the EU and the US. Other important considerations for vaccines are discussed below,

Drug Master File and Vaccine Antigen Master File

Vaccine antigen master files (VAMFs) and drug master files (DMFs) are complete dossiers on APIs or vaccine components. VAMFs and DMFs are "vehicles" used by the manufacturer to safeguard confidential information that is not available to third parties. These "master files" are designed to help both manufacturers and Competent Authorities reduce the number of submissions and assessments and ensure vaccine consistency. While a DMF in the US is more open to various components of the vaccine (like cell line, active substance, etc.), in the EU, such master files are not applicable for biological substances like vaccines and their components. This is due to a recommendation from the EU that the manufacturer have complete knowledge about the components, process, etc. of a complex product like a vaccine. Only antigens used in vaccines by the same manufacturer or MAH are allowed to use a VAMF.

If an antigen used in one component of a combination vaccine is also part of the other vaccine by the same manufacturer or MAH, this antigen can be subject to VAMF certification in the EU whereby the Competent Authority reviews and issues a VAMF certificate. In the EU, information on the scientific requirements and evaluation of the VAMF can be found in *Guideline on the Scientific Data Requirements for a Vaccine Antigen Master File* (EMEA/CPMP/BWP/3734/03). The guideline also clarifies the number of certificates required for certain vaccines, e.g., Polio (3); 23-valent Pneumococcal polysaccharide (23), etc. A manufacturer may choose to apply for VAMF certification at the Community level through EMA. A positive assessment of the submission results in the issuance of a VAMF certificate that can be used in all vaccines containing the same antigen. The certificate is also valid in all EU Member States. The procedural guidance is mentioned in *Guideline on requirements for Vaccine Antigen Master File (VAMF) certification* (EMEA/CPMP/BWP/4548/03).

In the US, the relevant regulation applicable to all vaccine components is 21 CFR 314.420 subpart G. The structure and content of DMFs are discussed under *Guideline for Drug Master files,* September 1989. In principle, in the US, it is possible to submit a DMF for any component of the vaccine (e.g., an adjuvant). However, FDA's guidance (*Cooperative Manufacturing Arrangements for Licensed Biologics*, 2008) recommends that for biologics, only certain information should be cross referenced to a DMF, e.g., container closure, etc.

Canada also has developed a Drug Master File system that allows sponsors to submit information on biological products to Health Canada. The guidance document (5 September 2008) on DMFs in Canada can be accessed at www.hc-sc.gc.ca/dhp-mps/prodpharma/applic-demande/guide-ld/chem/draft_ebauche_dmf_fmm_guide_ld-eng.php.

GMOs, DNA and Peptide Vaccines

Vaccine research in the past decade or more has focused on alternatives to the classic vaccine antigen approach. Newer vaccines are being developed that are genetically modified organisms (GMOs), DNA vaccines or peptide vaccines. These new types of vaccines present a challenge for both regulators and vaccine manufacturers. Usually, GMO vaccine candidates contain a vector or backbone that can be an attenuated virus or bacteria that contains a heterologous antigen or gene. These vaccine candidates are treated as GMOs and require environmental risk assessment in addition to the stringent quality, safety and efficacy assessment for both marketing authorization and clinical trial approval.

In the EU, special regulations and guidelines are in place for medicinal products using GMOs: Regulation (EC) No 726/2004, Directive 2001/18/EC and Directive 2008/27/EC (amending the previously mentioned directive) and guidelines such as *Environmental Risk Assessments for Medicinal Products Consisting of, or Containing, Genetically Modified Organisms (GMOs)* (EMEA/CHMP/BWP/473191/2006). Readers also are advised to refer to the *Guideline on quality, nonclinical and clinical aspects of live recombinant viral vectored vaccines* (EMA/CHMP/VWP/141697/2009). Usually, a GMO vaccine product requires more time for clinical trial assessment and includes additional reviews during license approval, e.g., in Germany a 90-day assessment of the CTA for a product containing a GMO in contrast to only 30 days for other medicinal products like conventional vaccines (**Figure 25-3**). As every country has different regulations and pathways, sponsors should check with their respective Competent Authority for more details on GMOs.

Assessing the environmental risks posed by a GMO product due to its release and/or excretion is an important aspect of the application. Live attenuated vaccines (not always GMOs) are subject to critical environmental assessment as they may find their way into the environment (*Environmental risk assessment of medicinal products for human use,* CHMP/SWP/4447/00). Recently, two products have been approved that are GMOs or produced from a GMO (Flublok,® approved in 2013, is a recombinant trivalent vaccine against influenza; Immojev,® approved in Australia, is a live attenuated chimeric vaccine against Japanese encephalitis).

WHO has issued a *Guideline for assuring the quality and nonclinical safety evaluation of DNA vaccines,* TRS 941 (2007). Although a concept paper was released by EMA on guidance for DNA vaccines, there is no specific guidance on the subject yet. Until such specific guidance is available, the *Note for guidance on the quality, preclinical and clinical aspects of gene transfer medicinal products* (CPMP/BWP/3088/99) should be followed. The US has published guidance on the development of plasmid vaccines: *Considerations for Plasmid DNA Vaccines for Infectious Disease Indications.* A guideline from WHO is available on *Production and quality control of synthetic peptide vaccines* TRS 889 (1997) *Annex 1*. Similar guidelines are not available from any other regulatory authority.

Therapeutic Vaccines

Therapeutic vaccines have seen a high interest in terms of new products being tested. Most of the research focuses on cancer and other life-threatening indications. Some of the products may involve genetically modified cells as therapeutic vaccines.

FDA published its expectations through guidance on the clinical considerations for therapeutic cancer vaccines in 2011, *Guidance for Industry: Clinical Considerations for Therapeutic Cancer Vaccines.* FDA also recently published *Draft Guidance for Industry: Immunogenicity Assessment for Therapeutic Protein Products.* The guideline suggests a risk-based approach to evaluating and mitigating immune responses to therapeutic proteins that may adversely affect their safety and efficacy.

Therapeutic vaccines currently are classified as ATMPs or advanced therapy medicinal products in the EU. Therapeutic vaccines are relatively new, and there are not many regulations in this field at this time. In the EU, no specific EMA guidelines have been issued on therapeutic vaccines. However, there are applicable guidelines on ATMPs, biologicals, cell-based products, etc. As all cancer therapies can be submitted through the Centralised Procedure, any cancer vaccine also will be regulated through the Centralised Procedure. If specific guidelines are not available, guidelines for similar products/indications should be followed, e.g., in this particular case, *Guideline on evaluation of anticancer medicinal products in men.* Until a guideline specific to cancer vaccines is available in the EU, manufacturers are advised to adhere to the US guideline.

Risk Management Plans and Pharmacovigilance of Vaccines

Compared to drugs, vaccines are generally safe medicinal products. Therefore, serious adverse events that are clinically relevant usually are rare and unlikely to be seen during vaccine development where exposure to vaccines is limited. Therefore, post-licensure monitoring of vaccines through Risk Management Plans (RMPs) and pharmacovigilance (PV) are important elements of the vaccine licensing process. Although RMPs and PV plans are required for all medicinal products, PV plans and RMPs for vaccines are unique in the following ways:

- Vaccines are given to healthy people, including children; consequently there is low tolerance for risks.
- There is no immediate benefit as diseases can be very rare, sometimes nonexistent (e.g., polio in the EU and US).
- Vaccines are provided to large populations.
- The population is very sensitive to a vaccine scare.

Vaccine dossiers, like those for other medicinal products, need to contain RMPs according to the *Guideline on Risk management systems for medicinal products for human use* (EMEA/CHMP/96268/2005). The RMP template also is provided by EMA. In the EU, PV for vaccines follows the procedures noted in Eudravigilance for all medicinal products. All adverse events in the EU are reported to either Member State Competent Authorities or centrally to Eudravigilance (http://eudravigilance.ema.europa.eu/human/index.asp). It is important to note that vaccine failures are considered adverse reactions. *Eudralex, The Rules Governing Medicinal Products in the European Union, Volume 9*, contains EU pharmacovigilance requirements (*Volume 9A* for human products and *Volume 9B* for veterinary products). *Volume 9A* describes overarching rules for PV procedures, documentation, etc. The regulation was adopted in December 2010 to overhaul the PV system and took effect from July 2012. One result of the revision is implementation of Good Pharmacovigilance Practices or GVPs. Detailed discussion on GVP is not possible here. The regulation is applicable to all medicinal products, including vaccines. Guidance for vaccine pharmacovigilance also was updated under the GVPs and issued as a draft guidance for public consultation (*Guideline on good pharmacovigilance practices (GVP): Product-or population-specific considerations I: Vaccines for prophylaxis against infectious diseases*, April 2013, (EMA/488220/2012)). This guidance also discusses adjuvants, preservatives, etc., that are normally inherent in vaccines, as these components may be responsible for adverse events.

A QP for Pharmacovigilance (QPPV) is essential for companies marketing their products in the EU. The requirements for this key role are described in detail in *Volume 9A*. The QPPV is tasked with establishing and maintaining the marketing authorization holder's pharmacovigilance system, overseeing product safety profiles, preparing periodic and other safety reports and acting as a central point of contact with authorities on a 24-hour basis.

In the US, however, there is a specific Vaccine Adverse Event Reporting System (VAERS) for adverse events in

Figure 25-3. Clinical trial approval timelines in Germany for Vaccines and Biotech products

Graphic display of the periods and process of clinical trial authorisations for Allergens, Vaccines and Biotech Products

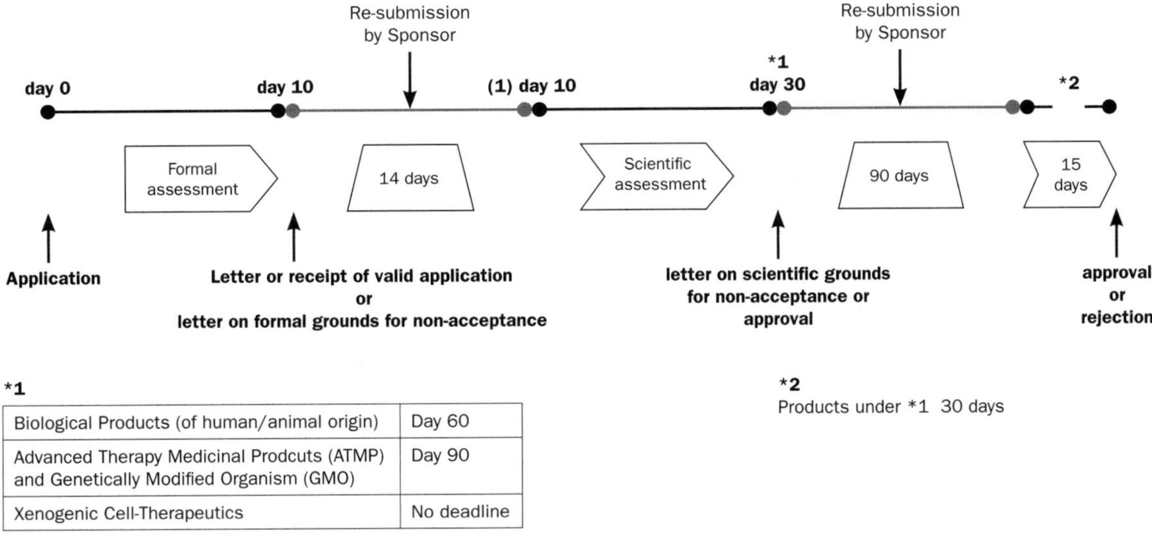

Biological Products (of human/animal origin)	Day 60
Advanced Therapy Medicinal Prodcuts (ATMP) and Genetically Modified Organism (GMO)	Day 90
Xenogenic Cell-Therapeutics	No deadline

Source Paul-Ehrlich Institute, Germany

vaccines. Risk management plans at FDA are known as Risk Evaluation and Mitigation Strategies or REMS. There are three guidances issued for medicinal products on this topic:

- *Guidance for Industry: Premarketing Risk Assessment* (Premarketing Guidance) (March 2005)
- *Guidance for Industry: Good Pharmacovigilance Practices and Pharmacoepidemiologic Assessment* (Pharmacovigilance Guidance) (March 2005)
- *Guidance for Industry: Development and Use of Risk Minimization Action Plans* (RiskMAP Guidance) (March 2005)

The pharmacovigilance system for vaccines in the US, VAERS, receives, compiles and analyzes vaccine adverse events. VAERS is managed by the Centers for Disease Control and FDA. Adverse events are reported to VAERS using a special form known as the VAERS-1 form. Regulations for postmarketing safety reporting for vaccines are mentioned under 21 CFR 600.80 and 81. FDA has issued specific guidance on postmarket safety reporting for vaccines (and drugs) in *Draft Guidance for Industry: Postmarketing Safety Reporting for Human Drug and Biological Products Including Vaccines* (2001).

Pricing, Reimbursement and Policymaking

Most vaccines are provided to children through their national immunization programs and are provided free of charge, but the government or insurance companies often pay for the vaccines. There are various models of cost sharing/reimbursement depending on the country. Therefore, vaccine pricing and reimbursement are also important elements of regulatory activities. Reimbursement and pricing are determined at a national level. Countries generally use some form of health technology assessment upon which to base their decisions.

Although vaccines are regulated by the Competent Authority, usually there is a national committee of experts that provides vaccine recommendations for the country. These recommendations generally are used as a national policy and are important to the reimbursement decision by the government. Well-known national committees include the Vaccines and Related Biologics Advisory Committee in the US and the Joint Committee on Vaccination and Immunization (JCVI) in the UK.

Summary

- General guidelines that are applicable to medicinal products also apply to vaccines.
- Biological and biotechnological product guidelines and those specifically for vaccines are more relevant than some medicinal product guidelines. Guidelines also are available for different disciplines such as the quality, nonclinical and clinical aspects of vaccine development.
- WHO and ICH are international institutions involved in the harmonization of vaccine guidelines.
- Successful global vaccine development can be pursued if WHO and ICH guidelines are followed throughout product development.

- WHO also issues guidelines for specific vaccines that are useful for both industry and Competent Authorities.
- In the EU, organizations at both the national and European level are involved in the regulation of vaccines.
- In the US, vaccines are regulated under the CFR for biologics.
- Every country has a specific lot release procedure that is followed for every vaccine and every lot.
- In the EU, lot release is done by any one laboratory of the OMCL.
- Adjuvant and immunomodulators are widely used in vaccines, with more adjuvants licensed in Europe than in the US.
- Seasonal influenza vaccines follow a well-defined path; pandemic influenza vaccines follow a core pandemic dossier approach.
- Vaccines that contain live virus vectors also are regulated as GMOs. Both licensure and clinical assessments of these products add complexity due to environmental assessments.
- DMF and VAMF may be used effectively in combination vaccines.
- Vaccines also are subject to pharmacovigilance and risk management procedures.
- The US has a specific vaccine adverse effects monitoring group called VAERS.
- In the EU, the pharmacovigilance system is undergoing a complete overhaul.
- Every EU Member State makes policies on vaccinations and reimbursement.

References

1. US Centers for Disease Control. Ten great public health achievements—United States, 1900–1999. MMWR 1999;48:241–3. CDC website. www.cdc.gov/mmwr/preview/mmwrhtml/00056796.htm. Accessed 24 March 2013.
2. WHO: Requirements for the use of animal cells as in vitro substrates for the production of biologicals (Requirements for Biological Substances No. 50). WHO Technical Report Series, No. 878. 1998; Annex 1. WHO website, www.who.int/biologicals/publications/trs/areas/vaccines/cells/WHO_TRS_878_A1Animalcells.pdf. Accessed 24 March 2013.
3. Robinson S. et al. A European pharmaceutical company initiative challenging the regulatory requirement for acute toxicity studies in pharmaceutical drug development, *Regul. Toxicol. Pharmacol.* (2008), 50 (3): 345-52. NCBI website. www.ncbi.nlm.nih.gov/pubmed/18295384. Accessed 24 March 2013.
4. Minor PD. Vaccines against seasonal and pandemic influenza and the implications of changes in substrates for virus production. *Clin Infect Dis* 2010; 50: 560-565. Oxford Journals website. http://cid.oxfordjournals.org/content/50/4/560.full. Accessed 24 March 2013.

Chapter 26

Products Manufactured From Human Blood and Plasma

By Birgit Hausberger Mag. rer. nat. and Anna-Veronika Schrodt Mag. phil.

OBJECTIVES

- ❑ Understand the definition of human blood and plasma-derived products and their importance for therapeutic treatment
- ❑ Provide examples of human blood and plasma products
- ❑ Understand the importance of quality control of human blood and plasma derived products and related challenges
- ❑ Gain familiarity with the Plasma Master File
- ❑ Gain a basic understanding of important guidelines, regulations and recommendations
- ❑ Identify the responsible regulatory organizations and obtain insight into the regulatory process for human blood or plasma products of the major agencies in the EU, US, Canada and Japan

REGULATIONS AND GUIDELINES COVERED IN THIS CHAPTER

EU

- ❑ Directive 2001/83/EC of the European Parliament and of the Council of 6 November 2001 on the Community code relating to medicinal products for human use, as amended
- ❑ *Guideline on Requirements for Plasma Master File (PMF) Certification*, CPMP/BWP/4663/03
- ❑ *Guideline on the Scientific Data Requirements for a Plasma Master File (PMF)*, EMEA/CHMP/BWP/3794/03 Rev. 1
- ❑ *Guideline on the warning on transmissible agents in summary of product characteristics (SmPCs) and package leaflets for plasma-derived medicinal products*. EMA/CHMP/BWP/360642/2010

US

- ❑ *Public Health Service Act*, Subpart I
- ❑ 21 CFR, Subchapter F, Subpart A 600.3(h)
- ❑ *Federal Food, Drug, and Cosmetic Act* (*FD&C Act*)
- ❑ 42 US Code 262

Japan

- ❑ *Japanese Pharmaceutical Affairs Law* (*PAL*)
- ❑ *Law Concerning Securing a Stable Supply of Safe Blood Products (Blood Law)*
- ❑ *Request of promoting proper use of fresh frozen blood plasma* 0709-1, 0709-2 and 0709-3

Canada

- ❑ *Food and Drugs Act* R.S.C., 1985, c. F-27

- ❑ Regulations C.R.C., c. 870, Divisions 4 and 8 of Part C
- ❑ Regulations Amending the Food and Drug Regulations (Human Plasma Collected by Plasmapheresis) SOR/2006-353
- ❑ *Guidance Document: Human Plasma Collected by Plasmapheresis* 08-102026-988
- ❑ Annex 2 to the Current Edition of the Good Manufacturing Practices Guidelines Schedule D Drugs (Biological Drugs)—GUI-0027

Introduction

Plasma

Human blood consists of blood cells and blood plasma, a yellow liquid that makes up approximately 60% of blood volume and holds the blood cells. Plasma consists mainly of water (92% by volume) and contains dissolved proteins (i.e., albumins, globulins and fibrinogen) and electrolytes, among many other components.

As plasma is not bound to a specific blood group, it can be universally deployed.

Human plasma for fractionation may be obtained as plasma donation by aphaeresis, a process by which blood is removed from the donor, the plasma is separated from the formed elements and the red blood cells are returned to the donor ("source plasma"), or it can be obtained as a by-product of whole blood donations ("recovered plasma").

Plasma-derived Products

The World Health Organization (WHO) defines plasma products as medicinal products obtained by a (large-scale) process by which plasma is separated into individual protein fractions that are further purified for medicinal use.[1] Other terms for plasma products are plasma derivatives, hemoderivatives or plasma-derived products.

Using either alcohol precipitation and subsequent biochemical separation techniques or chromatographic capture techniques, proteins are extracted from pooled plasma and used in the manufacture of therapeutic products, such as coagulation factors, fibrin sealants, coagulation inhibitors, immunoglobulins, albumin, etc.

Unlike "traditional" pharmaceutical drugs, plasma-derived therapies are often subject to changes that require regulatory activities prior to implementation since even minor changes in the manufacturing process may inadvertently result in significant and potentially dangerous differences in the final product.

Even though requirements relating to the quality and safety of the source material are often similar in different regions, regulatory approaches remain rather different.

Control of Starting Material and Manufacture

Due to the biological nature of the source material, plasma-derived products are subject to special controls to ensure the source material is free from disease-transmitting agents. To control the quality and safety in the manufacturing processes for plasma-derived products, it is essential to control the source material and its origin and to implement additional procedures for virus removal and virus inactivation.

In the mid-1980s, when plasma-derived products were identified as having caused widespread transmission of human immunodeficiency virus (HIV) and hepatitis C (HCV) virus, specific steps were introduced into the manufacturing process to inactivate or remove these and other blood-borne viruses. The period during which infectious donations are not detected has since been shortened by the introduction of the use of nucleic acid amplification technology (NAT) for viral DNA and RNA testing.

As knowledge of blood-transmittable diseases expands, safety measures continue to be adapted. At the start of the new millennium, the discovery that variant Creutzfeldt-Jakob Disease (vCJD) is transmissible through blood transfusions intensified concerns about possible unidentified ways in which the disease might spread. This led to more stringent measures to prevent the potential transmission of vCJD through human blood and plasma-derived products. Living in the UK is a recognized risk factor for vCJD. While the UK itself decided to no longer fractionate from UK plasma, other countries have introduced donor exclusion criteria, which during the risk period, prevent donors who have spent long periods in the UK from donating blood or plasma for fractionation.

The following procedures for virus inactivation/removal[2] are designed to ensure the safety of plasma derivatives:

- precipitation with ethanol
- heating in aqueous solution
- heating of lyophilised products
- solvent detergent treatment
- virus reduction filtration
- low pH

In addition, Good Manufacturing Practices (GMPs) should be adopted at all levels of the manufacturing process to avoid transmission of infectious agents.

WHO

The development of global guidelines and ensuring their appropriate use is one of the core functions of WHO. WHO provides technical guidance and quality assurance tools to regulatory authorities, National Control Laboratories

(NCLs) and manufacturers to support implementation of quality and safety systems for the production and control of blood products worldwide. Some of the most recent guidelines and recommendations related to human blood and plasma products are listed below:

- *WHO Recommendations for the Production, Control and Regulation of Human Plasma for Fractionation*
- *WHO Guidelines on Tissue Infectivity Distribution in Transmissible Spongiform Encephalopath*ies (2006)
- *WHO Guidelines on viral inactivation and removal procedures intended to assure the viral safety of human blood plasma products*, Technical Report Series (TRS) 924, Annex 4 (Adopted by ECBS 2001)
- *WHO Requirements for the collection, processing and quality control of blood, blood components and plasma derivatives*, TRS 840, Annex 2 (Adopted by ECBS 1992)
- *Regulation and licensing of biological products in countries with newly developing Regulatory Authorities*, TRS 858, Annex 1 (Adopted by ECBS 1994)
- *WHO Guidelines for national authorities on quality assurance for biological products*, TRS 822, Annex 2 (Adopted by ECBS 1991)
- *Quality and safety of blood products and related substances*, AIDE-MEMOIRE, WHO Ensuring the Quality and Safety of Plasma Derived Medicinal Products, Information Sheet

According to WHO, the main challenges and issues regarding human blood and plasma products are the need to:[3]

- strengthen national regulatory authorities on quality assurance systems for the control of quality and safety of blood products and in vitro diagnostic devices
- assure quality and safety of blood and plasma globally to prevent transmission of blood-borne viral diseases via blood products
- prioritize the development of WHO International Reference Materials of interest in regions and countries with limited resources
- facilitate the access to and the appropriate use of WHO International Reference Materials by NCLs or designated laboratories and manufacturers in developing countries
- promote support for the implementation of new manufacturing technologies to avoid viral contamination and other infectious agents via blood products

To improve cooperation and information-sharing among the leading regulatory agencies around the globe, the blood regulatory network was established in 2006.

Blood Regulators Network (BRN)

The Blood Regulators Network (BRN) is comprised of leading international regulatory authorities responsible for the regulation of blood, blood products and related in vitro diagnostic devices (IVD). The BRN provides a forum for the exchange of information and opinion among members on blood-related issues. The BRN focuses on scientific assessment of current and emerging threats to safety and availability of blood and blood products and assessment of the impact of new blood-related technologies, and also explores opportunities for regulatory cooperation and collaboration, where possible.

The objectives of the blood regulators network are to:

- identify issues
- share expertise and information
- promote convergence of regulatory policy
- propose solutions to specific issues, especially emerging public health challenges

EU

Special provisions for plasma-derived products were only brought into European Community legislation in 1989 by Council Directive 89/381/EEC, which extended the scope of Directives 65/65/EEC and 75/319/EEC and laid down requirements for medicinal products derived from human blood or human plasma.[4] In 2001, Council Directive 89/381/EEC was incorporated into Directive 2001/83/EC[5] on the Community code relating to medicinal products for human use, which lays down the general rules for Marketing Authorisation, authorization procedure, manufacture and importation, labeling, pharmacovigilance and advertising.

Medicinal products derived from human blood and human plasma are defined in Article 1(10) of Directive 2001/83/EC as follows: "Medicinal products based on blood constituents which are prepared industrially by public or private establishments, such medicinal products including, in particular, albumin, coagulating factors and immunoglobulin's of human origin."[6] The initial scope of Directive 2001/83/EC did not cover whole blood, plasma or blood cells of human origin.

The Community code requires the manufacturer to demonstrate its ability to attain batch-to-batch consistency and the absence of specific vial contamination.

Beginning in 2002, Directive 2001/83/EC was amended by the following directives to reflect new requirements relating to the source material for medicinal products derived from human blood and human plasma:

- Directive 2002/98/EC of the European Parliament and of the Council of 27 January 2003, also called the *Blood Directive*, applies both to blood and blood components for transfusion, as well as to human plasma for fractionation: "This Directive shall apply to collection and testing of human blood and blood components, whatever their intended purpose."[7] It replaces Article 109 of Directive 2001/83/EC with regard to the requirements for testing and collection of human blood and plasma. For all subsequent steps after collection and testing (e.g., processing, freezing, storage and transport to the manufacturer), requirements as laid down in Directive 2001/83/EC still apply.

It is important to note that Member States may introduce more stringent measures with regard to the quality and safety of blood and blood components, provided these measures comply with the treaty.

- Commission Directive 2003/63/EC of 25 June 2003 replaced Annex I to Directive 2001/83/EC and introduced the concept of the Plasma Master File (see below).[8]
- Directive 2004/27/EC of 31 March 2004 of the European Parliament and of the Council extended the scope of Directive 2001/83/EC to "plasma which is prepared by a method involving an industrial process" and amended the Community code with regard to Official Medicines Control Laboratories.[9]
- Commission Directive 2004/33/EC of 22 March 2004 defines certain technical requirements for blood and blood components, including eligibility of donors and storage, transport and distribution conditions.[10]
- Commission Directive 2005/61/EC of 30 September 2005 defines traceability requirements and reporting requirements in the event of serious adverse events and reactions.[11]
- Commission Directive 2005/62/EC of 30 September 2005 lays down standards and specifications relating to a quality system for blood establishments.[12]

Additional mandatory quality standards for plasma-derived medicinal products are provided in the *European Pharmacopoeia* monograph "Human plasma for fractionation" (No. 0853) and specific monographs for plasma-derived medicinal products.[13]

Guidance for GMP and other production and quality requirements

Annex 14 to the EU *Guidelines for Good Manufacturing Practice (GMP) for Medicinal Products for Human and Veterinary Use*[14] applies to medicinal products derived from human blood or plasma, fractionated in or imported into the EU/EEA. It was recently revised in the light of the above-mentioned directives. The requirements for collection and testing of starting materials derived from human blood and plasma are defined in Directive 2002/98/EC and relevant implementing directives, but for all subsequent steps after collection and testing (e.g., processing, freezing, storage and transport to the manufacturer) the requirements of Directive 2001/83/EC apply and must therefore be done in accordance with the principles and guidelines of GMP. The Committee for Medicinal Products for Human Use (CHMP) Biologics Working Party (BWP) was established to provide recommendations to the European Medicines Agency's (EMA) scientific committees and to establish guidelines related to quality and safety aspects of biological and biotechnological medicinal products. Among others, the BWP published *Note for Guidance on Plasma-derived medicinal products* (CPMP/BWP/269/95), which was recently replaced by the *Guideline on plasma-derived medicinal products,*[15] which provides guidance on source material, manufacture, quality control, virus inactivation/removal processes and risk assessment for virus transmission. The guideline emphasizes the importance of virus inactivation/removal steps: "For all plasma-derived medicinal products, it is an objective to incorporate effective steps for inactivation/removal of a wide range of viruses of diverse physico-chemical characteristics. (An effective step is defined in the Note for Guidance CPMP/BWP/268/95.) Thus it is desirable in most cases to incorporate two distinct effective steps which complement each other in their mode of action such that any virus surviving the first step would be effectively inactivated/removed by the second; at least one of the steps should be effective against non-enveloped viruses."[16]

Official Control Authority Batch Release (OCABR)

Official Medicines Control Laboratories (OMCL) are laboratories nominated by the national authority responsible for the quality control of medicines in their respective country. Their role is to support the regulatory authorities in controlling the quality of medicinal products available on the market.

Article 114 of Directive 2001/83/EC, as amended by Directive 2004/27/EC, states that "the competent authorities may require the marketing authorization holder for medicinal products derived from human blood or human plasma to submit samples from each batch of the bulk and/or the medicinal product for testing by an Official Medicines Control Laboratory or a laboratory that a Member State has designated for that purpose before being released into free circulation, unless the competent authorities of another Member State have previously examined the batch in question and declared it to be in conformity with the approved specifications."[17] OCABR performed by any given Member State thus must be mutually recognized by all other Member States requiring OCABR for that product.

Moreover, it is important to mention that the labeling of human blood and plasma products should indicate the risk of transmission of infective agents. Therefore, in 1994, the Committee for Proprietary Medicinal Products (now CHMP) recommended a standard text for the Summary of Product Characteristics (SmPC) and the user Package Leaflet to inform doctors and patients about the risk of transmission of infective agents associated with the administration of any human blood or plasma-derived medicinal products.

This warning text on transmissible agents has been reviewed and updated by the Blood Products Working Group (BPWG) and Biotechnology Working Party (BWP) in the core SmPCs for specific plasma-derived medicinal products approved since June 2000. The text can be modified if certain warnings are not valid for a specific product.

Additionally, since potential safety problems may be batch-related, health professionals are strongly advised to record the name and batch number of the product every time a plasma-derived medicinal product is administered to a patient in order to maintain a link between the patient and the batch of the product. Patients also are made aware of this recommendation through the warning statement in the user Package Leaflet.

Guideline on the warning on transmissible agents in summary of product characteristics (SmPCs) and package leaflets for plasma-derived medicinal products[18]

This guideline provides standard texts for warning statements on transmissible agents to be included in SmPCs and Package Leaflets for plasma-derived medicinal products. The original guideline[19] was adopted by CHMP in October 2003 and came into operation in May 2004. In 2011, the guideline was revised to include an update related to vCJD and new information concerning albumin as an excipient.

The Plasma Master File

In 2003, the European Commission introduced the concept of the Plasma Master File (PMF). In spite of the fact that the same plasma often is used in the manufacture of several medicinal products, the information relating to the source material was previously provided as part of each marketing authorization dossier. To simplify procedures for both the approval of and subsequent changes to human plasma-derived medicinal products, the plasma-related information could thereafter be provided as a separate file, evaluated centrally by the EMA:

> "A PMF should serve as a stand-alone document, which is separate from the marketing authorization dossier and through which a harmonized control of the relevant information regarding starting material used for the manufacture of plasma-derived medicinal products could be achieved."

As a first step, the PMF is assessed in a system analogous to the Centralised Procedure, and a certificate of compliance to Community legislation is issued. As a second step, the certificate of compliance is presented to the Competent Authority granting the medicinal products' marketing authorization(s). The Competent Authority shall take into account the effect of the certification of the PMF on the concerned medicinal product(s) without performing a reassessment of the PMF. In 2004, the BWP issued a guideline for the submission and evaluation (First Step) for PMF certification[21] as well as a guideline on the scientific data requirements for a PMF,[22] which was revised in 2006.

A PMF should include:

- a list of all products to which it applies, including, for example, medical devices incorporating stable derivatives of human blood or plasma, as well as active substances, excipients, stabilizers sold to other manufacturers
- information on centers or establishments in which blood or plasma collection is conducted
- annual reporting on epidemiological data for each center, as required per the *Guideline on epidemiological data on blood transmissible infections*[23]
- information on centers or establishments in which testing of blood/plasma is performed
- information on centers or establishments in which blood and/or plasma is stored
- information on establishments involved in the transport of plasma
- selection/exclusion criteria for blood/plasma donors
- information on system in place to ensure traceability
- information on the methods used for plasma testing, including validation data on tests performed on plasma pools
- information on the bags and bottles used for collection of blood/plasma
- procedures for any inventory hold period
- a characterization of the procedure or preparation and sampling of the plasma pool
- information on the system in place between the blood establishment(s), the product manufacturer and/or the PMF holder to ensure the fulfilment of Good Practice Requirements

Guidance on scientific and procedural requirements for the "Second Step" is provided in a Commission guideline.[24]

The PMF shall be updated and re-certified on an annual basis. Variations to the PMF must be submitted in accordance with Commission Regulation (EC) No 1234/2008 of 24 November 2008.[25]

If a marketing authorization holder decides not to use the PMF certification procedures, the information described in EMEA/CHMP/BWP/3794/03 should be provided in Module 3, section 3.2.S. of the documentation for the medicinal product.

The manufacturing process starting from the pooled plasma is not part of the PMF dossier; this should be described in the relevant sections of the dossier for each individual medicinal product.

In addition to quality control by the manufacturer, human blood and plasma products are subject to quality control by OMCLs.

US

Biologics are regulated and licensed under *Public Health Service Act*, Subpart I—Biological Products.

Biologics, including human blood and blood products, are defined in 21 CFR, Subchapter F, Subpart A 600.3(h),[26] as medicinal products used to prevent, treat or cure diseases or injuries of man, derived from or made with the aid of living organisms. Biologics are, in addition, classified and regulated as drugs under the *Federal Food, Drug, and Cosmetic Act* (*FD&C Act*).

The Regulation of Biological Products 42 US Code 262[27] defines a biological product as "a virus, therapeutic serum, toxin, antitoxin, vaccine, blood, blood component or derivative, allergenic product, protein (except any chemically synthesized polypeptide), or analogous product, or arsphenamine or derivative of arsphenamine (or any other trivalent organic arsenic compound), applicable to the prevention, treatment, or cure of a disease or condition of human beings."

A new human blood and blood product application must follow the Biologics License Application (BLA) process described in 21 CFR Part 601.[28] Changes to the licensed product, production process, quality control, equipment or facility subsequently must be approved by CBER.

Center for Biologics Evaluation and Research (CBER)

The Center for Biologics Evaluation and Research (CBER) is the center within FDA that regulates biological products for human use under applicable federal laws, including the *Public Health Service Act* and the *Federal Food, Drug and Cosmetic Act*. CBER protects and advances the public health by ensuring that biological products are safe and effective. CBER also is responsible for ensuring the safety of blood and blood products. CBER regulates the collection of blood and blood components used for transfusion or for the manufacture of pharmaceuticals derived from blood and blood components, such as clotting factors, and establishes standards for the products themselves. CBER also regulates related products, such as cell separation devices, blood collection containers and HIV screening tests used to prepare blood products or to ensure the safety of the blood supply. CBER develops and enforces quality standards, inspects blood establishments and monitors reports of errors, accidents and adverse clinical events.

There are product-specific offices within CBER. The Office of Blood Research and Review (OBRR) consists of three divisions:

- Division of Emerging Transfusion
- Division of Blood Applications
- Division of Hematology

CBER also works closely with other parts of the Public Health Service (PHS) to identify and respond to potential threats to blood safety, to develop safety and technical standards, to monitor blood supplies and to help industry promote an adequate supply of blood and blood products.[29]

The following measures are taken to provide safe blood and blood products:

- Blood donors are asked specific and very direct questions about risk factors that could indicate possible infection with a transmissible disease. This "up-front" screening eliminates approximately 90% of unsuitable donors.
- FDA requires blood centers to maintain lists of unsuitable donors to prevent the use of collections from them.
- In accordance with 21 CFR, Subchapter F, Subpart E 610.40, blood donations are tested for several different infectious agents using FDA-licensed test kits.

Plasma collection facilities are licensed independently from the final product; the responsibility for ensuring the quality of the plasma lies mostly with the collector.

Blood Establishment Registration and Product Listing

Blood establishments require a separate registration and licensing form (Form FDA 2830) and are subject to separate CGMP requirements for blood and blood components, as described in FDA's *Guideline for Quality Assurance in Blood Establishments*. There are also special guidelines for the inspection of blood banks. In addition, FDA inspects all blood facilities at intervals of at least two years, and "problem" facilities are inspected more often.

Regulation of the Blood Supply

FDA is responsible for regulatory oversight of the US blood supply. FDA promulgates and enforces standards for blood collection and for the manufacture of blood products, including both transfusible components of whole blood, pharmaceuticals derived from blood cells or plasma and related medical devices. FDA also inspects blood establishments and monitors reports of errors, accidents and adverse clinical events.

To increase the effectiveness of regulation of the blood industry, FDA has established the following initiatives.

Blood Action Plan

Created in 1997 to increase the effectiveness of scientific and regulatory actions and to ensure greater coordination, the Blood Action Plan addresses highly focused areas of concern, such as emergency operations, response to emerging diseases and updating regulations.

FDA Blood Products Advisory Committee

The Blood Products Advisory Committee (BPAC) reviews and evaluates available data concerning the safety, effectiveness and appropriate use of blood, products derived from blood and serum or biotechnology, which are intended for use in the diagnosis, prevention or treatment of human diseases, and, as required, any other product for which FDA has regulatory responsibility, and advises the FDA commissioner of its findings.

FDA Transmissible Spongiform Encephalopathies Advisory Committee

The Transmissible Spongiform Encephalopathies Advisory Committee (TSEAC) reviews and evaluates available scientific data concerning the safety of products that may be at risk for transmission of spongiform encephalopathies having an impact on public health as determined by the FDA commissioner.

Lot Release

Licensed biological products including products from human blood or plasma regulated by CBER undergo a special lot release under 21 CFR 610.2[30] because of their complexity. Samples of any lot of any licensed product together with the protocols showing results of applicable tests may at any time be required to be sent to the CBER director. Upon notification by the CBER director, a manufacturer shall not distribute a lot of a product before the lot has been released by the CBER director: provided that the CBER director shall not issue such notification except when deemed necessary for the product's safety, purity or potency.[31]

There are various guidelines/recommendations regarding biologics with special focus on human blood and plasma products. A list of current CBER guidelines is published quarterly in the *Federal Register* and also is available on CBER's website.

A few examples are listed below.

Draft Guidance for Industry: Revised Preventive Measures to Reduce the Possible Risk of Transmission of Creutzfeldt-Jakob Disease and Variant Creutzfeldt-Jakob Disease by Blood and Blood Products

This guidance is an amendment to the *Guidance for Industry: Revised Preventive Measures to Reduce the Possible Risk of Transmission of Creutzfeldt-Jakob Disease (CJD) and Variant Creutzfeldt-Jakob Disease (vCJD) by Blood and Blood Products*, dated May 2010 (2010 CJD/vCJD guidance) and contains revised recommendations for the labeling of plasma-derived products, including albumin and products containing plasma-derived albumin, to reflect current understanding of vCJD transmission through blood. This guidance is intended for manufacturers of plasma-derived products, including albumin, and products containing plasma-derived albumin.[32]

Guidance for Industry: Nucleic Acid Testing (NAT) to Reduce the Possible Risk of Human Parvovirus B19 Transmission by Plasma-Derived Products

This guidance provides recommendations to manufacturers of plasma-derived products for performing nucleic acid testing (NAT) for human parvovirus B19 as an in-process test for source plasma and recovered plasma used in the further manufacturing of plasma-derived products.[33]

Japan

The Japan Ministry of Health, Labour and Welfare (MHLW) is the governmental body for the regulatory system in Japan. It is organized into several departments; the Pharmaceutical and Food Safety Bureau (PFSB) handles blood and blood products.

PFSB consists of five divisions, one of which is the Blood and Blood Products division, which is responsible for the following functions:

- regulating blood collection services
- promoting blood donations
- assuring proper use of blood products and a stable supply of blood products
- maintaining a stable supply of blood products
- promoting, improving and coordinating the production and marketing of biological products

To harmonize government services, the Pharmaceutical and Medical Devices Agency (PMDA) was established in April 2004. PMDA has reorganized from the Offices of Biologics I and Biologics II, respectively, into new entities known as the Office of Cellular and Tissue-based Products and the Office of Vaccines and Blood Products. As of 1 October 2012, the Office of Vaccines and Blood Products is responsible for the regulatory oversight of vaccines, blood products and antitoxins.

In addition, the Pharmaceutical Affairs and Food Sanitation Council (PAFSC) serves as an advisory body to MHLW and reviews and discusses important pharmaceutical and food sanitation-related matters. The PAFSC has 17 committees and 18 subcommittees. The Committee on Blood Products has two subcommittees: Safety of Blood Products and Proper Use of Blood Products.[34]

Pharmaceutical Laws

Pharmaceutical administration in Japan is based on the following laws and regulations:

- *Pharmacists Law*

- *Law Concerning the Establishment for Pharmaceuticals and Medical Devices Organization*
- *Law Concerning Securing Stable Supply of Blood Products*
- Amends the *Pharmaceutical Affairs Law* (*PAL*) (Law No. 145), Law No. 96 of 2003 and Law No. 160 of 1956 to secure the safe supply of blood and blood products. The amendments concern regulations and approval application procedures for both drugs and devices where biologic products such as blood are involved.
- *Poisonous and Deleterious Substances Control Law*
- *Narcotics and Psychotropics Control Law*
- *Cannabis Control Law*
- *Opium Law*
- *Stimulants Control Law*

Detailed regulations are prepared by the government in the form of ministerial ordinances and notices for the enforcement and management of these laws.

Japanese PAL

The *PAL* regulates the manufacture, import and sale of drugs and medical devices. The basic purpose of the law is to ensure the safety, efficacy and quality of medical products in Japan. In 2003, the *PAL* defined a new category of "biologically derived products," named "specific biologically derived products," for so-called products that mainly use human blood- and tissue-based raw materials or ingredients, e.g., coagulation factors, human albumin serum, etc.

PAL states that safety measures must depend on product characteristics. These products are specially labeled with "特生物 (Specific biologically derived)," written in black on a white background framed by a black line. The production number/code also is indicated. Additionally, blood products and recombinant blood products that are substitutes for blood products should indicate the country where the blood and raw materials were collected and a distinction between "donated blood" and "non-donated blood." These allow free choice for patients who use these products.

The stable supply of the products concerned and their appropriate use are regulated under the *Law Concerning Securing a Stable Supply of Safety Blood Products (Blood Law)*, which also includes the above-mentioned labeling requirements.[35]

Request of Promoting Proper Use of Fresh Frozen Blood Plasma 0709-1, 0709-2 and 0709-3

This document requires local authorities and associations to promote proper use of fresh frozen blood plasma.

Canada

Health Canada's Biologics and Genetic Therapies Directorate (BGTD) is the Canadian federal authority that regulates human blood and plasma products. BGTD is organized into three centres:

- The Centre for Vaccine Evaluation (CVE)
- The Centre for Evaluation of Radiopharmaceuticals and Biotherapeutics (CERB)
- The Centre for Blood and Tissues Evaluation (CBTE)

The Centre for Blood and Tissues Evaluation (CBTE)

The Centre for Blood and Tissues Evaluation (CBTE) is responsible for the following products: blood and blood components, coagulation factors, immune globulins and other plasma derivatives and their recombinant analogues, cells and cell-based medicines, tissues and organs, xenografts and semen for in vitro fertilization. In addition, CBTE evaluates safety and clinical data for these products.

The Bureau of Biologics and Radiopharmaceuticals is responsible for the review and approval of all drug submissions for biologicals (Schedule D). Schedule D biological products include human blood and plasma products.

All drugs marketed in Canada are subject to the *Food and Drugs Act* (R.S.C., 1985, c. F-27) and *Regulations* (C.R.C., c. 870). For regulatory requirements specific to biological drug products (Schedule D to the regulations), please refer to Divisions 4 and 8 of Part C of the regulations.

CPID Certified Product Information Document—Chemical Entities

The CPID-CE is a condensed version of the Quality Overall Summary and represents the final, agreed data from the drug submission review (e.g., identification of the manufacturer(s), drug substance/drug product specifications, stability conclusions).The CPID-CE constitutes part of the Notice of Compliance (NOC) package and serves as an official reference document during the course of postapproval inspections and postapproval change evaluations by Health Canada.

As part of the New Drug Submission process, biologics manufacturers also must supply Product Specific Facility Information that outlines the method of manufacture of the biologic in significant detail, since slight variations can result in a different final product. Further, an inspection of the manufacturing facility, known as an On-Site Evaluation (OSE), is completed to assess the production process and facility since these aspects also have a significant impact on the product's safety and efficacy. If there is sufficient evidence to support safety, efficacy or quality claims for a New Drug Submission (NDS) or a Supplement to a New Drug Submission (S/NDS), the product is issued an NOC and a Drug Identification Number (DIN), indicating that the biologic is approved for sale in Canada.

Lot Release

Each lot of a Schedule D (biologic) drug is subject to the Lot Release Program before sale in Canada. The Lot Release Program derives its legislative authority from section C.04.015 of the *Food and Drug Regulations*. Products are assigned to one of four Evaluation Groups, with each group having different levels of regulatory oversight (testing and/or protocol review) based on the degree of risk associated with the product. The graduated risk-based approach to testing and oversight allows BGTD to focus ongoing testing on products for which enhanced surveillance is indicated, such as vaccines and blood products. The criteria used to determine the appropriate Evaluation Group include, but are not limited to, the nature of the product, the target population, the lot testing history in BGTD and the manufacturer's production and testing history.

Health Canada, in collaboration with the Public Health Agency of Canada, also monitors biologic adverse events, investigates complaints and problem reports, maintains postapproval surveillance and manages recalls, as required.[36]

Regulations Amending the Food and Drug Regulations (Human Plasma Collected by Plasmapheresis) SOR/2006-353

The objective of Regulation SOR/2006-353 is to maximize the safety and quality of human plasma collected by plasmapheresis and to maximize the safety of the donors participating in plasmapheresis. The regulation also reflects the current practice of plasma collection and methods of testing as well as a list of transmissible diseases for which tests should be performed.[37]

Guidance Document: Human Plasma Collected by Plasmapheresis 08-102026-988

The document provides regulatory guidance to Canadian establishments that collect human plasma by plasmapheresis for use in the manufacture of human drugs.[38]

Annex 2 to the Current Edition of the Good Manufacturing Practices Guidelines Schedule D Drugs (Biological Drugs)—GUI-0027

The purpose of this guideline is to provide additional interpretive guidance for Part C, Division 2, of the *Food and Drug Regulations* for Schedule D (biological) drugs. These guidelines are designed to facilitate compliance by the regulated industry and to enhance consistency in the application of the regulatory requirements. The guidance provided in this annex is applicable to the manufacture and control of bulk intermediates and finished Schedule D (biological) drugs, including: vaccines; fractionated plasma products (human, animal); antigens; allergens; hormones; cytokines; enzymes and products of prokaryotic and eukaryotic cell cultures (including monoclonal antibodies and products derived from rDNA technology). Interpretation of Health Canada/Health Products and Food Branch Inspectorate GMP requirements for the collection and processing of human blood and blood components is not within the scope of this guidance.[39]

Australia

The Therapeutic Goods Administration (TGA) is the regulatory agency responsible for regulating biologics, medicines and medical devices. TGA is a division of the Australian Government Department of Health and Ageing. In addition to evaluating therapeutic goods before they are marketed and monitoring products once they are on the market, TGA also assesses the suitability of medicines and medical devices for export from Australia.

TGA manages a number of committees, which provide independent advice on different areas of therapeutic goods administration (e.g., Advisory Committee on Prescription Medicines, Committee on Biologicals, Advisory Committee on Medical Devices).

Blood and blood components are not biologicals for the purposes of the *Therapeutic Goods Act* of 1989 (*TG Act*); they are regulated as medicines under Part 3-2 of the act. The legislation also allows the secretary to declare specific therapeutic goods as biologicals. Goods declared not to be biologicals are regulated by TGA as either a medicine or a medical device, but are not included in the Biologicals Regulatory Framework. These products are included in the Therapeutic Goods (products that are not biologicals) Determination No. 1 of 2011.[40]

The following products are currently declared not to be biological:

- haematopoietic progenitor cells (used for haematopoietic reconstitution), other than those that are excluded from regulation (see above)
- samples of human cells or tissues that are solely for diagnostic purposes in the same individual
- blood and blood components
- IVDs
- biological medicines including:
  - vaccines (that do not contain viable human cells)
  - recombinant products
  - plasma-derived products (or that contain plasma-derived products)

Figure 26-1 shows the relationship between products that are excluded as therapeutic goods, and those that are and are not included as biologicals.

Any product for which therapeutic claims are made by the manufacturer must be entered in the Australian Register

Figure 26-1. Regulatory Framework for Biologicals in Australia

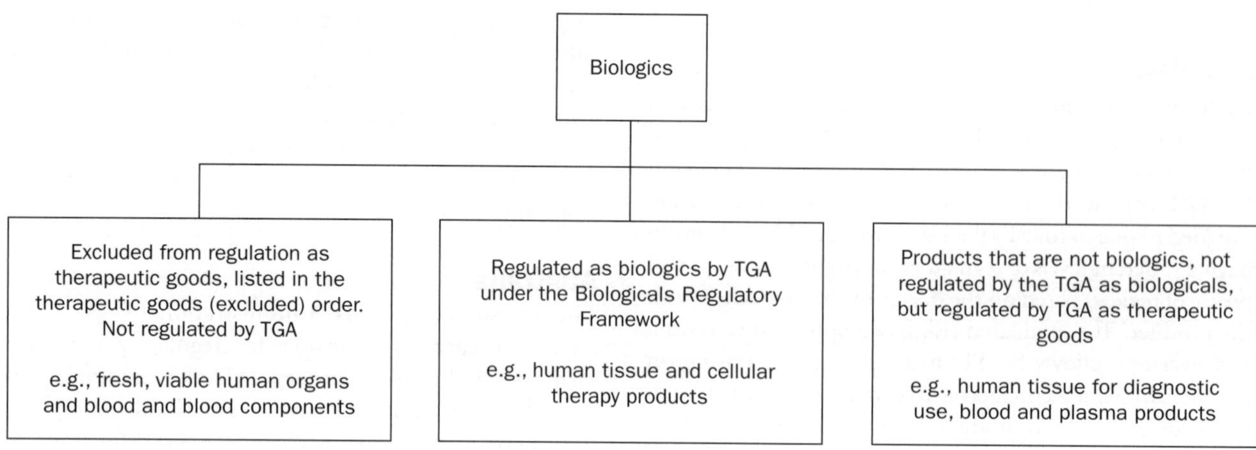

of Therapeutic Goods (ARTG) before it can be imported, exported or supplied for use in Australia.

Some basic TGA regulations with regard to human blood and plasma products are mentioned below.

TG Act 1989, Act No. 21 of 1990 as Amended

Blood, blood components and plasma derivatives are regulated under the *TG Act*. Plasma derivatives are prescription medicines subject to full regulation under provisions requiring standards, licensing of manufacture and inclusion in ARTG after the manufacturing, preclinical and clinical data are reviewed.[41]

Therapeutic Goods Order No. 81 Standards for Blood and Blood Components, Therapeutic Goods Act 1989, Section 10

Therapeutic Goods Order Number 81 states that blood and blood components must meet the requirements of the European Directorate for the Quality of Medicines and Healthcare of the Council of Europe document *Guide to the preparation, use and quality assurance of blood components* and must only be manufactured from blood that tests negative for HIV-1 and HCV using Nucleic Acid Amplification Technology.

Furthermore, the Therapeutic Goods Order contains two additional donor exclusion criteria relating to residence in the UK.

Guidance on donor selection, testing and minimising infectious disease transmission via therapeutic goods that are human blood and blood components, human tissues and human cellular therapy products describes in detail the requirements for donor selection, testing and minimizing infectious disease transmission via therapeutic goods that are human blood and blood components, human tissues and human cellular therapy products.[42]

TG Act 1989 Therapeutic Goods (Manufacturing Principles) Determination No. 1 of 2007

The *TG Act* determines that manufacturer(s) of plasma require a license under Chapter 3, Part 3-3 Section 36(1) of the act. Plasma, in this context, means "plasma, separated from human donor blood, intended for a number of purposes including the production of further blood components."[43]

Australian Code of Good Manufacturing Practice for Human Blood and Tissues

Manufacturers of blood and blood components and plasma must comply with the Australian GMP code and the relevant technical master file lodged by the manufacturer.

Hong Kong

The Department of Health (DH) is responsible for overseeing safety, efficacy and quality of all medicines marketed in Hong Kong. Medicines can be divided into Chinese medicines and non-Chinese medicines (or Western medicines) as they are regulated under different ordinances, i.e., *Chinese Medicine Ordinance* (Cap. 549) and *Pharmacy and Poisons Ordinance* (Cap.138) respectively.

Upon registration, a registration number will be assigned by the Pharmacy and Poisons Board (PPB), e.g., HK-12345, that is required to be printed on the medicine label. This allows the public to check the registration number on the label to see whether the medicine is registered.[44]

Pharmacy and Poisons Ordinance (Cap. 138)

According to the *Pharmacy and Poisons Ordinance* (Cap. 138), medicines to be applied to human or animal bodies for the diagnosis, treatment, relief or prevention of diseases must be registered with the PPB prior to marketing. The *Pharmacy and Poisons Ordinance* deals with blood products derived from human blood or manufactured by biotechnology e.g., albumin, fibrin, plasma proteins, etc.

"Poison" means a substance that is specified in the Poisons List under the *Poisons List Regulation* (Cap. 138). The packaging of the substance must be labeled with the term "poison," which does not imply that the substance is poisonous.

According to legislation in Hong Kong, medicines are classified into three main categories according to the severity of the diseases they are intended for and the magnitude of their side effects. Medicines in different categories have to be sold by different registered retailers under different specified conditions. For registration of products containing biologics, including human blood and plasma products, the *Guidance Notes on Registration of Pharmaceutical Products/Substance* apply.

The following information needs to be submitted:

- official evidence of registration approval of the product (e.g., original or certified true copies of free sale certificates) in two or more of the following countries: Australia, Austria, Belgium, Bulgaria, Canada, Cyprus, Czech Republic, Denmark, Estonia, Finland, France, Germany, Greece, Holland, Hungary, Ireland, Italy, Japan, Latvia, Lithuania, Luxembourg, Malta, Poland, Portugal, Romania, Slovak Republic, Slovenia, Spain, Sweden, Switzerland, UK and US
- signed expert evaluation reports on the product's safety, efficacy and quality; curriculum vitae of the expert
- EU Risk Management Plan (EU-RMP) and/or FDA Risk Evaluation and Mitigation Strategy (REMS); information on whether any of the risk management plan activities and mitigation strategies will be implemented in Hong Kong
- proposed package insert of the product; where the package insert is in the form of a patient information leaflet, a prescribing information leaflet for Health Professionals for use in Hong Kong also should be submitted
- clinical and scientific documentation substantiating the product's safety and efficacy[45]

(For a complete list, please refer to the above-mentioned guidance.)

India

The Ministry of Health and Welfare, the department of the Drug Controller General of India (DCGI) and the Central Drugs Standard Control Organization (CDCSO) are responsible for Biologic License Applications (BLA). BLAs are handled as New Drug Applications (NDAs) as long as they do not contain genetically modified organisms (GMOs). Marketing authorization applications for biologics or blood products must be submitted to CDSCO. The dossier should be submitted in CTD format; see guidance for preparation of the quality information for drugs.

There are only a few regulations for biologic products in India:

- *Drug and Cosmetics Act* of 1940
  The objective of the act is to regulate the import, manufacture, distribution and sale of drugs. Under the provisions of this act, the Central Government appoints the Drugs Technical Advisory Board to advise the central government and the state governments on technical matters arising out of the administration of this act. The board can constitute subcommittees for the consideration of a particular matter. Biologicals and special products are handled under schedule C.
- *Guidance for Industry: Preparation of the Quality Information for Drug* QI/71108
- *Guidance for submission of biological applications*

Haemovigilance Programme

The Indian Pharmacopoeia Commission in collaboration with the National Institute of Biologicals launched the Haemovigilance Program (biovigilance program) in December 2012 to collect and analyze data with respect to biologicals and haemovigilance.

Special scope:

- to track adverse reactions/events and incidents associated with biologicals, blood transfusion and blood product administration (haemovigilance) as well as tissue organ and cell therapy transplantation
- to help identify trends, recommend best practices and interventions required to improve patient care and safety, while reducing overall cost of the healthcare system[46]

Russia

The Ministry of Health and Social Development of the Russian Federation (Minsotsrazvitiye) is the federal executive authority in charge of:

- pharmaceutical industry: quality, efficiency and safety of pharmaceutical products
- medical and biological evaluation of the impact of hazardous factors of physical and chemical natures on the human body

The regulatory authority is the federal Service on Supervision in the Sphere of Public Health Services and Social Development (Roszdravnadzor).

The National Center of Pharmaceutical Products Expertise (FGU) is the key government body responsible for quality, safety and efficacy review.

Federal Law on Licensing of Certain Types of Activities

This federal law regulates the licensing system in Russia.

According to the law, the list of licensed types of activities has been reduced; however, the licensing of medicinal and pharmaceutical activities has been retained. This law introduces a uniform procedure for issuing licenses.

Packaging and Labeling Requirements

Drugs derived from human blood, blood plasma, organs and tissues should contain the following inscription on the secondary (consumer) packaging: "There are no HIV-1, HIV-2, hepatitis C virus antibodies and the hepatitis B virus surface antigen."

Special Dossier Requirements

A Normative Documentation (ND) in Russian language summarizing module 3 and the labeling for a specific product (based on the Russian Pharmacopeia and if necessary European Pharmacopoeia and US Phamacopeia) need to be provided. The ND forms the basis for local batch release of biological products, whereby each batch is checked/retested against the ND.

Mandatory testing for different groups of biological products is laid down in industrial standards.

Argentina

The National Administration of Drugs, Foods and Medical Devices (ANMAT), created in 1992, is the Argentinean regulatory agency. It operates under the authority of the Ministry of Health Secretariat of Policies, Regulation and Institutes' standards and guidelines.

The requirements for the registration of biologics, including plasma-derived products, are laid down in Order 7075/11 of October 2011.

For the registration of biologics, the dossier should be organized in five chapters, similar to the CTD structure:

- Chapter 1: Administrative information
- Chapter 2: Summaries of the Quality, Preclinical, and Clinical documentation
- Chapter 3: Information related to Quality
- Chapter 4: Preclinical Information
- Chapter 5: Clinical Information

For plasma-derived products, Chapter 3 should provide information on the origin of the blood or plasma used as source material, quality specifications and detection of adventitious agents, and demonstrate freedom from adventitious agents or the ability to eliminate or reduce them during the manufacturing process.

Brazil

The National Health Surveillance Agency (ANVISA) was established in 1999 as the Brazilian regulatory agency responsible for medicinal products for human use. Its mission is "to protect and promote health, ensuring the hygiene and safety of products and services and taking part in developing access to it."

Resolution RDC No. 46, adopted in May 2000, sets standards for production processes, quality control and distribution of plasma-derived products. This resolution requires that serological testing of single donations be performed in accordance with the European Pharmacopoeia Monograph "Human Plasma for Fractionation," current edition.

In December 2010, ANVISA adopted Resolution RDC No. 55, which addresses registration requirements for biologicals. Requirements specific to hemoderivatives are detailed in Resolution RDC No. 55 chapter III, section III, Article 32.

In addition to serological testing of single donations and manufacturing pools for HIV-1/-2, HCV, HBsAg and syphilis, testing also is required on the finished product.

When registering a plasma-derived product, the applicant must present a list of plasma collection sites, a list of the serological tests and NAT tests (including their validation), as well as a description of any virus removal or virus inactivation procedures and their validation, among other requirements.

Resolution RDC No. 49, dated September 2011, provides requirements on post-registration changes and inclusions, suspension and reactivation of manufacturing and cancellations of biological product registration. Post-registration changes are classified into level 1 changes (minor changes waiving prior authorization for implementation), level 2 changes (moderate changes requiring authorization prior to implementation) and level 3 changes (major changes requiring authorization prior to implementation). Changes specific to plasma-derived products are listed in Chapter XVI (Change or Inclusion of Blood-Derived Excipient Manufacturing Site) and Chapter XVII (Change of Plasma Collection Centers).

Summary

Generally, plasma-derived products are subject to similar requirements to ensure the safety and quality of the starting material, during the manufacturing process and for batch release. Major discrepancies continue to persist, however, with regard to the detail of information to be provided to regulatory agencies.

While EU authorities emphasize traceability to facilitate rapid identification of affected products in the event of a failure at the collection center level (and vice versa), thus requiring information on the establishments supplying plasma to the fractionators to be part of the medicinal product's dossier, FDA views plasma sold to manufacturers as a licensed product in itself. For this reason, product dossiers for submission to FDA do not need to contain the same level of detail as EU dossiers.

Non-ICH countries have recently started to place a stronger emphasis on the publication of guidance documents that address safety issues of using plasma as source material for medicinal products; these are often based on existing EU, FDA or WHO requirements.

References

1. WHO *Recommendations for the Production, Control and Regulation of Human Plasma for Fractionation*. WHO website. http://apps.who.int/medicinedocs/en/m/abstract/Js19650en/. Accessed 4 April 2013.
2. *Guideline on plasma-derived medicinal products* EMA/CHMP/BWP/706271/2010. EMA website. www.ema.europa.eu/docs/en_GB/document_library/Scientific_guideline/2011/07/WC500109627.pdf. Accessed 4 April 2013.
3. WHO *Quality Assurance and Safety: Blood Products and related Biologicals*. WHO website. http://www.who.int/bloodproducts/en/. Accessed 29 March 2013.
4. Council Directive of 14 June 1989 extending the scope of Directives 65/65/EEC and 75/319/EEC on the approximation of provisions laid down by law, regulation or administrative action relating to proprietary medicinal products and laying down special provisions for medicinal products derived from human blood or human plasma (89/381/EEC). EUR-Lex website. http://eur-lex.europa.eu/LexUriServ/LexUriServ.do?uri=OJ:L:1989:181:0044:0046:EN:PDF. Accessed 4 April 2013.
5. Directive 2001/83/EC of the European Parliament and of the Council of 6 November 2001 on the Community code relating to medicinal products for human use. EMA website. www.emea.europa.eu/docs/en_GB/document_library/Regulatory_and_procedural_guideline/2009/10/WC500004481.pdf. Accessed 4 April 2013.
6. Ibid.
7. Directive 2002/98/EC of the European Parliament and of the Council of 27 January 2003 setting standards of quality and safety for the collection, testing, processing, storage and distribution of human blood and blood components and amending Directive 2001/83/EC. EUR-Lex website. http://eur-lex.europa.eu/LexUriServ/LexUriServ.do?uri=OJ:L:2003:033:0030:0040:EN:PDF. Accessed 4 April 2013.
8. Commission Directive 2003/63/EC of 25 June 2003 amending Directive 2001/83/EC of the European Parliament and of the Council on the Community code relating to medicinal products for human use. EUR-Lex website. http://eur-lex.europa.eu/LexUriServ/LexUriServ.do?uri=OJ:L:2003:159:0046:0094:en:PDF. Accessed 4 April 2013.
9. Directive 2004/27/EC of the European Parliament and of the Council of 31 March 2004 amending Directive 2001/83/EC on the Community code relating to medicinal products for human use. EUR-Lex website. http://eur-lex.europa.eu/LexUriServ/LexUriServ.do?uri=OJ:L:2004:136:0034:0057:EN:PDF. Accessed 4 April 2013.
10. Commission Directive 2004/33/EC of 22 March 2004 implementing Directive 2002/98/EC of the European Parliament and of the Council as regards certain technical requirements for blood and blood components. EUR-Lex website. http://eur-lex.europa.eu/LexUriServ/LexUriServ.do?uri=OJ:L:2004:136:0034:0057:EN:PDF. Accessed 4 April 2013.
11. Commission Directive 2005/61/EC of 30 September 2005 implementing Directive 2002/98/EC of the European Parliament and of the Council as regards traceability requirements and notification of serious adverse reactions and events. EUR-Lex website. http://eur-lex.europa.eu/LexUriServ/LexUriServ.do?uri=OJ:L:2005:256:0032:0040:EN:PDF. Accessed 4 April 2013.
12, Commission Directive 2005/62/EC of 30 September 2005 implementing Directive 2002/98/EC of the European Parliament and of the Council as regards Community standards and specifications relating to a quality system for blood establishments. EUR-Lex website. http://eur-lex.europa.eu/LexUriServ/LexUriServ.do?uri=OJ:L:2005:256:0041:0048:EN:PDF. Accessed 4 April 2013.
13. European Pharmacopoeia Online. http://online.edqm.eu/EN/entry.htm. Accessed 29 March 2013.
14. EudraLex—Volume 4 Good manufacturing practice (GMP) Guidelines. EC website. http://ec.europa.eu/health/documents/eudralex/vol-4/index_en.htm . Accessed 29 March 2013.
15. Op cit 2.
16. Ibid.
17. Op cit 5.
18. *Guideline on the warning on transmissible agents in summary of product characteristics (SmPCs) and package leaflets for plasma-derived medicinal products*, EMA/CHMP/BWP/360642/2010 rev. 1. EMA website. www.ema.europa.eu/docs/en_GB/document_library/Scientific_guideline/2011/12/WC500119001.pdf. Accessed 4 April 2013.
19. *Note for Guidance on the warning on transmissible agents in summary of product characteristics (SPCs) and package leaflets for plasma-derived medicinal products*, CPMP/BPWG/BWP/561/03. EMA website. www.emea.europa.eu/docs/en_GB/document_library/Scientific_guideline/2009/09/WC500003590.pdf. Accessed 4 April 2013.
20. Op cit 18.
21. *Guideline on Requirements for Plasma Master File (PMF) Certification*, CPMP/BWP/4663/03. EC website. http://ec.europa.eu/health/files/eudralex/vol-2/c/466303en_08_2004_en.pdf. Accessed 4 April 2013.
22. *Guideline on epidemiological data on blood transmissible infections*, EMA/CHMP/BWP/548524/2008. EMA website. www.ema.europa.eu/docs/en_GB/document_library/Scientific_guideline/2010/10/WC500097728.pdf. Accessed 4 April 2013.
23. Ibid.
24. *Guideline on Plasma Master File (PMF) and Vaccine Antigen Master File (VAMF)*. EC website. http://ec.europa.eu/health/files/eudralex/vol-2/c/2ndstepvamfpmf_08_2004.pdf. Accessed 29 March 2013.
25. Commission Regulation (EC) No 1234/2008 of 24 November 2008 concerning the examination of variations to the terms of marketing authorizations for medicinal products for human use and veterinary medicinal products. EUR-Lex website. http://eur-lex.europa.eu/LexUriServ/LexUriServ.do?uri=OJ:L:2008:334:0007:0024:en:PDF. Accessed 4 April 2013.
26. 21 CFR, Subchapter F, Subpart A 600.3(h). FDA website. www.accessdata.fda.gov/scripts/cdrh/cfdocs/cfcfr/cfrsearch.cfm?fr=600.3. Accessed 4 April 2013.
27. 42 U.S.C. 262. GPO website. www.gpo.gov/fdsys/pkg/USCODE-2010-title42/pdf/USCODE-2010-title42-chap6A-subchapII-partF-subpart1-sec262.pdf. Accessed 4 April 2013.
28. 21 CFR Part 601. FDA website. www.accessdata.fda.gov/scripts/cdrh/cfdocs/cfcfr/CFRsearch.cfm?CFRPart=601. Accessed 4 April 2013.
29. About the Center for Biologics Research and Evaluation. FDA website. www.fda.gov/AboutFDA/CentersOffices/OfficeofMedicalProductsandTobacco/CBER/default.htm. Accessed 29 March 2013.
30. 21 CFR 610.2. FDA website. www.accessdata.fda.gov/scripts/cdrh/cfdocs/cfcfr/CFRSearch.cfm?fr=610.2. Accessed 4 April 2013.
31. Ibid.
32. *Draft Guidance for Industry: Revised Preventive Measures to Reduce the Possible Risk of Transmission of Creutzfeldt-Jakob Disease and Variant Creutzfeldt-Jakob Disease by Blood and Blood Products*. FDA website. www.fda.gov/downloads/biologicsbloodvaccines/guidancecomplianceregulatoryinformation/guidances/ucm213415.pdf. Accessed 4 April 2013.

33. *Guidance for Industry: Nucleic Acid Testing (NAT) to Reduce the Possible Risk of Human Parvovirus B19 Transmission by Plasma-Derived Products.* FDA website. www.fda.gov/biologicsbloodvaccines/guidancecomplianceregulatoryinformation/guidances/blood/ucm071592.htm. Accessed 4 April 2013.
34. English regulatory information task force Japan Pharmaceutical Manufacturers Association "Pharmaceutical administration and regulation in Japan," March 2012. JPMA website. www.jpma.or.jp/english/parj/1203.html. Accessed 4 April 2013.
35. Law Concerning Securing a Stable Supply of Safety Blood Products. See Yasuda N presentation "Regulatory framework for blood and blood components in Japan," October 2012. ICDRA website. http://icdra.ee/attachments/article/18/5-Naoyuki-Yasuda.pdf. Accessed 4 April 2013.
36. Drugs and Health Products. Health Canada website. www.hc-sc.gc.ca/dhp-mps/index-eng.php. Accessed 29 March 2013.
37. Regulations Amending the Food and Drug Regulations (Human Plasma Collected by Plasmapheresis) SOR/2006-353. Canada Gazette website. http://canadagazette.gc.ca/archives/p2/2006/2006-12-27/html/sor-dors353-eng.html. Accessed 4 April 2013.
38. *Guidance Document: Human Plasma Collected by Plasmapheresis,* 08-102026-988. Health Canada website, www.hc-sc.gc.ca/dhp-mps/brgtherap/applic-demande/guides/plasmapheresis/plasma-eng.php. Accessed 4 April 2013.
39. Annex 2 to the Current Edition of the Good Manufacturing Practices Guidelines Schedule D Drugs (Biological Drugs) (GUI-0027). Health Canada website. www.hc-sc.gc.ca/dhp-mps/compli-conform/gmp-bpf/docs/gui-0027_annexe_d-eng.php. Accessed 4 April 2013.
40. *Australian Regulatory Guidelines for Biologics, Part 1: Introduction to the Australian Regulatory Guidelines for Biologicals.* TGA website. www.tga.gov.au/pdf/biologicals-argb-p1.pdf. Accessed 4 April 2013.
41. *Therapeutic Goods Act* of 1989, Act No. 21 of 1990 as amended. WHO website. http://apps.who.int/medicinedocs/documents/s18007en/s18007en.pdf. Accessed 4 April 2013.
42. Therapeutic Goods Order No. 81 Standards for Blood and Blood Components, Therapeutic Goods Act 1989, Section 10. Australian Government ComLaw website. www.comlaw.gov.au/Details/F2008L04724. Accessed 4 April 2013.
43. *Therapeutic Goods Act* 1989 Therapeutic Goods (Manufacturing Principles) Determination No. 1 of 2007. Australian Government ComLaw website. www.comlaw.gov.au/Details/F2007L04726. Accessed 4 April 2013.
44. Hong Kong Department of Health homepage. www.dh.gov.hk. Accessed 29 March 2013.
45. Ibid.
46. India Ministry of Health and Family Welfare homepage. www.mohfw.nic.in. Accessed 29 March 2013.

Chapter 27

Principles of Orphan Drugs

Updated by Nicole Beard MSc, PhD

OBJECTIVES

- Examine the characteristics of orphan diseases, in particular their rarity
- Obtain a basic understanding of the principles for orphan drug designation and authorization
- Understand the differences between current orphan laws
- Understand the incentives introduced to stimulate development of drugs for orphan diseases

REGULATIONS AND GUIDELINES COVERED IN THIS CHAPTER

- *Orphan Drug Act* of 1983, Public Law 97-414, with amendments in 1985, 1988 and 1992
- Regulation (EC) 141/2000 of the European Parliament and of the Council of 16 December 1999 on orphan medicinal products
- Regulation (EC) No 726/2004 of the European Parliament and of the Council of 31 March 2004laying down Community procedures for the authorisation and supervision of medicinal products for human and veterinary use and establishing a European Medicines Agency
- *Guideline on aspects of the application of Article 8(1) and (3) of Regulation (EC) No 141/2000: Assessing similarity of medicinal products versus authorised orphan medicinal products benefiting from market exclusivity and applying derogations from that market exclusivity* (September 2008)
- Australian Regulatory Guidelines for Prescription Medicines (June 2004) (Appendix 8 was updated in May 2011)
- Japanese National Institute for Biomedical Innovation: Services to promote development of medicinal products for rare diseases

Introduction

Orphan drugs (or orphan medicinal products) are intended for the treatment of orphan diseases, which typically are understood to be rare diseases. In most legislation, the orphan principle is limited to drugs only. There are exceptions. For instance, in the US, the definition of orphan products was extended to products other than drugs, such as medical devices and medical foods (e.g., parenteral nutrition).

Orphan legislation originated in the US in the early 1980s. At that time, US Representative Henry Waxman was contacted by the mother of a boy suffering from Tourette syndrome—a neuropsychiatric disorder characterized by vocal and motor tics. Waxman, chairman of the House Energy and Commerce Committee's Subcommittee on Health and the Environment, held a hearing to assess the extent of the rare disease problem. Jack Klugman, the star of the weekly television medical drama, "Quincy," heard about this problem and decided to create an episode of the show on the orphan disease problem using the example of Tourette syndrome. The show triggered thousands of letters asking how one could help. On this basis, Waxman introduced an orphan drug bill. Another hearing was held, and Jack Klugman testified before the committee. The support of the popular actor turned out to be important for the introduction of the bill, which was put on hold on several occasions during the legislative process. Additional "Quincy" episodes on this topic, as well as intense press coverage such as full-page advertisements in major newspapers by rare-disease activists, were finally successful: the *Orphan Drug Act* (*ODA*) became law in 1983.

Subsequently, orphan drug legislation was introduced in Japan and Australia (1993 and 1997, respectively) and the EU in 2001. There are other countries or regions where particular orphan drug principles were introduced—e.g., Switzerland and Singapore. This chapter presents the most important principles of orphan drug legislation.

Regulatory Procedure

Essentially, all existing legislation provides a stepwise approach for authorization of orphan drugs. First, orphan designation has to be obtained for a product under development for a specified orphan disease. As soon as the nonclinical and clinical development has been completed, a marketing authorization for this orphan drug may be granted by the health authorities.

It is evident from this procedure that orphan designation cannot be obtained *posthoc*, meaning after the product has been authorized for the respective orphan indication. In 1988, the US *ODA* was amended to require sponsors to apply for orphan designation before submitting a marketing application. Similarly, the EU legislation explicitly states that the request for designation must be submitted before the application for marketing authorization. In Australia, authorization prior to 1 January 1998, the date when Orphan Drug Policy became effective, is the relevant cut-off date.

The request for designation in the US should include a description of the rare disease as well as a demonstration that its prevalence is below the defined threshold, a description of the product, the scientific rationale for the drug's use for this condition and, if applicable, a demonstration of the medical plausibility as well as some formal information. Essentially the same information is required for designation in the EU. The seriousness of the disease must be demonstrated, information on alternative treatment should be provided and the justification for the potential benefit for the patients. Furthermore, an overview of the drug development process is requested.

Interestingly, in Switzerland, according to Article 13 of the *Therapeutic Products Act* (*TPA*), a reduced assessment for a new drug substance or an extension of its indication—with the exception of oncological medicinal products—is possible for products that have been designated or authorized as "orphan drugs" by the European Medicines Agency (EMA) or by the US Food and Drug Administration (FDA), if the sponsor demonstrates the product intended for the Swiss market is identical to the reference product.

To receive orphan drug designation in Australia, the product must not have been rejected on safety grounds by the Australian Therapeutic Good Administration (TGA), FDA, the UK's Medicines and Healthcare products Regulatory Agency (MHRA), Sweden's Medical Products Agency (MPA), the Netherlands' Medicines Evaluation Board (MEB) or EMA.

In Japan, the applicant should have a clear product development plan and scientific rationale to support the need for the drug of interest.

After designation is obtained, the product can be authorized as an orphan drug (or orphan medicinal product in the EU nomenclature). It should be noted that authorization of orphan drugs generally follows the same regulatory procedures and principles as those for non-orphan drugs. Quality, safety and efficacy must be demonstrated adequately. However, some requirements of the approval process are eased. For instance, in certain cases, it is acceptable for studies to be statistically underpowered due to the fact that fewer patients are available. Still, statistical significance should be demonstrated.

Depending on the country or region, orphan drugs automatically qualify for special authorization processes, such as accelerated or priority review. This is discussed in more detail in the section on incentives for orphan drugs.

Australia's TGA usually will accept the same data submitted to FDA if the product has been registered as an orphan drug in the US, as long as additional, country-specific information on manufacturing and labeling is provided. In cases where the authorization was rejected by FDA due to safety concerns, TGA will accept the application if it includes additional data that address the objections raised by FDA. This means implicitly that in absence of such information,such authorization requests may not be submitted to TGA.

Orphan Diseases

Orphan drugs (or orphan medicinal products) are intended for the treatment, diagnosis or prevention of orphan diseases. The word orphan is derived from the Greek word "orphanos"—a child who has lost one or both parents or a parent who has lost a child.[1] One general understanding of an orphan disease is that it describes diseases neglected by doctors—orphans of the medical community. In a stricter sense, it designates diseases that affect only a small number of individuals. In fact, the latter principle is a cornerstone in the definition of an orphan disease in Australia, Japan, the US and the EU, as outlined in the following section.

Still, there are other reasons that a disease may be neglected by the pharmaceutical industry or medical community. One is that a drug might be intended for the treatment of disease but no return on the investment to develop the drug can be expected. Such principles are explicitly included in the legislation in the US and the EU, but in reality, the return on investment is only of minor relevance and therefore not discussed here in detail (in fact, no examples for drugs based on this justification exist in the EU and there is only one in the US).

A particular case for such a disease could be if it is endemic to countries with little economic power or lacking a substantial pharmaceutical industry. This is typically the case for many tropical diseases. For instance, hundreds of millions of people in Africa are infected with the malaria parasite *Plasmodium falciparum* annually. Since resistance of the parasite to currently existing drugs is increasing, there is an urgent medical need for new drugs. However, the efforts of most pharmaceutical companies are limited because the threat of malaria tropica in major pharmaceutical markets is primarily infected travelers. Currently, it appears there is a trend for pharmaceutical companies to concentrate more on tropical diseases than in recent decades. In addition, FDA issues priority review vouchers to sponsors of certain tropical disease product applications that sponsors may use themselves or transfer to another manufacturer.

No general criteria for orphan diseases (except the rarity of the condition) exist in countries with particular orphan legislation. Some legislation requests that the medical need be demonstrated. The EU *Orphan Regulation* states that the applicant shall demonstrate that the condition is life-threatening, seriously debilitating and/or serious and chronic. In addition, there should be no satisfactory method of diagnosis, treatment or prevention authorized in the EU or—in case such methods exist—the product in question must offer significant benefit to the patients (significant benefit might be greater efficacy, an improved safety profile, improved pharmacokinetic properties, compliance-promoting features or evidence of fewer interactions with food or medicinal products). The latter principle of lack of treatment alternatives or superiority to other treatments for the orphan disease also is included in the Japanese orphan legislation, but not the Australian legislation. This principle was not included in the original US *ODA* legislation; however, a 1992 amendment to the act requires a demonstration of clinical superiority to any authorized orphan drug for the same disease (it should be noted that non-orphan drugs also might be available for the treatment of orphan diseases, e.g., for historical reasons).

The scope of an orphan disease also might be viewed differently in different countries or regions. For instance, there is an important distinction in the definition of orphan diseases or conditions in the US and the EU. In the EU, the use of subgroups or degrees of severity is strongly discouraged to prevent a sponsor from defining a subgroup of a disease that fulfills the orphan criteria simply to take advantage of the incentives, despite the fact that the product is expected to be active in the broader population. In such a circumstance, the sponsor normally should apply for the broader condition. It should be noted that there are examples where subgroups received orphan designation in the EU, but the number is limited and the designation process is typically more cumbersome. The US legislation also states that the plausibility of a subset has to be demonstrated, but the EU interpretation is stricter. For example, "treatment of stage III and IV melanoma" has been recognized as an orphan disease in the US. In the EU, the applicant would have to demonstrate why the drug is not expected to be active in the treatment of stage I and II melanoma. If this is not possible, the application would have to be extended to "treatment of melanoma" (which does not fulfill the EU prevalence criteria).

Prevalence of Orphan Diseases

The common characteristic for an orphan disease is rarity, i.e., the prevalence mustfall below a certain threshold. However, there is no generally accepted definition of such an epidemiological threshold.

The epidemiological threshold for orphan diseases is no more than 200,000 cases in the US, not more than 2,000 cases in Australia and a maximum of 50,000 cases in Japan. Interestingly, these figures refer to absolute patient numbers. Consequently, the fraction of patients suffering from the orphan condition in relation to the total population varies with changes in the total population number. For instance, when the orphan legislation was introduced, the US population comprised approximately 250 million people. This meant the prevalence (i.e., total number of cases of the disease in the population at a given time, or the total number of cases in the population, divided by the number of individuals in the population) for an orphan disease was not more than 8.0 per 10,000 people. Today, while the population has increased to more than 300 million, the prevalence has decreased to 6.7 per 10,000 people. Thus, that the relative rarity of an orphan disease is apparently increasing with an increasing population.

In contrast, the EU threshold is defined on the basis of the prevalence rather than total patient number. Orphan diseases from an EU perspective affect not more than five people per 10,000 in the general population (this threshold also applies in Switzerland). This is a reasonable approach given the ongoing expansion of the EU and consequent continuing population increase. When the orphan legislation was introduced in 2001, the total EU population was approximately 400 million, corresponding to a maximum of 200,000 patients suffering from a particular orphan disease. Today, approximately 500 million people live in EU Member States, resulting in a maximum number of approximately 250,000 patients per orphan disease. If the threshold were defined on the basis of total patient

Table 27-1. Epidemiologic Thresholds of Orphan Diseases in Various Countries/Regions

Country/Region	Number of Cases	Prevalence
US	200,000	6.5 per 10,000*
Japan	50,000	1.5 per 10,000*
Australia	2,000	1.0 per 10,000*
EU	250,000#	5.0 per 10,000
WHO Definition	4.3 – 6.6 mio#	up to 10 per 10,000

* calculated on the basis of number of cases and current population
\# calculated on the basis of prevalence and current population

numbers, the possibility exists that drugs would lose their orphan status if the total population increased, despite the fact that the prevalence of the disease is unchanged.

Table 27-1 presents an overview and comparison of the different prevalence criteria. These data show that the strictest criteria are in Australia (1.0 per 10,000) while the World Health Organization's (WHO) definition is the most liberal (up to 10 per 10,000.)

Incentives

Each country with established orphan medicinal product legislation offers incentives to companies that develop drugs to treat orphan disorders. These measures are intended to motivate companies to invest in these diseases by negating the impact of expected low product sales due to the rarity of the disease. Several measures explicitly address this economic issue:

- market exclusivity
- fee reductions
- tax incentives
- support of research and development activities

One of the most important incentives is market exclusivity granted to the sponsor for the orphan drug's use in the treatment, prevention or diagnosis of the orphan disease after the product is authorized. The exclusivity period is 10 years in the EU and seven years in the US. In the EU, the exclusivity includes not just the product itself, but also similar products, to protect the sponsor from "me-too" approaches. Note that this protection does not apply to cases where a similar product offers significant benefit for patients. In Japan, the applicant will be granted a 10-year period of marketing exclusivity during which no generic/biosimilar versions of the drug may be placed on the market. However, 10 years is the maximum period of marketing exclusivity; it is possible that the Ministry of Health, Labour and Welfare (MHLW) could reduce this period, depending on circumstances. In contrast, no particular exclusivity is included in the Australian legislation.

For obvious reasons, such exclusivity is of particular importance for products not covered by any patent since it protects the sponsor against potential imitators.

Japan offers sponsors unique financial support, allowing them to receive financial aid from the government for collecting supporting data, such as clinical trials, bridging studies, etc.

Tax incentives are another incentive for the development of orphan products. In the US, sponsors may claim 50% of clinical trial costs as a credit against taxes owed. In Japan, the applicant may receive tax exemptions of up to 6% of research costs and 10% of corporate tax. No uniform tax regulation exists in the EU. Instead, tax incentives are determined at the national level in the different Member States. For instance, in France, sponsors of orphan medicinal products are exempted from taxes on direct sales or distribution of medicines. Similarly, special reimbursement procedures for orphan medicinal products are defined on a national level (e.g., in Italy, reimbursement is granted for all orphan drugs authorized under the EU Centralised Procedure). Tax incentives are not included in the Australian orphan legislation.

Several measures have been introduced to simplify the development and authorization processes for orphan drugs. These include Scientific Advice from the regulatory bodies or eligibility for particular authorization procedures.

Scientific Advice or protocol assistance is offered to sponsors of orphan drugs by FDA, MHLW and EMA but not by TGA. Orphan drug sponsors can obtain written recommendations from FDA concerning clinical and preclinical studies in order to register the new drug. In the EU, free Scientific Advice also is offered by EMA for the development of orphan medicinal products. This is called "protocol assistance." In addition, several EU Member States offer free Scientific Advice for orphan medicinal products independent of the Community-wide EMA advice. Similarly, MHLW offers free consultation services specifically for orphan drug designation applicants. In contrast, no such procedures are offered by Australian authorities.

FDA offers a Fast Track approval procedure to evaluate registration files. This procedure involves close sponsor

Table 27-2. Overview of Different Orphan Drug Legislation

	US	Japan	Australia	EU
Legal basis	*Orphan Drug Act* (1983)	*Orphan Drug Regulation* (1993)	*Orphan Drug Policy* (1998)	Regulation 141/2000/EC (2000)
Competent Authority	Food and Drug Administration (FDA) Office of Orphan Products Development (OOPD)	Ministry of Health, Labour and Welfare (MHLW) Orphan Drug Division	Therapeutic Goods Administration (TGA)	European Medicines Agency (EMA) Committee for Orphan Medicinal Products (COMP)
Prevalence threshold	200,000 patients	50,000 patients	2,000 patients	5 patients per 10,000 in the general population (corresponding to approx. 250,000 cases in total)
Prevalence per 10,000	6.5	1.5	1.0	5
Absence of adequate treatment alternatives	No	Yes	No	Yes
Market exclusivity	7 years	10 years	No particular exclusivity period	10 years
Tax incentives	50% for clinical studies	Exemptions of up to 6% of research costs and 10% of corporate tax	No	National measures of the different Member States
Fee reduction	No		100% waiver of evaluation fee	100% waiver of fees for Scientific Advice Fee reduction for pre- and post-authorization activities (including marketing authorization fees)
Research grants	Yes	Financial support of development	No	EU framework programs and national funding
Authorization peculiarities	Fast-track procedure	Fast-track approval process	Priority review	Centralised Procedure

interaction with FDA, resulting in an improved understanding of the information needed for registration and a chance to obtain marketing authorization faster and, potentially, with a less-comprehensive development program (Accelerated Approval).

Orphan products automatically qualify for the Centralised Procedure in the EU, which covers all EU Member States (plus Liechtenstein, Iceland and Norway). In fact, this procedure is mandatory for orphan medicinal products. The idea is that a product intended to treat a rare disease should be available to all patients. In Australia, orphan products are eligible for priority review. This means that marketing authorization applications are handled as quickly as possible, but there are no abbreviated timelines such as those in the US legislation for Priority Review or in the EU for accelerated assessment. In Switzerland, products for the treatment of rare diseases are eligible for a simplified authorization procedure. The application will be placed on a fast-track approval process in Japan, which generally proceeds much more smoothly than that of regular drugs. In theory, the fast-track approval process takes 10 months, while the approval for regular drugs takes 12 to 24 months.

Research grants are another means of supporting the development of drugs for the treatment of orphan diseases. For instance, in the US, FDA's Office of Orphan Products Development (OOPD) funds development through clinical study grants. Academic institutions and other responsible organizations are eligible for such grants, and small companies also are encouraged to apply. In the EU, an orphan drug sponsor can apply for framework programs and national grants. No such support is available for the development of orphan drugs in Australia.

Summary

Orphan drug legislation always consists of the combination of the product, the intended therapeutic indication and the orphan disease. Such legislation has been introduced in the US, Japan, Australia and the EU. Each piece of legislation defines the orphan disease by its rarity (although the thresholds vary significantly). Other characteristics, such as severity of the disease, are included in the definition of an orphan disease in some countries.

In general, the Australian orphan legislation is similar to that in the US, while the principles in effect in the EU share many characteristics with the Japanese regulation. Prevalence thresholds are different in all four countries/regions.

It appears there is only moderate benefit resulting from the orphan legislation in Australia. This is due to the fact that no market exclusivity or tax incentive is granted, while they have the most stringent prevalence threshold for the orphan condition. It is difficult to say where the orphan incentives are most pronounced: market exclusivity extends the longest in Japan and the EU. On the other hand, these areas have a more challenging definition of an orphan condition than the US.

A comparison of different features of orphan drugs and orphan diseases in different countries/regions is presented in **Table 27-2**.

Overall, it appears that orphan legislation has stimulated product development in these neglected therapeutic fields. Today, there are more than 400 orphan drugs authorized in the US. In the 12 years since orphan legislation was introduced in the EU, 83 orphan drugs have been authorized. Of course it is difficult to say whether this development would have taken place without orphan legislation. But, the large number of development projects under an orphan designation clearly indicates that these principles are appreciated by the pharmaceutical and biotech industries.

References

1. Aaronson JK. "Rare diseases and orphan drugs." *Br. J. Clin. Pharmacol.* 2006:(61)243-245.

Chapter 28

Combination Products

By Robert Laughner, MS, RAC (US, EU, CAN)

OBJECTIVES

- ❑ Review the conceptual and regulatory definitions of a combination product
- ❑ Understand different regulatory schemes for combination products across countries
- ❑ Understand the mechanism by which combination products are classified
- ❑ Describe how jurisdiction and review are assigned by regulatory authorities
- ❑ Understand manufacturing requirements for combination products

REGULATIONS AND GUIDELINES COVERED IN THIS CHAPTER

US

- ❑ *Safe Medical Devices Act* of 1990
- ❑ 21 CFR 3, Product Jurisdiction
- ❑ 21 CFR 820, Quality System Regulations
- ❑ 21 CFR 211, Current Good Manufacturing Practice

Canada

- ❑ Health Canada Policy, *Drug/Medical Device Combination Products*

EU

- ❑ Medical Devices Directive (Directive 93/42/EC), Article 4

International

- ❑ ISO 13485, *Medical Device–Quality Management Systems*
- ❑ ICH, *Pharmaceutical Development Q8(R2)*
- ❑ ICH, *Quality Risk Management Q9*
- ❑ ICH, *Pharmaceutical Quality System Q10*

Introduction

Combination products raise more challenges than any other category of regulated products. As they involve two or more regulated product categories, combination products contain all of the challenges presented by their individual components as well as new issues that arise from the combination. Often, the barriers to combination product development and regulation arise from differences in "cultural" perspective as much as from scientific and/or technical challenges.

Companies typically are either drug/biologic or medical devices companies. Most regulatory authorities regulate all three product categories, but each category is often regulated by a separate group, each having distinct requirements, laws and guidelines. This dichotomy leads to insular viewpoints based on each group's goals and expectations. Significant effort often is required to explain why a particular requirement may need to be modified to accommodate these novel products.

As a distinct regulatory entity, combination products are a relatively new concept. The first national law directly related to combination products was introduced in the US

Table 28-1. Combination Product Types

Type of Combination	Description	Examples
Single-entity (a.k.a. integral)	Two or more components combined as integral parts of a single unit.	• prefilled syringes • metered dose inhalers • transdermal patches • antimicrobial wound dressings • drug-eluting stents • antimicrobial catheters • medicated toothpastes
Co-packaged (a.k.a. kits)	Two or more components that are distinct entities that are combined in the same package.	• convenience kits • drug dispensing devices • drug vial/syringe packages • iontophoresis systems
Co-labeled (a.k.a. cross-labeled, virtual)	Two or more components that are distinct in form and packaging, but are to be used together according to their labeling.	• companion diagnostic tests • photodynamic therapies

with the *Safe Medical Devices Act* of 1990. To date, most countries do not have formal laws or regulations dealing specifically with combination products.

Definition of a Combination Product

The combination of drug, device and/or biologic can come in many forms. In general, they can be broken down into three categories based on how the components are combined, as defined in **Table 28-1**.

These three categories represent the conceptual ways in which the different product categories can be combined, but few countries have defined these combination product types in laws or regulations. The US currently is the only country that specifically addresses all three product types as combination products. Canada and the EU also have definitions for combination products, but they are more limited in scope. At the time of publication, other countries, such as Australia and Japan, have not provided formal definitions for combination products.

US Definition

The US currently has the most robust definition for combination products, which incorporates all of these concepts. 21 CFR 3.2(e) provides four definitions for a combination product:

1. a product comprised of two or more regulated components, i.e., drug/device, biologic/device, drug/biologic or drug/device/biologic, that are physically, chemically or otherwise combined or mixed and produced as a single entity
2. two or more separate products packaged together in a single package or as a unit and comprised of drug and device products, device and biological products, or biological and drug products
3. a drug, device or biological product packaged separately that, according to its investigational plan or proposed labeling, is intended for use only with an approved, individually specified drug, device or biological product, where both are required to achieve the intended use, indication or effect and where, upon approval of the proposed product, the approved product labeling would need to be changed, e.g. to reflect a change in intended use, dosage form, strength, route of administration or significant change in dose
4. any investigational drug, device or biological product packaged separately that, according to its proposed labeling, is for use only with another individually specified investigational drug, device or biological product where both are required to achieve the intended use, indication or effect

Canadian Definition

Health Canada's Therapeutic Products Directorate issued a policy document in 2005 titled *Drug/Medical Device Combination Products*, which defines a combination product as "a therapeutic product that combines a drug component and a device component (which by themselves would be classified as a drug or a device), such that the distinctive nature of the drug component and device component is integrated in a singular product." This definition covers the concept of a single-entity combination product. Co-packaged and co-labeled products are not identified specifically as combination products in Canada. The individual components of these products are regulated separately as a drug, device or biologic, based on their type.

EU Definition

While the EU does not have a general definition of combination products, the concept of a single-entity combination product is captured in the *Medical Devices Directive* (*MDD,* Directive 93/42 EC). According to the directive, where a device incorporates as an integral part a substance which, if used separately, may be considered to be a medicinal product and is liable to act on the body with action ancillary to that of the device, that device must be assessed and authorized in accordance with the *MDD*. All medical devices of this type are placed in the highest risk category in the EU, regardless of the class of the device without the medicinal component. As in Canada, there is no formal definition for co-packaged or co-labeled products. The individual components are regulated as appropriate for their type.

Determining a Regulatory Pathway

Determining a regulatory pathway is one of the first and most important steps for bringing any regulated product to market. Unfortunately, with multiple components that may be regulated differently and inconsistent definitions across countries, a sponsor may find itself in the position of having a product that is regulated as a drug/biologic in one country and a device in another country. One combination product could even require two entirely different submissions.

To reduce this uncertainty, the most important part of determining how a combination product is regulated is to establish its primary mode of action. A mode of action is a means by which a product achieves its therapeutic effect, so the primary mode of action is that mode that makes the most important contribution to the overall therapeutic effect. It is helpful to review combination products that already have been authorized by a regulatory authority to understand how their designation may have been determined. The US Food and Drug Administration (FDA) has published examples of approved combination products. While specific to the US, these examples demonstrate how a regulator may determine a product's primary mode of action. Examples, including some from FDA's list, are presented in **Table 28-2**.

The determination of both individual modes of action and the primary mode of action must come from a sound understanding of how a product fulfills its intended purpose, with as much sound scientific support as possible. If this firm foundation is established early, it is much easier to determine how that product should be regulated. Without this foundation, doubts about the product's primary mode of action may arise, and the product will likely default to the pathway that offers the greatest level of review and control to a regulatory authority, especially for products with novel combinations or therapeutic functions.

A product's pathway is chosen based on its primary mode of action: the primary or principal mechanism by which a product achieves its therapeutic function. If the primary mode is that of a device, such as in a drug-eluting

Table 28-2. Combination Product Designation Examples

Combination Product	Modes of Action	Primary Mode of Action	Comment
Paclitaxel-eluting Coronary Stent	1. Device—stent maintains vessel luminal diameter 2. Drug—paclitaxel inhibits neointimal production	Device	Coronary stents maintain vessel diameter with or without the addition of a drug. Paclitaxel reduces vessel re-occlusion due to proliferation of the intima through the stent.
Fentanyl-delivering Iontophoretic Transdermal System	1. Drug—Fentanyl provides analgesia 2. Device—patient-controlled transdermal delivery of drug	Drug	Device provides a convenient and controlled method to administer the drug.
Absorbable Surgical Hemostatic Agent	1. Device—collagen forms a physical barrier to blood flow 2. Biologic—thrombin activates fibrin to initiate clot formation	Device	Collagen provides the physical basis for clot formation, while the thrombin component speeds the natural conversion of fibrinogen to fibrin.
Anti-EGFR Antibody and EGFR Expression Diagnostic Test	1. Biologic—anti-EGFR antibody competitively inhibits EGFR signaling 2. Device—tests for EGFR expression within tumor cells	Both	Separate biologic and device regulatory approvals. Products are labeled to be used together for the targeted treatment of EGFR expressing tumors.

coronary stent or an antimicrobial-coated central venous catheter, the product likely will be regulated as a device. If the primary mode is that of a drug, such as a prefilled syringe, metered dose inhaler or almost any single-entity drug delivery device, the product likely will be regulated as a drug. Depending on the regulatory authority, this process of determining a product's designation as a drug or a device based on its primary mode of action may or may not be a formal procedure in the country's regulation.

Product Designation and Premarket Review

A combination product's designation determines its method of premarket review. This designation process varies by country and depends on the extent of the country's combination product regulation. For most countries, this will simply mean a submission to the authority that has responsibility for the component with the primary mode of action. This sometimes also will involve consultation with the regulatory authority or a particular committee or group within the authority to solicit their input on the sponsor's recommended designation. Currently, there are only two countries that have a regulation or a policy for officially designating a combination product prior to submission. As combination product-specific submissions do not exist at this time, a product that is designated as a drug generally will follow drug submission regulations and guidelines, and a product designated as a device generally will follow device submission regulations and standards.

US Designation and Review

The US has two general approaches for designating a combination product. The more informal approach is for a sponsor to submit a standard product application. If FDA has made a designation determination on a related product, the sponsor should submit its documentation in the same manner as the predecessor product. If the sponsor is confident in its determination of the product's primary mode of action, it may simply submit a product application to the center within FDA that it believes has jurisdiction for the component with the primary action. A product that has a drug or biologic component as the primary mode of action will be submitted to the Center for Drug Evaluation and Research (CDER) or the Center for Biologics Evaluation and Research (CBER), respectively. A product that has a device as the primary mode of action will be submitted to the Center for Devices and Radiological Health (CDRH). This is a simple approach, but if a center believes the sponsor's determination is incorrect, it will choose a different designation and the product will be handed to a different center for review.

The more formal approach in the US is to go through the Request for Designation (RFD) process. The RFD is an application to FDA's Office of Combination Products (OCP) where a sponsor provides its rationale for a product's modes of action and requests OCP's determination for the product's primary mode of action. OCP reviews the document and renders a binding jurisdictional determination on the product, including both the product's primary mode of action and the assignment to the center that will have primary responsibility for the product's review. There are three potential benefits of this approach. First, it gives a sponsor the option of a formal and binding determination on a product's designation prior to submission. This determination may be received while the product is still in early development or even at a conceptual level and may affect whether a sponsor chooses to pursue development of the product at all. Second, it allows the sponsor's product designation to be evaluated by a group that is largely independent of the center(s) that will ultimately be reviewing their product. Finally, the RFD process allows the sponsor to appeal a determination if it believes OCP's decision is inaccurate.

Regardless of the center to which the combination product is assigned, supporting centers will be given a collaborative or consultative role in the product's review. For example, a drug-eluting coronary stent has both device and drug actions, with the device component fulfilling the primary role. In this case, CDRH would have primary jurisdiction of the product, and CDER would support CDRH by reviewing the drug-specific portions of the application.

Canadian Designation and Review

Canada also has two general approaches for designating a combination product. A sponsor may proceed through a standard product submission if it is confident in its determination of the product's primary mode of action. Since both drugs and devices are handled through the Therapeutic Products Directorate (TPD), a product that has a drug or a device as the primary mode of action will be submitted to the same place with a different application. This is a simple approach, but if TPD believes the sponsor's determination is incorrect or that the sponsor should have received a formal classification decision, it will issue the sponsor a Screening Deficiency Notice.

The more formal approach in Canada is to submit a written request for a classification decision to the relevant bureau director detailing the product, its components, the mechanisms of action for each component and the sponsor's supported recommendation for the principal mechanism of action. The bureau will use the criteria in the policy document to designate the product based on its principal mechanism of action. If the bureau cannot come to a decision alone or in consultation with other relevant bureaus, the request will be forwarded to the Therapeutic Products Classification Committee (TPCC), which will review the matter and render a classification decision within 30 days. If the sponsor disagrees with the classification, it can initiate a Request for Reconsideration by sending a Letter of Intent to the director general.

Regardless of the principal mechanism that is chosen or the bureau with primary jurisdiction, the ancillary component of the product must meet acceptable standards of safety, efficacy and quality. To this end, TPD will undertake the review with any expertise necessary to effectively assess the benefit:risk profile of the product. Input from resources from one bureau or a team of resources from multiple bureaus may be used and can lead to requests for additional information to support the safety, efficacy and/or quality of the ancillary component. The review criteria, timelines and fees will be based on the product's principal mechanism and submission type. Finally, a classification decision made during an investigational testing application could be changed for a marketing submission if new information becomes available.

Manufacturing Combination Products

The manufacture of combination products can be a very confusing landscape to navigate. The regulatory requirements to ensure the quality of drugs and biologics versus medical devices evolved independently to address similar goals but different needs for each product category. As a combination product generally is regulated according to its primary mode of action, the manufacturing requirements typically will follow the requirements for the primary component. However, the ancillary component(s) still are expected to meet a sufficient level of safety and quality. While the US is the only country that has attempted to codify this dichotomy into defined manufacturing requirements for combination products, sponsors in other countries can consult international standards to determine the manufacturing requirements for combination products in those markets.

There are two separate, widely accepted international standards governing the manufacture of both medical devices and drugs/biologics. For medical devices, ISO 13485 *Medical Device—Quality Management Systems* is the most common set of manufacturing standards largely accepted in most major markets. For pharmaceuticals, the current ICH quality guidelines for pharmaceuticals provide a framework for the manufacture of pharmaceutical products that integrates well with the basic framework provided in ISO 13485 for the manufacture of medical devices. Some of these parallels include risk management practices (ICH *Quality Risk Management Q9*), designing quality into the product from the beginning based on the desired final performance of the product (ICH *Pharmaceutical Development Q8*) and manufacturing control based on quality systems (ICH *Pharmaceutical Quality Systems Q10*). Many countries recognize, in whole or in part, both ISO 13485 and ICH guidelines Q8, Q9 and Q10, including the US, EU, Canada, Japan and others. Even in countries that have their own requirements or only partially recognize these documents, they represent the most common industry standards for medical devices and pharmaceuticals and, as such, provide a solid foundation for further discussion and negotiation with a regulatory authority on the manufacturing requirements for a combination product.

Summary

Combination products can provide tremendous benefit to patients and at the same time present substantial challenges in their development, manufacture and regulation. While the few available combination product regulations, policies and guidances provide a conceptual background to understanding combination products, it is important for the sponsor to sufficiently understand both the components of its combination product and the applicable regulatory definitions in a given country to determine how a product may be regulated and what regulatory pathway is pursued. Since a product may be regulated under more than one scheme, it is important to know the regulatory requirements for the components, as well as any requirements or guidances that may be unique to combination products. This enables an effective discussion with a given regulatory authority to determine the requirements that are most appropriate for ensuring that these non-standard products have the necessary level of safety, efficacy and quality.

References

1. *Safe Medical Devices Act* of 1990.
2. 21 CFR 3, Product Jurisdiction. FDA website. http://www.accessdata.fda.gov/scripts/cdrh/cfdocs/cfcfr/CFRSearch.cfm?CFRPart=3. Accessed 2 April 2013.
3. 21 CFR 820, Quality System Regulation. FDA website. http://www.accessdata.fda.gov/scripts/cdrh/cfdocs/cfcfr/CFRSearch.cfm?CFRPart=820. Accessed 2 April 2013.
4. 21 CFR 211, Current Good Manufacturing Practice. FDA website. http://www.accessdata.fda.gov/scripts/cdrh/cfdocs/cfcfr/CFRSearch.cfm?CFRPart=211. Accessed 2 April 2013.
5. Health Canada Policy, *Drug/Medical Device Combination Products*. Health Canada website. http://www.hc-sc.gc.ca/dhp-mps/prodpharma/applic-demande/pol/combo_mixte_pol_2006-eng.php. Accessed 2 April 2013.
6. Council Directive 93/42/EC of 14 June 1993 concerning medical devices (Medical Devices Directive) . Eur-Lex website. http://eur-lex.europa.eu/LexUriServ/LexUriServ.do?uri=CELEX:31993L0042:en:NOT. Accessed 2 April 2013.
7. ISO 13485 Medical Device—Quality Management Systems. ISO website. http://www.iso.org/iso/catalogue_detail?csnumber=36786. Accessed 2 April 2013.
8. ICH. *Pharmaceutical Development Q8*. ICH website. http://www.ich.org/fileadmin/Public_Web_Site/ICH_Products/Guidelines/Quality/Q8_R1/Step4/Q8_R2_Guideline.pdf. Accessed 2 April 2013.
9. ICH. *Quality Risk Management Q9*. ICH website. http://www.ich.org/fileadmin/Public_Web_Site/ICH_Products/Guidelines/Quality/Q9/Step4/Q9_Guideline.pdf. Accessed 2 April 2013.
10. ICH. *Pharmaceutical Quality Systems Q10*. ICH website. http://www.ich.org/fileadmin/Public_Web_Site/ICH_Products/Guidelines/Quality/Q10/Step4/Q10_Guideline.pdf. Accessed 2 April 2013.

Chapter 29

Cosmetic Products

Updated by Marcela Saad, MSc, PharmD, RAC (Global)

OBJECTIVES

- ❑ Understand the history of cosmetic products
- ❑ Understand what cosmetic products are
- ❑ Understand how cosmetics are regulated
- ❑ Learn the critical requirements for placing a cosmetic in different markets

REGULATIONS AND GUIDELINES COVERED IN THIS CHAPTER

Canada

- ❑ *Cosmetic Regulations* to the *Food and Drugs Act*

EU

- ❑ Council Directive 76/768/EEC of 27 July 1976 on the approximation of the laws of the Member States relating to cosmetic products, as amended
- ❑ Council of Europe, Committee of Ministers, Resolution CM/ResAP(2012)1 on safety criteria for cosmetic products intended for infants

US

- ❑ *Tamper-Resistant Packaging Act* of 1980
- ❑ 21 CFR 700.25 Tamper-resistant packaging requirements for cosmetic products

A Piece of History

In ancient cultures, women added rouge (minerals crushed into power) to their faces and applied various minerals to adorn their eyes and to add color to their hair. As history evolved, cosmetics started to reach both male and female audiences. Interestingly, the trend among the European aristocracy was to use thick white powder on their faces and bosoms. However, one hidden reason was that the powder was used to cover scars from diseases such as smallpox.

Elizabeth I used white lead on her face, to create a look known as "the Mask of Youth" because she did not want people to see her age.

During the Victorian era, cosmetics were not used as uniformly. Simplicity and natural beauty were in favor at the time.

During the early part of the 20th century, makeup made a big comeback, especially in the US and Europe, due to the influence of ballet and theater stars. The idea was to use as much makeup as possible to achieve a glamorous look. Movie stars later became the trendsetters when it came to makeup styles, with the use of vibrant red lipstick and dramatic eye makeup.

The health of the beauty industry declined in the 1970s as the growth of cosmetics sales failed to keep pace with overall growth in personal spending.

Also, consumers considered cosmetics companies outdated, uncreative and dogmatic, and manufacturers received negative publicity regarding the safety of cosmetics ingredients, animal testing, microbial contamination and the possibility of cosmetics causing acne. In response, manufacturers introduced new products, especially in skin care and sunscreen lines. Manufacturers started to emphasize cost controls and quality and be more selective about the products they manufactured based on customer research.

Cosmetic lines since have expanded into the ethnic, teen and men's markets. "Natural" ingredients have been incorporated into cosmetics to satisfy a growing interest in organic products.

Today, makeup is used in a variety of different ways. Some people prefer dramatic looks, while others prefer a natural look. One thing is true; there is an alternative for most consumer preferences.[1]

Regulatory Overview

In general, cosmetic products are substances or mixtures intended to be placed in contact with various external parts of the human body, primarily intended to clean, perfume, protect or maintain them in good condition, or promote attractiveness, alter appearance or correct body odors. The exact definition differs according to national legislation. In most countries, a product is either a cosmetic or another type of product (e.g., a medicinal product) and must comply with the laws applicable for that product type. There are, however, some exceptions. For example, in the US, cosmetic products intended to cure, treat or prevent disease or to affect the body's structure or function, in addition to their intended cosmetic benefit, are regulated as cosmetic-drug products. Such products must comply with the regulatory requirements of each category. (Details are in the Regulatory Process section below.)

Depending on local regulations, the following products usually are defined as cosmetics:

- creams, emulsions, lotions, gels and oils for the skin (hands, face, feet, etc.)
- face masks
- tinted bases (liquids, pastes, powders)
- makeup powders, after-bath powders, hygienic powders, etc.
- toilet soaps, deodorant soaps, etc.
- perfumes, toilette waters and eau de cologne
- bath and shower preparations (salts, foams, oils, gels, etc.)
- depilatories
- deodorants and antiperspirants
- hair care products
    - hair tints and bleaches
    - products for waving, straightening and fixing
    - setting products
    - cleansing products (lotions, powders, shampoos)
    - conditioning products (lotions, creams, oils)
    - hair dressing products (lotions, lacquers, brilliantines)
- shaving products (creams, foams, lotions, etc.)
- products for making up and removing makeup from the face and the eyes
- products intended for application to the lips
- products for care of the teeth and the mouth, including mouthwashes
- products for nail care and makeup
- products for external intimate hygiene
- sunbathing products
- products for tanning without the sun
- skin-whitening products
- anti-wrinkle products

This list was taken from Annex I to Council Directive 76/768/EEC of 27 July 1976 on the approximation of the laws of the Member States relating to cosmetic products (EU *Cosmetics Directive*), as amended, hence the exact classification in other countries/regions may be slightly different. Common to most regions is the fact that unlike medicinal products, medical devices and biologics, cosmetics are not always subject to premarketing review and approval. In addition, cosmetics normally are not subject to postmarketing surveillance. Note that this is not a general rule since each region may regulate products differently. In most instances, although manufacturers must comply with Good Manufacturing Practices (GMPs),[2] it is not necessary to request country-specific inspection and GMP certification, but there are exceptions (e.g., the EU, Brazil, etc.).

There are various borderline products:[3]

- glue for artificial nails
- sculptured nails
- nail hardeners
- nail strengtheners
- products intended to remove corns and callosities (hard skin)
- products intended to soften callosities
- products for foot care containing antimycotic or other antimicrobial substances
- products reducing hair loss and stimulating hair growth
- products to whiten teeth
- products for the care of gingiva (gums) and to alleviate gum irritation
- products for sensitive teeth
- anticaries products
- antiplaque products
- products to clean the ear and nose
- anti-aging products
- exfoliants
- products to improve impure and blemished skin
- products for the care of the décolleté
- products for permanent makeup and tattooing
- products for the care of tired and heavy legs
- body massage/anti-cellulite products
- products with antimicrobial or antiseptic properties
- products with soothing, anti-irritant properties
- hyperaemic products; pre- and post-sport massage
- products for external intimate hygiene
- products to facilitate sexual intercourse; lubricating agents for condoms

- products against sexual impotence (external use)
- products with essential oils
- pure essential oils; products marketed in the context of aromatherapy
- insect repellents

This list is from a Council of Europe publication, *Cosmetic Products—Borderline Situations,* so again, the situation in other countries or regions may be somewhat different. In Mexico, for example, some dental products (teeth whiteners) are considered health products and are classified as medical devices.

Latin American countries developed their own regulations governing cosmetic products. Basically, the Latin American countries adapted the EU guidelines. Some countries (e.g., Brazil, Argentina and Mexico) have more cosmetics regulation than others. In all countries, market authorization approval is specified on a national basis.

Similarly to marketing approval, exact labeling requirements differ from country to country. In general, the following information should appear on the label:

- name and address of the manufacturer, packer and/or distributor if different (In the EU, for example, the address of the office/entity where the product information package can be consulted is underlined.)
- package contents, either by weight or volume, i.e., net quantity of contents
- shelf life or date of expiry (Note, in the EU, the shelf life is termed the date of minimum durability, which, if greater than 30 months (supported by stability data), can be replaced by a symbol denoting the period of time (months and/or years) that the product remains safe for use after opening. Brazil and other Latin countries, follow the same principle, but have not adopted symbols.)
- precautions for use and applicable warning statements
- batch or lot number
- function of the product, unless it is obvious from its presentation
- Declaration of Ingredients or ingredients list

Label texts should be in the language of the country in which the product is being sold. Any advertising must be factual and supported by appropriate data.

In the US,[4] liquid oral hygiene products (e.g., mouthwashes and breath fresheners) and cosmetic vaginal products also must comply with the *Tamper-Resistant Packaging Act* of 1980[5] and the *Federal Anti-Tampering Act* of 1983, and therefore, require tamper-resistant packaging.[6]

In general, advertising of cosmetics is allowed. However, any claims or statements should be based on factual evidence and should not be misleading. In addition, advertising statements should not indicate any medical or healing functions, unless such claims are allowed by the local regulation.

With respect to safety and quality, GMP is mandated for cosmetic products in the EU and other countries. However, in the markets where GMP is not required, products still must be clean and free from filth and foreign residuals. In addition, they must be manufactured, prepared, preserved, packed and stored under sanitary conditions.[7] Appropriate safety testing is encouraged in most jurisdictions and is mandatory in others (e.g., the EU). If products have not been tested for safety, this fact should be clearly stated on the labeling to allow consumers to make educated choices about these products.

Special care must be taken to control and eliminate adulterated and misbranded products. Generally, products are adulterated if they contain poisonous substances, filth, illegal additives, were manufactured or held under unsanitary conditions or if they are packaged in containers composed of any poisonous or deleterious substance that may render the contents injurious to health.[8] Products are misbranded if their labeling is false and misleading.[9] For this reason, some jurisdictions conduct inspections of manufacturing facilities and complaint records.[10]

Although adverse event reporting is not carried out in the same rigorous manner as for medicinal products, all substantiated and documented reports by qualified medical specialists should be collected. This process allows better oversight, especially in the case of any suspected health issues or hazards.

Animal testing is not prohibited in all jurisdictions; testing of cosmetic ingredients on animals should be replaced, wherever possible, with validated, alternative methods as soon as they become available.

Starting 13 July 2013, a new *European Cosmetic Products (Safety) Regulation* (EC/1223/2009) entered into force. It created a new notification procedure, which requires every product placed on the market to be notified to the European Commission. In addition, under Directive 2012/21/EU, various hair dye substances are due to be restricted from 1 September 2013.

In most jurisdictions, certain substances are prohibited and/or restricted. Restricted substances can be used only under specified conditions and limitations. Some countries publish lists of permitted ingredients, such as preservatives, excipients and other ingredients. When in doubt, it is always preferable to communicate with the specific regulatory authority and confirm that the components of a product's formulation do not contain any prohibited or restricted ingredients.

Regulatory Process

Some countries do not require registration of cosmetic products. Products placed on the market that conform to local cosmetic regulations do not need preapproval, and an evaluation is not carried out by the authorities prior to marketing these products. In many countries, however, a manufacturer wishing to place products on the market must notify the local authorities. It may be beneficial, especially in the case of misuse, to inform the authorities and/or poison centers of the substances, ingredients and quantities used in cosmetic products.

US

Cosmetic products are regulated by the US Food and Drug Administration's (FDA) Center for Food Safety and Applied Nutrition (CFSAN). CFSAN is responsible for assuring that cosmetics are safe and properly labeled. The two most important laws pertaining to cosmetics marketed in the US are the *Federal Food, Drug, and Cosmetic Act* (*FD&C Act*) and the *Fair Packaging and Labeling Act* (*FPLA*).

According to the *FD&C Act*, cosmetic products and ingredients do not require FDA approval before they enter the market. However, color additives (other than those used in most hair dyes) are an exception. It is important to point out that companies and individuals who market cosmetics in the US have the legal responsibility to ensure the safety of their products. FDA encourages cosmetic firms to report product formulations through the Voluntary Cosmetic Registration Program (VCRP), but companies are not legally required to inform FDA about their products and safety data.

FDA can inspect manufacturing facilities to determine whether proper controls and practices are being followed. FDA also works with US Customs and Border Protection to examine imported cosmetics.

Not all "personal care products" are regulated as cosmetics. Following are personal care products that may or may not be considered cosmetics in the US:

- Products intended to cleanse or beautify are generally regulated as cosmetics. Some examples are skin moisturizers, perfumes, lipsticks, fingernail polishes, makeup, shampoos, permanent waves, hair colors, toothpastes and deodorants. These products and their ingredients are not subject to FDA premarket approval, with the exception of color additives (other than coal tar hair dyes). Cosmetic companies are legally responsible for the safety of their products and ingredients.
- Products intended to treat or prevent disease, or affect the structure or function of the body, are classified as drugs even if a product affects how you look. Some examples are treatments for dandruff or acne, sunscreen products, antiperspirants and diaper ointments. Generally, drugs must receive premarket approval by FDA or, if they are nonprescription drugs, they must comply with special regulations, called "monographs," for their category.
- Some are both cosmetics and drugs. Examples include anti-dandruff shampoos and antiperspirant-deodorants, as well as moisturizers and makeup with SPF (sun protection factor) numbers. They must meet the requirements for both cosmetics and drugs.
- Some may belong to other categories, including medical devices (e.g., certain hair removal and microdermabrasion devices), dietary supplements (e.g., vitamin or mineral tablets or capsules), or other consumer products (e.g., manicure sets).[11]

While the *FD&C Act* does not recognize the term "cosmeceutical," the cosmetics industry uses this word to refer to cosmetic products that have medicinal or drug-like benefits. If a product has drug properties, it must meet the regulatory requirements for drugs.

Although the *FD&C Act* does not specifically require the use of animals in cosmetic safety testing, FDA has consistently advised cosmetic manufacturers to employ whatever testing is appropriate and effective for substantiating the safety of their products. In some cases, after considering available alternatives, companies may determine that animal testing is necessary to ensure the safety of a product or ingredient. Failure to adequately substantiate the safety of a cosmetic product or its ingredients prior to marketing causes the product to be misbranded unless the following warning statement appears conspicuously on the principal display panel of the product's label: "Warning—The safety of this product has not been determined" (21 CFR 740.10).

Neither the *FD&C Act* nor the *FPLA* requires cosmetic labeling to undergo premarket approval by FDA. It is the manufacturer's and/or distributor's responsibility to ensure that products are labeled properly. If the manufacturer fails to comply with the labeling requirements, its product may be considered a misbranded product, subject to regulatory actions.

The following information must appear on the label's principal display panel:

- An identity statement—indicating the nature and use of the product, by means of either the common or usual name, a descriptive name, a fanciful name understood by the public, or an illustration (21 CFR 701.11).
- An accurate statement of the net quantity of contents—in terms of weight, measure, numerical count or a combination of numerical count and weight or measure (21 CFR 701.13).

The following information must appear on label information panel:

- Name and place of business—this may be the manufacturer, packer, or distributor (21 CFR 701.12).
- Distributor statement—if the name and address are not those of the manufacturer, the label must

say "Manufactured for..." or "Distributed by..." (21 CFR 701.12).

- Material facts—failure to reveal material facts is one form of misleading labeling and therefore makes a product misbranded (21 CFR 1.21). An example is directions for safe use, if a product could be unsafe if used incorrectly.
- Warning and caution statements—these must be prominent and conspicuous. The *FD&C Act* and related regulations specify warning and caution statements related to specific products (21 CFR 740). In addition, cosmetics that may be hazardous to consumers must bear appropriate label warnings (21 CFR 740.1). Flammable cosmetics are an example.
- Ingredients—if the product is marketed on a retail basis to consumers, even if it is labeled "For professional use only" or words to that effect, the ingredients must appear on an information panel in descending order of predominance (21 CFR 701.3). As an alternative, when cosmetics are distributed on a mail-order basis, the package mailed to the consumer may contain readily visible instructions for locating the ingredient declaration, such as in a product catalog (currently interpreted as including a website), or instructions for requesting a copy of the ingredient declaration. Mail-order distributors must respond promptly to such requests (21 CFR 701.3(r)). If the product is also an OTC drug, its labeling must comply with the regulations for both OTC drug and cosmetic ingredient labeling, as stated above.

The labels of all cosmetics, whether marketed to consumers or salons, must include a warning statement whenever necessary or appropriate to prevent a health hazard that may occur with use of the product (21 CFR 740.1). Cosmetics sold on a retail basis to consumers also must bear an ingredient declaration, with the names of the ingredients listed in descending order of predominance. The requirement for an ingredient declaration does not apply, for example, to products used at professional establishments or to product samples distributed free of charge. However, the requirement does apply if these products also are marketed on a retail basis, even if they are labeled "For professional use only."

As part of the prohibition against false or misleading information, no cosmetic may be labeled or advertised with statements suggesting that FDA has approved the product.[12]

Canada

The *Food and Drugs Act* and the *Cosmetic Regulations* govern the classification and labeling of cosmetic products in Canada. In addition, the act and regulations also address the issues of composition, safety and advertising.

Some products that other countries or regions consider to be cosmetics are actually regulated as nonprescription drugs or natural health products in Canada (e.g., fluoridated toothpaste, sunscreens, anti-acne products, antiperspirants, etc.). These products include therapeutic claims or contain certain ingredients not permitted in cosmetics. Nonprescription drugs and natural health products must go through a different approval process, requiring applications, site licensing and fees.

It is, however, important to note that according to the Canadian *Food and Drugs Act*, every cosmetic manufacturer and importer shall provide a list of documents to the Canadian health authorities:

(a) a notification form that needs to be signed by the manufacturer, importer or an authorized person or entity.

(b) a copy of the labels and inserts that must contain:

  (i) the name and address of the manufacturer that appears on the label of the cosmetic in accordance with section 20

  (ii) the name under which the cosmetic is sold

  (iii) cosmetic's purpose

  (iv) ingredient list* and exact concentration or concentration range

  (v) cosmetic's physical form

  (vi) the name and address in Canada of the manufacturer, importer or distributor

  (vii) if the cosmetic was not manufactured or formulated by the person whose name appears on the label, the name and address of the person who manufactured or formulated it[13]

  *Manufacturers must use the International Nomenclature of Cosmetic Ingredients (INCI), which also is used in the EU, US and Japan. The use of INCI provides consistent information to both health professionals and users.

The submission of the form does not imply that the product is approved or that it is in compliance with the requirements of the *Canadian Food and Drugs Act* and the *Cosmetic Regulations* or the *Consumer Packaging and Labelling Act and Regulations.*

It is the responsibility of the manufacturer and importer to ensure that their products are in compliance with these requirements before selling them in the Canadian market.

To help cosmetic manufacturers satisfy the requirements for sale of a cosmetic, Health Canada developed the Hotlist, an administrative list of substances that are restricted and prohibited in cosmetics. The Hotlist is a science-based document that is reviewed and updated a few times per year as new scientific data become available. In this way, the Hotlist serves to keep the cosmetic industry aware of new substances Health Canada considers inappropriate for cosmetic use, or which require avoidable hazard labeling. Manufacturers should check the Cosmetics Program website regularly, or contact Health Canada directly, for Hotlist updates.

As of 16 November 2006, Canadian cosmetic regulations require companies to declare product ingredients on the label or exterior wrapping of their cosmetics, with the purpose of enhancing safety and providing consumers with important information concerning the composition of cosmetics.

Additional information that must appear on the label of a prepackaged cosmetic in Canada is:

- the product's identification in English and French (Given that in Canada both English and French are official languages, the labels need to include texts in both languages. Supplementary French language labeling requirements may apply.)
- the declaration of the product's net quantity in metric units of measure in English and French
- the identity and principal place of business of the dealer in English or French

Specific labeling requirements also are mandatory for certain cosmetics, such as hair dye, genital deodorants, containers under pressure and others. It is important to remember that symbols and warning statements used on pressurized containers always must be included in the labels.

As in the US, responsibility for cosmetic safety rests primarily with the manufacturer. There are no requirements for specific testing to be carried out for cosmetics. Manufacturers may be required to submit safety data on any ingredient in response to concerns arising from its structural relationship to other substances posing potential health risks, complaints or other sources.

It is known that the definitions of "drug" and "cosmetic" share some characteristics. Nevertheless, it is important to understand that the requirements for drugs take precedence over the requirements for cosmetics in situations where the claims for a product are considered to be both drug and cosmetic in nature. Drug and cosmetic claims can only be made for drugs. Cosmetics may contain only cosmetic claims; otherwise the product will be considered a drug and must comply with the appropriate drug regulations.

Europe

The main aspects of the EU cosmetic industry's regulatory environment were described in the overview.

Latin America

Even though international standards form the basis for countless regulations in Latin America and elsewhere, these building blocks are frequently structured to each country's specific needs.

The regulatory environment in Latin America is structured as follows:

i. Caribbean countries include Anguilla, Antigua and Barbuda, Aruba, Bahamas, Barbados, the British Virgin Islands, the Cayman Islands, Cuba, Dominica, Dominican Republic, Grenada, Guadeloupe (Fr.), Haiti, Jamaica, Martinique, Montserrat, Netherland Antilles, Puerto Rico, Saint Kitts and Nevis, Saint Lucia, Saint Vincent and the Grenadines, and Trinidad and Tobago, the Turks and Caicos Islands and the US Virgin Islands. They all have individual laws and regulations for consumer products. Considering that several of the islands are associated with the EU or the US, they follow those regulatory structures.
ii. Central American countries are Belize, Costa Rica, El Salvador, Guatemala, Honduras, Nicaragua and Panama. They also have individual laws and regulations for products but in some cases little information is available.
iii. South America includes Argentina, Bolivia, Brazil, Chile, Colombia, Ecuador, Falkland Islands, French Guiana, Guyana, Paraguay, Peru, the Republic of Suriname, Uruguay and Venezuela. Most of these countries have individual laws and regulations for products; however, five (Argentina, Brazil, Paraguay, Venezuela and Uruguay) have entered into a common market arrangement similar to that of the EU, known as Mercosur. At this time, full harmonization is in not imminent.

Cosmetics regulations in the Mercosur countries share a number of key features:

- harmonized definition of cosmetics
- harmonized negative and positive lists
- harmonized labeling requirements (with certain exceptions)
- manufacturers' responsibility for safety of cosmetic products, but with registration of products prior to marketing

Note that in Mercosur countries, positive (approved) and negative (nonapproved) ingredient lists are published, similar to Health Canada's Hot List.

The most regulated countries in Latin America already implement a surveillance system named Cosmetovigilance, which refers to the postmarketing surveillance of any undesirable health-related effects possibly due to the use of cosmetic products. In Brazil, for example, it is mandatory to submit undesirable reaction reports to the authority.

GMP certification of a manufacturing facility is required in most Latin American countries. Some countries may accept GMP certifications issued by foreign regulatory bodies; however, other countries perform facility inspections and issue their own GMP certification in order to approve a cosmetic product registration. It is important to remember that physical presence in the country (subsidiary or partnership) is also mandatory in most Latin American markets. In some cases, market authorizations are owned by the company established locally.

Latin American countries classify products according to different grades, where products classified as Grade I require notification; this is a simple procedure that generally can be completed electronically. Products classified as Grade II are more complex and require market authorization approval.

Summary

For cosmetics, most jurisdictions do not require a preapproval process for products marketed in conformance with local regulations. Cosmetics are, however, required to have proper labels, including mandatory warnings where applicable, a disclosure of all ingredients and, in some instances (e.g., in the EU), the address where product information is available. It is worth noting that the definition of a cosmetic can be quite different from one country to another. For example, a product defined as a cosmetic in the EU could be considered an over-the-counter (OTC) or nonprescription drug in the US. Therefore, companies wishing to sell the same product in different regions must make appropriate changes to the label to ensure compliance with the local classification and regulations. Attention to country-by-country language is recommended to avoid misinterpretations.

Some regions, such as the EU, publish lists of permitted colors, preservatives and UV filters, as well as lists of restricted and banned substances. Such lists tend to be reviewed and updated on a regular basis. In the US, the number of substances banned or restricted for use in cosmetics is very small. However, the US list of positive cosmetic colorants is much shorter, and there is no positive list of preservatives. Latin American countries enforce both positive and negative lists of ingredients.

The development of new regulations, with an emphasis on consumer safety, will significantly affect the cosmetics law in all EU Member States. The introduction of the EU *Cosmetic Products Regulation* (Regulation (EU) 1223/2009) replaced the EU *Cosmetics Directive* (Directive 76/768/EEC) beginning 11 July 2013. Regulatory professionals should stay abreast of this new regulation as it may be a catalyst for similar regulatory changes in other countries.

References

1. History of Cosmetics. Health and Beauty Advice website. http://www.health-and-beauty-advice.com/cosmetics/history-of-cosmetics.php. Accessed 25 July 2013.
2. Regulatory Affairs Professionals Society. Chapter 31, Cosmetics. In: *Fundamentals of US Regulatory Affairs Eighth Edition.* Rockville, MD; 2013:383–390.
2. *Cosmetic Products—Borderline Situations.* Strasbourg, France: Council of Europe Publishing; 2001:200
3. Cosmetic Regulations to the *Food and Drugs Act.*
4. 21 CFR 700.25 Tamper-resistant packaging requirements for cosmetic products
5. *Tamper-Resistant Packaging Act* of 1980.
6. *Federal Anti-Tampering Act* of 1983, Public Law 98-217, amended Chapter 65 of 18 USC.
7. Regulatory Affairs Professionals Society. Chapter 34, Cosmetics. In: *Fundamentals of Canadian Regulatory Affairs Third Edition.* Rockville, MD; 2011:257–262.
8. *Federal Food, Drug, and Cosmetic Act* of 1938, Section 601.
9. *Federal Food, Drug, and Cosmetic Act* of 1938, Section 602.
10. Op cit 2.
11. Cosmetics Q&A: "Personal Care Products." FDA website. http://www.fda.gov/Cosmetics/ResourcesForYou/Consumers/CosmeticsQA/ucm136560.htm. Accessed 25 July 2013.
12. Cosmetic Labels and Labeling Claims. FDA website. http://www.fda.gov/Cosmetics/CosmeticLabelingLabelClaims/default.htm. Accessed 25 July 2013.
13. Canadian *Food and Drugs Act.*

Chapter 30

Food Supplements

Updated by Julia Hilscher, Dr

OBJECTIVES

- ❑ Understand what food supplements are
- ❑ Understand food supplement labeling and health claim requirements
- ❑ Learn general safety and notification requirements related to food supplements

REGULATIONS AND GUIDELINES COVERED IN THIS CHAPTER

- ❑ WHO, *Guidelines for Vitamin and Mineral Food Supplements*, CAC/GL 55-2005
- ❑ EU, Council Directive 76/768/EEC of 27 July 1976 on the approximation of the laws of the Member States relating to cosmetic products, as amended
- ❑ EU, Directive 2002/46/EC of the European Parliament and of the Council of 10 June 2002 on the approximation of the laws of the Member States relating to food supplements, as amended
- ❑ US, *Dietary Supplement Health and Education Act* of 1994

Introduction

Food supplements—also known as dietary supplements or nutritional supplements—are concentrated sources of nutrients or other substances with a nutritional or physiological effect that are taken orally to supplement the normal diet. Nutrients include vitamins, minerals, herbs or other botanicals and amino acids; examples are enzymes, organ tissues, glandulars and metabolites.[1] Food supplements can be used alone or in combination and usually are marketed in dose form, i.e., pills, tablets, capsules, liquids in measured doses, etc. The exact definition of food supplements differs by country, and products may be classified and regulated as either foods or drugs. Other classes of products with a food-like character include dietetic foods, foods for infants and young children and foods for special medical purposes.

Ideally, a diet should provide all the nutrients and other substances necessary for normal development and healthy life maintenance.[2] Some consumers, however, believe their diets require supplementation and choose to complement their intake of nutrients or other beneficial substances with food supplements. Food supplements also may be used when, for whatever reason, dietary intake is insufficient.[3]

Food supplements must be safe, both in quantity and quality. Although the ingredients in most food supplements are found in nature, in supplement form, they contain much higher concentrations. Water-soluble vitamins, such as vitamins B and C, if consumed in excess, are flushed out of the system and not stored in the body. However, although essential in small quantities, fat-soluble vitamins such as vitamin A, if consumed in excess, are stored in adipose tissue and can cause poisoning known as Hypervitaminosis A. It is important to note that hypervitaminosis can occur when large amounts of vitamin-rich foods are consumed regularly; however, most cases of vitamin toxicity result from an excessive intake of vitamin supplements.

Since food supplements contain concentrated nutrients obtained, for example, by extraction of common foods, but also from novel or not well-established foods, ingredients

Table 30-1. Recommended Daily Allowances (RDAs) of Vitamins and Minerals

Vitamin/Mineral	Amount (RDA)	Unit
Vitamin A	800	μg
Vitamin D	5	μg
Vitamin E	12	mg
Vitamin C	80	mg
Thiamine	1.1	mg
Riboflavin	1.4	mg
Niacin	16	mg
Vitamin B6	1.4	mg
Folic acid	200	μg
Vitamin B12	2.5	μg
Biotin	50	μg
Pantothenic acid	6	mg
Calcium	800	mg
Phosphorus	700	mg
Iron	14	mg
Magnesium	375	mg
Zinc	10	mg
Iodine	150	μg

Source: Annex I to Council Directive 90/496/EEC, as amended by Directive 2008/100/EC

need to comply with applicable local regulations, where implemented, governing novel foods.[4–6] Regulations and definitions on novel foods vary. In the EU, novel foods are defined as foods or food ingredients that were not used for human consumption to a significant degree before 15 May 1997. Novel foods fall into one of four categories, including foods and food ingredients produced using a process that is not currently used, where that process gives rise to significant changes in the composition or structure affecting nutritional value, metabolism or level of undesirable substances. In the EU, these foods and food ingredients require a registration or notification prior to being placed on the market.[7]

Recommended Daily Allowances (RDAs)

Competent Authorities have established what is known as the recommended daily/dietary allowance, or RDA (in the US and Canada, Dietary Reference Intakes or DRIs), for various vitamins and minerals.

In the EU, RDAs are provided in the Annex to Council Directive 90/496/EEC of 24 September 1990 on nutrition labeling for foodstuffs, as amended. Examples of EU RDAs are shown in **Table 30-1**.

The Food and Nutrition Board of the Institute of Medicine in the US has published DRI tables based on gender, status (e.g., pregnant/lactating), age and level of activity. These are shown in **Tables 30-2** and **30-3**.

Minimum and Maximum Amounts Based on Safety

Apart from the RDA, minimum and maximum amounts of vitamins and minerals in food supplements are also of interest. Limits per daily portion of consumption should be based on:

- upper safe levels of vitamins and minerals established by scientific risk assessment and based on generally accepted scientific data (gender, age, weight and level of activity may affect any upper limits set)
- intake of vitamins and minerals from other dietary sources[8]

Tolerable upper limits also are listed for various elements and vitamins. These are shown in **Tables 30-4** and **30-5.**

Quality Requirements

For prescription and over-the-counter drugs, defined systems are in place to demonstrate product quality (e.g., stability and consistency of manufacture) before they can be placed on the market. In addition, manufacturing facilities are inspected by the Competent Authority to ensure

Table 30-2. DRIs: Vitamins

Dietary Reference Intakes (DRIs): Recommended Dietary Allowances and Adequate Intakes, Vitamins
Food and Nutrition Board, Institute of Medicine, National Academies

Life Stage Group	Vitamin A (µg/d)[a]	Vitamin C (mg/d)	Vitamin D (µg/d)[b,c]	Vitamin E (mg/d)[d]	Vitamin K (µg/d)	Thiamin (mg/d)	Riboflavin (mg/d)	Niacin (mg/d)[e]	Vitamin B_6 (mg/d)	Folate (µg/d)[f]	Vitamin B_{12} (µg/d)	Pantothenic Acid (mg/d)	Biotin (µg/d)	Choline (mg/d)[g]
Infants														
0 to 6 mo	400*	40*	10	4*	2.0*	0.2*	0.3*	2*	0.1*	65*	0.4*	1.7*	5*	125*
6 to 12 mo	500*	50*	10	5*	2.5*	0.3*	0.4*	4*	0.3*	80*	0.5*	1.8*	6*	150*
Children														
1–3 y	300	15	15	6	30*	0.5	0.5	6	0.5	150	0.9	2*	8*	200*
4–8 y	400	25	15	7	55*	0.6	0.6	8	0.6	200	1.2	3*	12*	250*
Males														
9–13 y	600	45	15	11	60*	0.9	0.9	12	1.0	300	1.8	4*	20*	375*
14–18 y	900	75	15	15	75*	1.2	1.3	16	1.3	400	2.4	5*	25*	550*
19–30 y	900	90	15	15	120*	1.2	1.3	16	1.3	400	2.4	5*	30*	550*
31–50 y	900	90	15	15	120*	1.2	1.3	16	1.3	400	2.4	5*	30*	550*
51–70 y	900	90	15	15	120*	1.2	1.3	16	1.7	400	2.4[h]	5*	30*	550*
> 70 y	900	90	20	15	120*	1.2	1.3	16	1.7	400	2.4[h]	5*	30*	550*
Females														
9–13 y	600	45	15	11	60*	0.9	0.9	12	1.0	300	1.8	4*	20*	375*
14–18 y	700	65	15	15	75*	1.0	1.0	14	1.2	400[i]	2.4	5*	25*	400*
19–30 y	700	75	15	15	90*	1.1	1.1	14	1.3	400[i]	2.4	5*	30*	425*
31–50 y	700	75	15	15	90*	1.1	1.1	14	1.3	400[i]	2.4	5*	30*	425*
51–70 y	700	75	15	15	90*	1.1	1.1	14	1.5	400	2.4[h]	5*	30*	425*
> 70 y	700	75	20	15	90*	1.1	1.1	14	1.5	400	2.4[h]	5*	30*	425*
Pregnancy														
14–18 y	750	80	15	15	75*	1.4	1.4	18	1.9	600[j]	2.6	6*	30*	450*
19–30 y	770	85	15	15	90*	1.4	1.4	18	1.9	600[j]	2.6	6*	30*	450*
31–50 y	770	85	15	15	90*	1.4	1.4	18	1.9	600[j]	2.6	6*	30*	450*
Lactation														
14–18 y	1,200	115	15	19	75*	1.4	1.6	17	2.0	500	2.8	7*	35*	550*
19–30 y	1,300	120	15	19	90*	1.4	1.6	17	2.0	500	2.8	7*	35*	550*
31–50 y	1,300	120	15	19	90*	1.4	1.6	17	2.0	500	2.8	7*	35*	550*

NOTE: This table (taken from the DRI reports, see www.nap.edu) presents Recommended Dietary Allowances (RDAs) in **bold type** and Adequate Intakes (AIs) in ordinary type followed by an asterisk (*). An RDA is the average daily dietary intake level; sufficient to meet the nutrient requirements of nearly all (97-98 percent) healthy individuals in a group. It is calculated from an Estimated Average Requirement (EAR). If sufficient scientific evidence is not available to establish an EAR, and thus calculate an RDA, an AI is usually developed. For healthy breastfed infants, an AI is the mean intake. The AI for other life stage and gender groups is believed to cover the needs of all healthy individuals in the groups, but lack of data or uncertainty in the data prevent being able to specify with confidence the percentage of individuals covered by this intake.

[a] As retinol activity equivalents (RAEs). 1 RAE = 1 µg retinol, 12 µg β-carotene, 24 µg α-carotene, or 24 µg β-cryptoxanthin. The RAE for dietary provitamin A carotenoids is two-fold greater than retinol equivalents (RE), whereas the RAE for preformed vitamin A is the same as RE.

[b] As cholecalciferol. 1 µg cholecalciferol = 40 IU vitamin D.

[c] Under the assumption of minimal sunlight.

[d] As α-tocopherol. α-Tocopherol includes *RRR*-α-tocopherol, the only form of α-tocopherol that occurs naturally in foods, and the *2R*-stereoisomeric forms of α-tocopherol (*RRR*-, *RSR*-, *RRS*-, and *RSS*-α-tocopherol) that occur in fortified foods and supplements. It does not include the *2S*-stereoisomeric forms of α-tocopherol (*SRR*-, *SSR*-, *SRS*-, and *SSS*-α-tocopherol), also found in fortified foods and supplements.

[e] As niacin equivalents (NE). 1 mg of niacin = 60 mg of tryptophan; 0–6 months = preformed niacin (not NE).

[f] As dietary folate equivalents (DFE). 1 DFE = 1 µg food folate = 0.6 µg of folic acid from fortified food or as a supplement consumed with food = 0.5 µg of a supplement taken on an empty stomach.

[g] Although AIs have been set for choline, there are few data to assess whether a dietary supply of choline is needed at all stages of the life cycle, and it may be that the choline requirement can be met by endogenous synthesis at some of these stages.

[h] Because 10 to 30 percent of older people may malabsorb food-bound B_{12}, it is advisable for those older than 50 years to meet their RDA mainly by consuming foods fortified with B_{12} or a supplement containing B_{12}.

[i] In view of evidence linking folate intake with neural tube defects in the fetus, it is recommended that all women capable of becoming pregnant consume 400 µg from supplements or fortified foods in addition to intake of food folate from a varied diet.

[j] It is assumed that women will continue consuming 400 µg from supplements or fortified food until their pregnancy is confirmed and they enter prenatal care, which ordinarily occurs after the end of the periconceptional period—the critical time for formation of the neural tube.

SOURCES: *Dietary Reference Intakes for Calcium, Phosphorous, Magnesium, Vitamin D, and Fluoride* (1997); *Dietary Reference Intakes for Thiamin, Riboflavin, Niacin, Vitamin B_6, Folate, Vitamin B_{12}, Pantothenic Acid, Biotin, and Choline* (1998); *Dietary Reference Intakes for Vitamin C, Vitamin E, Selenium, and Carotenoids* (2000); *Dietary Reference Intakes for Vitamin A, Vitamin K, Arsenic, Boron, Chromium, Copper, Iodine, Iron, Manganese, Molybdenum, Nickel, Silicon, Vanadium, and Zinc* (2001); *Dietary Reference Intakes for Water, Potassium, Sodium, Chloride, and* Sulfate (2005); and *Dietary Reference Intakes for Calcium and Vitamin D* (2011). These reports may be accessed via www.nap.edu.

Source: DRI reports, www.nap.edu

compliance with Good Manufacturing Practice (GMP). Such systems and procedures have not yet been established for food supplements.

Quality assurance and substance purity approaches differ from country to country. In the EU, for example, the purity of some vitamins and mineral substances permitted for use in food supplements is not yet specified in legislation;[9] generally accepted purity criteria recommended by international bodies can be applied. In the US, under the *Dietary Supplement Health and Education Act* of 1994 (*DSHEA*),[10] the supplier is responsible for ensuring that a dietary supplement is safe before it is marketed.[11] The US Food and Drug Administration (FDA) is responsible for taking action regarding any unsafe dietary supplement product on the market, i.e., in the postmarket phase.

Generally, international purity criteria in the form of standards are acceptable locally. Since food supplements are classified as foods or drugs, manufacturers may wish to use quality systems and quality control methods commonly used in these sectors, such as compliance with GMP, Hazard Analysis Critical Control Points (HACCP) and Food and Agriculture (FAO) and World Health Organization (WHO) food standards (implemented by the Codex Alimentarius Commission (CAC)).[12] The International Organization for Standardization (ISO) also has published numerous standards related to food analysis composition and quality management, e.g., ISO 22000:2005, *Food safety management systems—Requirements for any organization in the food chain*. Although voluntary, ISO standards are recognized by the World Trade Organization (WTO) under the Technical Barriers to Trade (TBT) agreement and have been incorporated into national legislation in many countries.

Food Supplement Labeling

Since food supplements can be bought off the shelf, it is essential that any information relating to their nutrient content be presented clearly to allow consumers to make an informed choice and to ensure they are used properly and safely. Whether food supplements are regulated nationally

Table 30-3. DRIs: Elements

Dietary Reference Intakes (DRIs): Recommended Dietary Allowances and Adequate Intakes, Elements
Food and Nutrition Board, Institute of Medicine, National Academies

Life Stage Group	Calcium (mg/d)	Chromium (μg/d)	Copper (μg/d)	Fluoride (mg/d)	Iodine (μg/d)	Iron (mg/d)	Magnesium (mg/d)	Manganese (mg/d)	Molybdenum (μg/d)	Phosphorus (mg/d)	Selenium (μg/d)	Zinc (mg/d)	Potassium (g/d)	Sodium (g/d)	Chloride (g/d)
Infants															
0 to 6 mo	200*	0.2*	200*	0.01*	110*	0.27*	30*	0.003*	2*	100*	15*	2*	0.4*	0.12*	0.18*
6 to 12 mo	260*	5.5*	220*	0.5*	130*	11	75*	0.6*	3*	275*	20*	3	0.7*	0.37*	0.57*
Children															
1–3 y	700	11*	340	0.7*	90	7	80	1.2*	17	460	20	3	3.0*	1.0*	1.5*
4–8 y	1,000	15*	440	1*	90	10	130	1.5*	22	500	30	5	3.8*	1.2*	1.9*
Males															
9–13 y	1,300	25*	700	2*	120	8	240	1.9*	34	1,250	40	8	4.5*	1.5*	2.3*
14–18 y	1,300	35*	890	3*	150	11	410	2.2*	43	1,250	55	11	4.7*	1.5*	2.3*
19–30 y	1,000	35*	900	4*	150	8	400	2.3*	45	700	55	11	4.7*	1.5*	2.3*
31–50 y	1,000	35*	900	4*	150	8	420	2.3*	45	700	55	11	4.7*	1.5*	2.3*
51–70 y	1,000	30*	900	4*	150	8	420	2.3*	45	700	55	11	4.7*	1.3*	2.0*
> 70 y	1,200	30*	900	4*	150	8	420	2.3*	45	700	55	11	4.7*	1.2*	1.8*
Females															
9–13 y	1,300	21*	700	2*	120	8	240	1.6*	34	1,250	40	8	4.5*	1.5*	2.3*
14–18 y	1,300	24*	890	3*	150	15	360	1.6*	43	1,250	55	9	4.7*	1.5*	2.3*
19–30 y	1,000	25*	900	3*	150	18	310	1.8*	45	700	55	8	4.7*	1.5*	2.3*
31–50 y	1,000	25*	900	3*	150	18	320	1.8*	45	700	55	8	4.7*	1.5*	2.3*
51–70 y	1,200	20*	900	3*	150	8	320	1.8*	45	700	55	8	4.7*	1.3*	2.0*
> 70 y	1,200	20*	900	3*	150	8	320	1.8*	45	700	55	8	4.7*	1.2*	1.8*
Pregnancy															
14–18 y	1,300	29*	1,000	3*	220	27	400	2.0*	50	1,250	60	12	4.7*	1.5*	2.3*
19–30 y	1,000	30*	1,000	3*	220	27	350	2.0*	50	700	60	11	4.7*	1.5*	2.3*
31–50 y	1,000	30*	1,000	3*	220	27	360	2.0*	50	700	60	11	4.7*	1.5*	2.3*
Lactation															
14–18 y	1,300	44*	1,300	3*	290	10	360	2.6*	50	1,250	70	13	5.1*	1.5*	2.3*
19–30 y	1,000	45*	1,300	3*	290	9	310	2.6*	50	700	70	12	5.1*	1.5*	2.3*
31–50 y	1,000	45*	1,300	3*	290	9	320	2.6*	50	700	70	12	5.1*	1.5*	2.3*

NOTE: This table (taken from the DRI reports, see www.nap.edu) presents Recommended Dietary Allowances (RDAs) in **bold type** and Adequate Intakes (AIs) in ordinary type followed by an asterisk (*). An RDA is the average daily dietary intake level; sufficient to meet the nutrient requirements of nearly all (97-98 percent) healthy individuals in a group. It is calculated from an Estimated Average Requirement (EAR). If sufficient scientific evidence is not available to establish an EAR, and thus calculate an RDA, an AI is usually developed. For healthy breastfed infants, an AI is the mean intake. The AI for other life stage and gender groups is believed to cover the needs of all healthy individuals in the groups, but lack of data or uncertainty in the data prevent being able to specify with confidence the percentage of individuals covered by this intake.

SOURCES: *Dietary Reference Intakes for Calcium, Phosphorous, Magnesium, Vitamin D, and Fluoride* (1997); *Dietary Reference Intakes for Thiamin, Riboflavin, Niacin, Vitamin B_6, Folate, Vitamin B_{12}, Pantothenic Acid, Biotin, and Choline* (1998); *Dietary Reference Intakes for Vitamin C, Vitamin E, Selenium, and Carotenoids* (2000); and *Dietary Reference Intakes for Vitamin A, Vitamin K, Arsenic, Boron, Chromium, Copper, Iodine, Iron, Manganese, Molybdenum, Nickel, Silicon, Vanadium, and Zinc* (2001); *Dietary Reference Intakes for Water, Potassium, Sodium, Chloride, and* Sulfate (2005); and *Dietary Reference Intakes for Calcium and Vitamin D* (2011). These reports may be accessed via www.nap.edu.

Source: www.nap.edu

under food or drug laws, supplement labeling must comply with the requirements of the appropriate classification. For example, in the EU where food supplements are classified as foods, their labeling must comply with:

- Directive 2000/13/EC of the European Parliament and of the Council of 20 March 2000 on the approximation of the laws of the Member States relating to the labelling, presentation and advertising of foodstuffs, as amended
- Directive 2002/46/EC of the European Parliament and of the Council of 10 June 2002 on the approximation of the laws of the Member States relating to food supplements, as amended
- Regulation No. (EC) 1830/2003 of the European Parliament and of the Council of 22 September 2003 concerning the traceability and labelling of genetically modified organisms and the traceability of food and feed products produced from genetically modified organisms and amending Directive 2001/18/EC
- Regulation No. (EC) 1924/2006 of the European Parliament and of the Council of 20 December 2006 on nutrition and health claims made on foods, as amended

Similarly, local laws and regulations must be taken into account when placing food supplements on the market in different countries or regions. Basic information to incorporate into food supplement labeling includes:

- manufacturer name and address
- product's country of origin
- list of ingredients
- quantity of certain ingredients or categories of ingredients
- net quantity
- expiry date
- any special storage conditions or conditions of use
- recommended daily dose
- warning not to exceed the stated recommended daily dose
- statement that food supplements should not be used as a substitute for a varied diet
- statement that the products should be stored out of the reach of young children
- amount of the nutrients or substances with a nutritional or physiological effect present in the product
- vitamin and mineral information expressed as a percentage of the reference values per daily recommended amount

Table 30-4. DRIs: Tolerable Upper Intake Levels, Vitamins

Dietary Reference Intakes (DRIs): Tolerable Upper Intake Levels, Vitamins
Food and Nutrition Board, Institute of Medicine, National Academies

Life Stage Group	Vitamin A (μg/d)[a]	Vitamin C (mg/d)	Vitamin D (μg/d)	Vitamin E (mg/d)[b,c]	Vitamin K	Thiamin	Riboflavin	Niacin (mg/d)[c]	Vitamin B_6 (mg/d)	Folate (μg/d)[c]	Vitamin B_{12}	Pantothenic Acid	Biotin	Choline (g/d)	Carotenoids[d]
Infants															
0 to 6 mo	600	ND[e]	25	ND	ND	ND	ND	ND	ND	ND	ND	ND	ND	ND	ND
6 to 12 mo	600	ND	38	ND	ND	ND	ND	ND	ND	ND	ND	ND	ND	ND	ND
Children															
1–3 y	600	400	63	200	ND	ND	ND	10	30	300	ND	ND	ND	1.0	ND
4–8 y	900	650	75	300	ND	ND	ND	15	40	400	ND	ND	ND	1.0	ND
Males															
9–13 y	1,700	1,200	100	600	ND	ND	ND	20	60	600	ND	ND	ND	2.0	ND
14–18 y	2,800	1,800	100	800	ND	ND	ND	30	80	800	ND	ND	ND	3.0	ND
19–30 y	3,000	2,000	100	1,000	ND	ND	ND	35	100	1,000	ND	ND	ND	3.5	ND
31–50 y	3,000	2,000	100	1,000	ND	ND	ND	35	100	1,000	ND	ND	ND	3.5	ND
51–70 y	3,000	2,000	100	1,000	ND	ND	ND	35	100	1,000	ND	ND	ND	3.5	ND
> 70 y	3,000	2,000	100	1,000	ND	ND	ND	35	100	1,000	ND	ND	ND	3.5	ND
Females															
9–13 y	1,700	1,200	100	600	ND	ND	ND	20	60	600	ND	ND	ND	2.0	ND
14–18 y	2,800	1,800	100	800	ND	ND	ND	30	80	800	ND	ND	ND	3.0	ND
19–30 y	3,000	2,000	100	1,000	ND	ND	ND	35	100	1,000	ND	ND	ND	3.5	ND
31–50 y	3,000	2,000	100	1,000	ND	ND	ND	35	100	1,000	ND	ND	ND	3.5	ND
51–70 y	3,000	2,000	100	1,000	ND	ND	ND	35	100	1,000	ND	ND	ND	3.5	ND
> 70 y	3,000	2,000	100	1,000	ND	ND	ND	35	100	1,000	ND	ND	ND	3.5	ND
Pregnancy															
14–18 y	2,800	1,800	100	800	ND	ND	ND	30	80	800	ND	ND	ND	3.0	ND
19–30 y	3,000	2,000	100	1,000	ND	ND	ND	35	100	1,000	ND	ND	ND	3.5	ND
31–50 y	3,000	2,000	100	1,000	ND	ND	ND	35	100	1,000	ND	ND	ND	3.5	ND
Lactation															
14–18 y	2,800	1,800	100	800	ND	ND	ND	30	80	800	ND	ND	ND	3.0	ND
19–30 y	3,000	2,000	100	1,000	ND	ND	ND	35	100	1,000	ND	ND	ND	3.5	ND
31–50 y	3,000	2,000	100	1,000	ND	ND	ND	35	100	1,000	ND	ND	ND	3.5	ND

NOTE: A Tolerable Upper Intake Level (UL) is the highest level of daily nutrient intake that is likely to pose no risk of adverse health effects to almost all individuals in the general population. Unless otherwise specified, the UL represents total intake from food, water, and supplements. Due to a lack of suitable data, ULs could not be established for vitamin K, thiamin, riboflavin, vitamin B_{12}, pantothenic acid, biotin, and carotenoids. In the absence of a UL, extra caution may be warranted in consuming levels above recommended intakes. Members of the general population should be advised not to routinely exceed the UL. The UL is not meant to apply to individuals who are treated with the nutrient under medical supervision or to individuals with predisposing conditions that modify their sensitivity to the nutrient.

[a] As preformed vitamin A only.

[b] As α-tocopherol; applies to any form of supplemental α-tocopherol.

[c] The ULs for vitamin E, niacin, and folate apply to synthetic forms obtained from supplements, fortified foods, or a combination of the two.

[d] β-Carotene supplements are advised only to serve as a provitamin A source for individuals at risk of vitamin A deficiency.

[e] ND = Not determinable due to lack of data of adverse effects in this age group and concern with regard to lack of ability to handle excess amounts. Source of intake should be from food only to prevent high levels of intake.

SOURCES: *Dietary Reference Intakes for Calcium, Phosphorous, Magnesium, Vitamin D, and Fluoride* (1997); *Dietary Reference Intakes for Thiamin, Riboflavin, Niacin, Vitamin B_6, Folate, Vitamin B_{12}, Pantothenic Acid, Biotin, and Choline* (1998); *Dietary Reference Intakes for Vitamin C, Vitamine E, Selenium, and Carotenoids* (2000); *Dietary Reference Intakes for Vitamin A, Vitamin K, Arsenic, Boron, Chromium, Copper, Iodine, Iron, Manganese, Molybdenum, Nickel, Silicon, Vanadium, and Zinc* (2001); and *Dietary Reference Intakes for Calcium and Vitamin D* (2011). These reports may be accessed via www.nap.edu.

Source: DRI reports, www.nap.edu

In addition to these main points, labeling must comply with any existing national legislation.

Food supplement labeling, presentation and advertising must not include any statement or implication that a balanced and varied diet cannot provide appropriate quantities of nutrients in general. It also is important that there be no claim that the product has the property of preventing, treating or curing a human disease and no reference to such properties. Any nutrition and health claims must be based on scientific facts and/or clinical data.

Notification

Some jurisdictions require, on either a mandatory or voluntary basis, that Competent Authorities be notified about all food supplements to facilitate efficient monitoring of the supplements. This notification usually takes the form of forwarding a copy of the label and/or ingredient(s) list.

Some Competent Authorities, e.g., FDA, introduced dietary supplement serious adverse event reporting[13] and require product information such as labeling, claims, package inserts and accompanying literature, to better monitor food supplements on the US market.[14]

Borderline Issues

In many cases, the distinction between food supplements and medicinal products may overlap in so-called "borderline products." This overlap may relate to the definition of a medicine and/or food supplement in the national legislation or to concentrations of certain nutrients. If a product falls under both the food and medicinal products definition, it should be treated as a medicinal product and regulated as such. The effect of product classification is profound. The safety and efficacy of medicinal products must be supported by extensive documentation and clinical information before they can be registered and placed on the market. Classifying a product as a food supplement, on the other hand, can limit the claims made on the packaging materials, especially health claims. In formulating a regulatory strategy, these points should be taken into consideration.

Table 30-5. DRIs: Tolerable Upper Intake Levels, Elements

Dietary Reference Intakes (DRIs): Tolerable Upper Intake Levels, Elements
Food and Nutrition Board, Institute of Medicine, National Academies

Life Stage Group	Arsenic[a]	Boron (mg/d)	Calcium (mg/d)	Chromium	Copper (µg/d)	Fluoride (mg/d)	Iodine (µg/d)	Iron (mg/d)	Magnesium (mg/d)[b]	Manganese (mg/d)	Molybdenum (µg/d)	Nickel (mg/d)	Phosphorus (g/d)	Selenium (µg/d)	Silicon[c]	Vanadium (mg/d)[d]	Zinc (mg/d)	Sodium (g/d)	Chloride (g/d)
Infants																			
0 to 6 mo	ND[e]	ND	1,000	ND	ND	0.7	ND	40	ND	ND	ND	ND	ND	45	ND	ND	4	ND	ND
6 to 12 mo	ND	ND	1,500	ND	ND	0.9	ND	40	ND	ND	ND	ND	ND	60	ND	ND	5	ND	ND
Children																			
1–3 y	ND	3	2,500	ND	1,000	1.3	200	40	65	2	300	0.2	3	90	ND	ND	7	1.5	2.3
4–8 y	ND	6	2,500	ND	3,000	2.2	300	40	110	3	600	0.3	3	150	ND	ND	12	1.9	2.9
Males																			
9–13 y	ND	11	3,000	ND	5,000	10	600	40	350	6	1,100	0.6	4	280	ND	ND	23	2.2	3.4
14–18 y	ND	17	3,000	ND	8,000	10	900	45	350	9	1,700	1.0	4	400	ND	ND	34	2.3	3.6
19–30 y	ND	20	2,500	ND	10,000	10	1,100	45	350	11	2,000	1.0	4	400	ND	1.8	40	2.3	3.6
31–50 y	ND	20	2,500	ND	10,000	10	1,100	45	350	11	2,000	1.0	4	400	ND	1.8	40	2.3	3.6
51–70 y	ND	20	2,000	ND	10,000	10	1,100	45	350	11	2,000	1.0	4	400	ND	1.8	40	2.3	3.6
> 70 y	ND	20	2,000	ND	10,000	10	1,100	45	350	11	2,000	1.0	3	400	ND	1.8	40	2.3	3.6
Females																			
9–13 y	ND	11	3,000	ND	5,000	10	600	40	350	6	1,100	0.6	4	280	ND	ND	23	2.2	3.4
14–18 y	ND	17	3,000	ND	8,000	10	900	45	350	9	1,700	1.0	4	400	ND	ND	34	2.3	3.6
19–30 y	ND	20	2,500	ND	10,000	10	1,100	45	350	11	2,000	1.0	4	400	ND	1.8	40	2.3	3.6
31–50 y	ND	20	2,500	ND	10,000	10	1,100	45	350	11	2,000	1.0	4	400	ND	1.8	40	2.3	3.6
51–70 y	ND	20	2,000	ND	10,000	10	1,100	45	350	11	2,000	1.0	4	400	ND	1.8	40	2.3	3.6
> 70 y	ND	20	2,000	ND	10,000	10	1,100	45	350	11	2,000	1.0	3	400	ND	1.8	40	2.3	3.6
Pregnancy																			
14–18 y	ND	17	3,000	ND	8,000	10	900	45	350	9	1,700	1.0	3.5	400	ND	ND	34	2.3	3.6
19–30 y	ND	20	2,500	ND	10,000	10	1,100	45	350	11	2,000	1.0	3.5	400	ND	ND	40	2.3	3.6
61–50 y	ND	20	2,500	ND	10,000	10	1,100	45	350	11	2,000	1.0	3.5	400	ND	ND	40	2.3	3.6
Lactation																			
14–18 y	ND	17	3,000	ND	8,000	10	900	45	350	9	1,700	1.0	4	400	ND	ND	34	2.3	3.6
19–30 y	ND	20	2,500	ND	10,000	10	1,100	45	350	11	2,000	1.0	4	400	ND	ND	40	2.3	3.6
31–50 y	ND	20	2,500	ND	10,000	10	1,100	45	350	11	2,000	1.0	4	400	ND	ND	40	2.3	3.6

NOTE: A Tolerable Upper Intake Level (UL) is the highest level of daily nutrient intake that is likely to pose no risk of adverse health effects to almost all individuals in the general population. Unless otherwise specified, the UL represents total intake from food, water, and supplements. Due to a lack of suitable data, ULs could not be established for vitamin K, thiamin, riboflavin, vitamin B_{12}, pantothenic acid, biotin, and carotenoids. In the absence of a UL, extra caution may be warranted in consuming levels above recommended intakes. Members of the general population should be advised not to routinely exceed the UL. The UL is not meant to apply to individuals who are treated with the nutrient under medical supervision or to individuals with predisposing conditions that modify their sensitivity to the nutrient.

[a]Although the UL was not determined for arsenic, there is no justification for adding arsenic to food or supplements.

[b]The ULs for magnesium represent intake from a pharmacological agent only and do not include intake from food and water.

[c]Although silicon has not been shown to cause adverse effects in humans, there is no justification for adding silicon to supplements.

[d]Although vanadium in food has not been shown to cause adverse effects in humans, there is no justification for adding vanadium to food and vanadium supplements should be used with caution. The UL is based on adverse effects in laboratory animals and this data could be used to set a UL for adults but not children and adolescents.

[e]ND = Not determinable due to lack of data of adverse effects in this age group and concern with regard to lack of ability to handle excess amounts. Source of intake should be from food only to prevent high levels of intake.

SOURCES: *Dietary Reference Intakes for Calcium, Phosphorous, Magnesium, Vitamin D, and Fluoride* (1997); *Dietary Reference Intakes for Thiamin, Riboflavin, Niacin, Vitamin B_6, Folate, Vitamin B_{12}, Pantothenic Acid, Biotin, and Choline* (1998); *Dietary Reference Intakes for Vitamin C, Vitamin E, Selenium, and Carotenoids* (2000); *Dietary Reference Intakes for Vitamin A, Vitamin K, Arsenic, Boron, Chromium, Copper, Iodine, Iron, Manganese, Molybdenum, Nickel, Silicon, Vanadium, and Zinc* (2001); *Dietary Reference Intakes for Water, Potassium, Sodium, Chloride, and Sulfate* (2005); and *Dietary Reference Intakes for Calcium and Vitamin D* (2011). These reports may be accessed via www.nap.edu.

Source: DRI reports, www.nap.edu

Summary

Globally, food supplements still are subject to widely diverse country-by-country regulations. Most countries have clear definitions about what constitutes a food supplement in their territories; they are generally recognized as vitamins and minerals. RDAs/RDIs for these substances have been published but may differ slightly across regions. Nutrition and health claims usually are allowed on food supplement labels only if substantiated by evidence and according to local rules and regulations. Since food supplements can be bought off the shelf, it is imperative that labeling information be clear to allow consumers to make an informed choice when buying such products to ensure they are used properly and safely.

References

1. US, *Dietary Supplement Health and Education Act* of 1994. http://www.fda.gov/Food/DietarySupplements/default.htm. Accessed 8 April 2013.
2. Regulatory Affairs Professionals Society. Chapter 32 Food Supplements, Health Claims and Borderline Issues. In: *Fundamentals of EU Regulatory Affairs Sixth Edition.* Rockville, MD; 2012:311–318.
3. WHO, Guidelines for Vitamin and Mineral Food Supplements, CAC/GL 55-2005.
4. Regulation (EC) No 258/97 of the European Parliament and of the Council of 27 January 1997 concerning novel foods and novel food ingredients, as amended. Eur-Lex website. http://eur-lex.europa.eu/LexUriServ/LexUriServ.do?uri=CELEX:31997R0258:en:HTML. Accessed 28 July 2013.
5. Australia New Zealand Food Standards Code—Standard 1.5.1—Novel Foods—F2011C00564. Australian Government ComLaw website. http://www.comlaw.gov.au/Details/F2013C00142. Accessed 27 July 2013.
6. Canada Food and Drug Regulation Division 28 Novel Foods, as amended
7. Op cit 4.
8. Directive 2002/46/EC of the European Parliament and of the Council of 10 June 2002 on the approximation of the laws of the Member States relating to food supplements. Eur-Lex website. http://eur-lex.europa.eu/LexUriServ/LexUriServ.do?uri=CONSLEG:2002L0046:20060421:EN:PDF. Accessed 27 July 2013.
9. Op cit 2.
10. Op cit 1.
11. Ibid.
12. United States Pharmacopeial Convention, white paper, *Importance of Standards in Assuring Good Quality Food Ingredients and Foods*, 23 September 2009. USP website. http://www.usp.org/sites/default/files/usp_pdf/EN/members/foodsIngred.pdf. Accessed 27 July 2013.
13. US, *Dietary Supplement and Nonprescription Drug Consumer Protection Act* of 2006, as amended. FDA website. http://www.fda.gov/RegulatoryInformation/Legislation/FederalFoodDrugandCosmeticActFDCAct/SignificantAmendmentstotheFDCAct/ucm148035.htm. Accessed 27 July 2013
14. Op cit 1.

Chapter 31

Veterinary Medicinal Products

Updated by Jethro Ekuta, DVM, PhD, RAC, FRAPS

OBJECTIVES

- ❑ Gain a basic understanding of what a veterinary medicinal product is
- ❑ Understand the main differences between the registration of human medicinal products and veterinary medicinal products
- ❑ Learn about specific aspects of veterinary products
- ❑ Learn about veterinary pharmacovigilance and Good Manufacturing Practices

REGULATIONS AND GUIDELINES COVERED IN THIS CHAPTER

VICH & OTHERS

- ❑ OECD, *Good Laboratory Practice: OECD Principles and Guidance for Compliance Monitoring* (ENV/MC/CHEM(98)17)
- ❑ VICH GL1, *Validation of Analytical Procedures: Definition and Terminology* (Step 7)
- ❑ VICH GL2, *Validation of Analytical Procedures: Methodology* (Step 7)
- ❑ VICH GL3, *Stability Testing of New Veterinary Drug Substances and Medicinal Products (Revision)* (Step 9)
- ❑ VICH GL4, *Stability Testing for New Veterinary Dosage Forms* (Step 7)
- ❑ VICH GL5, *Stability Testing: Photostability Testing of New Veterinary Drug Substances and Medicinal Products* (Step 7)
- ❑ VICH GL8, *Stability Testing for Medicated Premixes* (Step 7)
- ❑ VICH GL9, *Good Clinical Practice* (Step 7)
- ❑ VICH GL10, *Impurities in New Veterinary Drug Substances (Revision)* (Step 9)
- ❑ VICH GL11, *Impurities in New Veterinary Medicinal Products (Revision)* (Step 9)
- ❑ VICH GL17, *Stability Testing of New Biotechnological/Biological Veterinary Medicinal Products* (Step 7)
- ❑ VICH GL18, *Impurities: Residual Solvents in New Veterinary Medicinal Products, Active Substances and Excipients* (Step 7)
- ❑ VICH GL22, *Studies to Evaluate the Safety of Residues of Veterinary Drugs in Human Food: Reproduction Testing* (Step 7)
- ❑ VICH GL23, *Studies to Evaluate the Safety of Residues of Veterinary Drugs in Human Food: Genotoxicity Testing* (Step 7)

- VICH GL24, *Pharmacovigilance of Veterinary Medicinal Products: Management of Adverse Event Reports (AERs)* Pending adoption of GL30 and GL35 (Step 4)
- VICH GL28, *Studies to Evaluate the Safety of Residues of Veterinary Drugs in Human Food: Carcinogenicity Testing* (Step 7)
- VICH GL29, *Pharmacovigilance of Veterinary Medicinal Products—Management of Periodic Summary Update Reports* (Step 7)
- VICH GL30, *Pharmacovigilance of Veterinary Medicinal Products: Controlled List of Terms* (Step 5)
- VICH GL31, *Studies to Evaluate the Safety of Residues of Veterinary Drugs in Human Food: Repeat-Dose (90 Days) Toxicity Testing* (Step 7)
- VICH GL32, *Studies to Evaluate the Safety of Residues of Veterinary Drugs in Human Food: Developmental Toxicity Testing* (Step 7)
- VICH GL33, *Studies to Evaluate the Safety of Residues of Veterinary Drugs in Human Food: General Approach to Testing* (Step 7)
- VICH GL35, *Pharmacovigilance of Veterinary Medicinal Products: Electronic Standards for Transfer of Data* (Step 3)
- VICH GL36, *Studies to Evaluate the Safety of Residues of Veterinary Drugs in Human Food: General Approach to Establish a Microbiological ADI* (Step 7)
- VICH GL37, *Studies to Evaluate the Safety of Residues of Veterinary Drugs in Human Food: Repeat-Dose Chronic Toxicity Testing* (Step7)
- VICH GL39, *Test Procedures and Acceptance Criteria for New Veterinary Drug Substances and New Medicinal Products: Chemical Substances* (Step 7)
- VICH GL40, *Test Procedures and Acceptance Criteria for New Biotechnological/Biological Veterinary Medicinal Products* (Step 7)
- VICH GL42, *Pharmacovigilance of Veterinary Medicinal Products: Data Elements for Submission of Adverse Event Reports (AERS)* Pending adoption of GL30 and GL35 (Step 5)
- VICH GL46, *Studies to Evaluate the Metabolism and Residue Kinetics of Veterinary Drugs in Food-Producing Animals: Metabolism Study to Determine the Quantity and Identify the Nature of Residues* (Step 4)
- VICH GL47, *Studies to Evaluate the Metabolism and Residue Kinetics of Veterinary Drugs in Food-Producing Animals: Comparative Metabolism Studies in Laboratory Animals* (Step 4)
- VICH GL48, *Studies to Evaluate the Metabolism and Residue Kinetics of Veterinary Drugs in Food-Producing Animals: Marker Residue Depletion Studies to Establish Product Withdrawal Periods* (Step 4)
- VICH GL49, *Guidelines for the Validation of Analytical Methods Used in Residue Depletion Studies* (Step 4)

EU

- Directive 2001/82/EC of the European Parliament and of the Council of 6 November 2001 on the Community code relating to veterinary medicinal products, as amended by Directive 2004/28/EC
- *The Rules governing Veterinary medicinal products in the European Community, Notice to Applicants, Medicinal products for Veterinary Use, Volume 6B, Presentation and content of the dossier—Part 1*
- *Note for guidance on minimising the risk of transmitting animal spongiform encephalopathy agents via human and veterinary medicinal products* (EMEA /410/01 Rev. 2)
- *Position paper on risk assessment of the use of starting materials of ruminant origin in veterinary medicinal products intended for use in ruminant species* (EMEA/CVMP/121/01)
- *Position paper on the assessment of the risk of transmission of animal spongiform encephalopathy agents by master seed materials used in the production of veterinary vaccines* (EMEA/CVMP/019/01)

- ❑ Regulation (EC) No. 470/2009 of the European Parliament and of the Council of 6 May 2009 laying down Community procedures for the establishment of residue limits of pharmacologically active substances in foodstuffs of animal origin
- ❑ *Policy for classification and incentives for veterinary medicinal products indicated for minor use minor species (MUMS)/limited markets* (EMEA/429080/2009)
- ❑ Directive 2004/10/EC of the European Parliament and of the Council of 11 February 2004 on the harmonization of laws, regulations and administrative provisions relating to the application of the principles of good laboratory practice and the verification of their application for tests on chemical substances
- ❑ Directive 2004/9/EC of the European Parliament and of the Council of 11 February 2004 on the inspection and verification of good laboratory practice (GLP)

US

- ❑ 21 CFR 589 Substances Prohibited From Use in Animal Food or Feed
- ❑ 21 CFR 314 Applications for FDA Approval to Market a New Drug
- ❑ Environmental Assessment for Amendments to 21 CFR 589 Substances Prohibited from Use in Animal Food or Feed, Final Rule
- ❑ *Minor Use and Minor Species Animal Health Act* of 2004 (*MUMS*)
- ❑ 21 CFR 58 Good Laboratory Practice for Nonclinical Laboratory Studies

Introduction

Veterinary medical products prevent, treat or diagnose diseases in animals. They include not only drugs, vaccines, devices and diagnostic test kits, but also such products as food additives and feed ingredients and animal grooming aids.[1] As is the case for human medical products, the safety assessment of veterinary medicinal products is based on a benefit:risk analysis. The safety of veterinary medicinal products depends on the target animal's level of tolerance to the ingredients, and for food-producing animals, the acceptable level of residue.[2] The safety of the person administering the veterinary product also should be taken into consideration.

Medicines, such as antibiotics, have had a major impact on animal health. These products have improved animals' quality of life and life expectancy and have underpinned the drive toward greater agricultural efficiency in the livestock sector.[3] Veterinary medicines have paved the way for large-scale production of meat and dairy products. These benefits to animals and to agriculture also have implications for public health, e.g., the use of antibiotics in livestock production can increase the likelihood of treatment failures due to antibiotic resistance when human medicinal products containing such antibiotics are administered for the treatment of a human disease.

Differences Between Human and Animal Medicinal Products

- Human medicines are developed for one species whereas veterinary medicines are developed for many animal species.
- There may be geographic differences related to distribution of animal species and prevalence of diseases.[4]
- Veterinary medicinal products normally are not part of national health schemes and are not reimbursed; therefore, the entire cost of treatment must be borne by the animal's owner.
- Some species may end up in the human food chain; hence, harmful drug residues in animals must be strictly controlled.
- Those who administer veterinary medicinal products must be safeguarded from possible harmful effects of such products.[5]
- Veterinary medicines may have a more direct effect on the environment than human products due to the fact that many animals receiving such medications are bred and raised on farms with direct contact with the soil and vegetation.

What are Veterinary Medicinal Products?

The exact definition of a veterinary medicinal product varies country by country; however, in general, it is any substance or combination of substances administered to animals for the purpose of:

- treating disease in animals
- preventing disease in animals
- making a medical diagnosis in animals
- restoring, correcting or modifying physiological functions in animals by exerting a pharmacological, immunological or metabolic action[6]

Veterinary medicinal products include therapeutics, vaccines, agents for reproduction management and certain dietary supplements. The exact definition of a veterinary medicinal product is laid down in national laws and regulations. National legislation must be consulted, especially for borderline products, such as vitamin and mineral supplements, insecticides applied to animals, noninsecticidal shampoos, teat dips applied after milking, antiseptics, herbal products, etc.

General Requirements

The exact requirements and processes in granting marketing authorization to a veterinary medicinal product are country-specific. Generally, a marketing authorization application includes, at a minimum, the following information:

- name and permanent address or registered place of business of the company seeking a marketing authorization and, if different, that of the manufacturer
- manufacturing sites and description of the manufacturing methods
- veterinary medicinal product name
- qualitative and quantitative particulars of the product, including the international nonproprietary name (INN) recommended by the World Health Organization (WHO) or its chemical name
- therapeutic indications, contraindications and adverse reactions
- dosage for the various animal species for which the veterinary medicinal product is intended
- pharmaceutical form and method and route of administration
- proposed shelf life and storage conditions
- any precautionary and safety measures to be taken related to waste disposal and any other potential risks
- withdrawal period for medicinal products intended for food-producing species
- description of testing methods employed
- results of pharmaceutical (physicochemical, biological or microbiological) tests, including any safety and residue tests, preclinical and clinical trials and any potential risks
- description of the pharmacovigilance system and, where appropriate, the risk management system in place and evidence of a qualified person responsible for pharmacovigilance
- summary medical information and a mock-up of the veterinary medicinal product's immediate packaging, outer packaging and package leaflet
- copies of any marketing authorization obtained in other countries
- for veterinary medicinal products intended for one or more food-producing species, information on the Maximum Residue Limits (MRLs)

This list, based primarily on EU requirements,[7] is not exhaustive. The national requirements in different countries may vary slightly. The complexity of the registration process and the data requirements depend on the type of application and the registration method.

Harmonization

As discussed in Chapter 1, harmonization efforts were initiated in the 1990s via the creation of the International Conference on Harmonisation (ICH, drugs) in 1990 and the Global Harmonization Task Force (GHTF, medical devices), conceived in 1992. These harmonization efforts were intended to avoid duplication of effort and ensure global acceptance of data created, respectively, for drug and medical device dossier applications. A similar body, the International Cooperation on Harmonisation of Technical Requirements for Registration of Veterinary Products (VICH), was officially launched in April 1996.[8] This is a trilateral (EU-Japan-US) program that aims to harmonize technical requirements for veterinary product registration.

After the first International Technical Consultation on Veterinary Drug Registration (ITCVDR) in 1983, several government and industry initiatives culminated in the formation of VICH. Topics of interest included residues of veterinary drugs in foods, standard requirements for veterinary product registration and mutual exchange of guidelines for consultation.

In January 1993, the Global Harmonization of Standards (GHOST) discussion document was published by the *Fédération Européenne de la Santé Animale* (FEDESA, now International Federation for Animal Health (IFAH)). This document set out a program for the international harmonization of registration requirements for veterinary pharmaceuticals and biologicals.[9] The *Office International des Epizooties* (OIE, now the World Organization for Animal Health) set up an ad hoc group on harmonization of veterinary medicinal products in 1994. This group decided that VICH would have a complementary role in food safety standards and that issues related to GLP and GMP that were already subject to mutual recognition agreements would not fall within VICH's responsibilities. A discussion document was prepared with the aim of prioritizing topics for consideration by VICH, highlighting ICH guidelines that could be adapted to the VICH program and detailing areas where there was a lack of harmonization among the EU, US and Japanese guidelines.

Objectives

VICH's objectives are similar to those of ICH:

- establish and implement harmonized regulatory requirements for veterinary medicinal products in the VICH regions, which meet high quality, safety

Figure 31-1. VICH Steering Committee and Expert Working Groups

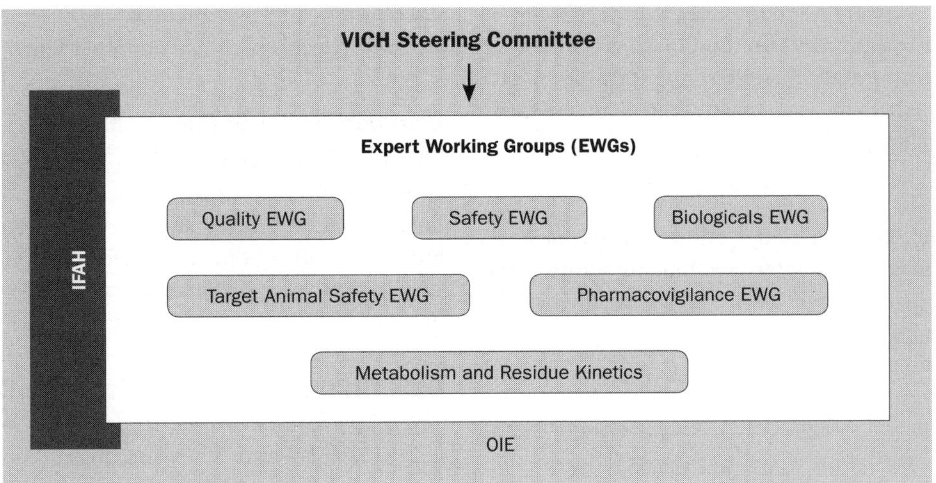

Source: http://www.vichsec.org

and efficacy standards and minimize the use of test animals and product development costs

- provide a basis for wider international harmonization of registration requirements
- monitor and maintain existing VICH guidelines
- ensure efficient processes for maintaining and monitoring consistent interpretation of data requirements following the implementation of VICH guidelines
- promote constructive dialogue between regulatory authorities and industry and provide technical guidance to enable response to significant emerging global issues and science that impact regulatory requirements within the VICH regions[10]

The VICH steering committee is empowered to drive the harmonization process. The steering committee is assisted by six Expert Working Groups (EWGs), each comprising six members (see **Figure 31-1**).

VICH EWGs address 10 topics:

1. quality
2. safety
3. ecotoxicity
4. Good Clinical Practice (GCP)
5. anthelmintics
6. pharmacovigilance
7. biologicals quality monitoring
8. antimicrobial resistance
9. target animal safety
10. metabolism and residue kinetics

Dossier Requirements

Although the registration procedures for veterinary medicinal products are generally the same as those described in Chapter 10 for human medicinal products, the dossier content differs slightly. While the exact requirements are determined on a local basis, the dossier for veterinary medicinal products normally includes:

- dossier summary—application form, medical summary information, labels, pack leaflet and other packaging texts and expert reports
- quality—physicochemical or biological test results
- safety—pharmacological, toxicological and environmental safety test results
- residues—residue study results and analytical methodology (not for immunological veterinary medicinal products)
- efficacy—preclinical and clinical trial results
- general conclusions for immunological veterinary medicinal products

Differences Between Human and Veterinary Dossiers

There are many parallels between human and veterinary marketing authorization application dossiers, especially in the areas of quality, safety and efficacy.[11] The main differences arise from the fact that certain animals may end up in the food chain; hence, emphasis is placed on protecting consumers from any potentially harmful residues from treatment with veterinary medicinal products. In addition, people administering veterinary medicinal products or coming into contact with the treated animal must be safeguarded from possible harmful effects.

Quality

The quality section of the dossier is essentially identical for both human and veterinary products. Standards and testing methods usually are based on the same quality guidelines. In the absence of specific veterinary guidelines, pharmaceutical assessors normally refer to the guidelines for human medicinal products. In most instances, there are strict rules governing transmissible spongiform encephalopathies (TSE), especially when bovine ingredients are used for bovine medicinal products.

Safety

A major difference between human and veterinary medicinal product dossiers is the safety section. In addition to active substance toxicology data, veterinary medicinal product dossiers include data on:

- target animal
- user safety
- environmental safety
- residues

The basic human and veterinary toxicology packages are very similar; however, specific studies on target species' metabolism and excretion are required in the veterinary dossier. In addition, a risk assessment of operator safety for those administering veterinary medicinal products may be required.[12] Veterinary medicinal products' effects on the environment are more direct than those of products for human use, with possible cumulative impact, and should be subject to a more rigorous environmental risk assessment (ERA). Direct contamination can occur via excretion by livestock and effects of pesticides and genetically modified organisms (GMOs), among others.

Residues

The most important difference between human and veterinary medicinal product dossiers is that information on product residues is required for veterinary medicinal products but not for human medicinal products. For products intended for food-producing animals, the veterinary dossier must include the following information on residues:

- studies on residue depletion in the appropriate tissues
- marker residue confirmation (not always the active substance)
- MRL information
- residue analytical methodology
- proposed post-therapy withdrawal period before any animal product is collected for human consumption[13]

Efficacy

The efficacy sections are similar for veterinary and human medicinal product dossiers and should include information on pharmacology and other preclinical studies as well as clinical trials. Veterinary product dossiers, however, also should include data on target species' safety (drug tolerance). Other relevant information includes existing resistance levels of the disease organism and its geographic distribution, and the potential for resistance development, especially to antimicrobial or anthelmintic drugs.

Common Technical Document

The use of the Common Technical Document (CTD)—essentially a single dossier structure for the EU, US and Japan—has not been applied to veterinary medicinal products in all regions. Discussions by the VICH Steering Committee concluded that, in the short term, priority must be given to harmonizing important guidelines.

Veterinary Medicinal Product Dossiers

Veterinary medicinal products can only be placed on the market after issuance of a marketing authorization based on evaluation of data submitted in the form of a dossier. The main data to be submitted are summarized in the section on Dossier Requirements. Following are data requirements for each dossier section based on VICH and national/regional standards.

Quality

The quality section of the veterinary medicinal product dossier usually contains the following information:

- composition
- manufacturing method description
- control of starting materials
- specific measure related to TSEs
- control tests of intermediates
- finished product control tests
- stability
- GMOs
- other relevant information

For medicinal products containing only substances of vegetable origin and immunologicals, the requirements may differ slightly. For example, the TSE section may be omitted for the former.

VICH Guidelines

VICH has published a series of quality guidelines covering:

- analytical validation
- impurities
- stability
- specifications

These guidelines can be found on the VICH website (http://www.vichsec.org[14]).

The composition section normally includes both qualitative and quantitative information about the active substance(s) and excipients, a brief description of the container and the composition and formula of any samples used in clinical trials in the target species. Development pharmaceutics should explain the choice of formulation, composition, substances and container and justify any overages, describing any tests conducted.[15]

Information on the method of manufacture should include the manufacturing formula and batch size. Manufacturing process information normally includes data on in-process controls and the pharmaceutical assembly process, as well as a manufacturing process flow chart. This should be complemented by process validation results.

All starting materials used in the manufacture of veterinary medicinal products, including starting materials used for the active ingredient(s), excipients and those used for the immediate packaging, should be controlled properly.

The occurrence of TSE in animals is handled differently in various regions. Some authorities may require specific measures related to preventing the transmission of TSEs to be included in the application dossier. National Competent Authorities in various countries have published their own guidance documents related to minimizing the risk of spreading TSE agents via human and veterinary medicinal products. Examples include the current EU *Note for Guidance on minimising the risk of transmitting animal spongiform encephalopathies agents via human and veterinary medicinal products*[16] and various position papers.[17] The US Food and Drug Administration (FDA) published rules in 1997 and 2008 to protect animals and consumers against bovine spongiform encephalopathy (BSE) by prohibiting the use of most mammalian protein in the manufacture of feeds for ruminant animals and by removing high-risk materials from all animal feed.[18] In 2008, FDA published a regulation that strengthened the 1997 rule, prohibiting the use in animal feed of tissues with the highest risk for carrying the agent thought to cause BSE, e.g., brain and spinal cord tissues.

Information on the control of intermediate products, if applicable, should distinguish between in-process controls and control tests on intermediate products. The control of the finished product normally includes data on product specifications and tests for release, control methods and test procedures such as identification tests, quantitative determination of active substance(s), purity tests and pharmaceutical tests. In addition, information on excipient(s) identification and determination usually is required. The scientific data should cover analytical validation of methods and comments on the choice of routine tests and standards, batch analysis data, results obtained and reference materials.[19]

All analytical procedures used for starting materials, intermediates or finished product(s) should be properly validated. VICH has published two guidelines on this topic: VICH GL1[20] on validation definitions and VICH GL2[21] on validation methods. These documents cover the four most common types of analytical procedures:

- identification tests
- quantitative tests for impurities
- limit tests for the control of impurities
- quantitative tests of the active moiety in samples of drug substance or drug product or other selected drug product components

Impurity testing of the active substance(s) and finished product(s) should be based on the VICH guidelines on impurity testing: VICH GL10 *Impurities in New Veterinary Drug Substances*,[22] VICH GL11 *Impurities in New Veterinary Medicinal Products*[23] and VICH GL18 *Impurities: Residual Solvents in New Veterinary Medicinal Products, Active Substances and Excipients*.[24]

Stability tests for the active ingredient and the finished product should be carried out under both normal and accelerated conditions. Data should cover analytical test procedures and validation. The information for the finished product also should include a section on shelf life and storage conditions. In addition, information about the product's shelf life after reconstitution and/or first opening normally is required. VICH has published a series of guidelines on stability testing:

- VICH GL3 *Stability Testing of New Veterinary Drug Substances and Medicinal Products*[25]
- VICH GL4 *Stability Testing: Requirements for New Dosage Forms*[26]
- VICH GL5 *Stability Testing: Photostability Testing of New Drug Substances and Products*[27]
- VICH GL8 *Stability Testing for Medicated Premixes*[28]
- VICH GL17 *Stability Testing of New Biotechnological/Biological Veterinary Medicinal Products*[29]

Release and testing specifications also need to be clearly outlined in a veterinary medicinal product application dossier. Several guidance documents have been published by national agencies and associations and VICH. The VICH guidelines cover test procedures and acceptance criteria for new veterinary drug substances and new medicinal products for both chemical substances (VICH GL39[30]) and biotechnological/biological veterinary medicinal products (VICH GL40[31]).

Some regions, e.g., the EU, require environmental risk assessments for marketing authorization applications for veterinary medicinal products containing or consisting of GMOs.[32] Applications may be complemented by other information such as data on metabolism and/or bioavailability.

Good Manufacturing Practice (GMP)

The principles of Good Manufacturing Practice (GMP) are applicable to all operations involving both the manufacture of finished veterinary products and the preparation of products for use in clinical trials. All analytical test procedures included in the dossier's quality section should be described in sufficient detail to enable authorities to evaluate and, if necessary, repeat any tests. All processes and tests used should be validated and the validation results included in the technical information.

Safety and Residues

Any potential risks to humans or the environment from use of the product should be demonstrated. These include not only adverse reactions in the target species but also aspects related to the safety of humans administering the product or handling treated animals, as well as risks associated with consuming food products derived from treated animals. When compiling this section, reference should be made to international and national guidelines on:

- establishment of MRLs of veterinary medicinal products in foodstuffs of animal origin
- environmental risk assessment for veterinary medicinal products

VICH has published several safety guidelines including:

- VICH GL33 *Studies to Evaluate the Safety of Residues of Veterinary Drugs in Human Food: General Approach to Testing*[33]
- VICH GL36 *Studies to Evaluate the Safety of Residues of Veterinary Drugs in Human Food: General Approach to Establish a Microbiological ADI*[34]
- VICH GL23 *Studies to Evaluate the Safety of Residues of Veterinary Drugs in Human Food: Genotoxicity Texting*[35]
- VICH GL22 *Studies to Evaluate the Safety of Residues of Veterinary Drugs in Human Food: Reproduction Texting*[36]
- VICH GL32 *Studies to Evaluate the Safety of Residues of Veterinary Drugs in Human Food: Developmental Toxicity Texting*[37]
- VICH GL31 *Studies to Evaluate the Safety of Residues of Veterinary Drugs in Human Food: Repeat-Dose (90 Days) Toxicity Testing*[38]
- VICH GL37 *Studies to Evaluate the Safety of Residues of Veterinary Drugs in Human Food: Repeat-Dose Chronic Toxicity Texting*[39]
- VICH GL28 *Studies to Evaluate the Safety of Residues of Veterinary Drugs in Human Food: Carcinogenicity Testing*[40]

Safety

Safety information normally would include data on the characteristics of the active substance, pharmacological studies (pharmacodynamics and pharmacokinetics), toxicological studies (e.g., single- and repeat-dose plus tolerance in the target species, among others), studies of other effects, user safety and environmental risk assessment.[41]

Data on the active substance should be detailed and usually include the substance's name (INN; International Union of Pure and Applied Chemistry (IUPAC); Chemical Abstract Service (CAS)) and its classification (therapeutic, pharmacological). In addition, other information such as the structural and molecular formulae, relative molecular mass, degree of impurity, qualitative and quantitative composition of impurities and physical properties (e.g., appearance, melting point, boiling point, vapor pressure, etc.) would be required. Data on the finished product normally would include information on the formulation, indication(s) and posology.[42]

Toxicological data should include all toxicology studies relevant to evaluating the product's safety. These studies normally would include:

- single-dose toxicity
- repeated-dose toxicity
- tolerance in the target species of animal
- reproductive toxicity, including teratogenicity
- effects on reproduction
- embryotoxicity/fetotoxicity, including teratogenicity
- mutagenicity
- carcinogenicity (if necessary)

Studies related to human safety also may be added. The omission of any studies should be duly justified. Tests should comply with VICH and national guidelines and regulations. Any other studies conducted, such as special studies (e.g., immunotoxicity, endocrine function tests, liver and renal function tests, etc.), tests in humans and/or microbiological studies, also should be described. User safety study results and environmental risk assessments also could be included in the safety section.[43] In addition to national and VICH guidelines, it may be useful to reference assessments by other official bodies such as the Joint FAO/WHO Expert Committee on Food Additives (JECFA), the Joint Meeting of the FAO Panel of Experts on Pesticide Residues in Food and the Environment (JMPR) and the WHO Expert Group on Pesticide Residues, where appropriate.

Residues

Information on residues is important for products intended for use in food-producing animal species. Such studies normally include:

- pharmacokinetics (absorption, distribution, biotransformation and excretion in the target species by the relevant route(s) of administration)
- depletion of residues
- MRLs
- withdrawal periods (calculated, whenever possible, using the statistical method recommended by the European Medicines Agency's Committee for Medicinal Products for Veterinary Use (CVMP)[44])

VICH has published a series of guidelines on metabolism and residue kinetics:

- VICH GL46 *Studies to Evaluate the Metabolism and Residue Kinetics of Veterinary Drugs in Food-producing Animals: Metabolism Study to Determine the Quantity and Identify the Nature of Residues*[45]
- VICH GL47 *Studies to Evaluate the Metabolism and Residue Kinetics of Veterinary Drugs in Food-producing Animals: Comparative Metabolism Studies in Laboratory Animals*[46]
- VICH GL48 *Studies to Evaluate the Metabolism and Residue Kinetics of Veterinary Drugs in Food-producing Animals: Marker Residue Depletion Studies to Establish Product Withdrawal Periods*[47]
- VICH GL49 *Guidelines for the Validation of Analytical Methods used in Residue Depletion Studies*[48]

Any analytical methods used in residue determination should be properly validated and adequately described.

Important aspects to consider when testing for residues are MRLs resulting from the use of a veterinary medicinal product (expressed in suitable units, e.g., mg/kg or µg/kg on a fresh weight basis) that may be legally permitted or recognized as acceptable in or on a food. MRLs are based on a Safety File, comprising a set of toxicology data, and a Residue File, describing a substance's residue nature, magnitude, metabolism and depletion. In order to establish appropriate withdrawal times, additional residue depletion studies or bioequivalence studies normally are necessary.

Establishment of MRLs for Major Species

The "no-observed-effect-level" (NOEL) is the highest drug dose that causes no observable effect and can be used to calculate the drug's acceptable daily intake (ADI). This is an estimate of the amount a person can ingest daily over a lifetime with no risk to the consumer.[49] In order to calculate the MRL, the total residues' (sum of the remaining unmetabolized parent compound and all its metabolites) distribution and depletion from the edible tissues of the treated animal species should be investigated. Using a marker residue, the ADI is distributed appropriately among the different animal produce (muscle, liver, kidney, fat, milk, eggs and honey) making up the daily "food basket" to obtain an MRL for each edible tissue. The total amount of residues in the food basket should not exceed the ADI. To exceed the ADI in relation to a particular substance, it would be necessary to consume more than 500g of meat (including offal and fat), 1.5 L of milk, two eggs and 20g of honey, each containing residues at the MRL, daily, for life.[50]

The rate of residue depletion should then be studied under controlled conditions and a withdrawal period set. This is the time required, after the last treatment, for the level of residues to fall below the MRL using statistical methods.

More information on MRLs can be found on national websites and those of the European Medicines Agency[51,52] and Health Canada.[53] The US Department of Agriculture's Food Safety and Inspection Service (FSIS) is responsible for inspecting meat and poultry product establishments at the federal level and for reporting any detected violative drug residues in meat and poultry to FDA's Center for Veterinary Medicine (CVM) for regulatory follow-up.[54]

Establishment of MRLs for Minor Species

Incentives not unlike those provided for human orphan drug products are made available to sponsors to address the shortage of drugs for treating relatively rare disorders of major veterinary species (minor use) and less-common animal species (minor species) under a veterinarian's care. In the US, the *Minor Use and Minor Species Animal Health Act* of 2004 (*MUMS*)[55] addresses this topic. In the EU, the European Medicines Agency has published, *Policy for classification and incentives for veterinary medicinal products indicated for minor use minor species (MUMS)/limited markets.*[56]

Efficacy

The efficacy section should contain preclinical and clinical testing information. Some of these tests are discussed in detail in the section on safety. Since many tests are similar to those for human medicinal products, see Chapter 10, which highlights issues for human medicinal product preclinical and clinical testing.

The preclinical testing section should include pharmacodynamic and pharmacokinetic data, i.e., absorption rate and extent, distribution, metabolism and excretion of the unchanged substance and/or metabolites. Other information may include target species tolerance and resistance to the active substance.

Clinical documentation should include information on the results and critical evaluations of dose determination and dose confirmation studies and clinical trials in the target species. This documentation should clearly demonstrate the active substance's therapeutic efficacy and safety. For veterinary medicinal products intended for long-term use, efficacy maintenance and the establishment of appropriate dosage regimes should be discussed. The possibility of resistance development also should be addressed. Suitable statistical methods should be used in any calculations.

Good Laboratory Practice

As discussed in Chapter 10, all preclinical studies should be conducted in conformity with Good Laboratory Practice (GLP) guidelines. GLP is a quality system applied to the organizational process and conditions under which non-clinical health and environmental safety studies are planned, performed, monitored, recorded, reported and archived.[57] GLP is outlined in the Organization for Economic

Co-operation and Development (OECD) Principles of GLP[58] and national regulations (US 21 CFR 58[59] and EU Directives 2004/10/EC[60] and 2004/9/EC[61]). OECD also has published a series of guidance documents on GLP implementation and monitoring that can be found at http://www.oecd.org.

For more information on GLP, please refer to Chapter 10.

Good Clinical Practice

All clinical trials must be conducted according to Good Clinical Practice (GCP) and GMP guidelines. VICH has published VICH GL9 *Good Clinical Practice*,[62] which can be used as a reference. This guidance covers topics such as adverse event reporting, regulatory requirements, audits, blinding, case report forms, disposal of animals and compliance. It also outlines the responsibilities of both the investigator and the sponsor, as well as the roles of contract research organizations (CROs) and monitors.

Authorization Procedures

As discussed in Chapter 10, authorization procedures for human medicinal products are determined at the national or regional (e.g., Centralised Procedure in the EU and Middle East) level(s). The same applies to veterinary medicinal products, which, in principle, follow registration procedures similar to those for human products. For more information about authorization procedures, see Chapter 10.

It is worth mentioning that in most countries, the evaluation of veterinary medicinal products is carried out by units within the Competent Authority distinct from those units accessing medicinal products for human use. Also, laws governing human medicinal products do not necessarily apply to veterinary medicinal products, which usually have their own set of regulations.

Postmarket Issues

Postmarket activities for veterinary medicinal products are similar to those for medicinal products for human use in many ways and include activities related to lifecycle management and pharmacovigilance. Marketing authorization holders (MAHs) for veterinary medicinal products must keep track of any changes in the postmarket phase by implementing a proper change control system. Minor changes to the product normally require notification only, whereas major changes may entail a new evaluation by the Competent Authority before the change can be implemented.

Pharmacovigilance

Veterinary medicinal product pharmacovigilance can be defined as the detection and investigation of the effects of the use of these products, mainly aimed at safety and efficacy in animals and safety in people exposed to the products.[63] The obligations for adverse reaction reporting for veterinary medicinal products are very similar to those for human medicines. The exact requirements are laid down in national laws and regulations. VICH has published a series of veterinary medicinal product pharmacovigilance reporting guidelines that also cover the management of Periodic Safety Update Reports (PSURs).[64] Other guidelines include VICH GL30 *Pharmacovigilance of Veterinary Medicinal Products: Controlled List of* Terms,[65] VICH GL35 *Pharmacovigilance of Veterinary Medicinal Products: Electronic Standards for Transfer of Data*[66] and VICH GL42 *Pharmacovigliance of Veterinary Medicinal Products: Data Elements for Submission of Adverse Event Reports.*[67]

The flow of information from the reporter to the MAH and/or the Competent Authority is vital to the pharmacovigilance reporting process. How this information is handled should be laid down in Standard Operating Procedures (SOPs). **Figure 31-2** shows the usual flow of information in a pharmacovigilance system.

Periodic Safety Update Reports (PSURs)

Pharmacovigilance reporting is important to guarantee the continued safety and efficacy of veterinary medicinal products on the market.[68] The International Birth Date (IBD), i.e., the date of initial product registration, is the basis for harmonizing PSUR reporting dates. The frequency of submitting update reports is subject to local regulatory requirements and regulations. After initial commercialization, PSURs normally are required every six month for the first two years, annually the following two years and every three years thereafter. According to VICH GL29, PSURs should contain:

1. MAH name and address responsible for the veterinary medicinal product detailed in the PSUR
2. clear identification of the veterinary medicinal product
3. time period covered by the PSUR (start and end dates)
4. Adverse Event Reports (AERs) for subject veterinary medicinal product and those for any same and/or similar pharmaceutical veterinary medicinal or biological products
5. line listing (per VICH GL 35) for AERs not yet submitted electronically at the time of PSUR submission
6. bibliographic listing of scientific articles published during the PSUR time period found in a widely accepted search engine that address AERs pertaining to the subject veterinary medicinal product and a brief statement assessing the relevance of these articles to the product
7. relationship of sales volume of veterinary medicinal product, by country, to the number of AERs

Figure 31-2. Information Flow in the Pharmacovigilance System

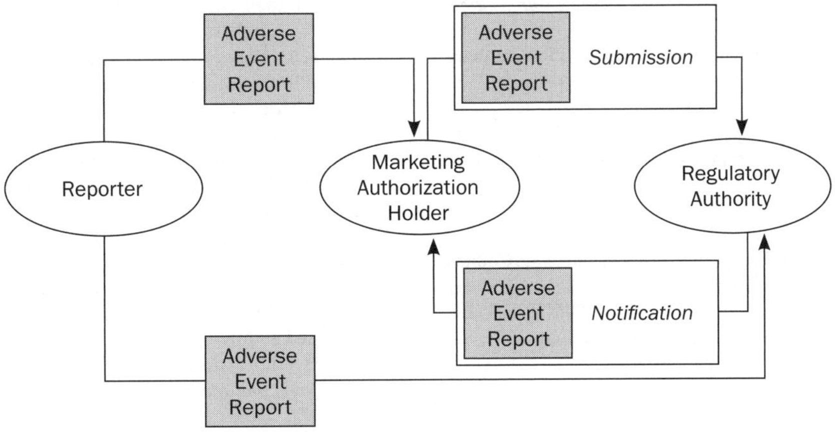

Source: VICH GL24, Pharmacovigilance of Veterinary Medicinal Products: Management of Adverse Event Reports (AERs)

8. an update of any Competent Authority-mandated or MAH regulatory actions for the subject product or related veterinary medicinal products (e.g., changes to the product, labeling changes and market suspensions) taken or pending for safety and effectiveness reasons during the reporting period
9. concise critical analysis and opinion on the subject veterinary medicinal product's risk:benefit profile and comments on important developments for:
   a. evidence of previously unidentified concerns
   b. changes in frequency of adverse events
   c. drug interactions
   d. human adverse events

The PSUR should be accompanied by a suitable discussion and conclusion, especially regarding changes to the label.

Postmarket Surveillance Studies

Postmarket surveillance studies may be initiated voluntarily by the MAH, or the requirements may be defined as postmarket commitments at the time authorization is granted. Alternatively, such studies may be required following evaluation of postmarket data, especially if there appear to be safety issues or higher than expected incidence of adverse events.

Reimbursement

Veterinary medicinal products normally are not part of national health schemes and are not reimbursed, and the entire cost of treatment must be borne by the animal's owner.

Conclusion

At the global level, the regulation of veterinary medicines is an important part of wider efforts in society to promote the health and well-being of animals. In this context, it is important to ensure the availability of high-quality, safe and effective medicines for veterinary use. Drugs administered to animals offer several challenges compared to human medicinal products. The veterinary market is fragmented by many animal species; animals may end up in the human food chain, so harmful drug residues must be strictly controlled, and the safety of individuals administering veterinary medicines or coming into contact with treated animals must be taken into consideration. In addition, animals treated with such veterinary medicinal products and bred outdoors come into direct contact with the soil and vegetation, resulting in adverse effects on the environment.

As with medicinal products for human use, the registration of veterinary medicinal products is governed by national laws and regulations. Companies operating at the global level need to have reliable and easy access to local regulatory information. To avoid duplication of effort and ensure global acceptance of data created for veterinary dossier applications, the VICH, a trilateral (EU-Japan-US) program, was initiated with the goal of harmonizing technical requirements for veterinary product registration.

Technical information presented to Competent Authorities in marketing authorization dossiers should take into account harmonized guidelines published by VICH and any national laws and regulations. More information about local requirements can be found on individual country's Competent Authority website.

References

1. Regulatory Affairs Professionals Society. Chapter 32, Veterinary Products. In: *Fundamentals of US Regulatory Affairs Eighth Edition,* Rockville, MD, 2013:391–400.
2. Regulatory Affairs Professionals Society. Chapter 35, Veterinary Products. In: *Fundamentals of Canadian Regulatory Affairs Third Edition,* Rockville, MD, 2011: 263–268.
3. Regulatory Affairs Professionals Society. Chapter 33 Veterinary Medicinal Products. In: *Fundamentals of EU Regulatory Affairs, Sixth Edition.* Rockville, MD, 2012:319–341.
4. Ibid.
5. Ibid.
6. Directive 2001/82/EC of the European Parliament and of the Council of 6 November 2001 on the Community code relating to veterinary medicinal products, as amended by Directive 2004/28/EC. EC website. http://ec.europa.eu/health/files/eudralex/vol-5/dir_2001_82/dir_2001_82_en.pdf. Accessed 29 July 2013.
7. Ibid, article 12(3).
8. What is VICH? Definition, history and objectives. VICH website. http://www.vichsec.org/en/what-is.htm . Accessed 29 July 2013.
9. Ibid.
10. Ibid.
11. Op cit 3.
12. Ibid.
13. Ibid.
14. VICH Topics—Expert Working Groups. VICH website. http://www.vichsec.org/en/topics.htm#1. Accessed 29 July 2013 2013.
15. EudraLex—*Volume 6 Notice to Applicants and Regulatory Guidelines for Medicinal products for Veterinary Use, Volume 6B, Presentation and content of the dossier* (March 2004). EC website. http://ec.europa.eu/health/documents/eudralex/vol-6/. Accessed 29 July 2013
16. *Note for guidance on minimising the risk of transmitting animal spongiform encephalopathy agents via human and veterinary medicinal products* (EMEA/410/01 rev 2). Eur-Lex website. http://eur-lex.europa.eu/LexUriServ/LexUriServ.do?uri=OJ:C:2011:073:0001:0018:EN:PDF. Accessed 29 July 2013.
17. a)*Position paper on the risk assessment of the use of starting materials of ruminant origin in veterinary medicinal products intended for use in ruminant species* adopted by the Committee for Veterinary Medicinal Products(2001). Eur-Lex website. http://eur-lex.europa.eu/LexUriServ/LexUriServ.do?uri=OJ:C:2001:286:0010:0011:EN:PDF Accessed 29 July 2013.; b) The *Position paper on the assessment of the risk of transmission of animal spongiform encephalopathy agents by master seed materials used in the production of veterinary vaccines* adopted by the Committee for Veterinary Medicinal Products (2001). EMA website. http://www.ema.europa.eu/docs/en_GB/document_library/Scientific_guideline/2009/10/WC500004601.pdf. Accessed 29 July 2013.
18. a) Substances Prohibited From Use in Animal Food or Feed—Final Rule, *Federal Register*: 25 April 2008 Volume 73, Number 81). FDA website. http://www.fda.gov/OHRMS/DOCKETS/98fr/08-1180.pdf. Accessed 29 July 2013.; b) Environmental Assessment for Final Rule—Substances Prohibited from Use in Animal Food or Feed, FDA-2002-N-0031-0129.
19. Op cit 15.
20. VICH GL1 *Validation of Analytical Procedures: Definition and Terminology* (Step 7, EWG consensus signed in 1997, Implemented in October 1999). VICH website. http://www.vichsec.org/pdf/gl01_st7.pdf. Accessed 29 July 2013.
21. VICH GL2 *Validation of Analytical Procedures: Methodology* (Step 7, EWG consensus signed in 1997, Implemented in October 1999). VICH website. http://www.vichsec.org/pdf/gl02_st7.pdf. Accessed 29 July 2013.
22. VICH GL10 *Impurities in New Veterinary Drug Substances (Revision)* (Step 9, January 2008). VICH website. http://www.vichsec.org/pdf/2000/GL10_ST7.pdf. Accessed 29 July 2013.
23. VICH GL11 *Impurities in New Veterinary Medicinal Products (Revision)* (Step 9, January 2008). VICH website. http://www.vichsec.org/pdf/2000/GL11_ST7.pdf. Accessed 29 July 2013.
24. VICH GL18 *Impurities: Residual Solvents in New Veterinary Medicinal Products, Active Substances and Excipients* (Step 7, EWG consensus signed in 1999, Implemented in July 2001). VICH wwebsite. http://www.vichsec.org/pdf/2000/Gl18_st7.pdf. Accessed 29 July 2013.
25. VICH GL3(R) *Stability: Stability Testing of New Veterinary Drug Substances and Medicinal Products (Revision)* (Step 9, January 2008). VICH website. http://www.vichsec.org/pdf/gl03_st7.pdf. Accessed 29 July 2013.
26. VICH GL4 *Stability Testing: Requirements for New Dosage Forms* (Annex to the parent stability guideline (VICH GL3), Step 7, EWG consensus signed in 1997, Implemented in May 2000). VICH website. http://www.vichsec.org/pdf/2007/GL03_ST7(R).pdf. Accessed 29 July 2013.
27. VICH GL5 *Stability Testing: Photostability Testing of New Drug Substances and Medicinal Products* (Step 7, EWG consensus signed in 1997, Implemented in May 2000). VICH website. http://www.vichsec.org/pdf/gl05_st7.pdf. Accessed 29 July 2013.
28. VICH GL8 *Stability Testing for Medicated Premixes* (Step 7, EWG consensus signed in 1998, Implemented in December 2000–June 2001). VICH website. http://www.vichsec.org/pdf/2000/GL08_ST7.pdf. Accessed 29 July 2013.
29. VICH GL17 *Stability Testing of New Biotechnological/Biological Veterinary Medicinal Products* (Step 7, EWG consensus signed in 1999, Implemented in July 2001). VICH website. http://www.vichsec.org/pdf/2000/Gl17_st7.pdf. Accessed 29 July 2013.
30. VICH GL39 *Test Procedures and Acceptance Criteria for New Veterinary Drug Substances and New Medicinal Products: Chemical Substances* (Step 7, EWG consensus signed in 2004, Implemented in November 2006). VICH website. http://www.vichsec.org/pdf/GL39-st7.pdf. Accessed 29 July 2013.
31. VICH GL40 *Test Procedures and Acceptance Criteria for New Biotechnological/Biological Veterinary Medicinal Products* (Step 7, EWG consensus signed in 2004, Implemented in November 2006). VICH website. http://www.vichsec.org/pdf/GL40-st7.pdf. Accessed 29 July 2013.
32. Op cit 15.
33. VICH GL33 *Studies to Evaluate the Safety of Residues of Veterinary Drugs in Human Food: General Approach to Testing* (Step 7, EWG consensus signed in 2001, Implemented in October 2003). VICH website. http://www.vichsec.org/en/GL33_st7-Rev2.doc. Accessed 29 July 2013.
34. VICH GL36 *Studies to Evaluate the Safety of Residues of Veterinary Drugs in Human Food: General Approach to Establish a Microbiological ADI* (Step 7, EWG consensus signed in 2002, Implemented in May 2005). VICH website. http://www.vichsec.org/pdf/05_2004/Gl36_st7_F_rev.pdf. Accessed 2 August 2013.
35. VICH GL23 *Studies to Evaluate the Safety of Residues of Veterinary Drugs in Human Food: Genotoxicity Testing* (Step7, EWG consensus signed in 2000, Implemented in August 2002). VICH website. http://www.vichsec.org/pdf/05_2004/GL23_st7-Rev.pdf. Accessed 2 August 2013.
36. VICH GL22 *Studies to Evaluate the Safety of Residues of Veterinary Drugs in Human Food: Reproduction Testing* (Step 7, EWG consensus signed in 2000, Implemented in August 2002). VICH website. http://www.vichsec.org/pdf/05_2004/GL22_st7-Rev.pdf. Accessed 2 August 2013.
37. VICH GL32 *Studies to Evaluate the Safety of Residues of Veterinary Drugs in Human Food: Developmental Toxicity Testing* (Step 7, EWG consensus signed in 2001, Implemented in October 2003 (Exc. EU)). VICH website. http://www.vichsec.org/pdf/05_2004/GL32_st7-Rev.pdf. Accessed 2 August 2013.
38. VICH GL31 *Studies to Evaluate the Safety of Residues of Veterinary Drugs in Human Food: Repeat-Dose Toxicity Testing* (Step 7, EWG consensus signed in 2001, Implemented in October 2003). VICH

website. http://www.vichsec.org/pdf/05_2004/GL31_st7-Rev.pdf. Accessed 2 August 2013.

39. VICH GL37 *Studies to Evaluate the Safety of Residues of Veterinary Drugs in Human Food: Repeat-Dose Chronic Toxicity Testing* (Step 7, EWG consensus signed in 2002, Implemented in May 2005). VICH website. http://www.vichsec.org/pdf/06_2004/GL37_st7-f.pdf. Accessed 2 August 2013.
40. VICH GL28 *Studies to Evaluate the Safety of Residues of Veterinary Drugs in Human Food: Carcinogenicity Testing* (Step 7, EWG consensus signed in 2001, Implemented in October 2003). VICH website. http://www.vichsec.org/pdf/11_2002/Gl28_st7.pdf. Accessed 2 August 2013.
41. Op cit 15.
42. Ibid.
43. Ibid.
44. Committee for Veterinary Medicinal Products, *Note for Guidance: Approach Towards Harmonisation of Withdrawal Periods* (April 1996). EMA website. http://www.ema.europa.eu/docs/en_GB/document_library/Scientific_guideline/2009/10/WC500004428.pdf. Accessed 2 August 2013.
45. VICH GL46 *Studies to Evaluate the Metabolism and Residue Kinetics of Veterinary Drugs in Food-producing Animals: Metabolism Study to Determine the Quantity and Identify the Nature of Residues* (Step 4, Released for adoption at Step 3 in September 2009). VICH website. http://www.vichsec.org/en/GL46-st7.doc. Accessed 2 August 2013.
46. VICH GL47 *Studies to Evaluate the Metabolism and Residue Kinetics of Veterinary Drugs in Food-producing Animals: Comparative Metabolism Studies in Laboratory Animals* (Step 4, Released for adoption at Step 3 in September 2009). VICH website. http://www.vichsec.org/en/GL47-st7.doc. Accessed 2 August 2013.
47. VICH GL48 *Studies to Evaluate the Metabolism and Residue Kinetics of Veterinary Drugs in Food-producing Animals: Marker Residue Depletion Studies to Establish Product Withdrawal Periods* (Step 4, Released for adoption at Step 3 in September 2009, still under discussion). VICH website. http://www.vichsec.org/en/GL48-st7.doc. Accessed 2 August 2013.
48. VICH GL49 *Guidelines for the Validation of Analytical Methods used in Residue Depletion Studies* (Step 4, Released for adoption at Step 3 in September 2009). VICH website. http://www.vichsec.org/en/GL49-st7.doc. Accessed 2 August 2013.
49. Op cit 3.
50. Ibid.
51. EMA. Maximum residue limits. http://www.ema.europa.eu/ema/index.jsp?curl=pages/regulation/document_listing/document_listing_000165.jsp&mid=WC0b01ac058002d89b. Accessed 2 August 2013.
52. Regulation (EC) No 470/2009 of the European Parliament and of the Council of 6 May 2009 laying down Community procedures for the establishment of residue limits of pharmacologically active substances in foodstuffs of animal origin. Eur-Lex website. http://eur-lex.europa.eu/LexUriServ/LexUriServ.do?uri=OJ:L:2009:152:0011:0011:EN:PDF. Accessed 2 August 2013.
53. Health Canada. Maximum Residue Limits (MRLs). Health Canada website. http://www.hc-sc.gc.ca/dhp-mps/vet/mrl-lmr/index-eng.php. Accessed 2 August 2013.
54. Op cit 1.
55. *Minor Use and Minor Species Animal Health Act* of 2004 (*MUMS*). GPO website. http://www.gpo.gov/fdsys/pkg/PLAW-108publ282/pdf/PLAW-108publ282.pdf. Accessed 2 August 2013.
56. EMEA/429080/09 Rev. 1 (July 2013). Revised policy for classification and incentives for veterinary medicinal products indicated for minor use minor species (MUMS)/limited markets. EMA website. http://www.ema.europa.eu/docs/en_GB/document_library/Regulatory_and_procedural_guideline/2009/10/WC500005157.pdf. Accessed 2 August 2013.
57. *Good Laboratory Practice: OECD Principles and Guidance for Compliance Monitoring* (ENV/MC/CHEM(98)17), Paris, France, Organisation for Economic Cooperation and Development, 1997, pp1-41. OECD website. http://search.oecd.org/officialdocuments/displaydocumentpdf/?cote=env/mc/chem(98)17&doclanguage=en. Accessed 2 August 2013.
58. Ibid.
59. *21 CFR 58* Good Laboratory Practice Regulations. FDA website. http://www.accessdata.fda.gov/scripts/cdrh/cfdocs/cfcfr/CFRSearch.cfm?CFRPart=58. Accessed 2 August 2013.
60. Directive 2004/10/EC of the European Parliament and of the Council of 11 February 2004 on the harmonisation of laws, regulations and administrative provisions relating to the application of the principles of good laboratory practice and the verification of their applications for tests on chemical substances. Eur-Lex website. http://eur-lex.europa.eu/LexUriServ/LexUriServ.do?uri=OJ:L:2004:050:0044:0044:EN:PDF. Accessed 2 August 2013.
61. Directive 2004/9/EC of the European Parliament and of the Council of 11 February 2004 on the inspection and verification of good laboratory practice (GLP). Eur-Lex website. http://eur-lex.europa.eu/LexUriServ/LexUriServ.do?uri=OJ:L:2004:050:0028:0043:EN:PDF. Accessed 2 August 2013.
62. VICH GL9 *Good Clinical Practice* (Step 7, EWG consensus signed in 1998, Implemented in July 2001). VICH website. http://www.vichsec.org/pdf/2000/Gl09_st7.pdf. Accessed 2 August 2013.
63. VICH GL24 *Pharmacovigilance of Veterinary Medicinal Products: Management of Adverse Event Reports (AERs)* (Step 5, October 2007, For implementation to be determined, Pending adoption of GL30 and GL35. Regulatory Authorities may consider implementation at an earlier stage as appropriate.) VICH website. http://www.vichsec.org/pdf/2007/1007/GL24-st7.DOC. Accessed 2 August 2013.
64. VICH GL29 (Step 7, EWG consensus signed in 2001, For implementation by June *Pharmacovigilance of Veterinary Medicinal Products—Management of Periodic Summary Update Reports* 2007). VICH website. http://www.vichsec.org/pdf/06_2006/GL29_st7.pdf. Accessed 2 August 2013.
65. VICH GL30 *Pharmacovigilance of Veterinary Medicinal Products: Controlled List of Terms* (Step 5, Recommended for adoption at step 6 in October 2007). VICH website. http://www.vichsec.org/en/GL30_st7Fin.pdf. Accessed 2 August 2013.
66. VICH GL35 *Pharmacovigilance of Veterinary Medicinal Products: Electronic Standards for Transfer of Data* (Step 3, Recommended for consultation at step 4 in October 2007). VICH website. http://www.vichsec.org/en/GL35-st7.doc. Accessed 2 August 2013.
67. VICH GL42 Pharmacovigilance of Veterinary Medicinal Products—Data Elements for Submission of Adverse Event Reports (Step 5, October 2007, For implementation to be determined, Pending adoption of GL30 and GL35). VICH website. http://www.vichsec.org/en/GL42-st7F.DOC. Accessed 2 August 2013.
68. Op cit 64.

Chapter 32

Botanical Drug Products and Traditional Medicine

By Mukesh Kumar, PhD, RAC

OBJECTIVES

- ❑ Understand what constitutes traditional medicine and botanical drug products
- ❑ Learn how traditional medicine and botanical drug products are regulated
- ❑ Understand how botanical drug products are developed for marketing approval
- ❑ Learn the key challenges in gaining approval for botanical drug products
- ❑ Learn strategic considerations for successful approval of a botanical drug product

Introduction

Products derived from plant sources are called herbal or botanical products. Products with a long history of human experience are called "traditional botanical products," while new products are called "modern botanical products." These products are marketed and used by consumers for various medicinal and non-medicinal benefits. The way these products are regulated varies depending on the intended application and country of marketing. This chapter provides the common definitions and describes regulatory pathways and development strategies for such products in the US and other regions. Botanical products are considered one of the most promising areas in the discovery of newer therapeutic products to treat a variety of diseases.

Traditional Medicines

Medicinal plants play an important role in several cultures and are widely used for both general health maintenance and specific therapeutic applications. Several well-documented traditional systems of medicine in the world are collectively referred to as "traditional medicine." While the majority of traditional medicines are based on medicinal plants, this system of medicine also involves chemical ingredients purified from natural resources, such as minerals and heavy metals, and includes non-medicinal practices such as exercise, yoga, meditation, acupuncture, movement therapies and dietary practices. The regulation of traditional medicine varies depending on the origin of the system, the country or region where it is used and the regulatory history of products comprising such systems. However, there are similarities across all traditional medical practices in terms of the definition of healthy and disease conditions, and the emphasis on the overall well-being of an individual rather than relief of symptoms alone.

Indian Traditional Medicine

Indian traditional medicine is based largely on an ancient system of disease prevention and treatment called Ayurveda, which uses a complex mixture of herbs and minerals along with dietary restrictions and exercise. The word "Ayurveda" means science of life (Ayu = life + Veda = knowledge/science). Ayurvedic medicine dominates traditional medicine in India with its 85% share of the market.[1] Ayurveda is one of the oldest systems of traditional medicine in the world, with a documented history of practice dating back almost 5,000 years. This system of medicine is based on ancient, sacred texts, such as the Vedas, Charak Samhita (at 1,200 years old, the most ancient treatise on healthcare and medicine) and Sushrut Samhita (surgery manual).[2] Treatment is based on a well-developed system that uses several botanical formulations.

The philosophy of Ayurveda goes beyond treating and curing disease to maintaining and improving health. Based on this philosophy, an individual's complete health status is assessed, and treatment is customized by the physician according to the patient's requirements. In this regard, Ayurvedic medicine is comparable to the field of personalized medicine. Though Ayurveda is designed to treat both acute and chronic illnesses, the popular belief is that it is more suitable for the latter. Hence, patients consulting Ayurvedic doctors most commonly seek treatment for chronic diseases, such as arthritis, skin diseases, gastrointestinal disorders, endocrinal diseases, diabetes and hypertension.

Ayurvedic literature describes the use of herbs, animal parts and minerals; however, the vast majority (more than 90% by some accounts) of Ayurvedic medicine is plant-based, with more than 2,660 herbs listed in traditional literature. Therefore, common medicinal products used in Ayurveda contain pure herbal and herb-mineral combinations. These products are available in various oral and topical formulations, such as pills, powders, wines, oils and creams or ointments. Some Ayurvedic formulations use heavy metals such as mercury or lead. In contrast to the Western medical community's belief that heavy metals are unsafe, Ayurveda recommends the use of heavy metal ashes to treat various chronic disorders. A small number of clinical studies have been conducted, primarily to evaluate safety issues associated with the use of heavy metals and minerals, but the results have been inconclusive.[3] In India, Ayurvedic medicine is regulated by the Department of Ayurveda, Yoga and Naturopathy, Unani, Siddha and Homoeopathy (AYUSH). AYUSH has developed monographs on several Ayurvedic herbs and traditional formulations under various initiatives, such as the *Indian Herbal Pharmacopoeia*, the *Ayurvedic Pharmacopoeia* and the Ayurvedic Formulary of India. In addition, several companies in India have built private chemical and germplasm libraries based on traditional Indian plants that can be used in drug leads. Ayurveda does not involve injectable products or drug-device combination products.

Ayurvedic medicine is taught at Ayurvedic medical schools that offer typical medical degree programs similar in format and nomenclature to Western or conventional medical schools. The minimum educational qualification for an Ayurvedic medical doctor is Bachelor of Ayurveda, Medicine and Surgery (BAMS), a four-and-a-half year medical degree program that involves a detailed study of the Ayurvedic principles of medicine, physiology, pharmacology, toxicology and allied fields. The degree program is followed by at least a one-year internship at an Ayurvedic hospital or clinic. There are more than 100 Ayurvedic medical colleges that graduate 15,000–20,000 doctors each year. There are more than 5,000 Ayurvedic hospitals in India, about half of which are run by the government, with both inpatient and outpatient facilities.

Traditional Chinese Medicine (TCM)

Traditional Chinese Medicine (TCM) is based on a broad range of medical practices sharing common theoretical concepts about how the human body and its surrounding environment interact to reflect an individual's well-being. TCM practices include herbal medicine, acupuncture, dietary therapy and Tui na and Shiatsu massage. The doctrines of TCM are based primarily on ancient books such as the *Yellow Emperor's Inner Canon* and the *Treatise on Cold Damage*, which have been modernized since the 1950s to integrate modern anatomical and pathological notions.

TCM's view of the body places little emphasis on anatomical structures, but is mainly concerned with the identification of functional entities (which regulate digestion, breathing, aging, etc.). While health is perceived as a harmonious interaction of these entities and the outside world, disease is interpreted as a disharmony in interaction. TCM is based on the ancient Chinese perception of humans as microcosms of the larger, surrounding universe, interconnected with nature and subject to its forces. The human body is regarded as an organic entity in which the various organs, tissues and other parts have distinct functions but are all interdependent. In this view, health and disease relate to the balance or imbalance of the functions. TCM aims to create overall well-being by preventing or curing diseases rather than reactively treating the symptoms of an ailment. TCM has been practiced for more than 3,000 years in China and Taiwan. A similar system of medicine is used in neighboring regions, such as Korea (Traditional Korean Medicine) and Japan (Kampo medicine).

TCM emphasizes individualized treatment. Practitioners traditionally use four methods to evaluate a patient's condition: observing (especially the tongue), hearing/smelling, asking/interviewing and touching/palpating (especially the pulse). A combination of therapeutic measures may be prescribed, the most common being Chinese herbal medicine and acupuncture. The Chinese *Materia Medica* (a pharmacological reference book used by TCM practitioners) contains hundreds of medicinal substances—primarily plants, but also some minerals and animal products—classified by their perceived actions in the body. Different parts of plants are used, such as the leaves, roots, stems, flowers and seeds. Typically, herbs are combined in formulas and used in teas, capsules, tinctures or powders. TCM does not involve injectable products, but does use devices, such as needles for acupuncture.

Traditional herbal medicine is regulated in China and Taiwan by a different process than that for chemical and biological drugs. The manufacturer of an herbal substance can claim its efficacy to treat an indication based on historical literature and is only required to meet the good manufacturing requirement as defined in Chinese regulations for TCM. The manufacturer is not required to prove the substance's safety due to the long history of human exposure. Over the last few years, the China Food and Drug Administration (CFDA, formerly State Food and Drug Administration) and the Taiwanese Department of Health (DOH) have implemented regulations requiring manufacturers to follow Good Manufacturing Practice (GMP) guidelines similar to those for pharmaceutical products. In addition, there have been efforts to control unsubstantiated medical claims about herbal products.

TCM is administered by trained TCM practitioners. TCM degree programs are offered by universities in China, Taiwan, Korea, Japan and the US. Most of these programs involve four to five years of study in concepts of medicine and the human body, followed by 6–12 months of internship. By some counts, approximately 10,000 TCM practitioners are in the US alone who treat close to one million patients each year. The exact numbers of practitioners in China, Korea, Taiwan and Japan are not available, but are estimated to be several tenfold the number in the US.

Traditional Medicine in the US

Traditional medicines from a variety of sources have been available in the US for several decades. In the US, various forms of traditional medicine are collectively called complementary and alternative medicine (CAM). Such medicines are not regulated directly by the US Food and Drug Administration (FDA), and there is no standardized, national system for credentialing CAM practitioners. The extent and type of credentialing vary widely from state to state and from one CAM profession to another. For example, some CAM professionals (e.g., chiropractors, acupuncturists) are licensed in all or most states, although specific requirements for training, testing and continuing education vary; TCM practitioners are not recognized in six states. FDA does not endorse any CAM medicine or practice due to the lack of rigorous, well-designed clinical trials to demonstrate the safety and efficacy of these products. FDA regulation of CAM practitioners is primarily via consumer complaints of injury upon use of a given treatment, or reports of false advertising.

In 1998, the National Institutes of Health (NIH) created the National Center for Complementary and Alternative Medicine (NCCAM). Its mission is to define, through rigorous scientific investigation, the usefulness and safety of complementary and alternative medicine interventions and their roles in improving health and healthcare in the US.[4] NCCAM conducts surveys of various CAM therapies in use, collects credible information for educating consumers and provides guidance about CAM patient resources. According to a survey conducted in 2007, about 38% of adults in the US use CAM either alone or in conjunction with conventional medicine. In addition, approximately 17% of adults use natural products, such as herbs for medicinal purposes.[5–7]

US regulations define a given botanical product based on its intended use. **Figure 32-1** describes the rationale for defining a product's US regulatory pathway based on its intended use. Several herbal products are available in the US as dietary supplements and for use in ethnic foods and cosmetics. These products are primarily available at ethnic stores, from private CAM practitioners or at health spas. Most are imported into the US. Most herbal products currently on the market are concentrated extracts, fluid extracts and tinctures. Some products, such as ginseng, have a much wider exposure due to its use in food products, such as soft drinks and energy bars.

There have been reports of CAM product contamination by drugs, toxins or heavy metals or the CAM product reportedly not containing the listed ingredients.[8] Some herbs are very powerful and can interact with drugs, resulting in serious side effects. For example, the Chinese herb ephedra (ma huang) has been linked to serious health complications, including heart attack and stroke.[9,10] In 2004, FDA banned the sale of ephedra-containing dietary supplements used for weight loss and performance enhancement,[11] but the ban does not apply to the use of ephedra in TCM remedies or herbal teas. Since no CAM product is currently approved by FDA as a medicinal product, these products cannot legally refer to any therapeutic or diagnostic claims. Another major regulatory issue with CAM products is their compliance with current Good Manufacturing Practices (CGMPs).

The US approach to herbal medicine is vastly different from that of Canada. In Canada, herbal products, called Natural Health Products (NHP), are regulated by a process very similar to that in the EU. NHPs can be introduced into the Canadian market either by establishing a reasonably long history of human use (Traditional Herbal Product) or by conducting a combination of clinical and nonclinical trials, along with published literature (Modern Herbal Product). Several herbal products reach the US via Canada when consumers purchase products in Canada and bring them back to the US for personal use.

Traditional Herbal Medicine in EU

Although there are very few popular traditional medicines that originated in European countries, the EU takes a very flexible approach to granting marketing approval to new and traditional plant-based medicines. Medicinal products that are made from substances derived from plants are known as "herbal medicinal products." Within this group of herbal medicinal products, those with a long tradition of use are called "traditional herbal medicinal products." EU legislation classifies traditional herbal medicinal products

Figure 32-1. US Regulatory Pathways for Marketing Botanical Drug Products

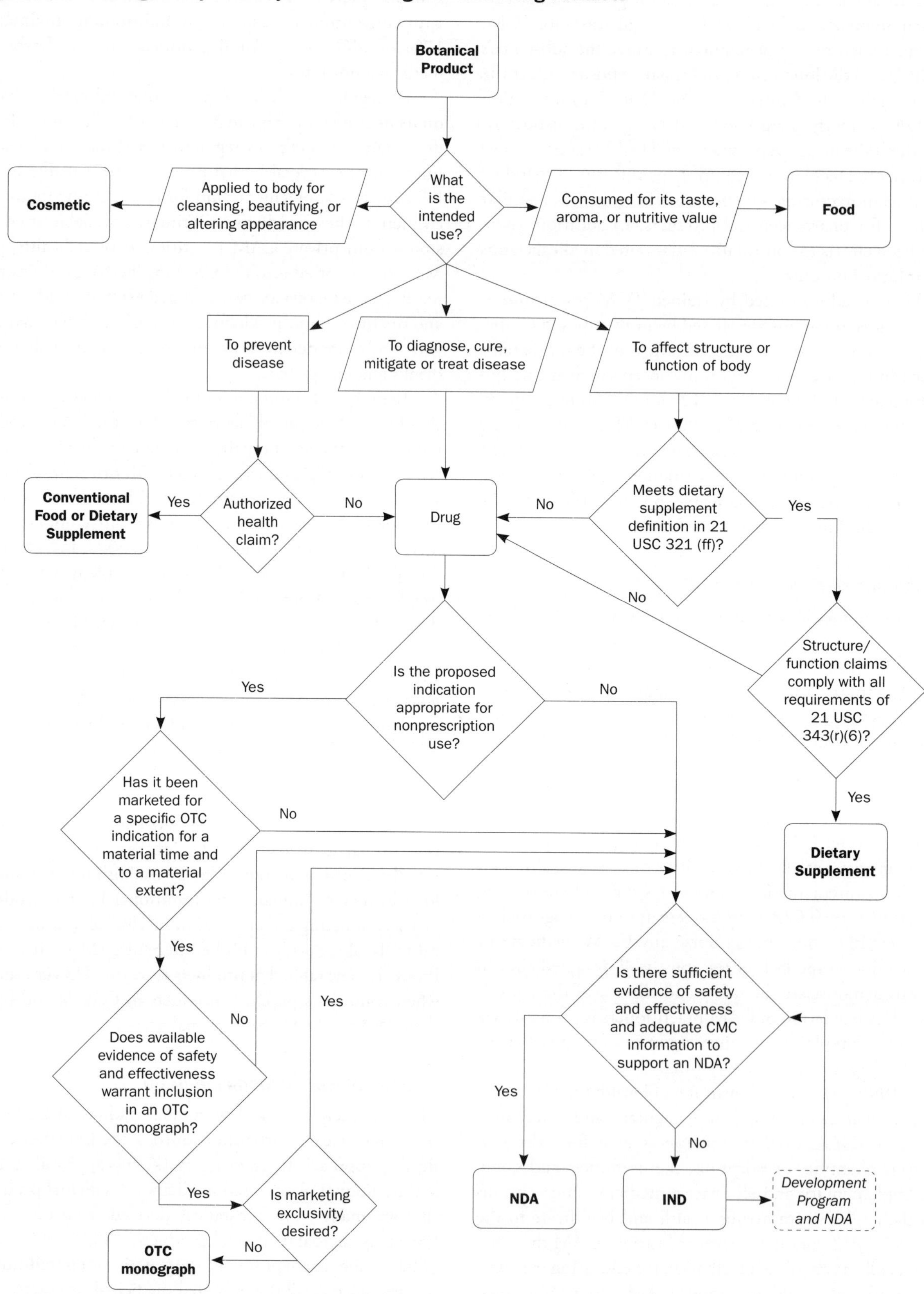

Adapted from Guidance for Industry: Botanical Drug Products, FDA, 2004.

as those products that have been used for at least 30 years, including at least 15 years within the EU, are intended to be used without the supervision of a medical practitioner and are not administered by injection.

In 2004, the EU enacted a special directive for traditional herbal medicines, the *Herbal Directive* (Directive 2004/24/EC), to create a lighter, simpler and less-costly registration procedure for them, while providing the necessary guarantees of quality, safety and efficacy. This regulation acknowledges that for traditional medicine that has been available in the EU for a long time, it is not necessary to conduct safety tests and clinical trials for registration. The EU asserts that the long history of use of such products makes it possible to replace additional testing requirements with documentation that indicates the product is not harmful in specified conditions of use and its efficacy is plausible on the basis of long-standing use and experience. However, since a long tradition of use does not exclude concerns about the product's safety, Competent Authorities of the Member States are entitled to ask for additional data, if deemed necessary. According to the directive adopted on 31 March 2004, all manufacturers of traditional herbal medicinal products that were marketed in the EU prior to 30 April 2004 had until 30 April 2011 to register any products if they wanted to continue marketing them in the EU.

In September 2004, the European Medicines Agency (EMA) created the Committee on Herbal Medicinal Products (HMPC) to assist the harmonization of procedures and provisions concerning herbal medicinal products laid down in EU Member States, and to further integrate herbal medicinal products into the European regulatory framework. As part of these objectives, HMPC provides EU Member States and European institutions with its scientific opinion on questions relating to herbal medicinal products. Other core tasks include the establishment of a draft "Community list of herbal substances, preparations and combinations thereof for use in traditional herbal medicinal products," as well as the establishment of Community herbal monographs. HMPC is composed of scientific experts in the field of herbal medicinal products.

For new herbal medicinal products, the EU offers three pathways for marketing approval:

1. Traditional use product—for products that have published evidence of at least 30 years of use worldwide, of which 15 years were in the EU.
2. Well-established product—for products with scientific literature establishing that the active ingredients of the product have been in well-established medicinal use within the EU for at least 10 years, with recognized efficacy and an acceptable level of safety.
3. Standalone product—full marketing authorization application consisting of only safety and efficacy data developed by the company itself or from a combination of its own studies and bibliographic data.

Regardless of the regulatory pathway for market approval, all herbal medicinal products must comply with CGMPs for herbal products. EU has published approximately 16 guidance documents describing the quality processes expected to be used in the herbal product manufacturing process.[12] In addition, the EU has published detailed Q&A documents addressing common questions raised by manufacturers of herbal products regarding regulators' CGMP expectations.

Traditional Medicine From the Rest of the World

Although the most common and popular traditional medicines have Indian and Chinese origins, several traditional medicines have been known to originate in South America, Africa and other regions. Most of the South American and African traditional medicines are herbal in nature. Unlike the Indian and Chinese traditional medicines, the practice of traditional medicine in South America and Africa is poorly documented and organized, with few training options. Due to this disorganized nature, such traditional medicines are best described as "Folk Medicine." Examples of folk medicines can be found in most cultures and societies. Folk medicine often coexists with Western medicine, but differs from formalized or institutionalized healing systems in the concepts of disease state and its treatment. Hence, folk medicine also is often referred to as CAM. Some examples of strong informal, and to some degree, institutionalized folk medicine traditions are: Traditional Brazilian medicine, Arabic indigenous medicine (Unani medicine and Ancient Greek medicine), Haitian folk medicine, Uyghur traditional medicine, various African herbal folk remedies, Celtic traditional medicine, Traditional Aboriginal Bush medicine and Georgian folk medicine. Since many folk medicine practitioners also may be trained in Western medical practices, theories and practices of folk medicine may influence, or be influenced by, the formalized medicine systems of the same culture.

Botanical Drug Products in the US

As mentioned above, FDA does not formally recognize or approve traditional medicine based on the history of use in the US or in other countries. There is no separate regulatory classification for traditional medicine, herbal or otherwise, in the US. If an herbal product is introduced into the US market with general health claims, it is classified as a dietary supplement and regulated by the Center for Food Safety and Applied Nutrition. However, FDA does have a formal process for marketing approval of medicinal products derived from plants, called Botanical Drug Products (BDPs). A BDP may be marketed under an over-the-counter (OTC) drug monograph or may require approval under a New Drug Application (NDA).

FDA's first and only formal detailed guidance on regulatory processes for BDP testing and marketing approval

Table 32-1. Direct to OTC Criteria for BDPs With Only Non-US Market Experience

1. Basic chemical and characterization information about the ingredients (detailed info on GACP and GMP validation) (could use national pharmacopeia as standard)
2. A list of all countries in which the BDP has been marketed
3. How the BDP has been marketed in each country (e.g., OTC general sales direct-to-consumer, sold only in a pharmacy)
4. The number of dosage units sold (cumulative and per patient)
5. Marketing exposure (e.g., race, gender, ethnicity) (relevance to US target population)
6. The use pattern in each country (most common use and known alternate uses)
7. Each country's system for identifying adverse drug experiences (ADEs), including method of collection
8. How long the BDP has been marketed in each country (minimum five or more years*)
9. All labeling used during the marketing period in any country, and the time period each was used**
10. All countries where the BDP is marketed only as a prescription drug and the reasons why
11. All countries where the BDP has been withdrawn from marketing or OTC marketing has been denied.

GACP = Good Agricultural and Collection Practices
GMP = Good Manufacturing Practices
**For multiple countries, at least one country must have five or more continuous years of marketing*
*** Provide product labels for each country*

was released in June 2004.[13] This guidance was prepared by working groups in the Medical Policy, Pharmacology and Toxicology, and Complex Drug Substances Coordinating Committees in the Center for Drug Evaluation and Research (CDER). This guidance describes the conditions under which a BDP may be marketed under an OTC monograph or when the BDP requires an NDA. FDA concurrently created a Botanical Review Team (BRT) to provide scientific expertise on BDPs through participation in all reviews, meetings and decisions regarding clinical trials and NDAs for BDPs. FDA's BDP guidance takes precedence over any other FDA guidance or regulation regarding testing and characterization of such products for marketing approval. It is essential for all BDP manufacturers to read these guidelines and the selected articles authored by BRT reviewers.

There have been a few publications in peer-reviewed journals by FDA experts that further clarify FDA's expectations regarding the scope and quality of data submitted to support BDP marketing approval.[14–16] Although FDA does not approve products solely on the basis of previous human experience with a given BDP in any country, including the US, it does appreciate the unique nature of such products in terms of identification and characterization of active ingredients and reduces its requirements for safety and efficacy testing in the light of previous human experience. For BDPs whose active ingredients have been marketed in the US over an extended period of time as dietary supplements, an applicant may submit reduced nonclinical safety and chemistry, manufacturing and control (CMC) information to support an Investigational New Drug (IND) application for a clinical trial and for an NDA. Review of recent decisions by FDA regarding BDPs and presentations and publications by FDA reviewers indicates there is significant flexibility in terms of the supporting data needed for a favorable decision by FDA regarding a given BDP.[17,18]

Despite the seemingly favorable regulatory environment in the US for BDPs, only two products have been approved under this category. Since 2004, more than a few hundred INDs were filed for such products, and several products have been tested in Phase 2 clinical trials; however, very few products reached the Phase 3 clinical testing phase. US regulatory requirements for BDP approval are described below, along with practical tips to meet these requirements based on the approval history of the two FDA-approved BDPs and information available about several INDs for BDPs under development.

OTC vs. NDA for Botanical Drug Products

Under US regulations, a new BDP can enter the market using two routes: as an OTC product, by petitioning for a new OTC monograph or modification of an existing monograph, or as a new product approved under an NDA. A botanical product that has been marketed in the US for more than five years for a specific OTC drug indication may be eligible for inclusion in an OTC drug monograph. The manufacturer would need to submit a petition in accordance with 21 CFR 10.30, amending the monograph to add the botanical substance as a new active ingredient. Even if the marketing history of the botanical substance is in a country other than the US, a manufacturer may petition for a new OTC monograph by submitting a Time and Extent Application (TEA), including detailed information about the BDP's marketing experience in that country. **Table 32-1** lists the information needed to support the non-US marketing experience.

Upon receiving the petition, FDA would submit the OTC monograph for approval, and if approved, the manufacturer could introduce the OTC product.

If the available evidence of safety and effectiveness does not warrant inclusion of the product in an OTC drug monograph, or if the proposed indication would not be appropriate for nonprescription use in the US, FDA would deny the OTC designation and require that the manufacturer submit an NDA to obtain market approval for the product. An NDA for a BDP is quite similar to that for a conventional drug in that the manufacturer needs to provide complete evidence of safety and effectiveness via nonclinical studies and clinical trials to support market approval. A botanical drug manufacturer still could seek approval for OTC use if the manufacturer can support the BDP's safety for use outside the supervision of a physician.

However, the NDA route offers some distinct practical advantages over approval as an OTC product. When a final OTC drug monograph is published for a specific use of a botanical drug, any person may market a product containing the same substance and for the same use, provided the labeling and other active ingredients (if present) are in accord with all relevant monographs and other applicable regulations. In contrast, when a product is approved under an NDA, the approval is specific to the drug product that is the subject of the application (the applicant's drug product), and the applicant is eligible for marketing exclusivity for five years (since most BDPs will be considered a new chemical entity) even in the absence of patent protection. During the period of market exclusivity, FDA will not approve, or in some cases even review, certain competitor products unless the second sponsor conducts all studies necessary to demonstrate the safety and effectiveness of its product and submits a full NDA. The market exclusivity period offers the distinct financial advantage of a prescription product with monopoly power. Since most BDPs are eligible for an NDA approval with minimal information, seeking approval as an OTC may put the applicant at a disadvantage because, unlike the NDA route, the OTC route will open the market to all competitors' products as well. This explains why there have been no known attempts by non-US BDP manufacturers to obtain OTC monographs for their products. **Figure 32-1** provides a schematic showing different regulatory approaches for marketing BDPs in the US, including OTC drug monograph and NDA procedures.

IND for Botanical Drug Products

Like conventional drugs, a BDP manufacturer needs to establish evidence of safety and efficacy of the investigational BDP via appropriately designed clinical trials, characterize the chemical nature of the formulation and implement CGMP to support an IND and eventually file an NDA for marketing approval. However, BDPs derived from traditional medicine may have the advantage of safety established via long human exposure, well-established manufacturing processes and basic chemical and physical characterization. Hence, these products could conceivably be approved by FDA in less time due to fewer requirements for clinical and preclinical studies compared to those for conventional drugs. **Table 32-2** lists the key strategic differences between a BDP and a conventional chemical drug. The key to success is using the available information strategically, identifying the gaps in the information for FDA acceptance and creating plans to fill those gaps.

A BDP follows a development pathway very different from that of a conventional drug.[19,20] A typical drug development pathway involves identification of the target indication and the potential chemical or biological agent (the lead molecule) to counter that target; development of the lead molecule; and finally, preclinical and clinical trials to demonstrate safety and efficacy. In contrast, a BDP derived from traditional medicine, i.e., where the product or its active ingredients have prolonged human experience, should be developed via a highly abbreviated development program. A typical BDP development program would follow this sequence of events: characterization of the active ingredients in the traditional product, meta-analysis of all previous human experience, gap analysis to identify additional elements needed for FDA review, IND for the clinical testing and preclinical studies, if needed, to address any safety issues identified in the clinical trials or un-addressed in all available information. **Table 32-3** lists

Table 32-2. Comparison of BDPs and Conventional Drugs

	Conventional Drugs	BDP
Chemical composition	Single or a few well-characterized components	Complex mixtures of numerous components
Manufacturing controls	CGMP	Extended to raw material production/harvesting
Human exposure	None or minimal	May be extensive
Market presence	Competing products	Dietary supplements
Clinical testing	Standard Phases 1-3 trials	Highly variable
Mass production	Standard processes	Lot to lot variations
Intellectual property issues	Patents and market exclusivity	Mostly market exclusivity alone

Table 32-3. Strategic Consideration for Developing a BDP for US Approval

Process	Conventional Development	BDP Development
Selection of the indication and need for special status	The most suitable indication is selected based on corporate mission and status of development. Available incentives identified, e.g., orphan or pediatric indication, tropical disease treatment, etc.	The indication is selected based on previous experience. Multiple indications are possible and are prioritized based on criteria similar to those for chemical drugs.
Preclinical design	Description of *in vitro* and animal studies required	Significantly reduced for products with long experience
CMC design and manufacturing plans	The manufacturing process and the analytical testing needed per Good Manufacturing Practices	Same as chemical drugs
Clinical plan	The description of clinical studies required per the current regulations for the indication selected	Fewer clinical studies needed, generally can start directly with a Phase 2 study
Regulatory steps and timelines	IND and NDA, FDA meetings	Similar steps as those for chemical drugs
Marketing plan	Although it might seem premature, it is best to consider marketing issues for the product as early as possible in the product lifecycle for periodic product viability assessment	Very similar to chemical drugs; however, physician surveys could help identify potential market issues postapproval
Postmarketing plan	Understanding postmarketing issues with similar approved products is critical for strategic planning	Similar considerations as those for chemical drugs
Tactical regulatory submissions	Similar regulatory filings in all countries	Most non-US regulators do not require a robust development plan for BDPs; hence, US regulatory submissions are always more complex compared to other countries

the key elements in the development program for a BDP compared to that for conventional chemical drugs.

In principle, the clinical and nonclinical testing program for a BDP is quite similar to that for chemical drugs. As with chemical drugs, BDP manufacturers must demonstrate product safety and efficacy via detailed animal and human testing. If such information is available from alternate credible sources, BDP developers can benefit from that. **Figure 32-2** describes three typical situations with BDPs. First, the manufacturer may be developing medicinal uses for a marketed botanical product. The marketed product may be available in the US as a dietary supplement or other mechanism, or the marketing experience may be from a non-US location. If detailed marketing information is available similar to that described in **Table 32-1** for OTC products, the manufacturer may be able to use previous human experience to support its claims for safety. In that case, only additional clinical trials to demonstrate the efficacy claims may be needed. Secondly, the manufacturer may be developing a non-marketed new botanical or a marketed botanical with safety issues. In these cases, a conventional development program involving preclinical and clinical studies may be needed. The manufacturer may be able to avoid some studies if there is previous experience with the ingredients. The third situation could be where the manufacturer is interested in pursuing a new use for a marketed botanical. In this case, additional clinical studies will be needed only to support the new case. The manufacturer could benefit from previous safety data from the marketed product in terms of reduced preclinical and clinical safety studies.

FDA accepts data from clinical trials all over the world, whether or not they are conducted under an IND application. However, it is easier for manufacturers to demonstrate applicability of their data from other countries to the US population by conducting confirmatory or bridging clinical trials in the US. Before these studies can be initiated, a manufacturer must file an IND application with FDA. Even for trials conducted in other countries, if the intent is to use those data in support of an NDA in the US, a manufacturer is encouraged to file an IND to solicit feedback and suggestions from FDA reviewers early in the clinical development plan. IND applications for BDPs are very similar in format and content to INDs for conventional drugs.

Chemistry, Manufacturing and Control (CMC) Information for BDPs

A major challenge in the development of a BDP is satisfying FDA's requirements for CMC information to support the IND and NDA. BDPs are different from chemical drugs in practically all aspects of their CMC information in terms of chemical components and content of each component in the final formulation, characterization of raw materials used and manufacturing principles. Per FDA's botanical product guidance, it is acceptable for a BDP to contain multiple components and for the CMC information to be less than perfect. The entire botanical extract is considered to be one active pharmaceutical ingredient (API) containing a mixture of known and unknown components. Characterization of the API in terms of multiple marker components is expected. The number of markers followed in the API could vary on a case-by-case basis, depending on the known components; however, sufficient general characterization to provide mass balance information is expected. The marker components can be used to establish the acceptance criteria for the API. Ideally, the manufacturer should pick marker components that also can be used for pharmacokinetic (PK) analysis in preclinical and clinical studies.

The characterization information should address the BDP's identity, purity, quality, strength, potency and consistency. FDA expects to see evidence that the manufacturer expended its best efforts to characterize the product by using a combination of tests such as spectroscopic and/or chromatographic fingerprints, chemical assays of characteristic markers and biological assays. A major concern with BDPs is the content of heavy metals and minerals, such as mercury and lead, in the finished product. The content of these elements must be evaluated and justified, if present. The acceptance criteria for the API ideally should be based on a combination of marker component levels, along with content of general components (such as protein, lipid, carbohydrate and amino acid content) and biological assays. The acceptable levels of known impurities such as pesticides, heavy metals and fertilizers should meet standards established for food products. Stability studies should track possible degradation products of the marker components.

One of the most important characteristics of a BDP is the use of plant raw material that could either come from a cultivated source or be collected from the wild. Strict quality control measures for each plant raw material need to be implemented. That includes genus/species identification by genotypic, phenotypic and chemical tests; growth conditions; processing methods; shipping and storage; and characterization of adulteration from other plant species. Traditional pharmacopoeial standards established in the country of origin are not sufficient for FDA; the characterization has to meet FDA requirements as specified in the guidance documents. Special care must be taken if endangered species or habitats are employed or if the raw material is collected from wild rather than cultivated plants. The manufacturer needs to demonstrate that plants are identified by trained personnel and, if possible, provide appropriate certificates of authenticity and analysis. Details about agricultural practices, such as qualification processes for the seeds, cultivation practices, management of soil, water and environmental contaminations, crop rotation, pesticides and fertilizers employed and hygienic practices should be compliant with Good Agricultural and Collective Practices (GACP) as defined by the US Department of Agriculture,[21,22] FDA[23] and EMA.[24] It is advisable to use multiple cultivars and regions for sourcing the botanical raw material to evaluate its variability.

Apart from raw material control and characterization, the manufacturer needs to establish appropriate analysis, quality control and quality assurance measures such as standard operating procedures, general methods of manufacture and qualitative and quantitative description (composition) of the finished product. Manufacturing must be done under CGMP conditions. Post-harvesting, processes for the raw material processing, quality control measures and use in manufacture follow similar principles as conventional drugs. The CGMP compliance of the extraction, purification, formulation, packaging and testing of the botanical API should be identical to that for chemical drugs.

It is important to remember that the CMC information for a given botanical API is vastly customized to the product. Discussions with FDA regarding the requirements for a given API are essential. It is evident from the review of the approval packages of the two BDPs approved by FDA that the agency is willing to relax its requirements in terms of CMC characterization in support of the NDA, provided the clinical safety and efficacy data are acceptable.

Clinical Studies With BDPs

Once the appropriate CMC information is collected, the sponsor should initiate clinical trials to demonstrate the formulation's safety and efficacy for the target indication. Even though a product may have a long market history, prior human experience with the marketed drug may be documented in many different forms and come from diverse sources, which may or may not meet modern quality standards. Also, botanical drug components could lead to dangerous drug-drug interactions. Hence, it is important to demonstrate safety and efficacy of the proposed product in high caliber clinical trials. Appropriately designed clinical trials should aim to reveal drug interactions and potential side effects and determine the appropriate treatment regimen for a product. For products with previous human use experience, it is possible to obtain a waiver from FDA regarding Phase 1 clinical studies and start the IND with Phase 2 clinical trials. The previous human use data could be provided in the same format as described in **Table 32-1** for OTC products. Additionally, PK analysis may be needed to establish the plasma level-biological response relationship.

Clinical studies should address several key aspects of the BDP's biological activity, such as the relative and absolute bioavailability using marker component, accumulation potential, effects of intrinsic (e.g., age, race, renal and hepatic insufficiency, etc.) and extrinsic factors (e.g., concomitant administration of inducer/inhibitor of metabolic enzymes and food) on the drug's PK. Additional clinical issues may be raised by FDA on a case-by-case basis. Again, based on the review of the approval packages for the two

Figure 32-2. Information Needed in an IND for a Botanical Drug Product
(Depending on marketing status of the ingredients)

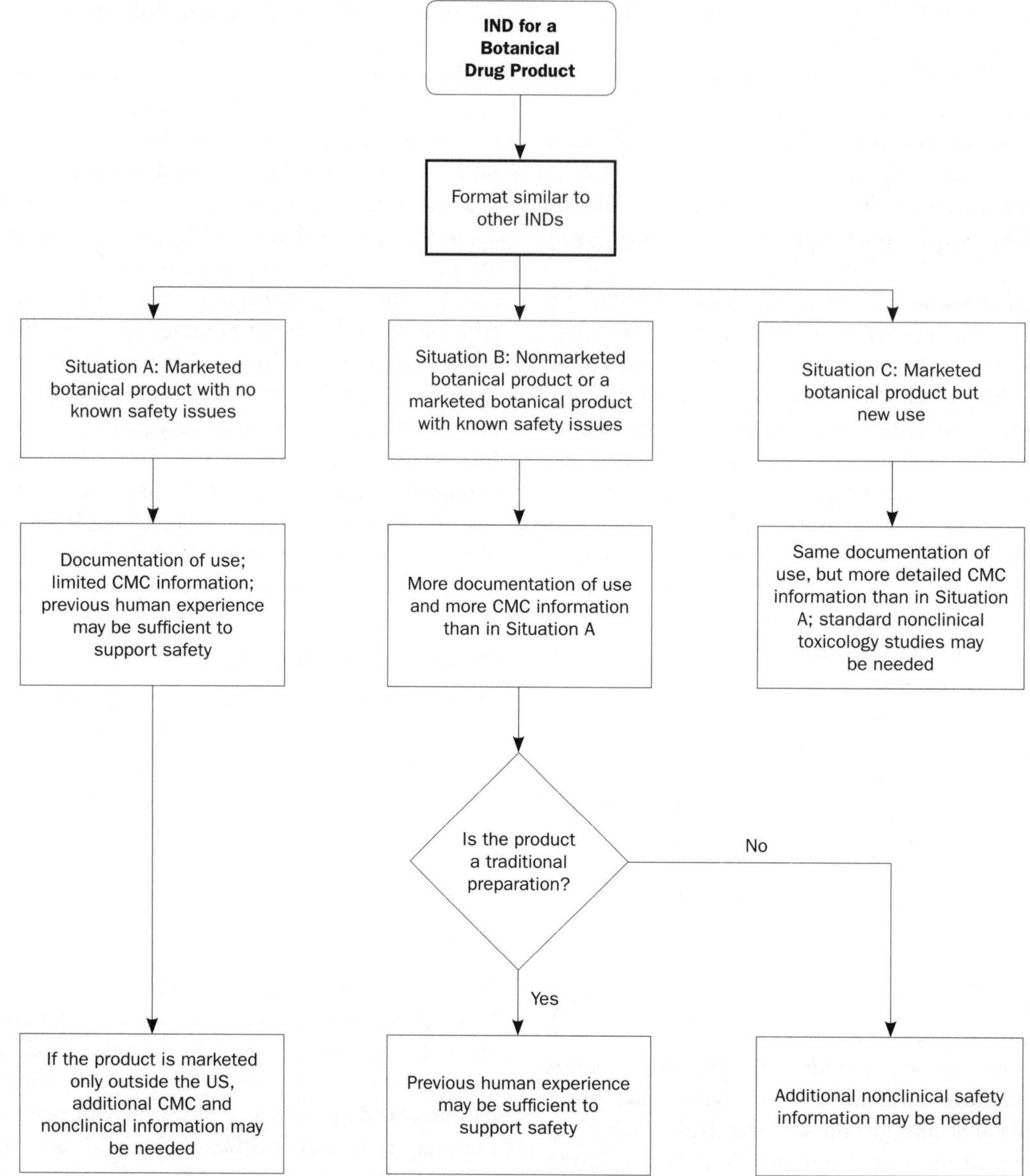

BDPs approved by FDA, it is evident the agency is willing to waive many clinical studies required for conventional drugs considering the historic human exposure of the API's ingredients. Hence, discussions with FDA review teams regarding clinical development plans are critical to the successful market approval of a given product.

Preclinical Studies to Support an NDA for a BDP

Classic toxicology studies to demonstrate safety, No Observed Adverse Event Level (NOAEL) determination and long-term toxicity studies may not be needed for BDPs with well-documented human use data. If not already available, a sponsor should plan to conduct laboratory studies to try to understand the product's mechanism of action. However, since BDPs are composed of multiple components, it might not be possible to identify all the APIs or determine the exact mechanism of action. Provided there are no safety concerns, a BDP could gain approval even if the mechanism of action is not confirmed.

The preclinical information needed for a BDP includes the comparative *in vivo* biotransformation pathways of the active and/or major ingredients, including metabolite profiles and metabolic enzymes in tested animals and humans. Biological activities of the major degradation/oxidation products of potential active components also should be evaluated, considering that metabolic breakdown products may play a role in various physiological functions. The sponsor should collect information on metabolic conversions (such as isomerization) in animals compared to humans and address how these changes impact the relevance of nonclinical studies. Blood levels of active and/or major constituents and their major biologically active metabolites should be assessed in conjunction with toxicology studies to demonstrate systemic exposure and to relate exposure levels to toxicity in both animals and humans. Chronic toxicology studies may be needed in two appropriate mammalian species (one non-rodent) with justification, using the same drug substance prepared and processed in the same manner as used in clinical trials in accordance with the ICH M3(R2) guidance document. Most of this information could be provided from peer-reviewed literature sources. Such data may need to be self-generated if not available in published peer-reviewed literature or if the published literature is for a product that differs greatly from the one being developed under the IND.

Practical Issues With Developing BDPs

A key claim for the safety of traditional drug products is their use by a large segment of the population for a very long time without any safety concerns. For FDA to accept that claim, a manufacturer needs marketing and sales data to show the number of doses sold, number of people for whom the drug has been prescribed, duration of market availability, populations exposed to the drug, etc. This kind of information may not have been collected and, even for well-established manufacturers, may be hard to compile.

As mentioned above, several traditional drugs contain heavy metals, such as mercury and lead, which are considered unacceptable in the US and, hence, such components either must be removed from the formulation or justified scientifically. Traditional medicine also is challenged by sometimes misplaced trust in the product's safety. Many people believe that because medicines are herbal (natural) or traditional, they are safe (or carry no risk of harm). However, traditional medicines and practices can cause harmful, adverse reactions if the product or therapy is of poor quality, or if it is taken inappropriately or in conjunction with other medicines. Increased patient awareness about safe usage, as well as additional training, collaboration and communication among providers of traditional and other medicines are important.

It can be difficult to assess the quality of finished herbal products because they are dependent on the quality of the source materials (which can include hundreds of natural constituents) and how elements are handled in production processes. In addition, botanical or herbal products are affected by the growth conditions of the source plants, such as weather, season, soil quality, use of fertilizers and irrigation conditions. Following GACP and CGMPs in the production of botanical products is difficult, but has been done successfully for many products. Key manufacturing issues are controlling variation in product lots, avoiding contamination with environmental agents such as pollutants and insects, ensuring quality control of raw material and process material and instituting quality assurance processes.

Botanical raw materials are collected from wild plant populations or cultivated medicinal plants. It may not be feasible to scale-up the manufacture of BDPs based on material harvested from the wild. Alternately, the expanding herbal product market could lead to over-harvesting of wild plants and threaten biodiversity. Poorly managed collection and cultivation practices could lead to the extinction of endangered plant species and the destruction of natural resources. Efforts to preserve plant populations and knowledge about the medicinal uses for BDPs are needed to sustain BDPs.

The biggest concern for a BDP developer is the protection of intellectual property. Since the efficacy of these products is based on historical literature, the products' very long history of use and their manufacture and sale by several vendors all claiming the same composition, it is very hard to enforce intellectual property rights (IPR). Most of these products are not eligible for traditional IPR protection methods, such as patents, and might be impossible to protect via trade secrets due to the wide availability of knowledge about production methods. However, FDA does offer market exclusivity to the first product of a class. By being the first to develop a BDP, a sponsor is guaranteed up to five years of marketing exclusivity during which FDA will not approve any other product claiming a similar composition and benefits. Also, since unapproved products cannot claim medical benefits, cannot be covered by insurance and have to be sold as dietary supplements with general health claims, the sponsor of the first NDA does have a significant advantage over the competition. That advantage, coupled with the fact that the investment in developing these products is far less than conventional drugs, makes it reasonable to expect a good return on investment.

Nonclinical pharmacology and toxicology information requirements for BDPs are far less stringent than those for synthetic or highly purified new drugs. A sponsor is required to list the general toxicity of the known components, the target organs and systems of toxicity, the relationship to dosage and duration of treatment to toxicity and the pharmacological activity.

In most cases, the long history of human exposure can be used to justify a waiver from FDA for conducting additional toxicology studies in initial clinical trials. However, if the product developed under an IND is new or different from the one with extensive human experience, nonclinical studies are needed before initiating human studies. Nonetheless, the number of nonclinical studies required could be far less than for a new chemical entity due to the nature of the product and its components. Based on safety incidents identified in the initial clinical trials, additional nonclinical toxicity studies might be needed.

To demonstrate safety in humans, a sponsor may present extensive previous human exposure to the traditional product using marketing data from all locations (domestic and international). Marketing information should include common dose and duration of treatment, approval status in other countries, number of doses sold, approximate number of people exposed to the drug, postmarketing safety information collected, if any, and status of large-scale manufacturing, storage and shipping capabilities. A major hurdle for traditional BDP products, since most are sold in non-US locations, is that a sponsor will need to translate all the supporting documents into English for FDA. Efforts must be made to create a persuasive case with traditional data and modern marketing data from the sponsor itself and from competitors for products that are either identical or similar in form, preferably for the same indication and route of administration. Exhaustive marketing data demonstrating extensive human exposure without any safety concerns also could help in obtaining a waiver of initial clinical trials and moving directly to pivotal trials in support of the NDA.

It is strongly recommended that sponsors prepare all available information and plans for the design of the proposed preclinical and clinical trials for the pre-IND meeting. By discussing the development program with FDA prior to implementation, the sponsor can receive critical feedback on the proposed studies and the acceptability of information. The sponsor should always request that representatives of the Botanical Review Team attend the meeting. All aspects of the product development plan should be discussed.

Conclusion

Botanical drug products hold great promise but also pose unique challenges in gaining acceptance by FDA. Manufacturers, who could be primarily from non-US regions, need training and guidance in developing therapeutic products acceptable to FDA reviewers. The highest barrier for developers is the requirement to establish new evidence based on clinical trials. Due to the high perception of efficacy in native populations, there is a strong placebo effect, leading to the failure of many products to meet the significant efficacy endpoint in a placebo-controlled study. Other challenges are lot-to-lot inconsistency in the finished product due to variations in the raw material, lack of good quality manufacturing and lack of validated human exposure data. Most quality issues can be addressed by applying GACP and CGMP principles and collecting efficacy and safety data via appropriately designed clinical trials.

The World Health Organization (WHO) has recognized the importance of botanical products and encourages its members to cooperate in promoting the use of traditional medicine in healthcare. It advises supporting traditional medicine and integrating it into national health systems through the implementation of national policies and regulations to ensure safety and quality. Botanical product guidance documents on supporting policies and pathways have been released by FDA and EMA. There is a concerted effort by regulators around the world to establish reliable scientific evidence for safe, effective and high-quality botanical products. Botanical products hold the promise of safe and effective treatments for a variety of ailments. In addition, it is expected that traditional medicine will evolve to produce better-quality products with modern scientific evidence of efficacy.

References

1. Ayurvedic Medicine: An Introduction. NIH, NCCAM website. http://nccam.nih.gov/health/ayurveda/introduction.htm. Accessed 15 August 2013.
2. Ayurveda. Wikipedia website. http://en.wikipedia.org/wiki/Ayurveda. Accessed 15 August 2013.
3. Op cit 1.
4. NIH, NCCAM website. http://nccam.nih.gov/. Accessed 15 August 2013.
5. "Complementary and Alternative Medicine Use Among Adults and Children: United States 2007," *National Health Statistics Reports* (December 2008). NIH, NCCAM website. http://nccam.nih.gov/sites/nccam.nih.gov/files/news/nhsr12.pdf. Accessed 15 August 2013.
6. Bardia A, et al. "Use of herbs among adults based on evidence-based indications: findings from the National Health Interview Survey." (2007), *Mayo Clin Proc.* 82(5):561-566.
7. Bent S. "Herbal Medicine in the United States: Review of Efficacy, Safety and Regulation." *J Gen. Intern. Med.* 23(6):854-859.
8. Podolsky D. "Herbal remedies with deadly ingredient still available on line" (21 March 2013). ConsumerReports.com website. http://www.consumerreports.org/cro/news/2013/03/herbal-remedies-with-deadly-ingredient-still-available-online/index.htm. Accessed 15 August 2013.
9. "Why is Ephedra banned by the FDA?" HHS.gov website. http://answers.hhs.gov/questions/7040. Accessed 15 August 2013.
10. Ehlers NR. Ephedra and the FDA. Harvard University website. http://dash.harvard.edu/bitstream/handle/1/8852148/Ehlers.html?sequence=2. Accessed 15 August 2013.
11. Ephedrine Alkaloid-Containing Dietary Supplements. FDA website. http://www.fda.gov/NewsEvents/Testimony/ucm115044.htm. Accessed 15 August 2013.
12. EU herbal guidance documents. EMA website. http://www.emea.europa.eu/ema/index.jsp?curl=pages/regulation/general/general_content_000365.jsp&mid=WC0b01ac0580029569. Accessed 31 July 2013.
13. *Guidance for Industry: Botanical Drug Products* (June 2004). FDA website. http://www.fda.gov/downloads/Drugs/GuidanceComplianceRegulatoryInformation/Guidances/UCM070491.pdf. Accessed 31 July 2013.
14. Chen ST, et al. "New Therapies from Old Medicines.", (2008) *Nat. Biotechnol.*, 26(10): 1077-83.
15. Chen ST. "Regulation of Research: Is it a Drug Trial or a Supplement Trial?" (2011) *Fitoterapia*, 82 (1): 14-16.
16. Wu KM, et al. "Current Regulatory Perspectives on Genetoxicity Testing for Botanical Drug Product Development in the USA." (2010) *Regul. Toxicol. Pharmacol*, 56(1): 1-3.

17. Drug Approval Package, Fulyzaq Delayed-Release Tablets. FDA website. http://www.accessdata.fda.gov/drugsatfda_docs/nda/2012/202292Orig1s000TOC.cfm. Accessed 15 August 2013.
18. Drug Approval Package Veregen Ointment. FDA website. http://www.accessdata.fda.gov/drugsatfda_docs/nda/2006/021902s000TOC.cfm. Accessed 15 August 2013.
19. Kumar M, Deo N, Midde N. "Developing Botanical Products for India for the US Market." (2009) *Regulatory Focus*, 14(8): 18-23.
20. Kumar M, Jethwani H. "Developing Traditional Chinese Medicines as Botanical Drugs for the US Market." (2009) *Regulatory Focus*, 14(8): 30-35.
21. Field Operations and Harvesting Harmonized Food Safety Standard. USDA website. http://www.unitedfresh.org/assets/Harmonized%20Standard%20-%20pre-farm%20gate%20130501.pdf. Accessed 15 August 2013.
22. Post Harvest Operations Harmonized Food Safety Standard., USDA website. http://www.unitedfresh.org/assets/pdfs/Post-harvest%20Operations%20Harmonized%20Standard%20120605.pdf. Accessed 15 August 2013.
23. *Guidance for Industry: Guide to Minimize Microbial Food Safety Hazards for Fresh Fruits and Vegetables*. FDA website. http://www.fda.gov/downloads/Food/GuidanceComplianceRegulatoryInformation/GuidanceDocuments/ProduceandPlanProducts/UCM169112.pdf. Accessed 15 August 2013.
24. Op cit 12.

Regulatory Affairs Comparative Matrix of the Regulations Across Product Lines

Useful Internet Addresses		
	Source	*Authorities and Standards Organizations*
Devices	www.imdrf.org www.iso.org www.iec.ch www.newapproach.org www.fda.gov	International Medical Device Regulators Forum (formerly Global Harmonization Task Force) International Organization for Standardization International Electrotechnical Commission New Approach Directives and related harmonised standards US Food and Drug Administration
Drugs	www.fda.gov www.ema.europa.eu www.ich.org www.who.int/ www.wipo.int www.tga.gov.au www.aesgp.eu www.hc-sc.gc.ca/index-eng.php www.picscheme.org/ www.swissmedic.ch www.vichsec.org	US Food and Drug Administration European Medicines Agency International Conference on Harmonisation World Health Organization World Intellectual Property Organization Australian Therapeutic Goods Administration Association of the European Self-Medication Industry Health Canada Pharmaceutical Inspection Convention and Pharmaceutical Inspection Cooperation Scheme Swiss Medicines Agency International Cooperation on Harmonisation of Technical Requirements for Registration of Veterinary Medicinal Products
Biologics		**Same as Drugs**

Introduction to Regulatory Affairs Drugs and Devices	
	Regulations and Guidelines
Devices	**US** • *Federal Food, Drug, and Cosmetic Act* of 1938, as amended by the *FDA Modernization Act* of 1997, Public Law 105-115 **GHTF/IMDRF** • SG2-N54R8:2006, *Medical Devices Post Market Surveillance: Global Guidance for Adverse Event Reporting for Medical Devices*, 20 November 2006 • SG5/N2R8:2007, *Clinical Evaluation*, May 2007 **EC** • Council Directive 93/42/EEC of 14 June 1993,concerning medical devices • MEDDEV 2.12-1 rev 8, Guidelines on a Medical Devices Vigilance System, January 2013
Drugs	**US** • *Federal Food, Drug, and Cosmetic Act* of 1938, as amended by the *FDA Modernization Act* of 1997, Public Law 105-115 **EU** • Commission Directive 2003/32/EC introducing detailed specifications as regards the requirements laid down in Council Directive 93/42/EEC with respect to medical devices manufactured utilising tissues of animal origin • Regulation (EC) No. 1829/2003 of the European Parliament and of the Council of 22 September 2003 on genetically modified food and feed **ICH** • *Pharmacovigilance Planning E2E*, Current Step 4 version, dated November 2004
Chapter 1 Main Topics	The main aim of drug regulation is to keep unsafe products off the market. It must be stressed, however, that no medicinal product is 100% safe. Tests carried out on a population of limited size, under controlled conditions, during clinical trials may fail to catch critical issues and adverse events. Once a product is on the market, unexpected adverse reactions may occur, or expected adverse events may occur at a higher incidence than expected. Hence, drug regulations call for drug monitoring in the post-authorization and postmarket phases. Most countries have enacted laws to regulate medical devices, food and food supplements and cosmetic products in addition to medicinal products. Non-harmonized registration requirements meant that manufacturers had to duplicate efforts to obtain approvals in different regions, which is time-consuming and expensive. Harmonization efforts include the creation of ICH and GHTF/IMDRF. Vigilance regulations for both drugs and medical devices have increased in importance. Both ICH and GHTF have published guidelines on pharmacovigilance/vigilance reporting and postmarket surveillance.

Clinical Trials	
	Regulations and Guidelines
	ICH • *Guideline for Good Clinical Practice E6(R1)*, Current Step 4 version, 10 June 1996 • *General Considerations for Clinical Trials E8,* Current Step 4 version, 17 July 1997 • *Structure and Content of Clinical Study Reports E3*, Current Step 4 version, 30 November 1995 • *Clinical Investigation of Medicinal Products in the Pediatric Population E11,* Current Step 4 version, 20 July 2000 • *Ethnic Factors in the Acceptability of Foreign Clinical Data E5(R1),* Current Step 4 version, 5 February 1998 • *Development Safety Update Report E2F,* Current Step 4 version, 17 August 2010 **EU** • Regulation (EC) No 1901/2006 of the European Parliament and of the Council od 12 December 2006 on medicinal products for paediatric use and amending Regulation (EEC) No 1768/92, Directive 2001/20/EC, Directive 2001/83/EC and Regulation (EC) No 726/2004 • Directive 2001/20/EC of the European Parliament and of the Council of 4 April 2001 on the approximation of the laws, regulations and administrative provisions of the Member States relating to the implementation of good clinical practice in the conduct of clinical trials on medicinal products for human use, Official Journal of the European Union, 2001 **US** • *Food and Drug Administration Safety and Innovation Act* (*FDASIA*) of 2012. • *21 CFR* Part 312, *Investigational New Drug Application* **Canada** • *Food and Drug Regulations*, Division 5, *Drugs For Clinical Trials Involving Human Subjects*, Canada, October 2012 **Australia** • *Access to Unapproved Therapeutic Goods, Clinical Trials in Australia*, Therapeutic Goods Administration, October 2004
Chapter 4 Main Topics	A clinical trial or study is any investigation in human subjects intended to discover the clinical, pharmacological or other pharmacodynamic effects of an investigational product(s); or identify any adverse reaction(s) to an investigational product(s); or study absorption, distribution, metabolism and excretion of an investigational product(s) with the objective of ascertaining the product's safety and/or efficacy. There are four clinical trial phases: • Phase 1—First-in-man trials, intended primarily to establish the drug's safety, tolerability and pharmacokinetic properties and establish a possible dose using placebo and/or double-blind techniques. These studies usually involve a few (20–80) healthy subjects. • Phase 2—Usually involves several hundred (200–500) patients in whom efficacy is tested while a more definitive therapeutic dose also is determined. In Phase 2, randomized, placebo-controlled studies are the standard design. • Phase 3—Trials with a larger population (1,000–5,000 patients) that primarily use double-blind, randomized, placebo- and/or active-controlled techniques to test for efficacy, benefits and possible side effects. • Phase 4—Postmarket studies that are performed after a license has been granted and only involve approved indications and conditions. Good Clinical Practices (GCP) are ethical and scientific guidelines that describe standards for designing, conducting, recording and reporting trials involving the participation of human subjects. GCPs include: • clinical trial design • clinical trial conduct • roles and responsibilities of involved parties • recording • reporting The development of Clinical Trial Registries reflects an increasing need to improve the transparency of clinical research, which can improve general knowledge on the ongoing research for certain diseases or pharmaceuticals. Sponsors usually are asked to provide specific information to the national or regional registries about their clinical trials.

Other Topics	
	Regulations and Guidelines
Advertising and Promotion	**EU** • Directive 2004/27/EC of the European Parliament and of the Council of 31 March 2004 amending Directive 2001/83/EC on the Community code relating to medicinal products for human use **US** • 21 CFR 314.550 Promotional materials (drugs) • 21 CFR 601.45 Promotional materials (biologics) **WHO** • Resolution WHA41.17, *Ethical Criteria for Medicinal Drug Promotion,* 1998 • Technical Report Series, No. 965, *The Selection and Use of Essential Medicines* **Other** • European Federation of Pharmaceutical Industries and Associations, European Code of Practice on the Promotion of Medicines, Update 2007 • International Federation of Pharmaceutical Manufacturers and Associations, Code of Pharmaceutical Marketing Practices • Pharmaceutical Research and Manufacturers of America (PhRMA) Code on Interactions with Healthcare Professionals, 2009
Chapter 6 Main Topics	Advertising prescription drugs and, in many cases, medical devices, is a highly regulated process in most countries. Advertisements for other product groups such as food supplements and cosmetics, although less strict, also are controlled. Although the exact definition is different across regions, advertising, as related to medicinal products or medical devices, generally can be understood to be the provision of any form of information, including door-to-door advertising or any activity that aims to promote the prescription, supply, sale or consumption of such products. **Forms of Advertising** • advertising of medicinal products, such as nonprescription drugs, which are freely available to the general public, whether over-the-counter or off-the-shelf • advertising of prescription-only drugs • advertising to the general public • advertising to healthcare professionals **Medical Representatives** Medical representative play a major role in the promotion of drugs and, therefore, should have an appropriate educational background, including sufficient medical and technical knowledge to present information on products. They should be adequately trained regarding appropriate ethical conduct, taking into consideration the WHO criteria. **Free samples** Free samples of legally available prescription drugs should be allowed only in modest quantities and only to prescribers, generally upon request.

	Regulations and Guidelines
Enforcement and Compliance	**ICH** • *Good Manufacturing Practice Guide for Active Pharmaceutical Ingredients Q7*, Current Step 4 Version, November 2000 • *Quality Risk Management Q9*, Current Step 4 Version, November 2005 • *Pharmaceutical Quality System Q10*, Current Step 4 Version, June 2008 • *Pharmacovigilance Planning E2E*, Current Step 4 Version, November 2004 • *Guideline for Good Clinical Practice E6(R1)*, Current Step 4 Version, June 1996 **GHTF/IMDRF** • SG4/N28R4:2008 *Guidelines for Regulatory Auditing of Quality Management Systems of Medical Device Manufacturers—Part 1: General Requirements* (August 2008) • SG3/N17:2008 *Quality Management System—Medical Devices—Guidance on the Control of Products and Services Obtained from Suppliers* (December 2008) • SG3/N15R8:2005 *Implementation of Risk Management Principles and Activities Within a Quality Management System* (May 2005) • SG3/N99-10:2004 *Quality Management Systems—Process Validation Guidance* (January 2004) **EU** • Regulation (EC) 726/2004 of the European Parliament and of the Council of 31 March 2004 laying down Community procedures for the authorisation and supervision of medicinal products for human and veterinary use and establishing a European Medicines Agency • Directive 2001/20/EC of the European Parliament and of the Council of 4 April 2001 on the approximation of the laws, regulations and administrative provisions of the Member States relating to the implementation of good clinical practices in the conduct of clinical trials for medicinal products for human use (*Clinical Trials Directive*) • Commission Directive 2005/28/EC of 8 April 2005 laying down principles and guidelines for good clinical practice as regards investigational medicinal products for human use, as well as the requirements for authorisation of the manufacturing or importation of such products (*Good Clinical Practice Directive*) • Commission Directive 2003/94/EC of 8 October 2003 laying down the principles and guidelines of good manufacturing practice in respect of medicinal products for human use and investigational medicinal products for human use (*Human GMP Directive*) • Commission Directive 91/412/EEC of 23 July 1991 laying down the principles and guidelines of good manufacturing practice for veterinary medicinal products (*Veterinary GMP Directive*) • Council Directive 92/25/EEC of 31 March 1992 on the wholesale distribution of medicinal products for human use • Directive 2004/10/EC of the European Parliament and of the Council of 11 February 2004 on the harmonization of laws, regulations and administrative provisions relating to the application of the principles of good laboratory practice and the verification of their applications for tests on chemical substances • Directive 2004/9/EC of the European Parliament and of the Council of 11 February 2004 on the inspection and verification of good laboratory practice • Council Directive 90/385/EEC of 20 June 1990 on the approximation of the laws of the Member States relating to active implantable medical devices (*AIMD Directive*) • Council Directive 93/42/EEC of 14 June 1993 concerning medical devices (*Medical Devices Directive*, *MDD*) • Directive 98/79/EC of the European Parliament and of the Council of 27 October 1998 on in vitro diagnostic medical devices (*IVD Directive*) **US** • *Federal Food, Drug, and Cosmetic Act* of 1938 (*FD&C Act*) • *Public Health Service Act* of 1944 (*PHS Act*) • 21 CFR 207 Registration of Producers of Drugs and Listing of Drugs in Commercial Distribution • 21 CFR 210 cGMP in Manufacturing, Processing, Packing, or Holding of Drugs and 211 cGMP for Finished Pharmaceuticals • 21 CFR 807 Establishment Registration and Device Listing for Manufacturers and Initial Importers of Devices • 21 CFR 820 Quality System Regulation • 21 CFR 803 Medical Device Reporting

<table>
<tr>
<td>Chapter 7
Main Topics</td>
<td>Enforcement can be defined as any action taken by a regulatory authority to protect the public from products of suspect quality, safety or efficacy, and may include activities such as:
• licensing
• inspections
• operations
• surveillance
• preclinical and clinical testing
• storage and distribution
• import control
• control of advertising and promotion

Competent Authorities exercise a legal right to control product use or sale within their jurisdictions by ensuring compliance with laws, regulations, standards and any postmarket commitments.

Pharmaceuticals and Biological Products
Regulatory compliance for pharmaceuticals and biologic products is enforced by inspections and monitoring. National legislation provides statutory powers to Competent Authorities to ensure compliance via such sanctions as monetary fines and/or imprisonment for noncompliance.

Inspections
Before medicinal products can be placed on the market, Marketing Authorization Holders, manufacturers, distributors or wholesalers, dealers and/or marketers must undergo several preapproval inspections by Competent Authorities. These cover all areas of GxPs related to the product's manufacture and distribution:
• Good Laboratory Practice
• Good Clinical Practice
• Good Manufacturing Practice
• Good Distribution Practice

Pharmacovigilance and Compliance
Pharmacovigilance inspections should be conducted to provide assurances that Marketing Authorization Holders are complying with their regulatory obligations and to facilitate compliance. The legal requirements for pharmacoviligance systems are specified in local laws and regulations.

Other Issues
Other postmarket issues include change control and monitoring advertising and promotion.

Medical Devices and In Vitro Diagnostic Devices
Like pharmaceutical products, medical devices must comply with national and regional laws and regulations enforced by monitoring and inspections. The innovative nature of the medical device industry creates unique legal and enforcement risks, compliance rules and industry codes of conduct. The areas to be inspected during the pre- and postmarket phases for drugs and devices are similar and cover preclinical and clinical testing, manufacturing process and controls, vigilance reporting, change control, quality systems and labeling and advertising activities.

Inspections
Inspections form part of both the pre- and postmarket phases of medical device manufacture. In many instances, inspections are carried out by third parties accredited by Competent Authorities, for example Notified Bodies in the EU or, less often, accredited firms in the US.

Quality Systems
Most jurisdictions require that medical device manufacturers implement a quality management system. ISO has published three standards on quality management:
• ISO 9000:2005 Quality management systems—Fundamentals and vocabulary
• ISO 13485:2003 Medical devices—Quality management systems system requirements for regulatory purposes
• ISO 14971:2007 Medical devices—Application of risk management to medical devices

Vigilance and Postmarket Surveillance and Compliance
Manufacturers placing medical devices on the market must have a vigilance system for collecting and evaluating reported incidents and taking any needed corrective action to prevent the recurrence of such incidents. For certain classes of products, such as diagnostic devices, where false positives and/or false negatives may occur, or long-term implantable devices and devices for home use, where the evaluation of performance from adverse event reports alone would not be sufficient, postmarket surveillance should be used.</td>
</tr>
</table>

Premarket Requirements (Drugs)	
	Regulations and Guidelines
Premarket Requirements/ Dossier Requirements	**ICH** • *Organization of the CTD for the Registration of Pharmaceuticals for Human Use M4(R3)*, Current Step 4 version, dated 13 January 2004 • *The Common Technical Document for the Registration of Pharmaceuticals for Human Use: Quality—M4Q(R1), Quality Overall Summary of Module 2 Module 3: Quality*, Current Step 4 version, 12 September 2002 • *The Common Technical Document for the Registration of Pharmaceuticals for Human Use: Safety—M4S(R2), Nonclinical Overview and Nonclinical Summaries of Module 2, Organization of Module 4*, Current Step 4 version, 20 December 2002 • *The Common Technical Document for the Registration of Pharmaceuticals for Human Use: Efficacy—M4E(R1), Clinical Overview and Clinical Summary of Module 2, Module 5 Clinical Study Reports*, Current Step 4 version, 12 September 2002 • *Impurities in New Drug Substances Q3A(R2),* Current Step 4 version, 25 October 2006 • *Specifications: Test Procedures and Acceptance Criteria for New Drug Substances and New Drug Products: Chemical Substances Q6A (including Decision Trees),* Current Step 4 version, 6 October 1999 • *Specifications: Test Procedures and Acceptance Criteria for Biotechnological/Biological Products Q6B*, Current Step 4 version, 10 March 1999 • *Pharmaceutical Development Q8(R2),* Current Step 4 version, August 2009 • *Safety Pharmacology Studies for Human Pharmaceuticals S7A,* Current Step 4 version, 8 November 2000
Chapter 9 Main Topics	Before granting marketing authorization, the Competent Authority evaluates a technical file (dossier), containing information pertaining to the results of preclinical and clinical testing and manufacturing. The Common Technical Document (CTD) provides a harmonized dossier structure accepted in the EU, US, Japan and many other countries. The CTD has five modules: **Module 1:** Administrative Information (country/region specific) **Module 2:** High Level Written and Tabulated Summaries **Module 3:** Chemistry, Manufacturing and Controls (CMC) **Module 4:** Nonclinical Information **Module 5:** Clinical Information

Authorization Procedures (Drugs)	
	Regulations and Guidelines
Authorization Procedures for Medicinal Products	**ICH** • *Guidance on Nonclinical Safety Studies for the Conduct of Human Clinical Trials and Marketing Authorization for Pharmaceuticals M3(R2,)* Current Step 4 version, 11 June 2009 • *Detection of Toxicity to Reproduction for Medicinal Products & Toxicity to Male Fertility S5(R2)*, Current Step 4 version, November 2005 • ICH, *Guidance on Genotoxicity Testing and Data Interpretation for Pharmaceuticals Intended for* • *Human Use S2(R1,)*Current Step 4 version, 9 November 2011 • *Guideline on the Need for Carcinogenicity Studies of Pharmaceuticals S1A*, Current Step 4 version, 29 November 1995 • *Safety Pharmacology Studies for Human Pharmaceuticals S7A*, Current Step 4 version, 8 November 2000 • *Note for Guidance on Toxicokinetics: The Assessment of Systemic Exposure in Toxicity Studies S3A*, Current Step 4 version, 27 October 1994 • *Pharmacokinetics: Guidance for Repeated Dose Tissue Distribution Studies S3B*, Current Step 4 version, 27 October 1994 • *Structure and Content of Clinical Study Reports E3*, Current Step 4 version, 30 November 1995 • *Guideline for Good Clinical Practice E6(R1)*, Current Step 4 version, 10 June 1996 • *Quality Risk Management Q9*, Current Step 4 version, 9 November 2005 • *Good Manufacturing Practice Guide for Active Pharmaceutical Ingredients Q7*, Current Step 4 version, 10 November 2000 **OECD** • OECD *Series on Principles of Good Laboratory Practice and Compliance Monitoring*, ENV/MC/CHEM(98)17, 1998. **EU** • Regulation (EC) No 726/2004 of the European Parliament and of the Council of 31 March 2004 laying down Community procedures for the authorisation and supervision of medicinal products for human and veterinary use and establishing a European Medicines Agency • Directive 2004/27/EC of the European Parliament and of the Council of 31 March 2004 amending Directive 2001/83/EC on the Community code relating to medicinal products for human use • Directive 2004/10/EC of the European Parliament and of the Council of 11 February 2004 on the harmonisation of laws, regulations and administrative provisions relating to the application of the principles of good laboratory practice and the verification of their applications for tests on chemical substances • Directive 2004/9/EC of the European Parliament and of the Council of 11 February 2004 on the inspection and verification of good laboratory practice (GLP) • *Volume 9A, The Rules Governing Medicinal Products in the European Union, Guidelines on Pharmacovigilance for Medicinal Products for Human Use* (version September 2008) **US** • FDA, 21 CFR 58 Good Laboratory Practice for Nonclinical Laboratory Studies • FDA, 21 CFR 314 Applications for FDA Approval to Market a New Drug

Chapter 10 Main Topics	Marketing Authorization Holders have certain legal responsibilities. The following list, although not exhaustive, includes the most important of those responsibilities: • The MAH is responsible for taking any technical and scientific progress into consideration and updating manufacturing and control operations. • When another organization, particularly a contract company, is the manufacturer, the MAH must ensure that a written agreement is in place to guarantee manufacturing operations comply with dossier rules and conditions and the manufacturer is obliged to inform the MAH of any changes before implementation. • If any information, including safety issues, which could lead to modification of the marketing authorization dossier or Summary of Product Characteristics (SmPC) is brought to the attention of the MAH, the Comptent Authorities must be informed immediately. • In most countries, marketing authorizations are issued for a limited time. The MAH is responsible for renewing the license before the marketing authorization's expiration date. The rules governing this vary from region to region. • In certain regions such as the EU, Canada, Switzerland, Australia, Japan and New Zealand, the MAH is required to have a qualified person for batch release. • In most countries, the MAH must have a qualified person in charge of pharmacovigilance. • The MAH must take full responsibility for medicinal product advertising. • The MAH must ensure all medicinal product documentation, including clinical trial information, is retained and archived. • Special requirements may apply to high-risk products such as immunological medicinal products and medicinal products derived from human blood or human plasma. Although the exact requirements and processes vary from country to country, in almost all regions, the requirements for new drug applications require at least: • nonclinical testing • application to begin clinical trials • new drug application, including results of nonclinical and clinical testing plus manufacturing information • pricing and reimbursement information • postmarketing activities Throughout this process, applicants are in frequent contact with the Competent Authorities.

Stability (Drugs)	
Stability	***Regulations and Guidelines***
	ICH • *Stability testing of new drug substances and products Q1A(R2),* February *2003* • *Stability Testing: Photostability testing of new drug substances and products Q1B.* November 1996 • *Stability testing of new dosage forms Q1C,* November 1996 • *Bracketing and matrixing designs for stability testing of new drug substances and products Q1D,* February 2002 • *Evaluation for stability data Q1E,* February 2003 • *Validation of analytical procedures: text and methodology Q2(R1),* November 1996 • *Impurities in new drug substances Q3A(R2),* October 2006 • *Impurities in new drug products Q3B(R2),* June 2006 • *Stability Testing of Biotechnological/Biological Products Q5C,* November 1995 • *Specifications: Test procedures and acceptance criteria for new drug substances and new drug products: Chemical substances Q6A,* October 1999 • *Specifications: Test procedures and acceptance criteria for biotechnological/ biological products Q6B,* March 1999)

Chapter 11 Main Topics	The purpose of stability testing is to provide evidence of how the quality of a drug substance or drug product varies with time because of environmental factors, such as temperature, humidity and light, and product-related factors, such as the drug substance's physical and chemical properties, interaction with the excipients, dosage form, manufacturing process and other factors. Stability testing also is used to establish a re-test period or shelf life for the drug substance and to determine the drug product's shelf life and recommendations for storage conditions. The world is divided into four climatic zones: I Temperate climate; II Subtropical and Mediterranean climate; III Hot and dry climate; IVa Hot and humid climate; and IVb Hot and very humid climate. The climate conditions in each zone have an effect on drug product stability. Stability study data generally should be provided on at least three primary drug substance batches and three primary drug product batches. Stability testing should be performed at batch release and at the end of the proposed drug product shelf life. Stability testing should be conducted on the drug substance in the packaged container closure system proposed for storage and distribution. The drug product batches should be of the same formulation and packaged in the same container closure system as proposed for marketing. Stability studies should be performed on each individual strength, dosage form and container type and size unless bracketing or matrixing is applied.

Quality Systems (Drugs)	
	Regulations and guidelines
Quality Systems and Inspection Processes—Pharmaceuticals	**ICH & WHO** • ICH, *The Common Technical Document for the Registration of Pharmaceuticals for Human Use: Quality—M4Q(R1), Quality Overall Summary of Module 2 Module 3: Quality*, Current Step 4 version, 12 September 2002 • *ICH, Quality Risk Management Q9*, Current Step 4 version, 9 November 2005 • ICH, *Pharmaceutical Development Q8(R2)*, Current Step 4 version, August 2009 • ICH, *Good Manufacturing Practice Guide for Active Pharmaceutical Ingredients Q7*, Current Step 4 version, 10 November 2000 • ICH, *Pharmaceutical Quality System Q10*, Current Step 4 version, 4 June 2008 • WHO, *Quality Assurance of Pharmaceuticals A compendium of guidelines and related materials, Volume 2, second updated edition, Good Manufacturing Practices and Inspection*, 2007 **EU** • Commission Directive 2003/94/EC of 8 October 2003 laying down the principles and guidelines of good manufacturing practice in respect of medicinal products for human use and investigational medicinal products for human use • Commission Directive 91/412/EEC of 23 July 1991 laying down the principles and guidelines of good manufacturing practice for veterinary medicinal products • *Volume 4, The Rules Governing Medicinal Products in the European Union, EU Guidelines to good manufacturing practice for medicinal products for human and veterinary use* (version December 2010) • Directive 2001/83/EC of the European Parliament and of the Council of 6 November 2001 on the Community code relating to medicinal products for human use, as amended by Directive 2004/27/EC and Regulation (EC) No 1901/2006 • Directive 2001/82/EC of the European Parliament and of the Council of 6 November 2001 on the Community code relating to veterinary medicinal products, as amended by Directive 2004/28/EC of the European Parliament and the Council of 31 March 2004 **US** • *Federal Food, Drug, and Cosmetic Act (FD&C Act)*, Section 501(a)(2)(b) • 21 CFR 210 Current Good Manufacturing Practice in the Manufacturing, Processing, Packaging or Holding of Drugs; General • 21 CFR 211 Current Good Manufacturing Practice for Finished Pharmaceuticals • 21 CFR 606 Current Good Manufacturing Practice for Blood and Blood Components **Canada** • *Food and Drug Regulations*, Division 2, Part C • *Good Manufacturing Practices (GMP) Guidelines*, 2009 Edition, Version 2 (4 March 2011)

<table>
<tr>
<td>Chapter 12
Main Topics</td>
<td>Human and veterinary drugs must meet minimum quality and safety requirements. Concerns over the rising costs of healthcare and escalation of the costs of R&D, coupled with the need to meet public expectations of safe and fast availability of new treatments, paved the way for rationalization and harmonization.

What began as harmonization of regulatory requirements for the development of a single market for pharmaceuticals in what is now the EU became the International Conference on Harmonisation (ICH), an initiative involving three regions: the EU, Japan and the US. Topics initially selected for harmonization included safety, quality and efficacy, to reflect the three basic criteria for approving and authorizing new medicinal products (www.ich.org). Recent emphasis on global cooperation has highlighted the importance of disseminating information and providing input beyond the ICH regions via international organizations such as the World Health Organization (WHO).

Good Manufacturing Practice (GMP)
"GMP" can be defined as "That part of Quality Assurance which ensures that products are consistently produced and controlled to the quality standards appropriate to their intended use." This is a requirement for both active ingredients and finished pharmaceutical products.

GMP assumes that licensed pharmaceutical products are manufactured by licensed manufacturers. To ensure compliance, manufacturers must be regularly inspected by Competent Authorities.

Inspections
Inspections can be considered part of the overall drug quality assurance system. They can be routine, precise and specific inspections; follow-up inspections; or quality systems inspections. The objective of inspecting pharmaceutical manufacturing plants is to enforce GMP compliance or to provide authorization for the manufacture of specific pharmaceutical products, usually in relation to an application for marketing authorization.

Mutual Recognition Agreements (MRAs)
MRAs on GMP and acceptance of inspections and quality systems among countries improve the pace of global trade. In most cases, each party evaluates the other during a transitional assessment period, which has a predefined timeframe. The assessment may include an appraisal of the other party's pharmaceutical legislation, guidances and systems; the findings usually are confirmed during compliance visits and joint inspections. If each party can confirm that the other's systems are equivalent with its own, an operational phase can begin.

Pharmaceutical Inspection Convention
The Pharmaceutical Inspection Convention and Pharmaceutical Inspection Co-operation Scheme (jointly referred to as PIC/S) are two international instruments among countries and pharmaceutical inspection authorities that together provide active and constructive cooperation in the field of GMP (www.picscheme.org/).</td>
</tr>
</table>

	Regulations and Guidelines
Generic Drug Products and Biosimilars	**WHO** • WHO Guidelines on Evaluation of Similar Biotherapeutic Products (SBPs), 22 April 2010 • WHO Informal Consultation on International Nonproprietary Names (INN) Policy for Biosimilar Products, Geneva, 4–5 September 2006 **EU** • EMA/393905/2006 Rev 2, European Medicines Agency: Questions and Answers on Generic Medicines , 22 November 2012, • Council Regulation No. (EEC) 1768/92 of 18 June 1992 concerning the creation of a supplementary protection certificate for medicinal products • Regulation (EC) No. 726/2004 of the European Parliament and of the Council of 31 March 2004 laying down Community procedures for the authorisation and supervision of medicinal products for human and veterinary use and establishing a European Medicines Agency • Directive 2001/83/EC of the European Parliament and of the Council of 6 November 2001 on the Community code relating to medicinal products for human use, as amended by Directive 2004/27/EC of the European Parliament and of the Council of 31 March 2004 and Annex 1 (Commission Directive 2003/63/EC of 25 June 2003) • Draft Guideline on Similar Biological Medicinal Products, CHMP/437/04 Rev 1 (22 May 2013) **US** • *Drug Price Competition and Patent Term Restoration Act* of 1984 (*Hatch-Waxman Act*), Public Law 98-417, 98 Statute 1585 • *Guidance for Industry: 180-Day Generic Drug Exclusivity Under the Hatch-Waxman Amendments to the Federal Food, Drug, and Cosmetic Act* (July 1998) • *Guidance for Industry: Court Decisions, ANDA Approvals, and 180-Day Exclusivity Under the Hatch-Waxman Amendments to the Federal Food, Drug, and Cosmetic Act* (March 2000) • *Patient Protection and Affordable Care Act* (March 2010), including the *Biologics Price Competition and Innovation Act* of 2009 • *Draft Guidance for Industry: Scientific Considerations in Demonstrating Biosimilarity to a Reference Product* (February 2012) • *Draft Guidance for Industry: Quality Considerations in Demonstrating Biosimilarity to a Reference Protein Product* (February 2012) • *Draft Guidance for Industry: Biosimilars: Questions and Answers Regarding Implementation of the Biologics Price Competition and Innovation Act of 2009* (February 2012) **Canada** • *An Act respecting food, drugs, cosmetics and therapeutic devices* (1920) (*Food and Drugs Act*) • *Federal Food and Drug Regulations* • Canadian Reference Product, 5 December 1995 • *Guidance for Sponsors: Information and Submission Requirements for Subsequent Entry Biologics (SEBs)* (5 March 2010
Chapters 13, 24 Main Topics	A generic medicine is a medicinal product that is similar to one already authorized ("reference medicinal product") and manufactured and distributed without patent protection on the active ingredient. Generics contain the same quantity of active substance(s), are used at the same dose to treat the same disease, and are equally safe and effective as originator products. The concept of generics arises from the fact that when the patent for an original, brand-name product patent expires, the medicine essentially becomes public property. Companies with appropriate expertise and manufacturing facilities may produce and market the product, provided they obtain the necessary authorizations from regulatory authorities. Developing copies (biosimilars) of well-known biopharmaceuticals (originators) is very challenging because minor molecular deviations from the reference product may affect the new product's efficacy and/or safety. Chapters 13 and 24 cover regulatory frameworks for generics and biosimilars, including: • definitions • data exclusivity • Supplementary Protection Certificates • Bolar (experimental and testing) provisions • bioequivalence • marketing authorization process • reference medicinal products • variations • pharmacovigilance

<table>
<tr><th></th><th>Regulations and Guidelines</th></tr>
<tr><td>Over-the-Counter Products (OTCs)</td><td>Australia
• Australian Regulatory Guidelines for Over-The-Counter Medicines (ARGOM), 2003 (draft revision published in 2013, but not yet implemented)

Canada
• Food and Drugs Act and Food and Drug Regulations, Part C

EU
• Directive 2004/27/EC of the European Parliament and of the Council of 31 March 2004 amending Directive 2001/83/EC on the Community code relating to medicinal products for human use
• EMA, Guideline on changing the classification for the supply of a medicinal product for human use, The Rules Governing Medicinal Products in the European Community Volume 2C: Guidelines (January 2006)

Japan
• Pharmaceutical Affairs Law, Act No. 145 of 1960, as amended

US
• Durham-Humphrey Amendment to the Federal Food, Drug, and Cosmetic Act, Public Law 82-215 (1951)</td></tr>
<tr><td>Chapter 14 Main Topics</td><td>The definition of an over-the-counter (OTC) drug and mode of dispensing can differ widely among regions and countries. Generally, OTC products can be defined as medications that can be purchased at a pharmacy, grocery or convenience store without a prescription. They are used to treat the symptoms of common ailments and are safe for general consumption if taken exactly as prescribed by the packaging.

To attain OTC status, products must meet certain conditions:
1. Self-medication in the form of nonprescription medicines should only be used for minor ailments.
2. Since the patient bears the full responsibility for his or her own treatment, the manufacturer and Competent Authorities are responsible for making sure the text used in the accompanying Patient Information Leaflet (PIL) is clear and understandable.
3. Self-medication normally should not be used for long periods of time to treat chronic conditions.
4. If patients experience any undesirable side effects, they should consult their doctors.
5. Self-medication must be used very carefully by pregnant or lactating women, babies and infants.

Switching Procedures
The switch from prescription to nonprescription status (Rx-to-OTC) is handled very differently by nations or regions. The decision for or against an Rx-to-OTC switch is made by the local Competent Authority.

Labeling and Advertising
Since OTC drugs are available without prescription, it is important that they be accompanied by adequate directions for use and warnings, to provide a high degree of consumer protection. The information to appear on the label and package leaflet is clearly specified in national laws.

Postmarket Surveillance/Enforcement
The increasing number of OTC drugs has created a growing need for systems to carefully monitor both their safety and their interaction with prescription drugs. This is especially important given the current trend of underreporting engendered by complicated systems, time lags and expenses associated with such systems.</td></tr>
</table>

Postmarket Requirements (Drugs)	
	Regulations and Guidelines
Pharmaceutical Postmarketing and Compliance	**ICH** • *Pharmaceutical Quality System Q10*, Current Step 4 version, 4 June 2008 • *Pharmaceutical Development Q8(R2)*, Current Step 4 version, August 2009 • *Quality Risk Management Q9*, Current Step 4 version, 9 November 2005 • *Post-Approval Safety Data Management: Definitions and Standards for Expedited Reporting E2D*, Current Step 4 version, 12 November 2003 **EU** • Regulation (EC) No 726/2004 of the European Parliament and of the Council of 31 March 2004 laying down Community procedures for the authorisation and supervision of medicinal products for human and veterinary use and establishing a European Medicines Agency • Directive 2001/83/EC of the European Parliament and of the Council of 6 November 2001 on the Community code relating to medicinal products for human use, as amended. • Commission Regulation (EC) No. 1084/2003 of 3 June 2003 concerning the examination of variations to the terms of a marketing authorisation for medicinal products for human use and veterinary medicinal products granted by a competent authority of a Member State • Commission Regulation (EC) No. 1085/2003 of 3 June 2003 concerning the examination of variations to the terms of a marketing authorisation for medicinal products for human use and veterinary medicinal products falling within the scope of Council Regulation (EEC) No. 2309/93 • Commission Regulation (EC) No. 1234/2008 of 24 November 2008 concerning the examination of variations to the terms of marketing authorisations for medicinal products for human use and veterinary medicinal products • *Guideline on dossier requirements for Type IA and Type IB notifications*, Revision 1 (July 2006) • Commission Regulation (EC) No. 540/95 of 10 March 1995 laying down the arrangements for reporting suspected unexpected adverse reactions which are not serious, whether arising in the Community or in a third country, to medicinal products for human or veterinary use authorised in accordance with the provisions of Council Regulation (EEC) No. 2309/93 **US** • 21 CFR 314.70 Supplements and other changes to an approved application • 21 CFR 314.81 Other postmarketing reports • 21 CFR 314.80 Postmarketing reporting of adverse drug experiences • *Guidance for Industry: SUPAC-IR: Immediate Release Solid Oral Dosage Forms, Scale-Up and Post-approval Changes: Chemistry, Manufacturing and Controls, In Vitro Dissolution Testing and In Vivo Bioequivalence Documentation*, US Food and Drug Administration, Center for Drug Evaluation and Research (CDER) (November 1995) • *Guidance for Industry: SUPAC-MR: Modified Release Solid Oral Dosage Forms: Scale-Up and Post-Approval Changes: Chemistry, Manufacturing and Controls, In Vitro Dissolution Testing and In Vivo Bioequivalence Documentation*, CDER (October 1997) • *Guidance for Industry: SUPAC-SS: Nonsterile Semisolid Dosage Forms; Scale-Up and Post-Approval Changes: Chemistry, Manufacturing and Controls, In Vitro Release Testing and In Vivo Bioequivalence Documentation*, CDER (May 1997) • *Guidance for Industry: Changes to an Approved NDA or ANDA*, CDER (April 2004) **Canada** • *Guidance for Industry: Changes in Product-Specific Facility Information*, Health Canada, Biologics and Genetic Therapies Directorate (BGTD) (July 2004) • Canadian Adverse Drug Reaction Monitoring Program: *Guidelines for the Voluntary Reporting of Suspected Adverse Reactions to Health Products by Health Professionals and Consumers* • *Guidance Document for Industry: Reporting Adverse Reactions to Marketed Health Products* MedEffect Canada (March 2011) **Australia** • *Australian Guideline for Pharmacovigilance Responsibilities of Sponsors of Registered Medicines Regulated by Drug Safety and Evaluation Branch*, Therapeutic Goods Administration (TGA)(July 2003; amended 31 May 2005) • *Australian regulatory guidelines for prescription medicines (ARGPM)*, appendices 12 and 13, TGA

Chapter 15 Main Topics	**Variations and Changes** Among the drivers of change are innovation, continual improvement, the results of process performance and product quality monitoring, and corrective and preventive actions (CAPA) (ICH *Pharmaceutical Quality System Q10*). To evaluate, approve and implement these changes properly, companies are obliged to have an effective change management system. In most territories, postapproval changes must be recorded and communicated to the Competent Authorities. *Pharmaceutical Quality System Elements* Some Q10 elements may be included already in regional GMP regulations; however, the Q10 model's intent is to enhance these elements to promote the lifecycle approach to product quality. The four basic elements are: • process performance and product quality monitoring system • CAPA system • change management system • management review of process performance and product quality **Pharmacovigilance** MAHs must have a pharmacovigilance system to ensure all information relevant to a medicinal product's balance of benefits and risks is fully and promptly reported to the Competent Authorities. In addition, the MAH generally is required to have a qualified person responsible for pharmacovigilance (QPPV) available at all times. **Sources of Individual Case Safety Reports (ICSR)** • unsolicited sources • solicited sources • contractual agreements • regulatory authority sources **Standards for Expedited Reporting** Reporting of all cases of adverse drug reactions (ADRs) that are both serious and unexpected should be expedited. *Minimum Criteria for Reporting* For the purpose of regulatory reporting, the minimum data elements for an ADR case are: • an identifiable reporter • an identifiable patient • an adverse reaction • a suspect product *Reporting Timeframes* According to ICH E2D, expedited reporting of serious and unexpected ADRs is required as soon as possible, but in no case later than 15 calendar days after initial receipt of the information by the MAH. The exact reporting timelines of other serious reports vary among countries. **Standard Operating Procedures (SOPs)** All postmarket activities for products manufactured in a GMP environment require relevant SOPs. The SOPs must be implemented, i.e., written and signed off and personnel trained on them. **Inspections** Inspectors may check the availability and status of SOPs, including training records. The handling of variations and change control is a typical area to be targeted during routine inspections. Inspectors also will check whether software in use has been validated properly.
	Regulations and Guidelines

Medical Devices	
	Regulations and Guidelines
Legal and Regulatory Requirements/ Premarket Evaluation	**GHTF/IMDRF** • GHTF/SG1/N071:2012, (revision of GHTF/SG1/N29:2005) *Definition of the Terms 'Medical Device' and 'In Vitro Diagnostic (IVD) Medical Device'* (May 2012) • GHTF/SG1/N055:2009, *Definitions of the Terms Manufacturer, Authorised Representative, Distributor and Importer* (March 2009) • GHTF/SG1/N68:2012, *Essential Principles of Safety and Performance of Medical Devices* (November 2012) • GHTF/SG1/N70:2011, *Label and Instructions for Use for Medical Devices* (September 2011) • GHTF/SG1/N78:2012, *Principles of Conformity Assessment for Medical Devices* (November 2012) • GHTF/SG1/N77:2012, *Principles of Medical Devices Classification* (November 2012) • GHTF/SG1/N011:2008, *Summary Technical Documentation for Demonstrating Conformity to the Essential Principles of Safety and Performance of Medical Devices (STED)* (February 2008) • GHTF/SG1/N044:2008, *Role of Standards in the Assessment of Medical Devices* (March 2008)
Chapter 16 Main Topics	According to GHTF/IMDRF, a medical device is any instrument, apparatus, implement, machine, appliance, implant, in vitro reagent or calibrator, software, material or other similar or related article: a) intended by the manufacturer to be used, alone or in combination, for human beings for one or more of the specific purpose(s) of: • diagnosis, prevention, monitoring, treatment or alleviation of disease, • diagnosis, monitoring, treatment, alleviation of or compensation for an injury, • investigation, replacement, modification, or support of the anatomy or of a physiological process, • supporting or sustaining life, • control of conception, • disinfection of medical devices, • providing information for medical or diagnostic purposes by means of in vitro examination of specimens derived from the human body; and b) which does not achieve its primary intended action in or on the human body by pharmacological, immunological or metabolic means, but which may be assisted in its intended function by such means. **Six Principles** GHTF has established six basic requirements that apply to all medical devices: 1. Medical devices should be designed and manufactured in such a way that, when used under the conditions and for the purposes intended, and taking into account the technical knowledge, experience, education or training of intended users, they will not compromise the clinical condition or the safety of patients, of users or, where applicable, other people. This should be considered in the context of the risk:benefit ratio. 2. The solutions adopted by the manufacturer for the design and manufacture of the devices should conform to the most current safety principles and should address the issue of residual risk and risk reduction. 3. Devices should achieve the performance intended by the manufacturer. 4. Device characteristics and performance should not be adversely affected to such a degree that the health or safety of the patient or the user are compromised during the lifetime of the device, under normal conditions of use. 5. The devices should be designed, manufactured and packed in such a way that their characteristics and performance are not affected under transport and storage conditions. 6. The benefits must be determined to outweigh any undesirable side effects for the performances intended.

Medical Devices	
	Regulations and Guidelines
Technical and Regulatory Requirements	**GHTF/IMDRF** • SG1-N11:2008 *Summary Technical Documentation for Demonstrating Conformity to the Essential Principles of Safety and Performance of Medical Devices (STED)* (February 2008) • SG1-N44:2008 *Role of Standards in the Assessment of Medical Device* (February 2008) • SG5 Guidance documents • SG1-N78:2012 *Principles of Conformity Assessment for Medical Devices* (November 2012) • SG1-N55:2009 *Definition of the Terms Manufacturer, Authorised Representative, Distributor and Importer* (March 2009) • SG3-N99-10 (Edition 2) *Quality Management Systems—Process Validation Guidance* (January 2004) • SG3-N15R8:2005 *Implementation of Risk Management Principles and Activities Within a Quality Management System* (May 2005) • SG3-N17R9:2008 *Quality Management System—Medical Devices—Guidance on the Control of Products and Services Obtained from Suppliers* (December 2008) **ISO** • ISO 14971 Application of Risk Management to Medical Devices
Chapter 17 Main Topics	**Essential Technical File Elements** The technical file is a means for manufacturers of all device classes to demonstrate a product's conformity to the *Essential Principles of Safety and Performance of Medical Devices.* The technical documentation should show how each medical device was developed, designed and manufactured, and should include descriptions and explanations necessary to understand the manufacturer's determination regarding conformity to the essential requirements. ***Premarket Phase*** The technical file for critical devices must be submitted to the regulatory authority for evaluation, while it is sufficient to have a copy of the files for less-critical devices readily available for inspection. ***Postmarket Phase*** The regulatory authority may, at any time, request a copy of the technical file for Class A and B (lower-risk) devices. The technical file must follow the lifecycle management (LCM) process in the postmarket phase. Changes that affect the quality system must be reported to the regulatory authority. **Content of the Summary Technical Documentation (STED)** • device description • product specification • reference to similar and previous generations of the device • labeling • design and manufacturing information • *Essential Principles* (EP) checklist • risk analysis and control summary • product verification and validation • Declaration of Conformity

<table>
<tr><th colspan="2">Medical Devices</th></tr>
<tr><th></th><th>Regulations and Guidelines</th></tr>
<tr><td>Device Quality Systems</td><td>ISO/WHO
• ISO 13485:2003—Medical devices—Quality management systems—Requirements for regulatory purposes
• ISO/TR 14969:2004—Medical devices— Quality management systems—Guidance on the application of ISO 13485: 2003
• World Health Organization, Medical Device Regulations: Global Overview and Guiding Principles, 2003

GHTF/IMDRF
• GHTF/SG3/N19:2012 Quality management system—Medical devices—Nonconformity Grading System for Regulatory Purposes and Information Exchange
• GHTF/SG3/N18:2010 Quality management system—Medical Devices—Guidance on corrective action and preventive action and related QMS processes (November 2010)
• GHTF/SG3/N17:2008 Quality Management System—Medical Devices—Guidance on the Control of Products and Services Obtained from Suppliers
• GHTF/SG3/N15R8 Risk Management Principles and Activities within a QMS (May 2005)
• GHTF/SG3/N99-10:2004 QMS—Process Validation Guidance (January 2004)</td></tr>
<tr><td>Chapter 18 Main Topics</td><td>A quality management system (QMS) is one of the five conformity assessment elements for medical devices (the others dealing with a system for postmarket surveillance, technical documentation, declaration of conformity and registration of manufacturers and their medical devices by the regulatory agency). A QMS is a set of interrelated or interactive processes to establish policy and objectives and to achieve those objectives in regard to quality.

The recognized international standard for medical device quality management systems is ISO 13485:2003 Medical devices—Quality management systems—Requirements for regulatory purposes. ISO 13485 was originally based on ISO 9001.

Although ISO 13485 is the recognized international standard for medical device quality systems, it is not accepted globally because:
1. It is a standard, and standards are voluntary in nature. A standard only becomes mandatory if required by regulation.
2. Some regulatory systems have their own versions of quality management system requirements (e.g., the US FDA has its own set of QMS requirements, the QSR). Still, most countries in the world use and accept ISO 13485 in some form or another.

Process validation uses objective evidence to prove that a process consistently produces a result or product meeting its predetermined requirements. This evidence must be documented in a protocol explaining the different validation steps and test parameters. Process validation is only one element of validation and includes facility and equipment validation, in addition to cleaning validation, analytical validation and computer validation.</td></tr>
</table>

<table>
<tr><th colspan="2">Medical Devices</th></tr>
<tr><th></th><th>Regulations and Guidelines</th></tr>
<tr><td>In Vitro Diagnostic Medical Devices</td><td>GHTF/IMDRF
• SG1-N45:2008 Principles of In Vitro Diagnostic (IVD) Medical Devices Classification (February 2008)
• SG1-N46:2008 Principles of Conformity Assessment for In Vitro Diagnostic (IVD) Medical Devices (July 2008)
• SG1-N68:2012 Essential Principles of Safety and Performance of Medical Devices (November 2012)
• SG1-N44:2008 Role of Standards in the Assessment of Medical Devices (March 2008)
• SG1-N063:2011 Summary Technical Documentation for Demonstrating Conformity to the Essential Principles of Safety and Performance of In Vitro Diagnostic Medical Devices (STED) (March 2011)
• SG2-N47R4:2005 Review of Current Requirements on Postmarket Surveillance (May 2005)
• AHWEG-UDI/N2R3:2011 Unique Device Identification System for Medical Devices (September 2011)</td></tr>
<tr><td>Chapter 19 Main Topics</td><td>An “in vitro diagnostic (IVD) medical device” is defined as a device that, whether used alone or in combination, is intended by the manufacturer for the in vitro examination of specimens derived from the human body solely or principally to provide information for diagnostic, monitoring or compatibility purposes (GHTF: SG1-N45:2008).
Examples include:
• reagents
• calibrators
• control materials
• specimen receptacles
• software and related instruments
• apparatus or other articles

IVD medical devices for self testing are intended by the manufacturer for use by lay people. In some jurisdictions, some classes of IVD medical devices may be covered by separate national regulations.

General Principles of Classification as proposed by GHTF
<table>
<tr><th>CLASS</th><th>RISK LEVEL</th><th>EXAMPLES</th></tr>
<tr><td>A</td><td>Low Individual Risk and Low Public Health Risk</td><td>Clinical chemistry analyzer, prepared selective culture media</td></tr>
<tr><td>B</td><td>Moderate Individual Risk and/or Low Public Health Risk</td><td>Pregnancy self testing, anti-nuclear antibody, urine test strips</td></tr>
<tr><td>C</td><td>High Individual Risk and/or Moderate Public Health Risk</td><td>blood glucose self testing, HLA typing, PSA screening, Rubella</td></tr>
<tr><td>D</td><td>High Individual Risk and High Public Health Risk</td><td>HIV blood donor screening, HIV blood diagnostic</td></tr>
</table>

Elements of Conformity Assessment:
The main elements of a conformity assessment system are:
• a quality management system (QMS)
• a postmarket surveillance (PMS) system
• summary technical documentation
• a Declaration of Conformity
• registration of manufacturers and their IVD medical devices with the regulatory authority</td></tr>
</table>

Medical Devices	
	Regulations and Guidelines
Postmarket Requirements	**EC** • MEDDEV 2.12/1: *Guidelines on a Medical Devices Vigilance System* (rev 8) (January 2013) **GHTF/IMDRF** • SG2-N8R4 *Guidance on How to Handle Information Concerning Vigilance Reporting Related to Medical Devices* (June 1999) • SG2-N79R11:2009 *Medical Devices: Post Market Surveillance: National Competent Authority Report Exchange Criteria and Report Form* (February 2009) • SG2-N54R8:2006 *Medical Devices Post Market Surveillance: Global Guidance for Adverse Event Reporting for Medical Devices* (November 2006) • SG2-N47R4:2005 *Review of Current Requirements on Postmarket Surveillance* (May 2005) • SG2-N57R8:2006 *Medical Devices Post Market Surveillance: Content of Field Safety Notices* (June 2006) **ISO** • ISO 13485:2003 *Medical devices—Quality management systems—Requirements for regulatory purposes* • ISO 14971:2007 *Medical devices—Application of risk management to medical devices* **US** • 21 CFR 803 Medical Device Reporting • Form FDA 3500A MedWatch Form – Mandatory Reporting
Chapter 22 Main Topics	**Vigilance Reporting** Manufacturers placing medical devices on the market must have a vigilance system in place for collecting and evaluating reported incidents and taking corrective action, if needed, to prevent the recurrence of such incidents. The main purpose of a medical device vigilance system is to improve protection of patients' and other users' health and safety by reducing the likelihood that a device incident will recur. **Postmarket Surveillance (PMS)** All regulatory systems recognize that adverse event reporting alone cannot capture all risks related to medical devices in the postmarket phase. For certain classes of products such as diagnostic devices, where false positives and/or false negatives may occur, or long-term implantable devices and devices for home use, evaluating the device's performance from adverse event reports alone would not be sufficient. To address this requirement, PMS activities are mandated in most countries. **Field Safety Corrective Action** Manufacturers placing medical devices on the market are obliged to put into place corrective and preventive action plans related to their products, if those devices pose a risk to users or other individuals. These plans include safety-related field corrective actions taken by the manufacturer to reduce the risk of harm to patients, operators or others and/or to minimize chances the event will recur.

High-Risk Products	
	Regulations and Guidelines
High-Risk Products: Products Derived From Biotechnology	**ICH** • *Viral Safety Evaluation of Biotechnology Products Derived from Cell Lines of Human or Animal Origin Q5A(R1)* (Current Step 4 version, September 1999) • *Quality of Biotechnological Products: Analysis of the Expression Construct in Cells Used for Production of r-DNA Derived Protein Products Q5B* (Current Step 4 version, November 1995) • *Quality of Biotechnological Products: Stability Testing of Biotechnological/Biological Products Q5C* (Current Step 4 version, November 1995) • *Derivation and Characterisation of Cell Substrates Used for Production of Biotechnological/Biological Products Q5D* (Current Step 4 version, July 1997) • *Comparability of Biotechnological/Biological Products Subject to Changes in Their Manufacturing Process Q5E* (Current Step 4 version, November 2004) • *Specifications: Test Procedures and Acceptance Criteria for Biotechnological/Biological Products Q6B* (Current Step 4 version, March 1999) • *Preclinical Safety Evaluation of Biotechnology-Derived Pharmaceuticals S6(R1)* (Current Step 4 version, June 2011) • *M4: The Common Technical Document* **EU** • Regulation (EC) No. 726/2004 of the European Parliament and of the Council of 31 March 2004 laying down Community procedures for the authorisation and supervision of medicinal products for human and veterinary use and establishing a European Medicines Agency • *The Rules Governing Medicinal Products in the European Union, Volume 2A,* Chapter 4 Procedures for Marketing Authorisation, Centralised Procedure • EMA/410/01 Rev.3*, Note for guidance on minimising the risk of transmitting animal spongiform encephalopathy agents via human and veterinary medicinal products*, March 2011 • Regulation (EC) No 1394/2007 of the European Parliament and of the Council of 13 November 2007 on advanced therapy medicinal products and amending Directive 2001/83/EC and Regulation (EC) No 726/2004. • Directive 2001/83/EC of the European Parliament and of the Council of 6 November 2001 on the Community code relating to medicinal products for human use, as amendedGuidance CHMP/QWP/227/02 Rev 3,*Guideline on Active Substance Master File Procedure* (October 2012) **US** • 21 CFR, Subchapter F Biologics, Part 600 Biological Products: General • 21 CFR 312 Investigational New Drug Application • *Guidance for Industry: Content and Format of Investigational New Drug Applications (INDs) for Phase 1 Studies of Drugs, Including Well-Characterized Therapeutic, Biotechnology-derived Products* (November 1995) • New Drug and Biological Drug Products; Evidence Needed to Demonstrate Effectiveness of New Drugs When Human Efficacy Studies Are Not Ethical or Feasible (Animal Efficacy Rule) (May 2002)
Chapter 23 Main Topics	Often, the terms "biotechnology" and "biological" are used synonymously or have overlapping definitions. Furthermore, definitions and regulatory requirements vary by region. **ICH** ICH has issued a range of guidelines pertaining to biologics, which are applicable in the EU, US, Japan and other countries that recognize ICH (e.g., Canada, Australia, New Zealand). The following topics are covered in this chapter for the EU, US, Japan, Canada, Asia Pacific, Latin America, Southern/Eastern Europe, Africa/Middle East and Russia/CIS: • introduction and history • current procedures and guidance • dossier requirements (quality, preclinical and clinical as well as specifics such as TSE, viral clearance, etc.) • advanced therapy medicinal products (ATMPs) • Drug Master File

	Regulations and Guidelines
Principles of Orphan Drugs	**EU** • Regulation (EC) 141/2000 of the European Parliament and of the Council of 16 December 1999 on orphan medicinal products • Regulation (EC) No. 726/2004 of the European Parliament and of the Council of 31 March 2004 laying down Community procedures for the authorisation and supervision of medicinal products for human and veterinary use and establishing a European Medicines Agency **US** • *Orphan Drug Act* of 1983, Public Law 97-414, with amendments in 1985, 1988 and 1992 • 21 CFR Part 316: Orphan Drug Regulations, 12 June 2013 **Australia** • *Australian Regulatory Guidelines for Prescription Medicines*, June 2004 (Appendix 8 updated May 2011)
Chapter 27 Main Topics	Orphan drugs (or orphan medicinal products) are intended for the treatment of orphan diseases, which are understood to be rare diseases. In most legislation, the orphan principle is limited to drugs only. There are exceptions. For instance, in the US, the definition of orphan products was extended to products other than drugs such as medical devices and medical foods (e.g., parenteral nutrition). Orphan diseases generally designate diseases that affect only a small number of individuals: that latter principle is a cornerstone in the definition of an orphan disease in Australia, Japan, the US and the EU, even though the exact meaning of "small number of individuals" varies per country/region. **Regulatory Procedure** A stepwise approach is employed for the authorization of orphan drugs in most jurisdictions: • obtaining orphan designation • applying for marketing authorization for the particular product The registration procedure generally follows the same principles as for non-orphan drugs. In some countries or regions, orphan drugs automatically qualify for particular authorization processes, such as accelerated or priority review. **Incentives** Each country with established orphan medicinal product legislation offers incentives to companies that develop drugs to treat orphan disorders. These measures are intended to motivate companies to invest in these products by negating the impact of expected low sales due to the rarity of the disease. Several measures that may be offered, depending on the country/region, explicitly address this economic issue: • market exclusivity • fee reductions • tax incentives • support of research and development activities

	Regulations and Guidelines
Food Supplements and Cosmetic Products	**Canada** • *Cosmetic Regulations* to the *Food and Drugs Act* **EU** • Council Directive 76/768/EEC of 27 July 1976 on the approximation of the laws of the Member States relating to cosmetic products, as amended. Recast in 2009 as Regulation (EC) No 1223/2009 of the European Parliament and of the Council of 30 November 2009 • Directive 2002/46/EC of the European Parliament and of the Council of 10 June 2002 on the approximation of the laws of the Member States relating to food supplements, as amended **US** • *Dietary Supplement Health and Education Act* of 1994 • *Tamper-Resistant Packaging Act* of 1980 • 21 CFR 700.25 Tamper-resistant packaging requirements for cosmetic products **WHO** • Guidelines for Vitamin and Mineral Food Supplements, CAC/GL 55-2005 (2005)

<table>
<tr>
<td>Chapters 29, 30
Main Topics</td>
<td>Food Supplements
Food supplements—also known as dietary supplements or nutritional supplements—are concentrated sources of nutrients or other substances with a nutritional or physiological effect, alone or in combination, usually marketed in dose form, i.e., pills, tablets, capsules, liquids in measured doses, etc., and used to supplement the normal diet. These nutrients can be vitamins, minerals, herbs or other botanicals, amino acids and substances such as enzymes, organ tissues, glandulars and metabolites. The exact definition differs by country, and products may be classified and regulated as either foods or drugs.

Recommended Daily Allowances (RDAs)
Competent Authorities have established what is known as the recommended daily/dietary allowance, or RDA, (in the US and Canada known as Dietary Reference Intakes (DRIs)) for various vitamins and minerals.

Minimum and Maximum Amounts Based on Safety
Apart from the RDA, minimum and maximum amounts of vitamins and minerals in food supplements have been established based on upper safe levels and the intake of vitamins and minerals from other dietary sources.

Cosmetic Products
In general, cosmetic products are substances or preparations intended to be placed in contact with various external parts of the human body, primarily intended to clean, perfume, protect or maintain them in good condition, or promote attractiveness, alter appearance or correct body odors.

Depending on local regulations, the following products are usually defined as cosmetics:
• creams, emulsions, lotions, gels and oils for the skin (hands, face, feet, etc.)
• face masks
• tinted bases (liquids, pastes, powders)
• makeup powders, after-bath powders, hygienic powders, etc.
• toilet soaps, deodorant soaps, etc.
• perfumes, toilette waters and eau de cologne
• bath and shower preparations (salts, foams, oils, gels, etc.)
• depilatories
• deodorants and antiperspirants
• hair care products:
   o hair tints and bleaches
   o products for waving, straightening and fixing
   o setting products
   o cleansing products (lotions, powders, shampoos)
   o conditioning products (lotions, creams, oils)
   o hair dressing products (lotions, lacquers, brilliantines)
• shaving products (creams, foams, lotions, etc.)
• products for making up and removing makeup from the face and the eyes
• products intended for application to the lips
• products for care of the teeth and the mouth including mouthwashes
• products for nail care and makeup
• products for external intimate hygiene
• sunbathing products
• products for tanning without the sun
• skin-whitening products
• anti-wrinkle products</td>
</tr>
</table>

	Regulations and guidelines
Veterinary Medicinal Products	**VICH & Others** OECD, OECD Series on Principles of Good Laboratory Practice and Compliance Monitoring (ENV/MC/CHEM(98)17) (1998) • VICH GL1, *Validation of Analytical Procedures: Definition and Terminology* (Step 7) • VICH GL2, *Validation of Analytical Procedures: Methodology* (Step 7) • VICH GL10, *Impurities in New Veterinary Drug Substances (Revision)* (Step 9) • VICH GL11, *Impurities in New Veterinary Medicinal Products (Revision)* (Step 9) • VICH GL18, *Impurities: Residual Solvents in New Veterinary Medicinal Products, Active Substances and Excipients* (Step 7) • VICH GL3, *Stability Testing of New Veterinary Drug Substances and Medicinal Products (Revision)* (Step 9) • VICH GL4, *Stability Testing for New Veterinary Dosage Forms* (Step 7) • VICH GL5, *Stability Testing: Photostability Testing of New Veterinary Drug Substances and Medicinal Products* (Step 7) • VICH GL17, *Stability Testing of New Biotechnological/Biological Veterinary Medicinal Products* (Step 7) • VICH GL39, *Test Procedures and Acceptance Criteria for New Veterinary Drug Substances and New Medicinal Products: Chemical Substances* (Step 7) • VICH GL40, *Test Procedures and Acceptance Criteria for New Biotechnological/Biological Veterinary Medicinal Products* (Step 7) • VICH GL9, *Good Clinical Practice* (Step 7) • VICH GL24, *Pharmacovigilance of Veterinary Medicinal Products: Management of Adverse Event Reports (AERs)* Pending adoption of GL30 and GL35 (Step 4) • VICH GL29, *Pharmacovigilance of Veterinary Medicinal Products—Management of Periodic Summary Update Reports* (Step 7) **EU** • Directive 2001/82/EC of the European Parliament and of the Council of 6 November 2001 on the Community code relating to veterinary medicinal products, as amended by Directive 2004/28/EC • *The Rules Governing Veterinary Medicinal Products in the European Community, Notice to Applicants, Medicinal Products for Veterinary Use, Volume 6B, Presentation and content of the dossier—Part 1* • Regulation (EC) No. 470/2009 of the European Parliament and of the Council of 6 May 2009 laying down Community procedures for the establishment of residue limits of pharmacologically active substances in foodstuffs of animal origin • *Revised Policy for classification and incentives for veterinary medicinal products indicated for minor use minor species (MUMS)/limited markets* (EMA/429080/2009 - Rev.1) • Directive 2004/10/EC of the European Parliament and of the Council of 11 February 2004 on the harmonization of laws, regulations and administrative provisions relating to the application of the principles of good laboratory practice and the verification of their application for tests on chemical substances • Directive 2004/9/EC of the European Parliament and of the Council of 11 February 2004 on the inspection and verification of good laboratory practice (GLP) **US** • 21 CFR 589 Substances Prohibited From Use in Animal Food or Feed • 21 CFR 314 Applications for FDA Approval to Market a New Drug • Environmental Assessment for Amendments to 21 CFR 589 Substances Prohibited from Use in Animal Food or Feed, Final Rule • *Minor Use and Minor Species Animal Health Act* of 2004 (*MUMS*) • *21 CFR 58* Good Laboratory Practice for Nonclinical Laboratory Studies

Chapter 31 Main Topics	Veterinary medical products prevent, treat or diagnose diseases in animals. They include not only drugs, vaccines, devices and diagnostic test kits, but also such products as food additives and feed ingredients and animal grooming aids. Safety assessment of veterinary products is based on a risk:benefit analysis. The safety of veterinary products depends on the target animal's level of tolerance of the ingredients and, for food-producing animals, the acceptable level of residue. The safety of the person administering the veterinary product also should be taken into consideration. **Differences Between Human and Animal Medicinal Products** • Human medicines are developed for one species, whereas the veterinary medicines market is fragmented by many animal species. • Veterinary medicinal products are normally not part of national health plans and are not reimbursed. • Some species may end up in the human food chain; hence, harmful drug residues must be strictly controlled. • Those administering veterinary medicinal products must be safeguarded from possible harmful effects. • Veterinary medicines may have a more direct effect on the environment than human medicines. **VICH** The International Cooperation on Harmonisation of Technical Requirements for Registration of Veterinary Medicinal Products (VICH) is a trilateral (EU-Japan-US) program that aims to harmonize technical requirements for veterinary product registration. Its objectives are: • establish and implement harmonized regulatory requirements • provide a basis for wider international harmonization of registration requirements • monitor and maintain existing VICH guidelines • ensure efficient processes for maintaining and monitoring consistent interpretation of data requirements **Dossier Requirements** • dossier summary: application form, medical summary information, labels, pack leaflet and other packaging texts and expert reports • quality: physicochemical or biological test results • safety: pharmacological, toxicological and environmental safety test results • residues: residue study results and analytical methodology (not for immunological veterinary medicinal products • efficacy: preclinical and clinical trial results • general conclusions for immunological veterinary medicinal products

Glossary

A

Abridged application
An application for marketing authorization based on demonstration of essential similarity or by detailed references to published scientific literature; does not contain the results of pharmacological and toxicological tests or the results of clinical trials. (EU)

Accelerated Assessment
A marketing authorization procedure designed to meet, in particular the legitimate expectations of patients and to take into account the increasingly rapid progress of science and therapies, for medicinal products of major interest from the point of view of public health and in particular from the view point of therapeutic innovation. (EU)

ACTD
ASEAN Common Technical Dossier

Active Pharmaceutical Ingredient
(API) Any drug component intended to furnish pharmacological activity or other direct effect in the diagnosis, cure, mitigation, treatment or prevention of disease; or to affect the structure or any function of the body of man or other animals.

ADI
Acceptable daily intake

ADME
Absorption, Distribution, Metabolism and Excretion

ADR
Adverse Drug Reaction

Adulterated
Product containing any filthy, putrid or decomposed substance; or prepared under unsanitary conditions; or not made according to GMPs; or containing an unsafe color additive; or does not meet the requirements of an official compendium.

AHWP
Asian Harmonization Working Party

AIMD
Active Implantable Medical Device

AIVC
Australian Influenza Vaccine Committee

ANDA
Abbreviated New Drug Application (US)

ANDS
Abbreviated New Drug Submission (Canada)

Animal Rule
Allows FDA to approve a product for which evidence of safety and efficacy has been based on data obtained in adequate and well-controlled animal trials.

ANMAT
National Administration of Drugs, Food and Medical Devices (Argentina)

Annual Report
An annual periodic report or progress report that must be submitted to FDA. It must include new safety, efficacy and labeling information; preclinical and clinical investigation summaries; CMC updates; nonclinical laboratory studies; and completed unpublished clinical trials.

ANSI
American National Standards Institute

ANVISA
National Health Surveillance Agency of Brazil

API
See Active Pharmaceutical Ingredient

AR
Authorized Representative

ARGOM
Australian Regulatory Guidelines for Over-the-Counter Medicines

ARTG
Australian Register of Therapeutic Goods

ASEAN
Association of Southeast Asian Nations. Comprised of Brunei Darussalam, Cambodia, Indonesia, Lao PDR, Malaysia, Myanmar, Philippines, Singapore, Thailand and Vietnam.

ASMF
Active substance master file (previously known as European Drug Master File (EDMF) (EU)

ATMP
Advanced therapy medicinal product

AusPAR
Australian Public Assessment Report

Ayurvedic Medicine
A type of complementary and alternative medicine (CAM) based on theories of health and illness and on ways to prevent, manage or treat health problems.

B

BA
Bioavailability

BACPAC
Bulk Actives Postapproval Changes (FDA)

BDP
Botanical Drug Product (FDA)

BE
Bioequivalence

BGTD
Biologics and Genetic Therapies Directorate (Canada)

Biologic
Any virus, therapeutic serum, toxin, antitoxin or analogous product applicable to the prevention, treatment or cure of diseases or injuries in man.

Biosimilars
New versions of existing biologics whose patents have expired. Also referred to as FOBs and SEBs.

BLA
Biologics License Application (US)

Blood Regulators Network
Comprised of leading international regulatory authorities responsible for the regulation of blood, products and related in vitro diagnostic devices.

BPAC
Blood Products Advisory Committee (FDA)

BPCA
Best Pharmaceuticals for Children Act (US)

BRN
See Blood Regulators Network

BSE
Bovine spongiform encephalopathy

BWP
Biologics Working Party (EU)

C

CAB
Conformity assessment body

CAC
Codex Alimentarius Commission

CADREAC
Collaboration Agreement between Drug Regulatory Authorities in EU Associated Countries

CADTH
Canadian Agency for Drugs and Technologies in Health

CAM
Complementary and Alternative Medicine

CAPA
Corrective and Preventive Actions

CAS
Chemical Abstract Service

CAT
Committee for Advanced Therapies (EU)

CBER
Center for Biologics Evaluation and Research (FDA)

CBTE
Centre for Blood and Tissues Evaluation (Canada)

CCDS
See Company Core Data Sheet

CCSI
See Company Core Safety Information

CDC
Centers for Disease Control and Prevention (US)

CDE
Center for Drug Evaluation (China)

CDEC
Canadian Drug Expert Committee (formerly the Canadian Expert Drug Advisory Committee (CEDAC))

CDER
Center for Drug Evaluation and Research (FDA)

CDRH
Center for Devices and Radiological Health (FDA)

CE Mark
Indicates product conforms with the essential health and safety requirements. (EU)

CEN
European Committee for Standardisation

CENELEC
European Committee for Electrotechnical Standardisation

Central Drugs Standard Control Organization
Regulatory body in India.

Centralised Procedure
A procedure to allow applicants to make an application directly to the European Medicines Agency, to be assessed by the CHMP or CVMP, to obtain a Marketing Authorisation (MA) that is valid throughout the EU. It is compulsory for medicinal products manufactured using biotechnological processes, but may also be used for other innovative products, on a voluntary basis. Centrally authorized products may be marketed in all Member States.

CERB
Centre for Evaluation of Radiopharmaceuticals and Biotherapeutics (Canada)

Certificate of Suitability (CEP)
Certificate that the substance's quality is suitably controlled by the relevant monographs of the European Pharmacopoeia with, if necessary, an annex appended to the certificate. Can be granted for APIs or excipients and for substances or preparations with risk of transmitting agents of TSE.

CFDA
China Food and Drug Administration

CFR
Code of Federal Regulations (US)

CFSAN
Center for Food Safety and Applied Nutrition (FDA)

CHMP
See Committee for Medicinal Products for Human Use (EU)

CIOMS
Council for International Organisations of Medical Sciences

CIS
Confederation of Independent States comprised of Armenia, Azerbaijan, Belarus, Georgia, Kazakhstan, Kyrgyzstan, Moldova, Russia, Tajikistan, Turkmenistan, Ukraine and Uzbekistan.

CJD
Creuzfeldt-Jakob Disease

CMC
Chemistry, Manufacturing and Controls

CMDCAS
Canadian Medical Devices Conformity Assessment System

CMP
Certificate of Medicinal Product (EU)

CMS
Concerned Member State (EU)

Committee for Medicinal Products for Human Use
(CHMP) A scientific committee within the European Medicines Agency that provides scientific advice on questions relating to the evaluation of medicinal products for human use.

Committee for Veterinary Medicinal Products
(CVMP) A scientific committee within the European Medicines Agency that provides scientific advice on questions relating to the evaluation of veterinary medicinal products.

Company Core Data Sheet
Includes product information relating to safety, indications, dosing, pharmacology and other information.

Company Core Safety Information
Contains the core safety data about the product that is required to be on the product's label in each country. This safety information is obtained from worldwide case reporting and screening of all product safety information.

Competent Authority
A Competent Authority is the governmental authority responsible for the authorization and supervision of medicinal products.

Conformity assessment
A procedure to enable public authorities to ensure that industrial products, including medical devices, placed on the market conform to the requirements as expressed in the provisions of the directives, particularly regarding the health and safety of users and consumers.

CPP
Certificate of a Pharmaceutical Product

Crisis Management Plan
Comprises various methods to respond to a crisis and establish metrics to deal with crises, including defining what scenarios constitute a crisis and possible response mechanisms. A crisis management plan should include possible worst-case scenarios and solutions in the form of a contingency plan.

CRO
Contract research organization

CTA
Clinical Trial Application

CTD
Common Technical Document

CVE
Centre for Vaccine Evaluation (Canada)

CVM
Center for Veterinary Medicine (FDA)

CVMP
See Committee for Medicinal Products for Veterinary Use (EU)

D

Dear Healthcare Professional Letter
Correspondence mailed by a manufacturer and/or distributor to physicians and/or other healthcare professionals to convey important information about drugs.

Decentralised Procedure
Procedure which may be used for medicinal products for which there is no existing Marketing Authorisation in any EU Member State. The applicant can select the Reference Member State and list the Concerned Member States.

Declaration of Conformity
A document whereby the manufacturer ensures either that the product safety component satisfies the essential requirements of the applicable directives, or that the product is in conformity with the type for which a type-examination certificate has been issued and satisfies the essential requirements of the applicable directives. (EU)

Declaration of Helsinki
Ethical principles for medical research involving human subjects. Trials conducted under Good Clinical Practice generally follow the *Declaration of Helsinki.*

DIN
Drug Identification Number (Canada)

Directive
An EC decision that is binding on EC institutions and Member States and must be transposed into national legislation. However, the way in which it is implemented is left to the discretion of each Member State. (EU)

DMF
Drug Master File

DQ
Design Qualification

DRI
Dietary Reference Intake

Drug
Any article intended for use in the diagnosis, cure, mitigation, treatment or prevention of disease in man.

Drug & Cosmetics Act
Primary law governing medical products in India.

DSHEA
Dietary Supplement Health and Education Act (US)

DSUR
Development Safety Update Report (EU)

DTC
Direct-to-consumer

E

EC
European Community; also refers to European Commission

eCTD
Electronic Common Technical Document

EDMF
European Drug Master File

EDQM
See European Directorate for the Quality of Medicines

EEA
See European Economic Area

EEC
See European Economic Community

EFPIA
See European Federation of Pharmaceutical Industries and Associations

EFTA
European Free Trade Association, composed of Iceland, Liechtenstein, Norway and Switzerland.

EMA
See European Medicines Agency

EP
Essential Principles

EPAR
See European Public Assessment Report

EP Checklist
A list of Essential Principles indicating their applicability to a particular device and justification for those not considered to be applicable.

ERA
Environmental Risk Assessment

Essential Requirements
The technical requirements with which a medical device must comply in order to be CE marked.

EU
See European Union

Eudamed
European Databank on Medical Devices

EudraCT
Database of all clinical trials commencing in the Community from 1 May 2004 onwards. It was established in accordance with Directive 2001/20/EC.

European Commission
(EC) A body with powers of initiation, implementation, management and control. It is composed of 20 members, called commissioners, appointed to five-year terms by Member States after they have been approved by the European Parliament.

European Community
(EC) The collective body formerly designated as the European Economic Community (EEC). The plural term European Communities also is widely used.

European Council
The European Council is the Heads of State or Government of the European Union Member States, who meet regularly. It is another and the most senior manifestation of the Council of the European Union.

European Directorate for the Quality of Medicines
(EDQM) The EDQM is part of the administrative structure of the Council of Europe. Its responsibilities include the Technical Secretariat of the European Pharmacopoeia Commission, certification for Ph.Eur.'s monograph suitability program, developing the European network of the Official Medicines Control Laboratories (OMCL) and providing the secretariat for this network.

European Economic Area
(EEA) A free-trade area, in all but agriculture, comprising the Member States of the EU plus Iceland, Liechtenstein and Norway. Previously called the European Economic Space.

European Federation of Pharmaceutical Industries and Associations
(EFPIA) Represents more than 2,000 pharmaceutical companies involved in research, development and manufacturing medicinal products for human use in the EU.

European Medicines Agency
(EMA) Agency responsible for coordinating the scientific evaluation of the safety, efficacy and quality of human and veterinary medicinal products that undergo the Centralised Procedure as well as for arbitration during the Mutual Recognition Procedure.

European Pharmacopoeia
(Ph.Eur.) Pharmacopée Européenne is a pharmacopoeia whose monographs are common to all concerned EU countries.

European Public Assessment Report
(EPAR) The EPAR highlights CHMP's scientific conclusion at the end of the Centralised Procedure and summarizes the grounds for the CHMP Opinion regarding granting a Marketing Authorisation for a specific medicinal product. It is made available by European Medicines Agency for public information, after deletion of commercially confidential information.

European Union
(EU) The EU is composed of 28 Member States (Austria, Belgium, Bulgaria, Croatia, Cyprus, Czech Republic, Denmark, Estonia, Finland, France, Germany, Greece, Hungary, Ireland, Italy, Latvia, Lithuania, Luxembourg, Malta, the Netherlands, Poland, Portugal, Romania, Slovakia, Slovenia, Spain, Sweden and the United Kingdom).

EWG
Expert Working Group

Excipient
An ingredient contained in a drug formulation that is not a medicinally active constituent.

F

F&DA
Food and Drugs Act. Primary law governing medical products in Canada.

F&EC
Facility and equipment controls

Falsified Medicines
Products that usually contain substandard or falsified ingredients, or no ingredients or ingredients, including active substances, in the wrong dosage thus posing an important threat to public health. (EU)

FAO
Food and Agriculture Organization of the United Nations

FAT
Factory Acceptance Test

Fast Track Approval
FDA program to facilitate the development and expedite the review of new drugs intended to treat serious or life-threatening conditions that demonstrate the potential to address unmet medical needs.

FD&C Act
Food, Drug, and Cosmetic Act. Primary law governing healthcare products in the US.

FDA
See US Food and Drug Administration

Field Safety Corrective Action
(FSCA) An action taken by a manufacturer to reduce the risk of death or serious deterioration in the state of health associated with the use of a medical device.

Field Safety Notice
(FSN) A communication to customers and/or users sent out by a manufacturer or its representative in relation to a Field Safety Corrective Action.

FIFARMA
Federación Latinoamericana de la Industria

FMA
Foreign Manufacturing Authorization (Japan)

FMEA
Failure Mode Effects Analysis

FOB
Follow-on biologic (*see* biosimilar)

Food Supplements
Also known as dietary supplements or nutritional supplements; concentrated sources of nutrients or other substances with a nutritional or physiological effect that are taken orally to supplement the normal diet.

FSCA
See Field Safety Corrective Action

FSN
See Field Safety Notice

G

GCC-DR
Gulf Central Committee for Drug Registration. Comprised of Bahrain, Kuwait, Oman, Qatar, Saudi Arabia and the United Arab Emirates.

GCDMP
Good Clinical Data Management Practice

GCP
Good Clinical Practice

GDP
Good Distribution Practice

GDP
Good Documentation Practice

Generic Drug
Drugs manufactured and approved after the original brand name drug has lost patent protection.

Genetically Modified Organism
(GMO) An organism in which the genetic material has been altered in a way that does not occur naturally by mating and/or natural recombination.

Genotoxicity tests
In vitro and *in vivo* tests designed to detect compounds that induce genetic damage directly or indirectly by various mechanisms.

GLP
Good Laboratory Practice

GMDN
Global Medical Device Nomenclature

GMO
See Genetically Modified Organism

GMP
Good Manufacturing Practice

GP
General public (Canada)

GPvP
Good Pharmacovigilance Practice

GRASE
Generally recognized as safe and effective (US)

GSL
General Sales List (UK)

GxP
Good Pharmaceutical Practices

H

HACCP
Hazardous Analysis Critical Control Points

Hatch-Waxman Act
Enacted in 1984, this act forms the basis for generic drug approval in the US.

Health Canada
Primary regulatory body for medicinal products in Canada.

HIPAA
Health Insurance Portability & Accountability Act (US)

HTA
Health Technology Assessment

Hotlist
An administrative list of substances that are restricted and prohibited in cosmetics (Canada)

HREC
Human Research Ethics Committee (Australia)

I

IB
Investigator's Brochure

IBD
International birth date

ICDRA
International Conference of Drug Regulatory Authorities

ICF
Informed Consent Form

ICH
International Conference on Harmonisation of Technical Requirements for Registration of Pharmaceuticals for Human Use (participants include the EU, US and Japan; observers include Australia and Canada).

ICSR
Individual case safety report

ICTRP
International Clinical Trial Registry Platform

IDMC
Independent Data Monitoring Committee

IEC
International Electrotechnical Commission; also Independent Ethics Committee

IFAH
International Federation on Animal Health

IFPMA
International Federation of Pharmaceutical Manufacturers & Associations

IGPA
International Generic Pharmaceutical Alliance

IMDRF
See International Medical Device Regulators Forum

IMPACT
International Medical Product Anti-Counterfeiting Task Force (WHO)

IMPD
Investigational Medicinal Product Dossier (EU)

IND
Investigational New Drug (US)

INN
International Nonproprietary Name

International Medical Device Regulators Forum
(IMDRF) A voluntary group of medical device regulators from around the world who have come together to build on the strong foundational work of the Global Harmonization Task Force on Medical Devices (GHTF) and aims to accelerate international medical device regulatory harmonization and convergence.

IPR
Intellectual property rights

IQ
Installation Qualification

IRB
Institutional Review Board

ISO
International Organization for Standardization

ISRCTN
International Standard Randomised Clinical Trial Number

IUPAC
International Union of Pure and Applied Chemistry

IVD
In vitro diagnostic medical device

J

JCVI
Joint Committee on Vaccination and Immunization (UK)

JECFA
Joint FAO/WHO Expert Committee on Food Additives

JMPR
Joint Meeting of the FAO Panel of Experts on Pesticide Residues in Food and the Environment

JPMA
Japan Manufacturers Association

L

LCM
Lifecycle management

M

MA
Marketing Authorization

mAb
Monoclonal antibodies

MAD
Mutual acceptance of data

MAH
See Marketing Authorization Holder

Marketing Authorization
(MA) Authorization issued by a Competent Authority to place a medicinal product on the market.

Marketing Authorization Holder
(MAH) The person who holds the marketing authorization for placing a medicinal product on the market and is responsible for the product's marketing.

MDDS
Medical Device Data Systems (FDA)

MDSAP
Medical Device Single Audit Program

MDUFMA
Medical Device User Fee and Modernization Act of 2004 (US)

MEB
Medicines Evaluation Board (Netherlands)

Memorandum of Understanding
(MOU) An agreement between two or more countries' regulatory authorities that allows mutual recognition of inspections.

MHLW
Ministry of Health, Labour and Welfare (Japan)

MHRA
Medicines and Healthcare products Regulatory Agency (UK)

MOU
See Memorandum of Understanding

MPA
Medical Products Agency (Sweden)

MRA
See Mutual Recognition Agreement

MRL
Maximum residue limit

MS
Member State

MTC
Mixed treatment comparisons

MUMS
Minor use, minor species

Mutual recognition agreement
(MRA) An international agreement by which two or more countries agree to recognize one another's conformity assessments.

Mutual Recognition Procedure
The Mutual Recognition Procedure, which is applicable to most conventional medicinal products, is one licensing procedure in the EU based on the extension of national marketing authorizations to one or more additional Member States. Applicants may select the Reference Member State that conducts the assessment and applicable Concerned Member States where the product would be put on the market if approved.

N

NAT
Nucleic acid amplification technology

NHI Drug Price List
National Health Insurance Price List (Japan)

NB
Notified Body

NCAR
National Competent Authority Report

NCCAM
National Center for Complementary and Alternative Medicine

NCE
New Chemical Entity

NCL
National Control Laboratories

ND
Normative Documentation (Russia)

NDA
New Drug Application (US)

NDS
New Drug Submission (Canada)

NF
National Formulary (US)

NHP
Natural Health Products (Canada)

NICE
National Institute for Health and Care Excellence (UK)

NICPBP
National Institute of the Control of Pharmaceutical and Biological Products (China)

NIH
National Institutes of Health (US)

NME
New molecular entity

NOAEL
No observable adverse effect level. The highest tested dose of a substance that has been reported to have no harmful (adverse) health effects on people or animals.

NOC
Notice of Compliance (Canada)

NOL
Non-objection Letter (Canada)

Novel Foods
Foods or food ingredients that have not been used for human consumption to a significant degree before 15 May 1997. (EU)

NPN
Natural Health Product Number (Canada)

Nuremburg Code of 1947
A set of research ethics principles for human experimentation that was created as a result of atrocities involving medical experimentation on humans during World War II.

O

OBBR
Office of Blood Research and Review (FDA)

OCABR
Official Control Authority Batch Release (EU)

OCP
Office of Combination Products (FDA)

ODA
Orphan Drug Act (US)

OECD
Organisation for Economic Co-operation and Development

OMA
Office of Medicines Authorization (Australia)

OMCL
Official medicines control laboratory

OOPD
Office of Orphan Products and Development (FDA)

OPDP
Office of Prescription Drug Promotion (FDA)

OQ
Operational Qualification

Orphan medicinal products
Drugs that cater to conditions with low prevalence and therefore lack commercial viability.

OTC
Over-the-counter (products available without a prescription)

OTCMES
OTC Medicines Section (Australia)

OVD
Optically Variable Devices

P

P&PC
Production and process controls

PAFSC
Pharmaceutical Affairs and Food Sanitation Council (Japan)

PAHO
Pan American Health Organization

PAI
Preapproval inspection

PAL
Pharmaceutical Affairs Law (Japan)

PBAC
Pharmaceutical Benefits Advisory Committee (Australia)

PBRER
Periodic Benefit-Risk Evaluation Report

PBS
See Pharmaceutical Benefits Scheme (PBS)

PD
See Pharmacodynamics

PDCO
Paediatric Committee (EU)

PDUFA
Prescription Drug User Fee Act of 1992 (US)

Periodic Safety Update Report
(PSUR) A periodic report on a medicinal product's worldwide safety experience submitted at defined post-authorization times.

PFSB
Pharmaceutical and Food Safety Bureau (Japan)

Pharmaceutical Benefits Scheme
(PBS) An Australian government initiative that provides affordable access for all residents to effective and cost-effective medicines.

Pharmacokinetics
(PK) The study of the processes of ADME of chemicals and medicines.

Pharmacodynamics
(PD) Study of the reactions between drugs and living structures.

Pharmacovigilance
(PV) The science and activities relating to the detection, assessment, understanding and prevention of adverse effects or any other drug-related problems.

PHS Act
Public Health Service Act (US)

PIC
Pharmaceutical Inspection Convention. The PIC and the Pharmaceutical Inspection Co-operation Scheme (PIC Scheme) operate together as PIC/S.

PIL
Patient information leaflet (EU)

PIP
Paediatric Investigation Plan (EU)

PK
See Pharmacokinetics

PMA
Premarket Approval. Marketing application required for Class III devices. (FDA)

PMDA
Pharmaceuticals and Medical Devices Agency (Japan)

PMF
Plasma Master File

PMOA
See Primary Mode of Action.

PMS
See Postmarketing Surveillance

POM
Prescription only medicine (UK)

Postmarketing surveillance
(PMS) After placing product on the market, the manufacturer must institute and update a systematic procedure that records, evaluates and reports any incidents, to proactively gather product experience in the postmarketing phase and to take any necessary corrective measures.

PQ
Performance Qualification

PQP
See Prequalification of Medicines Program

PRAC
Pharmacovigilance Risk Assessment Committee

PREA
Pediatric Research Equity Act (US)

Prequalification of Medicines Program
A service provided by the World Health Organization (WHO) to facilitate access to medicines that meet unified standards of quality, safety and efficacy for HIV/AIDS, malaria and tuberculosis.

Priority Review
FDA review category for drugs that appear to represent an advance over available therapy. NDA or BLA receives a faster review than standard applications.

Primary Mode of Action
(PMOA) The single mode of action of a combination product that provides the most important therapeutic action of the combination product; used to assign a combination product to a lead FDA center.

PSUR
See Periodic Safety Update Report

PV
See Pharmacovigilance

Q

QA
Quality assurance

QALY
Quality adjusted life year

QC
Quality control

QMS
Quality management system

QOS
Quality overall summary

QP
Qualified Person

QPPV
See Qualified Person for Pharmacovigilance (EU)

Qualified Person for Pharmacovigilence
(QPPV) Responsible for the overall pharmacovigilance for all medicinal products for which the company holds marketing authorizations within the EU.

QSR
Quality System Regulations

R

R&D
Research and development

RBP
Reference biotherapeutic product

RCT
Randomized controlled trials

RDA
Recommended daily/dietary allowance

Reference Listed Drug
Drug product listed in the Approved Drug Products with Therapeutic Equivalence Evaluations book (also known as the Orange Book). (FDA)

Reference Medicinal Product (EU)
(RMP) The originator product to which a generic drug must prove equivalence in order to obtain marketing authorization.

REMS
Risk Evaluation and Mitigation Strategy (US)

Request for Designation
(RFD) Process by which a company can obtain a formal agency determination of a combination product's primary mode of action and assignment of the lead agency center for the product's premarket review and regulation, or of the agency component that will have jurisdiction for any drug, device, or biological product where such jurisdiction is unclear or in dispute. (FDA)

RFD
See Request for Designation

RFID
Radio Frequency Identification

RMP
Reference medicinal product (EU)

RMP
Risk management plan

RMS
Reference Member State (EU)

RMS
Risk Management System

Rx-to-OTC Switch
The process of transferring FDA-approved prescription medications to nonprescription, over-the-counter (OTC) for the same dosage form, population and route of administration.

S

SAE
Serious adverse event

SBP
Similar biotherapeutic product

SEB
Subsequent entry biologic (Canada) (*see* biosimilar)

SIPD
Submission and Information Policy Division (Canada)

SMDA
Safe Medical Devices Act of 1990 (US)

SmPC
See Summary of Product Characteristics

SNDS
Supplementary New Drug Submission (Canada)

SOP
Standard operating procedure

SPC
See Supplementary Protection Certificates

Sponsor
Company, person, organization or institution conducting a clinical trial and/or filing for approval of a new medicinal product.

STED
Summary Technical Document

Summary of Product Characteristics
(SmPC) The definitive statement between the Competent Authority and the Marketing Authorisation Holder regarding the medicinal or veterinary product. It contains all information a prescriber/supplier needs for proper use of the medicinal or veterinary product. The content must be approved by the Competent Authority, and cannot be changed without the approval of the originating Competent Authority. (EU)

Supplementary Protection Certificates
(SPC) Provides 15 years of extended protection to originator pharmaceutical companies from first marketing approval in the EU.

SUPAC
Scale Up and Post Approval Changes (US)

SUSAR
Serious unexpected adverse reaction (EU)

SUSMP
Standard for the Uniform Scheduling of Medicines and Poisons (Australia)

T

TBT
Technical Barriers to Trade

TEA
Time and Extent Application (FDA)

TGA
Therapeutic Goods Administration (Australia)

TPCC
Therapeutic Products Classification Committee (Canada)

TPD
Therapeutic Products Directorate (Canada)

TCM
Traditional Chinese Medicine

Transmissible Spongiform Encephalopathies Advisory Committee
(TSEAC) reviews and evaluates available scientific data concerning the safety of products that may be at risk for transmission of spongiform encephalopathies having an impact on public health as determined by the FDA commissioner.

Treatment IND
Allows limited use of an unapproved drug for patients with a serious or life-threatening disease. (US)

TRIPS
World Trade Organization Agreement on Trade-Related Aspects of Intellectual Property Rights

TSE
Transmissible spongiform encephalopathies

TSEAC
See Transmissible Spongiform Encephalopathies Advisory Committee

U

UDI System
Unique Device Identification System

UNICEF
United Nations International Children's Emergency Fund

UPI
Unique Product Identifier (Australia)

US Agent
Identified representative of any foreign establishment engaged in the manufacture, preparation, propagation, compounding or processing of a device imported into the US. (FDA)

USP
United States Pharmacopeia

V

VAERS
Vaccine Adverse Event Reporting System (US)

VAMF
Vaccine Antigen Master File

VCRP
Voluntary Cosmetic Registration Program (FDA)

VHP
See Voluntary Harmonisation Procedure

VICH
International Cooperation on Harmonisation of Technical Requirements for Registration of Veterinary Medicinal Products

VMP
Validation Master Plan

Voluntary Harmonisation Procedure
(VHP) Intended to provide a coordinated assessment of multinational, multicenter clinical trials across the EU Member States.

VRBPAC
Vaccines and Related Biological Products Advisory Committee (FDA)

W

WHA
World Health Assembly

WHO
World Health Organization

WSMI
World Self-Medication Industry

WTO
World Trade Organization

Index

A

B

C

D

E

F

G

H

I

J

L

M

N

O

P

Q

R

S

T

U

V

W